# 21ST CENTURY GERMAN-ENGLISH ENGLISH-GERMAN DICTIONARY

LAUREL

Produced by The Philip Lief Group, Inc.

Published by
Dell Publishing
a division of
Bantam Doubleday Dell Publishing Group, Inc.
1540 Broadway
New York, New York 10036

Published by arrangement with
The Philip Lief Group, Inc.
6 West 20th Street
New York, NY 10011

ISBN: 0-440-22089-0

Printed in the United States of America

Published simultaneously in Canada

September 1996

10   9   8   7   6   5   4   3   2

OPM

# Contents

# Introduction

The *21st Century German-English/English-German Dictionary* is an invaluable reference source for today's students, business people, and travelers. Rather than wasting space on verbose, overly complicated definitions, the *21st Century German-English/English-German Dictionary* provides essential information in a brief, easy-to-use format.

The dual format of the *21st Century German-English/English-German Dictionary* eliminates the need to use two dictionaries: one volume for looking up words in German; and a separate one for looking up words in English. A student, for example, can use this dictionary to find the English translation to an unfamiliar German word—*and* to discover the correct way to express a certain English phrase in German. Because each entry is listed in both German and English, this dictionary is useful for every situation. Whether you are a business person checking the terms of a contract on an international deal, a foreign exchange student getting settled into a German dormitory, or a tourist trying to understand the items on a menu, the *21st Century German-English/English-German Dictionary* will help you find quick, clear translations from German to English—*and* from English to German.

Each entry in the *21st Century German-English/English-German Dictionary* appears in a concise, easy-to-follow format. The headwords are listed in alphabetical order, with a separate A-to-Z section for both the German-English and the English-German. The pronunciation, complete with syllable markings, appears in brackets after each headword, followed by its part of speech. (See Pronunciation Guide.) Entries for nouns also include an indication of gender, with *M* signifying a masculine word, *F* indicating a feminine word, and *N* representing a neuter word. Verbs are marked either *vt* (verb transitive) or *vi* (verb intransitive). Finally, a clear, succinct translation of each word appears, followed by a list of related forms and common phrases.

Reflecting current attitudes and ever-changing sensitivities in its choice of word list, definitions, translations, and pronunciations, the *21st Century German-English/English-German Dictionary* provides the most reliable and up-to-date information available. Whether for speaking, writing, or understanding, the *21st Century German-English/English-German Dictionary* successfully combines a simple, concise format with a contemporary slant, and will serve as an indispensable tool for every occasion.

# Pronunciation Guide

This dictionary represents a unique approach to phonetic pronunciation. It relies on plain, or readily understood, symbols and letters. There are no Greek symbols, and most people, whether English-speaking or German-speaking, should be able to easily sound out the words using this guide.

For English words, the pronunciation is based on conventional (unaccented) American English. The most common pronunciation has been chosen in any instance where there is more than one acceptable pronunciation.

The German language is very consistent with the sounds of its vowel groupings as well as consonants. This outline has very few, if any, exceptions. The groupings in the left column are the German language; their English counterparts are in the right hand column.

| VOWELS | ENGLISH EQUIVALENT |
|---|---|
| a = ah | cop, mop |
| e = eh | eh, hefty, heather |
| I = ee | seen, keen, mean |
| o = oh | phone, hope |
| u = oo | hoop, loop, soup |
| ä = eh | wet, met |
| ö = difficult to compare | like "Europe |
| ü = ooer | somewhat like "shooern" |
| ai = long I | fight, might |
| ei = uy | my, by, why |
| eu = oi | boy, toy, soy |
| ie = ee | eat, deep |
| au = ou | cow, how, now |

Whenever two consonants follow a vowel, it shortens the vowel sound somewhat, but not enough to really give it a different sound, just a quicker sort of pronunciation. For instance "haben" sounds like hah•ben, and machen is more like "makhen" with a quicker pronunciation. Whenever there is one consonant and then another vowel, it lengthens the vowels, as in the aforementioned example.

The consonant combinations are pronounced as follows:

| | |
|---|---|
| sch = always is pronounced "sh" | shook, shape, shirk |
| ch = is a throaty "kh" | German wihkh• tihg |
| sp, st, sch, is always "shp" "sht" "sh" | German spielen, streichen, Schule |

nd = can be nd or nt, as in the German word "land" = lahnt, or Ende is = ehndeh". The rule of thumb is: if there is another vowel after the nd is stays d, but sounds like a "t" when nd are the last two letters of the word. More examples are: Hund = nt sound; Mund = nt; finden = nd; Mandeln = nd.

| | |
|---|---|
| w = v sound always | wichtig = vihk• tihg |
| v = f sound in most cases, a few exceptions as noted in guide | viel = feel |
| f = f | |

z = ts in most cases, as in tse tse fly; in a consonant combination it stays "z"

j = English y in all cases: Ja, Jacht, jochen, they are all "y" sounds

b = can have a p sound as in "ab" sounds like "ap" in "abreißen" it is ahp-ruy-sen

ss = ß This is called an s-set, which looks like a capital B but it is a double s. abreißen could look like abreissen, but the ß is used, especially between two vowels.

qu in German is pronounced "kv"

th in German is pronounce "t"

h in German is pronounced at the beginning of words and between vowels in interjections, though it is often mute in English.

ung is always "oong"

ing is like it looks, "ing"

heit is always pronounced huyt; same for keit = kuyt

g = can sound like a k in some instances, as noted in the guide; especially when it is at the end of a word.

*Liaison*

In German, liaison is rarely used. Rather, it is common when speaking to pronounce each letter distinctly. There are no silent letters, and sounds aren't run together, as in the English dipthongs such as in "mail", or "fire". There isn't the "yer" or "yuh" elision as in English. The two vowels are separated, as in the German word "feier," which is pronounced "fai-air," with no "y" sound in between. Diphthongs *do* appear in the vowel combinations such as ai, au, ei, and they are pronounced the same in every instance.

A Glottal Stop, where the sound begins in the back of the throat, is used at the beginning of any word which starts with a vowel. It always is used in compounds between first and second elements when the second begins with a vowel.

*Basic pronunciation in this dictionary*

| Traditional English phonetics | Becomes | As in |
| --- | --- | --- |
| **VOWELS:** | | |
| æ | a | cat, ask |
| e | ai | gate, they, air |
| a, a: | ah | hot, father |
| | au | bought, haunt, war, fall |
| | e | fell, head |
| i, i: | ee | see, tea |
| | I | lid, damage |
| aï | uy | buy, lie, height, I |
| o | o | no, foe, road |
| u | oo | loop, chute, poor |
| | ou | now, out, town |
| | oi | boy, void |
| | uh | but, mother, hunt |
| | u | bird, aloof, alert, debris |
| | | book, put, could |

This neutral *u* sound is one of the most common vowel sounds in English, and it is used for many unstressed syllables.

| Traditional English phonetics | Becomes | As in |
|---|---|---|
| CONSONANTS | | |
| b | b | bat, be, able |
| d | d | dip, seed |
| f | f | fall, physic, laugh |
| g | g | gap, big |
| h | h | heat |
| | j | job, edge |
| k | k | cat, tick, kin, quit |
| l | l | lip, pull, help |
| m | m | ham, mat, limp |
| n | n | no, hang, bin |
| p | p | put, up |
| r | r | tar, ripe, part |
| s | s | sit, cite, hiss |
| t | t | hat, tin, butter |
| v | v | vine, have |
| w | w | why, wit |
| z | z | zoo, his, reads |
| | c | chin, itch |
| | sh | ash, action |
| | th | the, that |
| | zh | vision |
| | ng | bank, anger |

# Einführung

Das *deutsch-englische/englisch-deutsche Wörterbuch des 21.* Jahrhunderts ist ein unschätzbares Nachschlagwerk für Schüler, Geschäftsleute und Reisende. Statt Platz an weitschweifige, übermäßig komplizierte Definitionen zu verschwenden, bringt das *deutsch-englische/englisch-deutsche Wörterbuch des 21.* Jahrhunderts alle wesentlichen Informationen in einem kurzen, einfach zu gebrauchenden Format.

Durch das Doppelformat des *deutsch-englischen/englisch-deutschen Wörterbuch des 21.* Jahrhunderts erübrigt sich die Notwendigkeit für zwei Wörterbücher: eines, um deutsche Wörter und eines, um englische Wörter nachzuschlagen. Ein Schüler kann beispielsweise dieses Wörterbuch benutzen, um das englische Gegenstück eines unbekannten deutschen Wortes zu finden—*und* wie man einen bestimmten englischen Satz auf deutsch ausdrückt. Da jedes Wort sowohl auf deutsch als auch auf englisch erscheint, ist dieses Wörterbuch in jeder Situation nützlich. Ganz gleich, ob Sie in geschäftlicher Eigenschaft einen Ausdruck in einem internationalen Vertrag nachschlagen möchten, sich als Austauschstudent in einem deutschen Studentenheim niederlassen oder als Tourist versuchen, eine Speisekarte zu lesen, das *deutsch-englische/englisch-deutsche Wörterbuch des 21.* Jahrhunderts wird Ihnen helfen, schnelle, klare Übersetzungen vom Deutschen ins Englische—und vom Englischen ins Deutsche zu finden.

Jede Eintragung im *deutsch-englischen/englisch-deutschen Wörterbuch des 21.* Jahrhunderts erscheint in einem präzisen, leicht verständlichen Format. Die Stichworte sind in alphabetischer Reihenfolge aufgeführt, mit getrennten Abschnitten von A-Z für Deutsch-Englisch und für Englisch-Deutsch. Die Aussprache, komplett mit Silbenmarkierung, erscheint in Klammern nach jedem Stichwort, gefolgt von der Wortart (siehe Richtlinien zur Aussprache). Bei Hauptwörtern ist außerdem das Geschlecht angegeben, wobei M männliche, F weibliche und N sächliche Wörter kennzeichnet. Verben sind entweder als vt (transitives Verb) oder vi (intransitives Verb) markiert. Schließlich erscheint eine klare, knappe Übersetzung für jedes Wort, gefolgt von einer Liste verwandter Formen und typischer Sätze.

Aufgrund seiner Berücksichtigung gegenwärtiger Trends und Einfühlungsvermögen in die sich ständig verändernde Sprache bei der Auswahl der Wörter, Erklärungen, Übersetzungen und Aussprache bietet das *deutsch-englische/englisch-deutsche Wörterbuch des 21.* Jahrhunderts das zuverlässigste und aktuellste Nachschlagwerk, das es überhaupt gibt. Ganz gleich, ob es ums Sprechen, Schreiben oder Verstehen geht, im *deutsch-englischen/englisch-deutschen Wörterbuch des 21. Jahrhunderts* wird erfolgreich ein einfaches, präzises Format mit der Neigung zum Zeitgenössischen kombiniert, das als unentbehrliches Nachschlagwerk für jede Gelegenheit dienen wird.

# Richtlinien zur Aussprache

In diesem Wörterbuch wird eine eigene Art der phonetischen Aussprache benutzt. Es verläßt sich auf einfache, klar verständliche Symbole und Buchstaben. Es gibt keine griechischen Buchstaben, und die meisten Leute, ganz gleich, ob sie englisch oder deutsch sprechen, sollten in der Lage sein, die Wörter mit Hilfe dieser Richtlinien richtig auszusprechen.

Bei den englischen Wörtern basiert die Aussprache auf dem herkömmlichen amerikanischen Englisch. In Fällen, wo es mehr als eine akzeptable Sprechweise gibt, wurde die üblichste gewählt.

Die deutsche Sprache ist sehr konsequent in der Aussprache ihrer Vokale und Konsonanten. In diesem Umriß erscheinen sehr wenige Ausnahmen, wenn überhaupt welche. Die Gruppierungen in der linken Spalte sind für die deutsche Sprache, ihre englischen Gegenstücke erscheinen in der rechten Spalte.

| VOKALE | ENGLISCHES GEGENSTÜCK |
|---|---|
| ö–schwer zu vergleichen | wie ''*Eu*rope'' |
| ü = ooer | etwa wie ''sh*ooe*rn'' |
| ai = langes i | f*i*ght, m*i*ght |

Zwei Konsonanten, die einem Vokal folgen, verkürzen den Vokal etwas, doch nicht so sehr, daß ein ganz anderer Laut entsteht. Zum Beispiel klingt "haben" wie hah-ben, und machen mehr wie "makhen", mit einer schnelleren Sprechweise. Folgt ein weiterer Vokal einem Konsonanten, verlängert das den Vokal, wie im vorstehenden Beispiel gezeigt.

Konsonanten-Verbindungen werden wie folgt ausgesprochen:

| | |
|---|---|
| sch = wird immer "sh" ausgesprochen | shook, shape, shirk |
| ch = ist ein kehliges "kh" | deutsch: wichtig |
| sp, st, sch ist immer "shp" "sht" "sh" | deutsch: spielen, streichen, Schule |

nd = kann nd oder nt sein, wie im deutschen Wort "Land" = lahnt, oder Ende = ehndeh. Als Faustregel gilt:

Wenn dem nd ein weiterer Vokal folgt, bleibt es ein d, wenn nd jedoch am Ende des Wortes steht, klingt es wie t. Weitere Beispiele sind: Hund = klingt wie nt; Mund = nt, finden = nd, Mandeln = nd.

w = klingt immer wie v          wichtig = vihk-tihg

v = klingt meistens wie f, ein paar Ausnahmen, wie angegeben

f = f

z = ts in den meisten Fällen, wie in tse tse fly; in einer Konsonanten-Verbindung bleibt es "z"

j = immer wie das englische y: ja, Jacht, Joch, klingt immer "y"

b = kann wie p klingen, z.B. in "ab", klingt wie "ap" in abreißen (ahp-ruy-sen)

ss = ß "s-set" genannt, sieht wie ein großes B aus, ist aber ein Doppel-S. "abreißen" könnte wie "abreissen" aussehen, doch benutzt man das ß, besonders zwischen zwei Vokalen.

qu wird auf deutsch wie "kv" ausgesprochen

th wird in deutschen Wörtern wie "t" ausgesprochen

h wird am Anfang deutscher Wörter und zwischen Vokalen in Ausrufen ausgesprochen, während es im Englischen oft stumm ist.

ung ist immer "oong"

ing ist genau wie es aussieht "ing"

heit wird immer "huyt" ausgesprochen; das gleiche gilt für keit = kuyt

g = klingt manchmal wie k, wie angegeben, besonders wenn es am Ende eines Wortes steht

*Zusammenziehungen*

Im Deutschen wird jeder Buchstabe ausgesprochen. Es gibt keine stummen Buchstaben, und sie werden nicht zusammengezogen wie englische Doppellaute, z.B. "mail", "fire". Die "yer" oder "yuh" Elision wie im Englischen gibt es nicht. Die beiden Vokale werden getrennt, wie im deutschen Wort "Feier", das "fai-air" ausgesprochen wird, ohne "y"-Laut dazwischen. Doppellaute kommen in den Kombinationen ai, au, ei vor, und sie werden immer auf genau die gleiche Weise ausgesprochen.

     Ein Stimmritzenverschlußlaut, bei dem der Laut ganz hinten in der Kehle beginnt, wird am Anfang aller Wörter benutzt, die mit einem Vokal beginnen. Er wird immer in zusammengesetzten Wörtern zwischen dem ersten und dem zweiten Wort benutzt, wenn das zweite mit einem Vokal beginnt.

# A

**Aal** [ahl] *n* M eel

**Aasfresser** [ahs•FREH•sair] *n* M scavenger

**Ab- Verkürzung** [ahb•fair•KURTS•oong] *n* F abbreviation

**abbinden** [AP•BIN•den] *vt* strangulate; untie

**Abbruch** [AP•brookh] *n* M breakdown (machine)

**Abdomen** [AHB•do•muhn] *n* N abdomen

**Abdruck** [AP•druhk] *n* M imprint

**Abend** [AH•bent] *n* M evening

**Abendessen** [AH•bent•ES•sen] *n* N dinner

**Abendstern** [AH•bent•SHTAIRN] *n* M vespers

**Abenteuer** [AHB•ent•OI•air] *n* N adventure

**abenteuerlich** [ahb•ent•OI•air•LIK] *adj* adventurous

**aber** [AH•bair] *conj* but

**Abfälle** [ap•FEHL•eh] *npl* M trash

**abfahren** [AP•fahr•en] *vi* depart; leave; set out

**Abfahrt** [AP•fahrt] *n* F departure

**Abfall** [AP•fal] *n* M secession

**Abfälle** npl [AP•fahl] *n* M rubbish; descent; waste

**Abfassung** [AP•fah•soong] *n* F composition

**abflachen** [AP•flah•ken] *vt* flatten

**Abfluß** [AP•floos] *n* M drain

**Abfuhr** [AP•fuhr] *n* removal

**Abführmittel** [AP•fuhr•MI•tel] *n* N laxative

**abgehen** [AP•gai•ehn] *vi* deviate; go off; exit

**abgemagert** [AP•geh•mah•gairt] *adj* emaciated; shrunken

**abgenutzt** [AP•ge•nuhtst] *adj* hackneyed

**Abgeordneter** [AP•ge•OHRD•net•air] *n* M deputy

**abgerissen** [AP•geh•RIH•sen] *adj* ragged

**abgerissen** [AP•geh•RIH•sen] *adj* tattered

**Abgott** [AP•goht] *n* M idol

**abgrasen** [AP•grah•zen] *vt* graze

**Abgrund** [AP•gruhnt] *n* M abyss

**Abgrund** [AP•groont] *n* M chasm

**abhängen von** [AP•haing•en fuhn] *vi* depend

**abhalten** [AP•hal•ten] *vt* deter; hold off; keep off

**Abhandlung** [AP•hahnd•loong] *n* F treatise; dissertation; essay

**Abhang** [AP•hahng] *n* M slope

**abholen** [AP•ho•len] *vt* fetch

**abkommen** [AP•koh•men] *vi* come away; get away; take off

**abkühlen** [AP•koohl•ehn] *vt* chill

**abkürzen** [AHB•kuyurts•uhn] *vt* abbreviate

**Abkürzung** [AP•koorts•oong] *n* F shortcut

**abladen** [AP•lah•den] *vt* dump; unload; discharge

**ablaufen** [AP•lou•fen] *vi* expire; wear out

**ablehnen** [AP•lai•nen] *vt* refuse; decline; reject

**ablehnen** [AP•lai•nen] *vt* reject

**Ablehnung** [AP•lai•noong] *n* F denial

**ableiten** [AP•luy•ten] *vt* infer

**ablenken** [AP•lenk•en] *vt* deflect; turn away, aside or off

**ablösen** [AP•luh•zen] *vt* redeem; take off; detach

**Ablösung** [-oong] *n* F redemption

**ablohnen** [AP•loh•nen] *vt* pay off; dismiss

**Abnahme** [AP•nah•me] *n* F decrease

**abnehmen** [AP•nai•men] *vi* wane; decrease; lessen

**Abneigung** [AP•nuy•goong] *n* F dislike; reluctance; unwillingness

**Abordnung** [AP•ord•noong] *n* F delegation

**abraten** [AP•rah•ten] *vt* dissuade

**abreiben** [ap•ruy•ben] *vt* rub-down

**Abriß** [AP•ris] *n* M epitome; sketch; draft; summary

**abrupt** [AHB•roopt] *adj* abrupt

**abrüsten** [AP•ROOST•en] *vt* demobilize; disarm

**abrüsten** [AP•ROO•sten] *vt* disarm

**absagen** [AHP•zah•gehn] *vt* cancel; call off

**Absatz** [AP•tats] *n* M paragraph; break; pause

**abschätzen** [AP•shet•tsen] *vt* evaluate

**Abscheu** [ap•shoi] *n* M distaste

**abscheulich** [AB•shoy•lik] *adj* abominable

**abscheulich** [AP•shoi•lihk] *adj* hideous

**abscheulich** [AP•shoi•lihk] *adj* outrageous

**Abschied** [AP•sheed] *n* M leave

**abschießen** [AP•shee•sen] *vt* launch; discharge; shoot off

**abschließen** [AP•shlee•sen] *vt* transact; terminate; conclude

**Klammer** [KLAH•mair] *vt n* F clip

**abschöpfen** [AP•shuhp•fen] *vt* skim

**abschreiben** [AP•shruy•ben] *vt* transcribe

**abschwächen** [AP•shvehk•en] *vt* understate

**abschweifen** [AP•shvai•fen] *vt* digress

absehen von [AP•zai•en fon]
vt refrain

Absender [AP•zehn•dair] n M
sender

absetzen [AP•zets•en] vt
depose

Absicht [AP•zihkt] n F intent

absichtlich [AP•zihkt•lihk] adj
deliberate

absichtlich [AP•zihkt•lihk] adj
intentional

absolut unbedingt
[AHP•so•LOOT]
[uhn•buh•DINGKT] adj
absolute

absondern [AP•zohn•dairn] vt
dissociate

absondern [AP•zon•dairn] vt
seclude

absondern [AP•zohn•dairn] vt
secrete

absondern [AP•zohn•dairn] vt
sequester

Absonderung
[ap•ZOHN•dair•oong] n F
isolation

Absonderung [-oong] n F
sequestration

abstehen [AP•shtai•en] vi
desist

Absteig [AP•shtuyg] n M
descent

absteigen [AP•shtuy•ten] vi
dismount

Abstimmung [AP•shtihm•oong]
n F voting

absurd [ab•SOORD] adj
preposterous

Abtei [AB•tuy] n F abbey

Abtei [AB•tuy] n F abbey

Abteilung [AP•tuy•loong] n F
compartment; division

Abteilung [AP•tuy•loong] n F
department

Abteufer [AP•toi•fair] n M
sinker

abtrennen [AP•tren•nen] vt
sever

abtreten [AP•trai•ten] vt vi
cede

abwärts [AP•vairts] adj
downward

Abwanderung
[AP•vahn•dair•OONG] n F
drift

Abwasserkanal
[AP•vah•sair•kah•NAHL] n M
sewer

Abweichen [AP•vaiy•khen] n
N dissent

Abweichung [AP•vuyhk•oong]
n F variance

abweisen [AP•vai•sen] vt repel
refuse; turn down

abweisen [AP•vuy•zen] vt
repulse

abwenden [AP•ven•den] vt
divert; avert one's eyes

abwerfen [AP•vair•fen] vt
discard; release

abwesend [AHP•vai•zunt] adj
absent

abwischen [AP•vih•shen] vt
wipe

Abzeichen [AP•tsai•khen] n N
emblem; badge; stripe

abziehen [AP•tsee•en] vt
deduct

abziehen [AP•tsee•en] vt
subtract; pull down; deduct

Abziehen n N subtraction

**Abzug** [AP•tsoog] *n* M
deduction; withdrawal; retreat

**abzweigen** [AP•tsvai•gen] *vi*
diverge

**ach** [ahk] *excl* alas

**Achse** [AHK•seh] *n* F axis

**Achse** [AHK•seh] *n* F axle

**acht** [ahkht] *num* eight

**achte** [-eh] *num* eighth

**Achteck** [AHKt•ehk] *n* N
octagon

**achtsam** [AHKt•zahm] *adj* alert

**Achtung** [AHK•toong] *n* F
Attention

**achtzehn** [-tsain] *num* eighteen

**achtzehnte** [-tsainteh] *num*
eighteenth

**achtzig** [AHKHT•tsig] *num*
eighty

**Adel** [AH•del] *n* M gentry

**Adel** [AH•del] *n* M nobility

**Ader** [AH•dair] *n* F vein; artery;
vessel

**Adjektiv** [AD•yek•TEEV] *n* N
adjective

**Adler** [AHD•lair] *n* M eagle

**adlig** [AHD•lihg] *adj* noble

**Adoption** [AH•dop•tsee•OHN]
*n* F adoption

**Adreßbuch** [AH•dres•boohk] *n*
N directory

**Adresse** [AHD•res•uh] *n* F
address

**Adresse** [AH•dreh•seh] *n* F
return address

**Advent** [AHD•vent] *n* M
Advent

**Adverb** [AHD•fairb] *n* M
adverb

**Ächzen** [EHKS•sen] *n* N moan

**Ägyptien** [ai•GOOP•tee•en] *n*
Egypt

**ägyptisch** [ai•GOOP•tish] *adj*
Egyptian

**ähnlich** [AIN•lihk] *adj* similar;
*adv* similarly

**ähnlich sein** [-zuyn] *vt*
resemble

**Ähnlichkeit** [AIN•lihk•kuyt] *n*
resemblance

**Ähnlichkeit** [AIN•lihk•kuyt] *n*
F similitude

**Ähnlichkeit** [AIN•lihk•kuyt] *n*
F likeness

**älter, Ältere** [AIL•tair] [-e] *adj*
*n* M elder

**Älterer** [AIL•tair•air] *n* M
senior

**älteres Fräulein** [AIL•tair•es
FROI•luyn] *n* N spinster

**ältlich** [ELT•lihk] *adj* elderly

**Äquator** [EH•kva•tor] *n* M
equator

**Ärger** [AIR•gair] *n* F anger

**Ärger** [AIR•gair] *n* M huff

**ärgerlich** [AIR•gair•lik] *n*
annoying

**ärgerlich** [AIR•gair•lihk] *adj*
hot-tempered

**ärgerlich** [-lihk] *adj* irritating

**ärgerlich** [AIR•gair•lihk] *adj*
resentful

**ärgern** [AIR•gairn] *vt* aggravate

**ärgern** [AIR•gairn] *vt* annoy

**ärgern** [AIR•gairn] *vt* displease

**Ärgernis** [AIR•gair•nis] *n* N
nuisance

**Ärmel** [AIR•mel] *n* M sleeve

**Äthiopien**
[AI•tee•OH•PEE•uhn] *n*
Ethiopia

ätzend [EH•tsend] *adj* caustic

äußer [OI•sair] *adj* external

äußer; Äußere [OI•sair] [-e]
*adj n* N exterior

äußerlich [OI•sair•lihk] *adj*
outward

äußern [OI•sairn] *vi* utter

äußerst [OI•sairst] *adj* ultimate

äußerst [OI•sairst] *adj* utmost

äußerst; Äußerste [OI•sairst]
[-e] *adj n* N extreme

Affe [AH•fuh] *n* F ape

Affe [AH•feh] *n* M monkey

Afghanistan [af•GAH•ni•stahn]
*n* Afghanistan

Afrika [AH•free•kah] *n* Africa

aggressiv [ahg•GREHS•seev]
*adj* aggressive

ahnungslos [AHN•oongs•los]
*adj* unsuspecting

Ahorn [AH•horn] *n* M maple

AIDS [aids] *n* F AIDS

Akademie
[Ah•KAH•duh•MEE] *n* F
academy

akademisch
[AH•kah•DAIM•ish] *adj*
scholastic

Akt [ahkt] *n* M act

Aktentasche
[AHK•ten•TAH•scheh] *n* F
briefcase; portfolio

Aktionär [AHK•tsee•ON•air] *n*
M stockholder

aktiv tätig [ahk•TEEV] [tai•tig]
*adj* active

Akzent [AHK•tsent] *n* M accent

akzeptabel
[AHK•tsep•TAH•bel] *adj*
eligible

akzeptieren annehmen
[AHK•tsep•TEER•uhn]
[ahn•naim•uhn] *vt* accept

Alarm [AHL•arm] *n* M alarm

Albanien [AHL•bahn•eey•ehn]
*n* Albania

albern [AHL•bairn] *adj* foolish;
silly; absurd; inane

Algebra [AHL•geh•brah] *n* F
algebra

Algerien [ahl•GAIR•EEY•un] *n*
Algeria

Alkohol [AHL•koh•OHL] *n* M
alcohol; liquor

alkoholisch; Alkoholiker
[AHL•koh•HOL•ish]
[ahl•koh•hol•eek•air] *adj n* M
alcoholic

Allbekanntheit
[AL•beh•KAHNT•huyt] *n* F
notoriety

alle [AHL•leh] *adj* all

allein [ahl•LAIN] *adj adv* alone;
*adj* M solo

Alleinsein [ah•LUYN•zuyn] *n*
N privacy

Allergie [AHL•air•GEE] *n* F
allergy

allergisch [ahl•AIR•gish] *adj*
allergic

Allerheiligen
[AHL•air•HUY•LIH•gen]
Halloween

alles [AHL•es] *pr* everything

alles was [AH•les•VAHS]
whatever

allgemein [AL•geh•MUYN] *adj*
general

allmächtig [AL•MEHK•tig] *adj*
omnipotent

**alltäglich** [AL•TAIYG•likh] *adj* commonplace

**alltäglich** [AL•TAIG•lihk] *adj* trivial

**allwissend** [AHL•VIH•send] *adj* omniscience

**Alp** [alp] *n* M nightmare

**Alphabet** [AHL•fah•beht] *n* N alphabet

**als** [ahls] than

**alsbald** [ALS•balt] *adv* presently

**Alse** [AHL•seh] *n* F shad

**alt** [ahlt] *adj* old; stale

**Alter** [ahl•tair] *n* N age; old age

**altertümlich** [AL•tair•tOOM•lik] *adj* archaic

**altmodisch** [-moh•dish] *adj* old-fashioned; outmoded

**Altwaren** [AHLT•vahr•en] *npl* junk

**am Boden kriechen** [ahm BOH•den KREE•khen] *vi* grovel

**am Bord** [ahm BOHRD] *n* board (on board)

**am weitesten** [ahm VAI•test•EN] *adj adv* furthest; farthest

**Amateur** [AHM•eh•toor] *n* M amateur

**Ameise** [AH•mai•zeh] *n* F ant

**Amerika** [ah•MAIR•eek•ah] *n* N America

**Amnestie** [ahm•NEHST•ee] *n* F amnesty

**Amsel** [AHM•zel] *n* blackbird

**Amtsinsignien** [AMPTS•in•SIG•NEE•en] *npl* regalia

**Amtstracht** [AHMTS•trahkt] *n* F vestment; official attire

**amüsant** [AH•moo•SAHNT] *adj* entertaining

**amusieren** [AH•moo•SEEYR•ehn] *vt* amuse; entertain

**an bei zu auf** [ahn] [bai] [tsoo] [owf] *prep* at

**an Zahl übertreffen** [ahn TSAHL uh•bair•TREH•fen] *vt* outnumber

**Analogie** [AHN•eh•LOH•gee] *n* F analogy

**Analphabetentum** [AHN•ahl•FAH•bait•en•TOOM] *n* N illiteracy

**analphabetisch** *adj* illiterate

**Analyse** [AHN•eh•LOOZ•eh] *n* F analysis

**analysieren** [AHN•ih•LIH•ZEEYr•ehn] *vi* analyze

**Ananas** [AH•nah•NAHS] *npl* pineapple

**Anarchie** [AHN•ahr•KEE] *n* F anarchy

**anbauen** [AHN•BOU•en] *vt* cultivate; grow; raise

**anbeten** [AHN•BAIT•en] *vt* adore; worship

**Anbeter in** [-tair] [in] *n* M worshipper

**anbieten** [AN•bee•ten] *vt* offer; tender

**anbinden** [AHN•bin•den] *vt* tether; tie-up

**Anblick** [AHN•blihk] *n* M glimpse

**Anblick; Aspekt** [AHN•blik] [ah•shpekt] *n* M aspect

**Andenken** [AHN•daink•en] *n* N
keepsake; souvenir

**ander** [AHN•dair] *adj* other

**anderswo** [ahn•dairs•voh] *adv*
elsewhere

**anderweitig**
[AHN•dair•VUY•tig] *adj*
ulterior

**andeuten** [AHN•doi•ten] *vt*
imply; signify

**Andeutung** [AHN•doi•toong] *n*
F innuendo; hint; indication

**anerkennen**
[AHN•air•KEN•uhn] *vt*
acknowledge

**anfällig** *adj* susceptible

**Anfälligkeit**
[AHN•fehl•ig•kuyt] *n* F
susceptibility

**Anfänger** [AHN•feng•gair] *n* M
beginner

**anfänglich** [AHN•feng•lihk] *adj*
initial

**Anfall** [AHN•fal] *n* M stroke
(medical); fit; seizure

**Anfang** [AHN•fahng] *n* M
beginning

**Anfang** [AHN•fahng] *n* M
outset; beginning

**anfangen** [AHN•fahng•gen] *vt*
*vi* begin; commence

**anfangen beginnen**
[AHN•fahng•en]
[BEH•GIHN•nen] *vi* start

**angeboren**
[AHN•geh•BOHR•en] *adj*
inherent; innate

**Angeklagter**
[AHN•ge•KLOG•TE] *n* M
defendant

**Angelegenheit**
[AHN•geh•lAIG•en•HUYT] *n*
F affair (business); concern

**Angelpunkt**
[AHN•gel•POONKT] *n* M
hub; pivot

**angemessen**
[AHN•ge•MEH•sen] *adj*
pertinent

**Angemessenheit**
[AHN•geh•MEHS•sen•HUYT]
*n* F sufficiency

**angenehm** [AHN•geh•NAIM]
*adj* pleasant; agreeable;
comfortable

**angenommen**
[AHN•ge•NO•men] *adj*
hypothetical

**Angestellte**
[AHN•ge•SHTEL•teh] *n* M
employee

**angreifen** [AHN•grai•fen] *vt*
attack; *vi* tackle

**angreifend** [AHN•gruy•fend]
*adj* offensive

**Angriff** [AHN•grihf] *n* M
onslaught

**Angst** [ahng•st] *n* F anxiety;
dread

**Anhänger** [AHN•heng•air] *n* M
conformist

**Anhalt** [AHN•hahlt] *n* M
support hold; footing

**Anker** [AHN•kair] *n* M anchor;
lever

**anklagen** [AHN•klahg•gun] *vt*
accuse

**anklagen** {AHN•klah•gen] *vt*
indict

**Ankleiden** [AHN•kluy•den] *n* N
dressing

**ankommen** [AHN•koh•men] *vi*
arrive

**ankündigen**
[AHN•KOOND•ig•en] *vt*
advertise; announce

**Ankunft** [AHN•koonft] *n* F
arrival; coming

**Anlasser** [AHN•LAH•sair] *n* M
self-starter

**anmelden** [AN•MEHL•den] *vt*
announce; notify; report

**anmutig** [AHN•MOO•tig] *adj*
graceful

**annehmen** [AHN•NAIM•en] *vt*
adopt; assume

**Annehmlichkeit**
[AHN•NAIM•likh•kuyt] *n* F
convenience

**Anordnung** [AHN•ohrd•noong]
*n* F disposal

**anpassen** [AHN•pah•sen] *vt*
conform

**anreden** [AHN•raid•uhn] *vt*
address

**anregen** [AHN•rai•gen] *vt*
incite; stimulate

**anregend** [AHN•rai•gend] *adj*
suggestive

**Anregungsmittel**
[AHN•rai•goongs•MIH•tel] *n*
N stimulant

**Anrichte** [AHN•rihk•teh] *n* F
dresser; bureau (furniture)
chest of drawers

**Anrichtetisch**
[AHN•rihk•teh•TISH] *n* M
sideboard

**Anruf** [AHN•roof] *n* M phone
call

**anrufen Anruf** [AHN•roof•ehn]
[ahn•roof] *vt n* M call

**ansammeln**
[AHN•ZAHM•meln] *vt*
accumulate

**anschauen** [AHN•SHOU•en] *vt*
look at; view

**anscheinend**
[AHN•SHAI•nehnd] *adv*
apparently

**Anschlußgleis** [AHN•shluhs] *n*
N siding

**Ansehen** [AHN•zai•en] *n* N
credit

**ansengen** [AHN•zeng•en] *vt*
singe; scorch

**Ansichtskarte**
[AHN•ZIKTS•kahr•teh] *n* F
postcard

**Ansiedlung**
[AHN-ZEED-loong] *n* F
settlement

**anspornen** [AHN•shpor•nen] *vt*
urge

**Anspruch** [AHN•shpruct] *npl* M
claim; right

**anspruchslos**
[AHN•shproohks•los] *adj*
unassuming; undemanding

**anspruchsvoll**
[AHN•shprooks•VOL] *adj*
demanding

**anständig** [AHN•shten•dig] *adj*
decent

**anständig** [AHN•shten•dig] *adj*
modest

**anständig** [AHN•shten•dig] *adj*
reputable

**Anstand** [AHN•shtand] *n* M
decency

**Anstand** [AHN•shtahnd] *n* M
decorum

anstarren [AHN•stahren] vt
stare at

ansteckend [AHN•shtek•end]
adj contagious; infectious

Ansteckung
[AHN•SHTEHK•oong] n F
infection

anstelle [AHN•STELL•eh]
instead of; in place of

anstellen [AHN•SHTEL•en] vt
place; employ; hire

Anstellung sich verabreden
[AHN•SHTEL•lung]
[zik•VAIR•AP•rai•den] n vt F
appointment; to have an
appointment w/someone

anstiften [AHN•shtif•ten] vt
instigate

anstößig [AHN•shtuh•sig] adj
F obnoxious; offensive

Anstoß [AHN•shtohs] n M
umbrage

Anstrengung
[AHN•shtreng•oong] n F
strain

Anteil [AHN•tuyl] n N quota;
part; portion

Anthologie
[AHN•toh•loh•GEE] n F
anthology

antik [AHN•teek] adj antique

Antlitz [AHNT•lihts] n N
visage

Antrag [AN•trahg] n M petition

antreiben [AHN•truy•ben] vt
drive; propel

Antrieb [AHN•treeb] n M
incentive; stimulation

Antwort [AHNT•vorht] n
response; answer

antworten [AHNT•vohr•tehn]
vt answer; reply

anvertrauen
[AHN•FAIR•trou•en] vt
confide something to
someone; commit

Anwalt [AHN•vahlt] n M
solicitor; lawyer

anwenden [AHN•ven•den] vt
exert

anwesend Gegenwart bieten
[AHN•vai•zent]
[gai•gen•vahrt] [bee•ten] adj n
v F present

Anwesenheit
[AHN•VAI•zen•HUYT] n F
presence

Anzeichen [AHN•tsuy•khen] n
N symptom

Anzeige [AHN•tsaig•eh] n F
advertisement; classified ad

anzeigen [AHN•tsai•gen] vt
indicate; report (to the police)

Anzeiger [-air] n M indicator;
marker

anziehen [AHN•tsee•hen] vt
attract

anziehend [AHN•tsee•hend]
adj attractive

Anziehunskraft Reiz (m)
[AHN•TSEEH•oongs•krahft]
[raitz] n M attraction; force of
attraction

Anzug [AHN•tsoog] n M outfit

anzünden [AHN•tsuhn•den] vt
ignite

Anzünden n N ignition

Apfel [AHP•fel] n M apple

Apfelwein [AHP•fel•VUYN] n
M cider

Apotheke n F pharmacy

**Apotheker** [AH•poh•TAI•kair] *n* M druggist; pharmacist

**Apparat** [AH•pah•RAHT] *n* M gadget

**Appetit** [AH•puh•TEET] *n* M appetite

**Aprikose** [ah•PREE•KOH•ze] *n* F apricot

**April** [ah•PRIL] *n* M April

**Arbeit** [AHR•beit] *n* F employment; job; labor; work

**Arbeiten** *n* N working

**Arbeiter** [AHR•buy•tair] *n* M laborer; worker

**Arbeitgeber** [AHR•buyt•gai•bair] *n* M employer

**arbeitslos** [ahr•buyts•los] *adj* unemployed

**Arbeitslosigkeit** [-ig•kuyt] *n* F unemployment

**Arbeitstag** [AHR•buyts•tahg] *n* M workday

**Archäologie** [AHR•kai•oh•loh•gee] *n* F archaeology

**Architekt (in)** [AHR•kih•tekt] [-in] *n* M architect

**Architektur** [AHR•kee•tek•TOOR] *n* F architecture

**argumentieren** [AHR•gew•men•TEER•en] *vi* argue

**Argwohn** [AHRG•vohn] *n* M suspicion

**Arm** [ahrm] *n* M arm

**arm** [ahrm] *adj* needy; poor

**Armband** [AHRM•bahnt] *n* N bracelet

**Armbanduhr** [AHRM•bant•OOR] *n* F watch, observance

**Armbranduhr** [~•bahn•door] *n* F wristwatch

**Armee Heer (n)** [ahr•MEE] [hair] *n* F army

**armselig** [ARM•zee•lig] *adj* paltry

**Armut** [AHRM•oot] *n* F poverty

**Aroma Duft** [AH•ROH•mah] [dooft] *n* N aroma

**arrangieren ausrichten** [AHR•RANJ•jeer•en] [OWS•rik•ten] *vt* arrange

**arrogant** [AHR•ROH•gahnt] *adj* arrogant

**arrogant** [AHR•ROH•gant] *adj* overbearing

**Art 1** [ahrt] *n* F manner; species

**Art 2** [ahrt] *n* F sort

**Art sortieren** [ahrt] [sohr•teer•en] *n vt* F sort

**Artikel** [AHR•TEE•kel] *n* M article

**Arzt** [ahrtst] *n* M physician

**Arzt Ärztin** [ahrtst] [AIRTS•in] *n* M doctor

**Asche** [AH•sheh] *n* F ash; cinder

**Aschenbecher** [AH•shen•BREK•ker] *n* M ashtray

**Aschenputtel** [AHSH•ehn•PUH•tel] *n* N Cinderella

**Aspirine** [ASP•eer•EEN•eh] *n* F aspirin

**Astrologie** [AH•shtroh•loh•GEE] *n* F astrology

**Astronomie**
[AH•shtroh•noh•MEE] *n* F
astronomy

**Atelier** [AH•teh•LEER] *n* N
studio

**Atem** [AH•tem] *n* M breath

**atmen** [AHT•men] *vi* breathe

**auch** [ouhk] *adv* also; too

**auf** [ouf] *prep* on

**auf Computer umstellen** [ouf
KOM•POO•tair
oom•shtel•uhn] *vt* computerize

**auf dem elektrischen Stuhl
hinrichten** [ouf daim
el•EK•TRI•shen shtool
HIN•RIHK•ten] *vt* electrocute

**auf den Zehenspitzen** [ouf
dain TSAi•en•SHPIT•sen]
tiptoe

**auf halbem Weg** [ouf
HALB•en vaig] *adj* halfway

**auf keiner Landkarte
verzeichnet** [ouf KUYN•air
lAHNT•KAHR•teh
FAIR•TSUYHK•net]
uncharted

**aufbewahren**
[OUF•beh•VAHR•en] *vi*
preserve; keep; maintain

**aufblasen** [OUF•blah•zen] *vt*
inflate

**aufdecken** [OUF•dek•en] *vt*
uncover

**Aufdeckung** [OUF•dek•oong] *n*
F detection

**aufdrängen** [OUF•drehng•en]
*vt* impose

**aufeinanderfolgend**
[OUF•uyn•AHN•dair•FOL•gent]
*adj* consecutive

**Aufenthaltsort**
[OUF•ent•HALTS•ort] *n* M
sojourn

**auferlegen** [OUF•air•LAI•gen]
*vt* enforce; entail; impose

**aufessen** [OUF•es•sen] *vt*
consume

**auffangen** [OUF•fahng•en] *vt*
intercept

**aufflammen** [OUF•flah•men] *vt*
kindle

**auffüllen** [OUF•FUH•len] *vt*
replenish

**Aufgabe** [OUF•GAH•be] *n* F
task; resignation

**aufgeben 1** [OWF•gay•bun] *vt*
abandon; forgo

**aufgeben 2** [OUF•gai•ben] *vt*
relinquish; resign

**aufgedunsen**
[OWF•geh•DOONZ•en] *adj*
bloated; turgid

**aufgeregt** [OUF•ge•RAIGT]
*adj* excited

**aufgeschlossen**
[OUF•geh•SHLOH•sen] *adj*
open-minded

**aufhängen** [OUF•heng•en] *vt*
suspend

**aufhalten** [OUF•hal•ten] *vt*
detain; maintain; delay; halt;
stop; keep open

**aufhören** [OWF•hoor•ehn] *vt vi*
cease

**aufhören halten**
[OUF•her•ehn] [hahl•ten] *vt*
stop

**aufklären** [OUF•klair•en] *vt*
clarify; enlighten

**Aufklärung** [OUF•klair•oong] *n*
F reconnaissance;
enlightenment

**aufknöpfen** [OUF•knuhpf•en] *vt* unbutton

**aufknoten** [OUF•knoh•ten] *vt* untie

**Auflage** [OUF•lah•geh] *n* F imposition; condition

**auflauern** [OUF•lou•airn] *vt* waylay

**Auflehnung** [OUF•laihn•oong] *n* F mutiny

**auflesen** [OUF•lai•zen] *vt* glean; (col) pick up

**auflösen** [OUF•loo•zen] *vt* disintegrate; dissolve; esolve

**aufmachen** [OUF•mahk•en] *vt* undo

**aufmerksam** [OWF•mairk•zahm] *adj* attentive; mindful

**Aufmerksamkeit** [OWF•mairk•zahm•KUYT] *n* F attention

**Aufnahme** [OUF•nah•meh] *n* F photograph

**aufnehmen** [OUF•nai•men] *vt* record

**aufrecht** [OUF•rehkt] *adj* erect

**aufregen** [OUF•rai•gen] *vt* excite

**aufregend** [OUF•rai•gent] *adj* exciting

**Aufregung** [OUF•rai•goong] *n* F commotion; fuss

**aufreiben** [OUF•RUY•ben] *vt* fret

**aufrichten** [ouf•rikh•ten] *vt* cock (a gun)

**Aufruhr** [OUF•ruhr] *n* M revolt; riot; uproar

**aufs Spiel setzen** [OUFS shpeel ZET•tsen] gamble

**Aufsatz** [OUF•zahts] *n* M essay

**aufschneiden** [OUF•shnuy•den] *vt* slit

**aufschreien** [OUS•schruy•en] *vi* exclaim

**aufschwellen** [OUF•shvel•len] *vi* swell

**Aufseher** [OUF•zai•air] *n* M controller; overseer

**aufsenkrecht** [OUF•zenk•REHKT] *adj* upright

**aufspalten** [OUF•shpahl•ten] *vt* laminate

**Aufspürer** [OUF•shpoor•air] *n* M tracer

**aufständig** [OUF•SHTENd•ig] *adj* rebellious

**Aufstand** [OUF•shtant] *n* M rebellion

**Aufstehen** [OUF•shtai•hen] *n* N uprising

**aufsteigen** [OUF•shtuy•gen] *vi* climb; soar; be promoted

**aufstellen** [OUF•shtel•len] *vt* situate

**Aufstellung** [OUF•shtel•loong] *n* F disposition

**auftauchen** [OUF•TOU•khen] *vi* emerge

**Aufteilung** [OUF•TUY•loong] *n* F partition

**Auftrag** [OUF•trahg] *n* M commission

**Auftreffen** [OUF•tre•fen] *n* N impact

**auftreiben** [OUF•truy•ben] *vt* muster

**aufwärts** [OUF•vairts] *adv* upward; upward trend

**aufwecken** [OUF•vehk•en] *vt*
rouse; waken

**aufzählen** [OUF•tsai•len] *vt*
enumerate

**Aufzug** [OUF•tsoog] *n* M
elevator

**Augapfel** [OUG•ahp•fel] *n* M
eyeball

**Auge** [OU•ge] *n* N eye

**augenblicklich**
[OU•gen•BLIHK•lihk] *adj*
immediate; instant; in the
blink of an eye

**Augenbraue** [-brou•e] *n* F
eyebrow

**Augenlid** [OU•gen•lid] *n* N
eyelid

**Augenwimper** [-VIM•pair] *n* F
eyelash

**August** [ow•goost] *n* M August

**aus** [ous] *prep* from, out of; von
(place) ~\ from (place)

**aus dem Gleichgewicht
gebracht** [ous daim
gluyhk•geh•vihkt geh•brahkt]
unbalanced

**ausatem** [OUS•AHT•em] *vt*
exhale

**ausbilden** [ OUS•BIL•den]
train; educate

**Ausbildung** [OUS•bil•doong] *n*
F education

**ausborgen** [OWS•bohr•gen] *vt*
borrow

**ausbrechen** [OUS•brek•ken] *vt*
erupt; chip

**ausbreiten** [OUS•bruy•ten] *vt*
expand; spread

**Ausbreitung** [-oong] *n* F
expansion

**Ausbruch** [OUS•broohk] *n* M
eruption; outbreak; outburst

**ausbrüten** [OUS•bruh•ten] *vt*
hatch

**Ausdauer** [OUS•DOU•air] *n* F
endurance

**ausdehnen** [OUS•dai•nen] *vt*
enlarge; extend; dilate

**Ausdehnung** [OUS•dai•noong]
*n* F extension

**Ausdruck** [OUS•droohk] *n* M
euphemism; expression;
utterance

**ausdrücklich**
[OUS•DROOHK•lihk] *adj*
expressive

**ausdrucksvoll**
[OUS•DROOKS•fol] *adj*
demonstrative

**Ausdünstung**
[OUS•DUHNST•oong] *n* F
transpiration

**Ausfahrt** [OUS•fahrt] *n* F exit

**ausfeilen** [OUS•fuy•len] *vt*
chisel

**ausfindig machen**
[OUS•FIN•dig MAH•ken] *vt*
locate

**Ausflug** [OUS•floog] *n* M
excursion; outing

**Ausfluß** [OUS•floos] *n* M
emission

**ausführen** [OUS•foor•en] *vi*
perform

**Ausführung** [OUS•foor•oong]
*n* F performance

**Ausgabe** [OUS•gah•be] *n* F
edition; expenditure

**Ausgang** [OUS•gahng] *n* M
exit

**Ausgang haben** [OUS•gahng] [hah•ben] have the evening off; have a pass

**ausgearbeitet** [OUS•ge•ahr•buy•tet] *adj* elaborate

**ausgeben** [OUS•gai•ben] *vt* spend; expend

**ausgebraucht** [OUS•geh•brouhkt] *adj* used up

**ausgehungert** [OUS•ge•HOONG•airt] *adj* famished

**ausgenommen** [OUS•ge•NOH•men] *adj* exempt

**ausgeschlossen** [OUS•geh•SHLOH•sen] *adj* outgoing

**ausgesprochen** [OUS•geh•SHPROH•khen] *adj* pronounced

**ausgestorben** [OUS•ge•SHTOR•ben] *adj* extinct

**Ausgestoßener** [OUS•geh•SHTOH•SEN•air] *n* M outcast

**ausgestreckt** [OUS•geh•sHTREHKT] *adj* sprawl

**ausgezeichnet** [OUS•ge•TSAIHK•net] *adj* excellent

**Ausgleich** [OUS•gluyhk] *n* M equation

**ausgraben** [OUS•grah•ben] *vt* excavate; unearth

**aushelfen** [OUS•helf•uhn] *vi* accommodate

**Auskleidung** [OUS•kluy•doong] *n* F lining

**Ausladung** [OUS•lah•doong] *n* F discharge

**Ausländer** [OUS•len•dair] *n* M foreigner

**auslafen** [OUS•lau•fen] *vt* empty

**ausleeren** [OUS•lai•ren] *vt* evacuate

**ausleihen** [OUS•luy•en] *vt* lend

**ausliefern** [OUS•lee•fairn] *vt* extradite

**auslieren** [OUS•lee•ren] *vt* wear out

**auslöschen** [OUS•luh•shen] *vt* extinguish; obliterate

**Auslöser** [OUS•luh•zair] *n* M trigger

**Ausmaß** [OUS•mahs] *n* N magnitude

**Ausnahme** [OUS•nah•me] *n* F exception

**ausnahmslos** [OUS•nahms•los] *adv* invariably

**Ausnutzung** [OUS•nuhts•oong] *n* F exploit

**ausplaudern** [OUS•plou•dairn] *vt* tattle

**auspolstern** [OUS•pol•stairn] *vt* upholster

**auspressen** [OUS•preh•sen] *vt* squeeze

**Auspuff** [OUS•poof] *n* M exhaust

**ausräuchern** [OUS•ROI•khairn] *vt* fumigate

**Ausrede** [OUS•rai•de] *n* F excuse; plea

**Ausrufungszeichen** [OUS•ROOF•oongs•tSAIHK•en] *n* N exclamation point

**ausrüsten** [OUS•roo•sten] *vt*
equip

**Ausrüstung** [OUS•rooh•stoong]
*n* F equipment

**Aussätziger** [OUS•zets•ig•AIR]
*n* M leper

**Aussage** [OUS•sah•geh] *n* F
statement; testimony

**aussagen** [OUS•sah•gen] *vt*
say; declare; make a statement

**auscheiden** [OUS•shai•den] to
take out; excrete; ~ aus\ retire
from

**ausschließen** [OUS•shlee•sen]
*vt* preclude

**ausschweifend**
[OUS•shvai•fend] *adj*
dissolute

**Aussehen** [OWS•zai•hen] *n* N
appearance

**Außenabort** [OU•sen•AB•ort]
*n* M outhouse

**Außenseite** [OU•sen•SAi•teh] *n*
F outside

**Außenseiter** [OU•sen•SAI•tair]
*n* M outsider

**außer1** [OU•sair] *prep conj*
except

**außer2** [OU•sair] *adj* outer

**außer sich** [OU•sair ZIHK] *adj*
frantic

**außer Atmen** [OWS•air
AHT•men] *adj* breathless

**außerdem** [OU•sair•DAIM]
*adv* furthermore; moreover;
*adv prep* besides

**außerordentlich**
[OU•sair•or•DENT•lihk] *adj*
extraordinary

**außer sich vor Freude**
[OU•sair zihk for FROI•de]
*adj* overjoyed

**aussetzen** [OUS•ZETS•en] *vt*
abandon; submit

**Aussicht** [OUS•zihkt] *n* F
outlook; prospect; view
(bird's eye)

**aussöhnen** [OUS•zuh•nen] *vt*
reconcile

**Aussöhnung** [-oong] *n* F
reconciliation

**aussondern**
[OUS•SOHN•dairn] *vt* select;
separate out

**ausspeien** [OUS•SHPUY•en] *vt*
spout

**Aussprache**
[OUS•SHPRAH•khe] *n* F
pronunciation

**aussprechen**
[OWS•shprek•ken] *vi*
articulate

**ausspülen** [OUS•shpool•en] *vt*
gargle; rinse

**ausstatten** [OUS•shtah•ten] *vt*
furnish

**Ausstellung** [OUS•shtel•loong]
*n* F display; exhibit

**Aussteuer** [OUS•shtoi•air] *n* F
trousseau

**ausstrahlen** [OUS•shtrahl•en]
*vt* emit

**ausstrecken** [OUS•shtrehk•en]
*vt* stretch; extend

**ausstreuen** [OUS•shtroi•en] *vt*
disseminate; strew

**ausströmen** [OUS•shtroo•men]
*vi* emanate

**Austausch** [OUS•toush] *n* M
interchange

**austauschen**
[OUS•TOUSH•en] *vt* swap

**austeilen** [OUS•tai•len] *vt*
distribute
**Austeilung** [OUS•tai•loong] *n*
F distribution
**Auster** [OU•stair] *n* F oyster
**Australien**
[OW•SHTRAHL•LEE•en] *n*
Australia
**ausüben** [OUS•UH•ben] *vt*
wield
**Ausübung** [OUS•OO•boong] *n*
F exercise
**ausverharren**
[OUS•fair•HAAR•en] *vi*
persist
**auswärts** [OUS•vairts] *adv*
outwardly
**Auswanderer**
[OUS•vahn•dair•air] *n* M
emigrant
**auswandern** [OUS•vahn•dairn]
*vi* emigrate
**ausweichen** [OUS•vai•khen] *vt*
elude; *adj* evasive
**ausweisen** [OUS•vai•zen] *vt*
exclude

**auswendig lernen**
[OUS•vehn•dig•lair•nen] *vt*
memorize
**auswicklen** [OUS•vihk•eln] *vt*
unwrap
**auswringen** [OUS•vring•en] *vt*
wring (out)
**Auswuchs** [OUS•vuhks] *n* M
outgrowth; protuberance
**Auswurf** [OUS•voorf] *n* M
excrement
**ausziehen** [OUS•tsee•hen] *vt*
strip (clothes)
**Auto** [OW•toh] *n* N car
**Autobahn** [OW•toh•BAHN] *n*
F highway
**autodidaktisch**
[OU•to•DIH•DAHK•tish] *adj*
self-taught
**Autogramm** [OW•toh•grahm] *n*
N autograph
**automatisch**
[OW•toe•MAH•tish] *adj*
automatic
**Autorität** [OW•tohr•ri•TAIT] *n*
F authority
**Axt** [akst] *n* F axe

# B

**Baby** [BAI•bee] *n* N baby
**Bach** [bahk] *n* M brook;
stream
**backen** [BAHK•ken] *vt*
bake
**Backfett** [BAHK•fet] *n* N
shortening
**Bad** [bahd] *n* N bath

**Badeanzug**
[BAHD•eh•AHN•tsoog] *n* M
swimsuit
**Bademantel**
[BAHD•eh•MAHN•tel] *n* M
bathing suit
**Badende(r)** [BAH•den•deh]
[air] *n* F bather

**Baderobe** [BAHD•eh•roh•beh]
*n* F bathrobe
**Badewanne**
[BAHD•eh•VAHN•neh] *n* F
bathtub
**Badezimmer**
[BAHD•eh•TSIM•mair] *n* N
bathroom
**Bäcker (in)** [BEK•kair] [-in] *n*
M baker
**Bäckerei** [BEK•kair•AI] *n* F
bakery
**bähen** [BAI•hen] *vt* foment
**Bär** [bair] *n* M bear
**bagatellisieren**
[BAHG•ah•tel•ih•SEER•en] *vt*
minimize
**Bahn** [bahn] *n* F pathway; rail;
railway
**Bahnhof** [BAHN•hof] *n* M
railroad station
**Bahnwärter**
[BAHN•VAIR•tair] *n* M guard
**Basilienkraut**
[BAH•SIL•lee•en•krowt] *n* N
basil
**bald** [bahlt] *adv* soon
**Balg** [bahlg] *n* M urchin
**Balkon** [BAHL•kohn] *n* M
balcony
**Ball** [bahl] *n* M ball
**Ballade** [BAHL•LAHD•eh] *n* F
ballad
**Ballen** [bahl•len] *n* M bale
**Ballerina**
[BAHL•lair•REEN•eh] *n* F
ballerina
**Ballet** [BAHL•lai] *n* N ballet
**Balloon** [BAHL•lohn] *n* M
balloon

**Bambus** [BAHM•boos] *n* M
bamboo
**banal** [BAH•nahl] *adj* banal;
trite
**Banane** [bah•NAH•neh] *n* F
banana
**Band** [bahnt] *n* M ribbon; tape
**Bande** [BAHN•deh] *n* F bond;
mob; group
**Bank 1** [bahnk] *n* F (comm)
bank
**Bank 2** [bahnk] *n* M bench
**Bankhalter** [BAHNK•hahl•tair]
*n* M banker
**Banknote** [BAHN•knoh•teh] *n*
F bank note
**bankrott** [BAHNK•roht] *adj*
bankrupt
**Banner** [BAHN•nair] *n* N
banner
**Barbar** [BAHR•BAHR] *n* M
barbarian
**barbarisch** [BAHR•BAHR•ish]
*adj* barbarian
**barfuß** [BAHR•foos] *adj adv*
barefoot
**Bargeld** [BAHR•gelt] *n* N cash
**Barkellner -in** [BAHR•kel•nair]
[in] *n* M bartender
**barmherzig** [BAHRM•hair•tsig]
*adj* gracious; merciful
**Barmherzigkeit** [-kuyt] *n* F
mercy
**barok** [BAHR•rohk] *adj*
baroque
**Barok** [BAHR•rohk] *n* N
baroque\ ~zeit; *n* F baroque
period
**Barometer** [BAHr•oh•MAI•tair]
*n* N barometer

**Barrikade**
[BAHR•rih•KAH•deh] *n* F
barricade

**Bart** [bahrt] *n* M beard;
mustache

**Barthaar** [BAHRT•haar] *n* N
whisker

**Baseball** [BAIS•bal] *n* M
baseball

**Basis 1** [BAH•zis] *n* F base

**Basis 2** [BAH•zis] *n* F basis

**Baskenmütze**
[BAH•sken•MOO•tseh] *n* F
beret

**Baß** [bahs] *n* M bass (mus)

**Bastard** [BAH•shtahrd] *n* M
bastard

**Bataillon** [BAH•TAIY•yawn *n*
N battalion; squadron

**Batterie** [BAH•tair•REE] *n* F
battery

**Bauch** [bouhk] *n* M stomach

**Bauchung** [BOUKH•hoong] *n*
F bulge

**bauen** [BOU•ehn] *vt* build;
construct

**Bauer** [BOU•air] *n* M builder;
farmer; pawn; peasant

**Bauernbursche**
[BOU•airn•BOOR•sheh] *n* M
swain, young man

**Bauernhof** [BOU•airn•HOF] *n*
M farm

**Bauholz** [BOU•holts] *n* N
lumber; timber

**Baum** [boum] *n* M tree

**Baumherzigkeit**
[BOWM•HAIRTS•ig•kuyt] *n*
F charity

**Baumwolle** [BOUM•vol•eh] *n*
F cotton

**Bausch** [bousch] *n* M wad

**Bayonett** [BAIY•yawn•net] *n*
M bayonet

**beabnsichtigen**
[be•AP•ZIHK•TIG•en] *vt*
intend

**beachten** [beh•AHK•ten] *vt*
heed, obey, attend

**beachtlich** [be•AHKT•lihk] *adj*
respectable

**Beachtung** [beh•AKT•oong] *n*
F attention

**Beamte** [be•AHM•te] *n* M
servant (civil)

**Beamter** [beh•AHM•tair] *n* M
magistrate

**Beamter -in** [be•AHM•tair]
[-tin] *n* M clerk

**beantworten**
[beh•AHNT•VOHR•ten] *vt*
respond

**bearbeiten**
[beh•AHR•BUY•ten] *vt* edit

**beben** [BAI•ben] *vt* quiver

**Becher** [BEHK•air] *n* M
tumbler

**Bedarf** [beh•DAHRF] *n* M need

**bedauern 1** [beh•DOU•airn] *vt*
deplore

**bedauern 2** [beh•DOU•airn] *vt*
regret

**bedecken** [be•DEK•en] *vt*
cover; coat

**Bedefkung** [be•dek•oong] *n* F
covering

**bedeutend** [beh•DOI•tend] *adj*
M major

**bedeutsam** [beh•DOIT•zahm]
*adj* momentous

**Bedeutung** [beh•DOI•toong] *n*
F meaning; significance

**bedienen** [beh•DEEN•en] *vt*
tend (a machine)

**bedingte Haftenlasung**
[beh•DIHNK•te
HAHF•ent•LAH•soong] *n* F
parole (from prison)

**Bedingung** [beh•DING•oong] *n*
F condition; unter ~, daß\ on
condition that; requirement

**bedrohend** [beh•DROH•end]
*adj* menacing

**bedrücken** [beh•DRUHK•en] *vt*
oppress; vex

**bedrückt** [beh•DRUHK•en] *adj*
depressed

**Beeindruck** [be•UYN•druhk] *n*
M impression

**beeindrucken**
[be•UYN•DRUHK•en] *vt*
impress

**beenden** [beh•EN•den] *vt vi*
conclude

**beendigen** [beh•END•ig•en] *vt*
terminate

**beerdigen** [beh•air•DIG•gehn]
*vt* bury

**Beerdigung**
[beh•AIR•DIG•goong] *n* F
burial

**Beere** [BAIR•reh] *n* F berry

**befähigen** [be•FAI•HIG•en] *vt*
enable

**Befehl** [be•FAIL] *n* M
command

**befehlend** [be•FAI•lend] *adj*
imperative; command

**befestigen** [beh•FEST•IG•gen]
*vt* attach; fasten

**befestigt** [be•FEST•ikt] *adj*
fixed

**befeuchten** [beh•FOIK•ten] *vt*
dampen; moisten

**befleckt** [beh•FLEHKT] *adj*
spotted

**Beförderung**
[beh•FER•DAIR•oong] *n* F
promotion

**befragen** [beh•FRAHG•en] *vt*
interrogate

**Befragung** [-oong] *n* F
interrogation

**befreien** [beh•FRUY•en] *vt*
disengage; rid; liberate

**Befreiung** [behj•FRUY•oong] *n*
F emancipation; liberation

**befreunden** [beh•FROIN•den]
*vt* befriend

**befrieden** [beh•FREE•den] *vt*
pacify

**Befriedigung**
[be•FREE•di•goong] *n* F
gratification

**befruchten** [be•FROOHK•ten]
·*vt* fertilize

**begabt** [beh•GAPT] *adj* gifted

**Begabung** [beh•GAH•boong] *n*
F vocation

**begegnen** [beh•GAIG•nen] *vt*
meet, encounter

**Begegnung** [be•GAIG•noong]
*n* F encounter; meeting

**begehren** [be•GAIR•en] *vt*
covet

**begeistern**
[beh•GUY•STAIRN] *vt*
inspire

**begeistert** [be•GUY•STAIRT]
*adj* ecstatic; enthusiastic

**beginnen** [beh•GIN•ńen] *vt*
initiate; begin

**begleiten** [buh•GLAIT•uhn] *vt*
accompany

**Begleiter 1** [be•GLUY•tair] *n*
M escort

**Begleiter-in 2** [beh•GLAI•tair]
[in] *n* M companion

**Begleitung** [beh•GLUY•toong]
*n* F convoy

**begraben** [beh•GRAH•ben] *vt*
bury

**Begräbnis** [be•GREHB•nis] *n* N
funeral

**Begriff** [be•GRIF] *n* M concept;
idea; notion

**begrüßen** [beh•GRUH•sen] *vt*
greet

**Begrüßung** [be•GRUH•soong]
*n* F greeting

**begünstigen 1**
[bu•GUYNST•igun] *vt* abet

**begünstigen 2**
[bu•GUYNST•IGUN] *vt*
patronize

**Behälter** [beh•HAIL•tair] *n* M
container; receptacle

**behängen** [beh•HENG•en] *vt*
drape

**behaglich** [be•HAG•lihk] *adj*
cozy; snug

**behalten** [beh•HAHL•ten] *vt*
keep

**behandeln** [beh•HAHN•deln]
*vt* treat

**Behandlung**
[be•HAHND•loong] *n* F deal

**beharren** [beh•HAAR•en] *vi*
persevere

**beharrlich** [be•HAHR•lihk] *adj*
insistent

**Beharrlichkeit**
[beh•HAAR•LIHK•kuyt] *n* F
perseverance; persistence

**behaupten** [be•HOUP•ten] *vt*
purport

**behaupten** [beh•HOUP•ten] *vt*
claim

**Behauptung**
[beh•HOWP•toongk] *n* F
allegation; claim

**beherrschen** [beh•HAIR•shen]
*vt* dominate

**Behörde** [beh•HOORD•eh] *n* F
board (business/political)

**behindert** [beh•HIN•dairt] *adj*
handicapped

**Behinderung 1**
[beh•HIN•DAIr•oong] *n* F
handicap

**Behinderung 2**
[be•HIN•DAir•oong] *n* F
frustration; obstruction

**behutsam** [be•HOOT•zahm]
*adv* gingerly; carefully

**bei** [buy] *prep* by

**bei der letzten Ölung
gereichte Eucharistie** [buy
dair LEHTS•ten UHL•oong
geh•RUYHK•teh
oi•kahr•is•tee] viaticum

**Beiboot** [BUY•boht] *n* dinghy

**beide** [BAI•deh] *adj* both

**Beifall spenden** [BAI•fal
shpen•den] *vt* M applaud

**beige** [baizh] *adj* beige

**Beil** [buyl] *n* N hatchet, axe

**beiläufig** [BUY•loi•fig]
incidental

**Beileid** [BUY•luyd] *n* N
condolences

**Bein** [buyn] *n* N leg; auf
eigenen ~ en stehen\ to be
able to stand on one's own

feet; auf die ~e helfen\ to help
someone back on their feet

**beinahe** [BUY•nah] *adv* nearly

**Beiordnung**
[VUY•ORD•noong] *n* F
coordination

**beiseite** [BAI•SAi•teh] *adv*
aside

**beiseite schieben**
[BUY•ZUY•teh SHEE•ben] *vt*
shunt

**Beispiel** [BUY•shpeel] *n* N
example

**beißen 1** [BUY•sen] *vt* bite (as
food)

**beißen 2** [BUY•sen] *vt* bite (of
insect,snake)

**beissend** [BAIS•ehnt] *adj* acrid

**Beistand** [BUY•shtant] *n* M
succor

**Beitel** [BUY•tel] *n* M chisel

**Beitrag** [BUY•trahg] *n* M fee

**beitragen** [BUY•TRAH•gen] *vt*
contribute

**Beitragen** [BUY•TRAH•gen] *n*
N contribution

**beiwohnen** [BAI•VOH•nen] *vt*
attend

**bejarht** [beh•YAH•rt] *adj* aged

**bekannt** [beh•KAHNT] *adj*
conversant; familiar

**bekannt machen** [-MAH•ken]
*vt* familiarize

**Bekannte -er (M)**
[buh•KAHNT•uh] [-air] *n* F
acquaintance

**bekanntgeben**
[beh•KAHNT•GAI•ben] *vt*
disclose; notify

**bekanntmachen**
[beh•KAHNT•MAHK•en] *vt*
divulge; publicize

**Bekanntmachung**
[beh•KAHNT•MAHK•koong]
*n* F publication

**Bekehrte** [beh•KAIR•teh] *n* M
convert

**beklagen** [be•KLAH•gen] *vi*
complain

**beklagenswert**
[be•KLAHG•ens•VAIRT] *adj*
deplorable

**bekleiden** [beh•KLUY•den] *vt*
clothe

**bekommen** [beh•KOH•men] *vt*
get; obtain; receive

**bekümmern** [beh•KUH•mairn]
*vt* grieve

**bekümmert** [beh•KUHM•mairt]
*adj* sorrowful; solicitous

**belästigen** [beh•LEST•IG•en]
*vt* harass; molest; persecute

**belästigen Last**
[beh•LEST•IG•guhn] [lahst] *vt*
*n* F bother

**Belästigung 1**
[beh•LEHST•IG•oong] *n* F
intrusion

**Belästigung 2**
[beh•lEHST•IG•oong] *n* F
trouble

**belagern** [beh•LAHG•gairn] *vt*
besiege

**Belagerung**
[beh•LAH•GAIR•oong] *n* F
attack, siege

**belasten** [be LAHST•ehn] *vt*
burden

**Belastung** [be•LAH•stoong] *n* F
debit

**beleben** [beh•LAI•ben] *vt vi*
liven

**belehren** [be•LAIR•en] *vt*
instruct

**belehrend** [be•LAIR•end] *adj*
educational

**Belehrung** [beh•LAIR•oong] *n*
F instruction, education

**beleidigen** [beh•LUYD•ig•en]
*vt* offend

**Beleidigung**
[beh•LUY•dig•oong] *n* F
insult

**belesen** [be•LAI•zen] *adj*
erudite

**beleuchten** [be•LOIHK•ten] *vt*
illuminate, light up

**Beleuchtung**
[beh•LOIHK•toong] *n* F
lighting

**Belgien** [BEL•GEE•uhn] *n*
Belgium

**belgisch** [BEL•gish] *adj*
Belgian

**beliebt** [beh•LEEPT] popular; ~
bei\ popular with

**Beliebtheit** [beh•LEEPT•huyt]
*n* popularity

**belohnen** [beh•LOHN•en] *vt*
recompense

**Belohnung** [beh•LOHN•oong]
*n* F reward

**belüften** [beh•LUHF•ten] *vt*
ventilate

**Belüftung** [beh-] *n* F
ventilation

**bemerkenswert 1**
[beh•MAIRK•ENS•vairt] *adj*
notable; noteworthy

**bemerkenswert 2** [-svairt] *adj*
remarkable; striking

**bemerkenswert machen**
[beh•MAIRK•ENS•vairt
MAH•khen] *vi* signalize

**Bemerkung**
[beh•MAIRK•oong] *n* remark

**Bemühung** [be•MOO•hoong] *n*
F endeavor

**benachrichtigen**
[beh•NAHKT•RIHK•TIG•en]
*vt* inform

**benagen** [beh•NAH•gen] *vt*
nibble

**Benehmen** [beh•NAIM•en] *n* N
behavior; demeanor

**Benzin** [ben•ZEEN] *n* M
gasoline; petroleum

**beobachten**
[BAI•oh•BAHK•ten] *vt*
observe, watch

**beobachtend** [-tend] *adj*
observant

**Beobachter** *n* M observer

**Beobachtung**
[BAI•oh•BAHK•toong] *n* F
observance

**Beobachtung** F observation

**bequem** [be•KVAIM] *adj*
comfortable

**Bequemlichkeit**
[be•KVAIM•LIHK•kuyt] *n* F
ease, relaxation

**Beratung** [beh•RAHT•oong] *n*
F counsel

**berauben** [be•ROU•ben] *vt*
deprive

**berechnen** [beh•REKH•nen] *vt*
calculate

**berechtigt** [be•REHKT•igt] *adj*
entitled

**Berechtigung**
[beh•REKT•IG•oongk] *n* F
entitlement, right

**berechnen** [beh•REK•nehn] *vt*
F amend (law)

**Beredsamkeit**
[be•raid•ZAHM•kuyt] *n* F
eloquence

**beredt** [beh•RAIT] *adj* eloquent

**Bereich** [beh•RUYHK] *n* M
scope

**bereichern** [be•RUY•khairn] *vt*
enrich

**bereit** [beh•RUYT] *adj* ready,
prepared

**Bereitschaft 1**
[be•RUYT•shahft] *n* F
readiness

**Bereitschaft 2**
[be•RUYT•shahft] *n* F
willingness

**bereitwillig** [be•RUYT•vil•lig]
*adj* willingly

**bereuen** [beh•ROI•en] *vt* repent

**Berg** [BAIRG] *n* M mountain

**bergauf** [BAIRG•ouf] *adj*
uphill

**Bergbau** [BAIRG•bou] *n* M
mining

**bergig** [BAIRG•ig] *adj*
mountainous

**Bergspitze** [BAIRG•shpits•e] *n*
F hilltop

**Bericht** [beh•RIHKT] *n* M
report

**berichten** [beh•RIHK•ten] *vt*
relate, tell

**Berichterstatter**
[-air•SHTAH•tair] *n* M
reporter

**berichtigen** [buh•RIKT•ig•ehn]
*vt* adjust; rectify

**Bersteiger** [ßAIRG•shtuy•gair]
*n* M mountaineer

**bersten** [BAIR•sten] *vt* burst;
crack; break

**Berlin** [bair•LIN] *n* Berlin

**Berliner 1 (in)** [~er] *adj*
Berliner

**Berliner 2** *n* M jelly doughnut

**Beruf** [beh•ROOF] *n* M
occupation, career, profession;
calling

**beruflich** [beh•ROOF•LIHK]
*adj* professional

**beruhigen 1**
[beh•ROO•HIG•ehn] *vt/vi*
calm down

**beruhigen 2**
[beh•ROO•HIG•en] *vt*
reassure; comfort

**Beruhigung**
[be•ROO•hig•OONG] *n* F
comfort

**Beruhigungsmittel**
[be•ROO•HIG•oons•MIH•tel]
*n* N sedative

**beruhmt** [be•ROOMT] *adj*
famed; famous; illustrious

**berühmte Person**
[beh•ROOHM•teh Paiyr•zohn]
*n* F celebrity

**berühren** [beh•RUHR•en] *vi*
touch

**Berwerbung**
[beh•VAIR•boong] *n* F
application

**besänftigen**
[beh•ZENFT•ig•en] *vt* soothe;
comfort

**Besatzung** [beh•ZAHTS•oong]
*n* F garrison

**beschädigen**
[be•SHAI•DIG•en] *vt* deface;
vandalize; mar

**beschäftig** [beh•SHEFT•ig] *adj*
busy

**beschämt** [beh•SHAI•mt] *adj*
ashamed (to be)

**bescheinigen**
[beh•SHUYN•IG•ehn] *vt*
certify

**Bescheinigung**
[beh•SHUYN•IG•oong] *n* F
certificate

**beschleunigen**
[beh•SHLOI•NIG•en] *vt*
quicken

**beschlußfähige Anzahl**
[beh•SHLUHS•FAi•hig•eh
ahn•tsahl] *n* F quorum

**beschmutzen**
[beh•SHMUHTS•en] *vt*
pollute, defile

**beschneiden 1**
[beh•SHNUY•den] *vt* curtail,
end

**beschneiden 2**
[beh•SHNUY•den] *vt* trim

**Beschneidung**
[beh•SHNUy•doong] *n* F
circumcision

**beschränken**
[beh•SHRENK•en] *vt* restrict

**Beschränkung 1**
[beh•SHREHNK•oong] *n* F
limitation; restriction

**Beschränkung 2**
[beh•SHRENK•oong] *n* F stint

**beschreiben** [be•SHRUY•ben]
*vt* describe

**Beschreibung**
[be•SHRUY•boong] *n* F
description

**Beschriftung**
[beh•SHRIHFT•oong] *n* F
inscription

**beschuldigen**
[be•SHOOL•DIG•en] *vt*
impeach; incriminate

**beschützend**
[beh•SHUHTS•end] *adj*
protective

**Beschützer** [veh•SHUHTS•air]
*n* M protector

**Beschwerde**
[beh•SHVAIR•deh] *n* F
grievance; complaint

**beschwerlich**
[beh•SHVAIR•lihk] *adj*
troublesome; annoying

**beschwipst** [beh•SHVIHPST]
*adj* tipsy

**beschwören** [be•SHVOOR•en]
*vt* evoke

**bescwichtigen**
[beh•SHVIHK•tig•en] *vt*
placate

**beseitigen** [beh•SAIT•TIG•en]
*vt* redress

**Besen** [BAI•sen] *n* M broom

**besessen** [beh•ZEH•sen] *adj*
obsessive, possessed (by); wie
~\ possessed by

**Besessenheit**
[beh•ZEHS•en•HUYT] *n*
obsession

**besetzt** [beh•ZEHTST] *adj*
busy; enraged

**Besichtigung**
[beh•ZIHK•TIG•oong] *n* F
sightseeing

**Besichtigung Sicht**
[beh•ZIHK•TIG•oong] [zihkt]
*n* F view

**besiegen** [beh•ZEE•gen] *vt*
overthrow

**Besiegung** [be•ZEE•goong] *n* F
defeat
**besigen** [beh•ZEE•gen] *vt*
vanquish
**besinnungslos**
[beh•ZIHN•OONGS•los] *adj*
senseless
**Besitz** [be•ZITS] *n* M
possession; estate
**besitzen** [beh•ZITS•en] *vt*
occupy; possess
**Besitzer** [beh•TIHT•sair] *n* M
owner; landlord
**Besitzerin** [beh•ZIHTS•AIR•in]
*n* F landlady
**besoffen** [be•ZOH•fen] *adj*
drunk, inebriated
**Besoffenheit**
[beh•ZOH•fen•HUYT] *n* F
drunkenness; inebriation
**besonder** [beh•ZOHN•dair] *adj*
particular
**besonders** [be•ZON•dairs] *adv*
especially; [-s] particularly;
*adj* special
**Besonnenheit**
[beh•SON•en•HUYT] *n* F
discretion
**besorgt** [beh•ZOHRKT] *adj*
anxious
**Besorgung** [beh•ZOR•goong] *n*
F errand
**Besprechung**
[beh•SHPREHK•oong] *n* F
discussion
**bespritzen** [beh•SHPRITS•en]
*vt* spatter; splash
**besser** [BES•sair] *adj adv* better
**Besserwisser**
[BEHS•air•VIHS•air] *n* M
know-it-all

**best** [best] *adv* best
**bestätigen**
[be•SHTEH•TIG•en] *vt*
confirm; ratify; approve
**Bestätigung**
[beh•SHTAI•TIG•oong] *n* F
confirmation; ratification
**Bestandteil**
[beh•SHTAHNT•tuyl] *n* M
ingredient
**bestechen** [beh•SHTEH•khen]
*vt* bribe
**bestechend**
[beh•SHTEHK•end] *adj*
specious
**Bestechung** [beh•shtekh•oong]
*n* F bribe
**Besteck** [beh•SHTEHK] *n* N
silverware
**bestehen** [beh•SHTAi•en] *vi*
consist; subsist; exist
**Bestehen** *n no pl* N existence
**bestimmen** [be•SHTIM•men] *vt*
determine; specify
**bestimmt** [beh•SHTIMT] *adj*
bound; certain; definite;
express
**Besuch** [beh•ZOOHK] *n* M visit
**Besuchen** [-en] *n* N visitation
**Besucher in** [-air] [in] *n* M
visitor
**betäuben** [beh•TOI•ben] *vt*
stun
**Betäubung** [beh•TOI•boong] *n*
F daze
**betrachten** [be•TRAHK•ten] *vt*
contemplate
**Bete** [BEH•teh] *n* F beet
**beten** [BAI•ten] *vi* pray
**Beton** [be•TOHN] *n* M concrete

**Betonung** [beh•TOH•noong] *n*
F emphasis
**betrachten** [beh•TRAHK•ten]
*vt* regard
**Betrachtung**
[beh•TRAHK•toong] *n* F
speculation
**betreffen** [buh•TREF•uhn] *vt*
affect
**betreffend** [beh•TREF•end]
*prep* concerning
**betrüben** [beh•TRUH•ben] *vt*
sadden
**betrübt** [beh•TRUHPT] *adj*
sorry, remorseful
**Betrug** [be•TROOG] *n* M
deceit; fraud
**Betrüg** [beh•TROOG] *n* M
betrayal
**betrügen** [beh•TROO•gen] *vt*,
*vi* betray; defraud; swindle,
cheat
**Betrüger** [beh•TROOG•air] *n*
M cheater; impostor
**betrügerisch** [-air•is] *adj*
fraudulent
**betrügerisch**
[be•TROOG•air•ish] *adj*
deceitful
**betrunken** [beh•TRUHNK•en]
*adj* inebriated; intoxicated
**Bett** [beht] *n* N bed; bunk beds
**betten** [BET•ten] *vt* beg; make
a bed for
**Bettler** [BET•lair] *n* M beggar
**beugen** [BOI•gen] *vt* flex; *vt vi*
bow
**Beule** [BOI•le] *n* F dent, bump
**beunruhigen**
[beh•UHN•ROO•HIG•en] *vt*
perturb

**beunruhigend**
[beh•OON•ROO•HIG•ent] *adj*
disturbing
**Beurteilung**
[be•OOR•TUYL•oong] *n* F
diagnosis
**Beute** [BOI•teh] *n* F booty; loot
**Beutel** [BOI•tel] *n* F pouch; bag
**bevölkern** [beh•FUHL•kairn] *vt*
populate
**Bevölkerung** [-oong] *n* F
population
**bevorstehend**
[be•FOR•SHTAI•end] *adj*
forthcoming; imminent
**bevorzugt** [-oogt] *adj*
preferential
**Bevorzugung**
[beh•FOR•TSOOG•oong] *n* F
preference
**Bewahrung** [beh•VAHR•oong]
*n* F conservation
**bewässern** [beh•VEHS•sairn]
*vt* irrigate
**Bewässerung** [-oong] *n* F
irrigation, watering
**bewahren** [beh•VAHR•en] *vt*
preserve, prove oneself; pay
off
**bewegen** [beh•VAI•gehn] *vi vt*
budge
**bewegend** [beh•VAIG•end] *adj*
moving
**beweglich** [beh•VAIG•lihk] *adj*
mobile
**beweglich** [beh•vaig•lihk] *adj*
movable
**Bewegung** [beh•VAI•goong] *n*
F motion
**Bewegung** [beh•VAIG•oong] *n*
move (physical); persuade;
movement

**Beweis** [be•VAIS] *n* M
evidence; proof
**beweisen** [beh•VAI•zen] *vt*
prove
**Bewerbung** [beh•VAIR•boong]
*n* F solicitation
**bewerten** [beh•VAIR•ten] *vt*
appraise
**bewölkt** [beh•VOOLKT] *adj*
cloudy; overcast
**bewohnen** [beh•VOH•nen] *vt*
inhabit
**bewundern** [buh•VUHN•dairn]
*vt* admire
**bewußt** [beh•WOOST] *adj*
aware; conscious
**bezaubern** [beh•TSOW•bairn]
*vt* charm
**bezaubernd**
[beh•TSOW•bairnt] *adj*
charming; enchanting;
bewitching
**bezeichnen** [be•TSAIK•nen] *vt*
define; designate
**bezeichnend**
[beh•TSAIKh•nehnd] *adj n* F
characteristic, feature
**bezeugen** [beh•TSOI•gen] *vt*
testify
**Beziehung** [beh•TSEE•hoong]
*n* F relationship; connection
(often business)
**Bezirk** [beh•TSEERK] *n* M
district; ward
**bezwingen** [beh•TSVING•en]
*vt* conquer; defeat; quell
**BH Brusthalter** [BAI•hah]
[BROOST•hahl•tair] *n* M bra
**Bibel** [BEE•bel] *n* F Bible
**Biber** [BEE•bair] *n* M beaver
**Bibliothek** *n* F library

**Bibliothekar -in**
[bib•LEE•oh•TAIK•air -in] *n*
M librarian
**biegen** [BEE•gen] *vt* bend; flex
**Biegung** [BEE•goong] *n* F
inflection
**Biene** [BEE•neh] *n* F bee;
bumblebee
**Bienenkorb** [BEEN•en•kohrp]
*n* M hive; beehive
**Bier** [bee'ur] *n* N beer
**Bikini** [bee•KEE•nee] *n* M bikini
**Bilanz** [bee•LAHNTS] *n* F
balance-sheet
**Bild** [bild] *n* N picture; ein ~
machen\ to take a
picture/photograph
**Bildhauer** [BILD•hou•air] *n* M
sculptor
**bildlich** [BILD•lihk] *adj*
figurative
**Bildnis** [BILD•nis] *n* N portrait
**Bildwerk** [BILD•vairk] *n* N
imagery
**Billiardspiel**
[bil•YARDZ•shpeel] *n* N
billiards
**billig** [BIL•ig] *adj* cheap;
inexpensive
**Billigung** [BIL•ig•goong] *n* F
approval
**Billion Milliarde** [BEE•yohn]
[MILY•yard•eh] *n* F billion
**bin** [bin] *v* am; *1st pers sing.
pres* sein
**binden** [BIN•den] *vt* engage
**Bindestrich**
[BIHN•deh•SHTRIHK] *n* M
hyphen
**Bindfaden** [BINT•fah•den] *n* M
twine

**Biographie**
[BEE•oh•GRAHF•ee] *n* F
biography

**Biologie** [BEE•oh•loh•HEE] *n* F
biology

**Birke** [BEEYR•keh] *n* F birch

**Birma** [BEER•mah] *n* Burma

**birmanisch** [BEER•mahn•ish]
*adj* Burmese

**Birne 1** [BEER•neh] *n* F
lightbulb

**Birne 2** [BEER•neh] *n* F pear

**Birnstein** [beern•shtuyn] *n* M
pumice

**bis** [bihhs] *prep adv* till; until

**bis her** [bis hair] thus far

**Bischof** [BISH•hohf] *n* M
bishop

**bisher** [BIS•hair] *adv* hitherto

**bißchen** [BIS•shen] bit; a small
part

**bitte** [BIH•teh] *adj* pleased;
*interj* please

**Bitte** [BIH•teh] *n* F request

**bitten** [BIH•ten] *vt* ask; solicit

**bitter** [BIT•tair] *adj* bitter, sour

**Blätter** [BLEH•tair] *npl* foliage,
leaves

**Blase** [BLAH•zeh] *n* F blister

**blasen** [BLAH•zen] *vt* blow

**blaß** [blahs] *adj* pale

**Blatt** [blaht] *n* N blade

**Blatt** [blaht] *n* N leaf

**blau** [blauw] *adj* blue

**Blaue** [BLAUW•eh] *n* N blue

**Blechdose** [BLEHK•doh•zeh] *n*
F tin can

**Blei** [bluy] *n* N lead

**bleiben** [BLUY•ben] *vi* remain;
stay

**bleich** [bluyhk] *adj* pale; livid;
wan

**Bleichinstrumente**
[BLAIK•IN•shtroo•MEN•tch]
*n* F brass

**Bleichmittel** [BLAIK•mit•tel] *n*
bleach

**Bleiplatte** [BLUY•plah•te] *n* F
grid

**Bleistift** [BLUY•shtift] *n* M
pencil

**Bleistiftspitzer** [-shpits•air] *n*
M pencil sharpener

**Blick 1** [blihk] *n* M look; glance

**Blick 2** [blihk] *n* M visor; vista

**blind** [blint] *adj* blind

**Blindenschrift**
[BLINT•uhn•shrift] *n* F braille

**blinken** [BLINK•un] *vt* blink

**Blinken** [BLIHNK•en] *n* N
flash; twinkling

**Blinklicht** [BLINGK• likt] *n* N
blinker (car)

**blinzeln** [BLIN•zeln] *vi* wink

**Blitz** [blihts] *n* M lighting;
thunderbolt; flash

**Blitzlicht** [BLIHTS•lihkt] *n* N
flashlight

**Block** [blohk] *n* M block

**Blockade** [bloh•KAHD•eh] *n* F
blockade

**blöd** [bluht] *adj* silly

**blond** [blohnt] *adj* blonde

**bloß** [blohs] *adj* mere; *adv*
merely

**blühen** [BLOO•hen] *vi* bloom;
flourish

**Blume** [BLOO•me] *n* F flower

**Blumenblatt**
[BLOO•men•BLAHT] *n* N
petal

**Blumenhändler**
[BLOOM•en•HEN•dler] *n* M
florist
**Blumenkohl**
[BLOOM•ehn•KOHL] *n* M
cauliflower
**Bluse** [BLOOZ•eh] *n* F blouse;
tunic
**Blut** [bloot] *n* N blood
**Blüte** [BLOO•teh] *n* F blossom
**Blutegel** [BLUHT•ai•gel] *n* M
leech
**blüten** [BLOO•ten] *vi vt* bleed
**Bluterguß** [bloo•tair•goos] *n* M
bruise
**blütig** [BLOO•tig] *adj* bloody
**Blütung** [BLUH•toong] *n* F
hemorrhage
**bocken** [BOH•kehn] *vi* refuse to
move; buck
**Boden** [BOH•den] *n* M floor;
ground
**Bodensatz** [BOH•den•ZATS] *n*
M sediment
**Börse** [BER•seh] *n* F Stock
Exchange
**Börsenkurse**
[BER•sen•KER•seh] *n* F stock
market
**bösartig** [BUHS•ahr•tig] *adj*
vicious
**böse** [BOOZ•eh] *adj* angry;
mad; sinister; wicked
**böswillig** [BUHS•vihl•ig] *adj*
malignant
**Bogen** [BOH•gen] *n* M arch
**Bohne** [BOH•neh] *n* F bean
**bohren** [BOH•ren] *vt* bore
**Bohrer** [BOHR•air] *n* M drill
**Boje** [BO•heh] *n* F buoy

**bombardieren**
[BOHM•bahr•DEER•uhn] *vt*
bombard
**Bombe** [BOHM•beh] *n* F bomb
**Bombenangriff**
[BOHM•ben•AHN•grif] *n* M
bombing
**Bomber** [BOHM•bair] *n* M
bomber
**Bonus** [BOHN•oos] *n* M bonus
**boos** [booz] *npl* boos
(expression of disapproval)
**Boot** [boht] *n* N boat
**Bootfahren** [boht FAHR•ren] *n*
N boating
**Bordell** [BOHR•del] *n* N brothel
**Borke bellen** [BOHR•ke]
[bel•len] *n vi* F bark
**Borste** [BOHR•steh] *n* F bristle
**boshaft** [BOHS•hahft] *adj*
malicious; shrewish
**Boshaftigkeit**
[BOHS•HAHFT•ig•kuyt] *n* F
spite
**Bosheit** [BOZ•huyt] *n* F malice;
wickedness
**Bosnien** [BOHS•nee•uhn] *n*
Bosnia
**bosnisch** [BOHS•nish] *adj*
Bosnian
**Botanik** [boh•TAHN•ik] *n* F
botany
**Bote** [BOH•te] *n* M emissary;
messenger
**Botschaft** [BOHT•shahft] *n* F
message; embassy
**Botschafter** [BOHT•shahf•tair]
*n* M ambassador
**Boxen** [BOHKS•ehn] *n* N
boxing

**Boxer** [BOKS•air] *n* M boxer; pug

**Boykott** [BOI•koht] *n* M boycott

**Bräutigam** [BROW•tih•gahm] *n* M bridegroom; groom

**bräutlich** [BROIT•likh] *adj* bridal

**braten** [BRAH•ten] *vt* broil; fry; roast

**Bratensaft** [BRAH•ten•zahft] *n* F gravy

**Bratpfanne** [BRAHT•PFAHN•neh] *n* F skillet

**Brauch** [brouhk] *n* M custom; usage

**brauen** [BROW•ehn] *vt* brew

**Brauer** [BROW•air] *n* M brewer

**Brauerei** [BROW•air•AIY] *n* F brewery

**Braune** [BRAU•neh] *n* N brown

**braune** [BRAU•n] *adj* brown

**Braut** [browt] *n* F bride

**Brautjungfer** [BROWT•yoong•fair] *n* F bridesmaid

**brechen** [BREKH•ehn] *vt vi* break; violate; breach (in wall)

**breit** [brait] *adj* broad; wide

**Breite** [BRAI•teh] *n* F breadth; latitude; width

**Bremse bremsen** [BREHM•zeh] *n* F brake

**bremsen** [BREHM•zehn] *vt* brake

**brennbar** [BREN•bahr] *adj* flammable

**brennen** [BREH•nen] *vi vt* burn

**brennend** [BRE•nend] *adj* fiery

**brennend heiß** [BREN•nend huys] *adj* torrid; burning hot

**Brenner** [BREHN•nair] *n* M burner

**Brennerei** [BREN•air•uy] *n* F distillery

**Brennholz** [BREN•holts] *n* N firewood

**Brennofen** [BREN•oh•fen] *n* M furnace

**Brennstoff** [BREN•shtof] *n* M fuel

**Brett** [breht] *n* N board (wooden)

**Brief** [breef] *n* M letter

**Briefkasten** [BREEF•kah•sten] *n* M mailbox

**Brieftasche** [BREEF•tah•sheh] *n* F wallet

**Briefträger** [BREEF•trai•gair] *n* M mailman; postman

**Briefwechsel** [BREEF•veks•el] *n* M correspondence

**Brieschen** [BREES•khen] *n* N sweetbreads

**Brille** [BRIH•le] *n* F glasses

**bringen** [breeng•gen] *vt* bring

**Brise** [BREE•seh] *n* F breeze

**britisch** [BRIH•tish] *adj* British

**Brocken** [BROH•ken] *n* M scrap

**brodeln** [BROH•deln] *vt* simmer; bubble; foment; unrest (political)

**Brötchen** [BROO•tchuhn] *n* N bun, roll

**Brokat** [BROH•kaht] *n* M brocade

**Broker** [BROH•kair] *n* M broker; stockbroker

**Brokkoli** [BROH•kohl•lee] *n* F
broccoli

**Brombeere** [BROHM•bair•reh]
*n* F blackberry

**Bronze** [BROHN•tseh] *n* F
bronze

**bronze** [BROHN•tseh] *adj*
bronze (color)

**bronzefarben**
[BROHNTS•eh•fahr•ben] *adj*
bronze (material)

**Broschüre** [broh•sHOOR•eh] *n*
F brochure; pamphlet

**Brot** [broht] *n* N bread

**Bruch 1** [brookh] *n* M violation

**Bruch 2** [brookh] *n* M rupture;
break; breach (in wall)

**Brücke** [BROO•keh] *n* F bridge

**Bruder** [BROO•dair] *n* M
brother

**brüderlich**
[BROOH•dair•LIHK] *adj*
fraternal

**Brühe** [BROO•heh] *n* F broth;
clear soup; dishwater

**brüllen** [BROO•len] *vi* bellow;
roar; cry

**brüllend** [BROO•lend] *adj*
blatant

**Brummen** [BRUH•men] *n* N
growl

**Bündel** [BOON•del] *n* F bunch

**Bund** [[buhnt] *n* M alliance

**Brüssel** [BROO•sel] *n* Brussels

**Brust** [broost] *n* F bosom;
breast; chest

**Brustwarze**
[BRUHST•vahrt•seh] *n* F
nipple

**brutal** [broo•TAHL] *adj* brutal;
beastly

**brutal gemein** [broo•tAHL]
[geh•MAIN] *adj* beastly

**Buch** [bookh] *n* N book;
textbook; paperback

**Buchdruckerkunst**
[BOOHK•druhk•air•KUHNST]
*n* F typography

**Buche** [BOOK•eh] *n* F beech

**Buchhalter -in**
[BOOKH•hahl•tair] [-in] *n* M
bookkeeper

**Buchhaltung**
[BOOKH•hahl•toong] *n* F
bookkeeping

**Buchhandlung**
[BOOKH•hahnd•loong] *n* F
bookstore

**buchstabieren**
[BUHK•shtah•beer•en] *vi* spell

**Bucht** [bookt] *n* F bay; cove

**Buckel** [BUH•kel] *n* M hump

**bucklig** [BUHK•lig] *adj*
hunched

**Buddhismus** [boo•DIS•moos] *n*
M Buddhism

**Budget** [BOO•djeht] *n* N
budget

**Büffel** [BOOH•fel] *n* M buffalo

**Büffet** [BOOH•fai] *n* N buffet

**bügeln** [BOO•geln] *vt* iron;
press

**Bügelsäge** [BUH•gel•SAI•ge] *n*
F hacksaw

**Bühne** [BUH•neh] *n* F stage;
platform

**bühnenbegeistert**
[BUHn•en•BEH•guy•stairt]
*adj* stage-struck

**Bühneneingang**
[-n•UYN•gahng] *n* M stage
door

**Bulgarien**
[buhl•GAH•REE•uhn] *n*
Bulgaria

**Bumerang** [BOO•mair•rahng] *n*
M boomerang

**bummeln** [BOOM•eln] *vi*
dawdle; loiter; ramble

**Bummler** [BUHM•lair] *n* M
loafer

**Bund** [boont] *n* M alliance;
confederation

**Bündel** [BUHN•del] *n* N
bundle; sheaf; truss

**Bundes** [BOON•des] *adj*
federal; ~bank\ Federal Bank;
~ Post\ German Post Office; ~
republik\ Federal Republic of
Germany; ~ staat\ Federal
State; ~straße *n* F\ main
highway

**Bundesrat** [boon•des•raht] *n* M
federal

**Burg** [boorg] *n* F fortress

**Burg** [booyrg] *n* F castle

**Bürge** [BOOR•geh] *n* M
sponsor; bail; voucher

**bürgen** [BOOR•gen] *vi* vouch

**Bürger-in** [BOOr•gair•] [-in] *n*
M citizen

**Bürgermeister**
[BOOR•gair•MUY•stair] *n* M
mayor

**Bürgerrecht** [BOOR•gair•rehkt]
*n* N franchise

**Bürgersteig**
[BOOR•gair•shtuyg] *n* M
pavement; sidewalk

**Burggraben**
[BOORG•grah•ben] *n* M moat

**Büro** [byü•roh] *n* N bureau
(gov); office

**Bürokratie**
[byü•ROH•krah•TEE] *n* F
bureaucracy

**Bürste bürsten** [BOOR•shteh]
[-ehn] *n* F brush

**Bus** [boos] *n* M bus

**Buße** [BOO•seh] *n* F penance

**Büste** [BOOST•eh] *n* F bust (of
statue)

**Butler** [BOOT•lair] *n* M butler

**Butter** [BOO•tair] *n* F butter

# C

**Cafe ImbiB (m)** [ka•FAI]
[IM•bis] *n* N coffee shop

**Cambodien**
[KAHM•boh•DEE•ehn] *s*
Cambodia

**Campingplatz**
[KAMP•ing•PLAHTS] *n* M
campground

**Cape** [KAHP•eh] *n* N cape
(geog)

**CD** [tsai•dai] *n* compact disc

**Cedille** [seh•DEE•yeh] *n* F
cedilla

**Cello** [CHE•loh] *n* N cello

**Cembalo** [CHEM•bah•lo] *n* N
harpsichord

**Chamäleon**
[keh•MAIL•AI•ohn] *n* M
chameleon
**Chaos** [KAH•ohs] *n* N chaos
**Charakter** [kah•RAHK•taiyr] *n*
M character
**Charme** [SHAHR•meh] *n* F
charm
**Charterflug**
[CHAHR•tair•floog] *n* M
charter (flight)
**Chef** [shef] *n* M chef
**Chef in (f)** [shehf] [-in] *n* M
boss; chief
**Chemie** [khe•MEE] *n* F
chemistry
**Chemiker** [KEH•mee•kair] *n* M
chemist
**chemisch** [KHE•mish] *adj*
chemical
**Chemikalien**
[KHE•mi•KAHL•EE•yen] *n* pl
F chemical
**Chile** [CHI•lai] *n* Chile
**China** [KEE•nah] *s* China
**chinesisch** [kin•AI•zish] *adj*
Chinese
**Chinin** [KHI•neen] *n* N quinine
**Chlorophyll** [KLOR•oh•fil] *n* M
chlorophyll
**Cholera** [KOH•lair•ah] *n* F
cholera

**Chor** [kohr] *n* M choir; chorus
**Christentum** [KRIST•en•toom]
*n* N Christianity
**christlich** [KRIST•likh] *adj*
Christian
**Christ -in** [krist -en] *n* M
Christian
**Christus** [KRIST•oos] *n* M
Christ
**Chrom** [krohm] *n* N chrome
**Chronik** [KROH•neek] *n* F
chronicle
**chronologisch**
[KROH•noh•LOH•gish] *adj*
chronological
**Chrysanthemum**
[kri•SAHN•teh•moom] *n* N
chrysanthemum
**Clown** [kloun] *n* M clown
**Cocktail** [KAHK•tail] *n* N
cocktail
**College** [KAH•lej] *n* M
university; college
**Comicstrips**
[KAH•mik•SHTRIPS] *npl*
comics (comic strip)
**Computer** [kom•POO•tair] *n* M
computer
**Coup** [koo] *n* M coup
**Cowboy** [KOU•boi] *n* M
cowboy
**Curry** [KOO•ree] *n* N curry

# D

**da** [dah] *conj* as; since
**da; dort** [dah] [dohrt] *prep*
there

**da herum** [dah HAIR•oom]
thereabouts
**Dach** [dahk] *n* N roof

**Dachrinne** |DAHK•RIN•ne] *n* F
gutter

**Dachshund** |DAHKS•hoont] *n*
M dachsund

**Dachstroh** |DAHK•shtroh] *n* N
thatch; thatched roof

**Dachstube**
[DAHK•SHTOO•beh] *n* F
attic

**Dachziegel** |DAHK•TSEE•gel]
*n* M tile; tiled roof

**dadurch** |DAH•doorhk] *prep*
thereby

**Dämmerung** [DEHM•air•oong]
*n* F dusk; twilight

**Dänemark** |DAIN•eh•mahrk]
Denmark

**dagegen** [dah•GAI•gen] *adj*
opposed

**damals** [dahn] [DAH•mahls]
then

**Dame** |DAH•me] *n* F lady

**Damenkleid**
[DAH•men•KLUYD] *n* N
gown

**Damenunterwäsche**
[DAH•men•UHN•tair•VEH•she]
*npl* M lingerie

**Damhirschkuh**
[DAHM•heersh•koo] *n* M doe

**Damm** [dahm] *n* M dam

**Dampf** [dahmpf] *n* M fumes;
steam; vapor

**Dampfer** [DAMP•fair] *n* M
steam engine; steamer

**Dampfschiff** [DAHMPF•shihf]
*n* N steamboat; steamship

**danach** [DAH•nahk] *adv*
thereafter

**dankbar** [DAHNK•bahr] *adj*
grateful; thankful; *adv*
thankfully

**Dankbarkeit**
[DAHNK•bahr•kuyt] *n* F
gratitude

**danken** [DAHNK•en] *vt* thank

**Dankfest** [DANK•fest] *n* N
thanksgiving

**dann** [dahn] *adv* then; ~ und\
about then; ~ und wann\ now
and then

**daran1** [DAH•rahn] *adv* against
it/that; thereon

**daran2** *vi* ~ gehen\ to set about

**darauf** [DAHR•ouf] *adv* on
it/them; towards it/that/them;
thereupon

**darauf** [DAH•rouf] *prep* upon

**darauffolgend** [~ oh•glend]
*adj* after him/it/that

**darin** [DAH•rin] *adv* in there;
therein

**darlegen** [DAHR•lai•gen] *vt*
demonstrate

**Darlegung** [DAHR•LAI•goong]
*n* F demonstration

**Darm** [dahrm] *n* M bowels; gut;
intestine

**Darrofen** [DAHR•ro•fen] *n* M
kiln

**darstellbar**
[DAHR•SHTEL•bahr] *adj*
presentable

**darstellen** [DAHR•SHTEL•en]
*vt* depict; portray

**Darstellung** [-oong] *n* portrayal

**darunterliegend**
[dah•RUHN•TAIR•lee•gend]
*adj* underlying

**das Beste** [dahs BEH•steh] *n*
best

**das Ihrige** [dahs EER•ig•eh]
theirs

**das Jüngste Gericht** [dahs
YOONGST•eh ge•RIHKT]
doomsday
**Dasein** [DAH•zuyn] *n* N entity
**Dasein Wesen** [DAH•zain]
[VAI•zen] *n* N being
**Datum** [DAH•toom] *n* M date
**Dauer** [DOU•air] *n* F duration
**dauernd** [DOU•airnt] *adj*
continual
**dauernd** [DOU•airnd] *adj*
lasting
**dauernd ständig** [DOU•airnt]
[SHTEN•dig] *adj* chronic
**Dauerwelle**
[DOU•air•VEL•leh] *n* F perm
(hair)
**Daumen** [DOU•men] *n* M
thumb
**davon** [DAH•fon] *adv* from
there; thereof
**davon** *vi* ~ bleiben\ to keep
away
**davonlaufen**
[da•FON•LOU•fen] *vi*
runaway
**dazwischen kommen**
[dah•TSVISH•en koh•men] *vi*
intervene
**dazwischenliegend**
[dah•TSVISH•en•LEEG•end]
*adj* intermediate
**Debakel** [de•BAH•kel] *n* N
debacle
**Debatte** [dai•BAH•te] *n* F
debate, put something up for
discussion
**Debitor** [DE•bee•tor] *n* M
debtor
**Debüt** [dai•BOOH] *n* N debut
**Deck** [dek] *n* N deck

**Decke** [DEK•keh] *n* F blanket
**Deckel** [DEH•kel] *n* M lid;
cover
**decken** [DEH•ken] *vt* to cover
**Defekt** [DEH•fehkt] *n* M defect
**defensiv** [dai•fen•SEEV] *adj*
defensive
**Definition** [DE•fin•ITS•EE•ohn]
*n* F definition
**Deich** [daihk] *n* M embankment,
dike
**dekorativ** [DE•kor•ah•TEEV]
*adj* ornamental
**Delphin** [DEL•feen] *n* M
dolphin
**Demagoge** [DAI•mah•GOH•ge]
*n* M demagogue
**Demokrat** [DAI•moh•kraht] *n*
M democrat
**Demokratie**
[DE•moh•krah•TEE] *n* F
democracy
**demokratisch**
[DAI•moh•KRAH•tish] *adj*
democratic
**Demut** [DAI•muht] *n* F
humility
**demütig** [DAI•muh•tig] *adj*
humble
**demütigen** [-en] *vt* humiliate;
mortify; abase
**Demütigung** [-oong] *n* F
humiliation
**den Höhepunkt erreichen**
[dain
HOO•eh•POONKT•air•UYK•en]
*vi* culminate
**Denken** [DAINK•en] *n* N
reasoning
**denken** [DAINK•en] *vt vi*
think; *vt* imagine

**Denken** *n* N thinking

**Denker** [DEHNK•air] *n* M
speculator; thinker

**Denkmal** [DEHNK•mahl] *n* N
monument; memorial

**Denkschrift** [DEHNK•shrihft] *n*
F memoirs

**denkwürdig**
[DEHNK•voor•dig] *adv*
notably

**deportieren**
[dai•POR•TEER•en] *vt* deport

**Depression** [dai•PRES•EE•ohn]
*n* F depression

**deprimieren**
[de•PRI•MEER•en] *vt* depress

**deprimiert** [deh•PRIM•EERT]
*adj* dejected; depressed;
downcast

**der die das** the

**der die das welch daß** (conj°)
[dair] [dee] [dahs] [velkh]
[dahs] that

**derb** [dairb] *adj* blunt

**Deserteur** [DE•zehr•TOOR] *n*
M deserter

**deshalb** [DAIS•halb] therefore

**Desinfektionsmittel**
[DES•in•FEK•TEE•ONS•mi•tel]
*n* N disinfectant

**destillieren**
[dih•SHTIL•EER•en] *vt* distill

**deutlich** [DOIT•Likh] *adv*
clearly; conspicuous

**deutsch e** [doitsh (e)] *adj*
German

**Deutschland** [DOITSCH•lahnt]
*n* Germany

**Devisen** [ded•VEE•zen] *n* N
currency

**Dezember** [dai•TSEM•bair] *n*
M December

**Dezimalzahl**
[DETS•ee•MAHL•tsahl] *n* F
decimal

**Diabetiker**
[DEE•ah•BET•ee•kair] *n* M
diabetic

**Diät** [DEE•et] *n* F diet

**diagonal** [DEE•AHG•oh•nahl]
*adj* diagonal; transverse

**Dialekt** [DEE•ah•lekt] *n* M
dialect

**Dialog** [DEE•ah•lohg] *n* M
dialog

**Diamant** [DEE•ah•mahnt] *n* M
diamond

**dicht** [dihkt] *adj* dense; tight

**Dichte** [DIHKT•e] *n* F density

**Dichter** [DIHK•tair] *n* M poet

**Dichtheit** [DIHKT•huyt] *n* F
tightness

**Dichtung** [DIHK•toong] *n* F
fiction

**Dichtungsmanschette**
[DIHK•toongs•MAHN•shet•te]
*n* F gasket

**dick** [dik] *adj* fat; stout; thick

**dick machen** [dik•mah•khen] *vt*
fatten

**Dickdarm** [DIK•darm] *n* M
colon

**Dicke** [DIHK•eh] *n* F thickness

**dickflüssig** [DIHK•fluh•sig] *adj*
turbid

**dickköpfig** [DIK•kuhp•fig] *adj*
pig-headed

**die Augen öffnen** [dee
OU•gen UHF•nen] undeceive

**die Beine spreizen** [dee
BUY•neh SHPRUYTS•en]
straddle

**die Nase stecken** [dee NAH•zeh SHTEHK•en] pry

**die Oberhand gewinnen** [dee OH•BAIR•hahnt geh•VIN•nen] prevail

**die Treppe hinauf** [dee TREH•peh hin•OUF] upstairs

**die Treppe hinunter** [dee TREH•peh hin•OON•tair] downstairs

**die Türkei** [dee TOOR•kuy] *n* Turkey

**Dieb** [deeb] *n* M thief; robber

**Dieb Einbrecher** [deeb] [AIN•BREHK•air] *n* M burglar

**Diebstahl** [DEEB•shtahl] *n* M larceny; theft

**Diele** [DEE•leh] *n* F hallway; lounge

**dienen** [DEE•nen] *vt* serve; womit kann ich Ihnen ~\ how can I serve you?

**Diener** [DEE•nair] *n* M servant

**Dienstag** [DEENST•tahg] *n* M Tuesday

**dienstbar** [DEENST•bahr] *adj* subservient

**Dienststelle** [DEENST•ell•eh] *n* F agency

**diese; dieser; dies** [DEE•zeh] [-air] [-dees] these

**dieser diese** [DEE•zair] [dee•zeh] those; this

**Diktat** [dik•TAHT] *n* dictation

**Diktator** [DIK•tah•TOHR] *n* M dictator

**Diktatur** [DIK•tah•TOOR] *n* F dictatorship

**diktieren** [dik•TEER•ehn] *vt* dictate

**Dilemma** [DI•leh•MAH] *n* N dilemma

**Ding** [ding] *n* N thing

**Dinosaurier** [DEE•no•SOU•reer] *n* M dinosaur

**Diözese** [DEE•oh•TSEH•zeh] *n* F diocese

**Diplom** [dih•PLOHM] *n* N diploma

**Diplomat** [DI•ploh•MAHT] *n* M diplomat

**Diplomatie** [DI•ploh•MAH•tee] *n* F diplomacy

**diplomatisch** [DI•ploh•MAH•tish] *adj* diplomatic

**direkt** [DEE•rekt] *adj* direct

**direkt** [DEE•rekt] *adj* firsthand

**direkt** [DEE•rehkt] *adj* straightforward

**Direktor** [DEE•rek•tohr] *n* M director

**Diskant** [dih•SKANT] *n* M treble clef

**diskret** [dihs•KREHT] *adj* discreet

**diskutieren** [DIHSK•oo•teer•en] *vt* discuss

**disqualifizieren** [DIS•kvahl•if•its•EER•en] *vt* disqualify

**Dissident** [DIHS•ih•dent] *n adj* M nonconformist

**dissimulieren** [DIS•SIM•oo•LEER•en] *vt* dissimulate

**Distel** [DEE•stel] *n* F thistle

**Docht** [dohkt] *n* M wick

**Dörfler** [DERF•lair] *n* M villager

**Doktorat** [DOK•tor•AHT] *n* N
doctorate

**Dokument** [DOK•uy•MENT] *n*
N document

**Dollar** [DOL•lahr] *n* M dollar

**Dolmetscher** [DOHL•met•cher]
*n* M interpreter

**Dom** [dohm] *n* M cathedral

**Donner** [DON•nair] *n* M
thunder

**donnern; Donner**
[DOHN•nairn] [dohn•nair] *vi*
*n* M boom

**donnernd** [DON•nairnd] *adj*
thundering

**Donnerschlag** [-shlahg] *n* M
thunderclap

**Donnerstag** [-stahg] *n* M
Thursday

**doppel** [DOH•pel] *adj* double

**Doppelblick** [DOH•pel•BLIHK]
*n* M double vision

**Doppelehe** [DOH•pel•AIY•yeh]
*n* F bigamy

**doppelt1** [DOH•pelt] *adj* dual;
double; duplicate

**doppelt2** [DOH•pelt] *adv*
doubly

**Doppelzüngigkeit**
[DOH•pel•TSUHNG•ig•kuyt]
*n* F duplicity

**Dorf** [dohrf] *n* N village

**Dorn** [dorn] *n* M thorn

**dort drüben** [dohrt druh•ben]
over there; yonder

**Drache** [DRAH•khe] *n* M
dragon

**Dracheflieger**
[DRAH•keh•flee•GAIR] *n* M
dragonfly

**drängen** [DREHNG•en] *vt*
impel

**Draht** [draht] *n* M wire

**drahtig** [DRAHT•ig] *adj* wiry

**drahtlos** [-los] *adj* wireless

**Drahtzange**
[DRAHT•tsahn•geh] *n* F pliers

**Dramatiker**
[drah•MAH•ti•KAIR] *n* M
dramatist; playwright

**dramatisch** [drah•MAH•tish]
*adj* dramatic

**dramatisieren**
[DRAH•mah•ti•SEER•en] *vt*
dramatize

**draußen** [DROU•sen] *adj*
outdoor; outdoors

**drehen** [DRAi•en] *vt* turn; twist

**Drehkreuz** [DRAI•kroits] *n* N
wicket

**Drehpunkt** [DRAI•puhnkt] *n* M
pivot

**Drehstuhl** [-shtool] *n* M swivel
chair

**Drehung** [drai•hoong] *n* F
rotation

**Drehzapfen** [DRAI•tsahp•fen]
*n* M swivel

**drei** [druy] *num* three

**Dreieck** [DRUY•ehk] *n* N
triangle

**dreifach** [DRUY•fahk] *adj*
treble; triple

**Dreifuß** [DRUY•foos] *n* M
tripod

**dreimal** [DRUY•mahl] *adv*
thrice

**dreißig** [DRUY•sig] *num* thirty

**dreißigste** [DRUY•sig•steh]
*num* thirtieth

**dreizehn** [DRUY•tsain] *num*
thirteen

**dreizehnte** [-teh] *num*
thirteenth

**dreschen** [DREH•shen] *vt*
thresh

**Dreschen** *n* N threshing

**dringend 1** [DRIHNG•end] *adj*
pressing; urgent

**dringend 2** *adv* urgently

**dringend bitten** [DRIHNG•end
BIH•ten] *vt* implore

**Dringlichkeit**
[DRING•lihk•kuyt] *n* F
urgency

**dritte** [DRIH•teh] third

**drittens** [DRIH•tenz] thirdly

**Droge** [DROH•geh] *n* F drug

**Drogen 1** [DROH•gen] *npl*
dope; marcotics; drugs

**drogen 2** *vi* addicted

**drohen** [DROH•en] *vt* threaten

**drohend** [DROH•end] *adj*
ominous; threatening

**dröhnen** [DROH•nen] *vt* roar

**Drohung** [DROH•oong] *n* F
threat

**Drossel** [DROH•sel] *n* F thrush

**Druck** [druhk] *n* M pressure

**Druck** [druhk] *n* M print

**Druck** [druhk] *n* M stress

**drücken** [DROO•khen] *vt*
compress

**Drucken** [DRUHK•en] *n* N
printing

**Drucker** [-air] *n* M printer

**Druckfehler** [DRUHK•fair•lair]
*n* M misprint

**Drüse** [DRUH•ze] *n* F gland

**Dschungel** [DJUHN•gel] *n* M
jungle

**du** [doo] *pers pron* you
(familiar); thou

**du Sie** [doo] [zee] you

**du Sie selbst** [doo] [zee zelpst]
yourself

**Dublin** [DOOB•lin] *n* Dublin

**Dudelsackpfeifen**
[DOOD•del•ZAK•pfai•fen] *n*
F bagpipes

**Duett** [doo•et] *n* N duet

**Duft** [dooft] *n* M fragrance;
perfume

**duftend** [DOOFT•end] *adj*
fragrant

**dulden1** [DOOLD•uhn] *vi* give
in; acquiesce

**dulden2** [DOOLD•uhn] *vi*
tolerate

**Duldsamkeit**
[DULD•zahm•kuyt] *n* F
tolerance

**dumm** [doom] *adj* dumb; stupid

**Dummheit** [-huyt] *n* F stupidity

**Dummkopf** [DOOM•kohpf] *n*
M dummy

**dumpf** [duhmpf] *adj* stuffy

**Düne** [DOO•ne] *n* F dune

**Dung** [duhng] *n* M manure

**Dünger** [DOONG•air] *n* M
fertilizer

**dunkel** [DOON•kel] *adj* dark;
murky; obscure

**dunkelbraun**
[DOON•kel•braun] *adj*
brunette

**Dunkelheit** [DOONK•el•huyt]
*n* F darkness; obscurity

**dünn 1** [duhn] *adj* skinny; thin

**dünn 2** *adj* thinly

**Dünne** [DUH•neh] *n* F thinness

**Dunst** [duhnst] *n* M haze

**dunstig** [DUHNST•ig] *adj*
hazy; misty

**Duplikat** [DOOP•li•kaht] *n* N
counterpart

**durch** [doorhk] *prep adv*
through

**durch Rundfunk senden**
[doork ROONT•foonk
ZEN•den] *vt* broadcast

**durch Zwischenfragen
belästigen** [doorhk
tSVIHSH•en•FRAHGEN
beh•LEST•IG•en] *vt* heckle

**durchbohren**
[DOORHK•boh•ren] *vt* gore;
perforate; pierce

**durchdringen**
[DOORHK•dring•en] *vt*
penetrate; permeate

**durchdringend**
[DOORHK•dring•end] *adj*
strident

**durcheinander**
[DOORHK•uyn•ahn•dair] *adj*
distraught

**Durcheinander**
[DOORHK•uyn•ahn•dair] *n* N
muddle

**durcheinanderbringen**
[DOORHK•uyn•AHN•dair•
BRING•en] *vt* fluster; confuse

**durchfallen**
[DOORHK•fahl•en] *vt* fail

**durchführen**
[DOORHK•foor•en] *vt*
execute

**Durchführung 1**
[DOORHK•fuhr•oong] *n* F
transaction

**durchführung 2** *vt* taking
through; running through

**Durchgang** [DOOHRK•gahng]
*n* M gangway; passage

**durchgehend**
[DOORHK•gai•ehnd] *adj*
nonstop

**durchgescheuert**
[DOOHRK•ge•shoi•airt] *adj*
frayed

**durchgreifend**
[DOORKH•gruy•fend] *adj*
drastic

**Durchmesser**
[DOORHK•mes•air] *n* M
diameter

**durchnässen**
[DOORHK•nes•sen] *vt*
drench; soak

**durchschnittlich**
[DOORK•shnit•lik] *n* M
average

**Durchschnitt** [DOORK•shnit]
*adj* average

**Durchsicht** [DOORHK•zihkt] *n*
F revision

**durchsichtig**
[DOORHK•zihk•tig] *adj*
transparent

**durchsickern**
[DOOHRK•zihk•airn] *vi* ooze

**durchsieben**
[DOORHK•see•ben] *vt* sift

**durchstechen**
[DOORHK•shtehk•en] *vt*
puncture

**durchstreifen**
[DOORHK•shtruy•fen] *vt*
prowl

**dürfen** [DOOR•fen] *modal v* to
be allowed

**dürftig** [DERF•tig] *adj* tenuous

**Dürre** [DOOR•eh] *n* F drought

**Durst** [DOORST] *n* M thirst
**durstig** [DOOR•stig] *adj*
  parched
**Dusche** [DOO•sheh] *n* F shower
**düster** [DOO•stair] *adj* dim;
  dreary; gloomy; obscure;
  somber
**Düsterkeit** [DUH•stair•KUYT]
  *n* F gloom

**Dutzend** [DOO•tsend] *n* N
  dozen
**dynamisch** [duy •NAHM•ish]
  *adj* dynamic
**Dynamit** [DUH•nah•MEET] *n*
  N dynamite
**Dynastie** [DUH•nah•STEE] *n* F
  dynasty

# E

**e** [ai] e-elect
**Ebbe** [EB•be] *n* F ebb tide; tide
**eben** [AI•ben] *adj* smooth; even
**Ebene** [AI•ben•EH] *n* F level
**ebenfalls** [AI•ben•fals] *adv*
  ditto
**Ebenholz** [AI•ben•holts] *n* N
  ebony
**Ebenmaß** [AI•ben•mahs] *n* N
  proportion
**ebenso** [AI•ben•so] *adv*
  equally; just as (something)
**Eßwaren** [EHS•vah•ren] *npl*
  food; victuals
**Echo** [EH•kho] *n* N echo
**echt** [ekt] *adj* authentic;
  genuine; real; veritable; *adv*
  typically; ~ english\ typically
  English
**Echtheit** [EHKT•huyt] *n* F
  originality
**Ecke** [EK•eh] *n* F corner
**edel** [AI•del] *adj* precious
**Edelstein** [AI•del•shtuyn] *n* M
  gem
**Efeu** [EH•foi] *n* M ivy

**Egotist** [AI•go•TEEST] *n* M
  egotist
**Ehe** [AI•eh] *n* F marriage;
  matrimony
**Ehebruch** [AI•eh•brook] *n* M
  adultery
**ehedem** [AI•eh•DAIM] *adv*
  formerly; of old
**ehelich** [AI•eh•lihk] *adj* wedded
**ehemalig** [AI•eh•MAHL•ig] *adj*
  former
**eherbietig** [AIR•air•BEE•tig]
  *adj* reverent
**Ehre** [AIR•eh] *n* F honor
**ehren** [AIR•en] *vt* dignify;
  honor
**Ehrenmann** [AIR•en•mahn] *n*
  gentleman
**ehrenwert** [-vairt] *adj*
  honorable
**ehrlich** [AIR•lihk] *adj* honest;
  sincere; *adv* honestly;
  sincerely
**Ehrlichkeit** [-kuyt] *n* F honesty;
  sincerity

**ehrwürdig** [AIR•voor•dig] *adj*
reverend; venerable

**Ei** [uy] *n* N egg

**Eiche** [UY•che] *n* F oak

**Eichhörnchen**
[uyhk•HERN•chen] *n* N
squirrel

**Eid** [uyd] *n* M oath

**Eidechse** [UYD•ehks•eh] *n* F
lizard

**Eidotter** [UY•doh•tair] *n* M
yolk

**Eierfrucht** [UY•air•froohkt] *n* F
eggplant

**Eierstock** [UY•air•shtohk] *n* M
ovary

**Eierteig** [AIY•air•taig] *n* M
batter (cake)

**Eifer** [UY•fair] *n* M zeal;
passion

**Eiferer** [UY•fair•air] *n* M
fanatic; zealot

**Eifersucht** [UY•fair•suhkt] *n* F
jealousy

**eifersüchtig** [UY•fair•suhk•tig]
*adj* jealous

**eifrig** [UY•frig] *adj* eager;
zealous

**eigen** [UY•gen] *adj* own;
separate

**Eigenart** [UY•gen•ahrt] *adj*
characteristic; idiosyncratic

**Eigenbrötler**
[UY•gen•BRUHT•lair] *n* M
misfit

**eigenmächtig**
[AI•gen•MEK•tig] *adj*
arbitrary

**Eigenschaft** [UY•gen•shahft] *n*
F characteristic

**Eigensinn** [UYG•en•zin] *n* M
obstinacy

**eigensinnig** [UY•gen•zin•ig]
*adj* headstrong; opinionated;
stubborn

**eigentlich** [UY•gent•lik] *adv*
actually; essentially; virtually

**Eigentum** [UY•gen•toom] *n* N
ownership; property

**Eigentümer** [-air] *n* M
proprietor

**eigenwillig** [UY•gen•vih•lig]
*adj* willful

**Eikel** [UY•kel] *n* M disgust

**eikel** [UY•kel] *adj* disgusting

**Eile** [UY•le] *n* F hurry; haste

**eilig** [UY•lig] *adj* hurried;
hastily

**Eilzug** [UYL•tsoog] *n* M train
(express)

**Eimer** [UYM•uyr] *n* M bin (for
garbage); bucket; pail

**ein anderer neuer** [aiyn
AHN•dair•air] [noi•air] *adj*
another

**ein; eine; ein; 1** [ain] *art* a

**ein 2** *num* one

**ein-und-dreißigste**
[UYN•unt•DRUY•sig•steh]
thirty-first

**einatmen** [UYN•aht•men] *vt*
inhale

**einbahn** [UYN•bahn] *adj*
one-way

**einberechnet**
[UYN•be•REHK•net] *prep*
including

**Einbildung** [UYN•bil•doong] *n*
F imagination

**Einblick** [UYN•blihk] *n* M
insight

**Einbruch der Nacht**
[UYN•broohk dair nahkt] *n*
nightfall

**einbürgen** [UYN•boor•gen] *vt*
naturalize

**eindampfen** [UYN•dahmpf•en]
*vt* vaporize

**eindringen** [UYN•dring•en] *vi*
encroach

**Eindringling** [UYN•dring•ling]
*n* M intruder

**eindrucksvoll**
[UYN•druhks•fol] *adj*
impressive; spectacular

**einen Unterschied machen**
[UY•nen OON•tair•sheed
MAH•khen] *vt* differentiate

**einen Vertrag schließen**
[UY•nen fair•TRAHG
SHLEE•sen] *vi* contract

**einfach** [UYN•fahk] *adj* plain;
simple; *adv* plainly

**Einfachheit** [UYN•fahk•huyt] *n*
F modesty

**Einfall 1** [UYN•fall] *n* M
incursion; invasion; raid

**Einfall 2** [UYN•fal] *n* M whim

**Einfalt** [UYN•falt] *n* F
simplicity

**Einfaltspinsel**
[UYN•falts•PIN•zel] *n* M
simpleton

**Einfassung** [UYN•fah•soong] *n*
F fringe

**Einfließen** [UYN•flee•sen] *n* N
influx

**einflößen** [UYN•fluhs•sen] *vt*
instill

**Einfluß** [UYN•floos] *n* M
influence

**eingebildet**
[UYN•geh•BILD•et] *adj*
pretentious

**eingemauert**
[UYN•geh•MOU•airt] *adj*
walled

**eingestehen** [UYN•ge•shtai•en]
*vi* confess

**Eingeweide**
[UYN•geh•VAI•deh] *npl*
viscera; guts

**einhändig** [UYN•hen•dig] *adj*
single-handed

**einheimisch** [UYN•huym•ish]
*adj* indigenous; native

**einholen** [UYN•ho•len] *vt*
overtake

**einige** [AIN•ig•eh] *adj* any; *adv*
some

**Einigkeit** [AIN•igk•kait] *n* F
accord

**Einigung** [AIN•ig•oongk] *n* F
agreement

**einimpfen** [UYN•imp•fen] *vt*
implant; inoculate

**Einkaufen** [UYN•KOU•fen] *n*
N shopping

**einkaufen gehen** shopping
(to go)

**Einkommen** [UYN•koh•men] *n*
N income

**Einkommensquelle**
[UYN•koh•mens•KVEL•le] *n*
revenue

**Einkommensteuer**
[UYN•koh•men-] *n* F tax
(income)

**einladen** [UYN•lah•den] *vt*
invite

**Einladung** [UYN•lah•doong] *n*
F invitation

**Einlass Zutritt** [AIN•lahs]
[TSOO•trit] *n* M admission

**einleitend** [UYN•luy•tend] *adj*
preliminary

**Einleitung** [UYN•luy•toong] *n*
F overture

**einmal** [UYN•mahl] *adv* once

**Einmischung** [-oong] *n* F
interference

**einrechnen** [UYN•rehk•nen] *vt*
include

**Einrichtung** [UYN•rihk•toong]
*n* F installation

**einrücken** [UYN•ruhk•en]
indent

**eins** [uyns] *num* one

**einsam** [UYN•zahm] *adj* lone;
solitary; single

**einsam** [UYN•zahm] *adj* lonely;
solitary

**Einsamkeit** [-kuyt] *n* F
loneliness; solitude

**einsaugen** [UYN•zoug•gun] *vt*
absorb

**einschläfernd**
[UYN•shlai•fairnd] *adj*
soporific

**einschlagen** [UYN•shlah•gen]
*vt* envelop

**einschließen** [UYN•shlee•sen]
*vt* enclose

**einschneiden**
[UYN•shnuy•den] *vt* engrave

**einschränken** [UYN•shrenk•en]
*vt* confine

**einschreiben** [UYN•shruy•ben]
*vt* enroll

**einschrumpfen**
[UYN•shruhmp•fen] *vt* shrink

**Einschrumpfen** *n* N shrinkage

**einseitig** [UYN•sai•tig] *adj*
one-sided

**einsetzen1** [UYN•zets•en] *vt*
fix

**einsetzen2** [UYN•zets•sen] *vt*
insert; inset

**Einsetzung** [UYN•zet•soong] *n*
F appointment

**Einsiedler** [UYN•zeed•lair] *n* M
hermit; recluse

**einspritzen** [UYN•shprihts•en]
*vt* inject

**Einspruch** [UYN•shpruhk] *n* M
objection

**einstellen** [AIN•shtel•uhn] *vt* to
put in; adapt

**Einstellung** [AIN•shtel•oong] *n*
F employment

**einstimmig** *adj* unanimous

**Einstimmigkeit**
[UYN•shtim•ig•kuyt] *n* F
unanimity

**Eintauchen** [UYN•tou•khen] *n*
N dip

**eintauchen** [AIN•tou•kehn] *vt*
immerse

**eintauchen** [UYN•tou•khen] *vt*
steep

**einteilen** [UYN•tuy•len] *vt*
divide

**Einteilung** [UYN•tuy•loong] *n*
F division

**eintönig** [UYN•tuhn•ig] *adj*
monotonous

**Eintönigkeit** [-kuyt] *n* F
monotony

**eintragen** [UYN•trahg•en] *vt*
register

**Eintragung** [-oong] *n* F
règistration

**eintreten** [UYN•trai•ten] *vt*
enter

**eintunken** [UYN•tuhnk•en] *vt*
sop

**einverstanden**
[AIIN•faiur•SHTAHN•dehn]
*adj* agreeable

**Einwanderer**
[AIN•vahn•DAIR•air] *n* M
immigrant

**Einwanderung** [-oong] *n* F
immigration

**einweihen** [UYN•vuy•en] *vt*
induct

**Einweihung** [UYN•vuy•oong]
*n* F inauguration

**Einzahlung** [UYN•tsahl•oong]
*n* F payment; deposit

**Einzelhandel**
[UYN•zel•hahn•del] *n* M
retail trade

**Einzelheit** [UYN•tsel•huyt] *n* F
detail

**einzeln** [UYN•tseln] *adj*
individual; singular

**einziehen** [UYN•tsee•en] *vt*
confiscate

**einziehen** [UYN•tsee•en] *vt*
recruit

**einzig** [UYN•zig] *adj* only;
single

**Eis** [UYS] *n* N ice; ice cream

**Eisbahn** [UYS•bahn] *n* F rink

**Eisberg** [-bairg] *n* M iceberg

**Eisen** [UY•zen] *n* N iron

**Eisenbahn** [UY•zen•bahn] *n* F
railroad

**Eisenwaren**
[UY•zen•VAHR•en] *npl*
hardware

**eisig** [AI•sig] *adj* frigid; icy

**Eiswurfel** [UYS•voor•fel] *n* M
ice cube

**eitel** [UY•tel] *adj* conceited;
vain

**Eitelkeit** [UY•tel•kuyt] *n* F
conceit; vanity

**Eiweiß** [UY•vuys] *n* N protein

**ekelerregend**
[AI•kel•air•RAI•gend] *adj*
nauseous

**ekelhaft** [AI•kehl•hahft] *adj*
disgusting; revolting; nasty;
sickening

**elastisch** [eh•LAHS•tish] *adj*
elastic; flexible

**Elefant** [EL•eh•FAHNT] *n* M
elephant

**elegant** [EL•eh•GAHNT] *adj*
elegant

**Eleganz** [EL•eh•GAHNTS] *n* F
elegance

**elektrisch** [el•EK•trisch] *adj*
electric

**Elektrizität**
[EL•ek•tri•tsi•TAIT] *n* F
electricity

**elektronisch**
[EL•ek•TROHN•ish] *adj*
electronic

**Element** [EL•eh•ment] *n* N
element

**elementar** [EL•eh•men•tahr]
*adj* elementary

**Elen** [AI•len] *n* M elk

**elend** [AI•lend] *adj* miserable;
wretched

**Elend** [AIL•lend] *n* N misery

**elf** [elf] *num* eleven

**Elf** [elf] *n* M goblin

**Elfenbein** [ELF•en•BUYN] *n* N
ivory

**elfte** [-te] *num* eleventh

**elitär** [AI•lee•tair] *adj* elitist;
*adv* in an elitist fashion

**Elite** [AI•leet] *n* F elite

**Ellbogen** [EL•boh•gen] *n* M
elbow

**Eltern** [EL•tairn] *npl* parent

**Emaille** [EH•muy•le] *n* F
enamel

**Embargo** [em•BAHR•goh] *n* N
embargo

**Embryo** [em•BREE•o] *n* M
embryo

**Empfänger** [emp•FENG•air] *n*
M receiver

**Empfänger** *n* M recipient

**empfänglich** [emp•FENG•lihk]
*adj* hospitable; predisposed

**Empfang** [emp•fahng] *n* M
reception

**empfangen** [emp•FAHNG•en]
*vt* conceive

**empfehlen** [emp•FAI•len] *vt*
commend; recommend

**Empfehlung** [-loong] *n* F
recommendation

**empfindlich** [emp•FIND•lihk]
*adj* touchy; sensitive

**Empfindung** [emp•FIN•doong]
*n* F sentiment

**empört** [em•PERT] *adj*
indignant

**emporheben**
[em•POHR•HAI•ben] *vt*
elevate; uplift

**Emporkömmling**
[em•POR•KUHM•ling] *n* M
upstart

**emsig** [EM•zig] *adj* strenuous

**Ende 1** [EN•de] *n* N end; finish

**Ende 2** [EN•deh] *n* N upshot

**endlich** [END•lihk] *adv*
eventually; finally

**endlos** [END•los] *adj* endless;
unending

**Endnote** [END•no•te] *n* F
footnote

**Endstation**
[ENT•shah•TSEE•on] *n* M
terminal

**Energie** [EN•air•GEE] *n* F
energy

**energisch** [en•AIR•gish] *adj*
energetic

**eng** [ehng] *adj* narrow

**Engel** [EN•gehl] *n* M angel

**England** [EN•glahnt] *n* England

**englisch** [EN•glish] *adj* English

**engstirnig** [ENG•shteer•nig]
*adj* M bigot

**Engstirnigkeit**
[eng•SHTEERN•IG•kuyt] *n* F
narrow-minded

**Enkelkind** [AIN•kel•KINT] *n* N
granddaughter; grandson

**enorm** [ai•NOHRM] *adj*
enormous

**Entblößung** [ent•BLOO•song]
*n* F exposure

**entdecken** [ent•DEK•en] *vt*
discover; detect

**Entdeckung** [ent•DEH•koong]
*n* F discovery

**Ente** [EN•teh] *n* F duck

**entfalten** [ent•FAHL•ten] *vt*
unfold, develop, evolve

**entfernen** [ent•FAIR•nen] *vt*
remove

**entfernt** [ent•FAIRNT] *adj*
distant

**entfernt** [ent•FAIRNT] *adj*
removed

**Entfernung** [ent•FAIR•noong]
*n* M range

**entfrosten** [ent•FROHST•en] *vt*
defrost

**entführen** [ent•FUYR•en] *vt*
kidnap; abduct

**Entführer** *n* M kidnapper

**Entführung** [-oong] *n* F
kidnaping

**entgegengesetzt**
[ent•GAI•gen•ge•ZETST] *adj*
contrary

**entgegensetzen**
[ent•GAI•gen•ZETS•en] *vt*
oppose; set something against
something

**entgegenwirken**
[ent•GAI•gen•VEER•ken] *vt*
counteract

**Entgegnung** [ent•GAIG•noong]
*n* F argument

**entgleisen** [ent•GLAI•sen] *vi*
derail

**enthalten** [ent•HAHL•ten] *vt*
contain; comprise

**enthaupten** [ent•HOWP•ten] *vt*
behead

**Enthusiasmus**
[en•TOOZ•EE•AHs•moos] *n*
M enthusiasm

**entkorken** [ent•KOR•ken] *vt*
uncork

**entlang** [ent•LAHNG] *prep*
along

**entlangfahren**
[ent•LAHNG•FAHR•en] *vi*
coast

**entlassen** [ent•lah•sen] *vt*
dismiss

**Entlassung** [ent•LAH•soong] *n*
F dismissal; release

**entlasten** [ent•LAH•sten] *vt*
exonerate; unburden

**entlaufen** [ent•LOU•fen] *vi*
elope

**entleeren** [ent•LEER•en] *vt*
deflate

**entleihen** [ows•BOHR•gen]
[ent•LAI•hen] *vt* borrow

**Entlüfter** [ent•LUHF•tair] *n* M
ventilator

**entmutigen** [ent•MOO•tig•en]
*vt* discourage; dishearten

**entreißen** [ent•RUY•sen] *vt*
wrest

**entschädigen**
[ent•SHED•ig•en] *vt*
reimburse

**entscheidend** [ent•SHAI•dend]
*adj* decisive

**Entscheidung 1**
[ent•SHAI•doong] *n* F
decision

**Entscheidung 2**
[ent•SHUY•doong] *n* F
divorce

**Entscheidung 3**
[ent•SHUY•doong] *n* F option

**entschieden** [ent•SHEE•den]
*adj* resolute

**entschleiern** [ent•SHLUY•airn]
*vt* unveil

**Entschlossenheit**
[ent•shloh•sen•huyt] *n*
resolution

**entschuldigen**
[ent•SHOOLD•ig•oong] *vt*
excuse

**Entschuldigung**
[ent•shoold•ig•ungk] *n* F
apology; alibi

**entsetzlich** [ent•ZEHTS•lihk]
*adj* ghastly; frightening

**entspannen** [ent•SHPAH•nen]
*vt* relax

**Entspannung**
[ent•SHPAHN•oong] *n* F
recreation; relaxation

**entsprechen** [ent•SHPREK•en]
*vi* comply (with); correspond
(to)

**entsprechend**
[ent•SHPREK•ent] *adv*
corresponding; *adj* equivalent

**entstehen** [ent•SHTAI•en] *vi*
originate; come into being

**entstellen** [ent•SHTEL•en] *vt*
disfigure

**enttäuschen** [ent•TOI•shen] *vt*
disappoint

**enttäuschend** [ent•TOI•shent]
*adj* disappointing

**Enttäuschung**
[ent•TOI•shoong] *n* F
disappointment

**entwickeln** [ent•VIHK•eln] *vt*
develop

**Entwicklung** [ent•VIHK•loong]
*n* F development

**Entwicklung** [ent•vihk•loong] *n*
F evolution

**entwöhnen** [ent•VUH•nen] *vt*
wean; to break a habit (of)

**Entwurf** [ent•VOORF] *n* M
design; draft

**entwurzeln** [ent•VOORTS•eln]
*vt* eradicate

**entziffern** [ent•TSIF•airn] *vt*
decipher

**entzücken** [ent•TSUHK•en] *vt*
ravish

**entzückend** [ent•TSOOK•ent]
*adj* charming; delightful

**entzückt** [ent•TSOOKT] *adj*
delighted

**entzünden** [ent•TSUHN•den]
*vt* light; inflame

**Enzyklopädie**
[en•TSUY•klo•PAI•DEE•uh] *n*
F encyclopedia

**episch** [AI•pish] *adj* epic

**Epoche** [ai•POHK•eh] *n* F
epoch

**er** [air] he

**erbärmlich** [air•BAIRM•lihk]
*adj* depressing

**erbarmungslos**
[air•BAHRM•OONGS•los]
*adj* grim; merciless

**Erbe 1** [AIR•be] *n* M heir

**Erbe 2** [AIR•be] *n* N no pl
inheritance

**Erbeinheit** [AIRB•uyn•huyt] *n*
F gene

**erben** [AIR•ben] *vt* inherit

**Erbin** [AIR•bin] *n* F heiress

**erbittern** [air•BI•tairn] *vt*
exasperate

**Erbitterung**
[air•BIH•TAIR•oong] *n* F
rancor

**erbrechen** [air•BREHK•en] *vi*
throw up; vomit

**Erbschaft** [AIRB•shahft] *n* F
heritage

**Erbschaft** [AIRB•shahft] *n* F
inheritance

**Erbse** [AIRB•seh] *n* F pea

**Erbstück** [AIR•shtuhk] *n* N
heirloom

**Erdbeben** [AIRD•bai•ben] *n* N
earthquake

**Erdbeere** [AIRD•bair•eh] *n* F
strawberry

**Erdboden** [AIRD•boh•den] *n* M
soil

**Erde** [AIR•deh] *n* F earth

**Erdgeschoß**
[AIRD•ge•SHOHS] *n* N
ground floor

**erdichten** [AIR•DIHK•ten] *vt*
trump

**Erdkugel** [AIRD•koo•gel] *n* F
globe

**Erdnuß** [AIRD•noos] *n* F
peanut

**Erdnußbutter** [-boo•tair] *n* F
peanut butter

**Erdrosselung**
[air•DROH•SEL•oong] *n* F
strangulation

**Erdrutsch** [AIRD•ruhtch] *n* M
landslide

**Erdwall** [AIRD•vahl] *n* M
mound

**Ereignis** [air•UYG•nis] *n* N
event

**Ereignis** [air•UYG•nis] *n* N
happening

**Erektion** [air•EHK•TSEE•on] *n*
F erection

**erfahren 1** [air•FAHR•en] *adj*
experienced; sophisticated

**erfahren 2 lernen**
[air•FAHR•en] [lair•nen] *vt vi*
learn; experience; find out
(about)

**Erfahrung** [air•FAHR•oong] *n*
F experience

**Erfassung** [air•FAHS•oong] *n* F
coverage

**erfinden 1** [air•FIN•den] *vi*
contrive

**erfinden 2** [air•FIN•den] *vt*
devise; invent

**Erfinder** [~air] *n* M inventor

**erfinderisch**
[air•FIN•DAIR•ish] *adj*
imaginative; inventive

**Erfindung** [-oong] *n* F·
invention

**Erfolg** [AIR•Folg] *n* M success

**Erfolg haben** [AIR•folg
hah•ben] prosper

**erfolgreich** [air•FOLG•ruyhk]
*adj* prosperous; successful;
triumphant

**erfordern** [air•FOR•dairn] *vt*
require

**erforschen** [air•FOR•shen] *vt*
explore

**Erforschung** [air•FOR•shoong]
*n* F exploration

**erfreut** [air•FROIT] *adj* joyful

**Erfrierung** [air•FREER•oong] *n*
F frostbite

**erfrischen** [air•FRI•shen] *vt*
freshen; refresh

**erfrischend** [air•FRISH•end]
*adj* refreshing

**Erfrischung** [-oong] *n* F
refreshment

**erfüllen** [air•FUHL•en] *vt*
fulfill; accomplish

**Erfüllung** [-oong] *n* F
fulfillment; satisfaction

**ergänzen ganz** [air•GEN•zen]
[ghants] *vt adj* complete

**ergeben** [air•GAI•ben] *vt* yield

**Ergebnis** [air•GAIB•nis] *n* N
outcome

**ergeizig** [AIR•gaits•ig] *adj*
ambitious

**ergiebig** [AIR•gee•big] *adj*
yielding

**ergreifen** [AIR•GRUY•fen] *vt*
grasp; seize

**ergreifend** [air•GRUYF•end]
*adj* pathetic; touching

**Ergreifung** [-oong] *n* F seizure

**Erhaltung** [air•HAL•toong] *n* F
conservation

**erheben** [air•HAI•ben] *vt* exalt

**erheblich** [air•HAIB•likh] *adj*
considerable

**Erhebung** [air•HAI•boong] *n* F
uprising; upheaval

**erheiternd** [air•HUY•tairnd]
*adj* amusing; cheering;
exhilarating

**erhöhen** [air•HUH•en] *vt* raise;
heighten; increase

**Erhöhung** [air•HOO•oong] *n* F
eminence

**erholt** [air•HOLT] *adj* restful

**Erholung** [air•HOH•loong] *n* F
recovery

**erinnern** [air•nehrn] *vt* remind

**Erinnerung** [air•in•air•oong] *n*
F recollection; reminder;
reminiscence

**erkennen 1** [air•KEN•en] *vt*
discern; recognize; realize

**Erkennen 2** [air•KEN•nen] *n* N
recognition

**erklären** [air•KLAIR•en] *vt*
explain; pronounce

**Erklärung** [-oong] *n* F
explanation

**erklettern** [air•KLE•tairn] *vt*
climb; ascend

**erkranken** [air•KRAHNK•en]
*vi* sicken

**erkunden** [air•KUHN•den] *vt*
scouting

**Erlaß** [AIR•lahs] *n* M decree;
announcement; writ

**erläutern** [air•LOI•tairn] *vt*
illustrate

**Erläuterung** [-oong] *n* F
illustration

**erlangen** [air•LANG•en] *vt*
derive

**erlauben** [air•LOWB•ehn] *vt*
allow

**Erlaubnis** [air•LOUB•nis] *n* N
permission

**erleben** [air•LAI•ben] *vt*
undergo

**erleichtern** [air•LUYHK•tairn]
*vt* lighten; relieve

**Erleichterung**
[air•LUYHK•TAIR•oong] *n* F
relief

**Erleuchtung**
[air•LOIHK•toong] *n* F
inspiration

**Erlös** [air•LUHS] *n* M proceeds

**erlösen** [air•LUHS•en] save,
redeem

**Erlöser** [air•LUH•sair] *n* M
redeemer

**Ermäßigung**
[air•MES•IG•oong] *n* F
discount

**ermattet** [air•MAH•tet] *adj*
jaded

**ermorden** [air•MOHR•den] *vt*
assassinate

**Ermordung** [air•MORD•ung] *n*
F assassination

**ermüden** [air•MUH•den] *vi* tire

**ermüdend** [air•MUH•dend] *adj*
tiresome; wearisome

**Ermüdung** [air•MOO•doong] *n*
F fatigue

**ermutigen** [air•MOO•tig•en] *vt* encourage

**Ermutigung** [air•MOO•ti•goong] *n* F encouragement

**ernähren** [air•NAIR•en] *vt* nourish; nurture

**ernennen** [air•NEN•nen] *vt* appoint; nominate

**Ernennung** [-oong] *n* F nomination

**erneuern** [air•NOI•airn] *vt* renew; renovate

**Erneuerung** [air•NOI•AIR•oong] *n* F renewal

**erniedrigen** [air•NEED•RIG•uhn] *vt* abase

**erniedrigen** [air•NEED•RIG•uhn] *vt* humble, abase

**erniedrigend** [air•NEE•DRIG•ent] *adj* degrading

**ernst** [airnst] *adj* earnest; serious

**Ernst** *n* M seriousness

**Ernte** [AIRN•te] *n* F harvest

**ernten** [AIRN•ten] *vt* harvest; reap

**Ernüchterung** [AIR•NOOHK•tair•oong] *n* F disillusion

**Eroberer** [air•OH•BAIR•air] *n* M conqueror

**erobern** [air•OH•bairn] *vt* conquer

**Eroberung** [air•OH•BAIR•oong] *n* F conquest

**Eröffnung** [air•UHF•noong] *n* F opening

**erordieren** [air•OH•DEER•en] *vt* erode

**erpressen** [air•PREH•sen] *vt* extort

**Erpressung** [air•PRES•soong] *n* F blackmail

**erregt** [air•EHGT] *adj* elated; delighted

**Erregung** [air•RAI•goong] *n* F thrill; excite

**erröten** [air•ROOT•en] *vi* blush; redden

**Ersatzfüllung** [air•ZATS•FUH•loong] *n* F refill

**Ersatzmann** [AIR•zats•mahn] *n* M understudy

**erschaffen** [air•SHAH•fen] *vt* create

**Erschaffung** [air•SHAH•foong] *n* F creation

**erschallen** [air•SHAHL•len] *vt* peal; ring out

**erscheinen** [air•SHAI•nen] *vi* appear

**erschöpfen** [air•SHUHP•fen] *vt* deplete

**erschöpft** [air•SHUHPFT] *adj* exhausted; depleted; run-down

**Erschöpfung** [air•SHUHP•foong] *n* F exhaustion

**erschrecken** [air•SHREK•en] *vt* frighten; scare; startle; horrify; terrify; daunt

**erschreckend** [•end] *adj* alarming; frightening; scary

**Erschütterung** [air•SHUH•TAIR•oong] *n* F shock

**erst** [airst] *adj* first; premier

**erstaunen** [air•SHTOW•nehn] *vt* amaze; astonish

**erstaunlich** [air•SHTOWN•lik] *adj* amazing; stupendous

**erstechen** [air•SHTEHK•en] *vt* stab

**erster Klasse** [AIRST•air KLAH•se] *adj* first-class

**ersticken** [air•SHTIK•ehn] *vi vt* choke; *vt* stifle; suffocate

**Ersticken** *n* N suffocation; asphyxiation

**erstklassisch** [AIRST•KLAH•sish] *adj* classic

**erträglich** [air•TRAIG•lihk] *adj* tolerable

**Ertrag** [air•TRAG] *n* M output; yield; return

**ertrinken** [air•TRIN•ken] *vt* drown

**erwachen** [air•VAHK•en] *vi* wake

**Erwachsene -r** [Air•VAKS•EN•uh] [-air] *n* F adult

**erwähnen** [air•VAI•nen] *vt* mention

**erwarten** [air•VAHR•ten] *vt* expect

**erwartet** [-et] *adj* expecting

**Erwartung** [-oong] *n* F expectation

**Erweckung** [air•VEHK•oong] *n* F revival

**erweichen** [air•VUY•khen] *vi* relent

**erwerben** [air•VAIRB•uhn] *vt* acquire

**erwidern** [air•VEE•dairn] *vt* reply; reciprocate

**Erwiderung** [air•VEE•dair•oong] *n* retort

**erwischen** [air•VIH•shen] *vt* erase

**erwünscht** [air•VOONSHT] *adj* desirable

**erwürgen** [air•VOOR•gen] *vt* strangle

**Erz** [airts] *n* N ore

**erzählen** [air•TSAI•len] *vt* narrate

**Erzähler** [air•TSA•lair] *n* M narrator; story-teller

**erzählt** [air•TSAILT] told

**Erzählung** [air•TSAI•loong] *n* F narration; tale

**erzählungs** [air•TSAIL•oongs] *adj* narrative; tale

**erzeugen** [air•TSOI•gen] *vt* generate

**erzeugend** [air•TSOI•gend] *adj* productive

**Erzeuger** [air•TSOIG•air] *n* M manufacturer

**erzittern** [air•TSIH•tairn] *vi* tremble

**erzürnen** [air•TSUHR•nen] *vt* provoke

**erzwingen** [air•TSVING•en] *vt* coerce

**es** [es] *pron* it; (nom) he, she (acc) him, her

**Esel** [AIY•zel] *n* M donkey

**eskalieren** [ehsk•E•LEER•en] *vi* escalate

**essen** [ES•sen] *vi* eat

**Essen** [ES•sen] *n* N food

**Essenz** [ES•sents] *n* F essence

**Essig** [EH•sig] *n* M vinegar

**Eßlust** [ES•loost] *n* F gluttony

**Eßzimmer** [ES•tsim•air] *n* dining room

**Ethik** [AI•tik] *n* F ethic

**ethisch** [AI•tis] *adj* ethical

**ethnisch** [AIT•nish] *adj* ethnic

**Etikette** [AI•ti•ket•te] *n* F etiquette

**etwa** [EHT•vah] *adv* somewhat; about; approximately

**etwas 1** [EHT•vahs] *adj* slightly

**etwas 2** [EHT•vahs] something

**Eule** [OI•leh] *n* F owl

**Eure Majestät** [OI•reh•MAH•YES•tait] *n* F sire

**Europa** [OI•o•RO•pah] *n* Europe

**europäisch** [OI•ro•PAI•ish] *adj* European

**Europäische Gemeinschaft** [-e ge•MUYN•shahft] *n* F European Community

**Euter** [OI•tair] *n* N udder

**Evangelium** [AI•vahn•GAI•LEE•um] *n* N gospel

**eventuell** [AI•ven•too•EL] *adj* potential

**ewig** [AI•vig] *adj* eternal; *adv* forever

**Ewigkeit** [AI•vig•KUYT] *n* F eternity

**exekutiv** [EKS•ehk•OO•teef] *adj* executive

**Exemplar** [EKS•emp•lahr] *n* N specimen

**existieren** [EKS•i•STEER•en] *vi* exist

**exotisch** [EKS•o•tish] *adj* exotic

**Expedition** [EK•spe•DI•TSEE•on] *n* F expedition

**explodieren** [EKS•ploh•DEER•en] *vi* detonate; *vt* explode

**Explosion** [AIKS•plow•ZEE•ohn] *n* F explosion; blast

**Export** [EK•spohrt] *n* M export

**Extrakt** [EKS•trahkt] *n* M extract

**Extravertierter** [EK•strah•fer•TEER•tair] *n* M extrovert

**exzentrisch** [EK•sen•trish] *adj* M eccentric

**Exzenter** [EK•sen•tri•kair] *n* M eccentric

**Exzerpt** [EKS•sairpt] *n* N excerpt

# F

**Faß** [fass] *n* F barrel; cask; keg

**Fabel** [FAH•bel] *n* F fable

**fabelhaft** [FAH•bel•HAHFT] *adj* fabulous

**Fabrik** [fah•BREEK] *n* F factory

**fabrizieren** [fah•BRI•TSEER•en] *vt* fabricate

**Fach** [fahk] *n* M professional

**Facharbeiter**
[FAHK•ahr•BUY•tair] *n* M
workman

**Fachmann** [FAHK•mahn] *n* M
expert; specialist

**Fachschule** [FAHK•shoo•leh] *n*
F trade school

**Fackel** [FAH•kehl] *n* F torch

**fade** [FAH•de] *adj* insipid;
tasteless; dull

**Faden 1** [FAH•den] *n* M fathom

**Faden 2** [FAH•den] *n* M thread

**fadenscheinig** [-shuyn•ig] *adj*
threadbare

**fähig** [FAI•hig] *adj* able;
competent

**Fähigkeit** [FAI•hig•kait] *n* F
ability

**Fähigkeit** [FAIY•ig•kait] *n* F
capacity; competence

**Fähnchen** [FEHN•khen] *n* N
pennant; banner; flag

**Fahne** [FAH•neh] *n* F banner;
flag

**Fähre** [FAI•re] *n* F ferry

**fahren** [FAHR• en] go; drive;
sail

**fällig** [FEL•lig] *adj* due

**fälschen** [FAIL•shen] *vt* falsify

**färben** [FAIR•ben] *vt* tinge

**Fagott** [fah•GOHT] *n* N
bassoon

**Fahne** [FAH•ne] *n* F flag;
streamer

**Fahnestock** [-shtohk] *n* M
flagpole

**Fahrer** [FAHR•air] *n* M
chauffeur; driver

**Fahrkarte** [FAHR•kahr•teh] *n* F
ticket

**fahrlässig** [FAHR•les•sig] *adj*
reckless

**Fahrpreis** [FAHR•pruys] *n* M
fare

**Fahrrad** [FAHR•rahd] *n* N
bicycle

**Fahrt** [fahrt] *n* F drive

**Fahrwerk** [FAHR•vairk] *n* N
undercarriage

**Fahrzeug** [FAHR•tsoig] *n* N
vehicle

**Faktor** [FAHK•tor] *n* M factor

**Fakultät** [FAH•kool•tait] *n* F
dean; faculty

**Falke** [FAHL•ke] *n* M falcon;
hawk

**Fall 1** [fal] *n* M fall; downfall

**Fall 2[fahl]** *n* M instance; case

**Falle** [FAL•leh] *n* F trap

**falls** [fahls] case (in ~ of)

**Fallschirm** [FAHL•sheerm] *n* M
parachute

**falsch** [falsh] *adj* false; fake;
mistaken; phony; untrue

**falsch auslegen** [fahlsh
OUS•lai•gen] *vt* misconstrue

**falsch berichtigen** [fahlsh
beh•RIHK•TIG•en] *vt*
misinform

**falsch unrichtig** [fahlsh]
[UHN•rihk•tig] *adj* wrong

**falsch zählen** [fahlsh
TSAI•lehn] *vt* miscount

**Falschmeldung**
[fahlsh•MEL•doong] *n* F hoax

**falsh buchstabieren**
[-BOOHK•shtah•BEER•en] *vt*
misspell

**falsh urteilen** [-OOR•tuy•len]
*vt* misjudge

**Falte** [FAHL•te] *n* F fold; pleat;
tuck

**Familie** [fah•MEE•LEE•eh] *n* F
family

**Familienname**
[fah•MEE•LEE•EN•nah•me] *n*
M last name; surname

**Fanatiker** [fa•NA•TI•kair] *n* M
extremist

**Fang** [fahng] *n* M capture; arrest

**fangen** [FAHNG•ehn] *vt* catch;
capture

**Fangzahn** [FAHNG•tsahn] *n* M
fang; tusk

**fantastisch** [fahn•TAHST•ish]
*adj* fantastic

**Farbe** [FAHR•beh] *n* F color;
hue; tint

**farbenblind** [FAHR•ben•blint]
*adj* color-blind

**farbenfreudig**
[FAHR•ben•FROI•dig] *adj*
colorful

**Farbfernsehen**
[FAHRB•fairn•zeh•uhn] *n* N
color television

**Farbstoff** [FAHRB•shtohf] *n* M
dye

**Farn** [fahrn] *n* M fern

**Faschismus** [fah•SHEES•moos]
*n* M fascism

**Fashing** [FAH•shing] *n* M
carnival

**Faß** [fahs] *n* N vat

**Fassade** [fah•SAH•de] *n* F
facade

**fassen** [FAH•sen] *vt* to take
hold of; grab; seize; hold

**Fassung 1** [FAH•soong] *n* F
setting; frame

**Fassung 2** [FAH•soong] *n* F
version

**fast** [fahst] *adv* almost; nearly;
~nie\ hardly ever

**Fastenzeit** [FAHST•en•tsait] *n*
F Lent

**Fastnachtsdienstag**
[FAHST•nahkts•DEENST•tag]
*n* M Shrove Tuesday

**faszinieren**
[FAHS•tsin•EER•en] *vt*
fascinate; mesmerize

**faszinierend** [-d] *adj*
fascinating

**fasziniert** [FATS•in•eert] *adj*
spellbound

**faul** [foul] *adj* lazy; bad; idle

**Faulenzer** [FOUL•en•zair] *n* M
truant

**Faulpelz** [FOUL•pelts] *n* M
slacker

**Fauna** [FOU•nu] *n* F fauna

**Faust** [foust] *n* F fist

**Februar** [FAI•broo•ahr] *n* M
February

**Fechten** [FEHK•ten] *n* N
fencing (sport)

**Feder** [FAI•dair] *n* F feather;
plume; quill

**Federflocke**
[FAI•dair•FLOH•ke] *n* F fluff

**Fee** [fai] *n* F fairy

**Fegefeuer** [FAI•geh•FOI•air] *n*
purgatory

**Feger** [FAI•gair] *n* M sweeper

**Fehde** [FAI•deh] *n* F feud

**Fehdehandschuh**
[FAI•deh•HAHNT•shoo] *n* M
gauntlet

**Fehlbetrag** [FAIL•beh•trahg] *n*
M shortcoming

**fehlen** [FAI•len] *vi* fail; be lacking or missing

**fehlend** [FAI•lend] *adj* missing

**Fehler** [FAIL•air] *n* F blunder; error; flaw; mistake

**Fehlschlag** [FAIL•shlahg] *n* M miscarriage

**Feier** [FUY•air] *n* F celebration; ceremony

**feiern** [FUY•airn] *vt vi* celebrate

**feierlich** [FUY•air•lihk] *adj* solemn; grave

**feierlich begehen** [-beh•GAI•hen] *vi* solemnize

**Feierlichkeit** [fuy•air•lihk•kuyt] *n* F solemnity

**Feiertag** [FUY•air•tahg] *n* M holiday

**feig** [faig] *adj* cowardly

**Feige** [FUY•ge] *n* F fig

**Feigheit** [FAIG•huyt] *n* F cowardice

**Feigling 1** [FAIG•ling] *n* M coward

**Feigling 2** [fUYG•ling] *n* M quitter

**Feile** [FUY•le] *n* F file

**fein** [fuyn] *adj* fine; excellent; subtle; nicht~ genug sein\ not good enough

**Feind** [fuynd] *n* M enemy

**Feindschaft** [-shahft] *n* F hostility

**Feingefühl** [FUYN•geh•fuhl] *n* N sensitivity

**Feinheit** [FAIN•huyt] *n* F delicacy

**Feinkost** [FAIN•kost] *n* F delicatessen

**Feld** [feld] *n* N field

**Feldfrucht** [FELD•frookht] *n* F crop

**Feldwebel** [FELT•vai•bel] *n* M sergeant

**Fels** [fels] *n* M rock

**Felsblock** [FELS•blohk] *n* M boulder

**felsig** [FEL•sig] *adj* rocky

**Felsschlucht** [FELS•shlookht] *n* F canyon

**Fenster** [FEN•stair] *n* N window

**Fensterbrett** [FEN•stair•breht] *n* N sill

**Fensterladen** [-LAH•den] *n* M window shade

**Fensterscheibe** [-SHUY•be] *n* F windowsill

**fern** [fairn] *adj* far; remote; fern ~ hier\ far from here

**Ferne** [FAIR•neh] *n* F distance

**Fernglas** [FAIRN•glahs] *n* N binoculars

**Fernrohr** [FAIRN•rohr] *n* N telescope

**Fernsehen** [FAIRN•zai•hen] *n* N television

**Fernseher** [FAIRN•zai•air] *n* M television set

**Fernsehsendung** [FAIRN•zeh•zen•doong] *n* F broadcast

**Fest** [fest] *n* N festival

**fest** [fest] *adj* firm; solid; steadfast; steady

**fest werden lassen** [fehst VAIR•den LAH•sen] *vi* solidify

**Feste** [FEST•eh] *n* F fort

**Festessen** [FEST•essen] *n* N banquet

**festgefügt** [FEST•geh•FOOGT] *adj* coherent

**festgreifen** [FEST•gruy•fen] *vt* clutch

**Festigkeit** [FEST•ig•kuyt] *n* F consistency; solidity; steadiness

**Festigung** [FEST•Ig•oong] *n* F fortification

**Festland** [FEST•lahnd] *n* N mainland

**festlich** [FEST•lihk] *adj* festive

**Festmahl** [FEST•mahl] *n* M feast

**Festnahme** [FEST•nah•meh] *n* F detention

**festsetzen** [FEST•zets•en] *vt* fix; arrange; stipulate

**Festsetzung** [FEST•ZETS•tsoong] *n* F determination

**feststellen** [FEST•SHTEL•ehn] *vt* check; diagnose

**fettleibig** [FEHT•laib•ig] *adj* obese

**feucht** [foikht] *adj* damp; humid; moist

**Feuchtigkeit** [FOIHK•tig•kuyt] *n* F humidity; moisture

**feudal** [FOI•dahl] *adj* feudal

**Feuer** [FOI•air] *n* N fire; bonfire; blaze

**Feuerwehrmann** [-mahn] *n* M fireman

**Feuerwehrwache** [FOI•air•VAIR•VAH•hke] *n* F fire station

**Feuerwerk** [FOI•air•VAIRK] *n* N fireworks

**Fichte** [FIHK•teh] *n* spruce

**Fieber** [FEE•bair] *n* N fever

**fieberisch** [FEE•bair•ish] *adj* feverish

**Fiedel** [FEE•del] *n* F fiddle

**fiel** [feel] fell; fallen

**Figur** [fig•OOR] *n* F figure; physique

**Film** [film] *n* M film; movie

**Filter** [FIL•tair] *n* M filter; strainer

**Filz** [filts] *n* M felt

**Finanz** [fee•NAHNTS] *n* F finance

**Finanzabteilung** [fee•NANTS•AP•TUYL•oong] *n* F treasurer

**finanziell** [fee•NAHN•TSEE•el] *adj* financial

**Finger** [FING•air] *n* M finger

**Fingerabdruck** [FIN•gair•AP•droohk] *n* M fingerprint

**Fingergelenk** [FIHNG•air•GE•lehnk] *n* N knuckle

**Fingerhut** [FING•air•HOOT] *n* M thimble

**Fingerspitze** [FIN•gair•SHPIH•tse] *n* F fingertip

**Fink** [feenk] *n* M finch

**Finner** [FIN•nair] *n* Finn

**finnisch** [FIN•nish] *adj* Finnish

**Finnland** [FIN•lant] Finland

**finster** [FIN•stair] *adj* dark; gloomy; glum

**finster anblicken** [FIHN•stair AHN•blihk•en] *vt* scowl; frown

**Firme** [FEER•me] *n* F company

**Fisch** [fish] *n* M fish

**Fischen** [FISH•en] *n* N fishing

**Fischer** [FISH•air] *n* M
fisherman

**fiskalisch** [FISK•ahl•ish] *adj*
fiscal

**Fixierung** [FIKS•EER•oong] *n*
F fixation

**flach** [flahk] *adj* flat

**Fläche** [FLEK•uh] *n* F acre;
tract

**Fläschchen** [FLEHSH•khen] *n*
N vial

**Flamingo** [FLA•meen•go] *n* M
flamingo

**Flamme** [FLAH•me] *n* F flame

**Flanell** [FLA•nel] *n* M flannel

**Flasche** [FLAH•shuh] *n* F
bottle; flask

**Flattern** [FLAH•tairn] *n* N
flicker

**flattern** [FLAH•tairn] *vi* flutter

**Flaum** [floum] *n* M floss

**Flechse** [FLEHKS•eh] *n* F
sinew

**flechten** [FLEKH•ten] *vt* braid

**Flechte** [FLEKH•tuh] *n* F braid

**Fleck** [flehk] *n* M spot; stain

**flecken** [FLEHK•en] *vt* speckle

**fleckenlos** [-los] *adj* stainless

**Flecktyphus** [FLEHK•tuh•fuhs]
*n* M typhus

**Fledermaus** [FLAI•dair•mows]
*n* F bat

**flehen um** [FLAI•hen oom] *vt*
invoke

**Fleiß** [flais] *n* M diligence

**fleißig** [FLAI•sig] *adj* diligent

**Fleisch** [fluysh] *n* N flesh; meat

**Fleischerei** [FLAISH•air•ai] *n* F
butcher shop

**fleischfressend**
{FLUYSH•fres•sent} *adj*
carnivorous

**fleischig** [FLUYSH•ig] *adj*
fleshy

**Fleischklößchen** [-kluhs•chen]
*n* N meatball

**fleischlich** [FLUYSH•likh] *adj*
carnal

**Fleischspieß** [FLUYSH•shpees]
*n* M skewer

**fleißig** [FLUY•sig] *adj*
hardworking; industrious

**flexibel** [FLEHKS•EE•bel] *adj*
flexible

**Fliegen** [FLEE•gen] *n* N fly

**fliegende Untertasse**
{FLEE•gen•de
OON•tair•TAH•se] *n* F flying
saucer

**fliehen** [FLEE•en] *vi* flee

**fließend** [FLEE•send] *adj* fluent

**flink** [flihnk] *adj* nimble; agile

**Flinkheit** [FLINK•huyt] *n*
quickness

**Flint** [flint] *n* M flint

**Flirt** [fleert] *n* M flirt

**Flitter** [FLIH•tair] *n* M spangle

**Flittergold** [FLIH•tair•gold] *n*
N tinsel

**Flocke** [FLO•ke] *n* F flake

**Flößer** [FLUH•sair] *n* M rafter

**Flöte** [FLOO•te] *n* F flute

**Floh** [floh] *n* M flea

**Flora** [FLO•rah] *n* F flora

**Floß** [flohs] *n* N raft

**Flosse** [FLOH•se] *n* F fin

**Flotte** [FLO•te] *n* F fleet

**Flußkrebs** [FLOOS•krebs] *n* M
crayfish

**Fluch** [floohk] *n* M curse

**fluchen** [FLOO•ken] *vt vi*
blaspheme

**Flucht** [floohkt] *n* F escape

flüchtig [FLUHK•tig] *adj*
transient

Flüchtling [FLUHKT•leeng] *n*
M fugitive

Flüchtlinge [FLUHKT•ling•eh]
*n* F runaway

Flug [floog] *n* M flight

Flugbahn [FLOOG•bahn] *n* F
trajectory

Flügel [FLUH•gel] *n* M wing

Flughafen [FLOOG•hah•fuhn]
*n* M airport

Flugreise [FLOOG•ruy•zeh] *n* F
voyage

Flugschlag [FLOOG•shlahg] *n*
M volley

Flugzeug [FLOOG•tsoig] *n* N
airplane; plane

Flugzeughalle
[FLOOG•tsoig•hahl•e] *n* F
hangar

Flunder [FLOON•dair] *n* M
flounder

fluoreszierend
[FLOO•or•es•TSEEr•end] *adj*
fluorescent

Fluorid [FLOO•or•id] *n* N
fluoride

Fluß 1 [floos] *n* M fluency

Fluß 2 [fluhs] *n* M river; course
of a river

Flüßchen [FLOOS•khen] *n* N
creek

flüssig [FLOOS•ig] *adj* liquid;
fluid

Flüssigkeit; flüssig
[FLUH•sig•KUYT] *n* F liquid;
fluid

Flut [floot] *n* F flood; flow

fördern [FER•dairn] *vt* promote

Fötus [FUH•toos] *n* M fetus

fokal [FO•kahl] *adj* focal

Fokus [FO•koos] *n* M focus

Folge [FOHL•geh] *n* F
sequence; sequel

folgen [FOL•gen] *vt* follow;
come after; obey

folgend [FOL•gent] *adj*
following; ensuing

Folie [FO•lee•uh] *n* F foil

Folterknecht [-knehkt] *n* M
torturer

Folterung [FOL•tair•oong] *n* F
torture

foppen [FOHP•pen] *vi* tease

Form [form] *n* F form

Formalität [FOR•mahl•i•TAIT]
*n* F formality

Formel [FOR•mel] *n* F formula

formell [FOR•mel] *adj* formal

Formular [FORM•oo•lahr] *n* N
blank; form

Forscher [FOR•shair] *n* M
explorer

Forschung [FOR•shoong] *n* F
research

fortan [FORT•an] *adv*
henceforth

fortschleppen
[FOHRT•shleh•pen] *vt* trudge

Fortschritt [FORT•shrit] *n* M
headway

Fortschritt [FORT•shriht] *n* M
progress

fortschrittlich [-lihk] *adj*
progressive

Fortsetzung [FORT•zets•oong]
*n* F continuation

Fortsetzungen
[FORT•zet•tsoon•gen] *npl*
serial

Fossil [FOH•sil] *n* N fossil

**Foto** [FO•to] *n* N photo; photograph

**Fracht** [frahkht] *n* F cargo; freight

**Frack** [frahk] *n* M evening gown

**Fräulein** [FROI•luyn] *n* N Miss

**Frage** [FRAH•geh] *n* F question; query

**Fragebogen** [-BOH•gen] *n* M questionnaire

**fragen** [FRAH•gen] *vt* ask

**fragen nach** [FRAH•gen nahk] *vi* inquire (of)

**Fragezeichen** [-TSUY•khen] *n* N question mark

**fraglich** [FRAHG•lihk] *adj* questionable

**Fragment** [FRAHG•ment] *n* N fraction; fragment

**Fraktur** [FRAHK•toor] *n* F fracture

**Fraktura** [FRAHK•toor•eh] *n* F invoice

**Franc** [frahnk] *n* M franc

**Frankreich** [FRAHNK•ruyhk] *n* N France

**französisch** [frahn•TSOO•zish] *adj* French

**Frau** [frou] *n* F wife

**Frau Weib** [frou] [vaib] *n* F woman

**Frauenstimmrecht** [FROU•en•SHTIM•rehkt] *n* N suffrage

**frech** [frekh] *adj* brash

**frei** [fruy] *adj* free

**Freibad** [FRUY•bahd] *n* N swimming pool

**freie Zeit** [FRUY•e tsait] *n* leisure

**freier Platz** [FRUY•air plahts] *n* M vacancy

**freier Wille** [FRUY•air vil•eh] *n* M free will

**freigestellt** [FRUY•geh•shtelt] *adj* optional

**Freihandel** [FRUY•han•del] *n* M free trade

**Freiheit** [FRUY•huyt] *n* F freedom; liberty

**freimütig** [FRUY•moo•tig] *adj* outspoken

**freindlich** [FUYND•lihk] *adj* hostile

**freisprechen** [FRAI•shprek•uhn] *vt* acquit

**Freitag** [fruy•tahg] *n* M Friday

**freiwillig** [FRUY•vil•lig] *adj* voluntary

**Freiwilliger in** [-air] [in] *n* M volunteer

**Freiwilligkeit** [FRUY•vihl•ig•KUYT] *n* spontaneity

**Freizeit** [FRUY•tsuyt] *n* F pastime

**fremd** [frempt] *adj* foreign

**Fremder** [FREMPT•air] *n* M stranger

**Fremdheit** [FREMPT•huyt] *n* F strangeness

**fressen** [FREH•sen] *vt* devour

**Frettchen** [FRET•chen] *n* N ferret

**Freude** [FROI•deh] *n* delight; joy

**Freude** [FROI•deh] *n* F rejoicing

**fruen** [FROI•ehn] *vi* to be pleased

**Freuerzeug** [FOI•air•tsoig] *n* N
lighter

**Freund** [froind] *n* M friend; pal

**Freundin** [FROIN•din] *n* F
girlfriend

**freundlich** [FROIND•lihk] *adj*
friendly; genial; kindly

**Freundlichkeit** [-kuyt] *n* F
kindness

**Freundschaft** [FROINT•shahft]
*n* F friendship

**Frevel** [FRAI•vel] *n* M outrage

**Frieden** [FREE•den] *n* M peace

**Friedhof** [FREED•hohf] *n* M
cemetery

**friedlich** [FREED•lihk] *adj*
peaceful

**frieren** [FREER•en] *vt* freeze

**Frikadelle** [FRIH•keh•dehl•eh]
*n* F hamburger

**frisch** [frish] *adj* fresh

**Frische** [FRI•she] *n* F freshness

**Friseur** [FRIH•zoor] *n* M barber

**Friseur-in** [FRIH•zoor -in] *n* M
hairdresser

**Frist** [frihst] *n* respite

**Fröhlichkeit**
[FRUH•lihk•KUYT] *n* F glee

**froh** [froh] *adj* glad

**fromm** [frohm] *adj* devout;
pious

**Frosch** [frohsh] *n* M frog

**Frost** [frohst] *n* M frost

**frostig** [FROST•ig] *adj* frosty

**Frucht** [froohkt] *n* F fruit

**fruchtbar** [FROOHKT•bahr]
*adj* fertile

**Fruchtbarkeit** [-kuyt] *n* F
fertility

**Fruchtfleisch** [FRUHKT•fluysh]
*n* N pulp

**früh** [frooh] *adj* early

**früher** [FRUH•hair] *adj* prior;
earlier

**Frühling** [FRUH•ling] *n* M
spring

**frühreif** [FRUH•ruyf] *adj*
precocious

**Frühstück** [FROO•shtookh] *n* N
breakfast

**frustrieren** [FROO•streer•en] *vt*
frustrate

**Fuchs** [FOOKS] *n* M fox

**fügsam** [FOOG•zahm] *adj*
docile; tractable

**fühlen** [FUH•len] *vt* feel

**führen** [FUH•ren] *vt* take; lead;
guide; carry

**Führer** [FUH•rer] *n* M leader;
guide

**füllen** [FOOL•en] *vt* fill

**Füllung** [FOOL•oong] *n* F
filling; stuffing

**Fund** [foond] *n* M find

**Fundgrube** [FUNT•groo•beh] *n*
F quarry

**fünf** [foonf] *num* five

**Fünflinge** [FUHNF•ling•eh] *n* F
quintuplet

**fünfte** [FOONF•te] *num* fifth

**fünfzehn** [FOONF•tsain] *num*
fifteen

**fünfzehnte** [-te] *num* fifteenth

**fünfzig** [FOONF•tsig] *num* fifty

**fünfzigste** [FOONF•tsig•ste]
*num* fiftieth

**funkeln** [FOONK•eln] *vi* glitter;
sparkle

**funkelnd** [FOONK•elnt] *adj*
sparkling

**Funken 1** [foon•ken] *npl* embers

**Funken 2** [fuhn•ken] *n* M spark

**funktionieren**
[FUHNK•TSEE•on•EER•oong]
*vt* operate
**für** [foor] *prep* for
**Furcht** [foorhkt] *n* F fear
**furchtbar** [FOORHKT•bahr]
*adj* formidable; terrible; awful
**fürchterlich**
[FOORHK•tair•lihk] *adj*
dreadful
**furchtlos** [FOORHKT•los] *adj*
fearless
**Furnierholz** [foor•NEER•holts]
*n* N veneer; plywood

**Furt** [foort] *n* F ford
**Fuß** [foos] *n* M foot
**Fußball** [FOOS•bal] *n* M
football
**Fussel** [FUH•sel] *n* F lint
**Fußgänger** [FOOS•geng•air] *n*
M pedestrian
**Fußspur** [FOOS•shpoor] *n* F
footprint
**Fußweg** [FOOS•vaig] *n* M
footpath
**Futter** [FUH•tair] *n* N feed;
fodder; forage
**Futteral** *n* N[fuh•tair•ahl] case

# G

**Gabe** [GAH•beh] *n* F gift;
present; dowry
**Gabel** [GAH•bel] *n* F fork;
pitchfork
**gackern** [GAH•kairn] *vi* cackle
**gähnen** [GAI•nen] *vi* yawn
**Gälisch** [GAI•lish] *adj n* M
Gaelic
**Gänseblümchen**
[GENS•eh•BLOOM•khen] *n*
N daisy
**gären** [GAIR•en] v ferment
**Gästezimmer**
[GEST•eh•TSIM•air] *n* N
guestroom
**Galgen** [GAHL•gen] *n* M
gallows
**Galle** [GAHL•leh] *n* F bile; gall
**Gallenblase**
[GAHL•len•blah•zuh] *n* F
bladder

**Gallerie** [GAH•lair•ee] *n* F
gallery
**Gallerte** [GAHL•air•te] *n* F
jelly
**Galon** [GAH•lohn] *n* M gallon
**Galopp** [GAH•lohp] *n* M gallop
**Gang 1** [gahng] *n* M corridor
**Gang 2** [gahng] *n* M way of
walking; gait; errand
**Gang 3** [gahng] gang; mob
**Gangster** [GAHNG•stair] *n* M
gangster; racketeer
**Gans** [gants] *n* F goose
**ganz 1** [gahnts] *adj* entire;
whole
**ganz 2** [gants] *adv* quite; totally
**Ganze** [GAHNTS•e] *n* N
entirety
**Garage** [gah•RAH•jeh] *n* F
garage
**Garantie** [gahr•AHN•tee] *n* F
guarantee

**Garderobe**
[GAHR•deh•ROH•beh] *n* F
wardrobe

**Garnele** [gar•NEL•eh] *n* F
shrimp

**Garten** [GAH•ten] *n* M
backyard; garden

**Gas** [gahs] *n* N gas

**gasartig** [GAHS•ahr•tig] *adj*
gaseous

**Gaserzeuger**
[GAHS•air•TSOI•gair] *n* M
generator

**Gast** [gahst] *n* M guest

**Gastgeber** [GAHST•gai•bair] *n*
M host

**Gastgeberin** [-in] *n* F hostess

**Gasthaus -hof** [GAHST•hous]
[-hohf] *n* N inn; guest house

**Gastlichkeit**
[GAHST•lihk•kuyt] *n* F
hospitality

**Gastwirt** [GAHST•veert] *n* M
innkeeper

**Gatte** [GAH•teh] *n* M spouse

**Gattin** [GAH•tin] *n* F wife

**gaukeln** [GOU•keln] *vt* juggle

**Gaumen** [GOU•men] *n* M
palate

**Gauner** [gou•nair] *n* M crook

**Gaunerei** [GOU•nair•uy] *n* F
trickery

**Gaze** [GAH•tse] *n* F gauze

**Gebärmutter**
[GEL•BAIR•muh•tair] *n* F
womb

**Gebäude** [geh•BOU•deh] *n* N
building

**geben** [GAI•ben] *vt* give; ~was
gibst\ what's the matter/what's
up

**Geber** [GAI•bair] *n* M donor;
dealer (cards)

**Gebet** [BEH•bait] *n* N prayer

**Gebiet** [GEH•beet] *n* N territory

**Gebiß** [GEH•bis] *n* N bit

**geboren; geboren am** (born
on) [geh•BOH•ren] [ahm] *adj*
born (to be)

**Gebot** [GEH•boht] *n* N bid

**Gebrauch** [GEH•brouhk•en] *n*
M use

**gebrauchen** [GEH•brouhk•en]
*vt* use

**gebraucht** [GEH•brouhkt] *adj*
second-hand

**Gebrauchwagen** [-VAH•gen]
*n* M used car

**Gebrechlichkeit**
[ge•BREHK•lihk•kuyt] *n* F
infirmity

**Geburt** [geh•BOORT] *n* F birth;
childbirth

**Geburt Christi** [geh•BOORT
KHRI•stee] *n* F Nativity

**Geburtenregelung**
[geh•BOORT•en•RAI•gel•oong]
*n* F birth control

**Geburtenziffer**
[geh•BOOR•ten•TSIF•fair] *n*
F birthrate

**Geburtstag**
[geh•BOORTS•tahg] *n* M
birthday

**Gebüsch** [geh•BOOSH] *n* N
bush; shrubbery

**Gedächtnis** [geh•DEHKT•nis] *n*
N memory

**Gedanke** [geh•DAHNK•eh] *n*
M thought

**gedankenlos**
[geh•DAHNK•en•los] *adj*
thoughtless; unthinking

**Gedankenlosigkeit** [-ig•kuyt] *n* F thoughtlessness

**gedankenvoll** [geh•DAHNK•en•fol] *adj* thoughtful

**gedeihen** [geh•DUY•en] *vt* thrive

**Gedicht** [geh•DIHKT] *n* N poem

**Gedränge** [geh•DREHNG•eh] *n* N throng; crowd

**Geduld** [ge•DOOLD] *n* F ` patience

**geduldig** [geh•DOOL•dig] *adj* tolerant; patient

**geeignet** [ge•AIG•net] *adj* proper

**gefährden** [ge•FAIR•den] *vt* endanger; jeopardize

**gefährlich** [ge•FAIR•lihk] *adj* dangerous; hazardous

**Gefälle** [ge•FEHL•eh] *n* F pitch

**gefällig** [geh•FEL•ig] *adj* pleasing

**Gefälligkeit** [ge•FEL•ig•kuyt] *n* F facilities

**Gefängnis** [geh•FENG•nis] *n* N jail; prison

**Gefahr** [ge•FAHR] *n* F danger; hazard; menace

**Gefallen** [ge•FAL•en] *n* M favor

**gefallen** [geh•FAHL•en] *vt* please

**Gefangene** [geh•FANG•en•eh] *n* M prisoner

**Gefangener** [geh•FAHNG•ehn•air] *n* M captive

**geflogen** [ge•FLO•gen] *vt* flown

**Geflügel** [ge•FLOO•gel] *n* N fowl; poultry

**geflügelt** [geh•FLUH•gelt] *adj* winged

**Gefolge** [geh•FOL•geh] *n* N retinue

**Gefrierkammer** [ge•FREER•kah•mair] *n* M freezer

**Gefühl** [ge•FOOL] *n* N feeling

**Gefühl** [geh•FUHL] *n* N sensations

**gefunden** [ge•FUHN•den] found

**gegeben** [geh•GAI•ben] given

**gegen** [gai•GEN] *prep adv* against

**Gegend** [gai•GENT] *n* F area; region

**gegensätzlich** [gai•gen•zets•lihk] *adj* inconsistent

**Gegensatz** [GAI•gen•ZATS] *n* M converse

**gegenseitig** [GAI•gen•sai•tig] *adj* reciprocal

**Gegenstand** [GAI•gen•shtahnd] *n* M item

**Gegenteil** [GAI•gen•tuyl] *n* M opposite; reverse

**gegenüberliegend** [GAI•gen•UH•bair•LEE•gend] *adj* opposing

**Gegenüberstellung** [-shtehl•oong] *n* F opposition

**gegenwärtig** [GAI•gen•vair•tig] *adj* current

**Gegenwert** [GAI•gen•vairt] *n* M equivalent

**Gegestand** [GAI•gen•shtant] *n* M subject

**Gegner** [GAIG•nair] *n* M foe; opponent

**Gehalt** [geh•HALHT] *n* N salary; stipend

**Geheimnis** [geh•HUYM•nis] *n* N secret; mystery

**geheimnisvoll** [ge•HUYM•nis•fol] *adj* secretive; mysterious

**Geheimschrift** [geh•HUYM•shrift] *n* F code

**gehemmt** [geh•HEMPT] *adj* self-conscious

**gehen** [gai•HEN] *vi* go; walk

**Gehetze** [geh•HETS•eh] *n* F hustle

**Gehirn** [geh•HEERN] *n* N brain

**gehören** [geh•HER•en] *vi* pertain

**gehören zu** [geh•HOOR•ren tsoo] *vi* belong

**gehorchen** [ge•HOHR•chen] *vt* obey

**Gehorsam** [geh•HOR•zahm] *n* M obedience

**gehorsam** *adj* obedient

**Geier** [GUY•air] *n* M vulture

**geil** [guyl] *adj* lecherous

**Geisel** [GUY•zel] *n* M hostage

**Geist** [guyst] *n* M ghost; spirit

**Geisterglaube** [-air•GLOU•beh] *n* M spiritualism

**geistesabwesend** [GUYST•uhs•AHP•vaiz•uhnt] *adj* absent-minded

**Geisteskrankheit** [GUYST•es•KRAHN•kuyt] *n* F insanity

**geistig** [GUYST•ig] *adj* mental; spiritual

**Geistigkeit** [GUYST•ig•kuyt] *n* F spirituality

**geistlich** [GUYST•likh] *adj* clerical

**Geistlichkeit** [GUYST•likh•huyt] *n* F clergy

**Geiz** [guyts] *n* M meanness; stinginess

**Geizhals** [GUYTS•hahls] *n* miser

**geizig** [GUYTS•ig] *adj* miserly; stingy

**Geizkragen** [GUYTS•krah•gen] *n* M tightwad

**gekochtes Ei** [geh•KOHK•tes uyy] *n* N boiled egg

**Gelächter** [geh•LEHK•tair] *n* N guffaw; laughter

**Gelände** [geh•LEND•eh] *n* N terrain

**Geläute** [geh•LOI•teh] *n* M chime

**Gelassenheit** [ge•LAH•sen•huyt] *n* F composure

**Gelatine** [JEL•ah•TEEN•e] *n* F gelatin

**gelaunt** [ge•LOUNT] *adj* disposed

**gelb** [gelp] yellow

**Gelbsucht** [GELB•zoohkt] *n* F jaundice

**Geld** [gehld] *n* N money

**geldlich** [GEHLD•lihk] *adj* monetary

**Gelege** [ge•LAI•ge] *n* N clutch

**Gelegenheit** [geh•lai•gehn•HUYT] *n* F chance; occasion; opportunity

**gelegentlich** [-lihk] *adj* occasional; *adv* occasionally

**Gelehrsamkeit**
[ge•LAIR•zahm•KUYT] *n* F
learning

**gelehrt 1** *adj* scholarly

**gelehrt 2** [geh•LAIRT] *pp*
taught

**Gelehrter** [geh•LAIR•tair] *n* M
scholar

**Geleise** [geh•LUY•zeh] *n* F rut

**Gelenk** [ge•LEHNK] *n* N hinge

**geliebt** [geh•LEEPT] *adj*
beloved

**Geliebte** [geh•LEEP•teh] *n* F
belly

**gelingen** [geh•LING•en] *vi*
succeed

**gellen** [GEL•len] *vi* bray; yell

**gelten als** [GEL•ten ahls] *vi*
repute

**Gemälde** [geh•MAIL•de] *n* N
painting

**gemäßigt** [geh•MAI•sikt] *adj*
temperate; moderate

**Gemäßigte** [geh•MEH•sikteh] *n*
F moderate

**gemein** [geh•MUYN] *adj* cruel;
mean; vile

**Gemeinde** [geh•MUYN•deh] *n*
township

**gemeinsam** [ge•MUYN•zam]
*adj* common; joint; mutual

**Gemeinschaft**
[ge•MUYN•shahft] *n* F
community

**Gemeinschaftskonto**
[-s•KOHN•to] *n* N joint
account

**Gemüse** [geh•MUH•zeh] *n* F
vegetable

**Gemütlichkeit**
[geh•MOOT•lik•kuyt] *n* F
bliss

**genäht** [geh•NAIT] *adj* sewn

**genau** [ge•NOU] *adj* exact

**genau gleich** [ge•NOU gluyhk]
*adj* identical

**genau prüfen** [geh•NOU
pruh•fen] *vt* scrutinize

**genau richtig** [guh•NOU]
[rik•tig] *adj* accurate

**Genauigkeit**
[geh•NOU•ig•kuyt] *n* F
precision

**genehmigen** [ge•NAIM•ig•en]
*vt* approve

**Genehmigung**
[geh•NAIM•ig•OONG] F
permit; approval

**geneigt** [geh•NAIKT] *adj* bent;
prone

**Generation**
[gen•AIR•aht•TSEE•on] *n* F
generation

**genesend** [geh•NAI•sent] *adj*
convalescent

**Genesung** [geh•NAI•zoong] *n*
F convalescence

**genetisch** [ge•NEH•tish] *adj*
genetic

**genial** [GEE•nee•al] *adj*
ingenious

**Genick** [GEH•nik] *n* N scruff

**Genie** [jen•EE] *n* F genius

**genießbar** [ge•NEES•bahr] *adj*
enjoyable; edible

**genießen** [ge•NEE•sen] *vt*
enjoy

**Genosse** [ge•NO•se] *n* M
fellow

**genug** [geh•NOOG] *adj*
enough; plenty

**genügen** [geh•NUHG•en] *vi*
suffice

**genügend** [guh•NOOG•uhnt] *adj* adequate

**genügend** [geh•NOO•gend] *adj* sufficient

**Geographie** [GEH•oh•GRAH•fee] *n* F geography

**Geologie** [GAI•oh•LOH•gee] *n* F geology

**Geometrie** [GAI•oh•meh•TREE] *n* F geometry

**geometrisch** [GAI•oh•MEH•trish] *adj* geometric

**Gepäck** [geh•PEK] *n* N baggage; luggage

**Gepard** [GEH•pahrd] *n* M cheetah

**Geplapper** [geh•PLAH•pair] *n* N patter

**gerade 1** [geh•RAH•de] *adv* directly; precisely

**gerade 2** [ge•RAH•de] *adj* straight; just

**gerade** [gch•RAH•deh] *adj* straight

**gerade machen** [-MAH•khen] *v* straighten

**Gerät** [geh•RAIT] *n* N device; utensil; tackle (fishing)

**Gerät** [geh•REHT] *n* N utensil

**geräumig** [geh•ROI•mig] *adj* roomy

**Gerberei** [GAIR•bair•ruy] *n* F tannery

**gerecht** [ge•REHKT] *adj* fair; righteous

**Gereizheit** [ge•RUYTS•huyt] *n* F pique

**Gericht** [ge•RIHKT] *n* N court

**gerichtlich** [ge•RIHKT•lihk] *adj* judicial

**Gerichtshof** [geh•RIHKTS•hohf] *n* M tribunal

**Gerichtsort** [geh•RIHKTS•ort] *n* M venue

**geringer** [geh•RING•air] *adj* lesser

**geringschätzen** [ge•rING•SHEHTS•en] *vi* depreciate

**geringst** [geh•RINGST] *adj* least

**gerinnen lassen** [geh•RIN•en lah•sen] *vt* curdle

**gern** [gairn] *adj* willingly

**gern essen** [gairn ES•sen] *vt* relish (condiment)

**gerne** [GAIRN•e] *adv* gladly

**Gerste** [GAIR•steh] *n* F barley

**Gerstenkorn** [GAIRST•en•kohrn] *n* N sty

**Geruch** [geh•ROOK] *n* M odor; scent

**Gerücht** [geh•RUHKT] *n* M hearsay; *n* N rumor

**gesamt** [geh•ZAHMT] *adj* total

**Gesamtheit** [-huyt] *n* F totality

**Gesandter** [ge•ZAHN•tair] *n* M envoy; ambassador

**Gesang** [ge•ZANG] *n* M song; lieder

**Geschäft** [geh•SHEFT] *n* N business

**Geschäftsabschluß** [~AB•shluss] business deal

**Geschäft einkaufen gehen** [geh•SHEHFT] [UYN•kou•fen gai•en] *n v* N shop

**geschäftlich** [geh•SHEFT•lik] *adj* business

**Geschäftsimmer** [~TSIM•mer] office

**Geschäftsmann -frau** [geh•SHEFTS•mahn] [ -frow] *n* M businessman ~woman

**Geschenk** [geh•SHAINK] *n* N gift

**Geschichte** [geh•SHIHK•te] *n* F history; story

**Geschicklichkeit** [ge•SHIK•LIK•kuyt] *n* F craft; skill

**geschickt** [ge•SHIKT] *adj* skilled; skillful

**geschickt klug** [geh•SHIKT] [kloog] *adj* clever

**Geschirr** [geh•SHEER] *n* N harness

**Geschirrspülmaschine** [geh•SHEER•SHPOOl•mah•SHEEN•eh] *n* F dishwasher

**Geschlecht** [geh•SHLEHKT] *n* N gender; sex

**Geschlechts** [ge•SHLEHKTS] *adj* genital

**Geschmack** [ge•SHMAHK] *n* M flavor

**geschmiedig** [geh•SHMEE•dig] *adj* pliable

**geschmolzen** [geh•SHMOHLTS•en] *adj* molten

**Geschöpf** [ge•SHUHPF] *n* N creature

**Geschoß** [geh•SHOHS] *n* N missile

**Geschrei** [geh•SHRUY] *n* N whoop

**geschrumpft** [geh•SHRUHMPFT] *adj* shrunk

**Geschützfeuer** [geh•SHUHTS•foi•air] *n* N gunfire

**Geschwafel** [geh•SHVAH•fel] *n* N gibberish

**Geschwindigkeit** [geh•SHVIN•dig•kuyt] *n* F rate

**Geschwindigkeit** [geh•SHVIHNDIG•kuyt] *n* F speed; velocity

**Geschwindigkeitsgrenze** [-GREHN•zeh] *n* F speed limit

**Geschworenen** [-en] *npl* jury

**Geschworener** [geh•SHVOHR•en•air] *n* M juror

**Geschwür** [geh•SHVOOR] *n* N ulcer

**Geschwürbildung** [-BILD•oong] *n* F ulceration

**gesellig** [geh•ZEL•lig] *adj* sociable; social

**Gesellschaft** [geh•ZEHL•shahft] *n* F institute; society; assembly

**Gesetz** [geh•ZETS] *n* N law; statute

**gesetzestreu** [geh•ZETS•es•troi] *adj* law-abiding

**Gesetzgebung** [ge•ZETS•GAI•boong] *n* F legislation

**Gesetzgebungs** [ge•ZETS•GAI•boongs] *n* F legislature

**gesetzlich** [ge•ZETS•lihk] *adj*
lawful; legal

**gesetzt** [geh•ZETST] *adj* staid

**Gesicht** [ge•ZIHKT] *n* N face

**Gesichtsfarbe**
[geh•ZIHKTS•fahr•be] *n* F
complexion

**Gesichtspunkt** [geh•ZIHKTS-]
*n* M point of view

**Gesims** [ge•SIMS] *n* N cornice

**gespannt** [geh•SHPAHNT] *adj*
tense

**Gespenst** [geh•SHPEHNST] *n*
N specter

**gesponnen** [geh•SHPON•nen]
*pret pp* spun

**gesprächig** [geh•SHPREHK•ig]
*adj* talkative

**Gestalt** [ge•SHTAHLT] *n* F
form; guise; semblance

**Gestank** [geh•SHTANK] *n* M
reek; stench

**Geste** [GEH•ste] *n* F gesture

**Gestell** [geh•SHTEL] *n* N rack

**Gestell** [geh•SHTEL] *n* N
trestle

**gestern** [GEH•stairn] *adv*
yesterday

**gestikulieren**
[geh•SHTIHK•oo•LEER•en]
*vi* gesticulate

**gestört** [geh•SHTOORT] *adj*
deranged

**Gesträuch** [geh•SHTROIHK] *n*
N underbrush

**gesund** [geh•ZUHNT] *adj*
healthy; wholesome

**Gesundheit** [geh•ZUHNT•huyt]
. *n* F health

**Getöse** [ge•TOO•seh] *n* N din;
tumult

**Getränk** [geh•TRENK] *n* N
drink; beverage

**Getreide** [geh•TRUY•deh] *n* F
cereal; grain

**getrennt** [ge•TRENT] *adj*
estranged; separate

**getrocknet** [geh•TROHK•net]
*adj* dried

**Getue** [geh•TOO•eh] *n* M
bustle

**Gewächshaus**
[ge•VEHKS•hous] *n* N
greenhouse

**Gewährung** [ge•vair•oong] *n* F
grant

**Gewalt** [geh•VAHLT] *n* F
violence

**gewaltig** [geh•VAHL•tig] *adj*
monumental; tremendous

**gewaltig** [-tig] *adj* violent

**gewaltsam**
[geh•VAHLT•zahm] *adj*
oppressive

**gewann** [geh•VAHN] *pp* won

**gewähren** [geh•VAIR•ren] *vt*
donate; bestow

**Gewebe** [geh•VAI•beh] *n* N
tissue; web; webbing

**Gewehr** [geh•VAIR] *n* N rifle

**Gewerkschaft**
[geh•VAIRK•shahft] *n* F
trade-union

**Gewerkschaftsbund**
[geh•VAIRK•shahfts•buhnt] *n*
M labor union

**gewesen** [geh•VAIY•zen] *pp*
been

**Gewicht** [geh•VIHKT] *n* weight

**gewillt** [geh•VIHLT] *adj*
willing

**Gewinn** [geh•VIN] *n* M profit

**gewinnbringend** [-bring•end] *adj* profitable

**gewinnen 1** [geh•VIN•nen] *vt* win

**gewinnen 2** [guh•VIN•nen] *vt* acquire

**Gewinner in** [geh•VIN•nair] [in] *n* M winner

**Gewissen** [geh•VIS•sen] *n* N conscience

**gewissenhaft** [ge•VIS•en•hahft] *adj* conscientious

**Gewitter** [geh•VIH•tair] *n* N thunderstorm

**gewitterschwül** [geh•VIH•tair•shvuhl] *adj* thunderous

**gewöhnlich 1** [ge•VUHN•lihk] *adj* ordinary; usual

**gewöhnlich 2** [geh•VUHN•lihk] *adv* normally

**Gewölbe springen** [geh•VUHL•beh] [shpring•en] *n vi* N vault

**Gewohnheit** [ge•VOHN•huyt] *n* F habit

**gewohnt** [geh•VOHNT] *adj* usual; accustomed; wont

**gewunden** [geh•VUHN•den] *adj* spiral

**gewunden** [geh•VUHN•den] *adj* tortuous

**Gewürz** [geh•VOORTS] *n* N spice

**Gewürzgurke** [ge•VOORTS•goor•keh] *n* pickle

**Gewürznelke** [geh•VOORTS•nel•keh] *n* F clove

**Gezeiten** [geh•TSAIT•en] *adj* tidal

**Gicht** [gihkt] *n* F gout

**Giebel** [GEE•bel] *n* M gable

**Gier** [geer] *n* F greed

**Gier** [geer] *n* F lust

**gierig** [GEER•ig] *adj* greedy; gluttonous; voracious

**gießen** [GEE•sen] *vt* pour

**Gift** [gihft] *n* N poison; venom

**giftig** [GIHF•tig] *adj* poisonous; toxic; venomous

**gigantisch** [GI•gahn•tish] *adj* gigantic

**Gigue** [geeg] *n* F jig

**Giraffe** [jeer•AH•fe] *n* F giraffe

**Girlande** [GEER•lahn•de] *n* F garland

**Gischt** [gihsht] *n* F sprayer

**Gitter** [GIH•tair] *n* N grate; lattice; trellis

**Gitterfenster** [GIH•tair•FEN•stair] *n* N grille

**glänzend** [GLEHN•tsend] *adj* brilliant; flashy; splendid

**Glanz** [glahnts] *n* M brilliance; glamor; glare; gloss; luster

**Glas** [glahs] *n* N glass

**glasartig** [GLAHS•ahr•tig] *adj* glassy; vitreous

**Glasharmonika** [HAHR•moh•NEE•kah] *n* F harmonica

**Glasur** [GLAH•zoor] *n* F glaze; icing

**glatt** [glaht] *adj* glossy; sleek; slick; slippery

**Glaube** [GLAU•beh] *n* M belief; creed; faith

**glauben an** [GLAU•ben ahn] vt vi believe

**glaubwürdig** [GLOUB•voor•dig] adj believable; credible

**gleich** [gluyhk] adj equal; like

**gleichfalls** [gluyhk•fals] adv likewise

**Gleichgewicht** [GLAIK•geh•vikt] n N balance

**gleichgültig** [GLUYK•gool•tig] adj complacent; indifferent; nonchalant

**Gleichheit** [GLUYHK•huyt] n F equality

**gleichsam** [GLAIK•zahm] adj alike

**gleichzeitig** [GLUYHK•tsai•tig] adj simultaneous

**gleichzeitig sein** [GLUYHK•tsai•tig zuyn] vi synchronize

**gleiten** [GLUY•ten] vi glide; slide

**Gletscher** [GLEHT•chair] n M glacier

**Glied** [gleed] n N limb; link

**Gliederung** [GLEE•dair•oong] n F organization

**glitschig** [GLIHT•chig] adj slippery

**glitzern** [GLIH•tsairn] vi glisten

**Glitzern** [GLIH•tsairn] n N twinkle

**Glocke** [GLOS•keh] n F bell

**Glockenturm** [GLOW•ken•toorm] n M belfry

**Glossar** [GLOH•sahr] n N glossary

**Glück** [gluhk] n N luck; fortune

**glucken** [GLOO•ken] vi cluck

**glücklich** [GLUHK•lihk] adv happily; fortunate; lucky

**glücklich, froh** [-froh] adj happy

**glücklich, heiter** [GLOOK•likh] [HUY•tair] adj cheerful

**glücklicherweise** [-air•VAI•ze] adv fortunately; luckily

**Glücklichkeit** [-kuyt] n F happiness

**Glücksfall** [GLUHKS•fal] n M godsend

**Glühen** [GLUH•hen] n N glow

**glühend1** [GLOO•hend] adj fervent; ardent

**glühend2** [GLUH•hend] adj glowing; blazing (as fire)

**Gnade** [GNAH•de] n F grace

**gnädige Frau** [GNAI•dig•eh frou] n F madam

**gönnerhaft** [GUH•nair•haft] adj patronizing

**Göttin** [GUH•tin] n F goddess

**göttlich** [GUHT•lihk] adj divine

**Göttlichkeit** [GUHT•lih•kuyt] n F divinity

**Gold** [golt] n M gold

**golden** [GOL•den] adj golden

**Goldfisch** [GOLD•fish] n M goldfish

**Golf 1** [gohlf] n M golf (sport)

**Golf 2** [gohlf] n M gulf

**Gong** [gohng] n M gong

**Gorilla** [goh•RIL•la] n M gorilla

**gotisch** [GO•tish] adj gothic

**Gott** [goht] n M God

**gottheit** [GOHT•huyt] n F deity

**gottlos** [GOHT•los] *adj*
godless; atheistic

**Gouverneur** [GOO•vair•noor] *n*
M governor

**Grab** [grahb] *n* N tomb; grave

**graben** [GRAH•ben] *vt* dig

**Graben** [GRAH•ben] *n* M ditch;
trench

**Grabschrift** [GRAHB•shrift] *n*
F epitaph

**Grabstätte** [GRAHB•shteh•teh]
*n* F sepulcher

**Grabstein** [-shtuyn] *n* M
tombstone

**gräßlich** [GREHS•lihk] *adj*
grisly

**Grad** [grahd] *n* M degree

**Gräfin** [GRAI•fin] *n* F countess

**Gramm** [grahm] *n* M gram

**Grammatik** [grah•MAH•teek] *n*
F grammar

**grammatisch** [grah•MAH•tish]
*adj* grammatical

**Granit** [GRAH•neet] *n* M
granite

**graphisch** [GRAH•fish] *adj*
graphic

**Gras** [grahs] *n* N grass

**grasbedeckt**
[GRAHS•be•dehkt] *adj* grassy

**Grashüpfer** [GRAHS•hoop•fair]
*n* M grasshopper

**Grasnarbe** [GRAHS•nahr•beh]
*n* F sod; turf

**gratulieren**
[GRAH•too•leer•en] *vt*
congratulate

**Grau** [grou] *n* M horror

**graue** [grou] *adj* gray

**Graue** [groue] *n* N gray

**grausam** [GROU•zahm] *adj*
ferocious

**Grausamkeit**
[GRAU•zahm•kuyt] *n* F
bitterness

**Gravieren** [grah•VEER•en] *n* N
engraving

**greifbar 1** [GRUYF•bahr] *adj*
handy; available (in stock)

**greifbar 2** [GRUYF•bahr] *adj*
tangible

**greifen** [GRUY•fen] *vt* grab

**grell** [grel] *adj* glaring; lurid

**Grenze** [GREHN•zeh] *n* F
boundary; border

**grenzenlos** [GREHTS•en•los]
*adj* interminable

**Grenzgebiet** [grents•ge•beet] *n*
N frontier

**Grenzstein** [GREHNTS•shtuyn]
*n* M landmark

**Griechenland**
[GREEHK•en•lahnt] *n* N
Greece

**griechisch** [GREEHK•ish] *adj*
Greek

**Griff** [grif] *n* M grasp; grip;
handle

**Griffigkeit** [GRIHF•ig•kuyt] *n*
F traction

**Grille** [GRIL•eh] *n* F cricket

**grillenhaft** [GRIH•len•hahft]
*adj* whimsical

**Grimasse** [GRI•mah•se] *n* F
grimace

**grimmig** [GRI•mig] *adj* fierce

**Grinsen** [GRIHN•zen] *n* N grin

**Grippe** [GRI•peh] *n* F flu;
influenza

**grob** [grohb] *adj* coarse; crude;
gross; rude; uncouth

**grölen** [GROOL•en] *vt vi* bawl

**Größe** [GROO•seh] *n* F
greatness; size

**größenteils** [GRUHS•en•tuyls]
*adv* largely; mostly

**groß** [grohs] *adj* big; great;
large; tall

**Groß Britanien** [GROHS
brih•TAH•nee•en] *n* Great
Britain

**großartig** [GROHS•ahr•tig] *adj*
grand; magnificent

**Großartigkeit**
[GROHS•ahr•tig•kuyt] *n* F
magnificence

**Großeltern** [GROHS•el•tairn]
*npl* M grandparents

**Großhandel**
[GROHS•hahn•del] *n* M
wholesale

**Großmutter** [GROHS•moo•tair]
*n* F grandmother

**Großräumspflug**
[GROHS•roims•pfloog] *n* M
bulldozer

**Großtat** [GROHS•taht] *n* F feat

**Großvater** [GROHS•fah•tair] *n*
M grandfather

**großzügig** *adj* generous

**Großzügigkeit**
[GROHS•tsoog•ig•kuyt] *n* F
generosity

**grotesk** [GROH•tesk] *adj*
grotesque

**grün** [gruhn] *adj* green

**Grüne** [GROO•ne] *n* N green

**Grund** [gruhnt] *n* M reason

**Grundbesitzer** [gruhnt-] *n* M
landowner

**gründen** [GROON•den] *vt*
establish

**Gründer** [gruhn•dair] *n* M
founder

**grundlegend**
[GROONT•laig•gent] *adj*
basic; fundamental

**grundlos** [GRUHNT•los] *adj*
groundless

**Grundschule**
[GRUHNT•shoo•le] *n* F grade
school

**Gründung** [GROON•doong] *n*
F constitution

**Grünland** [GRUHN•lahnt] *n*
Greenland

**Grunzen** [GRUHN•tsen] *n* N
grunt

**Gruppe 1** [GRUH•peh] *n* F
gang; group

**Gruppe 2** [GROO•peh] *n* F
band (musical)

**gucken** [GUH•ken] *vi* peek

**Guckloch** [GUHK•lohk] *n* N
peephole

**Guillotine** [GUY•o•teen] *n* F
guillotine

**Guitarre** [GI•tah•re] *n* F guitar

**gültig** [GOOL•tig] *adj* valid

**Gültigkeit** [GOOL•tig•kuyt] *n* F
validity

**Gummi** [GOO•mee] *n* N gum;
rubber

**Gummiband**
[GOO•mee•BAHNT] *n* N
elastic, rubber band

**günstig** [GOONST•igk] *adj*
advantageous; convenient;
favorable

**gurgeln** [goor•geln] *vi* gurgle

**Gurke** [GOOR•ke] *n* F
cucumber

**gurren** [GOO•ren] *vi* coo

**Gurt** [goort] *n* M girdle
**Gürtel 1** [goor•tel] *n* M belt
**Gürtel 2** [goor•tel] *n* M zone
**Guß** [goos] *n* M gush
**gut** [goot] *adj* good
**Gut** [goot] *n* N property; stock
**gutwohl** [goot] [vohl] *adj* well
**gutaussehend**
　　[GOOT•ous•SAI•hend] *adj*
　　good-looking

**Güterwagen**
　　[GUH•tair•VAH•gen] *n* M
　　truck
**gütig** [GOO•tig] *adj* benign;
　　kind; gracious
**Gutsbesitzer**
　　[GOOTS•beh•zits•air] *n* M
　　yeoman
**Gutsherr** [GOOTS•hair] *n* M
　　squire

# H

**Haar** [hahr] *n* N hair
**Haarbürste** [-BOOR•ste] *n* F
　　hairbrush
**haarig** [HAHR•ig] *adj* hairy
**Haarlocke** [HAHR•loh•ke] *n* F
　　curl
**Haarnadel** [-NAH•del] *n* F
　　hairpin
**Haarschneiden**
　　[HAAR•shnuy•den] *n* N
　　tonsure
**Haarschnitt** [-shnit] *n* M
　　haircut; hairstyle
**haben** [HAH•ben] *aux* have
**hacken** [HAH•ken] *vt* chop;
　　hack
**Hackmesser** [HAK•mes•air] *n*
　　F cleaver
**Häkelei** [HEK•e•luy] *n* F
　　crochet
**Hämorrhoiden**
　　[HEM•or•HOI•den] *npl*
　　hemorrhoids

**Händedruck** [HEHN•de•druhk]
　　*n* M handshake
**Händler** [HEND•lair] *n* M
　　dealer; trader
**Hängematte**
　　[HEHNG•eh•mah•te] *n* F
　　hammock
**hängen** [HENG•en] *vi* hang
**hängend** [HENG•end] *adj*
　　pending
**härten** [HAIR•ten] *vt* harden
**häßlich** *adj* ugly
**Häßlichkeit** [HEHS•lihk•kuyt] *n*
　　F ugliness
**häufig** [HOI•fig] *adj* frequent
**Häufigkeit** [HOI•fig•kuyt] *n* M
　　frequency
**Haus** [hous] *n* N house; home
**häuslich** [hois•lihk] *adj*
　　domestic
**Hafen** [HAH•fen] *n* M harbor;
　　port
**Hafendamm** [hah•fen•dahm] *n*
　　M jetty

**Hafer** [HAH•fair] *n* M oats

**Haferbrei** [hah•fair•bruy] *n* M porridge; oatmeal

**Hagel** [HAH•gel] *n* M hail

**Hagelstein** [HAH•gel•shtuyn] *n* M hailstone

**hager** [HAH•gair] *adj* haggard; gaunt; thin

**Hahn** [hahn] *n* M cock

**Hain** [huyn] *n* M grove

**Haiti** [HAI•tee] *n* Haiti

**Haken** [HAH•ken] *n* M hook

**halb** [halb] *adj* half

**halb offen** [HAHLB OHF•fuhn] *adj* ajar

**halbe Stunde** [HALB•E SHTUHN•de] *n* F half-hour

**halbes Liter** [HALB•es lee•tair] *n* pint

**halbieren** [HAHL•beer•en] *vt* halve

**Halbinsel** [HAHLB•in•zel] *n* F peninsula

**halbjährlich** [HALB•yair•lihk] *adj* semiannual

**Halbmast** [HALB•mahst] *n* M half-mast

**Halbmond** [HAHLB•mohnt] *n* M crescent

**Hallo** [HAH•lo] hello

**Halo** [HAH•lo] *n* M halo

**Hals** [hahls] *n* M neck; throat

**Halt** [hahlt] *n* M halt; hold

**haltbar** [HAHLT•bar] *adj* durable; tenable

**halten** [HAL•ten] *vt* deem

**Halter** [HAHL•tair] *n* M holder

**Haltestelle** [HAHLT•eh•shtel•leh] *n* F station

**Haltung** [HALT•oong] *n* F attitude

**Hammelfleisch** [HAH•mehl•fluysh] *n* N mutton

**Hammer** [HAH•mair] *n* M hammer

**Hand** [hahnt] *n* F hand

**Handel** [HAHN•del] *n* M commerce; trade

**Handeln** [HAHN•deln] *n* N trading

**handeln um** [HAHN•deln oom] *vi* haggle

**Handelswert** [HAHN•dels-] *n* M value (market)

**Handfläche** [HAHNT•flehk•eh] *n* F palm

**Handgelenk** [HAHNT•ge•lenk] *n* N wrist

**Handgranate** [hahnt•greh•nah•te] *n* M grenade

**handgreiflich** [HAHNT•gruyf•lihk] *adj* palpable

**Handlung** [HAHND•loong] *n* F action; plot; treatment

**Handschellen** [HAHNT•shnel•en] *npl* handcuff

**Handschrift** [HAHNT•shrihft] *n* F handwriting

**Handschuh** [HAHNT•shoo] *n* M glove; mitten

**Handtuch** [HAHNT•toohk] *n* N handkerchief

**Handvoll** [HAHNT•fol] *n* F handful

**Hang** [hahng] *n* M hillside

**Hansepflaster**
[HAHN•zeh•PFLAH•stair] *n*
M bandage

**Harfe** [HAHR•fe] *n* F harp

**harmlos** [HAHRM•los] *adj*
harmless

**Harmonie** [HAHR•moh•nee] *n*
F harmony

**harmonieren**
[HAHR•moh•NEER•en] *vt*
harmonize

**harmonisch** [hahr•MOHN•ish]
*adj* harmonious

**Harpune** [hahr•POON•e] *n* F
harpoon

**hart** [hahrt] *adj* hard; tough

**hartnäckig** [HART•nek•ig] *adj*
obstinate; persistent

**Hase** [HAH•zeh] *n* M hare;
rabbit

**Haselnuß** [HAH•zel•noos] *n* F
hazelnut

**Haspel** [HAH•spel] *n* F reel;
winch

**Haß** [hahs] *n* M hate; hatred

**hassen** *vt vi* [HAHS•sen] hate;
detest

**hasten** [HAHST•en] *vi* scurry

**hastig** [HAHST•ig] *adv*
hurriedly

**hastig** [HAHST•ig] *adj* rash

**Hauch** [houhk] *n* M puff; whiff

**hauchdünn** [HOUHK•doon]
*adj* flimsy

**Haue** *n* F spanking

**hauen** [HOU•en] *vi* swipe

**Haufen** [HOU•fen] *n* N cluster;
heap; pile

**Haupt** [Houpt] *n* N chief

**haupt** [houpt] *adj* main;
primary; staple

**hauptberuflich**
[HOUPT•be•ROOF•lihk] *adj*
full-time

**Hauptbuch** [HOUPT•boohk] *n*
N ledger

**Hauptgericht** [-geh•rihkt] *n* N
main course

**Hauptpunkt** [houpt•poonkt] *n*
M feature

**Hauptquartier**
[HOUPT•kvar•teer] *n* N
headquarters

**hauptsächlich**
[HOUPT•zehk•lihk] *adv*
primarily

**hauptsächlich**
[HOUPT•zehk•lihk] *adj*
principal

**Hauptstadt** [HOWPT•shtaht] *n*
F capital

**hauptstätdtisch**
[HOUPT•shteht•ish] *adj*
metropolitan

**Hauptverkehrszeit**
[HOUPT•vair•KAIRS•tsait] *n*
F rush-hour

**Haus** [hous] *n* N house

**Hausarbeit** [HOUS•ahr•buyt] *n*
F chores; housework

**Hausaufgabe**
[HOUS•ouf•gah•be] *n* F
homework

**Hausfrau** [HOUS•frou] *n* F
housewife

**hausieren gehen**
[HOUS•eer•en GAI•en] *vt*
peddle; sell

**Hauslehrerin**
[HOUS•lair•air•in] *n* F
governess

**Hausschuh** [HOUS•shoo] *n* M
slipper
**Haussuchungsbefehl**
[HOUS•zoo•khoongs•beh•FAIL]
*n* M search warrant
**Haustier** [HOUS•teer] *n* N pet
**Hauswirtschaft** *n* F
housekeeping
**Haut** [hout] *n* F skin
**Hautwasser** [HOUT•vah•sair] *n*
N lotion
**Hebamme** [heh•BAHM•eh] *n* F
midwife
**Heben** [HAI•ben] *n* N lift
**heben** [HAI•ben] *vt* raise
**Hecke** [HEHK•eh] *n* F hedge
**Hefe** [HAI•feh] *n* F yeast
**Heft 1** [hehft] *n* N hilt
**Heft 2** [hehft] *n* N notebook
**heftig** [HEF•tig] *adj* intensive
**heftig ziehen** [HEHF•tig
tsee•en] *vt* yank
**Heftigkeit** [HEF•tig•kuyt] *n* F
intensity; vehemence
**hei!** [huy] hey
**Heide** [HUY•de] *n* M pagan
**Heidekraut** [HUY•de•krout] *n*
N heather
**Heideland** [HUY•deh•lahnt] *n*
N moor
**Heidelbeere** [HAI•del•bair•reh]
*n* F blueberry
**heikel** [HUY•kel] *adj* fastidious;
tricky
**Heilbutt** [HUYL•buht] *n* M
halibut
**heilen** [HUY•len] *vt* heal
**heilig** [HUY•lig] *adj* holy;
sacred; saintly
**Heilige Schrift** [HUY•lig•eh -]
*n* F scripture

**Heiligengrab**
[HUY•lig•en•grahb] *n* N
shrine
**Heiliger** [HUY•lihg•air] *n* M
saint
**Heiligkeit** [huy•lig•kuyt] *n* F
holiness
**heiligt** [HUY•lihkt] *adj*
hallowed; holy
**Heilmittel** [HUYL•mit•el] *n* N
cure; remedy
**Heim** [huym] *n* M home
**Heimatland** [huym•at•lahnt] *n*
N homeland
**heimatlos** [HUY•maht•los] *adj*
homeless
**heimlich** [HUYM•likh] *adj*
clandestine; covert; furtive;
underhanded
**Heimlichkeit**
[HUYM•lihk•kuyt] *n* F stealth
**heimwärts** [HUYM•vairts] *adv*
homeward
**Heimweh** [HUYM•vai] *n* M
homesick
**heiser** [HUY•sair] *adj* hoarse
**heiß** [huys] *adj* hot
**heiter** [HUY•tair] *adj* jovial;
cheerful; serene
**Heiterkeit** [-kuyt] *n* F serenity
**Heizgerät** [-GEH•reht] *n* N
heater
**Heizkörper** [HUYTS•ker•pair]
*n* M radiator
**Heizplatte** [HUYTS•plah•te] *n*
F hot-plate
**Heizung** [huyts•oong] *n* F
heating
**Held** [held] *n* M hero
**Heldentum** [HELD•en•toom] *n*
N heroism

**Heldin** [HELD•in] *n* F heroine

**Helfer -in** [HEHL•fair -in] *n* M
helper

**hell** [hel] *adj* bright; light

**hellwach** [HEHL•vahk] *adj*
wide awake

**Helm** [helm] *n* M crest

**Helm** [hehlm] *n* M helmet

**Hemisphäre** [HEM•is•FAIR•e]
*n* F hemisphere

**hemmen** [HEM•men] *vt* inhibit;
clog (as a drain)

**hemmen, hindern** [HEM•men]
[HIN•dairn] *vt* block

**Hengst** [haingst] *n* M stallion

**Henne** [HEN•ne] *n* F hen

**herab** [hair•AP] *adv* down

**herabhängen**
[hair•AP•haing•en] *vi* dangle;
droop

**herablassend**
[hair•AP•lah•send] *adj*
condescending

**herabsetzen**
[hair•AP•zets•tsen] *vt* detract

**herabstoßen**
[hair•AP•shtoh•sen] *vi* pounce

**herabstoßen**
[hair•ap•shtoh•sen] *vi* swoop

**herantreten an**
[haiyr•AHN•trai•tuhn ahn] *vt*
accost

**heranwinken**
[hair•AHN•veenk•en] *vt*
beckon

**herausfordern**
[haiyr•OWS•for•dairn] *vt*
challenge

**Herausforderung**
[haiyr•OWS•for•oong] *n* F
challenge

**Herausgeber**
[hair•OUS•gai•bair] *n* M
editor; publisher

**herauslocken**
[hair•OUS•loh•ken] *vt* elicit

**herausstehen**
[hair•OUS•shtai•en] *vi*
protrude

**Herbst** [HAIR•bst] *n* M autumn

**Herd** [haird] *n* M stove

**Herde** [HAIR•deh] *n* F herd;
flock; drove

**Hering** [HAIR•eeng] *n* M
herring

**Hernie** [HEHR•nee•eh] *n* F
hernia

**Heroin** [HAIR•o•EEN] *n* N
heroin

**heroisch** [HAIR•o•ish] *adj*
heroic

**Herold** [HAIR•old] *n* M herald

**Herr** [hair] *n* M mister; lord; sir

**Herrin** [HAIR•in] *n* F mistress

**herrisch** [HAIR•ish] *adj*
imperious

**herrlich 1** [HAIR•lihk] *adj*
glorious; wonderful

**herrlich 2** [HAIR•lihk] *adv*
wonderfully

**herrschend** [HAIR•shent] *adj*
dominant

**Hersteller** [HAIR•shtel•lair] *n*
M producer

**Herstellung** [HAIR•shtel•oong]
*n* F manufacture; production

**herumbasteln**
[HAIR•oom•bah•steln] *vt*
tamper

**herumreden**
[HAIR•oom•rai•den] *vt*
quibble

**herumsuchen**
[HAIR•oom•zoo•khen] *vi*
grope
**herumtanzen**
[HAIR•oon•tahn•tsen] *vt* frisk
**herumwirbeln**
[HAIR•oom•veer•beln] *vt*
twirl
**heruntersteigen**
[HAIR•oon•tair•shtuy•gen] *vi*
descend
**hervorragen**
[HAIR•for•rah•gen] *vi* excel
**hervorragend**
[HAIR•vor•ah•gent] *adj*
eminent; outstanding
**herz** [hairts] *adj* cardiac
**Herz** [hairts] *n* N heart
**Herzanfall** [HAIRTS•ahn•fal] *n*
M heart attack
**herzlich** [HAIRTS•lihk] *adj*
heartwarming
**herzlos** [HAIRTS•los] *adj*
heartless
**Herzog** [HAIR•tsog] *n* M duke
**Herzogin** [HAIR•tsog•in] *n* F
duchess
**Herzschlag** [-shlahg] *n*
heartbeat
**heterosexuell**
[HE•tair•o•ZEKS•oo•el] *adj*
heterosexual
**Heu** [hoi] *n* N hay
**Heuchelei** [HOI•khel•uy] *n* F
hypocrisy
**Heuchler** [HOIHK•lair] *n* M
hypocrite
**heuchlerisch** [HOIHK•lair•ish]
*adj* hypocritical
**Heugabel** [hoi•gah•bel] *n* F
pitchfork

**heulen** [HOU•len] *vi* howl
**Heuschober** [HOI•sho•bair] *n*
M haystack
**heute** [HOI•teh] today
**heute abend** [HOI•te ah•bent]
tonight
**heute in 14 Tage** [HOI•te in
FEER•tsain TAH•ge] fortnight
**Hexe** [HEKS•eh] *n* F witch
**Hieb** [heeb] *n* M stroke
**hier** [heeyr] *adv* here
**Hierarchie** [HEEYR•ahr•KEE]
*n* F hierarchy
**hiermit** [HEEYR•mit] *adv*
hereby; herewith
**hiesig** [HEE•zig] local
**hiktisch** [HEK•tish] *adj* hectic
**Hilfe** [HIL•fuh] *n* F aid; help
**hilflos** [HILFS•los] *adj* helpless
**hilfreich** [HILF•ruyhk] *adj*
helping
**Hilfsgeistlicher**
[HILFS•gaist•lihk•air] *n* M
curate
**Himbeere** [HIM•bair•eh] *n* F
raspberry
**Himmel** [HIH•mel] *n* M heaven;
sky
**Himmelskörper**
[HI•mehls•ker•pair] *n* M orbit
**himmlich** [HIHM•lihk] *adj*
heavenly
**hinaus** [hin•OUS] *adv* out; *adv*
*prep* beyond
**hinauswerfen**
[hin•OUS•vair•fen] *vt* eject;
expel
**Hindernis** [HIN•dair•nis] *n* N
hindrance; obstacle
**Hindu** [HIN•doo] *n* M Hindu

**hineindrängen**
[hin•UYN•dreng•en] *vi* intrude

**hineinziehen**
[hin•UYN•tsee•en] *vt*
implicate

**hingestreckt** [HIN•geh•shtrekt]
*adj* prostrate

**hinkritzeln** [HIN•krits•eln] *vt*
scribble

**hinnehmen** [HIN•naim•uhn] *vi*
give in; acquiesce

**hinsichtlich** [HIN•zihkt•lihk]
*adj* regarding

**hinter** [HIN•tair] *adj* hind

**hinter den Kulissen** [HIN•tair
dehn KOO•lih•sen] *adj adv*
offstage

**hinter Hinterteil** [HIN•tair]
[-taiy•yul] *prep n* M behind

**Hintergrund** [HIN•tair•groont]
*n* M background (in the)

**hinterherlaufen**
[HIN•tair•hair•lou•fen] *vi* tag
along

**hinterlassen** [HIN•tair•las•sen]
*vt* bequeath

**Hinterseite** [HIN•tair•sai•teh] *n*
F rear

**Hinterteil** [HIN•tair•taiy•uhl] *n*
M buttock; posterior; rump

**hinüberbringen**
[hin•UH•bair•BRING•en] *vt*
transfer

**hinunter** [hin•OON•tair] *adv*
down

**Hinweis** [HIN•vuys] *n* M clue;
reference

**hinweisen** [HIN•vai•sen] *vt*
refer; allude; *vi* allusion

**Hinweiss** [HIN•vais] *n* M
allusion

**hinziehen** [HIN•tsee•en] *vi*
protract

**hinzufügen**
[HIN•tsoo•foog•uhn] *vt* add

**Historiker** [hi•STOH•ri•kair] *n*
M historian

**historisch** [hi•STOHR•ish] *adj*
historic

**Hitze** [HIHTS•e] *n* F heat

**Hitzewelle** [HIHTS•e•vel•eh] *n*
F heatwave

**hoch** [hohk] *adj* high

**Hochburg** [HOHK•boorg] *n* F
stronghold

**Hochebene** [hohk•ai•ben•eh] *n*
F plateau

**hochhalten** [HOHK•hahl•ten]
*vt* uphold

**hochheben** [HOHK•hai•ben] *vt*
heave

**hochmütig** [HOHK•moo•tig]
*adj* haughty

**hochnäsig** [HOHK•nai•sig] *adj*
stuck-up

**hochschätzen**
[HOHK•sheh•tsen] *vt*
appreciate

**hochscheiben** [hohk•shee•ben]
*vt* boost

**Hochschule** [HOHK•shoo•le] *n*
F high school

**Hochzeit** [HOHK•tsait] *n* F
wedding

**hochzeitlich** [HOHK•tsait•lihk]
*adj* nuptial

**Hochzeitsreise**
[HOHK•tsaits•ruy•ze] *n* F
honeymoon

**hochziehen** [HOHK•tsee•ehn]
*vt* hoist

hocken [HOK•en] *vi* cower; squat

Hocker [HOHK•air] *n* M stool

Hockey [HOHK•ee] *n* N hockey

höchst 1 [huhkst] *adj* highly

höchst 2 [huhkst] *adv* topmost

Höcker [HUH•kair] *n* M hunchback

höflich [HOOF•lihk] *adj* courteous; polite

Höflichkeit [HOOF•lihk•kuyt] *n* F courtesy; politeness

Höhe [HUH•eh] *n* F height

Höhepunkt 1 [HOO•eh•poonkt] *n* M climax

Höhepunkt 2 [HUH•eh•poonkt] *n* M heyday

höheres Dienstalter [HUH•air•es DEENST•ahl•tair] *n* N seniority

Höhle [HOOH•leh] *n* M cave; den

hohl [hohl] *adj* hollow

Höhle sich eingraben [HOO•leh] [zik AIN•grah•ben] *n* *vt* F burrow

Höhlenmensch [HOOH•lehn•mensh] *n* M caveman

Hölle [HUH•le] *n* F hell

höllisch [HUHL•ish] *adj* hellish

hören [HER•en] *vt* hear; *vi* listen

Hören [HER•en] *n* N hearing

Hörer [HER•rair] *n* M receiver (telephone)

Hof [hohf] *n* M courtyard; yard

Hoffnung [HOHF•noong] *n* F hope

hoffnungslos [-los] *adj* hopeless

Hoffnungslosigkeit [HOF•noongs•LOS•ig•kuyt] *n* F desperation

hoffnungsvoll [-s•fol] *adj* hopeful; promising

Hoheit [HOH•huyt] *n* F dignity; grandeur; highness

Hohlkehle [HOHL•kai•le] *n* F gorge

Hokuspokus [HO•kus•PO•kus] *n* M hocus-pocus

holländisch [HOHL•end•ish] *adj* Dutch

Holz [holts] *n* N wood

Holz schneiden [hohlts SHNUY•dehn] *vt* *vi* carve

Holzarbeiter [HOLTS•ahr•buy•tair] *n* M woodworker

Holzfäller [-fel•air] *n* M lumberjack

Holzkohle [HOHLTS•kohl•eh] *n* F charcoal

Holzschuh [HOHLTS•shoo] *n* M clog

Holzwerk [HOLTS•vairk] *n* N woodwork

homosexuell [hoh•mo•zehks•oo•EL] *adj* homosexual

Honig [HOHN•ig] *n* M honey

Horizont [HOR•ih•tsohnt] *n* M horizon

Hormon [HOR•mohn] *n* N hormone

Horn [horn] *n* N horn

Hornisse [HOR•nis•se] *n* F hornet

**Horoskop** [HOR•oh•skop] *n* N
horoscope

**Hort** [hohrt] *n* M hoard

**Hose** [HOH•ze] *n* F pants;
jeans; trousers; overalls

**Hosenträger**
[HOH•zen•TRAI•gair] *npl*
suspenders

**Hot Dog** hot dog

**Hotel** [HO•tel] *n* N hotel

**Hubschrauber**
[huhp•shrou•bair] *n* M
helicopter

**Huf** [hoof] *n* M hoof

**Hufeisen** [HOOF•uy•zen] *n* M
horseshoe

**Hüfte** [HUHF•te] *n* F hip

**Hügel** [HUH•gel] *n* M hill

**hügelig** [HUH•gel•ig] *adj* hilly

**Hühnchen** [HOON•chehn] *n* N
chicken

**Hühnerkorb** [HOO•nair•korp] *n*
M coop

**Hühnerstall** [HUHN•air•shtahl]
*n* M hen-house

**Hühnerstange**
[HUHN•air•shtahng•eh] *n* F
roost

**Hülle** [HUH•leh] *n* F wrapper

**hüllen** [HUH•len] *vt* wrap;
shroud

**Hülse** [HUHL•se] *n* F husk; pod

**hülsig** [HUHL•sig] *adj* husky

**humanitär** [HOO•man•i•TAIR]
*adj* humanitarian

**Hummer** [HUH•mair] *n* M
lobster

**Humor** [HOO•mor] *n* M humor

**humorvoll** [-fol] *adj* humorous

**humpeln** [HUHM•peln] *vi*
hobble

**Hund** [hoont] *n* M dog; hound

**Hunde** [HOON•deh] *adj*
canine

**Hundehütte**
[HUHN•de•HUH•te] *n* F
kennel

**Hundert** [huhn•dair] *n* N
hundred

**Hunderteilig Zentigrad**
[HOON•dairt•TAIL•lig]
[TSEHN•ti•grahd] *adj* *n* M
centigrade

**Hundertfüßer**
[HOON•dairt•FOOS•air] *n* M
centipede

**Hundertjahrfeier**
[HOON•dairt•YAHR•FUYU•air]
*n* F centennial

**hundertst** [HUHN•dairtst] *num*
hundredth

**Hundin** [HOON•din] *n* F bitch

**Hunger** [HUHNG•air] *n* M
hunger

**Hungern** [HUHNG•airn] *n* N
starvation

**Hungersnot** [HOONG•airs•not]
*n* F famine

**hungrig** [HUHN•grig] *adj*
hungry; ravenous

**hupen** [HOO•pen] *vi* honk

**hüpfen** [HUHP•fen] *vt* hop; *vi*
skip

**Hürde** [HUHR•de] *n* F hurdle

**Hure** [HOO•reh] *n* F whore

**Hurrikan** [HUHR•ih•kahn] *n* M
hurricane

**Husten** [HOO•sten] *n* M cough

**Hut** [hoot] *n* M hat

**Hüter** [HOO•tair] *n* M
custodian; guardian

**Hütte** [HUH•te] *n* F hut; shack

**Hyäne** [hee•AI•ne] *n* F hyena
**Hyazinth** [HEE•ah•TSUHNTH] *n* M hyacinth
**Hydrant** [hee•DRAHNT] *n* M hydrant
**hydraulisch** [hee•DRAUL•ish] *adj* hydraulic
**Hygiene** [HUY•jeen] *n* F hygiene
**Hymne** [HIM•ne] *n* F hymn
**Hypnose** [HUYP•no•ze] *n* F hypnosis

**hypnotisch** [HUYP•no•tish] *adj* hypnotic
**hypnotisieren** [HUYP•no•ti•SEER•en] hypnotize
**Hypothese** [HUH•po•TAI•ze] *n* F hypothesis
**Hysterie** [hi•STAIR•EE•eh] *n* F hysterics
**hysterisch** [hi•STAIR•ish] *adj* hysterical

# I

**ich** [eehk] I
**Ich** [eehk] *n* N self; ego
**ichbezogen** [EEK•beh•TSOH•gen] *adj* self-centered
**ideal; Ideal** [ih•DAI•al] *adj* N ideal
**Idealismus** [-is•mus] *n* M idealism
**idealistisch** [-IST•ish] *adj* idealistic
**Idee** [EE•dai] *n* F idea; hunch
**identifizieren** [-en] *vt* identify
**Identifizierung** [IH•dent•i•fi•TSEER•oong] *n* F identification
**Identität** [EE•den•ti•TAIT] *n* F identity
**Ideologie** [EE•dai•o•lo•GEE] *n* F ideology
**Idiot** [IH•dee•ot] *n* M idiot
**idiotisch** [IH•dee•oh•tish] *adj* idiotic

**erzeugnis** [AIR•tsoig•nis] *n* N produce
**Igel** [EE•gel] *n* M hedgehog
**ignorieren** [IG•nor•eer•en] *vt* ignore
**ihn; ihm** [een] [eem] *pron* him
**ihr; dein; euer** [eer] [duyn] [oi•air] *pron* your; yours
**ihr, ihre** [eer] [eer•eh] *pron* their
**ihr, sie** [eer ][ zee] *pron* her
**ihrer, es** [eer•air [-e] [es] *pron* hers
**illegal** [IL•lai•gal] *adj* illegal
**Illusion** [il•LOO•ZEE•ohn] *n* F illusion
**im allgemeinen** [im AL•ge•muyn•en] *adv* commonly
**im allgemeinen** [im AL•geh•muyn•en] *adv* generally

**im Auftrag von** [im
OWF•trahg fun] *n* behalf
**im Ernst** [im AIRNST]
seriously
**im Fernsehen bringen** [im
FAIRN•zai•hen BRING•en] *vi*
televise
**im ganzen genommen** [im
GAHN•tsehn
guh•NOHM•ehn] *adv*
altogether
**im kürzem** [im KOORTS•em]
*adv* shortly; briefly
**im Stich lassen** [im SHTIHK
LAH•sen] *vt* forsake
**im Überfluß** [im UH•bair•fluhs]
*n* M plentiful
**Immatrikulation** [im•MAH•
TRIHK•oo•lah•tsee•ON] *n* F
matriculation
**immer** [IM•mair] *adv* always;
ever
**immer mehr** [IM•mair mair]
*adv* increasingly
**immer wieder** [IM•air
VEE•dair] *adv* continually
**Immergrün** [IM•air•GROON] *n*
N evergreen
**immerwährend**
[IM•mair•vair•END] *adj*
perpetual
**immun** [IM•moon] *adj* immune
**immun machen** *vt* immunize
**Immunität** [-i•TAIT] *n* F
immunity
**Impf** [impf] vaccine
**impfen** [imp•fen] *vt* vaccinate
**Import** [IM•port] *n* M import
**importieren** [IM•port•EER•en]
*vt* import

**impotent** [im•po•tent] *adj*
impotent
**improvisieren**
[IM•proh•vi•zeer•en] *vt vi*
improvise
**impulsiv** [im•PUHL•seev] *adj*
impulsive
**in; im; ins;** *prep,* in, into
**in Abrede stellen** [in AP•rai•de
SHTEL•en] *vt* disavow
**in Anbetracht** [in
AHN•be•trahkt] considering
**in den Schatten stellen** [in
dain SHAH•ten SHTEL•len]
*vt* overshadow
**in der Nähe** [in dair NAI•he]
*adj* nearby
**in Unordnung** [in
OON•ohrd•noong] *adj*
disorganized
**in Verlegenheit bringen** [in
fair•LAIG•en•HUYT]
[brihng•en] *vt* embarrass
**in wilde Flucht jagen** [in
VIL•deh FLOOHKT yah•gen]
stampede
**inbegriffen** [IN•be•grih•fen]
*adj* implicit
**Indien** [IN•dee•en] *n* India
**Indigo** [IN•di•go] *n* M indigo
**indirekt** [IN•dee•rekt] *adj*
indirect
**indisch** [IN•dish] *adj* Indian
**indisponiert**
[IN•dis•po•NEERT]
indisposed
**Indonesien** [in•do•NAI•see•en]
*n* Indonesia
**Industrie** [IN•doo•shtree] *n* F
industry

industriell [IN•duh•shtree•el]
*adj* industrial

Infanterie [IN•fahn•tair•ee] *n* F
infantry

Infinitiv infinitivisch
[IN•fin•i•TEEV] [-ish] *n* M
infinitive

infizieren [IN•fi•TSEER•en] *vt*
infect

Inflation [in•FLAH•TSEE•on] *n*
F inflation

Ingenieur [in•JEN•oor] *n* M
engineer

Ingwer [ING•vair] *n* M ginger

Inhaber [IN•hah•bair] *n* M
occupant

Inhalt [IN•halt] *n* M contents

Inhaltverzeichnis
[IN•hahlt•fair•TSAIHK•nis] *n*
N index

inner [IN•nair] *adj* inner; inside;
interior

innerhalb von [IN•nair•halb
fon] *prep* within

innerst [IN•nairst] *adj* inmost

ins Gefängnis werfen [ins
ge•FEHNG•nis vair•fen] *vt*
imprison

ins Pension gehen [ins
pen•SEE•on gai•en] retire

ins Wasser tauchen [ins
VAH•saiyr TOU•khen] *vt*
douse

Insasse [IN•sah•se] *n* M inmate

Insekt [in•ZEKT] *n* N bug;
insect

Insektengift [-en•gihft] *n* N
insecticide

Insel [IN•zel] *n* F island

Inspektor [ihn•SHPEHK•tor] *n*
M inspector

Instandhaltung
[in•SHTANT•hahlt•oong] *n* F
upkeep

Instinkt [IN•shtihnkt] *n* M flair;
instinct

Instrument [in•SHTROO•ment]
*n* N instrument

Integration
[IN•teh•grah•tsee•ON] *n* F
integration

intellektuell
[IN•tel•ehk•too•EL] *adj*
intellectual

intensiv [IN•ten•seev] *adj*
intensity

interessant [-ahnt] *adj*
interesting

Interesse [in•tair•ES•se] *n* F
interest

Internat [in•tair•NAHT] *n* N
boarding school

international
[IN•tair•nah•TSEE•on•ahl] *adj*
international

Interview [IN•tair•vyoo] *n* N
interview

intim [in•TEEM] *adj* intimate

Intoleranz [IN•tol•air•ants] *n* F
intolerance

intravenös [IN•trah•ven•UHS]
*adj* intravenous

Intuition [IN•too•its•EE•on] *n* F
intuition

investieren [IN•vest•EER•en]
*vt* invest

Investierung
[IN•vest•EER•oong] *n* F
investment

inwendig [IN•ven•dig] *adj*
internal

Irak [eer•AHK] *n* Iraq

**irakisch** [eer•AHK•ish] *adj* Iraqi

**Iran** [eer•AN] *n* Iran

**iranisch** [eer•AN•ish] *adj* Iranian

**irdisch** [EER•dish] *adj* earthly; mundane

**irgend jemand** [EEYR•geh•nt YAI•mahnt] *pron* anyone (anybody)

**irgendjemand** someone

**irgendwann** [-vahn] sometime

**irgendwie** [EEYR•gehnt•vee] *adv* anyway

**irgendwie** [EER•gent•vee] *adv* somehow

**irgendwo1** [EEYR•gehnt•voh] *adv* anywhere

**irgendwo2** [-voh] somewhere

**irgent etwas** [EEYR•gehnt EHT•vahs] *pron* anything

**Iris** [EER•is] *n* F iris

**irisch** [eer•ish] *adj* Irish

**Irland** [EER•lahnt] *n* Ireland

**Ironie** [EER•o•nee] *n* F irony

**ironisch** [EER•on•ish] *adj* ironic

**irreführend** [EER•eh•FOOR•end] *adj* misleading

**irrereden** [EER•eh•RAI•den] *vi* rave

**irreredend** [EER•eh•RAI•dent] *adj* delirious

**irrig** [EER•ig] *adj* devious

**Irrlehre** [EER•lai•re] *n* F heresy

**Islam** [EES•lahm] *n* M Islam

**Island** [EES•lant] *n* Iceland

**isolieren** [EE•so•LEER•en] *vt* isolate; insulate

**Isolierung** [EE•so•LEER•oong] *n* F insulation

**Italien** [ih•TAHL•ee•ain] *n* Italy

**italienisch** [ih•TAHL•ee•AIN•ish] *adj* Italian

**italisch** [ih•TAHL•ish] *adj* italic

# J

**ja** [yah] yes; yeah

**Jacke** [YAH•keh] *n* F jacket

**Jackpot** *n* M jackpot

**Jäger** [YAI•gair] *n* M hunter

**jährlich** [YAIR•lik] *adj* annual

**jämmerlich** [YEM•mair•lihk] *adj* rueful

**Jagd** [yagt] *n* F hunt

**Jagdhütte** [YAGD•huh•te] *n* F lodge

**jagen; Jagd** [YAH•gen] [yahgt] *vt n* M chase

**Jahr** [yahr] *n* N year

**Jahrestag** [YAHR•ehs•tahg] *n* M anniversary

**Jahreszeit** [YAHR•es•tsait] *n* F season

**Jahrhundert** [yahr•HOON•dairt] *n* N century

**Jahrtausend** [yahr•TOU•zent] *n* millenium

**Jahrzehnt** [yar•TSAINT] *n* N decade

**jammern** [YAH•mairn] *vi*
moan; lament; wail

**Januar** [YAH•noo•ahr] *n* M
January

**Japan** [YAH•pahn] *n* Japan

**japanish** [-ish] *adj* Japanese

**Jargon** [YAHR•gon] *n* M
jargon; lingo

**jauchzen** [YOWK•sehn] *vt*
cheer; rejoice

**Jawohl** [yah•vohl] yes; yes sir

**Jazzmusik** [JAZ•moo•SEEK] *n*
F jazz

**jede** [YAI•de] *adj* every

**jeden Tag** [-tahg] *adj* everyday

**jeder 1** [YAI•dair] *adj* either

**jeder 2; jede; jedes,** [yai•dair]
[-de] [-des] *adj* each

**jedermann** [-mahn] *pr*
everybody

**jedoch** [YAI•dohk] *conj*
however

**jemand** [YAI•mahnt] somebody

**jemanden zwingen**
[JAIY•mahn•den
TSVING•gen] *vt* bludgeon

**jenseits** [YAIN•saits] *adv prep*
beyond; on the other side of

**Jett** [jet] *n* M jet

**jetzt** [yehtst] *adv* now;
nowadays

**jeweilig** [yai•vail•lig] *adv*
respective

**Joch** [yohk] *n* N yoke

**Jockei** [YOHK•uy] *n* M jockey

**Jod** [yohd] *n* N iodine

**Jogging** [JOH•ging] *n* M
jogging

**Johannisbeere**
[yo•HAHN•is•BAIR•eh] *n* F
currant

**Joker** [JO•kair] *n* M joker

**Jongleur** [YON•gloor] *n* M
juggler

**Journalismus**
[jur•nahl•EES•moos] *n* M
journalism

**Journalist** [jur•nahl•EEST] n M
journalist

**jubeln** [YOO•beln] *vi* exult

**jubelnd** [YOO•belnd] *adj*
jubilant; joyful

**Jucken** [YUH•ken] *n* N itch

**juckend** [-d] *adj* itchy

**Jude** [YOO•deh] *n* M Jew

**judisch** [YOO•dish] *adj* Jewish

**Jugend** [YOO•gent] *n* F youth;
childhood

**Jugendjahre**
[YUH•gend•YAHR•eh] *npl* M
teens; teenagers

**jugendlich** [YOO•gent•lihk] *adj*
juvenile; youthful

**Jukebox** [YOOK•boks] *n* F
jukebox

**Juli** [YOO•lee] *n* M July

**jung** [yuhng] *adj* young

**Junge** [YOONG•geh] *n* M boy;
youngster

**Jünger** [YOONG•air] *n* M
disciple

**junger Hund** [YUHNG•air
huhnt] *n* M pup

**Jungfernschaft**
[YUHNG•fairn•shahft] *n* F
virginity

**Jungfrau** [YUHNG•frou] *n* F
virgin

**Junggeselle**
[YOONG•ge•zel•leh] *n* M
bachelor

**Jünglingsalter**
  |YOONG•lings•ahlt•air] *n* N
  adolescence
**Juni** [YOO•nee] *n* M June
**junior** |YOON•yor] *adj* junior
**Justiz** [YOO•steets] *n* M justice

**Juwel** [YOO•vel] *n* N jewel
**Juwelen** [YOO•vail•len] *npl*
  jewelry
**Juwelier** [-eer] *n* N jeweler
**Jux** [yuhks] *n* M spree

# K

**kabbeln** |KAH•beln] *vi*
  squabble
**Kabel** [KAH•bel] *n* N cable
**Kabine** [KAH•been•eh] *n* F
  cabin
**Kadaver** |kah•DAH•vair] *n* M
  carcass
**Kadett** |kah•DET] *n* M cadet
**Käfer** [KAIY•fair] *n* M beetle
**Käfig** [KAI•fig] *n* M cage
**Kaffee** [kah•FAIY] *n* M coffee
**Kaffeekanne**
  |kah•FAIY•KAH•neh] *n* F
  coffee pot
**Kaffeepause**
  |kah•FAIY•POU•ze] *n* F
  coffee break
**Kaffeetasse**
  |kah•FAIY•TAH•se] *n* F
  coffee cup
**kahl** [kahl] *adj* bald; hairless
**Kai** |kuy] *n* M wharf
**Kaigebühr** [KUY•ge•boor] *n* F
  dock
**Kaigeld** [KUY•geld] *n* N quay
**Kaiser** [KUY•zair] *n* M emperor
**Kaiserin** [KUY•zair•in] *n* F
  empress

**kaiserlich** [KUY•zair•lihk] *adj*
  imperial
**Kakao** [KAH•kou] *n* M cocoa
**Kaktus** [KAH•ktoos] *n* M
  cactus
**Kalb** [kahlb] *n* N calf
**Kalbfleisch** [KAHLB•fluysh] *n*
  N veal
**Kaleidoskop**
  [kah•LUYD•o•skohp] *n* N
  kaleidoscope
**Kalendar** [KAH•len•dar] *n* M
  calendar
**Kalium** [KAH•lee•oom] *n* N
  potassium
**kalt blütig** [KAHLT BLOO•tig]
  *adj* cold-blooded
**kalt** [kahlt] *adj* cold
**Kälte** [KAIYL•teh] *n* M cold;
  chill; coldness
**Kalzium** [KAHL•tsee•oom] *n*
  calcium
**Kamee** [kah•MEE] *n* F cameo
**Kamel** [KAH•mel] *n* N camel
**Kamerad** [KAH•mair•AHD] *n*
  M comrade
**Kameradschaft**
  [kah•mair•AHD•shahft] *n* F
  fellowship

**Kameramann**
[KAH•mair•uh•MAHN] *n* M
cameraman
**Kamin** [kah•MEEN] *n* M
fireplace; hearth
**Kamineinfassung**
[-UYN•fah•soong] *n* F
mantelpiece
**Kamm** [kahm] *n* M ridge
**Kamm kämmen** [kahm]
[KE•men] *n vt* M comb
**Kammer** [KAH•mair] *n* F
chamber; closet
**Kammerdiener**
[KAH•mair•DEEN•air] *n* M
valet
**Kampf** [kahmpf] *n* M fight;
combat; bout; strife
**kämpfen** [KEMPF•en] *vi* fight;
struggle
**kämpfen um** [KEMPF•en oom]
*vt* contest
**Kanadien** [kah•NAH•DEE•ehn]
*n* Canada
**Kanal** [kah•NAL] *n* M canal;
channel
**Kanalboot** [kah•NAHL•boht] *n*
N barge
**Kanarienvogel**
[kah•NAHR•ee•ehn•FOH•gel]
*n* M canary
**Kandidat** [KAHN•dee•DAHT]
*n* M candidate
**Känguruh** [KENG•uh•roo] *n* N
kangaroo
**Kanne** [KAHN•eh] *n* F can
**kannelieren**
[KAH•nehl•eer•EHN] *vt*
channel
**Kanone** [KAH•nohn•eh] *n* F
cannon

**Kanu** [kah•NOO] *n* N canoe
**Kanzel** [KAN•tsel] *n* F pulpit
**Kanzler** [KAHN•tslair] *n* M
chancellor
**Kapelle 1** [kah•PEHL•eh] *n* F
chapel
**Kapelle 2** [kah•PEHL•eh] *n* F
band, orchestra
**Kaper** [KAH•pair] *n* F caper
**Kapitän** [KAHP•ee•TAHN] *n*
M captain
**Kapital** [kah•PEE•tal] *n* N
capital; fund
**Kapitalanleger**
[KAH•pee•TAHL•ahn•LAI•gair]
*n* M investor
**Kapitalismus**
[KAH•pee•tahl•is•moos] *n* M
capitalism
**Kapitel** [kah•PEE•tehl] *n* M
chapter
**Kaplan** [KAHP•lahn] *n* M
chaplain
**Kappe** [KAH•peh] *n* M canopy
**Kapsel** [KAHP•sel] *n* F capsule
**Kapuze** [kah•poots•eh] *n* F
hood
**Kapuzinerkresse**
[kah•puh•tseen•air•kreh•seh] *n*
F nasturtium
**Karaffe** [kah•rah•fe] *n* F
decanter
**Kardinal** [kahr•din•ahl] *n* M
cardinal
**karibisches Meer**
[KAH•rib•ish•ehs MAIYR] *n*
N Caribbean (Sea)
**Karikatur**
[KAHR•ee•kah•TOOYR] *n* F
caricature; cartoon

**Karotte** [kah•ROHT•teh] *n* F
carrot

**Karpfen** [KAHRP•fehn] *n* M
carp

**Karren** [KAH•rehn] *n* M cart

**Karte** [KAHR•teh] *n* F card

**Kartentisch** [KAHR•ten-] *n* M
table (card)

**Kartoffel** [kahr•TOH•fel] *npl* F
potato

**Karton** [kahr•TOHN] *n* M
carton

**Kartonpapier**
[kar•TOHN•pah•PEER] *n* N
cardboard

**Karusell** [KAH•roo•sel] *n* N
merry-go-round

**Käse** [KAI•zeh] *n* M cheese

**Kaserne** [kah•SAIR•neh] *n* F
barracks

**Kasse 1** [KAH•seh] *n* F box
office

**Kasse 2** [KAH•seh] *n* F cash
register

**Kassenbestand**
[KAH•sen•BEH•shtand] *n* M
till

**Kassette** [KAH•set•teh] *n* F
cassette

**Kastanie** [KAH•stah•NEE•eh] *n*
F chestnut

**kastanienbraun**
[KAH•stahn•EE•en•BROUN]
*adj* maroon

**Kasten** [KAH•stehn] *n* M chest

**Katalog** [kah•tah•LOHG] *n* M
catalogue

**Katarakt** [KAH•tahr•ahkt] *n* M
cataract

**katastrophal**
[KAH•tah•SHTROH•fal] *adj*
disastrous

**Katastrophe**
[KAH•tah•SHTROH•feh] *n* F
catastrophe

**Kätzchen** [KETS•khen] *n* N
kitten

**Kategorie** [KAH•teh•gohr•EE]
*n* F category

**Kater** [KAH•tair] *n* M tomcat;
cat

**katolisch** [kah•TOH•lish] *adj n*
Catholic

**Katze** [KAHT•seh] *n* F cat

**Katzenjammer**
[KAHT•sen•YAH•mair] *n* M
hangover

**kauen** [KOU•ehn] *vt* chew;
munch

**Kauf** [kouf] *n* M purchase

**kaufen** [KOW•fun] *yt* buy

**Käufer -in** [KOI•fair] [ -in] *n* M
shopper

**Käufer -in** [KOI•fair] [-in] *n* M
buyer

**Kaufhaus** [KOUF•hous] *n* N
department store

**käuflich** [KOIF•lihk] *adj*
mercenary

**Kaufmann** [KOUF•man] *n* M
merchant

**Kaulquappe**
[KOUL•kvahp•peh] *n* F
tadpole

**kaum** [kowm] *adv* barely;
hardly

**Kaution** [KOW•tsee•ohn] *n* F
bail

**keck** [kek] *adj* flippant

**Kegel** [KAI•gel] *n* M cone

**kegeln** [KAI•geln] *vt* bowling

**Kehle** [KAI•leh] *n* F throttle

**Keil** [kuyl] *n* M wedge

**Keim 1** [kaim] *n* M bud; sprout; shoot

**Keim 2** [kuym] *n* M germ

**keimen** [KUY•men] *vi* germinate

**keimfrei** [KUYM•fruy] *adj* sterile

**keimfrei machen** [KUYM•fruy mahk•en] *vt* disinfect

**kein; keine** [kuyn -e] *pr ad* none

**Keks** [keks] *n* M cookie; cracker

**Kelle** [KEH•leh] *n* F trowel

**Keller** [KEL•lair] *n* M basement; cellar

**Kellner** [KEL•nair] *n* M waiter

**Kellnerin** [-in] *n* F waitress

**keltisch** [KEL•tish] *adj* Celtic

**Kenntnis** [KEHNT•nis] *n* F knowledge

**Kennwort** [ken•vort] *n* N password

**Kennzeichen** [KEN•tsai•ken] *n* N badge; distinguishing mark

**Kenya** Kenya

**keramisch** [KAIR•ahm•ish] *adj* ceramic

**Kerbe** [KAIR•beh] *n* F nick; notch

**Kerker** [KAIR•kair] *n* M dungeon

**Kerl** [kairl] *n* M guy

**Kern 1** [kairn] *n* M kernel

**Kern 2** [kairn] *n* M nucleus

**kernförmig** [KAIRN•fer•mig] *adj* nuclear

**Kerosin** [KAIR•oh•seen] *n* N kerosene

**Kerste** [KAIR•steh] *n* F candle

**Kessel** [KEH•sel] *n* M kettle

**Ketchup** [KEH•tchup] *n* M ketchup

**Kette** [KEH•teh] *n* F chain

**keuchen** [KOI•khen] *vi* pant

**keuchend** [koi•khend] *adj* wheezy

**Keule** [KOI•leh] *n* F club

**keusch** [koish] *adj* chaste

**Khaki** [KHA•kee] *n* N khaki

**kichern** [KEE•khairn] *vi* giggle

**Kiefer 1** [KEE•fair] *n* M jaw

**Kiefer 2** [KEE•fair] *n* F pine

**Kielwasser** [KEEL•vah•sair] *n* N wake

**Kies** [kees] *n* M gravel; grit

**Kieselstein** [KEE•sel•shtuyn] *n* M pebble

**Kilogramm** [KEE•lo•grahm] *n* N kilogram

**Kilometer** [KEE•lo•mai•tair] *n* M kilometer

**Kilowattstunde** [-VAHT•SHUHN•de] *n* F kilowatt

**Kilt** [kihlt] *n* M kilt

**Kind** [kint] *n* N child; kid

**Kinderbettchen** [KIN•dair•BET•khen] *n* N cot

**Kindergarten** [KIHN•dair•GAHRT•ten] *n* M kindergarten

**Kinderlied** [KIHN•dair•leed] *n* N nursery rhyme

**Kinderzimmer** [KIN•dair•TSIM•mair] *n* N nursery

**kindisch** [KINT•ish] *adj* childish

**Kinn** [kin] *n* M chin

**Kino** [KEE•noh] *n* N cinema; screen (movies)

**kippen** [KIH•pen] *vt* tilt; *vi* topple

**Kirche** [KEEUR•keh] *n* F
church

**Kirchengesang absingen**
[KEERKH•ehn•geh•ZAHNG]
[ap•zihng•ehn] *n vt* M chant

**Kirchenspaltung**
[KEER•khen•shpahl•toong] *n*
F schism

**Kirchenstuhl**
[KEER•khen•SHTOOL] *n* M
pew

**kirchlich** [KEERKH•lihk] *adj*
ecclesiastic

**Kirchturm** [KEERHK•toorm] *n*
M steeple

**Kirsche** [KEEYR•sheh] *n* F
cherry

**Kissen** [KIS•ehn] *n* N cushion;
pillow

**Kissenbezug** [-beh•tsoog] *n* M
pillowcase

**Kiste** [kis•teh] *n* F box; hutch

**Kitsch** [kihtsh] *n* M shoddy

**Kitt** [kit] *n* M putty

**kitzeln** [KEET•seln] *vt* tickle

**Kläger** [KLEH•gair] *n* M
plaintiff; prosecutor

**kläglich** [klaig•lihk] *adj* piteous

**klären** [KLAIR•en] *vt* purge

**Klage** [KLAH•ge] *n* F
complaint

**Klammer** [KLAH•mair] *n* F
bracket (in writing)

**Klammern** [KLAH•mairn] *npl*
parenthesis

**klammern** [KLAH•mairn] *vt*
staple

**Klamotten** [KLAH•moh•ten]
*npl* slop

**Klappe** [kla•pe] *n* F flap

**klappern** [KLAH•pairn] *vt*
rattle

**Klapperschlange**
[-SHLAHNG•eh] *n* F
rattlesnake

**Klapptür** [KLAHP•toor] *n* F
trap-door

**Klaps** [klahps] *n* M slap; smack

**klar** [klahr] *adj* lucid; clear

**klar** [klahr] *vt* clear

**Klarheit** [KLAHR•huyt] *n* F
clarity

**Klarinette** [KLAH•rin•et•eh] *n*
F clarinet

**Klasse** [KLAH•seh] *n* F class

**Klassenzimmer**
[KLAH•sen•TSIM•air] *n* N
classroom

**klassifizieren**
[KLAH•si•fi•TSEER•ehn] *vt*
classify

**klassifiziert**
[KLAH•sih•fi•TSEERT] *adj*
classified

**klassisch** [KLAH•sish] *adj*
classical

**Klassiker** [KLAH•sik•air] *n* M
classic

**Klatsch** [klahtsh] *n* M gossip

**Klatschbase**
[KLAHTCH•bah•zeh] *n* F
tattle-tale

**klatschen** [KLAHT•tsch•un] *vi*
*vt* blab

**klatschen** [KLAH•tsh•ehn] *vt*
clap

**Klaue** [KLOU•eh] *n* F claw

**klauen** [KLAU•en] *vt* claw (at)

**Klause** [KLOU•ze] *n* F clause

**Klaviatur** [klah•vee•ah•toor] *n* F
keyboard

**Klavier** *n* N piano
**Klavierspieler (in)**
[KLAH•vee•AIR•shpeel•air]
[in] *n* M pianist
**kleben** [KLAIY•ben] *vi* cling
**klebrig** [KLAI•brig] *adj*
tenacious
**Klebrigkeit** [-kuyt] *n* F tenacity
**Klebstoff** [KLAIYB•shtohf] *n*
M cement
**Klebstoff** [KLAIB•shtof] *n* M
glue
**Klebstoff** [KLAIB•shtohf] *n* M
paste
**Klee 1** [klai] *n̸* M clover
**Klee 2** [klai] *n* M trefoil
**Kleid** [kluyd] *n* N dress
**Kleiderbügel**
[KLUY•dair•boo•gel] *n* M
hanger
**Kleidung** [KLUY•doong] *n* F
clothing; clothes
**Kleidungsstück**
[KLUY•doongs•shtuhk] *n* N
garment
**Kleie** [KLAIY•uh] *n* F bran
**klein** [kluyn] *adj* little
**kleine Welle** [KLUY•neh
VEH•leh] *n* F ripple
**Kleinhändler**
[KLUYN•hend•LAIR] *n* M
retailer
**Kleinigkeit**
[KLUYN•ig•KUYT] *n* F trifle
**Klemmer** [KEHM•air] *n* F
clamp
**Klempner** [klehmp•nair] *n* M
plumber; plumbing
**Klima** [KLEE•mah] *n* N climate
**Klimaanlage**
[KLEE•mah•AHN•lahg•eh] *n*
F airconditioning

**Klingel** [KLIHNG•el] *n* N jingle
**klingeln** [KLIHNG•eln] *vi*
tinkle
**klingelte** [KLIHNG•el•teh] *past
tense* rang
**Klinik** [KLI•neek] *n* F clinic
**klinisch** [KLI•nish] *adj* clinical
**Klinke** [KLINNK•eh] *n* F jack;
latch
**Klippe** [KLIP•eh] *n* F cliff
**Klippfisch** [KLIP•fish] *n* M cod
**klopfen** [klohp•fen] *vt* rap; tap
**Klopfer** [KLOH•pfair] *n* M
knocker
**Kloster** [KLOH•staiyr] *n* N
cloister; convent; monastery
**Klotz** [klohts] *n* M log
**Klub** [kluhb] *n* M nightclub
**klug** [kloog] *adj* intelligent;
prudent
**Klugheit** [KLOOG•huyt] *n* F
intelligence; prudence
**Klumpen** [KLOOM•pen] *n* M
clump; lump
**knapp 1** [knahp] *adj* scarce; in
short supply
**knapp 2** [knahp] *adj* concise;
terse
**Knebel** [KNAI•bel] *n* M gag
**Knechtschaft**
[KNEHKT•shahft] *n* F
servitude
**kneten** [KNAI•ten] *vt* knead
**Knicker** [KNIH•kair] *n* M
skinflint
**Knie** [knee] *n* N knee
**knien** [KNEE•ehn] *vi* kneel
**Kniescheibe** [KNEE•shuy•be] *n*
F kneecap
**Knirps** [knEErps] *n* M tot;
whippersnapper

knirschen [KNEER•shen] *vt*
crunch; gnash

Knoblauch [KNOHB•louhk] *n*
M garlic

Knochen [KNOH•ken] *n* M
bone

Knopf [knohpf] *n* M button;
knob; stud

Knorpel [KNOR•pel] *n* M
gristle

knorrig [KNOH•rig] *adj* gnarled

Knoten [KNOH•ten] *n* M knot

knusprig [KNOO•sprig] *adj*
crisp

Koch [kokh] *n* M cook

kochen [KOKH•en] *vt* cook;
boil

Kochen [KOH•ken] *n* N
cooking

Köder [KOOH•dair] *n* M bait

kölnisches Wasser
[KUHLN•ish•es VAH•sair] *n*
N toilet water

Konditerei [KON•dit•tohr•AI] *n*
F bakery

König [KER•nig] *n* M king

Königin [KUHN•ig•en] *n* F
queen

königlich [KER•nig•lihk] *adj*
regal

Königreich [-ruyhk] *n* N
kingdom

konkurs [KOHN•koors] *adj*
bankrupt

können [KOOH•nen] *vi-aux* can

Können [KUH•nen] *n* N
proficiency

Körnchen [KERN•khen] *n* N
granule

Körper [KER•pair] *n* M body

körperbehindert
[KER•pair•beh•HIN•dairt] *adj*
disabled

körperlich [KER•poor•likh] *adj*
corporal

körperlich [KER•pair•lihk] *adj*
physical

korrupt [koh•ROOPT] *adj*
corrupt

Korruption
[koh•RUPT•TSEE•on] *n* F
corruption

köstlich [KOOST•lihk] *adj*
delicious; exquisite

Koffer [KOH•fair] *n* M trunk

Kohl [kohl] *n* M cabbage

Kohle [KOH•leh] *n* F coal

Kohlenstoff
[KOHL•ehn•shtohf] *n* M
carbon

Kokaine [koh•kuy•EEN•eh] *n* F
cocaine

Kokon [KO•kohn] *n* F cocoon

Koksnuß [KOH•kohs•NOOS] *n*
F coconut

Kolben [KOHL•ben] *n* M piston

Kolibri [KO•li•BREE] *n* M
hummingbird

Kolibri [KOH•lih•BREE] *n* M
woodpecker

Kollege [ko•LAI•ge] *n* M peer

Kollege -in [koh•LAIG•eh]
[-in] *n* M colleague

kollern [KOH•lairn] *vi* gobble

Kolonie [KOH•lohn•EE] *n* F
colony

kolossal [koh•LOH•sahl] *adj*
terrific

Koma [KO•mah] *n* N coma

Komet [KOO•met] *n* M comet

**Komiker** [KO•mik•air] *n* M
comedian

**komisch** [KOH•mish] *adj* funny

**Komma** [KO•mah] *n* M comma

**Kommandant**
[KO•man•DAHNT] *n* M
commander

**kommen** [KO•men] *vi* come

**kommentieren**
[KOH•men•TEER•en] *vi*
comment

**Kommentar** [ [KO•men•tahr] *n*
M comment

**Kommisar** [KO•mi•sahr] *n* M
commissioner

**Kommission** [KO•mi•SEE•on]
*n* F committee

**Kommunion**
[KO•moon•EE•on] *n* F
communion

**Kommunismus**
[ko•moo•NIS•moos] *n* M
communism

**Kommunist** [ko•moon•EEST] *n*
M communist

**Komödie** [ko•MOO•dee•eh] *n* F
comedy

**kompakt** [kom•PAKT] *adj*
compact

**Kompaß** [KOM•pahs] *n* M
compass

**Kompliment** [kom•PLI•MENT]
*n* M compliment

**komplizieren**
[KOM•pli•TSEER•en] *vt*
complicate

**kompliziert** [kom•PLI•tseert]
*adj* complex; complicated

**komponieren**
[KOM•pon•EER•en] *vt*
compose

**Komponist** [KOM•pon•IST] *n*
M composer

**Kompromiß** [KOM•pro•MIS] *n*
M compromise

**kompromißlos**
[KOHM•pro•MEES•los] *adj*
uncompromising

**Konditorei** [KON•dih•tor•UY]
*n* F pastry shop

**Konditorware**
[KOHN•dih•tor•VAHR•eh] *n*
F pastry

**Konditorwaren**
[KON•di•tohr•VAH•ren] *npl*
confectionery

**Konferenz** [KON•fair•ents] *n*
M conference

**Konflikt** [KON•fleekt] *n* M
conflict

**konfrontieren**
[KON•fron•TEER•en] *vt*
confront

**Konjugation**
[KON•yoo•gah•tsee•ON] *n* F
conjugation

**konjunktiv**
[KON•yuhnk•TEEV] *adj*
subjunctive

**konkrett** [KON•kret] *adj*
concrete

**konkurrieren**
[kon•koor•EER•en] *vi*
compete

**konkurrierend**
[KON•koo•EER•end] *adj*
competitive

**Konkurs** [KOHN•koors] *n* M
bankruptcy

**Konsequenz**
[KON•se•KVENTS] *n* F
consequence

**konservativ**
[KON•suyr•vah•TEEV] *adj*
conservative
**Konsonant** [KON•so•NAHNT]
*n* M consonant
**Konsortium**
[KON•sor•TEE•oom] *n* N
syndicate
**konstruieren**
[KON•shtroo•EER•en] *vt*
construe
**konstruieren bauen**
[KON•shtroo•eer•en]
[BOU•en] *vt* construct
**Konsulat** [KON•soo•laht] *n* N
consulate
**konsultieren**
[KON•sool•TEER•en] *vt*
consult
**Kontakt** [KON•tahkt] *n* M
contact
**Kontinent** [KON•ti•nent] *n* M
continent
**Konto** [kohn•toh] *n* N account
**Kontrast** [KON•trahst] *n* M
contrast
**kontrollieren**
[KON•trol•EER•en] *vt* control
**Kontroverse** [KON•tro•FAIRS]
*n* F controversy
**konvex** [KON•veks] *adj* convex
**konzentrieren**
[KON•tsen•TREER•en] *vt*
concentrate
**Konzert** [KON•tsairt] *n* N
concert
**koordinieren**
[KOH•ohr•di•NEER•en] *vt*
coordinate
**Kopf** [kopf] *n* M head

**Kopf hoch** [kopf hokh] cheer
up
**Kopfhörer** [-HER•air] *n* M
headphones
**Kopflehne** [-LAI•ne] *n* F
headrest
**Kopfschmerz** [-SCHMAIRTS]
*n* M headache
**Kopfstein** [KOHPF•shtuyn] *n*
M cobblestones
**Kopie** [koh•PEE] *n* F copy;
replica
**Koppelleine**
[KOP•pel•LUY•ne] *n* F leash
**Koralle** [koh•RAHL•eh] *n* F
coral
**Korb** [kohrp] *n* M basket;
hamper
**Korbball** [KORP•bal] *n* M
basketball
**Kord** [kohrd] *n* M corduroy
**Korea** [KOHR•ai•eh] *n* Korea
**Kork** [kohrk] *n* M cork
**Korkenzieher**
[KOHR•ken•TSEE•air] *n* M
corkscrew
**Korn** [kohrn] *n* N corn
**Kornkammer**
[KOHRN•kah•mair] *n* F
granary
**Korporation**
[KOR•pohr•ah•TSEE•on] *n* F
corporation
**Korrespondent -in**
[KOHR•es•PAHN•dent -in] *n*
M correspondent
**Korsika** [KOHR•si•kah] *n*
Corsica
**koscher** [KOH•shair] *adj* kosher
**Kosten** [KOH•sten] *n* N
expense

**kostspielig** [KOHST•shpeel•ig]
*adj* wasteful

**Kostüm** [koh•SHTOOM] *n* M
costume

**Kotelett** [KOH•te•let] *n* N
steak, chop

**Krach** [krahk] *n* M crack

**krächzen** [KREK•tsen] *vi*
croak; *vt* rasp

**kräftig** [KREHF•tig] *adj*
forceful; powerful; strong

**kräftigen** [KREHFT•ig•en] *adj*
invigorating

**Krähe** [KRAI•e] *n* F crow

**kränklich** [KREHNK•lihk] *adj*
sickly

**Kräuselung** [KROI•zel•oong] *n*
F kinky

**kräuter** [KROI•tair] *adj* herbal

**Kraft** [krahft] *n* F force; might;
power; vigor

**kraftlos** [-los] *adj* powerless

**kraftvoll** [KRAHFT•fol] *adj*
vigorous

**Kragen** [KRAH•gen] *n* M collar

**Krake** [KRAH•keh] *n* M
octopus

**Krampe** [KRAHM•pe] *n* F
cramp

**Krampf** [krahmpf] *n* M spasm

**Kranich** [KRAH•nihk] *n* M
crane

**krank** [krahnk] *adj* ill; sick

**Krankenhaus**
[KRAHNK•en•hous] *n* N
hospital

**Krankenschwester**
[KRAHNK•en•SHVEH•stair]
*n* F nurse

**Krankentrage**
[KRAHNK•en•trah•geh] *n* F
stretcher

**Krankheit** [KRAHNK•huyt] *n* F
disease; sickness

**Kranx** [krahnts] *n* M wreath

**Krater** [KRAH•tair] *n* M crater

**Kratze** [KRAHTS•eh] *n* F
rabble

**kratzen** [KRAH•tsen] *vt* scrape

**kratzend** [krahts•end] *adj*
grating

**Kratzer** *n* M scraper

**Krause** [KROU•zeh] *n* ruffle

**Kraut** [krout] *n* N herb

**Krautsalat** [krout•sah•laht] *n* M
slaw

**Kravatte** [krah•VAH•teh] *n* F
tie

**Krebs 1** [krehbs] *n* M cancer

**Krebs 2** [krebz] *n* M crab

**Kreditkarte**
[kre•DEET•KAHR•teh] *n* F
credit card

**Kreide** [KRUY•deh] *n* F chalk

**Kreis1** [kruys] *n* M circle

**Kreis2** [kruys] *n* M county

**kreischen** [KRUY•shen] *vi*
creak; screech; squawk

**kreisförmig** [KRUYS•foorm•ig]
*adj* circular

**Kreislauf** [KRUYS•louf] *n* M
circuit; circulation

**Krepp** [krep] *n* M crepe

**Kreuz** [kroits] *n* N cross

**kreuzen** [KROITS•en] *vt*
intersect

**Kreuzfeuer** [KROITS•foi•air] *n*
N crossfire

**Kreuzung 1** [KROITS•oong] *n*
F hybrid

**Kreuzung 2** [KROITS•oong] *n*
F intersection

**kreuzweise** [KROITS•vaiz•uh] *adv prep* across

**Kreuzworträtsel** [KROITS•vohrt•ret•sel] *n* N crossword (puzzle)

**Kreuzzug** [KROITS•oog] *n* M crusade

**Krickente** [KRIHK•en•teh] *n* F teal

**kriechen** [kree•khen] *vi* crawl

**Krieg** [kreeg] *n* M war

**Krieger** [KREEG•air] *n* M warrior

**kriegerisch** [KREEG•air•ish] *adj* warlike

**Kriegsmarine** [KREEGS•mah•REEN•eh] *n* F navy

**kriminell** [KRI•min•EL] *adj* criminal; delinquent

**Krippe** [KRIP•eh] *n* F crib

**Krise** [KREE•seh] *n* F crisis

**Kristall** [kri•STAHL] *n* M crystal

**Kritik** [krih•TEEK] *n* F criticism

**Kritiker** [krih•tih•KAIR] *n* M critic

**kritisch** [KRI•tish] *adj* crucial

**kritisieren** [KRI•tih•SEER•en] *vt* criticize

**kritzeln** [KRITS•eln] *vt* scrawl

**Krönung** [KROO•noong] *n* F coronation

**Kröte** [KRUH•teh] *n* F toad

**Krokodil** [KROH•koh•DEEL] *n* N crocodile

**Krone** [KROH•ne] *n* F crown

**Krücke** [KROO•keh] *n* F crutch

**Krug** [kroog] *n* M mug; jug

**Krume** [kroo•me] *n* F crumb

**krumm** [kroom] *adj* crooked

**krümmen** [KRUH•men] *vt* warp

**Krüppel** [KRUH•pel] *n* M cripple

**Kruste** [KROOST•eh] *n* F crust

**Kruzifix** [KROO•tsi•FIKS] *n* crucifix

**Kuß** [kuhs] *n* M kiss

**Kuba** [koo•ba] Cuba

**kubanisch** [KOO•bahn•ish] *adj* Cuban

**kubisch** [KOO•bish] *adj* cubic

**Küche** [KOO•khe] *n* F kitchen

**Kuchen** [KOOH•ken] *n* M cake

**Küchlein** [KOOKH•lain] *n* N chick

**Kugel1** [KOO•gel] *n* F ball; sphere; globe

**Kugel2** [KOO•gel] *n* F bullet

**Kügelchen** [KOO•gel•khen] *n* N pellet

**kugelförmig** [KOO•gel•ferm•ig] *adj* spherical

**Kugelschreiber** [KOO•gel•SHRUY•bair] *n* M pen

**Kuh** [koo] *n* M cow

**kühl** [kool] *adj* cool; chilly

**Kühle** [KOOL•eh] *n* F coolness

**Kühlung** [KUH•loong] *n* F refrigeration

**kühn** [koohn] *adj* bold; daring

**Kühnheit** [KOOHN•hait] *n* F boldness; courage; temerity

**Kult** [koolt] *n* M cult

**Kultiviertheit** [KUHL•tih•VEERT•huyt] *n* F sophistication

**Kulture** [KUHL•toor] *n* F
culture
**kulturell** [KUHL•toor•EL] *adj*
cultural
**Kummer** [KOO•mair] *n* M care;
grief; worry; bother
**Kunde** [KUHN•de] *n* M
customer
**Kunde -in** [KUHN•deh] [-in] *n*
M client
**Kundschaft** [KUHNT•shahft] *n*
F clientele
**Kundschaften**
[KUHNT•shahft•en] *npl* scout
**Kunst** [koonst] *n* F art
**Kunstfertigkeit**
[KUHNST•fair•tig•kuyt] *n* F
workmanship
**Kunstgriff** [KUHNST•grihf] *n*
M knack; sleight
**Künstler -in** [KOONST•lair]
[-in] *n* M artist
**künstlich** [KOONST•lik] *adj*
artificial
**Kunstseide** [KUHNST•zai•deh]
*n* F rayon

**Kupfer** [KOOP•fair] *n* N copper
**Kupon** [KOO•pon] *n* M coupon
**Kuppel** [KOO•pel] *n* F dome
**Kürbis** [KOOR•bis] *n* M gourd;
pumpkin
**Kurier** [KOO•reer] *n* M courier
**Kurort** [KOOR•ort] *n* M resort
**Kurve** [KOOR•veh] *n* F bend
**Kurve** [koor•ve] *n* F curve
**kurz** [koorts] *adj* brief; short;
concise
**Kürze** [KOOR•tseh] *n* F brevity
**Kurzgeschichte**
[-geh•shihk•teh] *n* F short
story
**Kurzschrift** [-shrift] *n* F
shorthand
**kurzsichtig** [KOORTS•zihk•tig]
*adj* nearsighted
**Kusine** [koo•ZEE•ne] *n* F
cousin
**Küste** [KOO•steh] *n* F coast;
shore
**Kutsche** [KOOTCH•eh] *n* F
carriage; coach
**Kuwait** *n* Kuwait

# L

**labil** [lah•BEEL] *adj* disoriented
**Labor** [lah•BOR] *n* N lab
**Laboratorium**
[lah•bor•ah•TOR•ee•oom] *n* N
laboratory
**Labour Party** Labor Party
**Labyrinth** [LAHB•rihnt] *n* N
maze
**Lachen** [lah•khen] *n* N laugh

**lächeln** [LEKH•eln] *vi* chuckle
**lachen** [LAH•khen] *vi* laugh
**lächerlich** [LEK•air•lik] *adj*
absurd; ridiculous
**Lack** [lahk] *n* M paint; lacquer;
varnish
**Ladenbesitzer**
[LAH•den•beh•ZITS•air] *n* M
shopkeeper

**Ladeninhaber**
[LAH•den•in•hah•bair] *n* M
tradesman
**Ladung 1** [LAH•doong] *n* F
subpoena
**Ladung 2** [LAH•doong] *n* F
load
**Lage** [LAH•geh] *n* F position
**Lage** [LAH•geh] *n* F situation
**Lager** [LAH•gair] *n* N
encampment
**Lager** [LAH•gair] *n* N lair
**Lager** [LAH•gair] *n* N store
**Lager lagern** [LAH•gair] [-n] *n*
*vi* N camp
**Lagerbestand**
[LAH•gair•be•SHTAHNT] *n*
M inventory
**Lagerhaus** [LAH•gair•hous] *n*
N depot
**Lagerhaus** [LAH•gair•hous] *n*
N warehouse
**Lagerraum** [LAH•gair•roum] *n*
M stockroom
**Lagerung** [LAH•gair•oong] *n* F
storage
**Lagerverwalter**
[-fair•VAHL•tair] *n* M
storekeeper
**Lagune** [lah•GOON•eh] *n* F
lagoon
**lahm** [lahm] *adj* lame
**lähmen** [LAI•men] *vt* paralyze
**Lähmung** [LAI•moong] *n* F
paralysis
**Laib** [laib] *n* M loaf
**Laich** [luyhk] *n* M spawn
**Lamm** [lahm] *n* N lamb
**Lampe** [LAHM•pe] *n* F lamp
**Lampenfieber**
[LAHM•pen•FEE•bair] *n* N
stage fright

**Land** [lahnt] *n* N country
**Land** [lahnt] *n* N land
**ländlich** [LEND•lihk] *adj* rural
**Länge 1** [LENG•eh] *n* F length
**Länge 2** [LEHN•ge] *n* F
longitude
**Landkarte** [LAHNT•kahr•te] *n*
F map
**Landmann** [LAHNT•mahn] *n*
M countryman
**Landschaft** [LAHNT•shahft] *n*
F scenery
**Landung** [LAHN•doong] *n* F
landing
**Landwirtschaft**
[LAHNT•veert•SHAH•FT] *n*
F agriculture; farming
**lang** [lahng] *adj* long
**Langboot** [LAHNG•boht] *n* N
galley
**Langeweile**
[LAHNG•geh•VAI•leh] *n* F
boredom
**langsam** [LAHNG•zahm] *adj*
slow; *adv* slowly
**langsam kochen**
[LAHNG•zahm koh•khen] *vt*
stew
**langweilig** [LAHNG•vai•lig]
*adj* boring; dull; tedious
**Lappen** [LAH•pen] *n* M lobe;
patch
**Lärm** [leeurm] *n* M noise;
clamor
**lärmend** [LAIRM•end] *adj*
tumultuous
**Larve** [LAR•ve] *n* F grub
**Lasche** [LAH•sheh] *n* F shackle
**lassen** [LAH•sen] *vt* let; leave;
stop
**Last** [lahst] *n* F load; burden

**lästig** [LEST•ig] *adj*
  inconvenient
**Lastwagen** [LAHST•vah•gen] *n*
  M van
**Latein; lateinisch** [lah•tuyn]
  [-ish] *adj n* Latin
**Lateinamerika**
  [-ah•MAIR•ih•ke] *n* N Latin
  America
**latent** [LAH•tent] *adj* latent
**Laterne** [lah•TAIR•ne] *n* F
  lantern
**Laternenpfahl**
  [lah•TAIRN•en•pfahl] *n* M
  lamppost
**Lauch** [louhk] *n* M leek
**lauern** [LOU•airn] *vi* skulk
**Lauf** [louf] *n* M course;
  sequence
**laufen** [LOU•fen] *vi* jog; run
**Laufen** [LOU•fen] *n* N running
**laufendes Band** [LOU•fen•des
  BAHNT] *n* N conveyer belt
**Läufer** [LOI•fair] *n* M racer;
  runner
**Laune** [LOU•ne] *n* F freak
**launenhaft** [LOU•nen•hahft]
  *adj* fickle
**launisch** [LOUN•ish] *adj*
  moody; wayward
**Laus** [lous] *n* F louse
**laut 1** [lowt] *adv* aloud; loud;
  noisy
**laut 2** [lowt] *prep* according to
**Laut** [lout] *n* M sound
**läuten** [LOI•ten] *vt* chime
**lautlos** [LOUT•los] *adj*
  soundless
**Lautsprecher** [-SHPREHK•air]
  *n* M loudspeaker

**lauwarm** [LOU•vahrm] *adj*
  lukewarm; tepid
**Lava** [LAH•vah] *n* F lava
**Lebanon** Lebanon
**Leben** [LAI•ben] *n* N life;
  existence
**lebend** [LAI•bend] *adj* living
**lebendig** [leh•BEND•ig] *adj*
  alive
**lebendig** [leh•BEHN•dig] *adj*
  spirited; lively
**lebendig** [lai•BEN•dig] *adj v*
  live
**Lebenserwartung**
  [-air•VAHR•toong] *n* F life
  expectancy
**lebenslänglich** [-LEHNG•lihk]
  *adj* lifelong
**lebenslängliche**
  **Freiheitsstrafe**
  [-IEHNG•lihk•eh
  FRUY•huyts•SHTRAH•feh] *n*
  F life sentence
**Lebenslauf** [LAI•bens•louf] *n*
  M lifespan
**Lebensmittel**
  [LAI•bens•MI•tel] *n* N
  groceries; viands
**Lebensmittelgeschäft**
  [-geh•shehft] *n* N grocery
**Lebensstil** [-SHTEEL] *n* M
  lifestyle
**lebenswahr** [lai•bens•VAHR]
  *adj* lifelike
**lebenswichtig**
  [LAI•bens•VIHK•tig] *adj* vital
**Leber** [LAI•bair] *n* F liver
**Lebewohl** [lai•be•vohl] *n* N
  farewell
**lebhaft 1** [LAIYB•hahft] *adj*
  brisk; skittish

**lebhaft 2** [LAIB•hahft] *adj*
vivacious

**Lebhaftigkeit** [-ig•KUYT] *n* F
vivacity

**leblos** [LAIB•los] *adj*
inanimate; lifeless

**lecken** [LEHK•en] *vt* lick

**lecker** [LEH•kair] *adj* luscious

**Leder** [lai•dair] *n* N leather

**leer** [lair] *adj* empty; vacant;
void

**leer an** [laiyr•ahn] *adj* devoid

**legalisieren**
[LAI•gal•i•SEER•en] *vt*
legalize

**Legat** [lai•GAHT] *n* N legacy

**legen** [LAI•gen] *vt* lay

**legendär** [le•gen•DAIR] *adj*
legendary

**legitim** [LEH•gi•TEEM] *adj*
legitimate

**Lehm** [laim] *n* M clay

**Lehre** [LAIY•reh] *n* F doctrine;
teaching; lore

**Lehren** [lair•en] *n* N teaching

**Lehrer –in** [LAIR•rair -in] *n* M
instructor; schoolteacher;
teacher

**Lehrsatz** [LAIYR•sats] *n* M
dogma

**Leibwache** [LAIB•vahk•eh] *n* F
bodyguard

**Leibweh** [LAIB•vai] *n* N gripe

**Leich** [laichk] *n* M cadaver;
corpse

**Leichenbeschauer**
[LUYK•en•beh•SHOU•air] *n*
M coroner

**Leichenbestatter**
[LUYHK•en•beh•SHTAH•tair]
*n* M undertaker

**Leichenschauhaus**
[LUYHK•en•SHOU•hous] *n*
N morgue

**Leichentuch**
[LUYHK•en•TOOHK] *n* N
shroud

**Leichenwagen**
[LUY•khen•VAH•gen] *n* M
hearse

**leicht** [luyhkt] *adj* easy; slight
*adv* easily; lightly

**leichter Tod** [LUYHK•tair
TOHD] *n* euthanasia

**leichtfertig** [LAIHKT•fair•tig]
*adj* frivolous; glib

**Leichtheit** [LUYHKT•huyt] *n* F
lightness

**leiden** [LUY•den] *vi* suffer

**Leiden** [LUY•den] *n* N
suffering; tribulation

**Leidenschaft** [LUY•den•shahft]
*n* F passion

**leidenschaftlich**
[LAID•en•SHAHFT•lihk]
passionate; impassioned

**leidenschaftslos**
[LUY•den•SHAHFTS•lohs]
*adj* dispassionate

**Leihen** [LUY•hen] *n* N loan

**Lein·**[lain] *n* M flax

**Leinen** [LUY•nen] *n* N linen

**Leinwand** [LUYN•vahnt] *n* F
screen

**leise** [LUY•zeh] *adj* quietly

**Leiste** [LUY•ste] *n* F groin

**Leistung** [LAIST•oong] *n*
excellence

**leitend** [LUY•tend] *adj* leading

**Leiter 1** [LUY•tair] *n* M
conductor; leader

**Leiter 2** [LUY•tair] *n* F ladder

**Leitstrahl** [LAIT•shtrahl] *n* M
beam

**Leitung** [LUY•toong] *n* F
conduct; guidance; leadership

**Lektion** [LEHK•tee•on] *n* F
lesson

**Lende** [LEHN•de] *n* F loin

**Lendenstück**
[LEHN•den•shtuhk] *n* N
sirloin

**Leopard** [AI•o•pahrd] *n* M
leopard

**Lepra** [LEH•prah] *n* F leprosy

**Lerche** [LAIR•khe] *n* F lark

**lesbisch** [LEZ•bish] *adj* lesbian

**lesen** [LAI•sen] *vt* read

**Leser** [LAI•zair] *n* M reader

**leserlich** [LAI•zai•lihk] *adj*
legible

**Lesung** [LAI•zoong] *n* F
reading

**Lethargie** [LEH•tahr•gee] *n* F
lethargy

**Lettein** [LEHT•tain] *n* Latvia

**letzt** [LEH•tst] *adj* final

**letzte** [LETS•ste] *adj* last

**letzter** [-air] *adj* latter

**leuchtend** [LOIHK•tend] *adj*
vivid; luminous

**Leuchter** [LOIHK•tair] *n* M
sconce

**Leuchtsignal** [LOIHKT•zig•nal]
*n* N flare

**Leuchtturm** [loihk•toorm] *n* M
lighthouse

**leugnen** [LOIG•nen] *vt* deny

**Leute** [loi•teh] *n* F people

**Leutnant** [LOIT•nant] *n* M
lieutenant

**liberal** [LIH•bair•ahl] *adj* liberal

**Libya** Libya

**lichtdurchlässig**
[LIHKT•doorhk•LEH•sig] *adj*
translucent

**Lichtfleck** [LIHKT•flek] *n* M
fleck

**Lichtung** [LIKHT•oong] *n* F
clearing

**lieb** [leeb] *adj* dear

**Liebe** [LEE•beh] *n* F love

**liebenswert** [LEEB•ehns•vairt]
*adj* likable

**liebenswürdig**
[LEEB•ens•VOOR•dig] *adj*
lovable

**lieber** [LEE•bair] *adv* rather;
preferably

**Liebesaffäre** [-ah•FAIR•reh] *n*
F love affair

**Liebesroman**
[LEEB•es•ROH•mahn] *n* M
romance

**liebevoll** [LEEB•eh•fol] *adj*
fond; devoted

**Liebhaber** [LEE•hab•air] *n* M
lover

**liebkosen** [LEEB•koh•sen] *vt*
fondle; caress

**Liebkosung** [LEEB•koh•zoong]
*n* F caress

**Liebling** [LEEB•ling] *n* M
darling

**lieblings** [LEEB•links] *adj*
darling; favorite

**Lied** [leed] *n* N song

**Liederlichkeit**
[LEE•dair•lihk•KUYT] *n* F
debauchery

**liefern** [LEEF•airn] *vt* deliver

**Lieferung** [LEE•fair•oong] *n* F
delivery

**Lieferwagen** [LEEF•air•vah•gehn] *n* M cart

**liegend** [LEE•gend] *adj* lying

**Liga** [LEE•gah] *n* F league

**Ligament** [LIHG•ah•ment] *n* N ligament

**Limonade** [LEE•mo•nah•deh] *n* F soda; pop

**Limonelle** [LEE•mon•el•le] *n* F lime

**Limousine** [LIH•moo•ZEEN•eh] *n* F sedan; limousine

**Linie** [LIHN•ee•eh] *n* F line; rank

**links** [links] left

**Links** [links] left-wing

**Linkshänder-in** [-HEN•dair -in] *n* M left-handed

**Linksradikale** [LINKS•RAH•di•KAHL•e] *n* M leftist

**Linse** [LIHN•ze] *n* F lens

**Lipenstift** [-shtift] *n* M lipstick

**Lippe** [LIH•peh] *n* F lip

**List** [lihst] *n* F trick; ploy

**Liste** [LIH•ste] *n* F list

**listig** [LIST•ig] *adj* crafty; wily

**literarisch** [LIH•tair•ahr•ish] *adj* literary

**Literatur** [LIH•tair•ah•TOOR] *n* F literature

**Litze** [LIH•tseh] *n* F strand

**Livree** [LIH•freh] *n* livery

**Lob** [lohb] *n* M praise

**Lobrede** [LOB•rai•de] *n* F eulogy

**Loch 1** [lohk] *n* N hole

**Loch 2** [lohk] *n* N leak

**locken** [LOH•ken] *vt* woo

**locker** [LOK•kair] *adj* lax

**locker** [LOK•air] *adj* loose; *adv* loosely

**lockern** [LOH•kairn] *vt* loosen; slacken

**lockig** [LOHK•ig] *adj* curly

**Lockspeise** [LOK•shuy•ze] *n* F decoy

**Lockung** [LOHK•oong] *n* F lure

**Lockvogel** [LOHK•fo•gel] *n* M stool pigeon

**Löffel** [LUH•fel] *n* M spoon

**Löffelvoll** [-fol] spoonful

**Löwin** [LUH•vin] *n* F lioness

**Logik** [LO•gihk] *n* F logic

**logisch** [LOH•gish] *adj* logical; consistent

**Logo** [LO•go] *n* logo

**Lohn1** [lohn] *n* M wage

**Lohn2** [lon] *n* M down payment

**Lohnliste** [LOHN•lih•steh] *n* F payroll

**Lohnscheck** [lohn•shek] *n* M paycheck

**Lokal** [LOH•kahl] *n* N bar; tavern

**Lokomotive** [LO•ko•mo•TEEV•eh] *n* F locomotive

**London** *n* London

**Lorbeer** [LOHR•bair] *n* M laurel

**Los** [los] *n* N lot

**löschen** [LUH•shen] *vt* put out; extinguish; quench

**lösen 1** [LUH•sen] *vt* cast off; undo

**lösen 2** [LUH•sen] *vt* solve

**Loskauf** [LOS•kouf] *n* M ransom

**losmachen** [LOS•mah•khen] *vt* detach

**losstürzen** [LOS•shtuhrts•sen]
  *vi* lunge
**Lösung** [LUH•zoong] *n* F
  solution
**Lösungsmittel** [-MIH•tel] *n* N
  solvent
**loswicklen** [LOS•vih•keln] *vt*
  unwind
**Lot** [loht] *n* N solder
**lotrecht** [LOHT•rehkt] *adj*
  vertical
**Löwe** [LUH•veh] *n* M lion
**Löwenzahn** [lew•ven•tsahn] *n*
  M dandelion
**Lücke** [LUH•keh] *n* F gap
**Luder** [LOO•dair] *n* N tramp
**Luft** [looft] *n* F air
**luftdicht** [LOOFT•dikt] *adj*
  airtight
**Lüfter** [LOOF•tair] *n* M fan
**luftgekühlt** [LOOFT•geh•koolt]
  *adj* air-conditioned
**Luftklappe**
  [LOOFT•KLAH•peh] *n* F
  choke (of car)
**Luftloch** [LUHFT•lohk] *n* N
  vent
**Luftpost** [LOOFT•pohst] *n* F
  airmail

**Luftreinigung**
  [LOOFT•RAIIN•ig•oongk] *n*
  F airconditioning
**Luftspiegelung**
  [LUHFT•shpeeg•el•oong] *n* F
  mirage
**Lüge** [LOO•ge] *n* F lie; fib
**Lügner** [LUHG•nair] *n* M liar
**Luke** [LUH•keh] *n* porthole
**Lümmel** [LUH•mehl] *n* M lout
**Lumpen** [LUHM•pen] *n* M rag
**Lunge** [LUHN•ge] *n* F lung
**Lungenentzündung**
  [LUHN•gen•ent•TSUHN•doong]
  *n* F pneumonia
**lustig** [LUHST•ig] *adj* hilarious;
  jolly; merry
**Lutschbonbon**
  [LUHTSH•bohn•bohn] *n* M
  lollipop
**luxus** [LOOKS•oos] *adj* fancy;
  luxurious
**Luxus** *n* M [LOOKS•oos]
  luxury
**lynchen** [LIHN•chen] *vt* lynch
**Lyrik** [LOOR•ihk] *n* F lyric;
  lyrics
**lyrisch** [LOOR•ish] *adj* lyrical

# M

**machen** [MAH•khen] *vt* do;
  make; matter
**Madaillon** [-yon] *n* N
  ·medallion
**Mädchen** [MEHD•chen] *n* N
  girl

**Mädchenname**
  [MEHD•chen•NAH•meh] *n* M
  maiden name
**Magd** [mahgt] *n* N maid
**Magen** [MAH•gen] *n* M
  stomach

**Magenschmerz** [-shmairts] *n*
M stomachache

**mager** [MAH•gair] *adj* lean

**mager** [MAH•gair] *adj* meager

**Magie** [MAH•jee] *n* F magic

**Magier** [MAH•geer] *n* M
magician

**magisch** [MAG•gish] *adj*
magical

**Magnet** [MAHG•neht] *n* M
magnet

**magnetisch** [-ish] *adj* magnetic

**Mahagonibaum**
[MAH•ha•gon•EE•boum] *n* M
mahogany

**mähen** [MAI•hen] *vt* mow

**mahlen** [MAHL•en] *vt* grind

**Mahlwerk** [MAHL•vairk] *n* N
grinder

**Mahlzeit** [MAHL•tsait] *n* F
meal

**Mähne** [MAI•neh] *n* F mane

**mahnen** [MAH•neṅ] *vt*
admonish

**Mai** [muy] *n* M May

**mainpulieren**
[MAHN•ip•yuu•LEER•en] *vt*
manipulate

**Majestät** *n* M majesty

**majestätisch**
[MAI•yeh•SHTEHT•ish] *adj*
majestic

**Makel** [MAH•kehl] *n* M stigma;
taint

**makellos** [MAH•kel•los] *adj*
immaculate

**Makkaroni**
[MAHK•kahr•OH•nee] *npl*
macaroni

**Makrele** [MAH•kreh•le] *n* F
mackerel

**Maler** [MAHL•air] *n* M painter

**malerisch** [MAH•lair•ish] *adj*
picturesque

**Mammut** [MAH•moot] *n* N
mammoth

**man** [mahn] *pron* you; one; they

**manchmal** [MAHNHK•mahl]
*adv* sometimes

**Mandarine**
[MAHN•dahr•EEN•eh] *n* F
tangerine

**Mandat** [MAHN•daht] *n* N
mandate

**Mandel** [MAHN•del] *n* F tonsil

**Mandelentzündung**
[-ent•TSUHN•doong] *n* F
tonsillitis

**Mangel** [MAHN•gel] *n* M
shortage; lack; deficiency

**mangelhaft** [MAHN•gel•hahft]
*adj* deficient

**Manie** [MAHN•ee] *n* F craze;
mania

**Mann** [mahn] *n* M husband;
man

**Mannigfaltigkeit**
[MAHN•ig•FAHL•tig•KUYT]
*n* F variety

**männlich** [MEN•lihk] *adj* male;
masculine; virile

**Männlichkeit** [-kuyt] *n* F
virility

**Mannschaft** [MAHN•shahft] *n*
F team; crew

**Manöver** [mahn•UH•fair] *n* N
maneuver

**Mantel** [MAHN•tel] *n* M
overcoat; cloak; cape
(clothing)

**Manuskript**
[MAHN•oo•skrihpt] *n* N
manuscript

**Marathonlauf**
[mahr•ah•TON•louf] *n* M
marathon

**Märchen** [MAIR•chen] *n* N
fairy tale

**Margarine** [mahr•gahr•EEN•eh]
*n* F margarine

**Marihuanahanf**
[MAH•ri•HUAN•ah•HAHNF]
*n* M marijuana

**Marine; See** [MAH•ree•ne]
[zee] *n* F marine

**marinieren**
[MAHR•ih•NEER•en] *vt*
marinate

**Marionette**
[MAH•ree•on•ET•te] *n* F
puppet

**Marke** [MAHR•keh] *n* F brand

**Markierung**
[MAHR•keer•oong] *n* F mark

**Markt** [mahrkt] *n* M market;
bazaar

**Marktpreis** [-pruys] *n* M
market value

**Marmelade**
[MAHR•meh•LAH•de] *n* F
jam; marmalade

**Marmor** [MAHR•mor] *n* M
marble

**Marotte** [MAH•roh•te] *n* F fad

**Mars** [mahrz] *n* M Mars

**Marschall** [MAHR•shal] *n* M
marshal

**marschieren** [MAHR•sheer•en]
*vt* march

**Märtyrer** [MEHR•tee•rehr] *n* M
martyr

**März** [mairts] *n* M march

**Masche** [MAH•sheh] *n* F mesh

**Maschine** [mah•SHEEN•eh] *n* F
machine

**Maschinengewehr**
[-geh•VAIR] *n* N machine
gun

**Maschinenschreiber**
[mah•SHEEN•en•SHRUY•bair]
*n* M typist

**Maschinerie**
[mah•SHEEN•air•EE] *n* F
machinery

**Maschinist** [mah•SHEEN•ist] *n*
M operator

**Masern** [MAH•sairn] *npl*
measles

**Maske** [MAHSK•eh] *n* F mask;
disguise

**Maskenball** [MAHSK•en•bal] *n*
M masquerade party

**Maß** [mahs] *n* N measure,
dimension

**Massage** [MA•sahj•eh] *n* F
massage

**Massaker** [MAHS•ah•kair] *n* N
massacre

**Maßanalyse**
[MAHS•ahn•ih•LUH•zeh] *n* F
quantitative

**Massenflucht**
[MAH•sen•FLOOHKT] *n* F
exodus

**Massenvernichtung**
[MAH•sen•vair•NIHK•toong]·
*n* F holocaust

**Mäßigkeit** [MAI•sig•kuyt] *n* F
temperance

**Mäßigung** [-IG•oong] *n* F
moderation

**massiv** [mah•SEEF] *adj* massive

**Maßnahme** [MAHS•nah•meh]
*n* F provision

**Maßstab 1** [MAHS•shtahb] *n* M canon

**Maßstab 2** [MAHS•shtahb] *n* M criterion

**Maßstock** [MAHS•shtohk] *n* M yardstick

**Mast** [mahst] *n* M mast; pylon

**Matematik** [MAH•teh•mah•TEEK] *n* F mathematics

**Material** [MAH•tair•ee•AHL] *n* N stuff

**Materialist** [MAH•tair•ee•ahl•EEST] *n* M materialist

**materialistisch** [-IST•ish] *adj* materialistic

**Matratze** [mah•TRAHTS•eh] *n* F mattress

**matrikulieren** [mah•TRIK•ool•EER•en] graduate

**Matrix** [mah•TRIKS] *n* F matrix

**Matrose** [mah•TROH•ze] *n* M sailor

**matt** [maht] *adj* languid

**Matte** [MAH•teh] *n* F mat

**Mauerblümchen** [MOU•air•BLUHM•chen] *n* N wallflower

**Maul** [moul] *n* N muzzle

**Maulbeerfeigenbaum** [MOUL•bair•FUYG•en•boum] *n* M sycamore

**Maulheld** [MOWL•held] *n* M bully

**Maultier** [MOUL•teer] *n* N mule

**Maulwurf** [MOUL•voorf] *n* M mole

**Maure** [MOU•reh] *n* M Moor

**Maurer** [MOU•rehr] *n* M mason

**Maus** [mous] *n* F mouse

**Mäuser** [MOI•zair] *npl* mice

**maximum** [MAHKS•ee•muhm] *adj* maximum

**Maximum** [MAHKS•ee•muhm] *n* N maximum

**Mayonnaise** [MUY•on•UYS•eh] *n* F mayonnaise

**Mechaniker** [meh•KAHN•ih•kair] *n* M mechanic

**mechanisch1** [-ish] *adj* mechanical

**mechanisch2** [meh•kahn•ish] *adj* rote

**Mechanismus** [-IS•moos] *n* M mechanism

**Medaille** [meh•DAI•yeh] *n* F medal

**Media** [MEH•dee•eh] *n* F media

**Medizin** [meh•dih•TSEEN] *n* F medicine

**medizinisch** [MEH•dih•TSEEN•ish] *adj* medical

**medizinisch behandeln** [beh•HAHN•deln] *vt* medicate

**Meer** [mair] *n* N ocean

**Meerenge** [MAIR•eng•eh] *n* F strait

**Meerrettich** [MAIR•reh•tihk] *n* M horseradish

**Meerschweinchen** [MAIR•shvain•khen] *n* N guinea pig

**Meerweib** [MAIR•vaib] *n* N mermaid

**Megaphon** [MEHG•ah•fohn] *n* N megaphone

**Mehl** [mail] *n* M flour
**Mehltaupilz** [MAIL•tou•pihlts] *n* M mildew
**mehr** [mair] *adj* more
**mehren** [MAIR•en] augment; multiply
**mehrfach** [MAIR•fahk] *adj* multiple; plural
**Mehrheit** [MAIR•huyt] *n* F majority
**Mehrwertssteuer** [MAIR•vairt•shtoi•air] *n* F tax (state tax)
**Mehrzahl** [MAIR•tsahl] *adj n* F plural
**Meile** [MAI•leh] *n* F mile
**mein** [muyn] *n* mine
**mein; meine** [muyn -e] *poss adj* my
**Meineid** [MUYN•uyd] *n* M perjury
**Meinung** [MUY•noong] *n* F opinion
**meist** [muyst] *adj* most
**Meister** [MUY•stair] *n* M master
**meistern** [MUY•stairn] *vi* cope
**Meisterstück** [MUY•stair•shtuhk] *n* N masterpiece
**Melancholie** [MEH•lahn•koh•lee] *n* F melancholy
**Melasse** [meh•LAH•seh] *n* F molasses
**Melodie** [MEH•lo•dee] *n* F melody; tune
**Melone** [meh•LOH•neh] *n* F melon
**Menge** [MENG•uh] *n* F crowd; multitude

**Mensch** *n* M human being
**Menschenfresser** [MEN•shen•FRES•sair] *n* M cannibal
**Menschenhaß** [MEHN•shen•hahs] *n* M misanthropist
**Menschenrecht** [-rehkt] *n* N human rights
**Menschentum** [MEHNSH•en•toom] *n* M manhood
**Menschenverstand** [MENSH•en•fair•SHTANT] *n* M common sense
**Menschheit** [MENSH•huyt] *n* F humanity; mankind
**menschlich** [MENSH•lihk] *adj* human; humane
**menschliche Arbeitskraft** [MENSH•lich•e AHR•buyts•krahft] *n* F manpower
**Mentalität** [men•tahl•i•TAIT] *n* F mentality
**merken** [maîrk•ehn] *vt* notice; feel; realize
**merklich** [MAIRK•lihk] *adj* noticeable
**Merkmal** [mairk•mahl] *n* N token
**Merkur** [MAIR•koor] *n* M mercury
**merkwürdig** [MAIRK•voor•dig] *adj* strange
**Messe** [MEH•seh] *n* F mass
**messen** [meh•sehn] *vt vi* measure; compete
**Messer** [MEH•sair] *n* N knife
**Messerwaren** [MES•air•VAHR•en] *npl* cutlery

**Meßgerät** [MES•ge•rait] *n* N gauge

**Messung** [MEHS•soong] *n* F measurement

**Metall** [meh•TAHL] *n* N metal

**metallen** [meh•TAHL•en] *adj* metallic

**Metapher** [meh•TAH•fair] *n* F metaphor

**Meteor** [MAI•tair•or] *n* M meteor

**Methode** [meh•TOH•de] *n* F method

**metrisch** [MEH•tris] *adj* metric

**Metzger** [MEHTS•gair] *n* M butcher

**Metzgerei** [MEHTS•gair•a] *n* F butcher (shop)

**Meuchelmord** [MOI•kel•mord] *n* M assassination

**mexicanisch** [MEHKS•ee•KAHN•ish] *adj* Mexican

**Mexico** [MEHKS•ee•koh] Mexico

**Miesepeter** [MEES•eh•PAI•tair] *n* M grouch

**Mietbetrag** [MEET•beh•trahg] *n* M rental

**Miete** [MEE•te] *n* F lease

**Mieter** [MEE•tair] *n* M tenant; lodger

**Migräne** [MEE•grain•eh] *n* F migraine

**Mikrochip** [MEE•kroh•chip] *n* M microchip

**Mikrophon** [MEE•kroh•fohn] *n* N microphone

**Mikroskop** [MEE•kroh•skohp] *n* N microscope

**mikroskopisch** [-ish] *adj* microscopic

**Mikrowelle** [MEE•kroh•VEL•leh] *n* F microwave

**Milch** [mihlk] *n* F milk

**mild** [mihld] *adj* meek

**mild sanft** [mild] [zahnft] *adj* bland

**militant** [mih•li•TAHNT] *adj* militant

**militarisch** [mihl•ih•TAHR•ish] *adj* military

**Miliz** [mihl•EETS] *n* F militia

**Million** [mil•EE•on] *num* F million

**Millionär** [-air] *n* M millionaire

**Milz** [mihlts] *n* F spleen

**Minderheit** [MIHN•dair•huyt] *n* F minority

**Minderjähriger klein** [MIHN•dair•YAIR•ig•air] [kluyn] *n* M minor

**mindest** [MIHN•dest] *adj* marginal

**Mineral** [MIHN•air•ahl] *n* N mineral

**Miniatur** [MIHN•ee•ah•TOOR] *n* N miniature

**Minimum** [MIHN•ee•moon] *n* N minimum

**Ministerium** [MIHN•ih•STAIR•ee•oom] *n* N ministry

**minus** [MEE•noos] *pre* minus

**Minute** [mih•NOOT•eh] *n* F minute

**Minze** [MIHN•zeh] *n* F mint

**mir; mich** [meer] [mihk] *pres prn* me

**mir; mich; ich; selbst** [meer]
[mihk] [eehk] [zelpst] *pr*
myself

**mischen** [MIH•shen] *vt* mix

**Mischling** [MISH•ling] *n* M
mongrel

**Mischmasch** [MISH•mash] *n* M
mess

**Mischung** [-oong] *n* F mixture

**Mißachtung** [MIS•ahk•toong] *n*
F disrespect

**mißbilligen** [MIS•BIL•ig•en] *vi*
disapprove

**Mißbilligung**
[MIS•BIL•IG•oong] *n* F
disapproval

**mißgestaltet**
[MIS•ge•SHTAHL•tet] *adj*
deformed

**Mißbrauch** [MIHS•brouhk] *n*
M abuse; misuse

**mißbrauchen** [MIS•brouk•uhn]
*vt* abuse

**Missetat** [MIH•seh•TAHT] *n* F
misdeed

**Mißgeschick**
[MISH•geh•SHIHK] *n* N
misfortune

**Mißgunst** [MIS•guhnst] *n* F
grudge

**mißhandeln** [MIHS•hahn•deln]
*vt* mistreat

**Mission** [MIH•see•OHN] *n* F
mission

**Missionar** [MIH•see•on•AHR] *n*
M missionary

**mißliche Lage** [MIS•lihk•eh
lah•geh] *n* F predicament

**Mißtrauen** [MIS•trou•en] *n* N
distrust; mistrust

**mißtrauisch** [MIS•trou•ish] *adj*
distrustful

**Mißverständnis**
[MIHS•fair•SHTEND•nis] *n* N
misunderstanding;
misconception

**mißverstehen**
[MIHS•fair•SHTAI•en] *vt*
misunderstand

**Mist** [mist] *n* M dung

**Mistkäfer** [MIHST•kai•fair] *n*
M scarab

**mit** [mit] *prep* with

**mit der Hand** [mit dair
HAHNT] *adj* manual

**mit einen ßrandmal zeichen**
[mit AI•nen BRAHNT•mahl
TSAI•ken] *vt* brand

**mit Fett gebießen** [mit FET
geh•BEE•sen] *vt* baste

**mit halbem Herzen** [mit
halb•en HAIR•tsen] *adj*
half-hearted

**mit Stacheln versehen** [mit
SHTAH•keln fair•ZEH•uhn]
*adj* barbed

**mit verblindenen Augen** [mit
FAIR•BLINT•en•un OW•gen]
*n* blindfold

**mitarbeiten** [MIT•ahr•buy•ten]
*vi* collaborate

**mitfühlend** [MIT•fuhl•end] *adj*
pitiful; sympathetic

**Mitglied** [MIT•gleed] *n* N
member

**Mitleid** [MIT•luyd] *n* N
compassion

**mitleidlos** [MIT•luyd•los] *adj*
ruthless

**mitleidsvoll** [mit•luyds•fohl]
*adj* compassionate

**Mitschuldiger-e**
[MIT•SHOOLD•igk•air] [uh]
*n* M accomplice

**Mittag** [MIH•tahg] *n* M noon

**Mittagessen** [MIH•tag•ES•sen]
*n* N lunch

**Mittagspause** [-POU•ze] *n* F
lunch hour

**mitte 1** [mih•teh] *adj* mid

**mitte 2** [mih•teh] *adj* medium

**Mitte** [MIH•teh] *n* F middle;
midst

**Mittel** [MIH•tel] *n* N means;
wherewithal

**Mittelalter**
[MIH•tel•AHL•TAIR] *n* N
Middle Ages

**mittelalterlich**
[MIH•tehl•AL•tair•LIHK] *adj*
medieval

**mittellos** [MIH•tel•los] *adj*
penniless

**mittelmäßig**
[MIH•tel•MAI•sig] *adj*
mediocre

**Mittelstand**
[MIH•tel•SHTAHNT] *n* M
middle class

**mitten unter** [MIH•tehn
oon•tair] *prep* among

**Mitternacht** [MIH•tair•nahkt] *n*
F midnight

**Mittlere Osten** [-OH•steň] *n*
Middle East

**Mittwoch** [MIHT•vohk] *n* M
Wednesday

**mitwirkend** [MIT•veer•kent]
*adj* auxiliary

**Möbel** [MUH•bel] *n* F furniture

**mobilisieren**
[MOH•bil•ih•SEER•en] *vt*
mobilize

**Mode** [MOH•de] *n* F fashion;
model; vogue

**modern 1** [MOH•dairn] *adj*
modern

**modern 2** [MO•dairn] *adj*
fashionable; up to date

**modernisieren**
[MOH•dairn•ih•SEER•en] *vt*
modernize

**Modezeichner**
[MOH•de•TSAIHK•nair] *n* M
designer

**modifizieren**
[MOH•dih•fih•TSEER•en] *vt*
modify

**modisch** [MOH•dish] *adj*
stylish

**mögen** [MUH•gen] modal *v*
might; to like to

**möglich** [MOOG•lihk] *adj*
possible; feasible

**möglicherweise** [-air•VUY•ze]
*adv* possibly; potentially

**Möglichkeit** [MOOG•likh•kuyt]
*n* F possibility; contingency

**Mohrrübe** [mohr•ROO•beh] *n*
F carrot

**Mörder** [MERD•air] *n* M killer

**Mörser** [MER•sair] *n* M mortar

**Mohn** [mohn] *n* M poppy

**Molen** [MOH•len] *n* molar

**Molkerei** [MOHL•kair•uy] *n* F
dairy

**Molluske** [MOHL•luhsk•eh] *n* F
mollusk

**Moment** [moh•MEHNT] *n* M
moment

**momentan** [MOH•men•TAHN]
*adj* momentary

**Monarch** [MOH•nahrk] *n* M
monarch

**Monarchie** [-KEE] *n* F
monarchy

**Monat** [MOH•naht] *n* M month

**monatlich** [MOH•naht•lihk] *adj*
monthly

**Mönch** [muhnhk] *n* M friar;
monk

**Mond** [mont] *n* M moon

**mond** [mont] *adj* lunar

**Mondlicht** [MOHND•lihkt] *n* N
moonlight

**Monolog** [MOHN•oh•lohg] *n*
M monologue; soliloquy

**Monopol** *n* M monopoly

**monopolisieren**
[MOHN•oh•pohl•ih•SEER•en]
*vt* monopolize

**Monotonie**
[MOH•noh•tohn•EE] *n* F
monotone

**Monsun** [MOHN•soon] *n* M
monsoon

**Montag** [MOHN•tahg] *n* M
Monday

**montieren** [MOHN•teer•en] *vt*
install

**Moorboden** [MOOR•boh•den]
*n* M quagmire

**Moos** [mohs] *n* N moss

**Moral** [mohr•AHL] *n* F morale;
morality

**moralisch** [mor•AHL•ish] *adj*
moral

**morbid** [MOHR•bihd] *adj*
morbid

**Mord** [mohrd] *n* M murder;
homicide

**Mörder** [MER•dair] *n* M
murderer

**mörderisch** [MER•dair•ish] *adj*
gory

**mörderlich** [MER•dair•lihk] *adj*
murderous

**Morgen** [MOHR•gen] *n* M
morning

**morgen** [MOR•gen] *adv*
tomorrow

**morgens** [MOR•genz] *adv* in
the morning

**Morgendämmerung**
[MOHR•gen•DEM•air•oong] *n*
F dawn

**Morokko** *n* Morocco

**Mosaik** [MOH•sai•ik] *n* N
mosaic

**Moschee** [MOH•shee] *n* F
mosque

**Moskow** Moscow

**moslem** [MOHS•lehm] *adj*
Muslim

**Motiv** [moh•TEEF] *n* N motive

**motivieren**
[MOH•tih•VEER•en] *vt*
motivate

**Motivierung** [-oong] *n* F
motivation

**Motor** [MOH•tohr] *n* M motor

**Motorboot** [MOH•tohr•boht] *n*
N motorboat

**Motorrad** [-rahd] *n* N
motorcycle

**Motte** [MOH•teh] *n* F moth

**Motto** [MOH•toh] *n* N motto

**Mücke** [MUHK•eh] *n* F
mosquito

**müde** [muh•deh] *adj* tired;
weary

**Müdigkeit** [MUH•dig•kuyt] *n* F
tiredness; weariness

**Mühe** [MOO•eh] *n* F effort

**Muhen** [MOO•hen] *n* N moo
(as a cow)

**Mühle** [MUH•leh] *n* F mill

**mühsam gehen** [MUH•zahm gai•en] *vi* plod

**Mulde** [MUHL•de] *n* F trough

**Müll** [muhl] *n* M garbage

**Mülleimer** [MUHL•uy•mair] *n* M garbage can

**Müllschaufel** [MUHL•shou•fel] *n* F dustpan

**Mumie** [MOO•mee] *n* F mummy

**Mund** [muhnt] *n* M mouth

**mundartlich** [MUHNT•ahrt•lihk] *adj* vernacular; slang

**Mundhöhle** [MUHNT•hooh•leh] *n* F cavity (dental)

**mündlich** [MUHND•lihk] *adj* verbal

**Mundvoll** [MUHNT•fol] *n* M mouthful

**Mundwasser** [MUHNT•vah•sair] *n* N mouthwash

**munter** [MOONT•air] *adj* animated; frisky

**Münze** [MOON•ze] *n* F coin

**mürbe 1** [MUHR•beh] *adj* mellow

**mürbe 2** [MUHR•beh] *adj* rotten, crumbling

**murmeln** [MOOR•meln] *vt* mumble; *vi* mutter

**Murmeln** [MOOR•meln] *n* N murmur

**murren** [MUHR•ren] *vi* grumble

**Muschel** [MUH•shel] *n* F mussel

**Muse** [MUH•ze] *n* F muse

**Museum** [moo•SEE•oom] *n* N museum

**Musik** [moo•SEEK] *n* F music

**musikalisch** [MOO•sih•KAHL•isch] *adj* musical

**Musike** [MOO•sih•kair] *n* M musician

**Muskel** [MOO•skel] *n* M muscle

**Muskeln** [MOO•skeln] *n* F brawn

**muskulös** [MUHSK•uh•luhs] *adj* muscular

**müssen** [MUH•sen] modal *v* must

**Muster** [MUH•stair] *n* N pattern

**Mut** [moot] *n* M courage

**mutig** [MOO•tig] *adj* valorous

**mutlos** [MOOT•los] *adj* despondent

**Mutter** [MUH•tair] *n* F mother

**mütterlich** [MUH•tair•lihk] *adj* maternal; motherly

**Muttermal** [MOO•tair•mahl] *n* M birthmark

**Mutterschaf** [MOO•tair•shahf] *n* N ewe

**Mutterschaft** [-shahft] *n* F motherhood

**mutwillig** [MOOT•vihl•ig] *adj* wanton

**Mütze** [MOOTS•eh] *n* F cap; bonnet

**Mysticker** [MIH•shtih•kair] *n* M mystic

**mystisch** *adj* mystical

**Mythologe** [MIH•toh•loh•GEH] *n* M mythology

# N

Nabel [NAH•bel] *n* M navel;
umbilicus

nach 1 [nahk] *prep* according

nach 2 [nahk] *prep adv* after

nach 3 [nahk] towards

nach innen introverted

nach innen gehend [nahk
IN•nen GAI•hen] *adj adv*
inward

nach innen richten [nahk
IN•nen RIHK•ten] introvert

nach Luft schnappen [nahk
LOOFT shnah•pen] *vt* gasp

nach, oben, auf [nahk oh•ben
ouf] up

nachahmen [NAHK•ah•men] *vt*
emulate; imitate

Nachahmer [NAHK•ahm•air] *n*
M mimic

Nachahmung
[NAHK•ah•moong] *n* M
imitation

Nachbar [NAHK•bahr] *n* M
neighbor

Nachbarschaft [-shahft] *n* F
neighborhood

nachdatieren
[NAHK•dah•TEER•en] *vt*
postdate

nachdenken [NAHK•daink•en]
*vt* ponder; contemplate

nachdenklich
[NAHK•denk•lihk] *adj*
pensive

Nachdenklichkeit
[NAHK•denk•lihk•KUYT] *n* F
thoughtfulness

nachfolgend [NAHK•fol•gend]
*adj* subsequent

Nachfrage [NAHK•frah•ge] *n* F
demand; inquiry

nachgeben [NAHK gai•ben] *vi*
give away; defer

nachgemacht
[NAHK•ge•mahkt] *adj*
counterfeit

nachhallend [NAHK•hahl•lend]
*adj* resonant

Nachkomme [NAHK•koh•me]
*n* M descendant

Nachkommen
[NAHK•koh•men] *npl* N
offspring

nachlässig [NAHK•leh•sig] *adj*
negligent; remiss

Nachlässigkeit
[NAHK•les•ig•kuyt] *n* F
negligence

Nachlaß [NAHK•lahs] *n* M
residue

Nachmittag [NAHK•mi•tagk] *n*
M afternoon

nachprüfen [NAHK•pruh•fen]
*vt* verify

Nachprüfung
[NAHK•pruh•foong] *n* F
review; verification

Nachricht [NAHKT•rihkt] *n* F
information

Nachrichten [NAHK•rihk•ten]
*npl* news; tidings

Nachrichtensendung
[NAHK•rihk•ten•zehn•doong]
*n* F newscast

**Nachruf** [NAHK•roof] *n* M
obituary

**nachsinnen** [NAHK•zin•nen] *vi*
meditate; speculate

**Nacht** [nahkt] *n* F night

**nächst** [naikst] *adj* next

**Nachteil** [NAHK•tuyl] *n* M
disadvantage

**nachteilig** [NAHK•tuyl•ig] *adj*
prejudiced

**Nachtigall** [NAHKT•ih•gahl] *n*
F nightingale

**Nachtisch** [NAHK•tish] *n* M
dessert

**nächtlich** [NEHKT•lihk] *adj*
nightly; nocturnal

**Nachtmusik**
[NAHKT•moo•seek] *n* F
serenade

**Nachtwächter** [nahkt-] *n* M
watchman

**nachzählen** [NAHK•tsai•len] *vt*
check; recount; tally

**nackt** [nahkt] *adj* naked; nude;
bare

**Nacktheit** [NAHKT•huyt] *n* F
nude; nudity; nakedness

**Nacktkultur**
[NAHKT•kuhl•toor] *n* F
nudist

**Nadel** [NAH•del] *n* F needle;
pin

**Nagel** [NAH•gel] *n* M nail; peg

**Nagel neu** [NAH•gel NOI] *adj*
brand-new

**Nagelpflege**
[NAHG•el•pflai•GEH] *n* F
manicure

**nagen an** [NAH•gen an] *vt*
gnaw

**Näharbeit** [NAI•ahr•buyt] *n* F
sewing

**Nähe** [NAI•he] *n* F proximity;
vicinity

**nämlich** [NAIM•lihk] *adv*
namely

**nahe** [nah•eh] *prep* by (near
to); *adj* near

**nähen** [NAI•hen] *vt* sew

**Näherin** [NAI•air•in] *n* F
seamstress

**Nähmaschine**
[-mah•SHEEN•eh] *n* F sewing
machine

**nahrhaft** [NAHR•hahft] *adj*
nourishing; nutritious

**Nahrung** [NAHR•oong] *n* F
nourishment; nutrition

**Naht 1** [naht] *n* F seam

**Naht 2** [naht] *n* F suture

**naiv** [nai•eev] *adj* naive; gullible

**Name** [NAH•meh] *n* M name

**Narbe** [NAHR•beh] *n* F scar

**narkotisch** [nahr•koh•tisch] *adj*
narcotic

**Narr** [nahr] *n* M fool; imbecile

**Narrenkappe**
[NAHR•ren•kah•pe] *n* F
dunce

**narrensicher**
[NAHR•en•ZIHK•air] *adj*
foolproof

**Narzisse** [NAHR•tsis•se] *n* F
daffodil

**Nase** [NAH•zeh] *n* F nose

**Nasen** [NAH•zen] *adj* nasal

**Nasenloch** [-lohk] *n* N nostril

**naß** [nahs] *adj* wet

**Nation** [nah•TSEE•on] *n* F
nation

**national** *adj* national

**Nationalität** [-ahl•ih•TAIT] *n* F
nationality

**Natrium** [nah•tree•oom] *n* N
sodium

**Natur** [NAH•toor] *n* F nature

**natürlich** [nah•TOOR•lihk] *adj*
natural; *adv* naturally

**Nautik** [NOU•teek] *n* F
navigation

**Nebel** [NAI•bel] *n* M fog; mist

**neben** [NAI•ben] *prep* beside;
next to

**nebenan** [NAI•ben•ahn] *adj*
next-door

**nebeneinanderstellen**
[NAI•ben•uyn•AHN•dair•
SHTEL•len] *vt* juxtapose

**Nebenfluß** [NAI•ben•floos] *n*
M tributary

**Nebengleis** [NAI•ben•gluys] *n*
N sidetrack

**Nebenhöhlenentzündung**
[NAI•ben•HUH•len•ent•
TSUHN•doong] *n* F sinusitis

**Neckerei** [NEK•kair•ai] *n* F
banter

**Neffe** [NEH•veh] *n* M nephew

**negativ** [NEHG•ah•TEEV] *adj*
negative

**Neger** [NAI•gair] *n* M Negro

**nehmen** [NAI•men] *vt* take

**Neid** [nuyd] *n* M envy

**neidisch** [nuy•dish] *adj* envious

**neigen** [NUY•gen] *vi* tend

**Neigung** [NAI•goongk] *n* F
affection; inclination;
penchant

**nein** [nain] *adv* no

**Nelke** [NEL•keh] *n* F carnation

**Neptun** *n* M Neptune

**Nerv** [nairf] *n* M nerve

**nervös** [nair•VUHS] *adj*
nervous

**Nerz** [nairts] *n* M mink

**Nessel** [NEH•sehl] *n* F nettle

**Nest** [nehst] *n* N nest

**net** [net] *adv* nicely

**nett** [net] *adj* kind; nice

**Netz** [nehts] *n* N net

**Netzwerk** [NEHTS•vairk] *n* N
network

**neu** [noi] *adj* new

**Neuerung** [NOI•air•oong] *n* F
innovation

**Neugier** [NOI•geer] *n* F
curiosity

**neugierig** [NOI•geer•ig] *adj*
curious; inquisitive; nosy

**Neuheit** [NOI•huyt] *n* F novelty

**Neujahr** [NOI•yahr] *n* N New
Year

**neulich** [NOI•lich] *adv* newly

**Neuling 1** [NOI•ling] *n* M
novice

**Neuling 2** [NOI•ling] *n* M colt

**neun** [noin] *num* nine

**Neunmalklug**
[NOIN•mahl•kloog] *n* M
wiseacre

**neunte** [NOIN•teh] *num* ninth

**neunzehn** [-tsain] *num* nineteen

**neunzig** [NOIN•tsig] *num*
ninety

**Neurose** [NOI•roh•ze] *n* F
neurosis

**neurotisch** [NOI•roh•tish] *adj*
neurotic

**neutral** [NOI•trahl] *adj* neutral

**neutralisieren**
[NOI•trahl•ih•SEER•en] *vt*
neutralize

**Neutralität** [-ih•TAIT] *n* F
neutrality

**nicht** [neekht] *adv* not

**nicht anerkannt** [NEEHKT
AHN•air•kahnt] *adj*
unacknowledged

**nicht anerkennen** [NIHKT
AHN•air•ken•nen] *vt* disown

**nicht anerkennen** [NIHKT
AHN•air•ken•nen] *vt* repudiate

**nicht beansprucht** [NEEHKT
beh•AHN•shpruhkt] *adj*
unclaimed

**nicht befriedigen** [NIHKT
beh•FREE•dig•en] *vt*
dissatisfy

**nicht bewußt sein** [NEEHKT
beh•VOOST zuyn] unaware

**nicht förmlich** [NIHKT
ferm•lihk] *adj* informal

**nicht gehorchen** [NIHKT
geh•HOHR•khen] *vt* disobey

**nicht nachgeben** [NEEHKT
NAHK•gai•ben] *adj*
unyielding

**nicht verantwortlich**
[NEEHKT
fair•AHNT•vort•lihk] *adj*
unaccountable

**nicht verfügbar** [NEEHKT
fair•FOOG•bahr] *adj*
unavailable

**nicht vergleichbar** [nihkt
fair•GLUYHK•bahr]
incomparable

**Nichtdasein** [NIHKT•dah•zuyn]
*n* N nonentity

**Nichte** [NIHK•teh] *n* F niece

**nichtig** [NIHK•tig] *adj* trivial;
null; of no consequence

**Nichtraucher**
[NEEHKT•rouhk•air] *n* M
nonsmoker

**nichts** [neekhts] *pr* nothing

**nichtsdestoweniger**
[NIHKTS•deh•stoh•VAIN•
ihg•air] *adv* nonetheless

**Nicken** [NIH•ken] *vt n* N nod

**nie** [nee] *adv* never

**Niedergang** [NEE•dair•gahng]
*n* M decadence; decline

**Niederlände**
[NEE•dair•len•deh] *npl*
Holland; Netherlands

**Niederschlag** *n* M precipitation

**niederschlagen**
[NEE•dair•SHLAH•gen] *vt*
precipitate

**niedrig** [NEED•rig] *adj* low;
*adv* lowly

**niedriger** [NEE•drig•air] *adj*
lower; inferior

**niemand** [nee•mahnt] *pron*
nobody

**Niere** [NEER•eh] *n* F kidney

**Nierenfett** [NEER•en•fet] *n* N
suet

**Nikotin** [NIH•koh•teen] *n* N
nicotine

**Nilpferd** [NIL•pfaird] *n* N
hippopotamus

**nippen an** [NIH•pen ahn] *vt* sip

**nirgendwo** [NEER•gent•voh]
*adv* nowhere

**Nische** [NIH•she] *n* F niche

**noch 1** [nohk] *conj* nor

**noch 2** [nohk] *adv* still; yet

**nördlich** [NERD•lihk] *adj*
northern

**nörgeln** [NER•geln] *vt* nag

**nominell** [NOH•mihn•EL] *adj*
nominal

**Nord** [nohrd] *n* M north

**Nord Amerika**
[-ah•MAIR•ih•kah] *n* North
America

**Nordirland** [-EER•lahnt] *n* N
Northern Ireland

**Nordpol** [NORD•pohl] *n* M
North Pole

**nordwärts** [-vairts] *adv*
northward(s)

**Norm** [norm] *n* F norm

**normal** [nor•MAHL] *adj* normal

**normalerweise**
[nor•MAHL•air•VUY•zeh]
*adv* normally; ordinarily

**Normung** [NOHR•moong] *n* F
standardization

**Norwegen** [NOR•vai•gen] *n*
Norway

**norwegisch** [NOR•vaig•ish] *adj*
Norwegian

**Not** [noht] *n* F hardship

**Notar** [NOH•tahr] *n* M notary

**Notausgang** [NOT•ous•gahng]
*n* M emergency exit

**Notfall** [NOT•fal] *n* M
emergency

**Notiz** [NO•teets] *n* F notice;
memo

**Notlage** [NOHT•lah•geh] *n* F
plight

**notorisch** [NO•tor•ish] *adj*
notorious

**notwendig** [NOHT•vehn•dig]
*adj* necessary

**Notwendigkeit**
[NOHT•vehn•dig•kuyt] *n* F
necessity

**November** [noh•FEM•bair] *n* M
November

**Nuance** [NOO•ahns•eh] *n* F
nuance

**nüchtern** [nuhk•tairn] *adj* sober

**nüchternd** [nd] *adv* soberly

**Nüchternheit**
[NUHK•tairn•huyt] *n* F
sobriety

**Nudel** [NOO•del] *n* F noodles

**Null** [nuhl] *num* zero

**Nummer** [NOO•mair] *n* F
number

**nun** [nuhn] *int* well

**Nuß** [nuhs] *n* F nut

**Nußknacker** [NUHS•knah•kair]
*n* M nutcrackers

**Nutzen** [NUH•tsen] *n* N use;
utility; benefit

**nützlich** [NOOTS•lik] *adj*
beneficial; useful

**Nützlichkeit** [-kuyt] *n* F
usefulness

**Nylon** [NEE•lon] *n* N nylon

**Nymphe** [NUHM•pfe] *n* F
nymph

# O

**Oase** [OH•ah•seh] *n* F oasis

**ob** [op] *conj* whether

**ob wenn** [op] [ven] *conj* if;
whether

**oben** [OH•ben] *adv* at the top; on the surface

**Ober** [OH•bair] *n* M waiter

**ober** [OH•bair] *adj* upper

**oberflächlich** [OH•bair•FLEHK•lihk] *adj* skin-deep

**Oberlicht** [OH•bair•lihkt] *n* N skylight

**Oberseite** [OH•bair•SUY•teh] *n* F upside

**Oberteil** [OH•bair•TUYL] *n* N top

**Objekt** [OB•yehkt] *n* N object

**Objektiv** [OB•yek•TEEV] *n adj* M objective

**Obmann** [op•mahn] *n* M foreman

**Observatorium** [ob•ZAIRV•ah•TOR•EE•oom] *n* N observatory

**Obst** [opst] *npl* F fruit

**Obstgarten** [OPST•gahr•ten] *n* M orchard

**obwohl** [op•VOHL] *conj* although; *adv* though

**ochrot** [HOHK•roht] *adj* N crimson

**Ochse** [OHKS•eh] *n* M ox

**oder** [oh•dair] *conj* or

**Ofen** [UHF•en] *n* M oven; stove

**offen** [OH•fen] *adj* frank; open; candid; *adv* openly

**öffnen** [UHF•nen] *vt* loosen

**offenbar** [OHF•fen•bahr] *adj* obvious; manifest

**offenbaren** [OHF•fen•bahr•en] *vt* reveal

**Offenbarung** [OH•fen•bahr•oong] *n* F disclosure; revelation

**Offenheit** [OH•fehn•hait] *n* F candor

**offensichtlich** [OF•fen•zihkt•lihk] *adj* obvious; evident; *adv* obviously

**Öffentlichkeit** [UHF•fent•luyhk•kuyt] *n* F limelight

**Öffnung** [UHF•noong] *n* F orifice

**offiziell** [of•FIH•TSEE•el] *adj* official

**Offizier** [oh•FIH•tseer] *n* M officer

**oft** [ohft] *adv* often

**ohne** [OH•neh] *prep* without

**ohneweiteres** [OH•neh•VAI•TAIR•es] *adj* offhand

**Ohr** [ohr] *n* N ear

**ohrenbetäubend** [OHR•en•be•TOI•bent] *adj* deafening

**Ohrring** [OHR•ring] *n* M earring

**okkult** [ok•KUHLT] *adj* occult

**Ökologie** [UH•ko•loh•GEE] *n* F ecology

**Ökonomie** [UH•ko•no•MEE] *n* F economy

**Oktober** [OHK•to•bair] *n* M October

**Öl** [uhl] *n* N oil

**ölig** [UHL•ig] *adj* oily; unctuous

**Olive** [oh•LEE•ve] *n* F olive

**Ölschacht** [UHL•shahkt] *n* M well (oil)

**Oma** [OH•ma] *n* F grandma

**Omelett** [OM•eh•let] *n* N omelet

**Omen** [OH•men] *n* N omen
**Onkel** [OHN•kel] *n* M uncle
**Opa** [OH•pah] *n* M grandpa
**Opal** [OH•pahl] *n* M opal
**Oper** [OH•pair] *n* F opera
**Opfer 1** [ohp•fair] *n* N offering;
sacrifice
**Opfer 2** [OHP•fair] *n* N victim
**Opportunist**
[OH•pohr•toon•EEST] *n* M
opportunist
**Optiker** [OP•tih•kair] *n* M
optician
**Optimismus**
[OP•ti•mihs•MOOS] *n* M
optimism
**Optimist** [OP•ti•MIHST] *n* M
optimist
**optimistisch** [-ish] *adj*
optimistic
**optisch** [OP•tish] *adj* optical
**Orakel** [OR•ah•kel] *n* N oracle
**orange** [OR•ahn•je] *adj* orange
**Orchester** [or•keh•stair] *n* N
orchestra
**orchestral** [OR•keh•strahl] *adj*
orchestral
**Orchidee** [OR•khi•dee] *n* F
orchid
**Orden** [OR•den] *n* N fraternity
**ordentlich** [OR•dent•lihk] *adj*
orderly
**ordinär** [OR•din•AIR] *adj*
vulgar
**ordinärscherzhaft**
[ORD•in•AIR•SHAIRTS•hahft]
*adj* scurrilous
**ordnen** [ord•nen] *vt* regulate
**Ordnung** [ORD•noong] *n* F
order

**Oregano** [or•EG•AN•oh] *n* M
oregano
**Organ** [OR•gan] *n* N organ
**organisch** [or•GAHN•isch] *adj*
organic
**organisieren**
[OR•gan•ih•SEER•en] *vt*
organize
**Organismus** [OR•gan•IS•moos]
*n* M organism
**Orgasmus** [or•GAHS•moos] *n*
M orgasm
**Orgie** [or•jee] *n* F orgy
**orientieren**
[OR•ee•en•TEER•en] *vt*
orientate
**Orientierung** [-oong] *n* F
orientation
**original** [OR•ig•ih•nahl] *adj*
original
**Original** [OR•ig•ih•nahl] N
original
**Ort** [ort] *n* M locality
**orthodox** [OR•to•dohks] *adj*
orthodox
**ortsfest** [ORTS•fehst] *adj*
stationary
**örtlich** [ERT•lihk] *adj* local
**Ost** [ost] *n* M East
**Ostern** [O•stairn] *n* N Easter
**Österreich** [OOST•air•raik] *n* N
Austria
**östlich** [UHST•lihk] *adj* eastern
**östlich morgenländisch**
[UHST•lihk] [MOR•gen•lend•
ish] *adj* oriental
**ostwärts** [OST•vairts] *adv*
eastward
**Otter** [OH•tair] *n* M otter
**Oval** [OH•fahl] *adj n* N
oval

**Ovation** [oh•VAH•TSEE•on] *n*
F ovation

**Ozean** [oh•TSEE•ahn] *n* M
ocean

# P

**Paar** [pahr] *n* N pair; couple

**Pacht** [pahkt] *n* F holding

**Pack** [pahk] *n* M pack

**Packkorb** [PAHK•korb] *n* M
crate

**Packpapier** [PAHK•pah•peer] *n*
N wrapping paper

**Paddelruder**
[PAH•del•ROO•dair] *n* N
paddle

**Päckchen** [PEHK•khen] *n* N
packet

**päpstlich** [PEPST•lihk] *adj*
papal

**Paket** [pah•KET] *n* N package;
parcel; bundle

**Pakistan** [PAH•kee•stahn] *n*
Pakistan

**Palastina** [PAH•lah•STEEN•ah]
*n* Palestine

**Palette** [PAH•leh•teh] *n* F
palette

**Palisade** [PAH•lih•sah•de] *n* F
stockade

**Palmsonntag**
[PAHLM•zon•tahg] *n* M Palm
Sunday

**Pampelmuse**
[PAHM•pel•moos] *n* F
grapefruit

**Panama** [PAH•nah•mah] *n*
Panama

**Panda** [PAHN•dah] *n* M panda

**Panik** [PAH•neek] *n* F panic

**Panther** [PAHN•tair] *n* M
panther

**Papa** [PAH•pah] *n* M papa

**Papagei** [PAH•pah•guy] *n* M
parrot

**Papier** [pah•peer] *n* N paper

**Papierdrachen**
[PAH•peer•DRAH•khen] *n* M
kite

**Papierkorb** [PAH•peer•kohrb] *n*
M wastepaper basket

**Pappel** [PAH•pel] *n* F poplar

**Papst** [pahpst] *n* M pope

**Parabel** [pah•RAH•bel] *n* F
parable

**Paradies** [PAHR•ah•DEES] *n* N
paradise

**Paradox** [PAHR•ah•DOHKS] *n*
N paradox

**Paraguay** [PAHR•ah•gwai] *n*
Paraguay

**parallel** [PAHR•ah•lehl] *adj*
parallel

**paranoid** [PAHR•ah•noid] *adj*
paranoid

**Pari** [PAHR•ee] *n* N par

**Parität** [PAHR•ee•TAHT] *n* F
parity

**Park** [pahrk] *n* M park

**parken** [PAHRK•en] *vt* park

**Parkplatz** [PAHRK•plahts] *n* M
parking

**Parkplatz** M parking lot
**Parlament** [PAHR•lah•ment] *n*
N parliament
**parlamentarisch**
[PAHR•lah•men•TAHR•ish]
*adj* parliamentary
**parochial** [PAH•roh•KEE•al]
*adj* parochial
**Parodie** [PAH•roh•DEE] *n* F
parody
**Partei Fest** [PAHR•tai] [fehst]
*n* F party
**Parteigänger**
[PAHR•tai•GEN•gair] *n* M
partisan
**Partisan** [PAHR•ti•zahn] *n* M
guerrilla
**Partner** [PAHRT•nair] *n* M
partner; mate
**Partnerschaft** [-shahft] *n* F
partnership
**Paß 1** [pahs] *n* M pass
**Paß 2** [pahs] *n* M passport
**Passagier** [PAH•sah•JEER] *n* M
passenger
**Passant** [pah•SAHNT] *n* M
passerby
**Passatwinde**
[PAH•saht•VIN•deh] *n* F
tradewind
**passen 1** [PAH•sen] *vi* fit (as
clothing); suit; be appropriate
**passen 2** [PAH•sen] *vi* pass
**passend** [PAH•send] *adj*
appropriate; becoming
**passieren** [PAH•seer•en] *vi*
happen
**passiv** [pah•SEEV] *adj* passive
**Pasta** [PAH•stah] *n* N pasta
**Pastellstift** [PAH•shtel•shtift] *n*
M crayon

**Pastete 1** [pah•STEH•teh] *n* F
pie
**Pastete 2** [pah•STAI•teh] *n* F
pâté
**pasteurisieren**
[PAH•shtoor•ih•SEER•en] *vt*
pasteurize
**Pastinak** [PAH•sti•NAHK] *n* M
parsnip
**Pate** [PAH•te] *n* M godfather
**Patent** [PAH•tent] *adj* patent
**Patentleder** [-LAI•dair] *n* F
patent leather
**Patentochter**
[PAH•ten•TOHK•tair] *n* F
goddaughter
**Pathologie** [PAH•tol•oh•GEE]
*n* F pathology
**Patient** [PAH•tsee•ENT] *n* M
patient
**Patin** [PAH•tin] *n* F godmother
**Patriot** [pah•TREE•oht] *n* M
patriot
**patriotisch** [-ish] *adj* patriotic
**Patriotismus** [-IS•moos] *n* M
patriotism
**Patron** [pah•TRON] *n* M patron
**Pause 1** [POU•ze] *n* F
intermission; pause
**Pause 2** [POU•zeh] *n* F break
(as work); recess
**pazifisch** [pah•TSIH•fish] *adj*
Pacific
**Pedal** [PEH•dahl] *n* N pedal
**Pedant** [peh•DAHNT] *n* M
pedant
**pedantisch** [-ISH] *adj* pedantic
**peinigen** [PUYN•ig•en] *vt*
torment; *vi* tantalize
**Peiniger** [-AIR] *n* M tormentor;
torturer

**peinlich genau** [PUYN•lihk geh•NOU] *adj* meticulous

**Peitsche** [PUYT•she] *n* F whip; scourge

**peitschen** [PAITCH•en] *vt* flog

**Peitschen** *n* N whipping

**Pelz** [pelts] *n* M fur

**pelzartig** [PELTS•ahr•tig] *adj* furry

**Pendant** [pen•DANT] *n* N pendant

**Pendel** [PEN•del] *n* N pendulum

**pendeln** [PEN•deln] *v* shuttle

**Penicillin** [PEN•ih•SIL•en] *n* N penicillin

**Penis** [PEE•nis] *n* M penis

**Pension 1** [pen•SEE•on] *n* F pension

**Pension 2** [pen•SEE•on] *n* N retirement

**per** [pair] *prep* by; per

**per Autostopp** [pair OU•to•SHTOP] hitchhike

**Perfektionist** [PAIR•fek•tsee•on•EEST] *n* M perfectionist

**Pergament** [PAIRG•ah•MENT] *n* N parchment

**periodisch** [PAIR•ee•OH•dish] *adj* periodic

**Perle** [PAIR•leh] *n* F bead; pearl

**Persenning** [PAIR•sen•ning] *n* F tarpaulin

**Persischer Golf** [PAIR•sish•air GOLF] *n* M Persian Gulf

**persönlich** [pair•ZUHN•lihk] *adj* personal

**Persönlichkeit** [pair•ZUHN•lihk•KUYT] *n* personality

**Person** [pair•ZOHN] *n* F person

**Personal** [PAIR•zon•al] *n* N personnel

**Perspektiv** [PAIR•shpek•TEEV] *n* M perspective

**Perücke** [pair•RUH•keh] *n* F wig

**Pessimismus** [PES•ih•MIS•moos] *n* M pessimism

**Pessimist** [PES•ih•MIST] *n* M pessimist

**pessimistisch** [-ish] *adj* pessimistic

**Pest** [pehst] *n* F pest

**Petersilie** [PAI•tair•ZEEL•lee•eh] *n* F parsley

**Pfad** [pfahd] *n* M trail

**Pfahl** [pfahl] *n* M picket

**Pfand** [pfahnt] *n* N pledge

**Pfandgut** [PFAHD•goot] *n* N mortgage

**Pfandhaus** [PFAHNT•hous] *n* N pawnshop

**Pfanne** [PFAH•neh] *n* F pan

**Pfannkuchen** [PFAHN•koo•khen] *n* M pancake

**Pfarrbezirk** [PFAHR•beh•TSEERK] *n* N parish

**Pfarrer** [PFAHR•air] *n* M minister; pastor; parson; rector

**Pfau** [pfou] *n* M peacock

**Pfederstärke** [-shtair•ke] *n* F horsepower

**Pfeffer** [PFEH•fair] *n* M pepper

**Pfefferkuchen** [PFEH•fair•KOO•khen] *n* M gingerbread

**Pfefferminze** [-MIN•tse] *n* F
peppermint

**pfeifen** [PFUY•fen] *vi* whistle

**Pfeil** [pfail] *n* M arrow

**Pfeiler** [PFUY•lair] *n* M pillar

**Pfeiler** [PFUY•lair] *n* M stilt

**Pfennig** [PFEN•nig] *n* M penny

**Pferd** [pfaird] *n* N horse

**Pferdchen** [PFAIRD•khen] *n* N
pony

**Pferdesschwanz**
[-es•SHVANTS] *n* M ponytail

**Pfingsten** [pfing•sten] *n* N
Whitsuntide

**Pfirsich** [PFEER•zish] *n* M
peach

**Pflanze** [PFLAHN•tseh] *n* F
plant

**Pflanzenwelt**
[PFLAHNTS•en•velt] *n* F
vegetation

**Pflaster** [PFLAH•stair] *n* N
plaster

**pflastern** [PFLAH•stairn] *vt*
pave

**Pflaume 1** [PFLOU•meh] *n* F
plum

**Pflaume 2** [PFLOUM•eh] *n* F
prune

**Pflege** [PFLAI•ge] *n* F keeping

**Pfleger in** [PFLAI•gair] [in] *n*
M keeper; orderly; nurse
(male)

**Pflicht** [pflihkt] *n* F duty

**Pflichtassistent**
[PFLIHKT•ah•sis•tent] *n* M
intern

**Pflug** [pfluhg] *n* M plow

**Pförtner** [PFURHT•nair] *n* M
janitor

**Pfosten** [PFOH•sten] *n* M pole;
stake

**Pfote** [PFOH•teh] *n* F paw

**Pfropfen** [PFROH•pfen] *n* N
graft

**Pfui** [PFOOY•ee] boo

**Pfund 1** [pfuhnt] *n* M pound
(weight)

**Pfund 2** [pfuhnd] *n* N quid,
pound (English currency)

**Pfütze** [PFUHTS•eh] *n* F
puddle

**Phänomen** [FAI•no•MEN] *n* N
phenomenon

**Phantasie** [FAHN•tah•ZEE] *n* F
fantasy; imagination

**phantastisch**
[FAHN•tah•STISH] *adj*
fantastic; quixotic

**Phantom** [FAHN•tom] *n* M
phantom; ghost

**Phase** [FAH•zeh] *n* F phase

**Philosoph** [FIL•oh•SOHF] *n* M
philosopher

**Philosophie** [-fee] *n* F
philosophy

**philosophisch**
[FIL•oh•SOH•fish] *adj*
philosophical

**Phonetik** [FOHN•eh•teek] *n* F
phonetics

**Photoapparat**
[FOH•toh•APP•ahr•AT] *n* N
camera

**Photograph (in)**
[FO•to•GRAHF -in] *n* M
photographer

**Photographie** [-fee] *n* F
photography

**Physik** *n* F physics

**Physiker** [FUH•zih•KAIR] *n* M
physicist

**Picke** [PIH•keh] *n* pick

**Pickel** [PIH•kel] *n* M pimple;
spot

**Picknick** [PIHK•nihk] *n* N
picnic

**piepsen** [PEEP•sen] *vi* peep

**piepsen** [PEEP•sen] *vi* squeak

**Piet** [PEE•eht] *n* M pier

**Pigment** [PIG•ment] *n* N
pigment

**Pilger** [PIL•gair] *n* M pilgrim

**Pille** [PIL•leh] *n* pill

**Pilot** [PEE•loht] *n* M pilot

**Pilz** [pihlts] *n* M mushroom

**Pinguin** [PIN•gween] *n* M
penguin

**Pinsel** [PIN•zel] *n* M paintbrush

**Pinzette** [PIN•tset•e] *npl* F
forceps; tweezers

**Pionier** [PEE•on•EER] *n* M
pioneer

**pirschen** [PEER•shen] *vi* stalk

**Pistole** [pi•STOHL•eh] *n* F gun;
pistol

**Pistolenhalfter**
[pih•STOHL•en•HAHLF•tair]
*n* F holster

**plädieren** [PLEH•deer•en] *vt*
plead

**plätschern** [PLEH•tschairn] *vi*
bicker

**Plakat** [plah•kaht] *n* N placard;
poster

**Plan** [plahn] *n* M plan; scenario

**Plan Entwurf** [plahn]
[ENT•voorf] *n* M blueprint

**Planet** [PLAH•net] *n* M planet

**Planke** [PLAHN•keh] *n* F plank

**Plantage** [PLAHN•taj] *n* F
plantation

**Planung** [PLAH•noong] *n* F
layout; plan

**Plappermaul** [PLAH•pair•maul]
*n* M chatterbox

**plappern** [PLAH•pairn] *vi*
babble

**plastisch Plastik** [PLAH•stish]
[-steek] *adj n* plastic

**Platin** [PLAH•teen] *n* N
platinum

**Platte** [PLAH•teh] *n* F plaque

**Plattenteller**
[PLAH•ten•TEL•air] *n* M
turntable

**plattiert** [PLAH•teert] *adj*
plated

**Platz** [plahts] *n* M location;
place

**Platzanweiser**
[PLAHTS•ahn•VUY•zair] *n*
M usher

**plaudern** [PLAU•dairn] *vi* chat

**Playboy** [PLAI•boi] *n* M
playboy

**plötzlich** [PLUHTS•lihk] *adj*
sudden; *adv* suddenly

**Plötzlichkeit** [-kuyt] *n* F
suddenness

**plumpsen** [PLUHMP•sen] *vi*
thump

**plündern** [PLUHN•dairn] *vt*
plunder; ransack

**Plus** [ploos] *n* N plus

**Pochen** [POHK•en] *n* N
pulsation

**pochen** [POH•khen] *vi* throb

**pochieren** [POH•cheer•en] *vt*
poach

**Podest** [PO•dest] *n* N pedestal

**Pöbelhaftigkeit**
[PUH•bel•HAHFT•ig•KUYT]
*n* F vulgarity; crudity
**Poesie** [POH•eh•ZEE] *n* F
poetry
**poetisch** [PO•eh•TISCH] *adj*
poetic
**Pokerspiel** [POH•kair•SHPEEL]
*n* N poker
**polar** [PO•lahr] *adj* polar
**Pole Polin** [POH•leh] [-lin] *n* M
Pole
**Polen** [POH•len] *n* Poland
**Polinesien**
[POL•ih•NAI•SEE•en] *n*
Polynesia
**polisch** [PO•lish] *adj* Polish
**Politik** [PO•li•TEEK] *n* F
politics
**Politiker** [PO•li•ti•KAIR] *n* M
politician
**politisch** [PO•lih•TISH] *adj*
political
**Politur** [POL•ih•TOOR] *n* F
polish
**Polizei** [PO•li•TSAI] *n* F police
**Polizeiwache**
[-TSAI•VAH•khe] *n* police
station
**Polizist** [POHL•i•TSIST] *n* M
policeman; cop; trooper
**Polizistin** [-in] *n* F
policewoman
**Pollen** [POL•len] *n* M pollen
**Pollution** [POL•loo•tsee•ON] *n*
F pollution
**Polo** [POH•loh] *n* N polo
**Polster** [POHL•stair] *n* N pad
**Polsterwaren**
[POL•stair•VAHR•en] *npl*
upholstery

**pommes frites** [POHM freet]
*npl* french fries
**populär** [POHP•oo•LAIR] *adj*
popular
**populär machen** [-MAH•khen]
*vt* popularize
**Pore** [POH•reh] *n* F pore
**porig** [POHR•ig] *adj* porous
**Pornographie**
[POR•no•grah•FEE] *n* F
pornography
**Portier** [POR•tee•AIR] *n* M
porter
**Portion** [POR•tsee•OHN] *n* F
portion; dose
**Portugal** [POR•too•GAHL] *n*
Portugal
**portugiese** [POR•too•GEE•zeh]
*adj* Portuguese
**Porzellan** [POHR•tsel•AHN] *n*
N china; porcelain
**Posaune** [POH•zou•neh] *n* F
trombone
**positiv** [POH•zih•TEEV] *adj*
positive
**Positur** [POH•zih•toor] *n* F
posture; stance
**Post** [pohst] *n* F mail; post
**postalisch** [POHST•ahl•ISH]
*adj* postal
**Postamt** [POHST•ahmpt] *n* N
post office
**Postgebühr** [-ge•BOOR] *n* F
postage
**postum** [POST•oom] *adj*
posthumous
**Pracht** [prahkt] *n* F splendor
**prachtvoll** [PRAHKT•fol] *adj*
gorgeous
**prädestiniert**
[PRAI•dehst•in•EERT] *adj*
predestined

**Prädikat** [PRAI•dih•kaht] *n* N
predicate

**prahlen** [PRAHL•len] *vi* brag;
boast; swagger

**prahlend** [PRAH•lend] *adj*
ostentatious

**Prahler** [PRAHL•lair] *n* M
doorman; bouncer

**Prahlerei** [PRAHL•lair] *n* F
*npl* bragging

**praktisch** [PRAHK•tish] *adj*
practical

**Prämie** [PRAI•mee•eh] *n* F
premium

**Präposition**
[PRAI•po•zits•EE•on] *n* F
preposition

**Präsident** [PRAI•zee•DENT] *n*
M president

**Präzedenzfall**
[PRAI•tseh•DENTS•fal] *n* M
precedent

**präzis** [prai•TSEES] *adj* precise

**predigen** [PRAI•dig•en] *vi*
preach

**Prediger** [-air] *n* M preacher

**Predigt** [PRAI•dihkt] *n* M
sermon

**Preis 1** [pruys] *n* M cost; price

**Preis 2** [pruys] *n* M prize;
reward

**Preis; Prämie** [prais]
[PRAI•me•eh] *n* M award

**Preiselbeere**
[PRUY•sel•BAIR•e] *n* F
cranberry

**preisen** [PRUY•sen] *vt* glorify

**Premiere**
[PRAI•meh•yee•AIR•eh] *n* F
premiere

**Presse** [PREH•seh] *n* F press

**pressen** [PREH•sehn] *vt* clench

**Prestige** [PREH•stee•jeh] *n* N
prestige

**pricklen** [PRIH•keln] *vi* tingle

**Priester** [PREE•stair] *n* M priest

**Priestershaft** [-shahft] *n* F
priesthood

**Primaten** [PREE•mah•ten] *npl*
primate

**Primel** [PREE•mel] *n* F
primrose

**primitiv** [prih•mih•teev] *adj*
primitive

**Prinz** [prints] *n* M prince

**Prinzessin** [PRIN•zes•sin] *n* F
princess

**Prinzip** [PRIHN•tseep] *n* N
principle

**Priorität** [PREE•or•ih•tait] *n* F
priority

**Prisma** [PRIHS•mah] *n* N prism

**Pristerseminar**
[PREE•stair•SEH•mihn•AHR]
*n* N seminary

**privat** [pree•VAHT] *adj* private

**Privatlehrer**
[pree•VAHT•lair•air] *n* M
tutor

**Privatschule** [pree•VAHT -] *n*
F school (boarding)

**Privileg** [PRIH•vih•LAIG] *n* N
privilege

**Privilegium**
[PRI•vih•LAIG•EE•oom] *n* N
prerogative

**Probe** [PRO•be] *n* F
experiment; rehearsal

**Probezeit** [PROH•beh•tsait] *n* F
probation

**Probierzimmer**
[PROH•beer•TSIM•air] *n* N
fitting room

**Problem** [proh•BLAIM] *n* N
problem
**Produkt** [proh•DOOKT] *n* M
product
**profan** [pro•FAHN] *adj* profane
**Professor** [proh•FEH•sor] *n* M
professor
**Profi** [PROH•fee] *n* M pro;
professional
**Profil** [PROH•feel] *n* N profile
**Programm** [PROH•grahm] *n* N
program
**Projekt** [proh•YEHKT] *n* N
project
**Proletariat**
[PROH•leh•TAHR•ee•aht] *n*
N proletariat
**Pronomen** [PRO•nohm•en] *n* N
pronoun
**Propaganda**
[PROH•pah•GAHN•dah] *n* F
propaganda
**Propeller** [pro•PEL•air] *n* M
propeller
**Prophet** [PRO•feht] *n* M
prophet
**Prosa** [pro•zah] *n* F prose
**Prost** [prohst] *excl* cheers
**Prostituierte**
[PRO•stih•TOO•EER•teh] *n* F
prostitute
**Protestant** [PRO•test•ANT] *n*
M Protestant
**protestieren**
[PROH•test•EER•en] *vt*
object; protest
**protoplasma**
[PRO•to•PLAHS•mah] *n* N
protoplasm
**Provinz** [PRO•vints] *n* F
province

**provinziell** [PRO•vin•TSEE•el]
*adj* provincial
**Prozent** [proh•TSENT] *n* M
percent
**Prozentgehalt** [-ge•HALT] *n*
M percentage
**Prozeß 1** [proh•TSEHS] *n* M
lawsuit; litigation
**Prozeß 2** [proh•TSEHS] *n* M
procedure; process
**Prüde** [PRUH•deh] *n* F prude
**prüfen** [PROO•fen] *vt* examine
**Prüfung** [PROO•foong] *n* F
exam; quiz; test
**Prügel** [PROO•gel] *n* F beating;
flogging
**Prunk** [pruhnk] *n* M pomp
**prunkhaft** [PRUHNK•hahft]
*adj* showy
**prunkvoll** [PRUHNK•vol] *adj*
grandiose; magnificent;
pompous
**Psalm** [pshalm] *n* M psalm
**Pseudonym** [SOO•do•NIM] *n*
N pseudonym
**Psychiater** [PSIH•kee•AH•tair]
*n* M psychiatrist
**Psychiatrie**
[PSUH•kee•ah•TREE] *n* F
psychiatry
**Psychologe** [psuh•kho•lo•ge] M
psychologist
**Psychologie** [-gee] *n* F
psychology
**psychologisch**
[PSUH•ko•LO•gish] *adj*
psychological
**Publikum** [PUHB•lih•koom] *n*
N public
**Pudding** [PUH•ding] *n* M
pudding
**Pudel** [POO•del] *n* M poodle

**puder** [POO•dair] *adj* powdered

**Pullover** [PUHL•oh•fair] *n* M sweater

**pulsieren** [PUHL•seer•en] *vt* pulsate

**Pulsschlag** [PULS•shlahg] *n* M pulse

**Pulver** [PUH•vair] *n* N powder

**Pumpe** [PUHM•peh] *n* F pump

**Punkt** [poonkt] *n* M dot; point

**pünktlich** [PUHNKT•lihk] *adj* punctual

**punktlos** [PUHNKT•los] *adj* pointless

**Punsch** [puhnsh] *n* M shrub

**Puppe** [POO•peh] *n* F doll

**purpurn** [POOR•poorn] *adj* purple

**Putter** [PUH•tair] *n* M putter

**putzen** [PUHTS•sen] *vt* clean; scrub; polish

**Putzfrau** [PUHTS•frou] *n* F cleaning lady

**Pyjama** [PEE•yah•mah] *n* M pajamas

**Pyramide** [PEER•ah•MEE•deh] *n* F pyramid

# Q

**Quadrant** [KVAHD•drahnt] *n* M quadrant

**Quadrat** [KVAHD•raht] *n* N square

**quälen** [KVAI•len] *vt* pester; haunt

**quaken** [KVAH•ken] *vt* quack

**Qual** [kvahl] *n* F pain; agony; anguish

**Qualifikation** [KVAL•if•ih•kahts•EE•on] *n* F qualification

**qualifizieren** [KVAL•ih•fi•TSEER•en] *vi* qualify

**Qualität** [KVAHL•ih•TAIT] *n* F quality

**qualitativ** [-tah•TEEV] *adj* qualitative

**Qualle** [KVAH•le] *n* F jellyfish

**Quantität** [KVAHN•ti•TAIT] *n* F quantity

**Quarantäne** [KVAR•ahn•TAIN•eh] *n* F quarantine

**Quart** [kvahrt] *n* N quart

**Quartett** [KVAHR•teht] *n* N quartet

**Quarz** [kvahrts] *n* M quartz

**Quaste** [KVAH•steh] *n* F tassel

**Quatsch!** [KVAHTCH] *n* M *excl* rubbish!

**Quecksilber** [KVEHK•zil•bair] *n* N quicksilver

**Quelle** [KVEL•le] *n* F fountain; resource; source

**Querblende** [KVAIR•blen•deh] *n* F transom

**querfeldein** [KVAIR•feld•uyn] *adj* cross-country

**Querschiff** [KVAIR•shif] *n* N transept

**Querstraße** [KVAIR•shtrau•se] *n* F crossroads

**quetschen** [KVETSH•en] *vt*
swat
**Quintett** [KVIN•teht] *n* N
quintet
**Quitte** [KVIH•teh] *n* F quince

**Quittung** [KVIH•toong] *n* F
receipt
**Quotient** [KVO•tsee•ent] *n* M
quotient

# R

**Rabbiner** [rah•bin•nair] *n* M
rabbi
**Rabe** [RAH•beh] *n* M raven
**Rache** [RAH•khe] *n* F revenge;
vengeance
**rächen** [REK•ken] *vt* avenge
**rachsüchtig** [RAHK•tsuhk•tig]
*adj* vindictive
**Rad 1** [rahd] *n* N bike; bicycle
**Rad 2** [rahd] *n* N wheel; caster;
gearwheel
**Rad fahren** [rahd FAHR•en]
ride (bicycle)
**radikal** [RAH•dih•kahl] *adj*
radical
**Radio** [RAH•dee•o] *n* N radio
**Radius** [RAH•dee•oos] *n* M
radius
**Raffinerie** *n* F refinery
**raffinieren** [FAH•fin•EER•en]
*vt* refine
**raffiniert** *adj* refined
**Raffinierung** *n* F refinement
**Rahm** [rahm] *n* M cream
**Rahmen** [RAHM•en] *n* M
frame
**Rakete** [rah•KAI•teh] *n* F rocket
**Rand** [rahnt] *n* M margin; rim;
verge
**Rand** [rah•nt] *n* M border

**Range** [rahn•geh] *n* F brat
**Ranke** [RAHNK•eh] *n* F tendril
**Ränke schmieden** [RENK•e
SHMEE•den] *n* intrigue
**rar** [rahr] *adj* rare
**Rasen** [RAH•zen] *n* M lawn
**rasen** [RAH•zen] *vi* rush
**Rasen** [RAH•zen] *n* M turf
**rasend machen** [RAH•zend
MAH•ken] *vt* madden
**Rasenmäher** [-MAI•air] *n* M
lawn mower
**Rasiermesser**
[rah•SEER•MEH•sair] *n* N
razor
**Rasse** [RAH•seh] *n* F breed
(race)
**Rastlosigkeit**
[RAHST•los•ig•KUYT] *n*
restlessness
**Rat** [raht] *n* M advice; counsel
**raten** [RAHT•en] *vt* advise
**Ratgeber** [RAHT•gai•bair] *n* M
counselor
**Rathaus** [RAHT•hous] *n* N city
hall
**Ratte** [RAH•teh] *n* F rat
**rattern** [RAH•tairn] *vi* rumble
**Rätsel** [RET•sel] *n* N enigma;
puzzle; riddle

**Raub 1** [roub] *n* M prey
**Raub 2** [roub] *n* M robbery
**rauben** [ROU•ben] *vt* rob
**Räuber** [ROI•bair] *n* M robber
**Raubtier** [ROWB•teer] *n* N
beast
**Raubtier** [ROUB•teer] *n* N
predator
**Rauchabzug**
[ROUHK•ap•tsoog] *n* M
funnel
**rauchen** [ROU•shen] *vt vi*
smoke
**rauchen verboten** no smoking
**Rauchfang** [ROUHK•fahng] *n .*
M flue
**Rauferei** [ROU•fair•ai] *n* F
brawl
**rauh** [rouh] *adj* harsh; raucous;
rough
**rauh werden** [rou vair•den] *vi*
roughen
**Raum** [roum] *n* M space
**räumen** [ROI•men] *vi* vacate
**räumig** [ROIM•ig] *adj* spacious
**Raupe** [ROW•peh] *n* F
caterpillar
**rautenförmig**
[ROU•ten•FER•mig] *adj*
diamond-shaped
**Reagenzglas**
[RAI•ah•GENTS•glahs] *n* N
test tube
**reagieren** [RAI•ah•GEER•en]
*vi* react
**Reagierung** [-GEER•oong] *n* F
reaction
**reaktionär**
[rai•AHK•tsee•on•AIR] *adj*
reactionary

**Realismus** [RAI•al•IS•moos] *n*
M realism
**Realist** [RAI•ahl•IST] *n* M
realist
**realistisch** [RAI•al•IH•stish] *adj*
realistic
**Realität** [RAI•ahl•ih•TAIT] *n* F
reality
**Rebatte** [rai•BAH•teh] *n* F
rebate
**Rebe** [RAI•beh] *n* F vine
**Rebell** [REH•behl] *n* M rebel
**Rebhuhn** [RAIB•hoon] *n* N
partridge
**Rechenmaschine**
[REHK•ehn•MAH•SHEEN•eh]
*n* F calculator
**rechnen** [REHK•nen] *vt* reckon
**Rechnen** [REHK•nen] *n* N
reckoning
**Rechnung** [REHK•noong] *n* F
tab
**recht** [rehkt] *adj* right; *adv*
properly; really
**Rechteck** [REHKT•ehk] *n* N
rectangle
**rechtfertigen**
[REHKT•fair•ti•gen] *vtr*
justify
**Rechtsakademie**
[rehkts•ah•kah•dehm•EE] *n* F
law school
**Rechtsanwalt**
[REHKTS•ahn•vahlt] *n* M
lawyer
**Rechtschaffenheit**
[REHKT•SHAH•fen•huyt] *n* F
integrity; righteousness
**Rechtschreibung**
[REHKT•SHRUY•boon] *n* F
spelling

**rechtshändig**
[REHKTS•hen•dig] *adj*
right-hand .

**rechtsläufig** [REKHTS•loi•fig]
*adj adv* clockwise

**Rechtsprechung**
[REHKTS•shprehk•oong] *n* F
jurisdiction

**rechtzeitig** [REHKT•tsait•ig]
*adj* seasonable; timely

**redaktionell**
[reh•DAHK•TSEE•on•ell] *adj*
editorial

**Rede** [RAI•deh] *n* F speech;
discourse

**Redefreiheit**
[RAI•de•FRUY•huyt] *n* F free
speech

**reden** [RAI•den] *vi* talk

**Reden** [RAI•den] *n* N talking

**Redewendung**
[RAI•deh•VEN•doong] *n* F
phrase

**Redner** [RAID•nair] *n* M orator

**reflexiv** [RAI•fleks•EEV] *adj*
reflexive

**Reform** [RAI•form] *n* F reform

**Refraktion**
[RAI•frahk•TSEE•on] *n* F
refraction

**Regel 1** [RAI•gel] *n* F rule

**Regel 2** [RAI•gel] *n* F
menstruation

**regelmäßig** [RAI•gel•MAI•sig]
*adj* regular; *adv* regularly

**Regelung** [RAI•gel•oong] *n* F
regulation

**Regen** [rai•gen] *n* M rain

**Regen** *n* M rainfall

**Regenbogen** [-BOH•gen] *n* M
rainbow

**Regenguß** [RAI•gen•GOOS] *n*
M downpour

**Regenmantel**
[RAI•gen•MAHN•tel] *n* M
slicker

**Regentropf** [-trohpf] *n* M
raindrop

**Regierung** [REH•geer•oong] *n*
F government

**Regime** [reh•JEEM] *n* N regime

**Regiment** [REH•ji•MENT] *n* N
regiment

**regnerisch** [RAIG•nair•ish] *adj*
rainy

**Reh** [rai] *n* M deer

**Rehkalb** [RAI•kahlb] *n* N fawn

**Reibe** [RUY•be] *n* F grater

**Reibung** [RAI•boong] *n* F
friction

**Reich** [ruyhk] *n* N empire; realm

**reich** [ruyhk] *adj* rich; wealthy

**reich verziert** [ruyhk
FAIR•tseert] *adj* ornate

**reichen** [RUY•chen] *vt* reach

**reichlich** [RUYK•likh] *adj*
copious

**reichlich vorhanden**
[RAIK•lik]
[FOR•HAHN•duhn] *adj*
abundant

**Reichtum** [RUYHK•toom] *n* M
wealth; opulence; richness

**reif** [ruyf] *adj* mature; ripe

**Reife** [RUY•feh] *ñ* F maturity

**Reifen** [RUY•fen] *n* M tire

**Reifenpfanne**
[RUY•fen•PFAH•neh] *n* F tire
(flat)

**Reihe** [ruy•he] *n* F row; tier

**Reihenfolge**
[RUY•en•FOL•geh] *n* F
succession

**Reiher** [RUY•air] *n* M heron

**Reim** [ruym] *n* M rhyme

**rein 1** [ruyn] *adv* (col) short for herein, hinein

**rein 2** [ruyn] *adj* pure; plain; clear

**Reinheit** [RUYN•huyt] *n* F chastity; purity

**reinigen** [RUYN•ig•en] *vt* clean; purify; clear out

**Reiniger** [RUYYN•ig•en] *n* M cleaner

**Reinlichkeit** [RUYN•likh•kuyt] *n* F cleanliness

**reinrassig** [RUYN•rah•sig] *adj* thoroughbred

**Reis** [rais] *n* M rice

**Reise** [RUY•ze] *n* F journey; trip

**Reisebüro** [-BYUR•oh] *n* N travel agency

**reisen** [RUY•zen] *vi* travel

**Reisender** [-dair] *n* M traveler

**Reiseplan** [RUY•ze•plahn] *n* M itinerary

**Reisetasche** [RUY•zeh•TAH•sheh] *n* F valise

**Reiseziel** [RAI•ze•tseel] *n* N destination

**Reißverschluß** [RUYS•vair•SHLUHS] *n* M zipper

**reiten** [RUY•ten] *vi* ride; ride (horseback)

**Reiter** [RUY•tair] *n* M rider

**Reiterie** [RUY•tair•uy] *n* F cavalry

**Reiz 1** [ruyts] *n* F charm

**Reiz 2** [ruyts] *n* M stimulus

**reizbar** [RUYTS•bahr] *adj* irritable

**reizend** [RAI•tsent] *adj* cute; engaging

**reizlos** [RUYTS•los] *adj* unattractive

**reizvill** [RAITS•fohl] *adj* attractive

**reklamieren** [RAI•kla•MEER•en] *vt* reclaim

**religiös** [rai•LIG•ee•UHS] *adj* religious

**Religion** [rai•lig•ee•ON] *n* F religion

**Religionsgemeinschaft** [REH•lig•ee•ONS•geh•MUYN•shaft] *n* F sect

**Renaissance** [RAI•nah•SAHNS] *n* F renaissance

**Rennbahn** [REHN•bahn] *n* F speedway

**rennen** [REN•nen] *vi* sprint

**Renntier** [REHN•teer] *n* N reindeer

**reparieren** [REHP•ahr•eer•en] *vt* mend; repair

**Reptil** [rehp•TEEL] *n* N reptile

**Republik** [rai•POOB•leek] *n* republic

**Republikaner** [-KAHN•air] *n* M republican

**reservieren** [reh•zair•VEER•en] *vt* reserve

**resonant** [REH•zoh•NAHNT] *adj* sonorous

**Resonanz** [REH•soh•NANTS] *n* resonance

**respektvoll** [reh•SPEHKt•fol] *adj* respectful

**Rest** [rehst] *n* M remainder; rest

**Restaurant**
[REH•stau•RAHNT] *n* N
restaurant

**Restaurierung**
[REH•stou•EER•oong] *n*
restoration

**Festlichkeit** [FEHSt•lihk•kuyt]
*n* F revelry

**Resultat** [REH•zuhl•TAHT] *n* F
result

**retten** [REH•ten] *vt* rescue

**Rettich** [REH•tihk] *n* M radish

**Rettungsboot**
[REH•toongs•BOHT] *n* N
lifeboat

**Reue** [ROI•eh] *n* F remorse

**Revers** [reh•FAIRS] *n* N lapel

**revidieren** [RAI•vih•DEER•en]
*vt* revise

**Revolution**
[REH•vo•loo•tsee•ON] *n*
revolution

**revolutionär** [-air] *adj*
revolutionary

**Rezept** [rai•TSEPT] *n* N recipe

**rezitieren** [RAI•tsih•teer•en] *vt*
recite

**Rhabarber** [rah•BAHR•bair] *n*
M rhubarb

**Rhetorik** [REH•tor•ik] *n* F
oratory; rhetoric

**Rheumatismus**
[RHOI•mah•TIS•moos] *n* M
rheumatism

**Rhinozeros**
[RHEE•no•TSAIR•ohs] *n* N
rhinoceros

**Rhythmus** [RHIT•moos] *n* M
rhythm

**Richter** [RIHK•tair] *n* M judge;
referee

**richtig** [RIKH•tig] *adj* correct;
right

**richtig** [RIKH•tig] *adv*
correctly; properly

**Richtung** [RIHK•toong] *n* F
direction

**Riedgras** [REED•grahs] *n* N
reed

**Riemen** [REE•men] *n* M strap;
thong

**Riese** [REE•se] *n* M giant

**riesig** [REE•zig] *adj* huge;
monstrous

**Riff** [rihf] *n* N ledge; reef

**Rinde** [RIHN•deh] *n* F rind

**Rinder** [RIN•dair] *adj* bovine

**Rindfleisch** [RINT•flaish] *n* N
beef

**Ring** [ring] *n* M hoop

**ring** [-ring] key ring

**Ring** [ring] *n* M ring

**Ringelblume**
[RIHNG•el•BLOO•me] *n* F
marigold

**ringen** [RING•en] *vi* wrestle

**ringsherum etwa**
[RINGZ•hair•OOM] [et•vah]
*adv* around

**Rinne** [RIH•ne] *n* F groove

**Rippe** [RIH•peh] *n* F rib

**Rippenstoß**
[RIH•pen•SHTOHS] *n* M
nudge

**Risiko 1** [RIH•see•koh] *n* N
peril; risk

**Risiko 2** [RIH•see•koh] *n* N
venture

**Riß** [rihs] *n* M tear

**Ritter** [RIH•tair] *n* M knight

**ritterlich** [RIH•tair•LIHK] *adj*
gallant; chivalrous

**Ritterlichkeit**
[RIT•air•likh•KUYT] *n* F
chivalry

**Ritual** [RIH•too•al] *n* N ritual

**Rivale** [ree•VAHL•eh] *n* M rival

**Robe** [ROH•beh] *n* F robe;
evening gown

**Robinie** [ROH•bin•EE•eh] *n* F
locust

**Rock** [rohk] *n* M skirt

**Röhre** [ROOR•he] *n* F duct

**Roggen** [ROH•gen] *n* M rye

**roh** [roh] *adj* raw

**Rohling** [ROH•ling] *n* M ruffian

**Rohr** [rohr] *n* M cane; pipe;
tube

**Rohr** *n* N tubing

**Rohstoff** [ROH•shtohf] *n* M
raw material

**Rolladen** [rohl•LAH•den] *n* M
shutter

**Rolle** [ROH•leh] *n* F role

**Rolle** [ROHL•uh] *n* F coil

**Rollen** [ROL•len] *n* N lurch

**rollen** [ROL•len] *vi* roll

**Rollschuh laufen** skate (roller)

**Rollstuhl** [ROHL•shtool] *n* M
wheelchair

**Rolltreppe** [ROL•tre•peh] *n* F
escalator

**Roman** [ro•MAHN] *n* M novel

**romanisch** [ro•MAHN•ish] *adj*
Roman

**Romantik** [roh•MAHN•teek] *n*
F romanticism

**Romantiker** [-air] *n* M
romanticist

**romantisch** [roh•MAHN•tish]
*adj* romantic

**Röntgenstrahl**
[RUHNT•gen•shtrahl] *n* M
X-ray

**rosa; Rosa** [ROH•seh] *n* N pink

**Rose** [ROH•zeh] *n* F rose

**Rosenkranz**
[ROH•zen•KRAHNTS] *n* M
rosary

**rosenrot** [ROH•zen•ROHT] *adj*
rosy

**Rosine** [roh•ZEEN•eh] *n* F
raisin

**Roß** [rohs] *n* N steed

**Rost 1** [rohst] *n* M rust

**Rost 2** [rohst] *n* M grill

**rostbraun** [ROHST•broun] *adj*
russet

**Rostfraß** [ROHST•frahs] *n* M
corrosion

**rostig** [ROHST•ig] *adj* rusty

**rot** [roht] *adj* red

**Rotary-Club** [ROH•tahr•EE
kluhb] *n* rotary

**Röte** [RUH•teh] *n* F redness

**röten** [RUH•ten] *vt* redden

**Rothirsch** [ROHT•heersh] *n* M
stag

**Rotkehlchen** [ROHT•kail•khen]
*n* N robin

**Roulade** [ROO•lah•de] *n* F fillet

**Route** [RUH•te] *n* F route

**Routinesache**
[ROO•teen•ZAH•khe] *n*
routine

**Rübe** [roo•beh] *n* F turnip

**Rubin** [ROO•bin] *n* M ruby

**Rußland** [RUHS•lahnt] *n* Russia

**Ruck 1** [ruhk] *n* M hitch

**Ruck 2** [ruhk] *n* M spurt

**Rückblick** [ROOK•blihk] *n* M
flashback

**Rückenmark**
[RUHK•en•mahrk] n N spinal
cord

**Rückerstattung**
[RUHK•air•SHTAH•toong] n
F restitution

**Rückgang** [ROOK•gahng] n M
decay

**rückgrat** [RUHK•graht] spinal

**Rücksack** [ROOK•zak] n M
backpack; knapsack

**Rücksicht** [RUHK•zihkt] n
respect

**rücksichtslos**
[RUHK•zihkts•los] adj
inconsiderate

**rücksichtsvoll**
[ROOK•zihkts•fol] adj
considerate

**rückwärts** [ROOK•vairts] adv
adj backward

**rückwirkend**
[RUHK•veer•kend] adj
retroactive

**Rückwirkung**
[ROOK•veer•koong] n F
backlash

**Rückzahlung**
[RUHK•tsahl•oong] n F
refund

**Rückzug** [RUHK•tsoog] n M
retreat

**Ruder** [ROO•dair] n N helm;
oar; rudder

**rudimentär**
[RUH•dih•men•TAIR] adj
vestigial

**Ruf** [roof] n M reputation

**rufen** [ROO•fen] vi shout

**Ruhe** [ROO•he] n F repose;
tranquility; quietness

**ruhig** [ROO•hig] adj placid;
quiet; sedate; tranquil

**Ruhm** [room] n M fame; glory;
renown

**rühren** [RUHR•en] vt stir

**Rühren** n N stirring

**Rührseligkeit**
[RUHR•zai•LIG•kuyt] n F
sentimentality

**Ruine** [roo•EE•ne] n F ruin

**Rum** [room] n M rum

**Rumpf** [ruhmpf] n M hull

**rund** [ruhnt] adj round

**Runde** [RUHN•deh] n F patrol

**Rundfunk** [ROONT •foonks] n
F broadcast

**rundlich** [ROONT•likh] adj
chubby; plump

**Rundschreiben**
[RUHND•shruy•ben] n N
newsletter

**Runzel** [RUN•tsel] n F wrinkle

**runzeln** [RUHN•zeln] vt
wrinkle; pucker

**Ruß** [ruhs] n M soot; smoke

**Rußland** [RUHS•lant] n N
Russia

**Rüsselkäfer**
[RUH•sel•KAI•fair] n M
weevil

**rußig** [RUH•sig] adj sooty

**russisch** [RUHS•ish] adj
Russian

**Rüstung 1** [ROOS•toong] n F
armor; armament

**Rüstung 2** [RUH•stoong] n F rig

**Rute** [ROO•teh] n F rod

**rutschen** [RUHT•chen] vi skid

**Rutschen** [RUHT•chen] n N
slip

**rütteln** [RUH•teln] vt jiggle

# S

Saal [zahl] *n* M hall

sabbern [SAH•bairn] *vi* slobber

Säbel [zeh•bel] *n* M saber

Sabotage [SAH•boh•taj] *n* F
sabotage

Sachbücher [ZAHK•buh•kair]
*npl* nonfiction

sachdienlich [ZAHK•deen•lihk]
*adj* relevant

Sachkenntnis
[ZAHK•kehnt•nis] *n* F
know-how

Sachverhalt [ZAHK•fair•halt] *n*
M issue

Sack [sehk] *n* M sack

Sack; Beutel; Tüte [zak]
[BOI•tel] [TOOT•eh] *n* M bag

Sackgeschwulst
[sahk•ge•SHVOOLST] *n* F
cyst

sadistisch [sah•DIH•stish] *adj*
sadistic

sächlich [ZEHK•lihk] *adj* neuter

Safran [sah•FRAHN] *n* M
saffron

Saft [zahft] *n* M juice

saftig [ZAHFT•ig] *adj*
succulent; juicy

Säge [ZAI•geh] *n* F chain saw

Sage [ZAH•ge] *n* F legend;
myth

sagen [ZAH•gen] *vt* tell

sagenhaft [SAH•gen•hahft] *adj*
mythical

sahnig [ZAHN•ig] *adj* creamy

Saite [ZUY•teh] *n* F chord

Sakrament [SAH•krah•MENT]
*n* N sacrament

Sakristei [SAHK•rihst•UY] *n* F
vestry

Salat [sah•LAT] *n* M lettuce;
salad

Salbe [SAHL•beh] *n* F ointment

Salbei [SAL•buy] *n* M sage

Salbung [SAHL•boong] *n* F
unction

Salon [sah•LAHN] *n* M parlor

Salto [SAHL•toh] *n* M
somersault

Same [ZAH•me] *n* M seed

sammeln [ZAH•meln] *vt* collect

Samt [zahmt] *n* M velvet

sanft [zahnft] *adj* gentle; mild

Sarg [zarg] *n* M coffin

Satire [sah•TEER•eh] *n* F satire;
skit

Sattel [SAH•tel] *n* M saddle

Satz [zats] *n* M sentence

Satzbau [ZATS•bou] *n* M
syntax

Sau [zou] *n* F sow

sauber [ZAU•bair] *adj* clean;
neat; tidy

Sauberkeit [ZOU•bair•kuyt] *n*
F cleanliness; tidiness

säubern [ZOI•bairn] *vt* sweep;
clean

sauer [ZOU•air] *adj* sour; tart;
bitter

sauer, bissig [ZOU•air]
[BIS•ig] [ZOI•ruh] *adj* acid;
acidic

**Sauerstoff** [ZOU•air•SHTOHF] *n* M oxygen

**saufen** [ZOU•fen] *vt* drink; guzzle

**Säule** [ZOI•leh] *n* F column

**saugen** [zou•gen] *vt* suck

**Saugen** *n* N suction

**Säugetier** [ZOUG•eh•teer] *n* N mammal

**Saugheber** [ZOUG•hai•bair] *n* M siphon

**Säugling** *n* N infant

**Säuglingsalter** [ZOIG•lings•AHL•tair] *n* N infancy

**Saum** [zoum] *n* M hem

**Säure** [ZOI•ruh] *adj n* F acid

**sausen** [ZOU•zen] *vi* whiz

**sausend** [ZOU•zend] *adj* sweeping

**Schabe** [SHAH•beh] *n* F cockroach

**Schablone** [SHAH•bloh•neh] *n* F stencil

**Schachspiel** [SHAHK•shpeel] *n* N chess

**Schade** [SHAH•deh] *n* F pity

**Schaden** [SHAH•den] *n* M damage; harm

**Schadenersatz** [SHAHD•en•air•zahts] *n* M indemnity

**schadhaft** [SHAHD•hahft] *adj* faulty

**schäbig** [SHAI•big] *adj* shabby; sordid

**Schädel** [SHAI•del] *n* M skull

**schädigen** [SHAI•dig•en] impair

**schädlich** [SHEHD•lihk] *adj* harmful; detrimental; hurtful; noxious

**scharf** [shahrf] *adj* sharp; acrid

**Schärfe** [SHAIR•feh] *n* F edge

**schälen, Schale** [SHAI•len] [SHAH•le] *vt n* F peel

**schändlich** [SHEND•lihk] *adj* disgraceful; disreputable

**schätzen 1** [SHEH•tsehn] *vt* cherish

**schätzen 2** [SHEH•tsehn] *vt* appraise

**Schätzung 1** [shehts•oong] *n* F estimate; guess; appraisal

**Schätzung 2** [SHETS•oong] *n* F rating

**Schaffel** [SHAHF•fel] *n* N fleece

**Schakal** [shah•kahl] *n* M jackal

**Schal** [shahl] *n* M scarf

**schal** [shahl] *adj* vapid

**Schalldämpfer** [SHAHL•demp•fair] *n* M silencer

**schalldämpfig** [SHAHL•dempf•ig] *adj* soundproof

**Schalle 1** [SHAW•leh] *n* F bowl

**Schalle 2** [SHAHL•eh] *n* F clasp

**Schaltbrett** [SHAHLT•bret] *n* N switchboard

**Schalter 1** [SHAHL•tair] *n* M switch

**Schalter 2** [SHAHL•tair] *n* M ticket office

**Schaltjahr** [SHAHLT•yahr] *n* N leap year

**Schaluppe** [SHAH•luh•peh] *n* F sloop

**schamlos** [SHAM•los] *adj* flagrant

**Schande** [SHAHN•deh] *n* F
disgrace

**scharf** [SHAHRF] *adj* sharp;
acute; keen

**Scharfrichter**
[SHAHRF•RIHK•tair] *n* M
executioner

**Scharfsinn** *n* M widsom;
sagacity

**scharfsinnig** [SHARF•ZIN•ig]
*adj* wise; sagacious

**Scharlach** [SHAHR•lahk] *n* M
scarlet

**Schatten** [SHAH•ten] *n* M
shade

**Schattenbild**
[SHAH•ten•BIHLD] *n* N
silhouette

**Schatz** [shahts] *n* M treasure

**Schatzkammer**
[SHAHTS•KAH•mair] *n* F
treasury

**Schau** [shou] *n* F spectacle

**Schaubild** [SHOU•bild] *n* N
graph

**schaudern** [SHOU•dairn] *vi*
shudder

**Schaufel** [SHOU•fel] *n* F
shovel

**schaufeln** [SHOU•feln] *vt*
scoop

**Schaukelstuhl**
[SHOU•kel•SHTOOL] *n* M
rocking chair

**Schaum** [shoum] *n* M foam;
scum; froth

**Schaunummer**
[SHOU•nuh•mair] *n* F stunt

**Schauspiel** [SHOU•shpeel] *n* N
drama

**Schauspieler**
[SHOU•SHPEEL•air] *n* M
actor

**Schauspielerin**
[SHOU•SHPEEL•air•in] *n* F
actress

**Scheck** [shek] *n* M check
(currency)

**Scheckbuch** [SHEK•book] *n* N
checkbook

**Scheffel** [SHEH•fel] *n* M
bushel

**Scheibe 1** [SHUY•beh] *n* F disk

**Scheibe 2** [SHUY•beh] *n* F
pane

**Scheibe 3** [SHUY•beh] *n* F
slice

**Scheide** [SHUY•deh] *n* parting

**Schein** [shuyn] *n* M license

**scheinbar 1** [SHUYN•bahr] *adj*
apparent; ostensible

**scheinbar 2** [SHUYN•bahr] *adj*
imaginary

**scheinen** [SHUY•nen] *vi* seem

**Scheinwerfer**
[SHUYN•vair•fair] *n* N
floodlight; headlight

**Scheitelpunkt**
[SHUY•tel•PUHNKT] *n* M
zenith

**scheitern** [SHUY•tairn] *vi* fail

**scheitern lassen** [SHUY•tairn
lah•sen] *vi* strand

**schekkig** [SHEK•kig] *adj*
variegated

**Schelligkeit** [-ig•kuyt] *n* F
swiftness

**schelten** [SHEHL•ten] *vt* scold

**Schelten** *n* N scolding

**Schema 1** [SHAI•mah] *n* M
diagram; plan

**Schema 2** [SHAI•meh] *n* N
scheme

**Schenkel** [SHAINK•el] *n* M
thigh
**schenken** [shehn•ken] *vt*
donate; bestow
**Schere** [SHAIYR•eh] *n* F
clippers; scissors
**scheu** [shoi] *adj* bashful; shy
**Scheu** [shoi] *n* F shyness
**scheußlich** [SHOIS•lihk] *adj*
horrid
**Scheuerlappen**
[SHOI•air•LAH•pen] *n* M
swab
**Scheune** [SHO•neh] *n* F barn
**Schi** [shee] *n* M ski
**Schicht** [shihkt] *n* F layer; ply
**schicken** [SHIH•khen] *vi* send
**Schicksal** [SHIHK•zahl] *n* N
destiny; doom; fate
**schicksalhaft** [-hahft] *adj*
fateful
**schieben** [SHEE•ben] *vt* shove
**Schiedsrichter**
[sheeds•rihk•tair] *n* M umpire
**schief 1** [sheef] *adj* oblique
**schief 2** [sheef] *adj* wry; ironic
**Schiefer** [SHEE•fair] *n* M slate;
schist
**schielen** [SHEE•len] *vi* squint
**Schienbein** [SHEEN•buyn] *n* N
tibia
**schießen** [SHEE•sen] *vt* shoot
**Schießen** *n* N shooting
**Schießer** [shee•sair] *n* M
shooter
**Schießgewehr**
[SHEEHS•ge•vair] *n* N
shotgun
**Schießpulver**
[SHEES•puh•vair] *n* N
gunpowder

**Schiff 1** [shihf] *n* N schedule
**Schiff 2** [shihf] *n* N vessel
**Schiffahrt** [shif•FAHRT] *n* F
cruise
**schiffen** [SHIH•fen] *vt* navigate
**Schiffer** [SHIH•fair] *n* M
skipper
**Schiffsschnabel**
[SHIHFS•shnah•bel] *n* M
prow
**Schild** [shild] *n* N sign
**Schildkröte** [SHILD•kruh•teh]
*n* F tortoise; turtle
**Schimmelpilz**
[SHIH•mehl•PIHLTS] *n* M
mold
**Schimmer** [SHI•mair] *n* M
gleam; glimmer
**Schimpanse**
[SHIM•PAHN•zeh] *n* M
chimpanzee
**Schinken** [SHIHNG•ken] *n* N
ham
**Schirm** [sheerm] *n* M umbrella
**Schirmdach** [SHEERM•dahk] *n*
N penthouse
**Schlacht** [shlahkt] *n* F battle
**schlachten** [SHLAHK•ten] *vt*
slaughter
**Schlachtschiff**
[SHLAHKT•shif] *n* N
battleship
**Schlachtvieh** [SHLAHKT•fee]
*n* N steer
**Schläf** [shlaif] *n* M sleep
**schlafen** [SHLAH•fen] *vi* sleep
**schlafend** [SHLAH•fent] *adj*
asleep; sleeping
**Schläfchen** [shehf•chen] *n* N
nap

schlaff [shlahf] *adj* slack; limp

schlaflos [-los] *adj* sleepless

Schläfrigkeit [SHLAI•frig•KUYT] *n* F sleepiness

Schlaflosigkeit [SHLAHF•lohs•ig•KUYT] *n* F insomnia

schläfrig [SHLAIF•rig] *adj* drowsy; sleepy

Schlafzimmer [shlahf•tsim•mair] *n* N bedroom

Schlag 1 [shlahg] *n* M hit; knock; pat

Schlag 2 [shlahg] *n* M welt

schlagen 1 [SHLAH•gen] *vt* punch

schlagen 2 [SHLAH•gen] *vt* strike

Schlagen [SHLAH•gen] *n* N beating

Schläger [SHLAI•gair] *n* M racket

Schlaglicht [SHLAHG•lihkt] *n* N highlight

Schlagloch [SHLAHG•lohk] *n* N pothole

Schlagteig [SHLAHG•taig] *n* M batter (baking)

Schlagwort [SHLAHG•vort] *n* N slogan

Schlagzeile [SHLAHG•tsai•le] *n* F headline

Schlamm [shlahm] *n* M mud; silt

schlammig [SHLAHM•mig] *adj* muddy

Schlampe [SHLAHM•peh] *n* F slattern; slut

Schlamperei [SHLAHM•pair•ai] *n* F pigsty

schlampig [SHLAHM•pig] *adj* grubby

Schlange [SHLAHNG•eh] *n* F serpent

schlank [shlahnk] *adj* slim

schlau [shlou] *adj* cunning; shrewd

Schlauch [shlouhk] *n* M hose

schlecht [shlehkt] *adj* bad; badly

schlecht bezahlen [shlehkt BEH•tsahl•en] underpay

schlechte Laune [SHLEHK•te LOU•ne] *n* F ill will

schlechter [SHLEHK•tair] *adj* worse

schlechtest schlimmst [-tehst] [shlihmst] *adj* worst

Schlegel [SHAI•gel] *n* M mallet

schleichen [SHLUY•khen] *vi* creep; slink

Schleier [SHLUY•air] *n* M veil

Schleife [SHLAI•feh] *n* F bow (knot); bow tie

Schleim 1 [shluym] *n* M mucous

Schleim 2 [shluym] *n* M slime

schlendern [SHLEN•dairn] *vi* stroll

schleppen [SHLEH•pen] *vi* drag; haul

Schleppen [SHLEH•pen] *n* v N tow; towing

Schleuder [SHLOI•dair] *n* F sling

schlicht [shlihkt] *adj* homely

schließen [SHLEE•sen] *vt* interlock

schließlich [SHLEES•lihk] *adj* eventual

**schließen 1** [SHLEE•sen] *vt*
shut

**schließen 2** [SHLEE•sen] *vt vi*
conclude

**schließlich** [SHLEES•lihk] *adj*
ultimately

**Schlinge** [SHLIHNG•ge] *n* F
loop; noose

**schlitten** [SHLIH•ten] *n* M
sleigh

**Schlittenfahren**
[SHLIH•ten•FAH•ren] *n* N
sledding

**schlittern** [SHLIH•tairn] *vi*
slither

**Schlittschuh** [SHLIHT•shoo•
lou•fen] *n* n ice-skate

**Schlittschuh Rollschuh**
[ROHL•schoo] *n* M
rollerskate

**Schlittschuhlaufen**
[SHLIHT•shoo•LOU•fen] *n* N
ice skating

**Schloß 1** [shlohs] *n* N manor;
palace

**Schloß 2** [shlohs] *n* N lock

**Schlucht** [shluhkt] *n* M ravine

**Schluck** [shluhk] *n* M gulp

**Schluckauf** [SHUHK•ouf] *n* M
hiccup

**schlucken** [SHLUHK•en] *vt*
swallow

**schlummern** [SHLOO•mairn]
*vi* doze

**schlurfen** [SHLOOR•fen] *vi*
shuffle

**Schluß** [shloos] *n* M ending

**Schlüssel** [SHLUH•sel] *n* M
key

**schmackhaft** [SHMAHK•hahft]
*adj* tasty; palatable

**schmacklos** [SHMAHK•los] *adj*
gaudy; tasteless

**schmähen** [SHMAI hen] *vt*
revile

**Schmähschrift**
[SHMAI•shrihft] *n* F lampoon

**Schmalz** [shmahlts] *n* N grease;
lard

**Schmarotzer**
[shmah•ROHTS•air] *n* M
parasite

**schmecken** [SHMEHK•en] *vi*
taste

**Schmeichelei** [-uy] *n* F flattery

**schmeichelhaft** [-hahft] *adj*
flattering

**schmeicheln** [SHMUY•keln] *vt*
coax; flatter

**Schmelzen** [SHMEHL•tsen] *n*
N fusion

**schmelzen** [SHMEHL•tsen] *vt*
melt; *vi* thaw

**Schmerz** [shmairts] *n* N ache;
pain

**schmerzend** [SMAIRTS•end]
*adj* painful

**schmerzlich** [SHMAIRTS•lihk]
*adj* grievous

**schmerzlos** [-los] *adj* painless

**Schmetterlinge**
[SHMEH•tair•LING•geh] *n* F
butterfly

**Schmiede 1** [SHMEE•deh] *n* M
blacksmith

**Schmiede 2** [SHMEE•de] *n* F
forge

**Schmiede, Schweißeisen**
[SHMEE•deh]
[SHVUYS•uy•zen] *n* N
wrought iron

**Schmiedehammer**
[SHMEE•deh•HAH•mair] *n* M
sledge

**schmieren** [SHMEER•en] *vt*
lubricate

**Schmiermittel**
[SHMEER•mi•tel] *n* N
lubricant

**Schminke** [SHMIHNK•eh] *n* F
make-up

**schmollen** [shmohl•len] *vi* pout

**Schmuck** [shmuhk] *n* M
decoration; ornament; trinket

**schmucken** [SHMUH•ken] *vt*
decorate; garnish

**Schmutz** [shmuhts] *n* M dirt;
filth; grime

**schmutzig** [shmuhts•ig] *adj*
dingy

**schmutzig** [SHMUHTS•gi] *adj*
dirty; filthy; squalid

**Schnabel** [SHNAH•bel] *n* M
beak

**schnauben** [SHNOU•ben] *vt*
snort

**Schnauze** [SHNOU•tseh] *n* F
nozzle; snout

**Schnee** [shnai] *n* M snow

**Schneeball** [-bal] *n* M snowball

**Schneefall** [fahl] *n* M snowfall

**Schneeflocken** [-FLOH•ken] *n*
N snowflake

**Schneepflug** [-pfluhg] *n* M
snowplow

**Schneeregen** [SHNAI•rai•gen]
*n* M sleet

**Schneesturm** [shnai•shtoorm] *n*
M blizzard

**Schneewehe** [-vai•he] *n* F
snowdrift

**shneiden** [SHNUY•den] *vt* cut

**Schneider** [SHNUY•dair] *n* M
tailor

**schnell** [shnel] *adj* fast; quick;
*adv* quickly; rapidly

**schnell hinschreiben** [shnel
hin•SHRUY•ben] *vt* jot

**Schnitt 1** [shniht] *n* M section

**Schnitt 2** [shniht] *n* M cut

**Schnittlauch** [SHNIT•loukh] *n*
M chive

**Schnitzel** [SHNI•tsel] *n* cutlet

**Schnitzer** [SHNIT•sair] *n* M
solecism

**Schnuppe** [SHNUH•peh] *n* F
snuff

**schnuppern** [SHNUH•pairn] *vi*
snuffle

**Schnur** [shnoor] *n* F cord; string

**Schnurrbart** [SHNOOR•bahrt]
*n* M moustache

**schnurren** [SHNOOR•en] *vt*
purr

**Schnürsenkel**
[SHNOOR•zehnk•el] *n* M
shoelace

**Schober** [SHOH•bair] *n* M
stack

**schön** [shoon] *adj* beautiful;
fine; glamourous

**Schönheit** [SHOON•hait] *n* F
beauty

**Schönheitsfehler**
[SHOON•haits•FAIL•air] *n* F
blemish

**Schönheitsmittel**
[SHOON•huyts•MIT•el] *n* N
cosmetic

**Schöpfer** [SHUHPF•air] *n* M
creator

**schöpferisch**
[SHUHPF•air•ISH] *adj*
creative

**Schokolade**
[SHO•koh•LAH•deh] *n* F
chocolate

**schon** [shohn] *adv* already;
anyway

**schön** *adj* beautiful; fine; nice;
well

**Schoner** [shoh•nair] *n* M
schooner

**schonungslos**
[shohn•oongs•LOS] *adj*
relentless

**Schopf** [shohpf] *n* M tuft

**Schornstein** [SHOHRN•shtain]
*n* M chimney

**Schoß** [shohs] *n* M lap

**Schotte** [SHOH•teh] *n* M Scot

**Schottenmütze**
[SHOHT•en•MUHT•seh] *n* F
tam-o'-shanter

**Schotter** [SHOH•tair] *n* M
rubble

**schottisches Plaid**
[SHOHT•ish•es plahd] *n* N
plaid

**Schottland** [-lahnt] *n* M
Scotland

**schräg** [shreg] *adj* diagonal

**Schräge** [SHRAI•geh] *n* F slant

**Schrank** [shrahnk] *n* M cabinet;
cupboard

**Schranke** [SHRAHNK•e] *n* F
limit

**Schraube** [SHRAU•beh] *n* F
bolt

**schrauben** [SHROU•ben] *vt*
screw

**Schraubenschlüssel**
[SHROU•ben•SHLUH•sel] *n*
F wrench (tool)

**Schraubenzieher** [-TSEE•air]
*n* M screwdriver

**Schraubstock**
[SHROUB•shtohk] *n* M vice
(tool)

**Schreck** [shrehk] *n* M dismay;
fright

**Schrecken** [SHREHK•en] *n* M
terror

**schrecklich** [SHREHK•lihk] *adj*
dire; horrible; terrible

**Schrei** [shruy] *n* M cry; hoot;
outcry

**schreiben** [SHRUY•ben] *vt*
write

**Schreiben** *n* N writing

**Schreiber** [SHRUY•bair] *n* M
scribe

**Schreiber** [-air] *n* M writer

**Schreibmaschine**
[SHRUYB•mah•SHEEN•eh] *n*
F typewriter

**Schreibtisch** [SHRUYB•tish] *n*
M desk

**Schreibwaren**
[SHRUYB•vahr•ren] *npl*
stationery

**schreien** [SHRUY•en] *vi*
scream

**schreiten** [SHRUY•ten] *vi*
stride

**schrekhaft** [SHREHK•hahft]
*adj* fearful

**Schrift** [shrihft] *n* F script

**Schriftrolle** [-ROH•leh] *n* F
scroll

**Schriftsteller**
[SHRIHFT•shtehl•air] *n* M
novelist

**Schriftsteller-in**
[SHRIFT•shtel•lair] [ -in] *n* M
author

**schrill** [shril] *adj* shrill

**schriller Schrei** [SHRIHL•air shruy] *n* M shriek

**Schritt** [shriht] *n* M pace

**schroff** [shrohf] *adj* gruff; abrupt

**schrubben** [SHRUH•ben] *vt* scour; scrub

**Schrubber** [SHRUH•bair] *n* M mop

**schrumpeln** [SHRUHMP•eln] *vt* shrivel

**Schubkarren** [SHUHB•kahr•ren] *n* M wheelbarrow

**Schublade** [shoob•LAH•de] *n* F drawer

**schüchtern** [SHOOK•tairn] *adj* coy; timid

**Schuft** [shuhft] *n* M wretch

**Schuh** [shoo] *n* M shoe

**Schuhmacher** [-MAH•khair] *n* M shoemaker

**Schuld 1** [shoold] *n* F debt; liability

**Schuld 2** [shoold] *n* F guilt; fault; demerit

**schulden** [SHUHL•den] *vt* owe

**schuldig 1** [SHUHL•dig] *adj* guilty

**schuldig 2** [shuhl•dig] *adj* respect (with gehen)

**Schuldige -r** [SHOOLD•ig•e -air] *n* F culprit

**Schuldlosigkeit** [SHOOLD•los•ig•KUYT] *n* F innocence

**Schule** [SHOO•leh] *n* F school

**Schüler** [SHOO•lair] *n* M pupil; schoolboy

**Schulgeld** [SHOO•geld] *n* N tuition

**Schulleiter** [-LUY•tair] *n* M schoolmaster

**Schulter** [SHOOL•tair] *n* M shoulder

**Schulung** [SHOO•loong] *n* F discipline; training

**Schuppen 1** [SHUP•pen] *n* M hovel

**Schuppen 2** [SHOOP•en] *npl* dandruff

**schüren** [SHUHR•en] *vt* stoke

**Schurke** [SHOOR•keh] *n* M villain; scoundrel; rascal

**Schurkerei** [SHOOR•kair•uy] *n* F villainy

**schurkisch** [SHOOR•kish] *adj* villainous

**Schürze** [SHOOR•tseh] *n* F bib

**Schuß** [shuhsh] *n* M gunshot; shot

**Schußgarn** [SHUHS•garn] *n* N woof (weaving)

**Schüssel** [SHUH•sel] *n* F dish

**Schutz** [shuhts] *n* M custody; protection

**Schutzblech** [SHOOTS•blehk] *n* N fender

**schützen** [SHUH•tsen] *vt* protect

**Schutzmarke** [SHUTS•mahr•keh] *n* F trademark

**schwach** [shvahk] *adj* weak; faint

**Schwachsinniger** [SHVAHK•ZIN•ig•air] *n* M moron

**schwächen** [SHVEHK•en] *vt* weaken

schwächlich [shvehk•lihk] *adj*
weakly

Schwaden [SHVAH•den] *n* M
swathe

Schwager [SHVAH•gair] *n* M
brother-in-law

Schwägerin [SHVAI•gair•in] *n*
F sister-in-law

Schwalbe [SHVAHL•beh] *n* F
swallow

Schwamm 1 [shvahm] *n* M
sponge

Schwamm 2 [shvahm] *n* M
fungus

Schwammtaucher
[-TOU•khair] *n* M sponger

Schwan [shvahn] *n* M swan

schwanger *adj* pregnant

Schwangershaft
[SHVAHNG•air•shahft] *n* F
pregnancy

Schwank [shvahnk] *n* M farce

schwanken [SHVAHN•ken] *vi*
falter; fluctuate; sway

Schwanz [shvahnts] *n* M tail

schwänzen [SHVENT•tsen] *vt*
skip; cut; play hooky

Schwarm [shvahrm] *n* M
swarm

schwarz [shvahrts] *adj* black

schwärzen [SHVAIR•tsehn] *vt*
blacken

Schwarzer [SHVAHRTS• air] *n*
M black man

schwärzlich [SHVAIRTS•lihk]
*adj* swarthy

Schwarzmarkt
[SHVAHRTS•mahr•kt] *n* M
black market

Schwebe [SHVAI•beh] *n* F
poise

schweben [SHVAI•ben] *vi*
hover

Schwede; Schwedin
[shvai•deh] [in] *n* M Swede

Schweden [SHVAI•den] *n*
Sweden

schwedisch [-ish] *adj* Swedish

Schweifsäge [SHVAIF•seh•ge]
*n* F jigsaw (puzzle)

Schweigen [SHVAI•gen] *n* N
silence

schweigsam [SHVAIG•zahm]
*adj* slient; taciturn; *adv*
silently

Schwein [shvain] *n* N pig; hog

Schweinefett [SHVAIN•eh•fet]
*n* N lard

Schweinefleisch
[SHVAIN•eh•fluysh] *n* N pork

Schweinestall
[SHVAIN•eh•shtahl] *n* M sty

Schweiz [shvaits] *n* F
Switzerland

Schweizer in [SHVAITS•air]
[in] *n* M Swiss

Schwelle [SHVEH•leh] *n* F
threshold

Schwellen *n* N swelling

Schwengel [SHVENG•el] *n* M
crank

Schwenkung
[SHVAINK•oong] *n* F facing

schwer [shvair] *adj* heavy; *adv*
heavily

schwierig [SHVEER•ig] *adj*
difficult

schwerfällig [SHVAIR•fel•ig]
*adj* unwieldy

Schwerkraft [SHVAIR•krahft]
*n* F gravity

Schwert [shvairt] *n* N sword

**schwerwiegend**
[SHVAIR•WEE•gend] *adj*
weighty

**Schwester** [SHVEH•stair] *n* F
sister

**schwieger** [SHVEE•gair]
in-laws

**Schwiegermutter**
[SHVEE•gair -] *n* F
mother-in-law

**Schwiegersohn** [SHVEE•
gair -] *n* M son-in-law

**Schwiegertochter**
[SHVEE•giar•TOHK•tair] *n* F
daughter-in-law

**Schwiegervater** [SHVEE•
gair -] *n* M father-in-law

**schwierig** [SHVEER•ig] *adj*
trying

**Schwierigkeit**
[SHVEER•ig•kuyt] *n* F
difficulty

**Schwimmbad** [SHVIM•bahd] *n*
N pool; swimming pool

**Schwimmbrille**
[SHVIM•BRIL•le] *n* F
goggles

**schwimmen** [SHVIH•men] *vi*
swim

**Schwimmen** *n* N swimming

**Schwimmer** [-air] *n* M
swimmer

**Schwimmweste**
[SHVIHM•vehst•eh] *n* F life
jacket

**Schwindel** [SHVIHN•del] *n* N
swindle

**schwindelend** [SHVIN•delnd]
*adj* dizzy

**Schwindelgefühl**
[SHVIN•del•GEH•fuhl] *n* N
vertigo

**schwinden** [SHVIN•den] *vi*
dwindle; swoon

**schwindlig** [SHVIND•lig] *adj*
giddy

**schwingen** [SHVING•en] *vi*
oscillate

**schwingen** [SCHVING•en] *vi*
swing

**Schwirren** [SHVEER•en] *n* N
twang

**schwirren** [SHVEER•en] *vi*
whir; zip

**Schwitzen** [SHVITS•en] *n* N
perspiration

**schwitzen** *vt* perspire; *vi* sweat

**schwören** [SHVUHR•en] *vi*
swear

**Schwung** [shvuhng] *n* M vim

**Schwur** [shvoor] *n* M vow

**sechs** [zehks] *num* six

**Sechseck** [ZEHKS•ehk] *n* N
hexagon

**sechste** [-teh] *num* sixth

**sechszehn** [-tsain] *num* sixteen

**sechszehnte** [-teh] *num*
sixteenth

**sechzig** [ZEHKS•ig] *num* sixty

**sechzigst** [ZEHK•sikst] *adj*
sixtieth

**See 1** [zeh] *n* M lake

**see 2** [zeeh] *adj* naval

**See 3** [zee] *n* F sea

**Seefahrer** [ZEE•FAHR•air] *n*
M navigator

**Seehund** [ZEE•huhnt] *n* M seal

**seekrank** [ZEE•krahnk] *adj*
seasick

**Seele** [ZEE•leh] *n* F soul

**Seeräuber** [ZEE•ROI•bair] *n* M
pirate

**Seesack** [ZEH•zahk] *n* M kit

**Segel** *n* N sailboat

**Segeljacht** [ZAI•gel•YAHKT] *n* F yacht

**segeln** [ZAI•geln] *vi* sail; sailing

**Segeltuch** [ZAI•gel•TOOKH] *n* N canvas

**segnen** [SAIG•nen] *vt* bless

**Segnung** [ZAIYG•noong] *n* F benediction

**Segnung** [SAIG•noong] *n* F blessing

**sehen** [ZAI•ehn] *vi* see

**Seher** [ZAI•hair] *n* M seer

**Sehkraft** [ZEH•krahft] *n* F eyesight; vision

**Sehne** [ZAIN•eh] *n* F tendon

**Sehnsucht** [ZAIN•zoohkt] *n* F nostalgia

**Sehnsucht** [ZAIN•zoohkt] *n* F yearning

**sehnsüchtig** [ZAIN•zuhk•TIG] *adj* wistful

**sehr** [sair] *adv* very

**Sehschlitz** [ZEE•shlihts] *n* M loophole

**Seide** [ZUY•deh] *n* F silk

**seiden** [ZUY•den] *vt* silken

**Seidenpapier** [ZUY•den•pah•peer] *n* N tissue paper

**Seidespunkt** [ZAI•des•POONKT] *n* M boiling point

**Seife** [zuy•feh] *n* F soap

**Seifenblase** [ZAI•fehn•BLAH•zeh] *n* F bubble

**Seifenschaum** [ZAI•fen•SHOUM] *n* M lather

**Seifenwasser** [ZUY•fen•VAH•sair] *n* N suds

**Seil** [zuyl] *n* N rope

**Seilrolle** [SUYL•ROL•le] *n* F pulley

**sein 1** [zain] *aux v* be

**sein 2** [zuyn] his

**sein, ihr, dessen, deren** [-deh•sen] [-dair•en] its

**seitdem** [TSAIT•daim] *adv* since

**Seite 1** [SAI•te] *n* F facet; side

**Seite 2** [SAI•teh] *n* F page

**Seitenblick** [ZAI•ten•BLIHK] *n* M leer

**Seitenschiff** [SAIT•ehn•SHIF] *n* N aisle

**seitlich** [SAIT•lihk] *adj* sideways

**seitwärts wenden** [SAIT•vairts•VEN•den] *vi* swerve

**Sekretärin** [SEK•reh•TAIR•in] *n* F secretary

**Sekretion** [SEH•kreht•TSEE•on] *n* F secretion

**Sekt** [sehkt] *n* M champagne

**sektiererisch** [SEHK•teer•AIR•ish] *adj* sectarian

**Sektor** [SEHK•tor] *n* M sector

**sekundär** [SEH•kuhn•DAIR] *adj* secondary

**Selbst** [zelpst] *n* N self

**Selbstachtung** [-AHK•toong] *n* F self-respect

**selbständig** [ZELPS•SHTEN•dig] *adj* distinct

**Selbstbedingung**
[ZELBST•beh•DING•oong] *n*
F cafeteria

**selbstbeherrscht**
[-beh•HAIRSHT] *adj*
self-control

**Selbstbiographie**
[ZELBST•bee•oh•gahf•FEE] *n*
F autobiography

**selbstgemacht**
[ZELPST•ge•mahkt] *adj*
homemade

**Selbstmord** [ZELPST•mohrd] *n*
M suicide

**selbstsicher** [ZELBST•zikh•air]
*adj* confident

**Selbstsucht** [-zoohkt] *n* F
selfishness

**selbstsüchtig** [-ZUHK•tig] *adj*
selfish

**Selbstverteidigung**
[-VAIR•TUY•dig•oong] *n* F
self-defense

**selbstvertrauerisch**
[ZELPST•fair•TROU•air•ish]
*adj* self-confident

**selten** [SEL•ten] *adv* seldom

**Seltenheit** [SEL•ten•huyt] *n* F
rarity

**seltsam** [ZELT•zahm] *adj*
queer; odd

**Seltsamkeit**
[ZELT•zahm•KUYT] *n* F
oddity

**Semmel** [ZEH•mehl] *n* F muffin

**Senat** [SEH•naht] *n* M senate

**Senator** [SEHN•ah•tor] *n* M
senator

**Sendschreiben**
[ZEND•shruy•ben] *n* N letter;
epistle

**Sendung** [ZEN•doong] *n* F
commercial

**Senf** [zehnf] *n* M mustard

**senil** [SEHN•eel] *adj* senile

**Senilität** [-ih•tait] *n* F senility

**senkrecht** [ZEHNK•rehkt] *adj*
vertical; perpendicular

**Senkrechte** [ZEHNK•rehkt•eh]
*n* F (math) vertical;
perpendicular

**Sense** [ZEHN•zeh] *n* F scythe

**sensibel** [sen•SEE•bel] *adj*
sensitive

**Sensibilität**
[SENS•ih•bil•ih•TAIT] *n* F
sensibility

**Separatismus**
[SEP•ahr•ah•TIS•moos] *n* M
separatism

**September** [ZEP•tem•BAIR] *n*
September

**septisch** [SEP•tish] *adj* septic

**Serie** [SAIR•ee•EH] *n* F series

**Serum** [SAIR•oom] *n* N serum

**Service** [SAIR•vees] *n* N setting

**Servierbrett** [SAIR•veer•bret] *n*
N tray

**Servierplatte** [SAIR•veer] *n* F
platter

**Serviette** [SER•vee•eh•TEH] *n*
F napkin

**Seuche** [ZOI•khe] *n* F
epidemic; plague

**seufzen** [ZOIF•sen] *vi* sigh

**sexuell** [ZEHKS•oo•EL] *adj*
sexual

**shnappen** [SHNAH•pen] *vt*
snatch; nab

**Sibylle** [SIH•bil] *n* F sibyl

**sich** [zihk] herself; himself

**sich abmühen** [zihk AP•muh•ehn] *vi* toil

**sich ansiedeln** [zihk AHN•zee•deln] *vi* settle

**sich anvertrauen** [zikh AHN•fair•trou•en] *vi* confide

**sich anwerben lassen** [zikh AHN•vair•ben lah•sen] *vt* enlist

**sich beeilen** [zihk be•UY•len] *vt* hasten

**sich bemächtigen** [zihk beh•mehk•tig•en] *vt* usurp

**sich bemühen** [zihk beh•MUH•en] *vi* strive

**sich benehmen** [zik beh•NAIM•en] *vi* behave

**sich bewerben um auflegen** [zik•beh•VAIR•ben•oom] [OWF•lai•gen] *vt* apply

**sich drehen** [zihk DRAI•hen] *vi* revolve

**sich ducken** [zihk DOOK•en] *vi* cringe

**sich einlassen auf** [zihk UYN•lah•sen ouf] indulge

**sich einmischen** [zihk uyn•MIH•shen] *vi* interfere

**sich einmischen** [zihk uyn•MIH•shen] *vi* meddle

**sich ekeln** [zihk AI•keln] *vt* nauseate

**sich enthalten** [zik ent•HAULT•uhn] *vt* abstain

**sich entkleiden** [zihk ent•KLUY•den] *vi vt* undress

**sich entscheiden** [zihk ent•SHUY•den] *vt* decide

**sich entschuldigen** [zik ent•SHOOLD•IG•en] *vi* apologize

**sich erbrechen** [zihk AIR•brehk•en] *vi* spew

**sich erheben** [zihk AIR•hai•ben] *vi* rise

**sich erholen** [zihk air•HOH•len] *vi* recuperate

**sich erinnern** [zihk air•IN•nairn] *vi* recollect

**sich erinnern an** [zihk air•IN•airn ahn] *vi* remember

**sich freuen** [zihk FROI•en] *vi* rejoice

**sich fürchten** [zik FOOR•k•ten] *vt* afraid (to be)

**sich gewöhnen** [zik guh•VUHN•uhn] *vt* accustom

**sich hüten vor** [zik HOO•ten for] *vi* beware (of)

**sich in Positur setzen** [zihk in POH•zih•TOOR ZEHT•tsen] *v* pose

**sich in Verbindung setzen** [zikh in fair•BIN•doong ZET•tsen] *vt* contact

**sich irren** [zihk •EER•en] *vi* err

**sich krümmen** [zihk KRUH•men] *vi* squirm

**sich krümmen** [zihk KRUH•men] *vi* writhe

**sich kümmern um** [zihk KUH•mairn oom] *vi* worry

**sich lehnen** [zihk LAI•nen] *vi* recline

**sich leisten** [zik LAIST•en] *vt* afford

**sich nähern** [zik NAI•hairn] *vt* approach

**sich paaren** [zihk PAH•ren] *vt* breed (animals)

**sich rühmen** [zik ROO•men] *vi* boast

**sich rühmen** [zihk RUH•men]
*vt vi* vaunt

**sich schlecht benehmen** [zihk
schlehkt beh•NAI•men] *vi*
misbehave

**sich sehnen** [zihk ZAI•nen] *vi*
yearn

**sich sehnen nach** [zihk
ZAI•nen nahk] *vi* crave

**sich selbst** [zihk ZELPST] *pron*
oneself

**sich (selbts)** [zihk ZEHLBST]
itself

**sich senken** [zihk ZEHNK•en]
*vi* sag

**sich senken** [zihk ZENK•en] *vi*
subside

**sich sorgen um** [zikh
ZOHR•gehn •oom] *vi* care
(about)

**sich spezialisieren** [zihk
SHPETS•ee•ahl•ih•SEER•en]
*vi* specialize

**sich trennen** [zihk TREN•nen]
*vt* secede

**sich ungeschikt anstellen**
[zihk UHN•ge•SHIHKT
AHN•shtel•en] *vt* fumble

**sich unterhalten sprechen**
[zikh OON•tair•HAL•ten]
[shprek•en] *vi* converse

**sich unterscheiden** [zihk
OON•tair•SHUY•den] *vi*
differ

**sich verabreden**
[zik•vair•AP•RAI•den] *vt* to
have an appointment
w/someone

**sich vergegenwärtigen** [zihk
vair•GAI•gen•VAIR•TIG•en]
*vt* visualize

**sich verlassen** [zihk
fair•LAH•sen] *vi* rely

**sich verlaufen** [zihk
fair•LOU•fen] *vi* stray

**sich vermischen** [zihk
vair•MIH•shen] *vi* mingle

**sich verschlectern** [zihk
fair•SHLEHK•tairn] *vi*
deteriorate

**sich verstellen** [zihk
fair•SHTEL•len] *vi* dissemble

**sich vollsaugen** [zihk
fol•SOU•gen] *vi* soak

**sich vorstellen** [zihk
for•shtel•len] *vt* introduce

**sich vorstellen** [zihk
for•SHTEL•en] *vt* imagine

**sich wälzen** [zihk VAIL•tsen]
*vi* wallow

**sich wehren** [zihk•VAIR•en] *vi*
fend

**sich weiden an** [zihk VAI•den
ahn] *vi* gloat

**sich zanken** [zihk
TSAHNK•en] *vi* wrangle

**Sichel** [SEE•khel] *n* F sickle

**sicher** [ZIH•kair] *adj* safe

**sicher** *adv* safely

**Sicherheit 1** [ZIKH•air•huyt] *n*
F certainty; safety; security

**Sicherheit 2** [ZIKH•air•huyt] *n*
F collateral

**Sicherheitsnadel** [-NAH•del] *n*
F safety pin

**sicherlich** [zikh•air•likh] *adv*
certainly

**sichern** [ZIHK•airn] *vt* secure

**Sicht** [zihkt] *n* F sight

**sichtbar** [ZIHKT•bahr] *adj*
visible

**Sichtbarkeit**
[ZIHKT•bahr•KUYT] *n* F
visibility

**sie ihnen** [zee] [ee•nen] them

**sie selbst** [zee zelbst] *prn*
themselves

**Sieb** [seeb] *n* N sieve

**sieben** [ZEE•ben] *num* seven

**siebte** [ZEEB•teh] *num* seventh

**siebzehn** [ZEEB•tsain] *num*
seventeen

**siebzehnte** [-teh] *num*
seventeenth

**siebzig** [ZEEB•tsig] *num*
seventy

**siebzigste** [-steh] *num*
seventieth

**sieden** [ZEE•den] *vt* seethe

**Sieg** [seeg] *n* M triumph;
victory

**Siegel** [SEE•gel] *n* N signet

**Sieger** [ZEE•gair] *n* M
champion

**Sieger in** [ZEE•gair] [in] *n* M
victor

**siegreich** [ZEEG•ruyhk] *adj*
victorious; winning

**Signal** [sig•NAHL] *n* N signal

**Signalhorn** [zig•NAHL•horn] *n*
N bugle

**Silbe** [SIHL•beh] *n* F syllable

**Silber** [ZIL•bair] *n* N silver

**Silberschmied** [-SHMEED] *n*
M silversmith

**simpel** [SIM•pel] *adj* rustic

**Sinfonie** [SIN•fohn•EE] *n* F
symphony

**singen** [zingen] *vi* sing

**Singvogel** [ZING•fo•gel] *n* M
song-bird

**sinken** [zinken] *vi* M sink

**Sinn1** [zihn] *n* M mind

**Sinn2** [zihn] *n* M sense

**sinnlos** [ZIN•los] *adj* fatuous

**Sinus** [SEE•noos] *n* M sinus

**Sirene** [see•RAI•neh] *n* F siren

**Sirup** [SEER•uhp] *n* M syrup

**Sittenlosigkeit**
[ZIT•ten•LOS•ig•KUYT] *n* F
immorality

**Sittich** [SIH•tihk] *n* M parakeet

**Sitz** [zits] *n* M seat

**sitzen** [ZITS•en] *vi* sit

**Sitzen** [ZITS•en] *n* N seating

**sitzen lassen** [ZIHT•tsen
lah•sen] *vt* jilt

**sitzend** [ZITS•end] *adj*
sedentary

**Sitzender** [ZITS•end•AIR] *n* M
sitter

**Sitzstange** [ZITS•shtahng•eh] *n*
F perch

**Sitzung** [ZITS•oong] *n* F
session

**Skandal** [SKAHN•dahl] *n* N
cover-up

**Skelett** [SKEHL•et] *n* N
skeleton

**skeptisch** [SKEHP•tish] *adj*
incredulous; skeptical

**Skizze** [SKIH•tse] *n* F outline;
sketch

**Sklave** [SKLAH•veh] *n* M slave

**Sklaverei** [SKLAV•air•uyy] *n* F
bondage

**sklavisch** [SKLAH•vish] *adj*
servile; slavish

**Skorpion** [SKOR•pee•on] *n* M
scorpion

**Skrupel** [SKROO•pel] *n* M
scruple

**Skulptur** [SKUHLP•toor] *n* F
sculpture

**Smaragd** [zmahr•AKT] *n* M
emerald

**Smoking** [SMOH•keeng] *n* M
tuxedo

**so** [soh] M so

**so** [so] thus

**Socke** [ZOHK•eh] *n* F sock

**Soda** *n* F soda

**Sodawasser**
[SO•dah•VAH•sair] *n* N soda
water; fizz

**Sofa** [SOH•fah] *n* N couch; sofa

**sofort** [so•FOHRT] *adv*
immediately; promptly

**sofortig** [so•FORT•ig] *adj*
prompt

**sogleich** [so•GLUYHK] *adv*
readily

**Sohle** [SOH•leh] *n* F sole

**Sohn** [zohn] *n* M son

**solch** [zolhk] *adv* such

**Soldat** [SOHL•daht] *n* M
soldier

**Solidarität**
[SOL•id•DAHR•ih•TAIT] *n* F
solidarity

**sollen** [ZOHL•len] *modal aux*
should; *aux v* ought

**Sommerhaus**
[ZOH•mair•HOUS] *n* N
cottage

**Sonate** [soh•NAH•teh] *n* F
sonata

**sonderbar** [ZOHN•dair•bahr]
*adj* odd

**Sonett** [SOHN•et] *n* N sonnet

**sonnen** [SON•nen] *adj* solar

**Sonnenbräunung**
[ZON•en•BROIN•oong] *n* F
tan

**Sonnenschirm**
[ZOHN•en•SHEERM] *n* M
parasol

**Sonnenwende**
[ZOHN•en•VEN•deh] *n* F
solstice

**Sonntag** [ZOHN•tahg] *n* M
Sunday; Sabbath

**sonst** [zohnst] *adv* else;
otherwise

**Sopran** [SOH•prahn] *n* M
soprano; treble voice

**sorgen für das Essen**
[ZOHR•gehn fuyr dahs
EHS•sehn] *vt* cater (banquet
etc)

**sorgenfrei** [ZOR•gehn•fruy] *adj*
carefree

**sorgfältig** [ZORG•faiyl•tig] *adj*
careful; thorough; painstaking

**Sorglosigkeit**
[ZORG•los•ig•KUYT] *n* F
recklessness

**Sorte** [ [SOHR•teh] *n* F brand

**Sortiment** [SOR•tee•ment] *n* N
set

**Souverän** [SUH•vair•EHN] *n*
M sovereign

**Sovjet** [SOHV•yet] Soviet

**Sozialismus**
[SOH•tsee•al•IS•moos] *n* M
socialism

**Sozialist** *n* M socialist

**Soziologie**
[SOH•tsee•ol•oo•GEE] *n* F
sociology

**spärlich** [SHPAIR•lihk] *adj*
sparse

**spät** [shpait] *adj* late; tardy

**Spalte** [SHPAHL•te] *n* F
crevice; fissure

**Spaltung 1** [SHPAHL•toong] *n* F splitting

**Spaltung 2** [SHPAHL•toong] *n* F cleavage

**Spange** [SHPAH•ngeh] *n* F brooch; buckle

**Spanier in** [SHPAH•ee•air] [in] *n* M Spaniard

**Spanisch** [SHPAHN•ish] *n* Spanish

**spanisch** [SPAHN•ish] Hispanic

**Spanne** [SHPAHN•neh] *n* F span

**Spannung 1** [SHPAHN•oong] *n* F suspense; tension

**Spannung 2** [SHPAH•noong] *n* F voltage

**Spargelk** [SHPAHR•gel] *n* F asparagus

**sparren** [shpahr•ren] *vi* spar

**sparsam** [SHPAHR•zam] *adj* frugal

**Sparsamkeit** [SHPAHR•zahm•KUYT] *n* F thrift

**Spaß** [shpahs] *n* M fun; jest

**spaßen** [SHPAH•sen] *vi* frolic

**Spaten** [SHPAH•ten] *n* M spade

**spazieren** [shpah•TSEER•en] *vi* walk

**Spaziergang** [SHPAH•tseer•gahng] *n* M promenade

**Speck** [shpek] *n* M bacon

**Speer** [shpeer] *n* M lance; spear

**Speiche** [SHPUY•khe] *n* F spoke

**Speicher** [SHPUY•khair] *n* M loft

**Speisekarte** [SHPUY•zeh•KAHR•teh] *n* F menu

**speisen** [SHPUY•sen] *vi* dine

**Speiseröhre** [SHPUY•ze•RUH•re] *n* F gullet

**Speiseschrank** [SHPUY•zeh•shrahnk] *n* M pantry

**Spektrum** [SHPEHK•troom] *n* N spectrum

**spekulativ** [SHPEHK•yoo•lah•TEEV] *adj* speculative

**spenden** [SHPEHN•den] *vt* dispense

**Spender** [SHPEHN•dair] *n* M dispenser

**Sperling** [SHPAIR•ling] *n* M sparrow

**Sperre** [SHPAIR•reh] *n* F barrier

**Sperrstunde** [SHPAIR•shtoon•de] *n* F curfew

**spezifisch** [shpe•TSIHF•ish] *adj* specific

**Sphäre** [SFAIR•eh] *n* F sphere

**Spiegel** [shpee•gel] *n* M mirror

**Spiegelung** [SHPEE•gel•OONG] *n* F reflection

**Spiel** [shpeel] *n* N game

**spielen** [SHPEEL•en] *vt* play

**Spieler** [SHPEE•lair] *n* M player

**Spielergebnis** [SHPEEL•air•GAIB•nis] *n* N score

**spielerisch** [-air•ish] *adj* playful

**Spielzeug** [SHPEEL•tsoig] *n* N
toy; plaything

**Spinat** [shpih•NAHT] *n* spinach

**Spinne** [SHPIN•neh] *n* F spider

**spinnen** [SHPIN•nen] *vt* spin

**Spinner** [SHPIHN•air] *n* M
spinner

**Spinngewebe**
[SHPIN•ge•WAI•beh] *n* N
cobweb

**Spinnrad** [SPHIN•rahd] *n* N
spinning wheel

**Spion** [SHPEE•on] *n* M spy

**Spionage** [SHPEE•on•ajz] *n* F
espionage

**spionieren**
[SHPEE•on•EER•en] *vi* spy

**Spirale** [shpee•RAHL•eh] *n* F
spire

**spitze** [SPHITS•eh] *adj* colossal

**Spitze 1** [SPHITS•eh] *n* F lace

**Spitze 2** [SPHIHT•seh] *n* F
peak; pinnacle; tip

**spitzig** [SPHITS•ig] *adj* pointed

**Spitzmaus** [SHPITS•mous] *n* F
shrew

**Spitzname** [SHPITS•nah•meh]
*n* M nickname

**splissen** [SPLIH•sen] *vt* splice

**Splitter** [SHPLIT•tair] *n* M
chip; sliver; splint; splinter

**spontan** [SPHON•tahn] *adj*
spontaneous

**Sporn** [shporn] *n* M spur

**Sport** [shport] *n* M sport

**Sport lehren** [shpohrt laiyr•en]
*vt* coach (sports)

**Sportler** [SHPORT•lair] *n* M
sportsman

**Spott** [shpoht] *n* M mockery;
ridicule

**spotten** [SHPOH•ten] *vi* flout;
jeer

**Sprache** [SHPRAH•khe] *n* F
language; parlance

**Sprachwissenschaft**
[SHPRAHK•VIH•sen•shahft]
*n* F linguistics

**sprechen** [SHPREHK•en] *vi*
speak

**Sprechender**
[SHPREHK•en•dair] *n* M
talker

**Sprecher** *n* M speaker

**sprenkeln** [SPHRENK•eln] *vt*
sprinkle

**Sprichwort** [SHPRIHK•vort] *n*
N proverb

**springen** [SHPRING•gehn] *vi*
*vt* bounce; leap

**Spritz** [shprihts] *n* M hairspray

**Spritzbrett** [SHPRITS•bret] *n*
M dashboard

**Spritze** [SHPRITS•eh] *n* F
syringe

**spritzen 1** [SHPRITS•en] *vi*
spray; squirt

**spritzen 2** [SHPRITS•en] *vt* spit

**Sproß** [shprohs] *n* M sprout

**Sprühregen** [SHPRUH•rai•gen]
*n* M drizzle

**Sprung** [shproong] *n* M jump;
bounce

**spucken** [SHPUHK•en] *vi* spit

**spuken** [SHPOO•keñ] *vi* spook

**Spule** [SHPOO•leh] *n* F spool

**spülen** [SHPOOL•en] *vt* flush

**Spülstein** [SHPUHL•shtuyn] *n*
M kitchen sink; sink =

**Spur** [shpoor] *n* F vestige

**Spur, Gleisa** [shpoor] [gluys] *n*
F track (train)

**Spur, nachspüren** [shpoor]
[NAHK•shpoor•en] *n* F *v*
trace

**Spürhund1** [SHPOOR•hoont] *n*
M beagle

**Spürhund2** [SHPOOR•huhnt] *n*
M sleuth

**Staat** [shtaht] *n* M state

**Staatsgeschirr**
[SHTAHTS•geh•SHEER] *n* N
trappings

**Staatsgut** [SHTAHTS•goot] *n*
N domain

**Staatsmann** {-mahn] *n* M
statesman

**Staatszimmer** [-tsim•mair] *n* N
stateroom

**Stab 1** [shtahb] *n* M baton

**Stab 2** [shtahb] *n* M slat

**stabil** [shtah•BEEL] *adj* stable;
sturdy; *adv* steadily

**stabilisieren**
[SHTAH•bih•lih•seer•en] *vt*
stabilize

**Stabilität**
[SHTAH•bil•ih•TAIT] *n* F
stability

**Stachelschwein**
[SHTAH•khel•shvain] *n* N
porcupine

**Stadion** [shtah•DEE•ohn] *n* N
stadium

**Stadt** [shtahdt] *n* F borough;
city; town

**städtisch** [SHTEHT•ish] *adj*
civic; urban; municipal

**stämmig** [SHTEM•ig] *adj*
stocky

**ständig** [SHTEN•dig] *adj*
constant; permanent

**stärken** [SHTAIR•ken] *vt*
fortify; *vi* strengthen

**Stärkungsmittel**
[SHTAIR•koongs•MIH•tel] *n*
N tonic

**Staffellauf** [SHTAH•fel•louf] *n*
M relay

**Stahl** [shtahl] *n* M steel

**Stall** [shtahl] *n* M stable

**Stamm 1** [shtahm] *n* F clan

**Stamm 2** [shtahm] *n* M stem

**Stamm 3** [shtahm] *n* M tree
(family)

**Stammbaum**
[SHTAHM•boum] *n* M
pedigree

**Stammbuch** [SHTAHM•book]
*n* N album

**Stand** [shtand] *n* M stall

**Standard** [shtahn•dahrd] *n* M
standard

**standardisieren**
[SHTAND•dard•ih•seer•en] *vt*
standardize

**Standbild** [SHTAHNT•bild] *n*
N image

**Standpunkt**
[SHTAHNT•poonkt] *n* M
attitude

**Stanniol** [SHTAHN•ee•ol] *n* N
tinfoil

**stark** [shtahrk] *adj* strong;
intense; potent

**starr 1** [shtahr] *adj* rigid

**starr 2** [shtahr] *adj* torpid

**starren** [SHTAH•ren] *vi* gaze

**Starrsinn** [SHTAHR•zin] *n* M
stubbornness

**Startpunkt**
[SHTAHRT•puhnkt] *n* M
starting point

**statisch** [SHTAH•tish] *adj* static

**Statistik** [SHTAH•tihst•eek] *n* F statistics

**statt** [shtaht] *adv* instead

**stattlich** [SHTAHT•lihk] *adj* portly; stately

**Statue** [SHTAH•too•eh] *n* F statue

**Status** [SHTAH•toos] *n* M status

**Staub** [shtoub] *n* M dust

**Staubsauger** [SHTOUB•zou•gair] *n* M vacuum

**Stauer** [SHTOUR•air] *n* M stevedore

**staunen** [SHTOU•nen] *vi* gape

**Stauung** [SHTOU•oong] *n* F congestion

**stechen** [SHTEHK•en] *vt* prick; *vt* prod

**stechen** [SHTEHK•en] *vt* sting

**Stechpalme** [STEHK•pahl•me] *n* F holly

**Steckdose** [SHTEHK•do•zeh] *n* F socket

**stecken** [SHTEK•en] *vt* thrust; stick into

**Steckenpferd** [SHTEHK•en•pfaird] *n* N hobby

**Steckmücke** [SHTEHK•muh•keh] *n* F gnat

**Stehen** [SHTAI•hen] *n* N standing

**stehlen** [SHTAI•len] *vt* steal

**steif 1** [shtuyf] *adj* prim

**steif 2** [shtuyf] *adj* steep

**steif 3** [shtuyf] *adj* stiff

**steifen** [SHTUY•fen] *vt* stiffen

**Steifheit** [SHTUYF•huyt] *n* F rigidity; stiffness

**Steigbügel** [SHTUYG•buh•gel] *n* M stirrup

**steigernd** [STUY•gairnt] *adj* cumulative

**Steigerung** [SHTAI•gair•oong] *n* F gain

**Steigung** [SHTUY•goong] *n* F upgrade

**Steilufer** [SHTAIYL•oof•air] *n* N bluff

**Stein** [shtuyn] *n* M stone

**steinern** [shtuyn•airn] *adj* stony

**Steinwerk** [-vairk] *n* N stonework

**Stelle** [SHTEL•leh] *n* F site; place; stead

**stellen** [SHTEL•len] *vi* put

**Stellvertreter** [SHTEL•fair•TRAI•tair] *n* M representative

**Stellvertretung** [SHTEL•vair•trai•toong] *n* F proxy

**Stemmeisen** [SHTEM•uy•sen] *n* N crowbar

**Stempel** [SHTEM•pel] *n* M stamp

**Stengel** [SHTEN•gel] *n* M stalk

**Stenographin** [SHTEHN•oh•GRAH•fin] *n* F stenographer

**Steppdecke** [SHTEP•DEHK•ke] *n* F quilt

**sterben** [SHTAIR•ben] *vi* die

**sterbend** [SHTAIR•bent] *adj* dying

**sterblich** [SHTAIRB•lihk] *adj* mortal

**Sterblicher** [SHTAIRB•lihk•air] M mortal

**Sterblichkeit** [SHTAIRB•lihk•kuyt] *n* F mortality

**Stereo** [SHTAIR•ee•oh] *n* N stereo

**Stereotypie** [-tuh•PEE] *n* F stereotype

**sterilisieren** [SHTAIR•ih•lih•SEER•en] *vt* sterilize

**Sterilität** [SHTAIR•il•ih•TAIT] *n* F sterility

**Sterling** [SHTAIR•ling] *n* M sterling

**Sternbild** [SHTAIRN•bild] *n* N constellation

**Sterne** [SHTAIR•neh] *n* F star

**Sternkunde** [SHTAIRN•koon•deh] *n* F astronomy

**Stethoskop** [SHTEHT•oh•skohp] *n* N stethoscope

**Steuer** [SHTOI•air] *n* F income tax; tax

**Steuerbord** [SHTOI•air•bord] *n* N starboard

**steuern** [SHTOI•airn] *vt* steer

**Steuerzahler** [SHTOI•air•tsahl•air] *n* M taxpayer

**Stewardeß** [SHTEH•vard•EHS] *n* F stewardess

**Stich 1** [shtihk] *n* M jab

**Stich 2** [shtihk] *n* M stitch

**Stichprobe** [STIHK•proh•beh] *n* F test (blood)

**Stickerei** [SHTIH•kair•UY] *n* F embroidery

**Stickstoff** [SHTIHK•shtohf] *n* M nitrogen

**Stiefel** [SHTEE•fel] *n* M boot

**Stiefkind** [SHTEEF•kint] *n* N stepchild

**Stiefmutter** [-muh•tair] *n* F stepmother

**Stiefmütterchen** [SHTEEF•muh•tair•chen] *n* N pansy

**Stiefsohn** [-zohn] *n* M stepson

**Stieftochter** [-TOHK•tair] *n* F stepdaughter

**Stiefvater** [-FAH•tair] *n* M stepfather

**Stiege** [SHTEE•geh] *n* F stair

**Stiel** [shteel] *n* M stem

**Stier** [shteer] *n* M bull

**Stift** [shtihft] *n* M spike

**Stift** [shtihft] *n* M tack

**Stifter** [SHTIF•tair] *n* M benefactor

**Stiftung** [SHTIF•toong] *n* F donation

**Stigma** [SHTIG•mah] *n* N stigma

**Stil** [shteel] *n* M style

**still** [shtil] *adj* calm; still

**Stille** [SHTIL•le] *n* F stillness; hush; quiescence

**stillen** [SHTIH•len] *vt* stanch

**stillschweigend** [SHTIL•SHVAI•gend] *adj* tacit

**Stillstand** [SHTIL•shtant] *n* M stoppage

**Stillstand stehen** [SHTIL•stahnt] [SHTAI•hen] *n vi* M stand

**Stimm** [shtim] tuning

**Stimme** [SHTIM•meh] *n* F
voice

**Stimmenzählung**
[SHTI•men•TSAI•loong] *n* F
poll

**stimmlich** [SHTIM•lihk] *adj*
vocal

**Stimmung** [SHTIH•moong] *n* F
mood

**stinken** [SHTINK•en] *vi* stink

**Stinktier** [SHTINK•teer] *n* N
skunk

**Stipendium**
[shti•PEHN•DEE•oom] *n* N
scholarship

**Stirn** [shteern] *n* M forehead

**Stirnrunzeln**
[SHTEERN•roonts•eln] *n* N
frown

**Stock 1** [shtohk] *n* M staff; stick

**Stock 2** [shtohk] *n* M story (of
house)

**stocken** [SHTOHK•ken] *vi* balk

**stockend** [SHTOHK•end] *adj*
stagnant

**Stockung** [SHTOHK•oong] *n* F
holdup

**Stoff** [sthohf] *n* M cloth

**Stöhnen** [SHTUH•nen] *n* N
groan

**Stöpsel** [SHTUHP•sel] *n* M
plug; stopper

**Stör** [shter] *n* M sturgeon

**stören** [SHTOOR•en] *vt* disturb

**Störung** [SHTOOR•oong] *n* F
disturbance; harassment

**Störungssucher**
[SHTUHR•oongs•ZOO•kair] *n*
M troubleshooter

**Stoff** [shtohf] *n* M fabric;
material

**Stoffrest** [SHOHF•rehst] *n* M
remnant

**Stoiker** [SHTO•ih•kair] *n* M
stoic

**Stoizismus** [-TSEES•moos] *n*
M stoicism

**Stola** [SHTOH•lah] *n* F stole

**stolpern** [SHTOHL•pairn] *vi*
stumble

**stoltz** [shtolts] *adj* proud

**Stolz** [shtolts] *n* M pride

**stolzieren** [SHTOLTS•eer•en]
*vt* flaunt; brag

**stopfen** [SHTOHP•fen] *vt* darn

**Stoppel** [SHTOH•pel] *n* F
stubble

**Stoppuhr** [SHTOHP•oor] *n* F
timer; stopwatch

**Storch** [shtorhk] *n* M stork

**Stoß** [shtohs] *n* M jerk; jolt;
bump

**stoßen** [SHTOH•sen] *vt* poke;
push

**stoßen** [SHTOH•sen] *vt* thrust;
bump

**Stoßstange**
[SHTOHS•SHTAH•ngeh] *n* F
bumper (of car)

**stottern** [SHTOH•tairn] *vi*
stammer; stutter

**Sträfling** [STREF•ling] *n* M
convict

**Strafe** [SHTRAH•feh] *n* F
penalty; punishment

**strafen** [SHTRAH•fen] *vt*
punish; penalize

**Straffälliger**
[SHTRAHF•fel•ig•air] *n* M
misdemeanor

**Straflosigkeit**
[SHTRAHF•los•ig•KUYT] *n*
F impunity

**strafmildernde**
[SHTRAHF•mihl•dairn•deh]
*adj* mitigating

**strafrechtlich**
[shtrahf•rehkt•lihk] *adj* penal

**Straftäter** [SHTRAHF•tai•tair]
*n* M delinquent

**Strahl** [shtrahl] *n* M ray

**Strahlen** [SHTRAHL•en] *n* N
radiance

**strahlend** [SHTRAHL•end] *adj*
radiant

**Strahlung** [SHTRAHL•oong] *n*
F radiation

**stramm** [shtrahm] *adj* stalwart

**Strand** [shtrahnt] *n* M beach;
seashore

**Strang** [shtrahng] *n* M skein

**Straße** [SHTRAH•seh] *n* F
street; avenue; road

**Straße Autobahn**
[SHTRAH•se] [ou•to•bahn] *n*
F highway

**Straßenbahn**
[SHTRAH•sen•bahn] *n* F
streetcar; tram

**Straßenbahnwagen**
[SHTRAH•sen•bahn•VAH•gen]
*n* M trolley

**Strategie** [SHTRAH•teh•GEE]
*n* F strategy

**strategisch** [shtrah•TAIG•ish]
*adj* strategic

**Stratosphäre**
[SHTRAH•toh•SFAIR•eh] *n* F
stratosphere

**Strauch** [shtrouhk] *n* M shrub

**Strauß** [shtrous] *n* M ostrich

**Strebe** [SHTRAI•beh] *n* F strut

**streckbar** [SHTREHK•bahr] *adj*
tensile

**Strecke** [SHTREHK•e] *n* F
distance; extent

**Streich** [shtruyhk] *n* M prank

**streichen** [SHTRAI•ken] *vt*
delete

**streif** [shtruyf] *adj* starchy

**Streifen** [SHTRUY•fen] *n* M
strip; stripe

**Streiker** [SHTRUYK•air] *n* M
striker

**Streit 1** [shtruyt] *n* M discord

**Streit 2** [shtuyt] *n* M fight;
quarrel

**streitbar** [SHTRUYT•bahr] *adj*
martial

**streng** [shtreng] *adj* severe;
stern; strict

**Strenge** [SHTRENG•eh] *n* F
rigor

**Streu** [shtroi] *n* F litter

**streuen** [SHTROI•en] *vt* scatter

**Strich** [shtrihk] *n* M streak

**Strichjunge**
[SHTRIHK•yuhng•eh] *n* M
pimp

**Strichpunkt** [STRIHK•puhnkt]
*n* M semicolon

**Strick** [shtrihk] *n* M halter

**stricken** [SHTRIHK•en] *vt* knit

**Stricken** [SHTRIHK•en] *n* N
knitting

**Strickjacke** [SHTRIK•yah•kch]
*n* F cardigan

**Strohhalm** [SHTROH•halm] *n*
M straw (drinking)

**Strolch** [shtrohlk] *n* M hoodlum

**Strom 1** [shtrom] *n* M current
(of river)

**Strom 2** [shtrom] *n* M charge
(electrical); electrical cable

**Stromschnelle**
[SHTROHM•shnel•eh] *n* F
chute

**Stromverbraucher**
[SHTROHM•vair•BROUHK•air]
*n* M outlet

**Strophe** [SHTROH•feh] *n* F
stanza

**Strudel** [SHTROO•del] *n* M
whirlpool

**Struktur** *n* F structure

**strukturell**
[SHTRUHK•toor•EL] *adj*
structural

**Strumpfband**
[SHTRUHMPF•bahnd] *n* N
garter

**Strümpfe** [SHTRUHMP•feh] *n*
F stocking

**Strumpfhose**
[SHTRUHMPF•hoh•ze] *n* F
pantyhose

**Strumpfwaren**
[SHTRUHMPF•vahr•en] *npl*
hosiery

**Stück1** [shtook] *n* N chunk;
piece

**Stuck2** [shtuhk] *n* M stucco

**Stückchen** [SHTUHK•chen] *n*
N morsel

**Student in** [SHTOO•dent] *n* M
student; freshman; sophomore;
undergraduate

**Studentenwohnheim**
[SHTOO•dent•en•VOHN•huym]
*n* N dormitory

**studieren** [SHTOO•deer•en] *vi*
study

**Stufe 1** [SHTOO•fe] *n* F grade

**Stufe 2** [SHTOO•feh] *n* F step

**Stufe** [SHTOO•fe] *n* F degree

**stufenweise**
[SHTOO•fen•VAI•ze] *adj*
gradual

**Stuhl** [shtool] *n* M chair;
armchair

**Stulpe** [SHTOOL•pe] *n* F cuff

**stumm** [shtuhm] *adj* mute

**Stummel 1** [SHTOO•mehl] *n* M
butt (of cigarette)

**Stummel 2** [SHTOO•mehl] *n* M
stump

**Stummer** [SHTUHM•air] *n* M
mute

**stumpf** [shtuhmpf] *adj* obtuse

**Stumpf** [shtumpf] *n* M stub

**Stumpfheit** [shtuhmpf•huyt] *n*
F stupor

**Stunde** [SHTUHN•de] *n* F hour

**Stundenglas** [-en•glahs] *n* N
hourglass

**stündlich** [SHTUHND•lihk] *adj*
*adv* hourly

**stur** [shtoor] *adj* stolid

**Sturm** [SHTOORM] *n* M storm;
gale; tempest

**stürmisch** [shtoorm•ish] *adj*
stormy; tempestuous

**Sturtz** [shtuhrts] *n* M tumble;
fall

**Stute** [SHTOO•teh] *n* F mare

**Stütze** [SHTOOTS•eh] *n* F
brace; prop

**stützen** [SHTUHTS•en] *vt*
sustain

**subjektiv** [SOOB•yehkt•EEV]
*adj* subjective

**sublim** [SOOB•leem] *adj*
sublime

**Substantiv** [SUHB•shtan•teev]
*n* N noun

Substanz [soob•SHTAHNTS] *n*
F matter; substance

Suche [ZOO•khe] *n* F quest

suchen [ZOO•khen] *vt* search;
seek

Sucht [sookt] *n* F addiction

Süchtige-r [SUHK•tig•uh] [-air]
*n* F addict

Süchtiger [TSOOK•tig•air] *n* M
drug addict

Süd Amerika [SUHD
ah•MAIR•ih•kah] *n* South
America

südlich [SUHD•lihk] *adj* south

südöstlich [SUHD•UHST•lihk]
*adj* southeast

Südstaatler
[SUHD•SHTAHT•lair] *n* M
southerner

südwärts [SUHD•vairts] *adv*
southward

südwestlich
[SUHD•VEHST•lihk] *adv*
southwest

Summe [SOOM•eh] *n* F amount

Summe [ZUH•meh] [ *n* F total

Summen [ZOO•men] *n* M buzz
(of insect)

summen [ZUH•men] *vt* hum

Sumpf [zoompf] *n* M bog;
marsh; swamp

sumpfig [-ig] *adj* marshy

Sünde [ZUHN•deh] *n* F sin

sündenlos [ZUHN•den•los] *adj*
sinless

Sünder [ZUHN•dair] *n* M
sinner

Suppe [ZUH•peh] *n* F soup

Suppenkelle
[ZUH•pen•KEL•le] *n* F
ladle

surren [ZOOR•en] *vi* zoom

süß [zuhs] *adj* sweet

süßen [ZUH•sen] *vt* sweeten

Süßigkeit [-ig•KUYT] *n* F
sweetness

Süßigkeiten
[ZOOS•ig•KAIT•ehn] *n* F
candy

Süßkartoffel
[ZUHS•KAHR•toh•fel] *n* F
sweet potato

Süßwasser [ZOOS•vah•sair] *n*
N freshwater

Symbol [SIM•bohl] *n* N symbol

symbolisch [-ish] *adj* symbolic

symmetrisch [sih•MAI•trish]
*adj* symmetrical

Sympathie [SIM•pah•TEE] *n* F
sympathy

symptomatisch
[SIMP•toh•MAH•tish] *adj*
symptomatic

Synagoge [SIN•ah•GOH•geh] *n*
F synagogue

synchronisiert
[SOON•kroh•ni•seert] *adj*
dubbed

Synonym [SIH•noh•NIM] *n* N
synonym

synonymisch [-ish] *adj*
synonymous

Synthese [SIN•tai•zeh] *n* F
synthesis

Syrien [SUHR•ee•en] *n* Syria

Syrier in [SUHR•ee•air] [in] *n*
M Syrian

System [sis•TAIM] *n* N system

systematisch [-AHT•ish] *adj*
systematic

Szene [TSAI•neh] *n* F scene

# T

**Tabak** [tah•BAHK] *n* M tobacco

**Tabakhändler** [-HEND•lair] *n* M tobacconist

**tabellarisieren** [TAH•bel•ih•SEER•en] *vt* tabulate

**Tabelle** [tah•BEL•leh] *n* F chart; graph

**Tablette** [tahb•LEH•teh] *n* F tabloid

**Tachometer** [TAHK•oh•MAI•tair] *n* N tachometer

**Tadel** [TAH•del] *n* M reproof

**tadeln** [TAH•deln] *vt* reprove

**Täfelchen** [TEH•fel•khen] *n* N tablet

**Tafel1** [TAH•fel] *n* F blackboard; panel

**Tafel2** [TAH•fel] *n* F slab

**tafelförmig** [TAH•fel•FERM•ig] *adj* tabular

**Taft** [tahft] *n* M taffeta

**Tag** [tahg] *n* M day

**Tagebuch** [TAHG•eh•boohk] *n* N diary; journal

**Tagesbericht** [TAHG•es•BEH•rihkt] *n* M bulletin

**Tagesbruch** [TAHG•es•BROOHK] *n* M daybreak

**Tagesordnung** [tAHG•ehs•ORD•noongk] *n* F agenda

**täglich** [TAIG•lihk] *adj* daily

**Tagung** [TAH•goong] *n* F convention

**Taifun** [TAI•foon] *n* M typhoon

**Taille** [TAI•leh] *n* F waist

**Takt** [tahkt] *n* M tact

**Taktik** [TAHK•teek] *n* F tactics

**taktil** [TAHK•teel] *adj* tactile

**taktisch** [-ish] *adj* tactical

**Tal** [tahl] *n* N valley

**Talent** [tah•LENT] *n* N talent

**Talg** [tahlg] *n* M tallow; candle wax

**Talk** [tahlk] *n* M talcum

**Tandem** [TAHN•dem] *n* N tandem

**Tangente** [TAHN•gen•teh] *n* F tangent

**Tangier** [TAHN•geer] *n* Tangiers

**Tank** [tahnk] *n* M tank (army); tank (gasoline)

**Tanker** [tahnk•air] *n* M tanker (ship)

**Tanne** [TAH•ne] *n* F fir

**Tante** [TAHN•te] *n* F aunt

**Tanz tanzen** [tahnts] *n* M dance

**tanzen** [tahnts•en] *vt vi* dance

**tänzeln** [TEHN•tseln] *vi* prance

**Tänzer -in** [TEN•tsair] [-in] *n* M dancer

**Tapete** [tah•PAI•teh] *n* F wallpaper

**tapfer** [TAHP•fair] *adj* brave; courageous

**Tapferkeit** [TAHP•fair•kuyt] *n* F bravery; prowess; valor

**Tara** [TAHR•ah] *n* F tare
(weight)

**Tasche** [TAH•sheh] *n* F
handbag; pocket; pocketbook

**Taschendieb**
[TAH•shen•DEEB] *n* M
pickpocket

**Taschenmesser** [-MEH•sair] *n*
N pocketknife

**Tasse** [TAH•seh] *n* F cup;
teacup

**Tat** [taht] *n* M act; deed

**tat** [taht] did (*pret* of tun)

**Tätigkeit** [TAI•tig•KUYT] *n* F
function

**Tatsache** [TAHT•zah•ke] *n* F
fact

**Tatsachen** [TAHT•sah•khen]
*npl* data

**tatsächlich** [TAHT•zehk•lihk]
*adv* indeed; virtually; virtual

**Tau** [tou] *n* M dew

**taub** [toub] *adj* deaf

**taub machen** [toub MAHK•en]
*vt* deafen

**Taube** [TOU•be] *n* F dove;
pigeon

**Tauchen** [TOU•khen] *n* N dive

**Taucher** [TOU•khair] *n* M
plunger

**Taufe** [TOW•feh] *n* F baptism

**taufen** [TOW•fen] *vt* baptize;
christen

**taumeln** [TOUM•eln] *vi* stagger

**Tausch** [toush] *n* M exchange

**täuschen** [TOI•shen] *vt*
deceive; hoodwink

**Täuschung** [TOI•shoong] *n* F
deception; delusion

**tausend** [TOU•zent] *num*
thousand

**tausendste** [-steh] thousandth

**Taxi** [TAHKS•ee] *n* N cab; taxi

**Technik** [tehk^•NEEK] *n* F
engineering

**Techniker** [TEHK•nih•kair] *n*
M technician

**technisch** [TEHK•nish] *adj*
technical

**Tee** [tee] *n* M tea

**Teegebäck** [TAI•geh•BEK] *n* N
scone

**Teegesellschaft**
[-geh•ZEHL•shahft] *n* F tea
party

**Teekanne** [tEE•KAHN•neh] *n*
F teakettle; teapot

**Teelöffel** [TEE•LUH•fel] *n* M
teaspoon

**Teer** [tair] *n* M tar

**Teich** [tuyhk] *n* M pond

**Teig** [tuyg] *n* M dough

**Teil** [tuyl] *n* M component; part;
portion

**Teilchen** [TUYL•khen] *n* N
particle

**Teilnahme** [TUYL•nah•meh] *n*
F participation

**teilnehmen** [TUYL•nai•men] *vi*
participate

**Teilnehmer** [TUYL•nai•mair] *n*
M participant

**teilweise** [-VAI•zeh] *adj*
partial; *adv* partially

**teilzeitig** [TUYL•TSAI•tig] *adj*
*adv* part-time

**Telefon** [TEHL•eh•FOHN] *n* N
phone; telephone

**Telefonnummer** [-NUH•mair]
*n* F telephone number

**Telefonzelle**
[TEHL•eh•FOHN•TSEL•le] *n*
F pay phone; phone booth

**Telegramm**
[TEHL•eh•GRAHM] *n* N
telegram

**Telegraph** [TEH•leh•GRAHF]
*n* M telegraph

**Telephonist in**
[TEHL•eh•fon•EEST] [in] *n*
M telephone operator

**Teller** [TEL•air] *n* M plate

**Tempel** [TEM•pel] *n* M temple

**Temperament**
[TEM•pair•ah•MENT] *n* N
temper; temperament

**Temperatur**
[TEMP•air•ah•TOOR] *n* F
temperature

**Temple** [TEM•pl] *n* M temple

**Tendenz** [TEN•dents] *n* F
tendency; trend

**Tennis** [tehn•is] *n* M tennis

**Tenor** [TEN•or] *n* M tenor

**Teppich** [TEHP•pikh] *n* M
carpet; rug

**Termin** [TAIR•meen] *n* M
deadline

**Terpentin** [TAIR•pen•TEEN] *n*
N turpentine

**Terrasse** [tair•AH•seh] *n* F
terrace

**terrorisieren**
[TAIR•or•ih•SEER•en] *vt*
terrorize

**Testament** [TEHST•ah•MENT]
*n* N testament

**Tetanus** [TEH•tah•NOOS] *n* M
tetanus

**teuer** [TOI•air] *adj* costly;
expensive

**Teufel** [TOI•fel] *n* M devil;
fiend

**Teufelchen** [TOI•fel•khen] *n* N
imp

**Teufelskerl** [TOI•fels•kaiy•rel]
*n* M daredevil

**teuflisch** [TOIF•lish] *adj*
fiendish

**Text** [tekst] *n* M text

**Textilwaren**
[teks•TEEL•VAHR•ren] *npl*
M textile

**Textur** [TEKS•toor] *n* F fiber;
texture

**Theater** [TAI•ah•TAIR] *n* N
theater

**theatralisch**
[TAI•ah•TRAHL•ish] *adj*
theatrical

**Theke** [TAI•ke] *n* F counter

**Thema** [TAI•meh] *n* N theme;
topic

**Theologie** [TAI•oh•loh•GEE] *n*
theology

**Theorem** [TAI•or•em] *n* N
theorem

**theoretisch** [TAI•or•EHT•ish]
*adj* theoretical

**Theorie** [TAI•or•EE] *n* F theory

**therapeutisch**
[TAIR•ah•POI•tish] *adj*
therapeutic

**Thermometer**
[TAIR•moh•MAI•tair] *n* N
thermometer

**Thermostat**
[TAIR•moh•STAHT] *n* M
thermostat

**These** [TAI•zeh] *n* F thesis

**Thron** [trohn] *n* M throne

**Thunfisch** [TOON•fish] *n* M
tuna; tuna fish

**Thymian** [TIH•mee•ahn] *n* M
thyme

**Tiara** [TEE•ahr•ah] *n* F tiara

**Ticken** [TIK•en] *n* N tick

**ticken** [TIH•ken] *vi* tick (clock)

**tief** [teef] *adj* deep; profound

**Tiefe** [TEE•feh] *n* F depth

**Tier** [teeyr] *n* N animal

**tierärztlich** [TEER•airtst•lihk]
*adj* veterinary

**Tierarzt** [TEER•ahrtst] *n* M
veterinarian

**Tierkreis** [TEER•kruys] *n* M
zodiac; *adj* zodiacal

**Tiger** [TEE•gair] *n* M tiger

**Tigerin** [TEE•gair•in] *n* M
tigress

**tilgen** [TIL•gen] *vt* eliminate;
liquidate; raze

**Tinktur** [TINK•toor] *n* F
tincture

**Tinte** [TIHN•te] *n* F ink

**Tirade** [tee•RAH•deh] *n* F tirade

**Tisch** [tish] *n* M table

**Tischgast** [TISH•gahst] *n* M
diner

**Tischgeschirr** [-geh•SHEER] *n*
N tableware

**Titel** [TEE•tel] *n* M heading;
title

**titular** [TEE•too•lahr] *adj* titular

**Toast** [tohst] *n* M toast

**toben** [TOH•ben] *vt* rant

**Toboggan** [toh•BOG•gahn] *n*
M toboggan

**Tochter** [TOHK•tair] *n* F
daughter

**Tod** [tohd] *n* M death

**Todesopfer**
[TOH•des•OHP•fair] *n* N toll

**Todesurteil**
- [TOH•des•OOR•tuyl] *n* N
sentence (death)

**tödlich** [TOOD•lihk] *adj*
deadly; fatal

**tödlich** [TUHD•lihk] *adj* fatal

**Toilette** [TOI•LEH•teh] *n* F
toilet

**Toilettenpapier** [-PAH•peer] *n*
N toilet paper

**Tomate** [to•MAH•teh] *n* F
tomato

**Tombola** [TOM•boh•lah] *n* F
raffle

**Ton** [tohn] *n* M tone

**Tonnage** [TON•nah•jeh] *n* F
tonnage

**Tonne** [TON•neh] *n* F ton

**Topas** [TOH•pahs] *n* M topaz

**Topf** [topf] *n* M jar; pot

**Töpferei** [TUHP•fair•uy] *n* F
pottery

**Topographie**
[TO•poh•grah•FEE] *n*
topography

**Tor** [tohr] *n* N gate

**Torf** [torf] *n* M peat

**Torheit** [TOR•huyt] *n* F folly

**torkeln** [TOR•keln] *vi* totter

**Tornado** [TOR•NAH•doh] *n* M
tornado

**Torpedo** [TOR•PEE•doh] *n* M
torpedo

**Torte** [TOHR•teh] *n* F cake; tart

**tot** [toht] *adj* dead

**total** [toh•tal] *adj* outright

**totalitär** [TO•tahl•ih•TAIR] *adj*
totalitarian

**töten** [TUH•ten] *vi* slay; *vt vi*
kill

**Totengräber**
[TOH•ten•GRAI•bair] *n* M
sexton

**Totschlag** [TOHT•shlahg] *n* M
manslaughter

**Tour** [toor] *n* F tour

**Tourist** [toor•IST] *n* M tourist

**Toxin** [TOHKS•in] *n* N toxin

**Trachea** [TRAHK•ai•eh] *n* F
trachea

**Tradition** [TRAH•dits•EE•on] *n*
F tradition

**tragbar** [TRAHG•bahr] *adj*
portable

**tragen 1** [TRAH•gehn] *vt* carry

**tragen 2** [TRAH•gen] *vt* wear

**Träger** [TRAI•gair] *n* M girder

**tragisch** [TRAH•gish] *adj* tragic

**Tragödie** [trah•GUH•DEE•eh] *n*
F tragedy

**Trainer** [TRAI•nair] *n* M coach;
trainer

**Traktor** [TRAHK•tor] *n* M
tractor

**trampeln** [TRAHM•peln] *vi*
trample

**Tramper** [TRAHM•pair] *n* M
hitchhiker

**Trance** [trahns] *n* F trance

**Trank** [trahnk] *n* M potion

**Transit** [TRAHN•seet] *n* M
transit

**transitiv** [TRAHN•sih•TEEV]
*adj* transitive

**transpirieren**
[TRAHNS•peer•EER•en] *vi*
transpire

**transportieren**
[TRANS•por•TEER•en] *vt*
transport

**Trapez** [TRAH•peez] *n* N
trapeze

**Traube** [TROU•be] *n* F grape

**Traubenzucker**
[TROU•ben•TSOO•kair] *n* M
glucose; dextrose

**Trauer** [TROU•air] *n* F
mourning

**trauern** [TROU•airn] *vt* mourn

**Traum** [troum] *n* M dream

**Träumerei** [TROI•mair•uy] *n* F
daydream

**träumerisch** [TROU•mair•ish]
*adj* dreamy

**traurig** [TROU•rig] *adj* sad

**Traurigkeit** [-kuyt] *n* F sadness

**Travestie** [TRAH•veh•stee] *n* F
travesty

**Treffen** [TREH•fen] *n* N rally

**Treibsand** [TRUYB•zahnt] *n* M
quicksand

**trennbar** [TREN•bahr] *adj*
separable

**trennen** [TREH•nen] *vt*
disconnect; segregate

**trennend** [TREN•end] *adv*
separately

**Trennung** [-oong] *n* F
separation

**Treppe** [TREH•peh] *n* F stair

**treu** [troi] *adj* faithful; loyal

**treu bleiben** [TROI•BLAI•bun]
*vi* abide (by)

**Treue** [TROI•e] *n* F fidelity;
loyalty

**Tribun** [TREE•boon] *n* M
tribune

**Trick** [trihk] *n* M trick; ruse

**Triebkraft** [TREEB•krahft] *n* F
impetus

**Triebwerk** [TREEB•vairk] *n* N
gear

**trillern** [TRIH►lairn] *vt* trill;
warble

**Trinkgeld** [TREENK•geld] *n* N
gratuity

**Trio** [TREE•oh] *n* N trio

**Tritt 1** [trit] *n* M footstep; kick

**Tritt 2** [triht] *n* M tread (stairs)

**Trittleiter** [TRIHT•luy•tair] *n* F
stepladder

**trocken** [TROH•ken] *adj* dry

**trocken dürr** [TROH•k•nen]
[dooyr] *adj* arid

**trocknen** [TROHK•nen] *vt*
dehydrate

**Trockner** [TROHK•nair] *n* M
dryer

**Tröpfeln** [TRUHP•feln] *n* N
drip

**Trommel** [TROH•mel] *n* F
drum

**Trommelfell** [TROM•mel•FEL]
*n* M tympani

**Trommeln** [TROHM•meln] *n* N
tattoo

**Trommler** [TROHM•lair] *n* M
drummer

**Trompete** [trom•PAI•teh] *n* F
trumpet

**Tropen** [TROH•pen] *npl* M
tropic

**Tropfen** [TROHP•fen] *n* M
drop

**tropfen** [TROHP•fen] *vt* seep;
run (nose)

**tröpfeln** [TRUHP•feln] *vi*
trickle

**Trophäe** [troh•FAI] *n* F trophy

**tropisch** [TROH•pish] *adj*
tropic

**Trost** [trohst] *n* M solace

**trösten** [TRUHST•en] *vt* trust,
comfort

**Trott** [troht] *n* M trot

**trotten** [TROH•ten] *vi* trot

**Trotz** [trohts] *n* M defiance

**trotz** [trohts] *prep* despite; *adv*
notwithstanding

**trotzdem** [TROHTS•daim] *adv*
nevertheless

**trotzen** [TROTS•en] *vt* defy

**trösten** [TRUHST•en] *vt*
console

**Tröstung** [TRUHST•oong] *n* F
consolation

**trübe** [TROO•beh] *adj* dismal

**trüben** [TRUH•ben] *vt* tarnish

**Trübsinn** [TRUHB•zin] *n* M
mope; sulk

**trug** [troog] *pp* wore (*pret* of
tragen)

**Trupp** [truhp] *n* M troop

**Truppe** [TROO•peh] *n* F cast
(of a play)

**Truthahn** [TROO•tahn] *n* M
turkey

**Tscheche** [TSCHEK•e] *n* M
Czech

**tschechisch** [TSCHEK•ish] *adj*
Czech

**Tschechoslowakei**
[TSCHEK•oh•sloh•vahz•KUY]
*n* F Czechoslovakia

**tuberkulös**
[TOO•bair•kuh•LUHS] *adj*
tubercular

**Tuberkulose** [-LOH•zeh] *n* F
tuberculosis

**Tuch** [toohk] *n* N towel

**Tuch** [tookh] *n* N cloth

**tüchtig** [TOOK•tig] *adj* efficient

**Tüchtigkeit** [TOOK•tig•kuyt] *n*
F efficiency

**Tüll** [tuhl] *n* M tulle

**Tulpe** [TUHL•peh] *n* F tulip

**Tummelplatz**
[TUH•mel•PLAHTS] *n* M
playground

**Tümmler** [TUHM•lair] *n* M
porpoise

**Tumor** [TOO•mor] *n* M tumor

**Tun** [toon] *n* N occurrence;
doings

**tun, machen** [toon] [MAH•ken]
*vtg* do

**tun haben** *vtg* be busy

**Tünche** [TUHN•che] *n* F
whitewash

**Tunnel** [TUHN•nel] *n* M tunnel

**Tür** [toor] *n* F door

**Turbine** [TOOR•BEEN•eh] *n* F
turbine

**Türke** [TOOR•keh] *n* M Turk

**Türkis** [TOOR•kis] *n* M
turquoise

**türkisch** [TOOR•kish] *adj*
Turkish

**Turm** [toorm] *n* M tower

**Türmatte** [TOOR•mah•te] *n* F
doormat

**Türmchen** [TERM•khen] *n* N
turret

**Turner-in** [TOOR•nair-in] *n* M
gymnast

**turnerisch** [TOORN•air•ish] *adj*
gymnastics

**Turnhalle** [TOORN•hahl•e] *n* F
gym; gymnasium

**Turnier** [toor•NEER] *n* N
tournament

**Türstufe** [TOOR•SHTOO•feh]
*n* F doorstep

**Tüte** [TOOT•eh] *n* F bag

**Tweed** [tveed] *n* M tweed

**Typ** [tuhp] *n* M type

**typhös** [TUH•fuhs] *adj* typhoid

**typisch** [TUHP•ish] *adj* typical

**Tyrann** [TEER•ahn] *n* M tyrant;
despot

**Tyrannie** [TEER•ahn•ee] *n* F
tyranny

**tyrannisch** [TEER•ahn•ish] *adj*
tyrannical; domineering

# U

**übbel** [OO•bel] *adj* evil

**Übelkeit** [UH•behl•kuyt] *n* F
nausea

**Übeltat** [UH•bel•taht] *n* F
malpractice

**übender** [UH•ben•dair] *adj*
practicing

**über** [UH•bair] *adj* over; *prep*
via

**über Bord** [UH•bair BORD]
*adv* overboard

**über oben** [OOB•air] [O•bun]
*adv* above

**überall** [OO•bair•AL] *adv*
everywhere

**überall** [UH•bair•AHL] *adj*
overall

**Überbleibsel**
[UH•bair•bluyb•zel] *n* N
leftovers

**überbuchen**
[UH•bair•BOO•khen] *vt*
overbook

**überfallen** [UH•bair•FAHL•len]
*vt* invade

**Überfluß** [OO•bair•FLOOS] *n*
M glut

**überfluten**
[UH•bair•FLUH•ten] *vt*
overrun

**Übergang** [UH•bair•GAHNG]
*n* M transition

**übergespannt**
[UH•bair•GEH•shpahnt] *adj*
overdrawn

**Übergewicht**
[UH•bair•GEH•vihkt] *n* N
overweight

**übergreifen auf**
[UH•bair•GRUY•fen ouf] *vt*
overlap

**überhaufen**
[OO•bair•HOU•fen] *vt* clutter

**überhören**
[UH•bair•HUHR•ren] *vt*
overhear

**überholen** [UH•bair•HOH•len]
*vt* overhaul

**überlasten** [UH•bair•LAH•sten]
*vt* overwork

**überlaufen lassen**
[UH•bair•LOU•fen LAH•sen]
*vt* spill

**überleben** [UH•bair•LAI•ben]
*vt* outlive

**Überleben** [UH•bair•LAI•ben]
*n* N survival

**überleben** *vt* survive

**Überlebender** [-dair] *n* M
survivor

**überlegen** [OO•bair•LAI•gen]
*vt* M consider

**überlegen** [UH•bair•LAI•gen]
*vt* reconsider

**übermäßig** [OO•bair•MAI•sig]
*adj* excess

**übermäßig** [UH•bair•MAI•sig]
*adj* hyperactive

**übermäßig** [UH•bair•MAIS•ig]
*adj* undue

**übermannen**
[UH•bair•MAH•nen] *vt*
overwhelm

**übermitteln** [OO•bair•MIT•eln]
*vt* convey

**übernacht** [UH•bair•NAHKT]
*adj* overnight

**überqueren**
[UH•bair•KVAIR•en] *vt*
traverse

**überreden** [UH•bair•RAI•den]
*vt* persuade

**überschreiten**
[OO•bair•SHRUY•ten] *vt*
exceed

**überschreiten**
[UH•bair•SHRUY•ten] *vt*
overstep

**überschreiten**
[UH•bair•SHRUY•ten] *vt*
transcend

**Überschrift**
[OOH•bair•SHRIFT] *n* F
caption

**überschwemmen**
[OO•bair•SHVEM•en] *vt* float

**überschwemmen**
[UH•bair•SCHVEM•men] *vt*
inundate

**Überschwemmung**
[OO•bair•SHVE•moong] *n* F
deluge

**Überschwemmung**
[UH•bair•SHVEM•moong] *n*
F overflow

**übersee** [UH•bair•ZEE] *adj adv*
overseas

**übersehen 1** [UH•bair•ZAI•en]
*vt* overlook

**übersehen 2** [UH•bair•ZEH•en]
*vt* oversee

**übersenden**
[UH•bair•ZEN•den] *vt*
transmit

**Übersender** [-dair] *n* M
transmitter

**übersetzen** [OO•bair•ZETS•en]
*vt* decode; translate

**Übersetzer in** [ -in] *n* M
translator

**Übersetzung**
[UH•bair•ZEHTS•oong] *n* F
interpretation; translation

**überströmen**
[UH•bair•SHTRUH•men] *vt*
suffuse

**Überstundenlohn**
[UH•bair•SHTUHN•den•lohn]
*n* M overtime

**überteuern** [UH•bair•TOI•airn]
*vt* overcharge

**übertragen**
[OO•bair•TRAH•gen] *vt*
assign

**übertragen auf**
[OO•bair•TRAH•gen ouf] *vt*
communicate

**übertreiben** [OO•bair•truy•ben]
*vt* exaggerate; overdo

**Übertreibung** [-oong] *n* F
exaggeration

**übertreten** [UH•bair•TRAI•ten]
*vt* transgress

**Übertretung**
[UH•bair•TRAI•toong] *n* F
transgression; trespass

**überwachsen**
[UH•bair•VAHKS•sen] *adj*
overgrown

**überwältigen**
[UH•bair•VAIL•tig•en] *vt*
overpower

**überwältigend**
[UH•bair•VAIL•tig•end] *adj*
overwhelming

**überweisen** [OO•bair•VAI•zen]
*vt* endorse

**überwiegen**
[UH•bair•VEE•gen] *vt*
outweigh

**überwiegend**
[UH•bair•VEE•gent] *adj*
prevalent

**überwinden**
[UH•bair•VIN•den] *vt*
overcome

**überwintern**
[UH•bair•VIN•tairn] *vi*
hibernate

**überzeugen** [OO•bair•tsoi•gen]
*vt* convince

**überzeugend**
[OO•bair•TSOI•gent] *adj*
convincing; persuasive

**Überzeugung**
[UH•bair•TSOIG•oong] *n* F
persuasion

**überziehen** [UH•bair•TSEE•en]
*vt* overdraw

**Überzieher** [UH•bair•TSEE•air]
*n* M topcoat

**üblich** [UHB•lihk] *adj* habitual;
usually

**Übrigbleibsel**
[UH•brig•BLUYB•zel] *n* N
remains

**Übung** [UH•boong] *n* F practice

**Uhr** [oor] *n* F clock; o'clock;
timepiece

**Ulme** [OOL•meh] *n* F elm

**um über** [oom] [oob•air] *prep*
about

**umarmen** [OOM•ARM•en] *vt*
cuddle

**Umarmung**
[OOM•AHR•moong] *n* F
embrace; hug

**umbauen** [UHM•BOU•en] *vt*
remodel

**umbringen** [OOM•BRING•en]
*vt vi* kill

**umdrehen** [OOM•DRAI•hen]
*vi* veer

**umfahren** [OOM•FAHR•en] *vi*
commute

**Umfang** [OOM•fahng] *n* M
girth

**umfassen** [OOM•FAH•sen] *vt*
encompass

**umfassend** [OOM•FAHS•end]
*adj* comprehensive; extensive

**Umgangssprache**
[UHM•GAHNGS•shprah•khe]
*n* F slang

**umgangssprachlich**
[OOMG•GAHNGZ•shprahk•
likh] *adj* colloquial

**Umgebung 1**
[OOM•GAI•boong] *n* F
environment

**Umgebung 2**
[UHM•GAI•boong] *n* F
outskirts

**Umgestalter**
[OOM•geh•SHTAHL•tair] *n*
M transformer

**Umgießen** [OOM•GEE•sen] *n*
N transfusion

**umherstreifen**
[UHM•hair•SHTRUY•fen] *vt*
straggle

**umklammern**
[OOM•KLAH•mairn] *vt* close;
clasp

**umkommen** [UHM•KOH•men]
*vi* perish

**Umkreis** [OOM•kruys] *n* M
circumference; perimeter

**umlaufen** [OOM•LOUF•ehn] *vi*
*vt* circulate

**Umleitung** [OOM•LUY•toong]
*n* F detour

**Umschlag** [OOM•shlahg] *n* M
envelope

**umschreiben** [uhm•shruy•ben]
*vt vi* rewrite

**umsetzen** [OOM•ZET•sen] *vt*
turnover

**umsiedeln** [-eln] *vi* migrate

**Umsiedler** [UHM•ZEED•lair] *n*
M migrant

**Umstände** [OOM•SHTEN•deh]
*n pl* F circumstances

**umstellen** [OOM•SHTEL•len]
*vt* transpose

**umstoßen** [OOM•SHTOH•sen]
*vt* upset

**umstürzlerisch**
[UHM•shtuhrts•lair•ish] *adj*
subversive; seditious

**umwandeln** [OOM•vahn•deln]
*vt* transform

**Umwandlung** [-loong] *n* F
transformation

**umwickeln** [OOM•vih•keln] *vt*
muffle

**Umzug** [UHM•tsoog] *n* M
parade; procession

**unabhängig** [UHN•ap•heng ig]
*adj* independent

**Unabhängigkeit**
[UHN•ap•HENG•ig•kuyt] *n* F
independence

**unachtsam** [UN•AHKT•zahm]
*adj* inadvertent

**unangenehm**
[OON•AHN•ge•naim] *adj*
embarrassing

**unangreifbar**
[UHN•AHN•gruyf•bahr] *adj*
unassailable

**unanständig**
[UHN•AHN•shten•dig] *adj*
indecent; obscene

**Unanständigkeit**
[UHN•AHN•shtehn•dig•kuyt]
*n* F obscenity

**unanwendbar**
[UHN•AHN•vend•bahr] *adj*
irrelevant

**unartig** [UHN•AHR•tig] *adj*
naughty

**unaufhörlich**
[UHN•OUF•her•lihk] *adj*
incessant; unceasing

**Unausgewogenheit**
[UHN•OUS•ge•VOH•gen•huyt]
*n* F imbalance

**unbarmherzig**
[UHN•BAHRM•hair•tsig] *adj*
pitiless

**unbeaufsightigt**
[UHN•be•OUF•zihk•tikt] *adj*
uncontrolled

**unbedacht** [UHN•be•DAHKT]
*adj* indiscreet

**unbedeutend**
[UHN•beh•DOIT•end] *adj*
petty

**unbedingt 1**
[UHN•beh•DINGKT] *adj*
categorical

**unbedingt 2**
[UHN•beh•DINKT] *adj*
unconditional

**unbeeinflußt**
[UHN•beh•UYN•floost] *adj*
unbiased

**Unbefugter**
[UHN•beh•FUHG•tair] *n* M
trespasser

**unbegrenzt**
[UHN•beh•GRENTST] *adj*
unbounded

**Unbehagen**
[OON•be•HAH•gen] *n* N
discomfort

**unbenutzt**
[UHN•beh•NUHTST] *adj*
unused

**unbequem** [UHN•be•KVAIM]
*adj* ill at ease

**unbequem** [UHN•beh•KVAIM]
*adj* uncomfortable

**unberührt** [UHN•beh•RUHRT]
*adj* untouched

**unbesiegbar**
[UHN•be•ZEEG•bahr] *adj*
invincible

**unbesiegt** [UHN•beh•SEEKT]
*adj* unconquered

**unbestimmt**
[UHN•be•SHTIMT] *adj*
indefinite

**unbestreitbar**
[UHN•beh•SHTRUYT•bahr]
*adj* undeniable

**unbewaffnet**
[UHN•beh•VAHF•net] *adj*
unarmed

**unbeweglich**
[UHN•be•VAIG•lihk] *adj*
immobile

**unbeweglich machen** *vt*
immobilize

**unbewußt** [UHN•beh•VUHST]
*adj* unconscious

**Unbewußtheit**
[UHN•beh•VUHST•huyt] *n* F
unconsciousness

**unbiegsam**
[UHN•BEEG•zahm] *adj*
unbending

**und** [oont] *conj* and

**undankbar**
[UHN•DAHNK•bahr] *adj*
thankless

**Undankbarkeit**
[UHN•DAHNK•bar•kuyt] *n* F
ingratitude; thanklessness

**undenkbar** [UHN•DENK•bahr]
*adj* unthinkable

**undeutlich** [UHN•DOIT•lihk]
*adj* vague; indistinct;
undistinguished

**unduldsam**
[UHN•DOOLD•zahm] *adj*
intolerant

**undurchdringlich**
[UHN•DOORHK•dring•lihk]
*adj* impervious

**undurchsichtig**
[UHN•DOORHK•sihk•tig] *adj*
opaque

**unehelich** [UHN•AI•eh•lihk]
*adj* illegitimate

**Unehre** [OON•AIR•eh] *n* F
dishonor

**unehrlich** [OON•AIR•lihk] *adj*
dishonest; corrupt

**unempfindlich**
[UHN•EMP•find•lihk] *adj*
insensitive

**unendlich** [UHN•END•lihk] *adj*
infinite

**Unendlichkeit**
[UHN•END•lihk•kuyt] *n* F
infinity

**unentshieden**
[UHN•ENT•shee•den] *adj*
undecided

**unentwegt** [-ENT•vaikt] *adj*
undeviating

**unerfahren** [uhn•AIR•fahr•en]
*adj* inexperienced

**unerfolgreich**
[uhn•AIR•folg•ruyhk] *adj*
unsuccessful

**unerläßlich** [uhn•AIR•les•lihk]
*adj* indispensable

**unerlaubt** [uhn•AIR•loupt] *adj*
illicit

**unermüdlich**
[uhn•AIR•muhd•lihk] *adj*
tireless; untiring

**unerprobt** [uhn•AIR•prohpt]
*adj* untried

**unersättlich**
[uhn•AIR•zets•lihk] *adj*
insatiable

**unersetzbar**
[uhn•AIR•zets•bahr] *adj*
irreplaceable

**unersetzlich**
[uhn•AIR•zets•lihk] *adj*
irreparable

**unerträglich**
[uhn•AIR•treg•lihk] *adj*
intolerable; unbearable

**unerzählt** [uhn•AIR•tsailt] *adj*
untold

**unfähig** [uhn•FAI•hig] *adj*
incapable; incompetent;
unable

**Unfähigkeit**
[uhn•FAI•hig•KUYT] *n* F
inability

**Unfall** [UHN•fal] *n* M accident;
mishap

**unfehlbar** [uhn•FAIL•bahr] *adj*
infallible

**unfreiwillig**
[UHN•FRUY•vil•lig] *adj*
involuntary

**unfruchtbar öde**
[oon•FROOKT•bahr]
[OO•deh] *adj* barren

**ungarisch** [UHN•gahr•ish] *adj*
Hungarian

**Ungarn** [UHN•gahrn] *n*
Hungary

**ungebildet** [uhn•GEH•bil•det]
*adj* uneducated

**ungebrochen**
[uhn•GEH•brohk•en] *adj*
unbroken

**Ungebühr** [uhn•GEH•boor] *n* F
misconduct

**Ungeduld** [uhn•GE•doold] *n* F
impatience

**ungeduldig** [-ig] *adj* impatient

**ungeeignet**
[UHN•ge•UYG•net] *adj*
inappropriate

**ungefähr** [UHN•geh•FAIR] *adv*
roughly

**ungefähr fast** [OON•ge•FAIR]
[fahst] *adv* approximately

**ungeheuer** [UHN•ge•HOI•air]
*adj* immense

**Ungeheur** [UHN•geh•HOI•air]
*n* N monster

**Ungeheurerlichkeit**
[-lihk•kuyt] *n* N monstrosity

**ungehorsam**
[OON•ge•HOHR•zahm] *adj*
disobedient

**ungekünstelt**
[UHN•geh•KUHN•stehlt] *adj*
unaffected

**ungenau** [UHN•ge•NOU] *adj*
inaccurate

**ungenügend**
[UHN•ge•NOOG•ent] *adj*
inadequate

**ungepflegt**
[OON•ge•PFLAIGKT] *adj*
dishevelled

**ungerechtfertigt**
[UHN•geh•REHKT•FAIR•tikt]
*adj* unwarranted

**ungeschickt**
[OON•geh•SHIKT] *adj*
awkward; clumsy

**ungeschult**
[UHN•geh•SHOOLT] *adj*
untrained

**ungesellig** [OON•geh•ZEL•ig]
*adj* antisocial

**ungestört**
[UHN•geh•SHTURHT] *adj*
undisturbed; untroubled

**ungestüm 1**
[UHN•geh•SHTOOM] *adj*
boisterous

**ungestüm 2**
[UHN•ge•STUHM] *adj*
impetuous

**ungesund** [UHN•geh•ZUHNT]
*adj* unwholesome

**ungewaschen**
[UHN•geh•VAH•shen] *adj*
unwashed

**ungewöhnlich**
[UHN•guh•VOON•lik] *adj*
abnormal; exceptional;
uncommon

**ungewohnt**
[UHN•ge•VOHNT] *adj*
unaccustomed

**Ungeziefer**
[UHN•geh•TSEE•fair] *n* N
vermin

**ungläubig** *adj* unbelieving

**Ungläubiger**
[UHN•GLOI•big•air] *n* M
unbeliever

**unglaublich**
[UHN•GLOUB•lihk] *adj*
incredible; unbelievable

**ungleich** [UHN•gluyhk] *adj*
unequal

**Ungleichheit**
[UHN•gluyhk•HUYT] *n* F
inequality

**Unglück** [UHN•glook] *n* N
adversity; disaster

**unglücklich** [UHN•gluhk•lihk]
*adj* unlucky; hapless

**ungültig** [UHN•guhl•tig] *adj*
invalid

**Unheil** [UHN•huyl] *n* N
mischief

**unheilbar** [UHN•huyl•bahr] *adj*
incurable

**unheimlich** [UHN•huym•lihk]
*adj* uncanny

**unhöflich** [UHN•huhf•lihk] *adj*
impolite; rude; uncivil

**uninteresiert**
[OON•in•TAIR•es•EERT] *adj*
disinterested; unconcerned

**Universität**
[OON•ee•vair•si•TAIT] *n* F
university; college

**unklug** [UHN•kloog] *adj*
imprudent; unwise

**unkontrollierbar**
[UHN•kohn•tro•LEER•bahr]
*adj* uncontrollable

**unkonventionell**
[UHN•kon•ven•TSEE•on•el]
*adj* unconventional

**Unkraut** [UHN•krout] *n* N tare;
weed

**unkrautartig** [-ahr•tig] *adj*
weedy

**unkultiviert**
[UHN•kool•tih•VEERT] *adj*
uncultured

**unkundig** [UHN•KUHN•dig]
*adj* ignorant

**unlogisch** [uhn•LOH•gish] *adj*
illogical

**unmenschlich**
[uhn•MEHNSH•lihk] *adj*
inhuman; cruel

**unmöglich** [uhn•MUHG•lihk]
*adj* impossible

**unnahbar** [uhn•NAH•bahr] *adj*
unapproachable

**unnötig** [uhn•NUH•tig] *adj*
needless

**unordentlich**
[uhn•OHR•dent•lihk] *adj*
messy

**Unordentlichkeit**
[uhn•OR•DENT•lihk•kuyt] *n*
F untidiness

**Unordnung** [oon•ORD•noong] *n* F disorder; clutter

**unorganisch** [uhn•OR•gahn•ish] *adj* inorganic

**unpassend** [uhn•PAH•send] *adj* unbecoming; unsuitable

**unpersönlich** [uhn•PAIR•SUHN•lich] *adj* impersonal

**Unrecht** [UHN•rehkt] *n* N injustice

**unregelmäßig** [UHN•RAI•gel•MAI•sig] *adj* irregular

**Unregelmäßigkeit** [-kuyt] *n* F irregularity

**unreif** [UHN•raif] *adj* immature

**unrein** [UHN•ruyn] *adj* impure; unclean

**Unreinheit** [UHN•ruyn•HUYT] *n* F impurity

**unrichtig** [UHN•rihk•tig] *adj* incorrect

**Unruhe** [UHN•roo•he] *n* F turmoil

**Unruhestifter** [UHN•roo•eh•SHTIF•tair] *n* M trouble maker

**unruhig** [UHN•roo•hig] *adj* restless; uneasy; turbulent

**unruhig sein** [OON•roo•hig•ZAIN] *vi* fidget

**uns 1** [uhns] *pron pl* ourselves

**uns 2** [uhns] *per pron* us

**unschätzbar** [UHN•shets•bahr] *adj* invaluable; priceless

**unscharf** [oon•shahrf] *adj* blurry

**unscheinbar** [uhn•SHUYN•bahr] *adj* inconspicuous

**unschicklich** [uhn•SHIHK•lihk] *adj* improper

**unschuldig** [uhn•SHOOL•dig] *adj* innocent

**unser** [UHN•sair] *poss adj* our; *poss* ours

**unsicher** [uhn•ZIHK•air] *adj* insecure; precarious; uncertain

**unsichtbar** [uhn•ZIHKT•bahr] *adj* invisible

**Unsinn** [OON•zin] *n* M nonsense; drivel

**unsittlich** [uhn•ZIT•lihk] *adj* immoral

**unsterblich** [uhn•SHTAIRB•lihk] *adj* immortal; undying

**Unsterblichkeit** [-kuyt] *n* MF immortality

**untätig** [uhn•TAI•tig] *adj* idle; inactive

**unten** [OON•ten] *adv* below; beneath

**unter** [UHN•tair] *prep* under; *prep* underneath

**unter Normalgröße** [-nor•MAHL•GRUH•seh] undersized

**Unterarm** [OON•tair•ARM] *n* M forearm

**Unterausschuß** [UHN•tair•OUS•shuhs] *n* M subcommittee

**Unterbau** [OON•tair•BOU] *n* M foundation

**unterbewußt** [UHN•tair•beh•VOOST] *adj* subconscious

**unterbieten** [-BEE•ten] *vt* undersell

**Unterbilanz**
[OON•tair•BEE•lants] *n* F
deficit

**unterbrechen**
[UHN•tair•BREHK•en] *vt*
interrupt

**Unterbrechung** [-oong] *n* F
interruption

**unterdessen**
[UHN•tair•DES•sen] *adv*
meanwhile

**unterdrücken**
[UHN•tair•DRUH•ken] *vt*
repress

**Unterdrückung**
[UHN•tair•DRUHK•oong] *n* F
oppression

**untergenommen**
[-geh•NO•men] *pp* undertaken

**untergeordnet**
[UHN•tair•GEH•ord•net] *adj*
subordinate

**untergrund**
[UHN•tair•GRUHNT] *adj*
underground

**Untergrundbahn**
[UHN•tair•GRUHNT•bahn] *n*
F subway

**unterhalb** [UHN•tair•HAHLB]
*prep* underneath

**Unterhalt** [UHN•tair•HAHLT]
*n* M sustenance

**Unterhaltung 1**
[OON•tair•HAL•toong] *n* F
conversation

**Unterhaltung 2**
[OON•tair•HAHL•toong] *n* F
entertainment

**Unterhemd** [OON•tair•HEMD]
*n* N undershirt

**Unterhose**
[UHN•tair•HOH•zeh] *n* F
underwear; panties

**unterirdisch**
[UHN•tair•EER•dish] *adj*
subterranean

**Unterjacke** [UHN•tair•YAH•ke]
*n* F jersey

**unterjochen**
[UHN•tair•YOHK•en] *vt*
subdue

**Unterkleidung**
[UHN•tair•KLUY•doong] *n* F
underclothes

**Unterlassung**
[OON•tair•LAH•soong] *n* F
failure; default

**unterminieren**
[UHN•tair•MIN•eer•en] *vt*
undermine

**Unternehmen 1**
[OON•tair•NAI•men] *n* N
enterprise; undertaking

**Unternehmen 2**
[OON•tair•NAI•men] *n* N
establishment

**unternehmen**
[UHN•tair•NAI•men] *vt*
undertake

**unternehmend**
[UHN•tair•NAI•mend] *adj*
enterprising

**Unternehmung**
[UHN•tair•NAI•moong] *n* F
venture (business)

**unterrichten**
[OON•tair•RIHK•ten] *vt*
educate; teach

**unterschätzen**
[UHN•tair•SHEHT•sen] *vt*
underestimate

**unterscheiden**
[OON•tair•SHUY•den] *vi*
discriminate; distinguish

**Unterschied**
[OON•tair•SHEED] *n* M
difference

**unterschiedslos**
[OON•tair•SHEEDS•los] *adj*
undiscriminating

**Unterschlagung**
[UHN•tair•SHLAHG•oong] *n*
F misappropriation

**Unterschrift**
[UHN•tair•SHRIHFT] *n* F
signature

**Unterseeboot**
[UHN•tair•ZEE•boht] *n* N
submarine

**Unterseite** [OON•tair•SAI•teh]
*n* F bottom

**unterstreichen**
[OON•tair•SHTRUY•khen] *vt*
emphasize; underline

**unterstützen**
[UHN•tair•SHTUHTS•en] *vt*
subsidize

**untersuchen**
[UHN•tair•ZOO•khen] *vt*
inspect; investigate

**Untersuchung 1**
[UHN•tair•ZOOHK•oong] *n* F
inspection; investigation;
inquisition

**Untersuchung 2**
[UHN•tair•ZOO•khoong] *n* F
scrutiny

**Untertauchen**
[UHN•tair•TOU•khen] *n* N
plunge

**untertauchen**
[UHN•tair•TOU•khen] *vt*
submerge

**Unterteilung**
[UHN•tair•TUY•loong] *n* F
subdivision

**unterweisen**
[UHN•tair•VAI•sen] *vt*
indoctrinate

**Unterwelt** [vehlt] *n* F
underworld

**unterwerfen**
[UHN•tair•VAIR•fen] *vt*
subjugate

**Unterwerfung 1**
[UHN•tair•VAIRF•oong] *n* F
subjection

**Unterwerfung 2**
[UHN•tair•VAIR•foong] *n* F
submission

**unterwürfig**
[UHN•tair•VOORF•ig] *adj*
menial

**unterzeichnen**
[UHN•tair•TSAIHK•nen] *vt*
subscribe

**Unterzeichner**
[UHN•tair•TSAIHK•nair (in)]
*n* M subscriber

**Unterzeichneter**
[-TSAIHK•neh•tair] *n* M
undersigned

**Unterzeichnung** [-noong] *n* F
subscription

**Untier** [OON•teer] *n* N brute

**untrennbar** [uhn•TREN•bahr]
*adj* inseparable

**untreu** [oon•TROI] *adj* disloyal

**Untreue** [uhn•TROI•eh] *n* F
infidelity

**untröstlich** [uhn•TRUHST•lihk]
*adj* heartbroken

**Untugend** [uhn•TOOG•end] *n*
F vice

**unveränderlich**
[uhn•FAIR•EN•dair•lihk] *adj*
unchangeable

**unverändert**
[uhn•FAIR•EN•dairt] *adj*
unchanged

**unverantwortlich**
[uhn•VAIR•AHNt•vort•lihk]
*adj* irresponsible

**unverdächtigt**
[uhn•FAIR•DEHK•tikt] *adj*
unsuspected

**unverdient**
[uhn•FAIR•DEENT] *adj*
unearned

**unverheiratet**
[oon•FAIR•HUY•air•ah•teht]
*adj* F celibate

**unvermeidlich**
[uhn•FAIR•MUYD•lihk] *adj*
inevitable; unavoidable

**unvernünftig**
[uhn•FAIR•NUHNF•tig] *adj*
irrational

**unverschämt**
[uhn•FAIR•SHEMT] *adj*
impertinent; insolent;
impudent

**unversehrt** [uhn•FAIR•SAIRT]
*adj* intact

**unvollendet** [uhn•FOL•EN•det]
*adj* incomplete

**unvollständig**
[uhn•FOL•STEHN•dig] *adj*
imperfect

**unvoreingenommen**
[uhn•FOR•UYN•ge•NO•men]
*adj* impartial

**unvorsichtig**
[oon•FOR•ZIKH•tig] *adj*
careless; unwary

**unwahrscheinlich**
[uhn•VAHR•SHUYN•lihk]
*adj* improbable

**unwesentlich**
[uhn•VAI•ZENT•lihk] *adj*
immaterial

**unwichtig** [uhn•VIHK•tig] *adj*
insignificant

**unwiderstehlich**
[uhn•VEE•dair•SAI•lihk] *adj*
irresistible

**unwillkommen**
[uhn•VIHL•ko•men] *adj*
unwelcome

**unwirksam**
[uhn•VEERK•zahm] *adj*
ineffective

**Unwissenheit**
[uhn•VIHS•sen•HUYT] *n* F
ignorance

**unwürdig** [uhn•VOOR•dig] *adj*
unworthy

**Unze** [UHN•tse] *n* F ounce

**unzeitig** [uhn•TSAIT•ig] *adj*
untimely

**unzerbrechlich**
[-tsair•BREHK•lihk] *adj*
unbreakable

**unzerstörbar**
[UHN•tsair•SHTER•bahr] *adj*
indestructible

**unzüchtig** [oon•TSOOK•tig]
*adj* bawdy; lewd; obscene

**unzufrieden**
[oon•TSOO•FREE•den] *adj*
displeased

**unzureichend**
[uhn•TSOO•RUYHK•end] *adj*
insufficient

**üppig 1** [UH•pig] *adj*
exuberant; profuse

**üppig 2** [UH•pig] *adj* opulent

**uralt** [OOHR•ahlt] *adj* ancient

**Uran** [OOR•ahn] *n* N uranium

**Urenkelin** [OOR•aink•el•in] *n* F great-granddaughter

**Urgroßeltern** [-EL•tairn] *npl* great-grandparents

**Urgroßenkel** *n* M great-grandson

**Urgroßmutter** [-MUH•tair] *n* F great-grandmother

**Urgroßvater** [OOR•gross•FAH•tair] *n* M great-grandfather

**Urheberrecht** [OOR•hai•bair•rekht] *n* N copyright

**Urin** [OOR•een] *n* M urine

**urinieren** [OOR•in•EER•en] *vi* urinate

**Urlaub** [OOR•loub] *n* M vacation

**Urne** [OOYR•neh] *n* F urn; casket

**Ursache** [OOYR•zah•keh] *n* F cause

**Ursprung** [OOR•shpruhng] *n* M origin

**ursprunglich** [OOR•SHPRUHNG•lihk] *adv* originally

**Urteilsspruch** [OOR•tuyls•SHPROOHK] *n* M verdict

# V

**väterlich** [FEH•tair•lihk] *adj* fatherly; paternal

**Vagabund** [VAH•gah•bunt] *n* M vagabond

**Valentinsgruß** [VAHL•en•teens•gruhs] *n* M valentine

**Vanillasoße** [van•EEL•ah•ZOH•se] *n* F custard

**Vanille** [vah•NIL•lah] *n* F vanilla

**Variete** [VAHR•EE•eh•tai] *n* N vaudeville; variety show

**Vase** [VAH•zeh] *n* F vase

**Vater** [FAH•tair] *n* M dad; father

**Vaterland** [FAH•tair•LANT] *n* N fatherland

**Vaterschaft** [VAH•tair•SHAHFT] *n* F paternity

**Vegetarier in** [VEH•geh•tahr•EE•air] [in] *n* M vegetarian

**Veilchen** [FUYL•khen] *n* N violet

**Vene** [VAI•neh] *n* F vein

**Ventil** [VEN•teel] *n* N valve

**Venusmuschel** [VEE•noos•MOOSH•ehl] *n* F clam

**verabscheuen** [fair•AB•shooi•un] *vt* abhor; loathe; detest

**verachten** [fair•AHK•ten] *vt*
despise; scorn

**Verachtung** [fair•AHK•toong]
*n* F contempt; disdain

**verächtlich 1** [fair•EHKT•lihk]
*adj* contemptible; despicable

**verächtlich 2** [fair•EHKT•lihk]
*adj* disparaging

**verächtlich behandeln**
[vair•EHKT•LIHK
beh•HAN•deln] *vi* snub

**veränderlich**
[fair•EN•dair•LIHK] *adj*
variable

**verändern** [fair•AIYN•dairn] *vt*
diversify; vary

**Veränderung**
[fair•EN•dair•oong] *n* F
variation

**verärgern** [vair•AIR•gairn] *vt*
irritate

**verärgert** [fair•AIR•gairt] *adj*
disgruntled

**verallgemeinern** [-airn] *vt*
generalize

**Verallgemeinerung**
[fair•AHL•ge•MUYN•AIR•
oong] *n* F generalization

**veraltet** [fair•AHL•tet] *adj*
obsolete; outdated

**Veranda** [fair•AHN•dah] *n* F
verandah

**veranschaulichen**
[fair•AHN•SHOU•lihk•en] *vt*
exemplify

**Veranstalter**
[fair•ahn•shtahl•tair] *n* M
promoter

**verantwortlich**
[fair•AHNT•VOHRT•lihk] *adj*
liable; responsible

**Verantwortlichkeit**
[vair•AHNT•VOHRT•lihk•
kuyt] *n* responsibility

**verarmt** [fair•ARMT] *adj*
destitute

**Verband** [fair•BANT] *n* M
band

**Verbandskasten**
[fair•BAHNTS•KAH•sten] *n* F
first aid

**verbannen** [fair•BAHN•nen] *vt*
banish

**Verbannung** [fair•BAHN•oong]
*n* F exile

**Verbeugung** [fair•BOI•goong]
*n* F bow

**Verbesserung**
[fair•BES•AIR•oong] *n* F
correction; improvement

**verbieten** [fair•BEE•ten] *vt*
forbid; prohibit

**Verbrecher** [fair•BREHK•en] *n*
M outlaw

**verbilligen** [fair•BIL•ig•ehn] *vt*
cheapen

**verbinden 1** [fair•BIN•den] *vt*
join; connect

**verbinden 2** [fairt•BIN•den] *vt*
associate

**verbindlich** [fair•BIND•lihk]
*adj* obliging

**Verbindung** [fair•BIN•doong] *n*
F conjunction; junction;
alliance

**Verbindung Gesellschaft**
[fair•BIN•doong]
[geh•ZEL•shahft] *n* F
association

**Verbitterung**
[fair•BIT•TAIR•oong] *n* F
bitterness

**verblassen** [fair•BLAH•sen] *vi*
fade

**verblüffen** [fair•BLUH•fen] *vt*
dazzle; dumbfound

**verborgen** [fair•BOHR•gen]
*adj* hidden

**verborgen liegen**
[fair•BOR•gen lee•gen] *vi* lurk

**Verborgenheit**
[fair•BOR•gen•HUYT] *n* F
secrecy

**Verbot** [FAIR•boht] *n* N ban;
prohibition

**Verbrauch** [fair•BROUKH] *n*
M consumption

**Verbrauchsgüter**
[fair•BROUKS•goo•tair] *n* M
consumer

**verbraucht** [fair•BROUKHT]
*adj* decrepit

**Verbrechen** [fair•BREK•en] *n*
N crime

**Verbrecher** [fair•BREHK•air] *n*
M felon; thug

**verbrecherisch Kriminal**
[fair•BREK•air•ish]
[KRI•min•AHL] *adj n* M
criminal

**verbrennen** [fair•BREHN•nen]
*vt* scorch

**Verbum** [FAIRB•oom] *n* N
verb

**verbuttern, Butterfaß**
[fair•BOO•tairn]
[BOO•tair•FAHS] *vt n* F
churn

**verdächtigen**
[fair•DEHK•tig•en] *vt* suspect

**verdammen** [fair•DAHM•en] *vt*
condemn; damn

**verdammt** [fair•DAHMT] *adj*
doomed; damned

**verdampfen** [fair•DAHMP•fen]
*vt* evaporate

**verdauen** [fair•DOU•en] *vt*
digest

**Verdauung** [fair•DOU•oong] *n*
F digestion

**Verdauungsstörung**
[fair•DOU•oongs•SHTOOR•
oong] *n* F indigestion

**verdecken** [fair•DEK•en] *vt*
conceal

**verderben 1** [fair•DAIR•ben] *vt*
spoil; debase

**verderben 2** [fair•DAIR•ben] *vt*
demoralize

**verderblich** [fair•DAIRB•lihk]
*adj* mischievous

**verderbt** [fair•DAIRPT] *adj*
degenerate

**verdichten** [fair•DIKH•ten] *vt*
condense

**verdicken** [fair•DIHK•en] *vt*
thicken

**verdienen** [fair•DEEN•en] *vt*
deserve; earn

**Verdienstlichkeit**
[fair•DEENST•lihk•kuyt] *n* F
merit

**verdienstvoll**
[fair•DEENST•fol] *adj*
deserving

**verdometschen**
[fair•DOL•met•chen] *vt*
interpret

**verdorben** [fair•dor•ben] *adj*
foul

**Verdorbenheit**
[fair•DOHR•ben•HUYT] *n* F
corruption

**verdorren** [fiar•DOR•ren] *vi*
wither

**verdrehen** [fair•DREH•en] *vt*
twist; distort

**Verdrehung** [fair•DRAI•hoong]
*n* F wrench

**verdreschen** [fair•DREH•shen]
*vt* thrash; wallop

**verdrießlich** [fair•DREES•lihk]
*adj* grumpy; grouchy

**verdummen** [fair•DUHM•men]
*vt* stupefy

**verdunkeln** [fair•DOONK•eln]
*vt* darken

**verdünnen** [fair•DAHN•en] *vt*
dilute

**verehren** [fair•AIR•en] *vt*
admire; revere; venerate

**Verehrung** [fair•AIR•oong] *n* F
reverence; veneration

**vereinbar** [fair•UYN•bar] *adj*
compatible

**vereinfachen**
[fair•UYN•FAHK•ehn] *vt*
simplify

**Vereinfachung**
[fair•UYN•FAHK•oong] *n* F
simplification

**vereinigen** [fair•UYN•IG•en] *vt*
consolidate; incorporate

**Vereinigung**
[fair•UYN•I•goong] *n* F guild

**vereiteln** [fair•UY•teln] *vt*
thwart

**vererbt** [fair•AIRPT] *adj*
hereditary

**Vererbung** [fair•AIR•boong] *n*
F heredity

**Verfahren** [fair•FAHR•en] *n* N
proceeding

**Verfahrensweise**
[fair•FAHR•ens•VAI•zeh] *n* F
policy

**verfallend** [fair•FAL•ent] *adj*
decadent

**verfaulen** [fair•FOUL•en] *vt*
rot; putrefy

**verfault** [fair•FOULT] *adj*
putrid

**verfeinern** [fair•FUYN•airn] *vt*
improve

**Verfinsterung**
[fair•FIN•stair•oong] *n* F
eclipse

**verfolgen** [fair•FOL•gen] *vt*
pursue; obsess

**Verfolger** [fair•FOL•gair] *n* M
follower

**Verfolgung** [fair•VOL•goong]
*n* F pursuit; prosecution

**verfügbar** [fair•FOOG•bar] *adj*
available

**verfügen** [fair•FOO•gen] *vt*
enact

**verführen** [fair•FER•en] *vt*
seduce

**Verführer** [fair•FER•hair] *n* M
seducer

**verführerisch** [-ish] *adj*
tempting; seductive

**Verführung** [-oong] *n* F
seduction

**vergänglich** [fair•GENG•lihk]
*adj* volatile

**vergangen 1**
[faiur•GAHNG•ehn] *adv* ago

**vergangen 2** [fair•GAHNG•en]
*adj* past

**vergeben** [fair•GAI•ben] *vt*
forgive

**vergeblich** [fair•GAIB•lihk] *adj*
useless; fruitless

**Vergebung** [fair•GAI•boong] *n*
F remission

**vergelten 1** [fair•GEL•ten] *vt*
render

**vergelten 2** [fair•GEL•ten] *vi*
retaliate

**Vergeltung** [fair•GEL•toong] *n*
F retaliation

**vergessen** [fair•GEH•sen] *vt*
forget

**Vergessenheit**
[fair•GEH•sen•HUYT] *n* F
oblivion

**vergeßlich** [fair•GEHS•lihk] *adj*
forgetful; oblivious

**vergewaltigen** [-en] *vt* rape

**Vergewaltigung**
[FAIR•geh•VAHL•tig•oong] *n*
F rape; abduction

**Vergiftung** [fair•GIHF•toong] *n*
F poisoning

**Vergleich** [fair•GLUYKH] *n* M
comparison

**vergleichen** [fair•GLAI•ken] *vt*
compare

**Vergnügen** [fairg•NOO•gen] *n*
N pleasure

**vergöttern** [fair•GUH•tairn] *vt*
idolize

**vergoldet** [fair•GOL•det] *adj*
gilded; gold-plated

**vergrößern 1**
[fair•GROO•sairn] *vt* enhance

**vergrößern 2**
[fair•GRUH•sairn] *vt* magnify

**Vergrößerungsglas** [-glahs] *n*
N magnifying glass

**vergütern** [fair•GOO•tairn] *vt*
compensate

**Vergütung** [fair•GOO•toong] *n*
F compensation

**Verhältnis 1** [fair•HELT•nis] *n*
N liaison

**Verhältnis 2** [fair•HAILT•nis] *n*
N ratio; relation

**verhaften** [fair•HAF•ten] *vt*
arrest

**verhandeln** [fair•HAHN•deln]
*vi* negotiate

**Verhandlung**
[fair•HAHND•loong] *n* F
negotiation

**verhaßt** [fair•HAHST] *adj*
hateful; odious

**verhauen** [fair•HOU•en] *vt*
spank

**verheiraten**
[fair•HUY•air•ah•ten] *vt* marry

**verheiratet**
[fair•HUY•air•ah•tet] *adj*
married

**verhindern** [vair•HIN•dairn] *vt*
hinder; impede; prevent

**Verhinderung**
[fair•HIN•dair•oong] *n* F
impediment

**verhöhnen** [fair•HUH•nen] *vt*
taunt

**verhungern** [fair•HUHNG•airn]
*vi* starve

**verjüngen** [fair•YUHNG•en] *vi*
rejuvenate

**Verkäufer** [fair•KOI•fair] *n* M
vendor

**Verkäufer** *n* M vendor (street)

**verkaufen** [fair•KOU•fen] *vt*
sell

**Verkehr 1** [fair•KAIR] *n* N
dealings; intercourse

**Verkehr 2** [fair•KAIR] *n* N
traffic

**verkehren Verdreher**
[fair•KAIR•en] [fair•drai•air]
*n* M pervert

**Verkehrsstraße**
[fair•KAIRS•SHTRAH•seh] *n*
F thoroughfare

**verkehrt** [fair•KAIRT] *adj*
perverse; topsy-turvy

**verklagen** [fair•klah•GEN] *vt*
sue

**verklammern**
[fair•KLAH•mairn] *vt* grapple

**verkörpern 1** [fair•KER•pairn]
*vt* embody

**verkörpern 2** [fair•KER•pairn]
*vt* impersonate

**verkrüppeln** [fair•KRU•peln] *vt*
stunt

**verkündigen**
[fair•KUHN•dig•en] *vt*
proclaim

**verkürzen** [fair•KOORTS•en]
*vt* shorten

**verlängern** [fair•lehn•gairn] *vt*
lengthen; prolong

**verlässig** [fair•LES•ig] *adj*
dependable

**Verlangen** [fair•LAHN•gen] *n*
N demand

**verlangen** [fair•LAHNG•en] *vi*
insist

**verlassen** [fair•LAH•sen] *adj*
forsaken

**verlegen 1** [fair•LAI•gen] *adj*
embarrassed

**verlegen 2** [fair•LAI•gen] *vt*
misplace

**Verlegenheit**
[fair•LAI•gen•huyt] *n* F
embarrassment

**verleihen** [fair•LUY•en] impart

**verletzen 1** [fair•LEH•tsen] *vt*
infringe

**verletzen 2** [fair•LEHT•sen] *vt*
injure

**Verletzung** [fair•LEHTS•oong]
*n* F hurt; injury

**verleumden** [fair•LOIM•den] *vt*
defame; malign

**Verleumdung**
[fair•LOIM•doong] *n* F libel;
slander

**verliebt** [fair•LEEPT] *adj* in
love (with); enamored

**verlieren** [fair•LEER•en] *vt*
forfeit; lose

**verlobt** [fair•LOPT] *adj*
engaged

**Verlobte** [-e] *n* F fiancée

**Verlobter** [fair•LOB•ptair] *n* M
fiancé

**Verlobung** [fair•LOH•boong] *n*
F engagement

**verlocken** [fair•LOHK•en] *vt*
wile

**verlockend** [fair•LO•kent] *adj*
enticing; inviting

**verloren** [fair•LOHR•en] *adj*
lost

**verlorene** [fair•LOR•ene] *adj*
prodigal

**Verlust** [fair•LUHST] *n* M loss

**vermählen** [fair•MAI•len] *vt*
wed

**vermehren** [fair•MAIR•en] *vt*
multiply

**Vermehrung, vermehren**
[fair•MAIR•oong] [-en] *n* F
increase; multiplication

**vermeiden** [fair•MAI•den] *vt*
avoid; dodge; evade;

shunvermieten [fair•mee•ten]
*vt* rent

**vermindern 1** [fair•MIN•dairn]
*vt* diminish; reduce

**vermischen 2** [fair•MISH•uhn]
*vt* blend

**vermitteln** [fair•MIHT•eln] *vt*
mediate

**vermitteln zwischen**
[fair•MIT•teln TSVI•shen]
go-between

**Vermittler** [-lair] *n* M mediator

**Vermittlung** [fair•MIT•loong] *n*
F intervention

**vermuten** [fair•MOO•ten] *vt*
presume

**vermutlich** [fair•MUHT•lihk]
*adj* presumably

**Vermutung** [fair•MOO•toong]
*n* F presumption

**Vernachlässigung**
[fair•NAHK•LES•ig•oong] *n* F
disregard; neglect

**vernichten** [fair•NIHK•ten] *vt*
decimate; devastate; demolish;
nullify

**vernichtend** [fair•NIHK•tend]
*adj* devastating

**vernünftig** [fair•NUHNF•tig]
*adj* judicious; rational;
reasonable; sensible

**Vernünftigkeit**
[fair•NUHNFT•ig•kuyt] *n* F
sense (common)

**Vernunftschluß**
[fair•NUHNFT•shluhs] *n* M
syllogism

**Verpacken** [fair•PAH•ken] *n* N
packing

**verpassen** [fair•PAH•sen] *vt*
miss

**Verpflichten** [fair•PFLIHK•ten]
*n* N obligation

**verpflichten** [fair•PLIHK•ten]
*vt* oblige

**Verpflichtung**
[fair•PFLIKH•toong] *n* F
commitment

**verplifchtend**
[fair•PFLIHK•tend] *adj*
obligatory

**Verräter** [fair•RAI•tair] *n* M
traitor

**verräterisch**
[fair•REH•TAIR•ish] *adj*
treacherous

**Verrat** [fair•RAHT] *n* M
treachery; treason; betrayal

**Verrater** [fair•RAH•tair] *n* M
traitor; betrayer

**Verrichtung** [fair•RIHK•toong]
*n* F execution

**verringern** [fair•RING•airn] *vi*
lessen

**verrücken** [fair•ROO•ken] *vt*
dislocate

**verrückt** [fair•ROOKT] *adj*
crazy; insane

**Verrückter** [fair•RUHK•tair] *n*
M madman

**Verruf** [fair•ROOF] *n* M
discredit; disrepute

**verrufen** [fair•ROO•fen] *adj*
infamous

**verrühren** [fair•RUHR•en] *vt*
scramble

**Vers** [fairs] *n* M verse

**versagen** [fair•SAH•gen] *vi*
misfire

**versammeln** [fair•ZAHM•meln]
*vt* assemble; gather;
congregate

**Versammlung**
[fair•ZAHM•loong] *n* F
congregation; gathering

**Versand** [fair•SANT] *n* M
transmission

**Versanstaltung**
[fair•AHN•SHTAHL•toong] *n*
F crush

**verschaffen** [fair•SHAH•fen] *vt*
procure

**Verscheidenheit**
[fair•SHEE•den•HUYT] *n* F
diversity

**verschieben 1** [fair•SHEE•ben]
*vt* postpone

**verschieben 2** [fair•SHEE•ben]
*vt* remit

**verschieden** [fair•shee•den] *adj*
different; diverse; varied;
various

**Verschiedenheit**
[fair•SHEED•en•huyt] *n* F
discrepancy

**verschlacken**
[vair•SHLAH•ken] *vi* slag

**verschlingen** [fair•SHLING•en]
*vt* engulf; *vi* intertwine

**verschmachten**
[fair•SHMAHK•ten] *vi* swelter

**verschmähen**
[fair•SHMAI•hen] *vt* spurn

**verschmelzen**
[fair•SHMEHLTS•en] *vt*
merge

**verschönen** [fair•SHOO•nen] *vt*
embellish

**verschonen Ersatz**
[fair•SHOH•nen] [air•zats] *vt*
*n* M spare

**verschroben** [fair•SHRO•ben]
*adj* cranky

**verschuldet** [fair•SHOOL•det]
*adj* indebted

**verschweißen**
[fair•SHVUY•sen] *vt* weld

**verschwenden**
[fair•SHVEN•den] *vt*
dissipate; squander; waste

**Verschwender**
[fair•SHVEN•dair] *n* M
spendthrift

**verschwenderisch**
[fair•SHVEN•DAIR•ish] *adj*
extravagant; lavish

**Verschwendung**
[fair•SHVEN•doong] *n* F
extravagance

**verschwinden**
[fair•SHVIN•den] *vi*
disappear; recede; vanish

**Verschwörung**
[fair•SHVOOR•oong] *n* F
conspiracy

**Versehen** [fair•SAI•en] *n* N
lapse

**versehentlich**
[fair•ZAI•ent•LIHK] *adj*
unawares

**versengen** [fair•ZEHNG•en] *vt*
scathe; sear

**versetzen 1** [fair•ZETS•en] *vt*
displace

**versetzen 2** [fair•ZETS•en] *vt*
transplant

**versichern** [fair•ZIHK•airn] *vt*
ensure; insure

**versichern** [fair•ZIHK•airn] *vt*
underwrite

**Versicherung**
[fair•zihk•air•oong] *n* F
insurance

**versiert** [fair•SEERT] *adj*
versed

**versklaven** [fair•SKLAH•ven]
*vt* enslave

**versorgen** [fair•ZOR•gen] *vt*
provide

**Versorger** [fair•OR•gair] *n* M
provider

**verspätet** [fair•SHPAI•tet] *adj*
belated

**Verspätung** [air•SHPAI•toong]
*n* F delay

**versperren** [fair•SHPAIR•en] *vt*
obstruct

**verspotten** [fair•SHPO•ten] *vt*
deride; mock

**Versprechen**
[fair•SHPREHK•en] *n* N
promise

**verstaatlichen**
[fair•SHTAHT•lihk•KEHN] *vt*
nationalize

**verständlich**
[fair•SHTEHND•lihk] *adj*
understandable

**verstärken 1** [fair•SHTAIR•ken]
*vt* intensify

**verstärken 2**
[fair•SHTAIR•khen] *vt*
reinforce

**Verstand** [fair•SHTANT] *n* M
comprehension; understanding

**Verstand** [fair•SHTANT] *n* M
wit

**verstaubt** [fair•SHTOUPT] *adj*
musty

**Verstauchung**
[fair•SHTOUHK•oong] *n* F
sprain

**verstauen** [fair•SHTOU•en] *vt*
stow

**Versteck** [fair•SHTEHK] *n* N
hiding

**verstecken** [fair•SHTEH•ken]
*vt* hide

**Versteckplatz** [-plahts] *n* M
hiding place

**verstehen** [fair•SHTAI•en] *vt*
comprehend; *vi* understand

**versteinert** [fair•SHTUYN•airt]
*adj* petrified

**Verstopfung**
[fair•SHTOHP•foong] *n* F
blockage

**verstorben** [fair•SHTOHR•ben]
*adj* deceased

**Verstoß** [fair•SHTOHS] *n* M
offense

**verstümmeln**
[fair•SHTUH•meln] *vt* maim;
mutilate

**Versuch** [fair•zoohk] *n* M trial

**versuchen** [fair•ZOO•ken] *vt*
attempt (to); try

**versuchen** [fair•ZOO•khen] *vt*
tempt

**Versuchung** [-oong] *n* F
temptation

**versunken** [fair•SUHN•ken] *adj*
rapt

**vertagen** [fair•TAHG•ehn] *vt vi*
adjourn

**vertauschen** [fair•TOW•shuhn]
*vi* alternate (with)

**verteidigen 1** [fair•TUY•dig•en]
*vt* defend

**verteidigen 2**
[fair•TUYD•ig•en] *vt*
vindicate

**Verteidigung**
[fair•TUY•DIG•oong] *n* F
defense

**vertiefen** [fair•TEEF•en] *vt*
deepen

**vertieft** [fair•TEEFT] *adj*
preoccupied

**Vertiefung** [fair•TEEF•oong] *n*
F dimple

**vertilgen** [fair•TIL•gen] *vt*
exterminate

**Vertrag** [fair•TRAHG] *n* M
contract; pact; treaty

**Vertragsbruch**
[fair•TRAHGZ•brookh] *n* M
breach (of contract)

**Vertrauen** [fair•TROU•en] *n* N
confidence; reliance; trust

**vertrauen** [fair•TROU•en] *vt*
trust

**vertrauenswürdig**
[fair•TROU•ens VOOR•dig]
*adj* trustworthy

**vertraulich** [fair•TROU•likh]
*adj* confidential

**Vertraute** [fair•TROU•te] *n* F
confidant

**Vertrautheit**
[fair•TROUT•huyt] *n* F
intimacy

**vertreiben1** [fair•TRUY•ben] *vt*
dispel

**vertreiben2** [fair•TRUY•ben] *vt*
evict; oust

**Vertreibung** [fair•TRUYB•ung]
*n* F abortion

**vertreten** [fair•TRAI•ten] *vt*
represent

**Vertreter 1** [fair•TRAI•tair] *n* M
delegate

**Vertreter 2 -in**
[fair•TRAI•tair] *n* M agent

**Vertretung** [-toong] *n* F
representation

**verübeln** [fair•UH•beln] *vt*
resent

**verüben** [fair•UH•ben] *vt*
perpetrate

**verunreinigen**
[fair•OON•ruyn•IG•en] *vt*
contaminate

**veruntreuen**
[fair•OON•TROI•en] *vt*
embezzle

**verursachen**
[fair•OOR•ZAH•ken] induce

**verurteilen**
[fair•oor•TUY•LEN] *vt*
denounce; repudiate

**Vervollständigung**
[fair•FOHL•SHTEN•dig•oong]
*n* F complement

**verwahrlostes Kind**
[fair•VAHR•los•tes kihnt] *n* N
waif

**verwalten** [fair•VAULT•ehn] *vt*
administer; govern; manage

**Verwalter** [fair•VAHL•tair] *n*
M manager; trustee; steward

**Verwaltung** [fair•VAHL•toong]
*n* F management

**Verwandlung**
[fair•VAHND•loong] *n* F
conversion

**verwandt** [fair•VAHNT] *adj*
related

**Verwandter** [fair•VANT•air] *n*
M relative

**Verwandtschaft**
[fair•VAHNT•shahft] *n* F kin

**verwechseln** [fair•VEKS•eln]
*vt* confound

**Verweigerung**
[fair•VAIG•air•oong] *n* F
refusal

**verweilen** [fair•VUY•len] *vi*
linger

**Verweis** [fair•VUYS] *n* M
reprimand

**verwelken** [fair•VEL•ken] *vt*
wilt

**verweltlichen**
[fair•VELT•lihk•en] *vt*
secularize

**verwendbar** [fair•VEND•bahr]
*adj* serviceable

**verwenden** [fair•VEN•den] *vt*
utilize

**verwickeln** [fair•VIHK•eln] *vt*
involve

**verwickelt** [fair•VIHK•elt] *adj*
intricate

**Verwirklichung**
[fair•VEERK•LIHK•oong] *n* F
realization

**verwirren** [fair•VEER•en] *vt*
confuse; distract; perplex;
tangle

**verwirrt** [fair•VEERT] *adj*
confusing; perplexed

**Verwirrung** [fair•VEER•oong]
*n* F confusion; disarray

**verwöhnen** [fair•VUH•nen] *vt*
pamper

**Verworfenheit**
[vair•VOR•fen•huyt] *n* F
turpitude

**verworren** [fair•VOR•ren] *adj*
promiscuous

**verwundbar**
[fair•VUHNT•bahr] *adj*
vulnerable

**verwüsten** [fair•VUH•sten] *vt*
ravage

**verzaubern** [fair•TSOU•bairn]
*vt* enchant

**verzeichnen**
[fair•TSAIHK•nen] *vt* itemize

**verzeihen** [fair•TSAI•en] *vt*
condone

**Verzeihung** [fair•TSAI•hoong]
*n* F pardon

**verzichten auf1**
[fair•TSIHK•ten ouf] *vt* quit

**verzichten auf2**
[fair•TSIHK•ten ouf] *vt* waive

**verzinnt** [fair•TSINT] *adj*
tinned

**verzögern** [fair•TSUH•gairn] *vt*
retard

**verzogen** [fair•TSOH•gen] *adj*
warped

**Verzückung**
[fair•TSOOK•oong] *n* F
ecstasy; rapture

**verzweifelt** [fair•TSVAI•felt]
*adj* desperate; forlorn

**Verzweiflung**
[fair•TSVAIF•loong] *n* F
despair

**Vestibül** [FEHST•ih•BUHL] *n*
N vestibule

**Veteran** [FEH•tair•AHN] *n* M
veteran

**Veto** [FAI•toh] *n* N veto

**Vetter** [fet•tair] *n* M cousin

**Viadukt** [FEE•ah•DOOHKT] *n*
M viaduct

**vibrieren** [fih•BREER•en] *vi*
vibrate

**Vibrieren** *n* N vibration

**Vieh** [fee] *n* N cattle; livestock

**Viehhof** [FEE•hof] *n* M
stockyards

**viel** [feel] *adj* much

**viele** [FEEL•eh] *adj* many;
several

**Vielfraß** [FEEL•frahs] *n* M
glutton
**vielleicht** [fee•LUYHKT] *adv*
perhaps
**vielseitig** [feel•sai•tihg] *adj*
miscellaneous
**vier** [feer] *num* four
**vierseitig** [FEER•suy•tig] *adj*
quadrilateral
**vierte** [-te] *num* fourth
**Viertel** [FEER•tel] *n* N quarter
**vierteljährlich**
[FEER•tel•YAIR•lihk] *adj*
quarterly
**Viertelscheffel**
[VEER•tel•SHEH•fel] *n* M
peck
**vierzehn** [FEER•tsain] *num*
fourteen
**vierzig** [FEER•tsig] *num* forty
**Villa** [FIL•la] *n* F mansion
**Villa** [FEE•la] *n* F villa
**Violine** [VEE•oh•LEEN•eh] *n* F
violin
**Violinist in** [-eest] [in] *n* M
violinist
**Viper** [FEE•pair] *n* F viper
**Virulenz** [FEER•uhl•ENTS] *n* F
virulence
**Virus** [fee•ruhs] *n* N virus
**visionär** [FIH•ZEE•on•AIR] *adj*
visionary
**Viskosität** [FIH•skoh•sih•TAIT]
*n* F viscosity
**visuell** [FIH•zoo•EL] *adj* visual
**Visum** [FEE•zoom] *n* N visa
**Vitalität** [FIH•tahl•ih•TAIT] *n* F
vitality
**Vitamin** [FEE•tah•MEEN] *n* N
vitamin

**Vitriol** [FEE•TREE•ol] *n* N
vitriol
**völlig 1** [FUHL•ligk] *adv*
absolutely; wholly; thoroughly
**völlig 2** [FUHL•ig] *adv* perfectly
**Vogel** [FOH•gel] *n* M bird
**Vogelbauer**
[FOH•gel•BOW•air] *n* N bird
cage
**Vokal** [FOH•kahl] *n* M vowel
**Volk** [FOLK] *n* N folk;
populace
**Volksstamm** [FOLKS•shtsahm]
*n* M tribe
**Volksverhetzung**
[FOLKS•vair•hets•oong] *n* F
sedition
**Volkszählung**
[fOLKS•TSAIYL•oong] *n* F
census
**voll** [fol] *adj* full
**vollbringen** [FOHL•bring•uhn]
*vt* accomplish
**vollenden** [FOL•end•en] *vt*
consummate
**voller Skrupel** [FOL•air -]
scrupulous
**vollkommen** [FOL•koh•men]
*adj* perfect
**Vollkommenheit** [-huyt] *n* F
perfection
**Vollmacht 1** [FOL•mahkt] *n*
warrant
**Vollmacht 2** [FOL•mahkt] *n* F
authority
**Vollmond** [FOL•mohnt] *n* M
full moon
**vollstopfen** [FOL•shtop•fen] *vt*
cram
**Volt** [fohlt] *n* N volt

**Volumen** [FOL•oom•en] *n* N
volume

**von** [fuhn] *prep* from; of

**von den Lippen ablesen** [fon
dain LIH•pen AP•lai•zen]
lip-read

**von Hand gemacht** [fon
HAHNT ge•MAHKT] *adj*
handmade

**von hier** [fon HEER] *adv* hence

**von Natur** [fon NAH•toor] *n* F
naturally

**vor Christus** [for KRIH•st•oos]
BC

**vor kurzem** [for KOORTS•em]
*adv* recent

**Vorabend** [FOR•ah•bent] *n* M
eve; evening

**Vorahnung** [VOR•ahn•oong] *n*
F foreshadow

**vorangehen** [for•AN•gai•en] *vt*
forego; precede

**vorausbezahlt**
[for•OUS•beh•TSAHLT] *adj*
prepaid

**voraussagbar** [-bahr] *adj*
predictable

**Voraussage** [for•OUS•SAH•ge]
*n* F forecast; foretell; predict

**Voraussagung** [-oong] *n* F
prediction

**voraussehen** [for•OUS•sai•en]
*vt* foresee

**voraussetzen**
[for•OWS•zets•en] *vt* assume

**Voraussetzung**
[for•OUS•zets•oong] *n* F
premise

**voraussichtlich**
[for•OUS•zihkt•lihk]
prospective

**Vorbedacht** [FOR•be•DAHKT]
*n* M foresight

**Vorbedingung**
[FOR•beh•DING•oong] *n* F
prerequisite

**Vorbehalt** [FOR•beh•HALT] *n*
M proviso; reservation

**vorbereiten** [-en] *vt* prepare

**Vorbereitung**
[FOR•beh•RUYT•oong] *n* F
preparation

**vorbeugend** [FOR•boi•gend]
*adj* preventive

**vorbildlich** [FOR•bild•lihk] *adj*
exemplary

**vorderst** [FOR•dairst] *adj*
foremost

**Vordertür** [FOR•dair•TOOR] *n*
F front door

**vorehelich** [FOR•ai•eh•lihk] *adj*
premarital

**voreingenommen**
[for•AIN•geh•NOH•men] *adj*
biased

**Vorfahr** [FOR•fahr] *n* M
ancestor

**Vorfahren** [FOR•fahr•en] *npl* N
forefather

**Vorfall** [FOR•fal] *n* M episode;
incident

**Vorgänger** [FOR•geng•air] *n*
predecessor

**vorgeben** [FOR•gai•ben] *vi*
pretend

**Vorgrund** [FOR•groont] *n* M
foreground

**Vorhaben** [FOR•ha•ben] *n* N
intention

**Vorhalle** [FOR•hahl•e] *n* F
lobby; porch; stoop

**Vorhang** [FOR•hahng] *n* M
curtain; drapes

**vorher** [FOR•hair] *adv* before;
previously

**Vorhergehen** [-GAI•en] *n* N
precedence

**vorherrschen** [FOR•hair•shen]
*vt* reign

**vorherrschend**
[FOR•hair•shend] *adj*
predominant; prevailing

**Vorkommen** *n* N occurence

**vorkommen** [FOR•koh•men] *vi*
occur

**Vorläufer** [VOR•loi•fair] *n* M
forerunner

**vorläufig** [FOR•loi•fig] *adj*
tentative

**Vorlage** [FOR•lahg•eh] *n* F bill

**Vorlegeschloß**
[FOR•laig•eh•SHOHS] *n* N
padlock

**Vorlesung** [FOR•lai•zoong] *n* F
recital

**Vorliebe** [FOR•lee•beh] *n* F
partiality

**vormittags** [FOR•mih•tahgz]
A.M.

**vorn vor** [forn] [for] *adv prep*
ahead (of)

**Vorname** [FOR•nah•me] *n* M
first name

**vorne** [FOR•ne] *adj* front

**vornehm** [FOR•naim] *adj* plush

**Vorort** [for•ort] *n* M suburb

**Vorrede** [FOR•rai•deh] *n* F
preface

**Vorschau** [FOR•shou] *n* F
preview

**Vorschlag** [FOR•shlahg] *n* M
proposal; proposition;
suggestion

**vorschlagen** [FOR•shlah•gen]
*vt* propose; suggest

**vorschreiben**
[FOR•schruy•ben] *vt* prescribe

**vorschreibend**
[FOR•shruy•bend] *adj*
mandatory

**Vorschrift** [FOR•shrift] *n* F
prescription

**Vorsicht** [FOR•zikht] *n* F
caution

**vorsichtig** [FOR•zikht•ig] *adj*
cautious; wary

**Vorsichtsmaßregel**
[FOR•zihkts•MAHS•rai•gel] *n*
F precaution

**Vorsilbe** [FOR•zil•beh] *n* F
prefix

**Vorsitzender**
[FOR•ZITS•ehn•dair] *n* M
chairman

**Vorsorge** [FOR•ZOR•geh] *n* F
providence

**Vorspeise** [FOR•SHPAI•zuh] *n*
F appetizer

**Vorspiel** [FOR•shpeel] *n* N
prelude

**Vorsprechen** [FOR•shpreh•ken]
*n* N audition

**Vorsprung** [FOR•shprung] *n* M
projection

**vorstädtisch**
[FOR•SHTEHT•ish] *adj*
suburban

**vorstehend** [FOR•SHTAI•end]
*adj* prominent

**Vorsteher** [fOR•SHTAI•air] *n*
M provost

**Vorstellung 1**
[FOR•SHTEL•oong] *n* F
introduction

**Vorstellung 2**
   [FOR•shtel•oong] *n* F
   presentation
**vortäuschen** [FOR•toi•shen] *vt*
   feign; simulate
**Vorteil** [FOR•tail] *n* M
   advantage
**Vorteil** [FOR•taiel] *n* M benefit;
   advantage
**Vortrag** [FOR•trahg] *n* M
   lecture
**Vorurteil** [for•OOR•tai•el] *n* M
   bias; prejudice
**vorwärts** [FOR•vairts] *adj*
   forward; *adv* onward
**vorwärtsbringen**
   [FOR•vairts•BRING•en] *vt/vi*
   advance
**Vorwand** [FOR•vahnt] *n* M
   pretext

**Vorwort** [FOR•vort] *n* N
   foreword
**Vorwurf 1** [FOR•voorf] *n* M
   motif
**Vorwurf 2** [FOR•voorf] *n* M
   reproach
**Vorwürfe machen**
   [FOR•woor•feh MAH•ken] *vt*
   blame; upbraid
**vorzeitig** [FOR•TSAI•tig] *adj*
   premature
**vorziehen** [FOR•TSEE•ehn] *vt*
   prefer
**vorzüglicher**
   [for•TSOOG•LIHK•air] *adj*
   preferable
**Vulkan** [FUL•kahn] *n* M
   volcano
**vulkanisch** [FUHL•kahn•ish]
   *adj* volcanic

# W

**waagerecht** [VAH•ge•REHKT]
   *adj* horizontal
**wach** [vahk] *adj* awake
**Wachhund** [VAHK•huhnt] *n* M
   watchdog
**Wachs** [vahks] *n* N wax
**wachsam** [VAHK•zahm] *adj*
   vigilant
**Wachsein** [VAHK•zuyn] *n* N
   vigil
**wachsen 1** [VAHKS•en] *vt*
   grow
**wachsen 2** [VAHKS•en] *vi*
   vegetate

**Wachsen** [VAHKS•en] *n* N
   growth
**Wachtel** [VAHK•tel] *n* F quail
**Wachtelhund**
   [WAHK•tel•HUHNT] *n* M
   spaniel
**wackeln** [VAH•keln] *vi* wag
**Wächter** [VEHK•tair] *n* M
   keeper; sentinel; warden
**wählen** [VAIY•len] *vi vt*
   choose; select; elect
**Wähler** [VAI•lair] *n* M voter
**wählerisch** [VAIL•LAIR•ish]
   *adj* selective

**Wählerschaft**
[VAIL•AIR•shahft] n F
constituent

**während** [VAIR•rent] prep
whereas

**wärme** [VAIR•meh] adj
thermal

**Wärme** [VAIR•meh] n F
warmth

**Wäsche** [VEH•sheh] n F
washing; laundry

**Wäscher** [VEHSH•air] n M
washer

**Wäschestärke**
[VEH•she•SHTAIR•keh] n F
starch

**wässerig** [VEH•sair•ig] adj
watery

**Waffe** [VAH•feh] n F weapon

**Waffel 1** [VAH•fel] n F wafer

**Waffel 2** [VAH•fel] n F waffle

**Waffenruhe**
[VAH•fehn•ROO•heh] n F
cease-fire; truce

**wagen** [VAH•gen] vt dare

**Wagen** [VAH•gen] n M wagon

**Wahl 1** [vahl] n F ballot

**Wahl 2** [vahl] n F choice;
election; selection

**Wahlkampf werben**
[VAHL•kam•pf] [vair•behn] n
vi M campaign

**Wahlstimme**
[VAHL•shtim•meh] n F vote

**Wahlzählung**
[VAHL•tsai•loong] n F returns
(election)

**Wahnsinn** [VAHN•zin] n M
frenzy; madness

**wahnsinnig** [VAHN•zin•ig] adj
demented; madly

**Wahnsinniger**
[VAHN•zin•ig•AIR] n M
lunatic

**Wahnvorstellung**
[VAHN•FOR•shtel•oong] n F
hallucination

**wahr** [vahr] adj true; truthful

**während** [VAIR•end] adv
while

**Wahrhaftigkeit**
[VAHR•hahft•ig•KUYT] n F
truthfulness

**Wahrheit** [VAHR•huyt] n F
truth

**wahrnehmen** [VAHR•nai•men]
vt perceive

**Wahrnehmung**
[VAHR•nai•moong] n F
perception

**Wahrsager** [VAHR•zah•gair] n
M soothsayer

**wahrscheinlich**
[vahr•SHUYN•lihk] adj likely;
probable; adv probably

**Wahrsheinlichkeit**
[vahr•SHUYN•LIHK•kuyt] n
probability

**Waidblau** [VAID•blou] n N
pastel

**Waise** [VAI•zeh] n F orphan

**Waisenhaus** [VAI•zehn•hous] n
N orphanage

**Wal** [vahl] n M whale

**Wald** [vahlt] n M forest

**Waldland** [VALT•lant] n N
woodland

**Wallfahrt** [VAHL•fahrt] n F
pilgrimage

**Walnuß** [VAHL•noos] n F
walnut

**Walzer** [VAL•tsair] n M waltz

**Wand** [vahnt] *n* F wall

**Wanderarbeiter**
[VAHN•dair•AHR•buy•tair] *n*
M hobo

**Wanderer** [-air] *n* M wanderer

**wandern** [VAHN•dairn] *vt*
hike; *vi* roam; wander

**Wandgemälde**
[VAHNT•geh•MAIL•deh] *n* N
mural

**Wandteppich**
[VAHNT•TEH•pihk] *n* M
tapestry

**Wange** [VAHNG•eh] *n* F cheek

**wann, wenn** [vahn] [vehn] *adv*
when; whenever

**Wanne** [VAH•neh] *n* F tub

**Wappenkunde**
[VAH•pen•KUHN•de] *n* F
heraldry

**Ware** [VAH•reh] *n* F
commodity

**Waren** [VAHR•en] *n* F
merchandise; *npl* wares

**warm** [vahrm] *adj* warm; hearty

**warnen** [VAHR•nen] *vt* warn

**Warnung** [VAHR•noong] *n* F
warning; premonition

**warten** [VAHR•ten] *vi* wait

**Warten** [VAHR•ten] *n* N
waiting

**Wartezimmer**
[VAHR•teh•TSIM•mair] *n* N
waiting room

**Wartung** [VAHR•toong] *n* F
maintenance

**warum** [VAH•room] why

**Warze** [VAHR•tseh] *n* F wart

**was** [vahs] *int* what

**Waschbär** [VASH•bair] *n* M
raccoon

**waschen** [VAH•shen] *vt* wash;
launder

**Waschmaschine** *n* F
washing machine

**Waschmittel** [VAHSH•mi•tel]
*n* N detergent

**Waschraum** [VAHSH•roum] *n*
M lavatory

**Wasser** [VAH•sair] *n* N water

**wasserdicht** [-dihkt] *adj*
waterproof; watertight

**Wasserfall** [-fal] *n* M waterfall

**Wasserfarbe** [-FAHR•beh] *n* F
watercolor

**Wasserrinne**
[VAH•sair•RIN•ne] *n* F
ravine; gully

**Wasserspeier**
[VAH•sair•SHPUY•air] *n* M
gargoyle

**Wassersport** [-shport] *n* M
water sports

**Wasserstoff**
[VAH•sair•SHTOF] *n* M
hydrogen

**Wasserstraße** [-SHTRAH•seh]
*n* F waterway

**waten** [VAH•ten] *vi* wade

**watscheln** [VAHTCH•eln] *vi*
waddle

**Wattierung** [vah•TEER•oong]
*n* F padding

**weben** [VAI•ben] *vt* weave

**Webmaschine**
[VAIB•mah•SHEEN•eh] *n* F
loom

**Wechsel wechseln**
[VEKH•sehl] [-n] *n vt vi* M
change

**Wechseljahre**
[VEHKS•el•YAHR•eh] *npl* F
menopause

**Wechselsprechanlage**
[VEHKS•el•SHPREHK•AHN•
lah•ge] *n* F intercom

**Wecker** [VEHK•air] *n* M alarm
clock

**weder** [VAI•dair] *adj* neither

**weg** [vaig] *adv* away; gone; off

**Weg** [vaig] *n* M lane; path

**wegätzen** [VAIG•ETS•tsen] *vt*
corrode

**wegen** [VAIY•gen] *prep*
because of

**weglassen** [VAIG•lah•sen] *vt*
omit

**Weglassung** [VAIG•lah•soong]
*n* F omission

**Wegnahme** [VAIG•nah•meh] *n*
F deprivation; privation

**wegschnitzen**
[VAIG•shnits•en] *vt* whittle

**wegwerfen 1** [VAIG•vair•fen]
*vt* fling

**wegwerfen 2** [VAIG•vair•fen]
*vi* throw out

**Weh** [vaih] *n* N pang

**wehe!** [VAI•eh] *excl* alas!

**wehen** [VAI•hen] *vt* waft

**Weiße** [VUY•seh] *n* F
whiteness

**weiblich** [VAIB•lihk] *adj*
female; feminine; womanly

**Weiblichkeit** [VUYB•lihk•kuyt]
*n* F womanhood

**weich** [vuyhk] *adj* soft

**weich machen** [VAICH
MAH•khen] *vi* soften

**Weiche** [VAIHK•e] *n* F flank

**Weichheit** [-huyt] *n* F softness

**Weide 1** [VAI•de] *n* F
pasture; meadow

**Weide 2** [VUY•deh] *n* F willow

**Weiden** [VUY•den] wicker

**weihen** [VAI•en] *vt* consecrate

**weihen** [VAI•hen] *vt* dedicate

**Weihnachten** [VUY•nakt•ehn]
*n* F Christmas

**Weihnachtszeit**
[VUY•nahkts•TSAIT] *n* F
Yuletide

**Weihrauch beräuchern**
[VUY•rouhk] [beh•ROUHK•en]
*n v* M incense

**Weihung** [VAI•hoong] *n* F
dedication

**weil** [VAIY•yel] *conf* because

**Weile** [VUY•le] *n* while

**Weiler** [VAI•lair] *n* M hamlet

**Wein** [vuyn] *n* M wine

**Weinberg** [VUYN•bairg] *n* M
vineyard

**Weinbrand** [vain•brahnt] *n* M
brandy

**weinen** [VUY•nen] *vi* sob;
weep

**weinend** [-end] *adj* weeping

**Weinglas** [-glahs] *n* N
wineglass

**Weinkeller** [-KEL•lair] *n* M
wine cellar

**Weinlesezeit**
[VUYN•lai•zeh•tsuyt] *n*
vintage

**weisaussagen**
[VAIS•ous•SAH•gen] *vt*
prophesy

**Weise** [VAI•zeh] *n* F mode

**weise** [VUY•zeh] *adj* wise

**Weisheit** [VUYS•huyt] *n* F
wisdom

**weiß** [vuys] white

**Weissagung**
[VAIS•zah•GOONG] *n* F
prophecy

**weiß werden** [vuys vair•den]
  *vi* whiten

**weit** [vait] *adj* vast; widely

**weit, offen** [vait, OH•fen] *adj*
  gaping

**weit verstreut** [vuyt
  fair•shtroit] *adv* widespread

**Weite** [VAI•teh] *n* F vastness

**weiter 1** [VAI•tair] *adj* farther:
  further

**weiter 2** [VAI•tair] *adv* forth

**weiterführen**
  [VAI•tair•FUHR•ren] *vt*
  prosecute

**weitergegen**
  [VAI•tair•GAI•en] *vi* proceed

**weitergehen**
  [VAI•tair•GAI•en] *vi* continue

**weitervermieten**
  [VAI•tair•FAIR•MEET•en] *vt*
  sublet

**Weizen** [VUYTS•en] *n* M
  wheat

**welch** [vehlk] which

**welch auch immer** whichever

**welchen** [VEHL•chen]
  whomever

**Welle** [VEH•leh] *n* F wave

**Wellenlänge** [-n•LENG•eh] *n* F
  wavelength

**wellig** [VEHL•ig] *adj* wavy

**Welt** [velt] *n* F world

**Weltbürger**
  [VELT•BOOR•gair] *n* M
  cosmopolitan

**weltlich** [VELT•lihk] *adj*
  secular

**weltlich** [VELT•lihk] *adj*
  worldly

**weltoffen** [VELT•of•en] *adj*
  cosmopolitan

**Weltraumfahrer**
  [VELT•rowm•FAHR•rair] *n*
  M astronaut

**weltumfassend**
  [VELT•oom•FAH•sent] *adj*
  global

**wem wen** [vaim] [vain] whom

**wenig** [VAIN•ig] *adj* few

**wenig** [VAIN•ig] *adj* less

**wer** [vair] who

**werden** [VAIR•den] *vi* become

**werden Wille** [VAIR•den]
  [vih•leh] *vi* *n* M will

**werfen** [VAIR•fen] *vt* cast;
  throw; toss

**Werfer** [VAIR•fair] *n* M pitcher

**Werkstatt** [VAIRK•shtaht] *n* F
  workshop

**Werkzeug 1** [VAIRK•tsoig] *n* N
  engine

**Werkzeug 2** [VAIRK•tsoig] *n* N
  tool

**Werkzeug vollenden**
  [VAIRK•tsoig] [FOL•EN•den]
  *n* *vt* N implement

**Wert** [vairt] *n* M value; worth

**wertlos** [VAIRT•los] *adj*
  worthless

**Wertschätzung**
  [vairt•shets•oong] *n* F esteem

**wertvoll** [VAIRT•fol] *adj*
  valuable

**Werwolf** [VAIR•vohlf] *n* M
  werewolf

**Wesen** [VAI•sen] *n* N essence

**wesentlich** [VAI•zent•LIHK]
  *adj* essential; integral;
  substantial

**Wesentliche**
  [VAI•sent•LIHK•e] *n* N gist

**wesentlichst**
[VAI•zent•LIHKST] *adj* prime

**weshalb** [VAIS•halb] *adv*
wherefore

**Wespe** [vehs•peh] *n* F wasp

**wessen** [VEH•sen] whose

**Weste** [VEH•ste] *n* F vest

**Westen** [VEH•sten] *n* M west

**Westländer** [-LEHN•dair] *n* M
westerner

**westlich** [VEHST•lihk] *adj*
western

**westwärts** [VEHST•vairts] *adj*
westward

**Wettbewerb** [VET•be•VAIRB]
*n* M competition

**Wette** [VET•teh] *n* F bet

**wetteifern** [VEHT•uy•fairn] *vi*
vie

**wetten** [VET•ten] *vt* wager

**Wetter** [VEH•tair] *n* N weather

**Wetteraussicht** [-OUS•zihkt] *n*
F weather conditions

**Wetterfahne**
[VEH•tair•FAH•neh] *n* F
weathervane

**Wettermantel**
[VEH•tair•MAHN•tel] *n* M
trench coat; raincoat

**Wettkampt** [VET•kahmpf] *n* M
contest

**Wettrennen** [VET•ren•nen] *n*
N race

**Wettstreit** [VEHT•shtruyt] *n* M
rivalry

**wetzen** [VEHT•sen] *vt* whet

**Whisky** [VIH•skee] *n* M
whiskey

**wichtig** [VIHK•tig] *adj*
important; significant

**Wichtigkeit** [VIHK•tig•kuyt] *n*
F importance

**Wichtigtuer** [VIK•tig•TOO•air]
*n* M busybody

**wicklen** [VIH•keln] *vt* wrap

**Widder** [VIH•dair] *n* M ram

**widerlegen**
[VEE•dair•LAI•gen] *vt*
disprove; *vi* refute

**widerlich 1** [VEE•DAIR•lihk]
*adj* loathsome; repugnant

**widerlich 2** [VEE•DAIR•lihk]
*adj* rancid

**widerrufen**
[VEE•DAIR•roo•fen] *vt*
revoke; repeal

**Widersee** [VEE•DAIR•zee] *n* F
undertow

**widerspiegeln**
[VEE•DAIR•shpee•geln] *vt*
reflect

**widersprechen**
[VEE•DAIR•shprek•en] *vt*
contradict; *vi* disagree

**widersprechend**
[VEE•DAIR•shprehk•end] *adj*
incompatible

**Widerspruch**
[VEE•DAIR•shproohk] *n* M
disagreement; contradiction

**Widerstand**
[VEE•DAIR•shtant] *n* M
resistance

**widerstehen**
[VEE•DAIR•shtai•en] *vt*
resist; withstand

**widerwärtig**
[VEE•DAIR•vair•tig] *adj*
repulsive

**Widerwille** *n* M unwillingness

**widerwillig**
[VEE•DAIR•vil•lig] *adj*
reluctant; unwilling

**widmen** [VEED•men] *vt* devote

**Widmung** [VEED•moong] *n* F
devotion

**wie** [vee] *adv* as; how

**wieder** [VEE•dair] *adv* again

**wieder anpassen** [VEE•dair
AHN•pah•sen] *vt* readjust

**wieder aufbauen** [VEE•dair
OUF•bou•en] *vt* reconstruct

**wieder erscheinen** [VEE•dair
air•SHUY•nen] *vt* reappear

**wieder hinstellen**
[HIN•shtel•len] *vt* replace

**wiederaufbauen**
[-OUF•bou•en] *vt* rebuild

**wiederaufnehmen**
[-OUF•nai•men] *vt* resume

**wiederbezahlen**
[-beh•TSAHL•en] *vt* repay

**wiedereinführen**
[-UYN•FUHR•en] *vt*
re-establish

**wiedereinbringen**
[-UYN•BRING•en] *vt* recoup

**wiedereintreten**
[VEE•dair•UYN•trai•ten] *vt*
re-enter

**wiedereröffnen**
[-air•UHF•nen] *vt* reopen

**wiedererwecken**
[-air•VEHK•en] *vt* resuscitate

**wiedererzeugen**
[-air•TSOI•gen] *vt* reproduce

**Wiedererzeugung** [-oong] *n*
reproduction

**Wiedergeburt**
[VEE•dair•geh•BOORT] *n* F
rebirth

**wiedergewinnen**
[-geh•VIN•nen] *vt* recover;
regain

**Wiedergutmachung**
[VEE•dair•GOOT•mahk•oong]
*n* F reparation

**wiederherstellen**
[-HAIR•shtel•len] *vt* restore

**wiederholen 1**
[VEE•dair•HOL•len] *vt*
rehearse

**wiederholen 2**
[VEE•dair•HOL•len] *vt* repeat;
reiterate

**Wiederholung** [-oong] *n*
repetition

**wiederkäuen**
[VEE•dair•KOI•en] *vt*
ruminate

**wiederkehren**
[VEE•dair•KAIR•ren] *vt* recur

**wiedervereinigen**
[VEE•dair•vair•uyn•ig•en] *vt*
rejoin; reunite

**Wiedervereinigung**
[VEE•dair•vair•uyn•ig•oong] *n*
F reunion

**Wiege** [VEE•ge] *n* F cradle

**wiegen** [VEE•gen] *vt* weigh

**Wiegenlied** [VEE•gen•LEED]
*n* N lullaby

**wiehern** [VEE•hairn] *vi* neigh

**Wiese** [VEE•zeh] *n* F meadow;
prairie

**Wiesel** [VEE•zel] *n* N weasel

**wild** [vilt] *adj* wild

**Wildbret** [VILD•breht] *n* N
venison

**Wildschwein** [VILT•shvain] *n*
N boar

**willen** [VIH•len] sake

**Willkommen** [VIL•kom•men] *n* N welcome

**wimmeln** [VIH•meln] *vi* teem

**wimmern** [VIM•mairn] *vt* whimper

**Wimper** [VIHM•pair] *n* F lash

**Wimperntusche** [VIHM•pairn•TUH•sheh] *n* F mascara

**Wind** [vint] *n* M wind

**winden** [VIN•den] *vi* wind; coil

**windig** [VIN•dig] *adj* windy

**Windmühle** [-MUH•leh] *n* F windmill

**Windpocken** [VINT•pok•ken] *n pl* chicken pox

**Windschlag** [-shlahg] *n* M windfall

**windschnittig** [vint•SHNIHT•tig] *adj* streamlined

**Windschutzscheibe** [-SHUHTS•shuy•beh] *n* F windshield

**Windstoß** [VIND•stohs] *n* M flurry; gust; squall

**Windung** [VIN•doong] *n* F coil (as rope or wire)

**Windung sich winden** [VIN•doong] [zihk] [vin•den] *n* F wind (as a clock)

**Wink** [veenk] *n* M hint; cue

**Winkel** [VEEN•kail] *n* M angle

**winseln** [VIN•zeln] *vi* squeal; whine

**Winter** [VIN•tair] *n* M winter

**winterhart** [VIN•tair•hart] *adj* perennial

**Winterschlaf** [VIN•tair•shlahf] *n* M hibernation

**wintrig** [VIN•trig] *adj* wintry

**winzig** [VIN•zig] *adj* tiny

**Wippen** [VIH•pen] *n* N seesaw

**wir** [veer] *pers pron* we

**Wirbel** [VEER•bel] *n* M vertebra

**wirbeln** [VEER•beln] *vi* gyrate; swirl; whirl

**Wirbelsäule** [VEER•bel•SOI•leh] *n* F spinal column

**Wirbelwind** [-vint] *n* M whirlwind

**wirklich** [VEER•klihk] *adj* really; substantive; truly

**wirksam** [VEERK•sahm] *adj* effective

**Wirkung 1** [VEER•koong] *n* F effect

**Wirkung 2** [VEER•koong] *n* F operation

**wirkungsvoll** [VEER•koongs•fol] *adj* telling

**wirtschaflich** economical

**Wirtschaft** [VEERT•shahft] *n* F economics

**Wirtschafterin** [VEERT•shahf•TAIR•in] *n* F housekeeper

**wirtschaftlich** [VEERT•shahft•lihk] *adj* economical

**wischen, Wischen** [VIH•shen] *vt n* N whisk

**Wischer** [VIH•shair] *n* M eraser

**Wischer** [VIH•shair] *n* M wiper

**wispern** [VIH•spairn] *vi* whisper

**wissen** [VIH•sen] *vt* know

**Wissenschaft** [VIH•sen•shahft] *n* F science

**Wissenschaftler** [-lair] *n* M
scientist

**wissenschaftlich** [-lihk] *adj*
scientific

**Witterungskunde**
[VIH•tair•OONGS•kuhn•deh]
*n* F meteorology

**Witwe** [VIT•veh] *n* F widow

**Witwer** [-air] *n* M widower

**Witz** [vihts] *n* M joke;
witticism; practical joke

**witzeln** [VITS•eln] *vt* joke;
quip

**witzig** [VIT•tsig] *adj* facetious;
witty

**witzige Bermerkung**
[VIT•sig•eh
beh•MAIRK•oong] *n* F
wisecrack

**wo, auch, immer** [voh ouhk
IM•mair] wherever

**wo ungefähr**
[-UHN•geh•FAIR]
whereabouts

**wo, wohin** [voh] [voh•HIN]
*prep* where

**Woche** [VOH•keh] *n* F week

**Wochentag** [-n•tahg] *n* M
weekday

**wodurch** [vo•DOORHK] *prep*
whereby

**wöchentlich** [VUH•kent•LIHK]
*adj* weekly

**Wörterbuch**
[VOOR•tair•BOOHK] *n*
dictionary

**Wörterverzeichnis**
[VER•tair•fair•TSUHK•nis] *n*
N vocabulary

**wogen** [VOH•gen] *vi* wave;
undulate

**wohlerzogen**
[VOHL•air•TSO•gen] *adj*
well-bred

**Wohlfahrt** [VOHL•fahrt] *n* F
welfare

**Wohlgefühl** [-geh•FUHL] *n* N
well-being

**wohlhabend** [-HAH•bend] *adj*
well-to-do

**Wohlstand** [vohl•SHTANT] *n*
M prosperity

**wohnen** [VOH•nen] *vi* live;
dwell; reside

**Wohnen** [VOH•nen] *n* N
lodgings

**Wohnhaus** [VOHN•hous] *n* N
tenement

**Wohnung** [VOHN•oongk] *n* F
abode; apartment; dwelling;
residence

**Wohnwagen**
[VOHN•VAH•gen] *n* M house
trailer

**Wohnzimmer**
[VOHN•TSIM•mair] *n* N
sitting room

**Wolf** [volf] *n* M wolf

**Wolke** [VOHL•keh] *n* F cloud

**Wolkenbruch**
[VOL•ken•BROOHK] *n* M
torrent

**Wolkenkratzer**
[VOL•ken•krah•tsair] *n* M
skyscraper

**wollen** [VOH•len] *aux verb*
want

**wollig** [VOHL•lig] *adj*
woolly

**Wollstoff** [VOHL•shtof] *n* M
woolen

**wollten** [VOHL•ten] *pret*
would

**wollüstig** [vohl•luhst•ig]
*adj* sensual; voluptuous

**Wort** [vort] *n* N word

**Wort Zeit Dauer**
[vohrt] [tsait] [DOU•air] *n* N
term

**Wortführer** [VORT•fer•air] *n*
M spokesperson

**wortreich** [VOHRT•ruyhk] *adj*
verbose

**Wortspiel** [VORT•shpeel] *n* N
pun; play on words

**Wortstreit** [VOHRT•shtruyt] *n*
M dispute

**wortwörtlich**
[VOHRT•vert•lihk] *adj*
literal

**Wucher** [VOO•kair] *n* M
loan-sharking; usury

**Wucherer** [VOO•kair•air] *n* M
usurer

**wund** [vuhnd] *adj* sore

**Wunde** [VUHN•deh] *n*
wound

**Wunder1** [VUHN•dair] *n* N
marvel; miracle

**Wunder2** [VUHN•dair] *n* N
prodigy

**Wunder, sich verwundern**
[VUHN•dair] [zihk] [vair-] *n*
N wonder

**wunderbar** [VUHN•dair•bahr]
*adj* wonderful; marvelous

**wunderlich 1**
[VUHN•dair•lihk] *adj*
miraculous

**wunderlich 2**
[VUHN•dair•lihk] *adj* quaint

**Wundermittel**
[VUN•dair•mih•tel] *n* N
panacea

**Wunsch; wünschen** [vuhnsh]
[-en] *n vi* M wish; desire

**würdig 1** [VOOR•dig] *adj*
dignified

**würdig 2** [VOOR•dig] *adj*
worthy

**würdigen** [woor•dig•en] *vt*
appreciate

**Wurf** [voorf] *n* M pelt

**Würfel 1** [VOOR•fel] *n* M
cube

**Würfel 2** [VOOR•fel] *npl*
dice

**Wurfmaschine**
[VOORF•mah•SHEEN•eh] *n*
F catapult

**Wurfspeer** [VOORF•shpair] *n*
M dart; javelin

**Würger** [VOOR•gair] *n* M
shrike; shrew

**Wurm** [voorm] *n* M worm

**Würze** [VOORTS•eh] *n* F
seasoning; zest

**Wurzel** [VOOR•tsel] *n* F root

**wüst** [voost] *adj* desolate

**Wüste** [VOO•ste] *n* F
desert

**Wut** [voot] *n* F rage

**Wutanfall** [VOOT•ahn•fahl] *n*
M tantrum

**wütend** [VOO•tend] *adj*
furious; rabid

**wütend machen** [voo•tend
mahk•en] *vt* enrage;
infuriate

**Wüterich** [VUH•tair•rihk] *n* M
tartar

# X

**Xenophobie** [ZEE•no•fo•BEE] *n* F xenophobe
**Xylographie** [ZEE•lo•grah•FEE] *n* F xylography

**Xylophon** [ZEE•loh•fohn] *n* N xylophone

# Z

**Zacke** [TSAH•keh] *n* F prong
**zäh machen** [TSAI mah•ken] *vt* toughen
**Zähigkeit** [TSAI•hig•kuyt] *n* F stamina; toughness
**zählen** [TSAI•len] *vt* count
**Zähler** [TSAI•lair] *n* M meter
**Zahl 1** [tsahl] *n* F number
**Zahl 2** [tsahl] *n* F pay; check (bill)
**zahlbar** [TSAHL•bahr] *adj* payable
**zahllos** [TSAHL•los] *adj* countless
**zahlreich** [TSAHL•ruyhk] *adj* numerous
**Zahlung** [TAHL•oong] *n* F payment
**Zahlzeichen** [TSAHL•tsai•khen] *n* N numeral
**zahm** [tsahm] *adj* tame
**Zahn** [tsahn] *n* M tooth
**zahnärztlich** [TSAHN•erts•lihk] *adj* dental
**Zahnartzt** [TSAHN•arhtst] *n* M dentist

**zahnen** [TSAH•nen] *vi* teethe
**Zahnpasta** [TSAHN•pah•steh] *n* F toothpaste
**Zahnstocher** [-SHTOHK•air] *n* M toothpick
**Zahnweh** [-vai] *n* N toothache
**Zaire** Zaire
**Zange** [TSAHN•geh] *n* F tongs
**Zank** [tsahnk] *n* M squabble
**Zäpfchen** [TSEHPF•khen] *n* N uvula
**Zapfen** [TSAHP•fen] *n* M spigot
**Zapfen zapfen** [TSAHP•fen] *n vt* M tap
**Zapfenstreich** [TSAHP•fen•struyhk] *n* M tattoo
**Zapfern** [TSAHP•fairn] *n* M faucet
**Zar** [tsahr] *n* M czar
**zart** [tsahrt] *adj* delicate; tender; *adv* gently
**Zartheit** [TSAHRT•huyt] *n* F tenderness
**zärtlich** [TSAIRT•lihk] *adj* endearing

**Zauber** [TSOU•bair] *n* M
magic; fascination

**Zauberer** [TSOU•bair•air] *n* M
sorcerer; wizard

**Zauberstab** [TSOU•bair•shtahb]
*n* M wand

**zaudern** [TSOU•dairn] *vi* tarry

**Zaum** [tsoum] *n* M curb

**Zaun** [tsoun] *n* M fence

**Zebra** [TSAI•brah] *n* N zebra

**Zecke** [TSEH•keh] *n* F tick
(insect)

**Zeder** [TSAIY•dair] *n* F cedar

**Zehe 1** [TSAI•heh] *n* F digit

**Zehe 2** [TSAI•eh] *n* F toe

**Zehennagel**
[TSAI•en•NAH•gel] *n* M
toenail

**zehn** [tsain] *num* ten

**zehnte** [TSAIN•teh] *num* tenth

**Zehnte** [TSAIN•teh] *n* M tithe

**Zeichen 1** [TSAI•khen] *n* N
note

**Zeichen 2** [TSAI•khen] *n* N
sign (street)

**Zeichenstetzung**
[TSAIHK•en•ZETS•oong] *n* F
punctuation

**Zeichnen** [TSAIHK•nen] *n* N
drawing

**zeichnen** [TSAIK•nen] *vi*
doodle

**Zeigefinger**
[TSAI•ge•FING•air] *n* M
index finger

**zeigen** [tsai•gen] *vi* show

**Zeiger** [TSAI•gair] *n* M pointer

**Zeit** [tsait] *n* F time

**Zeit zu gewinnen suchen**
[tsait tsoo ge•vin•nen
zoo•khen] *vi* temporize

**Zeitalter** [TSAIT•ahl•tair] *n* N
era

**Zeitdauer** [TSAIT•dou•air] *n* F
period

**Zeitform** [TSAIT•form] *n* F
tense

**zeitgenössisch**
[TSAIT•ge•NOOS•ish] *adj*
contemporary

**Zeitkarte** [TSAIT•kahr•teh] *n* F
season ticket

**zeitlich** [TSAIT•lihk] *adj*
temporal

**Zeitmesser** [TSAIT•meh•sair] *n*
M timekeeper

**Zeitschrift** [TSAIT•shrihft] *n* F
magazine; periodical

**Zeittabelle** [-tah•BEHL•eh] *n* F
timetable

**Zeitung** [TSAI•toong] *n* F
newspaper; gazette

**zeitweilig** [TSAIT•vai•lig] *adj*
temporary

**Zelle** [TSEL•leh] *n* F cell; booth

**Zelt** [tselt] *n* N tent; pavilion

**zensieren** [TSEHN•zeer•ehn] *vt*
censor

**Zensor** [TSEHN•sohr] *n* M
censor

**Zensur** [TSEHN•zoor] *n* F
censorship

**Zentimeter**
[TSEHN•tee•MAI•tair] *n* M
centimeter

**zentral** [TSEHN•trahl] *adj*
central

**Zentrum** [TSEHN•troom] *n* N
center

**Zephir** [TSEH•feer] *n* M zephyr

**Zeppelin** [TSEH•peh•LIN] *n* M
zeppelin

**Zepter** [TSEHP•tair] *n* N
scepter

**zerbrechen** [TSAIR•brehk•en]
*vt* disrupt

**zerbrechlich** [tsair•brehk•lihk]
*adj* fragile

**zerbrökeln** [TSAIR•brook•eln]
*vi* crumble

**zerdrücken** [TSAIR•druh•ken]
*vt* mash

**zereißen** [TSAIR•ruy•sen] *vt*
tear

**Zeremonie**
[TSAIR•eh•mohn•ee] *n* F rite

**zerfetzen** [TSAIR•fets•en] *vt*
shred

**zerfetzen** [TSAIR•fets•en] *vt*
slash

**Zerfressen** [TSAIR•freh•sen] *n*
N erosion

**zerhacken** [TSAIR•hahk•en] *vt*
mince

**zerklüftet** [TSAIR•kluhf•tet]
*adj* jagged

**zerklüftet** [TSAIR•kluhf•tet]
*adj* rugged

**zerknittern** [TSAIR•knih•tairn]
*vt* rumple

**zerkratzen** [TSAIR-] *vt* scratch

**zerlegen** [TSAIR•lai•gen] *vt*
dissect

**zermahlen** [TSAIR•mahl•len]
*vt* pulverize

**zermalmen** [TSAIR•mahl•men]
*vt* squelch

**zerquetschen**
[TSAIR•kveht•chen] *vt* squash

**zerren** [TSAIR•ren] *vt* tug; pull

**zersetzen** [TSAIR•ZETS•en] *vi*
decompose; rot

**zerspalten**
[TSAIR•SHPAHL•ten] *vt* split

**zerstäuben**
[TSAIR•SHTOI•ben] *vt*
spray

**zerstören**
[tSAIR•SHTUYR•uhn] *vt*
abolish; destroy

**zerstörend**
[TSAIR•SHTOOR•ent] *adj*
destructive

**Zerstörung**
[TSAIR•SHTOOR•oong] *n* F
destruction; havoc

**zerstreuen**
[TSAIR•SHTROI•en] *vt*
diffuse

**zerstreuen**
[TSAIR•SHTROI•en] *vt*
disperse

**Zettel** [TSEH•tel] *n* M label

**Zeuge** [TSOI•geh] *n* M witness

**Zeugnis** [TSOIG•nis] *n* N eye
witness

**Zickzack** [TSIHK•tsahk] *n* M
zigzag

**Ziege** [TSEE•ge] *n* F goat

**Ziegelstein**
[TSEE•gel•SHTAIN] *n* M
brick

**Ziegenpeter**
[TSEE•gen•PAI•tair] *n* M
mumps

**Ziehen** [TSEE•en] *n* N draw

**ziehen** [TSEE•en] *vt* pull

**Ziel 1** [tseel] *n* N aim

**Ziel 2** [tseel] *n* N goal; target

**ziemlich** [TSEEM•lihk] *adj*
reasonably

**Zifferblatt** [TSIF•air•blaht] *n* N
dial

**Zigarette** [TSIG•gahr•ET•eh] *n*
F cigarette

**Zigarre** [TSEE•gahr•eh] *n* F
cigar

**Zigeuner** [tsi•GOI•nair] *n* F
gypsy

**Zihnk** [tsink] *n* N zinc

**Zimmer** [TSIM•mair] *n* N room

**Zimmerkollege**
[-koh•LAIG•eh] *n* M
roommate

**Zimmermann Tischler**
[TSIM•maiyr•MAHN]
[TISH•lair] *n* M carpenter

**zimperlich** [TSIM•pair•lihk] *adj*
squeamish

**Zimt** [tsimt] *n* M cinnamon

**Zinn** [tsin] *n* N tin

**Zipfel** [tsip•fel] *n* M tag

**Zirkumflex**
[TSEER•koom•fleks] *n* M
circumflex

**Zirkus** [TSEER•koos] *n* M
circus

**zirpen** [TSEERP•ehn] *vi vt*
chirp

**zischen** [TSIH•shen] *vi* hiss;
sizzle

**Zitat** [TSI•taht] *n* F quotation

**Zither** [TSIH•tair] *n* F zither

**zitieren** [TSI•teer•ehn] *vt* cite;
quote

**Zitrone** [TSIH•trohn•e] *n* F
lemon

**Zitronenlimonade**
[TSIH•trohn•en•LEE•mo•
NAH•de] *n* F lemonade

**zittern** [TSIH•tairn] *vi* quake;
quaver; shiver

**Zittern** *n* N tremor

**zitternd** *adj* tremulous

**zivil** [TSI•vil] *adj* civil

**Zivilisation**
[TSI•veel•ih•zat•tsee•ohn] *n* F
civilization

**zivilisieren**
[TSI•vil•ih•ZEER•ehn] *vt*
civilize

**zögern** *vi* hesitate

**Zögern** *n* N hesitation

**zögern** [tsuh•gairn] *vi*
procrastinate

**zögernd** [TSUH•gairnd] *adj*
hesitant; *adv* reluctantly

**Zoll 1** [tsohl] *n* M inch

**Zoll 2** [tsol] *n* M toll

**Zollbrücke** [-BRUH•keh] *n* F
toll bridge

**zollfrei** [TSOHL•fruy] *adj*
duty-free

**Zolltarif** [TSOL•tahr•EEF] *n* M
tariff

**Zoo** [tsoo] *n* M zoo

**Zoologie** [TSOO•loh•GEE] *n* F
zoology

**zoologisch** [TSOO•loh•GISH]
*adj* zoological

**Zopf** [tsophf] *n* M tress

**Zorn** [tsorn] *n* M fury; wrath

**zu** [tsoo] *prep* unto; to

**zu Hause** [tsoo HOU•ze] *adj*
indoor

**zu Pferd** [tsoo -] *adj* horseback

**Zubehör** [TSOO•be•HOOR] *n*
N paraphernalia

**Zucht** [tsoohkt] *n* F stud
(animal)

**züchtigen** [TSOOKH•tig•ehn]
*vt* chastise

**Zucker** [TSOO•kair] *n* M sugar

**Zuckerdose** [-DOH•zeh] *n* F
sugar bowl

**Zuckerkrankheit**
[TSOO•kair•KRAHNK•huyt]
*n* F diabetes

**zufällig 1** [TSOO•fel•ig] *adj*
accidental; casual; random;
haphazard

**zufällig 2** [TSOO•fel•ig] *adj*
fortuitous

**Zufall** [TSOO•fal] *n* M
coincidence; fluke

**Zuflucht** [TSOO•fluhkt] *n* F
recourse; refuge

**Zufluchtsort**
[TSOO•floohkts•ohrt] *n* M
haven

**zufrieden** [TSOO•free•den] *adj*
M content

**zufügen** [TSOO•foo•gen] *vt*
inflict

**Zug 1** [tsoog] *n* M train

**Zug 2** [tsoog] *n* M trait

**Zugabe** [TSOO•gah•be] *n* F
encore

**Zugang** [TSOO•gahng] *n* M
entry; access

**zugeben** [TSOO•gaib•ehn] *vt*
admit

**Zugehörigkeit**
[TSOO•geh•HOOR•ig•kuyt] *n*
F membership

**Zügel** [TSUH•gel] *n* M rein

**Zugeständnis 1**
[TSOO•ge•SHTEND•nis] *n* N
concession

**Zugeständnis 2**
[TSOO•ge•SHTENT•nis] *n* N
confession

**zugestehen**
[TSOO•ge•SHTAI•en] *vt*
concede

**Zugleiter** [TSOOG•LUY•tair] *n*
M trainman

**Zuhörer** [TSOO•her•air] *n* M
listener

**zukünftig** [TSOO•kuhnf•tig]
*adj* future

**Zulassung, Räumung**
[TSOO•lahs•oong]
[ROIM•oong] *n* F clearance

**zum günstigen Preis** [tsoom
GOONST•ig•gen prais] *adj n*
bargain

**zum halben Preis** [tsoom
HALB•en pruys] half-price

**zum Teil** [TSOOM tuyl] *adv*
partly

**zumachen, schließen**
[TSOO•makh•en]
[SHLEE•sen] *vt* F close

**Zünddraht** [TSUHN•draht] *n* M
primer

**Zünder** [TSUHN•dair] *n* M
fuse; match; tinder

**Zünderkerze**
[TSUHN•dair•KAIR•tseh] *n* F
spark plug

**Zuneigung** [TSOO•nuy•goong]
*n* F liking

**Zunge** [TSUHNG•eh] *n* F
tongue

**zungenlahm** [-lahm] *adj*
tongue-tied

**zupfen** [TSUHP•fen] *vt* N
pluck; twitch

**zurechtlegen**
[TSOO•rehkt•LAI•gen] *vt*
dispose

**zurechtweisen**
[TSUHR•rehkt•VAI•sen] *vi*
rebuke

**züruck; hinter; Rücken**
[TSOO•rook] [HIN•tair]
[ROOK•ken] *adv adj n* M
back

**zurückbleiben**
[tsuh•RUHK•bluy•ben] *vi* lag;
rebound

**zurückfallen**
[tsuh•ROOK•fal•len] *vt*
relapse

**zurückgezogen**
[-geh•TSO•gen] *adj*
withdrawn

**Zurückgezogenheit**
[tsuhr•ook•ge•TSOHG•en•huyt]
*n* F seclusion

**zurückhalten**
[tsuh•ROOHK•hahl•ten] *vt*
restrain

**zurückhalten** [-HAHL•ten] *vt*
withhold

**zurückhaltend**
[tsoo•rook•hal•tend] *adj*
demure

**zurückholen** [-HOH•len] *vt*
retrieve

**zurückkehren** [-KAIR•en] *vi*
return

**zurückkehren**
[tsuh•ROOHK•KAIR•ren] *vt*
revert

**zurückkommen 1**
[tsoo•RUHK•KO•men] *vi*
comeback

**zurücknehmen 2**
[tsuh•RUHK•NAI•men] *vt*
retract

**zurückprallen**
[tsuhr•ROOK•PRAHL•len] *vt*
recoil

**zurückrufen**
[tsuhr•OOK•ROO•fen] *vi*
recall

**zurückziehen**
[tsuh•RUHK•TSEE•en] *vt*
withdraw

**Zurückziehung** [-hoong] *n* F
withdrawal

**zurückzucken**
[tsoo•ROOK•TSOO•ken] *vi*
flinch

**zusätzlich** [tsoo•ZETS•lik] *adj*
extra; additional

**zusammen** [tsoo•TSAH•men]
*prep* together

**Zusammenarbeit**
[tsoo•SAHM•en•AHR•buyt] *n*
F cooperation; teamwork

**zusammenarbeiten**
[tsoo•SAH•men•AHR•buy•ten]
*vi* cooperate

**zusammenbrechen**
[tsoo•TSAHM•en•BREHK•en]
*vi* collapse; succumb

**Zusammenbruch**
[tsoo•SAHM•en•BROOKH] *n*
M collapse

**zusammendrängen**
[tsoo•TSAHM•en•DRAING•en]
*vi* huddle

**zusammengesetzt**
[tsoo•SAHM•en•ge•ZETST]
*adj* compound

**Zusammenhang**
[tsoo•SAHM•en•hahng] *n* M
context

**zusammenkommen**
[tsoo•SAHM•en•koh•men]
convene

**zusammenlaufen**
[tsoo•SAHM•en•LOU•fen] *vi*
converge

**Zusammenlegung**
[tsoo•ZAHM•en•LAIG•oong]
*n* F merger

**zusammenprallen Stoß**
[tsoo•SAHM•ehn•PRAHL•ehn]
[shtohs] *vi n* M clash

**zusammensetzen**
[tsoo•SHAM•en•zets•en] *vt*
combine

**Zusammensetzung**
[tsoo•SAHM•en•ZETS•oong]
*n* F combination

**Zusammenstoß**
[tsoo•SAH•men•SHTOS] *n* M
crash

**zusammenstoßen**
[tsoo•SAH•men•SHTOH•sen]
*vi* collide (with)

**zusammentreffen**
[tsoo•SAHM•en•TRE•fen] *vi*
coincide

**zusammenziehen**
[tsoo•TSAH•men•TSEE•en] *vt*
tighten

**Zusammenziehung**
[tsoo•SAHM•en•TSEE•hoong]
*n* F contraction

**zusammenzucken**
[tsoo•TSAH•men•TSUHK•en]
*vt* wince

**Zusatzreifen** [TSOO•zats-] *n* M
tire (spare)

**Zuschauer** [TSOO•shou•air] *n*
M spectator; onlooker

**Zuschauer, Publikum**
[TSOO•show•air]
[POOB•lik•oom] *n* F audience

**zuschlagen** [TSOO•shlah•gen]
*vt* slam

**zuspitzen** [TSOO•shpit•sen] *vt*
taper

**zustimmen** [TSOO•shti•mehn]
*vi* agree; consent

**Zustimmung**
[TSOO•shtim•oong] *n* F
consent

**zuteilen** [TSOO•tuyl•en] *vt*
confer

**Zutritt** [TSOO•trit] *n* M
entrance

**zuverlässig** *adj* reliable

**zuverlässig**
[TSOO•fair•LEHS•ig] *adj*
trusty; staunch

**Zuverlässigkeit**
[TSOO•vair•LES•ig•kuyt] *n* F
reliability

**Zuwachs Hinzufügung**
[TSOO•vax]
[HIN•tsoo•FEEUG•uhn] *n* M
addition

**zuziehen** [TSOO•tsee•ehn] *vt*
incur

**Zwang** [tsvahng] *n* M constraint

**zwanzig** twenty

**zwanzigste**
[TSVAHN•tsig•steh] *num*
twentieth

**Zweck** [tsvehk] *n* M purpose

**zwecklos** [TSVEHK•los] *adj*
futile

**Zwecklosigkeit**
[TSVEHK•los•ig•KUYT] *n* F
uselessness

**zwei** [tsvai] *num* two

**zweideutig** [TSVAI•doi•tig]
*adj* ambiguous

**Zweifel** [TSVUY•fel] *n* M
doubt; misgivings

**Zweifel** [TSVAI•fel] *n* M qualm

**zweifelhaft** [TSVAI•fel•haft]
*adj* dubious

**zweifellos** [TSVAI•fel•los] *adv*
definitely

**zweifelnd** [TSVUY•felnd] *adj*
doubtful

**Zweig** [tsvaig] *n* M branch;
twig

**Zweikampf** [TSVAI•kahmpf] *n*
M duel

**zweimal** [TSVAI•mahl] twice

**zweireihig** [TSVUY•ruy•hig]
*adj* double-breasted

**zweisprachig**
[TSVAI•shprahk•ig] *adj*
bilingual

**zweite** [TSVAI•teh] *adj* second

**zweitens** [TSVAI•tenz] *adv*
secondly

**zweitrangig**
[TSVAIT•rahng•ig] *adj*
second-rate

**Zwerg** [tsvairg] *n* M dwarf

**Zwergrind** [TSVAIRG•rind] *n*
N runt

**Zwickel** [TSVIK•el] *n* M gusset

**Zwicken** [TSVIHK•en] *n* N
pinch; twinge

**Zwiebel** [TSVEE•bel] *n* F onion

**Zwilling** [TSVIH•ling] *n* M
twin

**zwingen** [TSVING•en] *vt*
compel

**zwingend** [TSVING•end] *adj*
compulsive; compelling

**zwischen** [TSVIH•schn] *prep*
*adv* between

**Zwischenraum**
[TSVISH•en•roum] *n* M
interval

**Zwischenzeit**
[TSVIHSH•en•tsait] *n* F
interim; meantime

**zwitschern** [TSVIHT•chairn] *vi*
twitter

**zwölf** twelve

**zwölfte** [TSVUHLF•teh] *num*
twelfth

**Zyklus** [TSEEK•loos] *n* M cycle

**Zykon** [TSEE•klohn] *n* M
cyclone

**Zylinder** [TSUHL•in•dair] *n* M
cylinder

**Zyniker** [TSUHN•eek•air] *n* M
cynic

**zynisch** [TSUHN•ish] *adj*
cynical

**Zypresse** [TSUH•pres•se] *n* F
cypress

# A

**a** [u or ai ] (before vowel or
silent 'h' ) an [en] art ein eine
ein

**A.M.** abbr vormittags

**abandon** [u•BAN•dun] vt
aufgeben

**abase** [u•BAIS] vt erniedrigen;
demutigen

**abbey** [a•BEE] n Abtei F

**abbreviate** [u•BREE•vee•ait] vt
abkürzen

**abbreviation**
[u•BREE•vee•AI•shn] n
Ab-Verkürzung F

**abdomen** [AB•du•men] n
Abdomen N

**abduct** [ub•DUHKT] vt
entführen

**abet** [u•BET] vt begünstigen

**abhor** [ub•HAUR] vt
verabscheuen

**abide (by)** [u•BUYD] vi treu
bleiben

**ability** [u•BI•li•tee] n
Fähigkeit F

**able** [AI•bl] adj fähig

**abnormal** [ab•NAUR•ml] adj
ungewöhnlich

**abode** [u•BOD] n Wohnung F

**abolish** [u•BAH•lish] vt
zerstören

**abominable** [u•BAH•mi•nu•bl]
adj abscheulich

**abortion** [u•BAUR•shn] n
Vertreibung F

**about** [u•BOUT] prep um; über

**above** [u•BUHV] adv über;
oben

**abrupt** [u•BRUHPT] adj
schroff; abrupt

**absent** [AB•sunt] adj abwesend

**absent-minded** [-MUYN•did]
adj geistesabwesend

**absolute** [AB•su•loot] adj
absolut ; unbedingt

**absolutely** [AB•su•LOOT•lee]
adv völlig

**absorb** [ub•ZAURB] vt
einsaugen

**abstain** [ab•STAIN] vi sich
enthalten

**absurd** [ub•SURD] adj
lächerlich

**abundant** [u•BUHN•dunt] adj
reichlich; vorhanden

**abuse 1** [u•BYOOS] n
Missbrauch M

**abuse 2** [u•BYOOZ] vt
missbrauchen

**abyss** [u•BIS] n Abgrund M

**academy** [u•KA•du•mee] n
Akademie F

**accent** [AK•sent] n Akzent M

**accept** [ak•SEPT] *vt*
akzeptieren; annehmen

**access** [AK•ses] *n* Zugang M

**accident** [AK•si•dunt] *n*
Unfall M

**accidental** [AK•si•DEN•tl] *adj*
zufällig

**accommodate**
[uh•KAH•mu•DAIT] *vt*
aushelfen

**accompany** [u•CUHM•pu•nee]
*vt* begleiten

**accomplice** [u•KAHM•plis] *n*
Mitschuldiger-e MF

**accomplish** [u•KAHM•plish] *vt*
vollbringen; erfüllen

**accord** [u•KAURD] *n*
Einigkeit F

**according** [u•KAUR•ding] *prep*
nach

**accost** [u•KAUST] *vt*
herantreten an (acc)

**account** [u•KOUNT] *n* Konto N

**accumulate**
[u•KYOO•myu•LAIT] *vt*
ansammeln

**accurate** [A•kyu•ret] *adj* genau;
richtig

**accuse** [u•KYOOZ] *vt* anklagen

**accustom** [u•KUH•stum] *vt* sich
gewöhnen

**ache** [aik] *n* Schmerz N

**acid** [A•sid] *adj* sauer; bissig; *n*
Säure F

**acknowledge** [ek•NAH•lij] *vt*
anerkennen

**acquaintance** [u•KWAIN•tuns]
*n* Bekannte -er (m) F

**acquiesce** [a•kwee•YES] *vi*
hinnehmen; dulden

**acquire** [u•KWUYUR] *vt*
erwerben; gewinnen

**acquit** [u•KWIT] *vt* freisprecher

**acre** [AI•kur] *n* Fläche F

**acrid** [A•krid] *adj* beissend;
scharf

**across** [u•KRAUS] *adv*
kreuzweise quer

**act** [akt] *n* Akt M

**action** [AK•shn] *n* Handlung F

**active** [AK•tiv] *adj* aktiv; tätig

**actor** [AK•tur] *n*
Schauspieler M

**actress** [AK•tris] *n*
Schauspielerin F

**actually** [AK•chu•lee] *adv*
eigentlich

**acute** [u•KYOOT] *adj* scharf

**adapt** [u•DAPT] *vt* einstellen

**add** [ad] *vt* hinzufügen

**addict** [A•dikt] *n* Süchtige-r F

**addiction** [u•DIK•shn] *n*
Sucht F

**addition** [u•DI•shn] *n* Zuwachs;
Hinzufügung (f) M

**additional** [u•DI•shun•ul] *adj*
zusätzlich

**address 1** [A•dres] *n* Adresse F

**address 2** [u•DRES] *vt* anreden

**adequate** [A•de•kwet] *adj*
genügend

**adjective** [A•jik•tiv] *n*
Adjektiv N

**adjourn** [u•JURN] *vt vi*
vertagen

**adjust** [u•JUHST] *vt* berichtigen

**administer** [ud•MI•ni•stur] *vt*
verwalten

**admire** [ud•MUYR] *vt*
bewundern

**admission** [ud•MI•shun] *n*
Einlass; Zutritt M

**admit** [ud•MIT] (let enter) *vt*
zugeben

**admonish** [ud•MAH•nish] *vt*
mahnen

**adolescence** [A•du•LE•suns] *n*
Jünglingsalter N

**adopt** [u•DAHPT] *vt* annehmen

**adoption** [u•DAHP•shun] *n*
Adoption F

**adore** [u•DAUR] *vt* anbeten

**adult** [u•DUHLT] *n* Erwachsene
-r (m) F

**adultery** [u•DUHL•tu•ree] *n*
Ehebruch M

**advance** [ed•VANS] *vt/vi*
vorwärtsbringen

**advantage** [ed•VAN•tej] *n*
Vorteil M

**advantageous**
[AD•VUN•TAI•jus *adj*
günstig

**Advent** [AD•vent] *n* Advent M

**adventure** [ed•VEN•chur] *n*
Abenteuer N

**adventurous** [ed•VEN•chu•rus]
*adj* abenteuerlich

**adverbe** [AD•vurb] *n*
Adverb M

**adversity** [ad•VUR•si•tee] *n*
Unglück N

**advertise** [AD•vur•TUYZ] *vt*
ankündigen

**advertisement**
[AD•vur•TUYZ•munt] *n*
Anzeige F

**advice** [ad•VUYS] *n* Rat M

**advise** [ad•VUYZ] *vt* raten

**affair** [u•FAIR] *n*
Angelegenheit F

**affect** [u•FEKT] *vt* betreffen

**affection** [u•FEK•shn] *n*
Neigung F

**afford** [uh•FAWRD] *vt* sich
leisten

**Afghanistan** [af•GA•ni•STAN]
*n* Afghanistan

**afraid** (to be) [u•FRAID] *adj*
sich fürchten

**Africa** [A•fri•ku] *n* Afrika

**after** [AF•tur] *prep adv* nach

**afternoon** [AF•tur•NOON] *n*
Nachmittag M

**again** [uh•GEN] *adv* wieder

**against** [uh•GENST] *prep adv*
gegen

**age** [aij] *n* Alter N

**aged** [AI•jud / aij'd] *adj* bejahrt

**agency** [AI•jun•cee] *n*
Dienststelle F

**agenda** [uh•JEN•duh] *n*
Tagesordnung F

**agent** [AI•junt] *n* Vertreter -in
(f) M

**aggravate** [A•gru•VAIT] *vt*
ärgern

**aggressive** [u•GRE•siv] *adj*
aggressiv

**ago** [uh•GO] *adv* vergangen

**agree** [uh•GREE] *vi* zustimmen

**agreeable** [u•GREE•u•bl] *adj*
einverstanden; angenehm

**agreement** [u•GREE•munt] *n*
Einigung F

**agriculture** [A•gri•CUL•chur] *n*
Landwirtschaft F

**ahead** (of) [uh•HED] *adv*
(prep) vorn; vor

**aid** [aid] *n* Hilfe F

**AIDS** [aids] *n* AIDS F

**aim** [aim] *n* Ziel N

**air** [air] *n* Luft F

**air•conditioning**
[-kuhn•DI•shuh•ning] *n*
Luftreinigung; Klimaanlage F

**air-conditioned**
[-kuhn•DI•shuhnd] *adj*
luftgekühlt

**airmail** [AIR•mail] (by ~ ) *n*
Luftpost F

**airplane** [AIR•plain] *n*
Flugzeug N

**airport** [AIR•paurt] *n*
Flughafen M

**airtight** [AIR•tuyt] *adj* luftdicht

**aisle** [uyl] *n* Seitenschiff N

**ajar** [uh•JAHR] *adj* halb; offen

**alarm** [u•LAHRM] (*vt*: alarmer)
*n* Alarm M

**alarm clock** [u•LAHRM
CLAHK] *n* Wecker M

**alas** [uh•LAS] *excl* ach

**Albania** [al•BAI•nee•yuh] *n*
Albanien

**album** [AL•bum] *n*
Stammbuch N

**alcohol** [AL•ku•HAL] *n*
Alkohol M

**alcoholic** [AL•ku•HAU•lik] *adj*
alkoholisch; *n* Alkoholiker M

**alert** [uh•LUHRT] *adj* achtsam

**algebra** [AL•je•bru] *n*
Algebra F

**Algeria** [AL•jee•ree•yu] *n*
Algerien

**alibi** [A•li•BUY] *n*
Entschuldigung F

**alike** [uh•LUYK] *adj* gleichsam;
lebendig

**all** [awl] *adj* alle

**allegation** [A•lu•GAI•shun] *n*
Behauptung F

**allergic** [u•LUR•jik] *adj*
allergisch

**allergy** [A•luhr•jee] *n* Allergie F

**alliance** [u•LUY•yuns] *n*
Verbindung F; Bund M

**allow** [uh•LOW] *vt* erlauben

**allude (to)** [uh•LOOD] *vi*
anspielen (auf)

**allusion** [u•LOO•zhuhn] *n*
Hinweiss hinweisen M

**almost** [AWL•most] *adv* fast

**alone** [uh•LON] *adj adv* allein

**along** [uh•LAWNG] *prep*
entlang

**aloud** [uh•LOWD] *adv* laut

**alphabet** [AL•fu•BET] *n*
Alphabet N

**already** [aul•RE•dee] *adv* schon

**also** [AWL•so] *adv* auch

**alternate (with)**
[AUL•tur•NAIT] *vi*
vertauschen

**although** [awl•THO] *conj*
obwohl

**altogether**
[AUL•too•GE•thuhr] *adv* im
ganzen genommen

**always** [AWL•waiz] *adv* immer

**am** [am] *v* bin

**amateur** [A•mu•CHUR] *adj n*
Amateur M

**amaze** [u•MAIZ] *vt* erstaunen

**amazing** [u•MAI•zing] *adj*
erstaunlich

**ambassador** [am•BA•su•dur] *n*
Botschafter M

**ambiguous** [am•BI•gyoo•wus]
*adj* zweideutig

**ambitious** [am•BI•shus] *adj*
ergeizig

**amend** (law) [u•MEND] *vt*
ändern; berechnen; *n*

**amendment** [u•MEND•ment] *n*
Berechtigung F

**America** [u•ME•ri•ku] *n*
Amerika N

**amnesty** [AM•ni•stee] *n*
Amnestie F

**among** [u•MUHNG] *prep*
mitten; unter •

**amount** [u•MOUNT] *n*
Summe F

**amuse** [u•MYOOZ] *vt*
amusieren

**analogy** [u•NA•lu•jee] *n*
Analogie F

**analysis** [u•NA•lu•sis] *n*
Analyse F

**analyze** [A•nu•LUYZ] *vt*
analysieren

**anarchy** [A•nahr•kee] *n*
Anarchie F

**ancestor** [AN•SE•stur] *n*
Vorfahr M

**anchor** [AN•kur] *n* Anker M

**ancient** [AIN•shunt] *adj* uralt

**and** [and] or [end] *conj* und

**angel** [AIN•jul] *n* Engel M

**anger** [ANG•gur] *n* Ärger F

**angle** [ANG•gl] *n* Winkel M

**angry** [ANG•gree] *adj* böse

**anguish** [AN•gwish] *n* Qual F

**animal** [A•ni•ml] *n* Tier N

**animate** [A•ni•mut] *adj* munter

**anniversary** [A•ni•VUR•su•ree]
*n* Jahrestag M

**announce 1** [u•NOUNS] *vt*
ankündigen

**announce 2 (notify; report)**
[u•NOUNS] *vt* anmelden

**annoy** [u•NOI] *vt* ärgern •

**annoying** [u•NOI•ying] *adj*
ärgerlich

**annual** [A•nyoo•ul] *adj* jährlich

**another** [u•NUH•thur] *adj* ein
anderer neuer

**answer** [AN•sur] *vt* antworten;
*n* Antwort F

**ant** [ant] *n* Ameise F

**anthology** [an•THAH•lu•jee] *n*
Anthologie F

**antique** [an•TEEK] *adj* antik

**antisocial** [AN•ti•SO•shul] *adj*
ungesellig

**anxiety** [ang•ZUY•yu•tee] *n*
Angst F

**anxious** [ANK•shus] *adj*
besorgt

**any** [E•nee] *adj* einige

**anyone** (anybody)
[E•nee•WUHN] *pron* irgend;
jemand

**anything** [E•nee•THING] *pron*
etwas; irgent

**anyway** [E•nee•WAI] *adv*
irgendwie

**anywhere** [E•nee•WAIR] *adv*
irgendwo

**apartment** [u•PAHRT•munt] *n*
Wohnung F

**ape** [aip] *n* Affe F

**apologize** [u•PAH•lu•JUYZ] *vi*
sich entschuldigen

**apology** [u•PAH•lu•jee] *n*
Entschuldigung F

**apparently** [u•PA•runt•lee] *adv*
anscheinend

**appear** [u•PEER] *vi* erscheinen

**appearance** [u•PEER•uns] *n*
Aussehen N

**appetite** [A•pu•TUYT] *n*
Appetit M

**appetizer** [A•pu•TUY•zur] *n*
Vorspeise F

**applaud** [u•PLAUD] *vt*
applaudieren; spenden

**applause** [u•PLAUS] *n*
Beifall M

**apple** [A•pl] *n* Apfel M; ~ tree\
Apfelbaum M

**application** [A•pli•KAI•shn] *n*
Berwerbung F

**apply** [uh•PLUY] *vt* sich
bewerben; um auflegen

**appoint** [u•POINT] *vt* ernennen

**appointment** [u•POINT•ment]
*n* Verbredung F; to have an
~w/someone\ Anstellung sich
verabreden

**appraisal** [u•PRAI•zl] *n*
Schätzung F

**appraise** [u•PRAIZ] *vt*
bewerten; schätzen

**appreciate** [u•PREE•shee•AIT]
*vt* hochschätzen; würdigen

**approach** [u•PROCH] *vt* sich
nähern; *n* (access) Gang M

**appropriate** [u•PRO•pree•IT]
*adj* passend

**approval** [u•PROO•vl] *n*
Billigung Genehmigung F

**approve** [uh•PROOV] *vt*
genehmigen; bestätigen

**approximately**
[u•PRAHK•su•mit•lee] *adv*
ungefähr fast

**apricot** [a•pri•KAHT] *n*
Aprikose F

**April** [AI•pril] *n* April M

**arbitrary** [AHR•bi•TRE•ree]
*adj* eigenmächtig

**arch** [ahrch] *n* Bogen M

**archaeology**
[AHR•kee•AH•lu•jee] *n*
Archäologie F

**archaic** [ahr•KAI•ik] *adj*
altertümlich

**architect** [AHR•ki•TEKT] *n*
Architekt (in) M

**architecture**
[AHR•ki•TEK•chur] *n*
Architektur F

**area** [A•ree•u] *n* Gegend F

**argue** [AHR•gyoo] *vi*
argumentieren

**argument** [AHR•gyu•mint] *n*
Entgegnung F

**arid** [A•rid] *adj* trocken; dürr

**arm 1** [ahrm] *n* Arm (anat) M

**arm 2** [ahrm] *n* Waffe
(weapon) F

**armchair** [AHRM•chair] *n*
Stuhl M

**armor** [AHR•mur] *n* Rüstung F

**army** [AHR•mee] *n* Armee;
Heer F

**aroma** [u•RO•mu] *n* Aroma N;
Duft M

**around** [u•ROUND] *adv*
ringsherum; etwa

**arrange** [u•RAINJ] *vt*
arrangieren; ausrichten

**arrangement** [u•RAINJ•ment]
*n* Anordnung F

**arrest** [u•REST] *vt* verhaften

**arrival** [u•RUY•vl] *n* Ankunft F

**arrive** [u•RUYV] *vi* ankommen

**arrogant** [A•ru•gent] *adj*
arrogant

**arrow** [A•ro] *n* Pfeil M

**art** [ahrt] *n* Kunst F

**article** [AHR•ti•kl] *n* Artikel M

**articulate** [ahr•TI•cyu•LAIT]
*vt/vi* aussprechen

**artificial** [AHR•ti•FI•shl] *adj*
künstlich

**artist** [AHR•tist] *n* Künstler
-in M

**as** [az] als; wie

**ash** [ash] *n* Asche F

**ashamed (to be)** [u•SHAIMD]
*adj* beschämt

**ashtray** [ASH•trai] *n*
Aschenbecher M

**aside** [u•SUYD] *adv* beiseite

**ask** [ask] *vt* fragen

**asleep** [u•SLEEP] *adj* schlafend

**asparagus** [u•SPA•ru•gus] *n*
Spargelk F

**aspect** [A•spekt] *n* Anblick;
Aspekt M

**aspirin** [A•sprin] *n* Aspirine F

**assassinate** [u•SA•si•NAIT] *vt*
ermorden

**assassination**
[u•SA•si•NAI•shun] *n*
Meuchelmord M;
Ermordung F

**assemble** [u•SEM•bl] *vt*
versammeln

**assembly** [u•SEM•blee] *n*
Versammlung; Gesellschaft F

**assign** [u•SUYN] *vt* übertragen

**associate** [u•SO•shee•AIT] *vt*
verbinden

**association** [u•SO•see•AI•shn]
*n* Verbindung; Gesellschaft F

**assume** [u•SOOM] *vt*
voraussetzen; annehmen

**astonish** [u•STAH•nish] *vt*
erstaunen

**astrology** [u•STRAH•lu•jee] *n*
Astrologie F

**astronaut** [A•stru•NAHT] *n*
Weltraumfahrer M

**astronomy** [a•STRAH•nu•mee]
*n* Astronomie; Sternkunde F

**at** [at] *prep* an; bei; zu; auf;

**attach** [u•TACH] *vt* befestigen

**attack** [u•TAK] *vt* angreifen

**attempt (to)** [u•TEMPT] *vt*
versuchen

**attend** [u•TEND] *vt* beiwohnen

**attention 1** [u•TEN•shn] *n*
Aufmerksamkeit; Beachtung F

**attention 2** [u•TEN•shn] *n*
Achtung F

**attentive** [u•TEN•tiv] *adj*
aufmerksam

**attic** [A•tik] *n* Dachstube F

**attitude** [A•ti•TOOD] *n*
Haltung M; Standpunkt F

**attract** [u•TRAKT] *vt* anziehen

**attraction** [u•TRAK•shn] *n*
Anziehunskraft; Reiz M

**attractive** [u•TRAK•tiv] *adj*
reizvill; anziehend

**audience** [AU•dee•uns] *n*
Zuschauer N; Publikum F

**audition** [au•DI•shun] *n*
Vorsprechen N

**August** [AU•gust] *n* August M

**aunt** [ant or ahnt] *n* Tante F

**Australia** [au•STRAIL•yu] *n*
Australien

**Austria** [AU•stree•u] *n*
Österreich N

**authentic** [au•THEN•tik] *adj*
echt

**author** [AU•thur] *n*
Schriftsteller M; ~in F

**authority** [u•THAU•ri•tee] *n*
Autorität; Vollmacht F

**autobiography**
[AU•to•buy•AH•gru•fee] *n*
Selbstbiographie F
**autograph** [AU•tu•GRAF] *n*
Autogramm N; Unterschrift F
**automatic** [AU•to•MA•tik] *adj*
automatisch
**autumn** [AU•tum] *n* Herbst M
**auxiliary** [awg•ZIL•yu•ree] *adj*
*n* mitwirkend
**available** [u•VAI•lu•bl] *adj*
verfügbar
**avenge** [u•VENJ] *vt* rächen
**avenue** [A•vu•NYOO] *n* Straße;
Allee F; Boulevard M
**average** [A•vur•ij] *adj*
durchschnittlich; *n*
Durchschnitt M

**avoid** [u•VOID] *vt* vermeiden
**awake** [u•WAIK] *adj* wach; *vi*
erwachen; *vt* waken
**award** [u•WAURD] *n* Preis M;
Prämie F; *vt* geben
**aware** [u•WAIR] *adj* bewußt
**awareness** [u•WAIR•ness] *n*
Bewußtsein N
**away** [u•WAI] *adv* weg; *vt*
put ~ \ weglegen
**awful** [AU•ful] *adj* furchtbar
schrecklich
**awkward** [AU•kwurd] *adj*
ungeschickt
**axe** [ax] *n* Axt; Beil (n) F
**axis** [AK•sis] *n* Achse F
**axle** [AK•sl] *n* Achse F

# B

**babble** [BA•bl] *n* Gemurmel N;
*vi* plappern
**baby** [BAI•bee] *n* Baby N;
~sitter\ *n* Babysitter (in)
M (F)
**bachelor** [BA•chu•lur] *n*
Junggeselle M
**back** [bak] *n* Rücken M; *adv*
züruckn; *adj* hinter; *vt*
zurücsetzen
**background (in the)**
[BAK•grownd] *n*
Hintergrund M
**backlash** [BAK•lash] *n*
Rückwirkung F
**backpack** [BAK•pak] *n*
Rücksack M

**backward** [BAK•wurd] *adv adj*
rückwärts
**backyard** [bak•YAHRD] *n*
Garten M
**bacon** [BAI•kun] *n* Speck M
**bad** {bad] *adj* schlecht
**badge** [baj] *n* Kennzeichen;
Abzeichen N
**badly** [BAD•lee] *adv* schlecht
**bag** [bag] *n* Sack; Beute; Tüte
M
**baggage** [BA•gij] *n* Gepäck N
**bagpipes** [BAG•puyps] *npl*
Dudelsackpfeifen F
**bail** [baiul] *n* Bürge M; Kaution
F; on ~ \ *vt* jegen Kaution
freibekommen

**bait** [bait] *n* Köder M
**bake** [baik] *vt* backen
**baker** [BAI•kur] *n* Bäcker in M
**bakery** [BAI•ker•ee] *n*
Bäckerei; Konditerei F
**balance** [BA•luns] *n*
Gleichgewicht N
**balance-sheet**
[BA•lens•SHEET] *n* Bilanz F
**balcony** [BAL•ku•nee] *n*
Balkon M
**bald** [bauld] *adj* kahl
**bale** [baiul] *n* Ballen M
**balk** [bauk] *vi* stocken
**ball** [bawl] *n* Ball M; to have a
~\ sich prima amüsieren
**ballad** [BA•lud] *n* Ballade F
**ballerina** [BA•lu•REE•nu] *n*
Ballerina F
**ballet** [BA•lai] *n* Ballet N
**balloon** [bu•LOON] *n*
Balloon M
**ballot** [BA•lut] *n* Wahl F
**bamboo** [bam•BOO] *n*
Bambus M
**ban** [ban] *n* Verbot N
**banal** [bu•NAL] *adj* banal
**banana** [bu•NA•nu] *n* Banane F
**band** [band] *n* Verband M;
Gruppe F
**bandage** [BAN•dij] *n*
Hansepflaster M
**banish** [BA•nish] *vt* verbannen
**bank** [bank] *n* Bank F
**bank note** [BANK•not] *n*
Banknote F
**banker** [BANG•kur] *n*
Bankhalter M
**bankrupt** [BANK•ruhpt] *adj*
bankrott; konkurs

**bankruptcy**
[BANK•RUHPT•see] *n*
Konkurs M
**banner** [BA•nur] *n* Banner N;
Fahne F
**banquet** [BANG•kwet] *n*
Festessen N
**banter** [BAN•tur] *n* Neckerei F
**baptism** [BAP•tizm] *n* Taufe F
**baptize** [bap•TUYZ] *vt* taufen
**bar** [bahr] (pub) *n* Lokal N
**barbarian** [bahr•BE•ree•un] *n*
Barbar M; *adj* barbarisch
**barbed** [bahrbd] *adj* mit
Stacheln versehen
**barber** [BAHR•bur] *n*
Friseur M
**bare** [bair] *adj* nackt
**barefoot** [BAIUR•fut] *adj adv*
barfuß
**barely** [BAIR•lee] *adv* kaum
**bargain** [BAHR•gin] *n* Preis; *vi*
zum günstigen
**barge** [bahrj] *n* Kanalboot N
**bark** [bahrk] *n* Borke F ; ~ at\
*vi* bellen
**barley** [BAHR•lee] *n* Gerste F
**barn** [bahrn] *n* Scheune F
**barometer** [bu•RAH•mi•tur] *n*
Barometer N
**baroque** [bu•ROK] *n* Barok N;
*adj* barok
**barracks** [BA•ruks] *npl*
Kaserne F
**barrel** [BA•rul] *n* Faß F; they
have us over a ~\ sie haben
uns in der Zange
**barren** [BA•run] *adj*
unfruchtbar; öde (landscape)
**barricade** [BA•ri•KAID] *n*
Barrikade F

**barrier** [BA•ree•ur] *n* Sperre F

**bartender** [BAHR•TEN•dur] *n* Barkellner -in M

**base** [bais] *n* Basis F

**baseball** [BAIS•bawl] *n* Baseball M

**basement** [BAIS•munt] *n* Keller M

**bashful** [BASH•ful] *adj* scheu

**basic** [bai•sik] *adj* grundlegend; the ~s\ das Westenliche

**basil** [baizl] *n* Bailienkraut N

**basis** [BAI•sis] *n* Basis F

**basket** [BA•skit] *n* Korb M

**basketball** [BA•skit•BAWL] *n* Korbball M

**bass (mus)** [bais] *n* Baß M

**bassoon** [bu•SOON] *n* Fagott N

**bastard** [BA•sturd] *n* Bastard M

**baste** [baist] *vt* mit Fett gebießen

**bat** [bat] *n* Fledermaus F

**bath** [bath] *n* Bad N

**bather** [BAI•thur] *n* Badende(r) F

**bathing suit** [BAI•thing ~ ] *n* Bademantel M

**bathrobe** [BATH•rob] *n* Baderobe F

**bathroom** [BATH•room] *n* Badezimmer N

**bathtub** [BATH•tuhb] *n* Badewanne F

**baton** [bu•TAHN] *n* Stab M

**battalion** [bu•TA•lyun] *n* Bataillon N

**batter** [BA•tur] *n* Eierteig; Schlagteig (baking) M

**battery** [BA•tu•ree] *n* Batterie F

**battle** [batl] *n* Schlacht F

**battleship** [BA•tl•SHIP] *n* Schlachtschiff N

**bawdy** [BAU•dee] *adj* unzüchtig

**bawl** [baul] *vt* brüllen; *vi* grölen

**bay** [bai] *n* Bucht F

**bayonet** [BAI•u•net] *n* Bayonett M

**bazaar** [bu•ZAHR] *n* Markt M

**BC** (before Christ) vor Christus

**be** [bee] (am, is are) *aux v* sein; he is (something) er ist ~

**beach** [beech] *n* Strand M

**bead** [beed] *n* Perle F

**beagle** [BEE•gl] *n* Spürhund M

**beak** [beek] *n* Schnabel M

**beam** [beem] *n* Leitstrahl M

**bean** [been] *n* Bohne F

**bear 1** [bair] *n* Bär M

**bear 2** [bair] *vt* tragen (burden, weight)

**beard** [beerd] *n* Bart M

**beast** [beest] *n* Raubtier N

**beastly** [BEEST•lee] *adj* brutal; gemein

**beat** [beet] *vt* schlagen

**beating** [BEE•ting] *n* Schlagen N; Prügel F

**beautiful** [BYOO•ti•ful] *adj* schön

**beauty** [BYOO•tee] *n* Schönheit F

**beaver** [BEE•vur] *n* Biber M

**because** [bi•CUHZ] *conj* weil

**because of** [bi•CUHZ UHV] *prep* wegen

**beckon** [BE•kun] *vt* heranwinken

**become** [bi•CUHM] *vi* werden

**becoming** [bi•CUH•ming] *adj*
  passend
**bed** [bed] *n* Bett N
**bedroom** [BED•room] *n*
  Schlafzimmer N
**bee** [bee] *n* Biene F
**beech** [beech] *n* Buche F
**beef** [beef] *n* Rindfleisch N
**beehive** [BEE•huyv] *n*
  Bienenstock M
**been** [bin] (past of be) gewesen
**beer** [bee'ur] *n* Bier N
**beet** [beet] *n* Bete F
**beetle** [beetl] *n* Käfer M
**before** [bi•FAWR] *adv* vorher
**befriend** [bu•FREND] *vt*
  befreunden
**beg** [beg] *vt* betten
**beggar** [BE•gur] *n* Bettler M
**begin** [bi•GIN] *vt vi* anfangen
**beginner** [bu•GI•nur] *n*
  Anfänger M
**beginning** [bi•GI•ning] *n*
  Anfang M
**behalf** [bi•HAF] *n* im Auftrag
  von
**behave** [bi•HAIV] *vi* sich
  benehmen
**behavior** [bi•HAI•vyur] *n*
  Benehmen N
**behead** [bi•HED] *vt* enthaupten
**behind** [bi•HUYND] *n*
  Hinterteil M; *prep adv* hinter
**beige** [baizh] *adj n* beige
**being** [BEE•ing] *n* Dasein;
  Wesen N
**belated** [bi•LAI•tid] *adj*
  verspätet
**belfry** [BEL•free] *n*
  Glockenturm M
**Belgian** [BEL•jun] *adj* belgisch

**Belgium** [BEL•jum] *n* Belgien
**belief** [bi•LEEF] *n* Glaube M
**believe** [bi•LEEV] *vt vi*
  glauben an
**bell** [bel] *n* Glocke F
**bellow** [BE•lo] *vi* brüllen
**belly** [BE•lee] *n* Geliebte F
**belong** [bi•LAUNG] *vi*
  gehören zu
**beloved** [bi•LUVHVD] *adj*
  geliebt
**below** [bi•LO] *adv* unten
**belt** [belt] *n* Gürtel M
**bench** [bench] *n* Bank M
**bend** [bend] *vt* biegen
**bend** [bend] *n* Kurve F
**beneath** [bi•NEETH] *adv* unter;
  unten
**benediction** [BE•ni•DIK•shun]
  *n* Segnung F
**benefactor** [BE•ni•FAK•tur] *n*
  Stifter M
**beneficial** [BE•nu•FI•shl] *adj*
  nützlich
**benefit** [BE•ni•FIT] *n*
  Vorteil M
**benign** [bi•NUYN] *adj* gütig
**bent** [bent] *adj* geneigt
**bequeath** [bi•KWEETH] *vt*
  hinterlassen
**beret** [bu•RAI] *n*
  Baskenmütze F
**berry** [BE•ree] *n* Beere F
**beside** [bi•SUYD] *prep* neben
**besides** [bi•SUYDS] *adv prep*
  außerdem
**besiege** [bi•SEEJ] *vt* belagern
**best 1** [best] *adj* das Beste; to
  be .~\ am besten
**best 2** [best] *adv* best

**bestow** [bi•STO] *vt* schenken
gewähren

**bet** [bet] *n* Wette F

**betray** [bi•TRAI] *vt* betrügen

**betrayal** [bi•TRAI•ul] *n* Betrüg;
Verrat M

**betrayer** [bi•TRAI•ur] *n*
Verrater M

**better** [BE•tur] *adj* besser

**between** [bi•TWEEN] *prep adv*
zwischen

**beverage** [BE•vu•rij] *n*
Getränk N

**beware** (of) [bi•WAIR] *vi* sich
hüten vor

**bewitching** [bi•WI•ching] *adj*
bezaubernd

**beyond** [bi•YAHND] *adv prep*
jenseits; hinaus

**bias** [BUY•us] *n* Vorurteil M

**biased** [BUY•ust] *adj*
voreingenommen·

**bib** *n* Schürze F

**Bible** [BUY•bl] *n* Bibel F

**bicker** [BI•kur] *vi* plätschern

**bicycle** [BUY•si•kul] *n*
Fahrrad N

**bid** [bid] *n vi* Gebot N

**big** [big] *adj* groß

**bigamy** [BI•gu•mee] *n*
Doppelehe; Bigamie F

**bigot** [BI•gut] *n* engstirnig M

**bike** [buyk] *n* Rad N

**bikini** [bi•KEE•nee] *n* Bikini M

**bile** [buyl] *n* Galle F

**bilingual** [BUY•LING•gwul]
*adj* zweisprachig

**bill** [bil] *n* Vorlage F

**billiards** [BIL•yurdz] *n*
Billiardspiel N

**billion** [BIL•yun] *num* Billion
Milliarde F

**bin** (for garbage) [bin] *n*
Eimer M

**binoculars** [bi•NAH•kyu•lurz]
*npl* Fernglas N

**biography** [buy•AH•gru•fee] *n*
Biographie F

**biology** [buy•AH•lu•jee] *n*
Biologie F

**birch** [burch] *n* Birke F

**bird** [burd] *n* Vogel M

**birdcage** [BURD•kaij] *n*
Vogelbauer N

**birth** [burth] *n* Geburt F

**birth control** [BURTH
kon•TROL] *n*
Geburtenregelung F

**birthday** [BURTH•dai] *n*
Geburtstag M

**birthmark** [BURTH•mahrk] *n*
Muttermal M

**birthrate** [BURTH•rait] *n*
Geburtenziffer F

**bishop** [BI•shup] *n* Bischof M

**bit** *n* Gebiß N

**bitch** [bich] *n* Hundin F

**bite** [buyt] *vt* beißen

**bitter** [BI•tur] *adj* bitter; sauer

**bitterness** [BI•tur•NIS] *n*
Grausamkeit; Verbitterung F

**blab** [blab] *vi vt* klatschen

**black** [blak] *n* Schwarzer; *adj*
schwarz

**black market** [BLAK
MAHR•kit] *n*
Schwarzmarkt M

**blackberry** [BLAK•BU•ree] *n*
Brombeere F

**blackbird** [BLAK•burd] *n*
Amsel

**blackboard** [BLAK•baurd] *n*
Tafel F

**blacken** [BLA•kun] *vt*
schwärzen

**blackmail** [BLAK•mail] *n*
Erpressung F

**blacksmith** [BLAK•smith] *n*
Schmiede M

**bladder** [BLA•dur] *n*
Gallenblase F

**blade** [blaid] *n* Blatt N

**blame** [blaim] *vt* Vorwürfe
machen

**bland** [bland] *adj* mild; sanft

**blank** [blank] *n* Formular N

**blanket** [BLANG•kit] *n*
Decke F

**blaspheme** [blas•FEEM] *vt vi*
fluchen

**blast** [blast] *n* Explosion F

**blatant** [BLAI•tunt] *adj*
brüllend

**blaze** [blaiz] *n* Feuer N

**bleach** [bleech] *n* Bleichmittel

**bleed** [bleed] *vi vt* blüten

**blemish** [BLE•mish] *n*
Schönheitsfehler F

**blend** [blend] *vt* vermischen

**bless** [bles] *vt* segnen

**blessing** [BLE•sing] *n*
Segnung F

**blind** [bluynd] *adj* blind

**blindfold** [BLUYND•fold] *n*
mit verblindenen Augen

**blink** [blink] *vt* blinken

**blinker** (car) [BLING•kur] *n*
Blinklicht N

**bliss** [blis] *n* Gemütlichkeit F

**blister** [BLI•stur] *n* Blase F

**blizzard** [BLI•zurd] *n*
Schneesturm M

**bloated** [BLO•tid] *adj*
aufgedunsen

**block 1** [blahk] *n* Block M

**block 2** (obstruct) [blahk] *vt*
hemmen; hindern

**blockade** [blah•KAID] *n*
Blockade F

**blockage** [BLAH•kij] *n*
Verstopfung F

**blonde** [blahnd] *adj* blond

**blood** [bluhd] *n* Blut N

**bloody** [BLUH•dee] *adj* blütig

**bloom** [bloom] *vi* blühen

**blossom** [BLAH•sum] *n* Blüte
F; *vi* blühen

**blouse** [blous] *n* Bluse F

**blow 1** [blo] (strike) *n*
Schlag M

**blow 2** [blo] (as wind) *vt* blasen

**bludgeon** [BLUH•jn] *vt*
jemanden; zwingen

**blue** [bloo] *adj n* blau; Blaue N

**blueberry** [BLOO•be•ree] *n*
Heidelbeere F

**blueprint** [BLOO•print] *n* Plan
Entwurf M

**bluff** [bluhf] *n* Steilufer N

**blunder** [BLUHN•dur] *n*
Fehler F

**blunt** [bluhnt] *adj* derb

**blurry** [BLU•ree] *adj* unscharf

**blush** [bluhsh] *vi* erröten

**boar** [baur] *n* Wildschwein N

**board 1** [baurd] *n* Brett (wood)
N; Behörde (council) F

**board 2** [baurd] *vt* am Bord

**boarding school**
[BAUR•ding ~ ] *n* Internat N

**boast** [bost] *vi* sich rühmen

**boat** [bot] *n* Boot N

**boating** [BO•ting] *n*
Bootfahren N

**body** [BAH•dee] *n* Körper M

**bodyguard**
[BAH•dee•GAHRD] *n*
Leibwache F

**bog** [bahg] *n* Sumpf M

**boil** [boil] *vt* kochen

**boiled egg** [boild ~ ] *n*
gekochtes Ei N

**boiling point** [BOI•ling ~ ] *n*
Seidespunkt M

**boisterous** [BOI•stu•rus] *adj*
ungestüm

**bold** [bold] *adj* kühn

**boldness** [BOLD•nes] *n*
Kühnheit F

**bolt** [bolt] *n* Schraube F

**bomb** [bahm] *n* Bombe F

**bombard** [BAHM•bahrd] *vt*
bombardieren

**bomber** [BAH•mur] *n*
Bomber M

**bombing** [BAH•ming] *n*
Bombenangriff M

**bond** [bahnd] *n* Bande F

**bondage** [BAHN•dij] *n*
Sklaverei F

**bone** [bon] *n* Knochen M

**bonfire** [BAHN•fuyur] *n*
Feuer N

**bonnet** [BAH•nit] *n* Mütze F

**bonus** [BO•nus] *n* Bonus M

**boo** [boo] *vt vi* Pfui

**book** [bük] *n* Buch N

**bookkeeper** [BÜK•KEE•pur] *n*
Buchhalter -in M (F)

**bookkeeping** [BÜK•KEE•ping]
*n* Buchhaltung F

**bookstore** [BÜK•staur] *n*
Buchhandlung F

**boom** [boom] *vi n* donnern
Donner M

**boomerang** [BOO•mu•RANG]
*n* Bumerang M

**boos** [booz] *npl* boos

**boost** [boost] *vt* hochscheiben

**boot** [boot] *n* Stiefel M

**booth** [booth] *n* Zelle F

**booty** [BOO•tee] *n* Beute F

**border** [BAUR•dur] *n* Rand M;
Grenze F

**bore** [baur] *vt* bohren

**boredom** [BAUR•dum] *n*
Langeweile F

**boring** [BAU•ring] *adj*
langweilig

**born** (to be) [baurn] *adj*
geboren; geboren am (born
on)

**borough** [BUH•ro] *n* Stadt F

**borrow** [BAH•ro] *vt* ausborgen;
entleihen

**Bosnia** [BAHZ•nee•u] *n*
Bosnien

**Bosnian** [BAHZ•nee•un] *adj n*
bosnisch

**bosom** [BU•zum] *n* Brust F

**boss** [baus] *n* Chef in M (F)

**botany** [BAH•tu•nee] *n*
Botanik F

**both** [both] *adj* beide

**bother** [BAH•thur] *vt*
belästigen; Last F

**bottle** [BAH•tl] *n* Flasche F

**bottom** [BAH•tum] *n*
Unterseite F

**boulder** [BOL•dur] *n*
Felsblock M

**bounce 1** [bouns] *vi vt* springen

**bounce 2** [bouns] *n* Sprung M

**bouncer** [BOUN•sur] *n*
Prahler M

**bound** [bound] *adj* (to be ~
for) bestimmt

**boundary** [BOUN•du•ree] *n*
Grenze F

**bout** [bout] *n* Kampf M

**bovine** [BO•vuyn] *adj* Rinder

**bow 1** [bou] *n* Verbeugung; *vt*
*vi* beugen

**bow 2** (knot) [bo] *n* Schleife F

**bow tie** [BOW tuy] *n*
Schleife F

**bowels** [boulz] *npl* Darm M

**bowl** [bol] *n* Schalle F

**bowling** [BO•ling]] *n* kegeln

**box** [bahks] *n* Kiste F

**box office** [BAHKS AW•fis] *s*
Kasse F

**boxer** [BAH•ksur] *n* Boxer M

**boxing** [BAH•ksing] *n* Boxen N

**boy** [boi] *n* Junge M

**boycott** [BOI•kaht] *n vt*
Boykott M

**bra** [brah] *n* BH Brusthalter M

**brace** [brais] *n* Stütze F

**bracelet** [BRAI•slit] *n*
Armband N

**bracket** (in writing) [BRA•kit]
*n* Klammer F

**brag** [brag] *vi* prahlen

**braid** [braid] *n vt* flechten
Flechte F

**braille** [brail] *n* Blindenschrift F

**brain** [brain] *n* Gehirn N

**brake** [braik] *n* Bremse F; *vi*
bremsen

**bran** [bran] *n* Kleie F

**branch** [branch] *n* Zweig M

**brand 1** [brand] *n* Marke;
Sorte F

**brand 2** [brand] *vt* (cattle etc)
mit einen ßrandmal zeichen

**brand-new** [brand•NOO] *adj*
Nagel neu

**brandy** [BRAN•dee] *n*
Weinbrand M

**brash; brash** *adj* frech

**brass** [bras] *n* Bleichinstrumente
F

**brat** [brat] *n* Range F

**brave** [braiv] *adj vt* tapfer

**bravery** [BRAI•vu•ree] *n*
Tapferheit F

**brawl** [braul] *n* Rauferei F

**brawn** [braun] *n* Muskeln F

**bray** [brai] *vi* gellen

**breach 1** (in wall) [breech] *n*
Bruch M; *vt* brechen

**breach 2** (of contract) [breech]
*n* Vertragsbruch M

**bread** [bred] *n* Brot N

**breadth** [bredth] *n* Breite F

**break 1** [braik] *vt vi* brechen; ~
down (vehicle)\ *vt* ausfallen;
~ in (interrupt)\ *vi*
unterbrechen; ~ in (illegally)\
*vi* einbrechen; ~ through\ *vi*
durbrechen

**break 2** [braik] *n* Bruch M

**breakdown** (machine)
[BRAIK•doun] *n* Abbruch M

**breakfast** [BREK•fust] *n*
Frühstück N

**breast** [brest] *n* Brust F

**breath** [breth] *n* Atem M

**breathe** [breeth] *vi* atmen

**breathless** [BRETH•lis] *adj*
außer Atmen

**breed 1** (animals) [breed] *vt*
sich paaren

**breed 2** (race) [breed] *n*
Rasse F

**breeze** [breez] *n* Brise F

**brevity** [BRE•vi•tee] *n* Kürze F

**brew** [broo] *vt* brauen

**brewer** [BROO•ur] *n* Brauer M

**brewery** [BROO•u•ree] *n*
Brauerei F

**bribe** [bruyb] *n* Bestechung F;
*vt* bestechen

**brick** [brik] *n* Ziegelstein M

**bridal** [BRUY•dl] *adj* bräutlich

**bride** [bruyd] *n* Braut F

**bridegroom** [BRUYD•groom]
*n* Bräutigam M

**bridesmaid** [BRUYDZ•maid] *n*
Brautjungfer F

**bridge** [brij] *n* Brücke F

**brief** [breef] *adj* kurz

**briefcase** [BREEF•kais] *n*
Aktentasche F

**briefly** [BREE•flee] *adv* im
Kürzen

**bright** [bruyt] *adj* hell

**brilliance** [BRIL•lyuns] *n*
Glanz M

**brilliant** [BRIL•lyunt] *adj*
glänzend

**bring** [bring] *vt* bringen

**brisk** [brisk] *adj* lebhaft

**bristle** [BRI•sl] *vi* Borste F

**British** [BRI•tish] *adj* britisch

**broad** [braud] *adj* breit

**broadcast** [BRAUD•kast] *n*
Fernsehsendung; Rundfunk F;
*vt* durch Rundfunk senden

**brocade** [bro•KAID] *n*
Brokat M

**broccoli** [BRAH•klee] *n*
Brokkoli F

**brochure** [bro•SHUR] *n*
Broschüre F

**broil** [broil] *vt* braten

**broker** [BRO•kur] *n* Broker M

**bronze** [brahnz] *n* Bronze F;
*adj* bronzefarben

**brooch** [broch] *n* Spange F

**brook** [brük] *n* Bach M

**broom** [broom] *n* Besen M

**broth** [brauth] *n* Brühe F

**brothel** [BRAH•thl] *n*
Bordell N

**brother** [BRUH•thur] *n*
Bruder M

**brother-in-law**
[BRUH•thur•in•LAU] *n*
Schwager M

**brown** [braun] *adj n* braun
Braune N

**bruise** [brooz] *n vt* Bluterguß M

**brunette** [broo•NET] *n*
dunkelbraun

**brush** [bruhsh] *n vt* Bürste
bürsten F

**Brussels** [BRUH•slz] *n* Brüssel

**brutal** [BROO•tl] *adj* brutal

**brute** [broot] *n* Untier N

**bubble** [BUH•bl] *n vi*
Seifenblase F

**buck** [buhk] *vi* bocken

**bucket** [BUH•kit] *n* Eimer M

**buckle** [BUH•kl] *n vt* Spange F

**bud** [buhd] *n vi* Keim M

**Buddhism** [BOO•DI•zm] *n*
Buddhismus M

**budge** [buhj] *vi vt* bewegen

**budget** [BUH•jit] *n* Budget N

**buffalo** [BUH•fu•LO] *n*
Büffel M

**buffet** [buh•FAI] *n* Büffet N

**bug** [buhg] *n* Insekt N

**bugle** [BYOO•gl] *n*
Signalhorn N

**build** [bild] *vt* bauen; ~ on\ *vt*
anhauen; ~ up\ *vi* enstehen

**builder** [BIL•dur] *n* Bauer M

**building** [BIL•ding] *n*
Gebäude N

**bulb** [buhlb] *n* Birne F (elec); *n*
Zweibel F (flower)

**Bulgaria** [BUHL•GAI•ree•u] *n*
Bulgarien

**bulge** [buhlj] *n* Bauchung F

**bull** [bül] *n* Stier M

**bulldozer** [BÜL•do•zur] *n*
Großräumspflug M

**bullet** [BÜ•lit] *n* Kugel F

**bulletin** [BÜ•lu•tin] *n*
Tagesbericht M

**bully** [BÜ•lee] *n* Maulheld M

**bumblebee** [BUHM•bl•BEE] *n*
Biene F

**bump** [buhmp] *n vt* stoßen
Stoß M

**bumper (of car)** [BUHM•pur]
*n* Stoßstange F

**bun** [buhn] *n* Brötchen N

**bunch** [buhnch] *n* Menge;
Bündel F

**bundle** [BUHN•dl] *n* Paket N

**bunk beds** [BUHNK ~] *npl*
Bett N

**buoy** [BOO•ee] *n* Boje F

**burden** [BUR•dn] *n* Last F; *vt*
belasten

**bureau 1** [BYÜ•ro] *n* Büro N

**bureau 2** (chest of drawers) *n*
Kommode F

**bureaucracy**
[byü•RAH•kru•see] *n*
Bürokratie F

**burglar** [BUR•glur] *n* Dieb;
Einbrecher M

**burial** [BU•ree•ul] *n*
Beerdigung F

**Burma** [BUR•mu] *n* Birma

**Burmese** [bur•MEEZ] *adj*
birmanisch

**burn** [burn] *vi vt* brennen;
verrbrennen; ~ up\ *vi*
auflodern

**burner** [BUR•nur] *n* Brenner M

**burning** [BURN•ing] *adj*
brennend

**burrow** [BUH•ro] *n vt* Höhle
sich eingraben F

**burst** [burst] *vt* bersten

**bury** [BU•ree] *vt* begraben;
beerdigen

**bus** [buhs] *n* Bus M

**bush** [büsh] *n* Gebüsch N

**bushel** [BÜ•shul] *n* Scheffel M

**business** [BIZ•nis] *n* Geschäft
N; *adj* geschäftlich

**businessman ~woman**
[BIZ•nis•MAN] *n*
Geschäftsmann —frau M

**bust** (of statue) [buhst] *n*
Büste F

**bustle** [BUH•sl] *n* Getue M

**busy** [BI•zee] *adj* beschäftig
besetzt

**busybody** [BIZ•ee•BAH•dee] *n*
Wichtigtuer M

**but** [buht] *conj* aber

**butcher 1** [BU•chur] *n*
Metzger M

**butcher 2 (shop)** [BU•chur] *n*
Metzgerei; Fleischerei F

**butler** [BUHT•lur] *n* Butler M

**butt** (of cigarette) [buht] *n*
Stummel M

**butter** [BUH•tur] *n vt* Butter F
**butterfly** [BUH•tur•FLUY] *n*
  Schmetterlinge F
**buttock** [BUH•tuk] *n*
  Hinterteil M
**button** [BUH•tn] *n* Knopf M
**buy** [buy] *vt* kaufen

**buyer** [BUY•ur] *n* Käufer -in
  (f) M
**buzz (of insect)** [buhz] *n*
  Summen M
**by 1** [buy] *prep* bei; ~ bus\ mit
  dem bus
**by 2** (near to) [buy] *prep* nahe

# C

**cab** [kab] *n* Taxi N
**cabbage** [KA•bij] *n* Kohl M
**cabin** [KA•bin] *n* Kabine F
**cabinet** [KA•bi•nit] *n*
  Schrank M
**cable** [KAI•bl] *n vi vt* Kabel N
**cackle** [KA•kl] *vi* gackern
**cactus** [KAK•tes] *n* Kaktus M
**cadaver** [ku•DA•vur] *n*
  Leich M
**cadet** [ku•DET] *n* Kadett M
**cafeteria** [KA•fi•TEE•ree•u] *n*
  Selbstbedingung F
**cage** [kaij] *n* Käfig M
**cake** [kaik] *n* Kuchen Torte
  (f) M
**calcium** [KAL•see•um] *n*
  Kalzium
**calculate** [KAL•kyoo•LAIT] *vt*
  berechnen
**calculator** [KAL•kyoo•LAI•tur]
  *n* Rechenmaschine F
**calendar** [KA•lin•dur] *n*
  Kalendar M
**calf** [kaf] *n* Kalb N
**call** [kaul] *n* Anruf M; *vt*
  anrufen; (visit) *n* Beutsch M
**calling** [KAU•ling] *n* Beruf M

**calm** [kahm] *adj* still
**calm down** [KALM DOUN] *vt*
  *vi* beruhigen
**Cambodia** [kam•BO•dyu] *s*
  Cambodien
**camel** [KA•mul] *n* Kamel N
**cameo** [KA•mee•O] *n* Kamee F
**camera** [KA•mu•ru] *n*
  Photoapparat N
**cameraman** [KA•mu•ru•MAN]
  *n* Kameramann M
**camp** [kamp] *n* Lager N; *vi*
  lagern
**campaign** [kam•PAIN] *n*
  Wahlkampf M; *vi* werben
**campground** [KAMP•ground]
  *n* Campingplatz M
**can 1** [kan] *n* Kanne F
**can 2** [kan] *vi aux* können
**Canada** [KA•nu•du] *s* Kanadien
**canal** [ku•NAL] *n* Kanal M
**canary** [ku•NA•ree] *n*
  Kanarienvogel M
**cancel** (call off) [KAN•suhl] *vt*
  absagen
**cancer** [KAN•sur] *s* Krebs M
**candid** [KAN•did] *adj* offen;
  ehrlich

**candidate** [KAN•di•DUT] *n*
Kandidat M

**candle** [KAN•dl] *n* Kerste F

**candor** [KAN•dur] *n*
Offenheit F

**candy** [KAN•dee] *n*
Süßigkeiten F

**cane** [kain] *n* Rohr M

**canine** [KAI•nuyn] *adj* Hunde

**cannibal** [KA•ni•bl] *n*
Menschenfresser M

**cannon** [KA•nun] *n* Kanone F

**canoe** [ku•NOO] *n* Kanu N

**canon** [KA•nun] *n* Maßstab M

**canopy** [KA•nu•pee] *n*
Kappe M

**canvas** [KAN•vus] *n*
Segeltuch N

**canyon** [KA•nyun] *n*
Felsschlucht F

**cap** [kap] *n* Mütze F

**capacity** [ku•PA•ci•tee] *n*
Fähigkeit F

**cape 1** (clothing) [kaip] *n*
Mantel M

**cape 2** (geog) [kaip] *n* Cape N

**caper** [KAI•pur] *n* Kaper F

**capital** [KA•pi•tl] *n*
Hauptstadt F

**capitalism** [KA•pi•tu•LI•zm] *n*
Kapitalismus M

**capsule** [KAP•sul] *n* Kapsel F

**captain** [KAP•tin] *n* Kapitän M

**caption** [KAP•shun] *n*
Überschrift F

**captive** [KAP•tiv] *n*
Gefangener M

**capture** [KAP•chur] *vt n* fangen
Fang M

**car** [kahr] *n* Auto N

**carbon** [KAHR•bun] *n*
Kohlenstoff M

**carcass** [KAHR•kus] *n*
Kadaver M

**card** [kahrd] *n* Karte F

**cardboard** [KAHRD•baurd] *n*
Kartonpapier N

**cardiac** [KAHR•dee•AK] *adj*
herz

**cardigan** [KAHR•di•gun] *n*
Strickjacke F

**cardinal** [KAHR•di•nl] *n*
Kardinal M

**care** [kair] *n* Kummer M; take ~
of \ bei

**care** (about) [kair] (I don't care)
*vi* sich sorgen um; es ist mir
egal

**career** [ku•REER] *n* Beruf M

**carefree** [KAIR•free] *adj*
sorgenfrei

**careful** [KAIR•ful] *adj*
sorgfältig; be ~\ aufpassen

**careless** [KAIR•lis] *adj*
unvorsichtig

**caress** [ku•RES] *n* Liebkosung
F; *vt* liebkosen

**cargo** [KAHR•go] *n* Fracht F

**Caribbean** (Sea)
[KU•ri•BEE•un] *n* karibisches
Meer N

**carnal** [KAHR•nul] *adj*
fleischlich

**carnation** [kahr•NAI•shun] *n*
Nelke F

**carnival** [KAHR•nu•vl] *n*
Fasching M

**carnivorous** [kahr•NI•vu•rus]
*adj* fleischfressend

**carp** [kahrp] *n* Karpfen M

carpenter |KAHR•pun•tur| *n*
Zimmermann; Tischler M

carpet |KAHR•put| *n*
Teppich M

carriage |KA•rij| *n* Kutsche F

carrot |KA•rut| *n* Karotte;
Mohrrübe F

carry |KA•ree| *vt* tragen

cart |kahrt| *n* Lieferwagen;
Karren M

carton |KAHR•tn| *n* Karton M;
Karikatur F

carve |kahrv| *vt vi* Holz
schneiden

case |kais| *n* Fall M

case (in ~ of) |kais| *n* falls

cash |kash| *n* Bargeld N

cash register |KASH
RE•jis•tur| *n* Kasse F

cask |kask| *n* Faß N

casket |KA•skit| *n* Urne F

cassette |ku•SET| *n* Kassette F

cast 1 |kast| (of play) *n* Truppe
F; *vt* besetzen

cast 2 |kast| *vt* werfen; ~ off \
abwerfen

castle |KA•sl| *n* Burg Schloß
(f) F

casual |KA•zhoo•ul| *adj* zufällig

cat |kat| *n* Katze F

catalogue |KA•tu•LAHG| *n vt*
Katalog M

catapult |KA•tu•PUHLT| *n*
Wurfmaschine F; *vt*
schleudern

cataract |KA•tu•RAKT| *n*
Katarakt M

catastrophe |ku•TA•stru•fee| *n*
Katastrophe F

catch |kach| *vt* fangen

categorical |KA•tu•GAU•ri•kl|
*adj* unbedingt

category |KA•tu•GAU•ree| *n*
Kategorie F

cater (banquet, etc) |KAI•tr|
*vt* sorgen für das Essen

caterpillar |KA•tur•PI•lur| *n*
Raupe F

cathedral |ku•THEE•drul| *n*
Dom M

Catholic |KATH•lik| *adj n*
katolisch

cattle |KA•tl| *npl* Vieh N

cauliflower
|KAH•lee•FLOU•ur| *n*
Blumenkohl M

cause |kauz| *n* Ursache F; *vt*
verusachen

caustic |KAU•stik| *adj* ätzend

caution |KAU•shun| *n vt*
Vorsicht F; *adj* vorsichtig

cavalry |KA•vl•ree| *n* Reiterie F

cave |kaiv| *n* Höhle M

caveman |KAIV•man| *n*
Höhlenmensch M

cavity |KA•vi•tee| *n*
Mundhöhle F

cease |sees| *vt vi* aufhören

cease-fire |SEES•FUYUR| *n*
Waffenruhe F

cedar |SEE•dur| *n* Zeder F

cede |seed| *vt vi* abtreten

cedilla |si•DI•lu| *n* Cedille F

celebrate |SE•li•BRAIT| *vt vi*
feiern

celebration |SE•li•BRAI•shun|
*n* Feier F

celebrity |si•LE•bri•tee| *n*
berühmte Person F

celibate |SE•li•but| *adj*
unverheiratet F

**cell** [sel] *n* Zelle F
**cellar** [SE•lur] *n* Keller M
**cello** [CHE•lo] *n* Cello N
**Celtic** [KEL•tik] *adj* keltisch
**cement** [si•MENT] *n* Klebstoff
M; *vt* kleben
**cemetery** [SE•mi•TE•ree] *n*
Friedhof M
**censor** [SEN•sur] *n* Zensor M;
*vt* zensieren
**censorship** [SEN•sur•SHIP] *n*
Zensur F
**census** [SEN•sus] *n*
Volkszählung F
**centennial** [sen•TEN•ee•ul] *n*
Hundertjahrfeier F
**center** [SEN•tur] *n* Zentrum N
**centigrade** [SEN•ti•GRAID] *n*
*adj* Hunderteilig; Zentigrad M
**centimeter** [SEN•ti•MEE•tur] *n*
Zentimeter M
**centipede** [SEN•ti•PEED] *n*
Hundertfüßer M
**central** [SEN•trul] *adj* zentral
**century** [SEN•chu•ree] *n*
Jahrhundert N
**ceramic** [si•RA•mik] *adj*
keramisch
**cereal** [SI•ree•ul] *n* Getreide F
**ceremony** [SE•ri•MO•nee] *n*
Feier F
**certain** [SUR•tn] *adj* bestimmt
**certainly** [SUR•tn•lee] *adv*
sicherlich
**certainty** [SUR•tn•tee] *n*
Sicherheit F
**certificate** [sur•TI•fi•kut] *n*
Bescheinigung F
**certify** [SUR•tu•FUY] *vt*
bescheinigen
**chain** [chain] *n* Kette F

**chain saw** [CHAIN sau] *n*
Säge F
**chair** [chai'ur] *n* Stuhl M; arm
~\ *n* Sessel M
**chairman** [CHAI'UR•mun] *n*
Vorsitzender M
**chalk** [chauk] *n* Kreide F
**challenge** [CHA•linj] *n*
Herausforderung F; *vt*
herausfordern
**chamber** [CHAIM•bur] *n*
Kammer F
**chameleon** [ku•MEEL•yun] *n*
Chamäleon M
**champagne** [sham•PAIN] *n*
Sekt M
**champion** [CHAM•pyun] *n*
Sieger M
**chance** [chans] *n* Gelegenheit F
**chancellor** [CHAN•su•lur] *n*
Kanzler M
**change** [chainj] *n* Wechsel M;
*vt vi* wechseln; ~ over\ *vi* sich
ustellen auf
**changing** [CHAINJ•ing] *adj*
sich verändernd
**channel 1** (TV radio)
[CHA•nul] *n* Kanal M
**channel 2** (water) [CHA•nul] *vt*
kannelieren
**chant** (rel) [chant] *n*
Kirchengesang M; *vt*
viabsingen
**chaos** [KAI•ahs] *n* Chaos N
**chapel** [CHA•pl] *n* Kapelle F
**chaplain** [CHA•plen] *n*
Kaplan M
**chapter** [CHAP•tur] *n*
Kapitel M
**character** [KA•ruk•tur] *n*
Charakter M

**characteristic**
[KA•ruk•tu•RI•stik] *n*
Eigenschaft F; *adj*
bezeichnend

**charcoal** [CHAHR•col] *n*
Holzkohle F

**charge** [charj] *n* Strom fordern
M; *vi vt* sorge; übernehmen

**charity** [CHA•ru•tee] *n*
Baumherzigkeit F

**charm** [chahrm] *n* Charme F;
Reiz (M; *vt* bezaubern

**charming** [CHAHR•ming] *adj*
entzückend

**chart** [chahrt] *n* Tabelle F

**charter (flight)** [CHAHR•tur] *n*
Charterflug M

**chase** [chais] *n vt* jagen Jagd M

**chasm** [KA•zm] *n* Abgrund M

**chaste** [chaist] *adj* keusch

**chastise** [cha•STUYZ] *vt*
strafen; züchtigen

**chastity** [CHA•sti•tee] *n*
Reinheit F

**chat** [chat] *vi* plaudern

**chatterbox** [CHA•tur•BAHKS]
*n* Plappermaul M

**chauffeur** [SHO•fur] *n*
Fahrer M

**cheap** [cheep] *adj* billig

**cheapen** [CHEE•pn] *vt*
verbilligen

**cheat** [cheet] *vt vi* betrügen;
schwindeln

**cheater** [CHEE•tr] *n*
Betrüger M

**check** [chek] *vt* feststellen

**check 1** (bill) [chek] *s* Zahl F

**check 2** (currency) [chek] *s*
Scheck M

**checkbook** [CHEK•buk] *n*
Scheckbuch N

**cheek 1** [cheek] *n* Wange F

**cheer 2** [cheer] *vt* jauchzen

**cheer up** *vi* Kopf hoch!

**cheerful** [CHEER•ful] *adj*
glücklich; heiter

**cheers (drinking toast)**
[cheerz] *excl* Prost

**cheese** [cheez] *n* Käse M

**cheetah** [CHEE•tu] *n*
Gepard M

**chef** [shef] *n* Chef M

**chemical** [KE•mi•kul] *n*
Chemikalien F; *adj* chemisch

**chemist** [KE•mist] *n*
Chemiker M

**chemistry** [KE•mi•stree] *n*
Chemie F

**cherish** [CHE•rish] *vt* schätzen

**cherry** [CHE•ree] *n* Kirsche F

**chess** [ches] *n* Schachspiel N

**chest** [chest] *n* Brust F;
Kasten M

**chest of drawers** [CHEST uhv
DRAW•urz] *n* Anrichte F

**chestnut** [CHEST•nuht] *n*
Kastanie F

**chew** [choo] *vt* kauen

**chick** [chik] *n* Küchlein N

**chicken** [CHI•kin] *n*
Hühnchen N

**chicken pox** [ ~ PAHKS] *n*
Windpocken N

**chief** [cheef] *n* Haupt N

**child** [chuyld] *n* Kind N

**childbirth** [CHUYLD•burth] *n*
Geburt F

**childhood** [CHUYLD•hud] *n*
Jugend F

**childish** [CHUYL•dish] *adj* kindisch

**Chile** [CHI•lee] *n* Chile

**chill** [chil] *n* Kälte M; *vi vt* abkühlen

**chilly** [CHI•lee] *adj* frostig; kühl

**chime** [chuym] *n* Geläute M; *vi* läuten

**chimney** [CHIM•nee] *n* Schornstein M

**chimpanzee** [chim•PAN•ZEE] *n* Schimpanse M

**chin** [chin] *n* Kinn M

**China** [CHUY•nu] *n* China

**china** [CHUY•nu] *n* Porzellan N

**Chinese** [chuy•NEEZ] *adj* chinesisch

**chip** [chip] *n* Splitter M; *vt* ausbrechen

**chirp** [churp] *vi* zirpen

**chisel** [CHI•zl] *n* Beitel M; *vt* ausfeilen

**chivalry** [SHI•vl•ree] *n* Ritterlichkeit F

**chive** [chuyv] *n* Schnittlauch M

**chlorophyll** [KLAU•ru•FIL] *n* Chlorophyll M

**chocolate** [CHAU•ku•lut] *n* Schokolade F

**choice** [chois] *n* Wahl F

**choir** [kwuyr] *n* Chor N

**choke 1** [chok] *vt* ersticken

**choke 2** (of car) [chok] *n* Luftklappe F

**cholera** [KAH•lu•ru] *n* Cholera F

**choose** [chooz] *vi vt* wählen

**chop 1** [chahp] *vt* hacken

**chop 2** (of meat) [chahp] *n* Kotelett

**chord** [kaurd] *n* Saite F

**chores** [chaurz] *npl* Hausarbeit F

**chorus** [KAU•rus] *n* Chor M

**Christ** [kruyst] *n* Christus M

**christen** [KRI•sn] *vt* taufen

**Christian** [KRI•schun] *n* Christ —in M; *adj* christlich

**Christianity** [KRI•schee•A•nu•tee] *n* Christentum N

**Christmas** [KRIS•mus] *n* Weihnachten F

**chrome** [krom] *n* Chrom N

**chronic** [KRAH•nik] *adj* dauernd; ständig

**chronicle** [KRAH•ni•kl] *n* Chronik F

**chronological** [KRAH•nu•LAH•ji•kl] *adj* chronologisch

**chrysanthemum** [kri•SAN•thi•mum] *n* Chrysanthemum N

**chubby** [CHUH•bee] *adj* rundlich

**chuck** [chuhk] *vt* werfen

**chuckle** [CHUH•kl] *vi* lächeln

**chunk** [chuhnk] *n* Stück N

**church** [church] *n* Kirche F

**churn** (butter) [churn] *n* Butterfaß F; *vt* verbuttern

**chute** [shoot] *n* Stromschnelle F

**cider** [SUY•dur] *n* Apfelwein M

**cigar** [si•GAHR] *n* Zigarre F

**cigarette** [SI•gu•RET] *n* Zigarette F

**cinder** [SIN•dur] *n* Asche F

**Cinderella** [SIN•du•RE•lu] *n* Aschenputtel N

**cinema** [SI•nu•mu] *n* Kino N

cinnamon [SI•nu•mun] *n*
Zimt M

circle [SUR•kl] *n* Kreis M

circuit [SUR•kit] *n* Kreislauf M

circular [SUR•cyu•lur] *adj*
kreisförmig

circulate [SUR•kyu•LAIT] *vi vt*
umlaufen

circulation
[SUR•kyu•LAI•shun] *n*
Kreislauf M

circumcision
[SUR•cuhm•SI•zhun] *n*
Beschneidung F

circumference
[sur•CUHM•fu•runs] *n*
Umkreis M

circumflex [SUR•cuhm•FLEKS]
*adj* Zirkumflex M

circumstances
[SUR•cum•STANS] *n*
Umstände F

circus [SUR•kus] *n* Zirkus M

cite [suyt] *vt* zitieren

citizen [SI•ti•zn] *n* Bürger
-in M

city [SI•tee] *n* Stadt F

city hall [SIT•tee HAL] *n*
Rathaus N

civic [SI•vik] *adj* städtisch

civil [SI•vl] *adj* zivil

civilization [SI•vi•li•ZAI•shun]
*n* Zivilisation F

civilize [SI•vi•LUYZ] *vt*
zivilisieren

claim [klaim] *n* Behauptung F;
*vt* behaupten

clam [klam] *n* Venusmuschel F

clamor [KLA•mur] *s* Lärm M

clamp [klamp] *n vt* Klemmer F

clan [klan] *n* Stamm F

clandestine [klan•DE•stin] *adj*
heimlich

clap [klap] *vi* klatschen

clarify [KLA•ri•FUY] *vt*
aufklären

clarinet [KLA•ri•NET] *n*
Klarinette F

clarity [KLA•ri•tee] *s* Klarheit F

clash [klash] *n* Stoß M; *vi*
zusammenprallen

clasp [klasp] *n* Schalle F; *vt*
umklammern

class [klas] *n* Klasse F; *vt*
klasifizieren

classic [KLA•sik] *n* Klassiker
M; *adj* erstklassisch

classical [KLA•si•kl] *adj*
klassisch

classified [KLA•si•FUYD] *adj*
klassifiziert

classified ad [KLA•si•FUYD
AD] *n* Anzeige F

classify [KLA•si•FUY] *vt*
klassifizieren

classroom [KLAS•rum] *n*
Klassenzimmer N

clause [klauz] *n* Klause F

claw [clau] *n* Klaue F; ~ at\ *vi*
klauen

clay [klay] *n* Lehm M

clean [kleen] *adj* sauber; *vt*
saubern

cleaner [KLEE•nur] *n*
Reiniger M

cleaning lady [KLEE•ning
LAI•dee] *n* Putzfrau F

cleanliness [KLEN•lee•nis] *n*
Reinlichkeit F

clear [kleer] *adj* klar; *vt*
reinigen; ~ up (issue)
aufklären

**clearance** [CLEE•runs] *n*
Zulassung Räumung F

**clearing** [KLEE•ring] *n*
Lichtung F

**clearly** [KLEER•lee] *adv*
deutlich; klar

**cleavage** [KLEE•vij] *n*
Spaltung F

**cleaver** [KLEE•vur] *n*
Hackmesser F

**clench** [klench] *vt* pressen

**clergy** [KLUR•jee] *n*
Geistlichkeit F

**clerical** [KLE•ri•kl] *adj* geistlich

**clerk** [clurk] *n* Beamter -in M

**clever** [KLE•vur] *adj* geschickt;
klug

**client** [KLUY•unt] *n* Kunde
-in M

**clientele** [KLUY•un•TEL] *n*
Kundschaft F

**cliff** [klif] *n* Klippe F

**climate** [KLUY•mit] *n* Klima N

**climax** [KLUY•maks] *n*
Höhepunkt M

**climb** [cluym] *n* Aufstieg M;
*vt/vi* erklettern

**cling** [kling] *vi* kleben

**clinic** [KLI•nik] *n* Klinik F

**clinical** [KLI•ni•kl] *adj* klinisch

**clip** [klip] *n* Klammer F; *vt*
abschneiden

**clippers** [KLI•purz] *npl*
Schere F

**cloak** [klok] *s* Mantel M

**clock** [klahk] *n* Uhr F

**clockwise** [KLAHK•wuyz] *adj*
*adv* rechtsläufig

**clog** [klahg] *n* Holzschuh M;
*vt/vi* hemmern

**cloister** [KLOI•stur] *n*
Kloster N

**close 1** [klos] *adj adv* knapp

**close 2** [kloz] *vt/vi* zumachen;
schließen

**closet** [KLAH•zit] *n* Kammer F

**cloth** [klauth] *n* Tuch N;
Stoff M

**clothe** [kloth] *vt* bekleiden

**clothes** [klothz] *npl* Kleidung F

**clothing** [KLO•thing] *n*
Kleidung F

**cloud** [kloud] *n* Wolke F

**cloudy** [KLOU•dee] *adj*
bewölkt

**clove** [klov] *n* Gewürznelke F

**clover** [KLO•vur] *n* Klee M

**clown** [kloun] *n* Clown M

**club** [kluhb] *n* Keule F; (card
suit) *npl* Kreuz

**cluck** [cluhk] *vi* glucken

**clue** [kloo] *n* Hinweis M

**clump** [kluhmp] *n* Klumpen M

**clumsy** [KLUHM•zee] *adj*
ungeschickt

**cluster** [KLUH•stur] *n*
Haufen N

**clutch 1** [kluhch] *n* Gelege N

**clutch 2** [kluhch] *vt* ( ~ at) *vi*
festgreifen

**clutter** [KLUH•tur] *vt n*
überhaufen Unordnung F

**coach 1** [koch] *n* Kutsche F;
Trainer M

**coach 2** (sports) [koch] *n vt*
Sport lehren

**coal** [kol] *n* Kohle F

**coarse** [caurs] *adj* grob;
(manners) gewöhnlich

**coast 1** [kost] *n* Küste F

**coast 2** [kost] *vi* entlangfahren

**coat** [kot] *n* Mantel M; (paint, etc) *vt* bedecken

**coax** [koks] *vt* schmeicheln

**cobblestones** [KAH•bl•STONZ] *npl* Kopfstein M

**cobweb** [KAHB•web] *n* Spinngewebe N

**cocaine** [ko•KAIN] *n* Kokaine F

**cock 1** [kahk] *n* Hahn M

**cock 2** (a gun) [kahk] *vt* aufrichten

**cockroach** [KAHK•roch] *n* Schabe F

**cocktail** [KAHK•tail] *n* Cocktail N

**cocoa** [KO•ko] *n* Kakao M

**coconut** [KO•ku•nuht] *n* Koksnuß F

**cocoon** [ku•KOON] *n* Kokon F

**cod** [kahd] *n* Klippfisch M

**code** [kod] *n vt* Geheimschrift F

**coerce** [ko•URS] *vt* erzwingen

**coffee** [KAU•fee] *n* Kaffee M

**coffee break** [KAU•fee BRAIK] *n* Kaffeepause F

**coffee cup** [KAU•fee KUP] *n* Kaffeetasse F

**coffee pot** [KAU•fee POT] *n* Kaffeekanne F

**coffee shop** [KAU•fee SHAHP] *n* Cafe Imbiß (m) N

**coffin** [KAU•fin] *n* Sarg M

**coherent** [ko•HEE•runt] *adj* festgefügt

**coil** [koil] *n* Rolle; Windung F; *vt vi* winden

**coin** [koin] *n* Münze F

**coincide** [KO•in•SUYD] *vi* zusammentreffen

**coincidence** [ko•IN•si•duns] *n* Zufall M

**cold** [kold] *n* Kälte F; *adj* kalt

**cold-blooded** [-BLU•did] *adj* kalt blütig

**collaborate** [ku•LA•bu•RAIT] *vi* mitarbeiten

**collapse** [ku•LAPS] *n* Zusammenbruch M; *vi* zusammenbrechen

**collar** [KAH•lur] *n* Kragen M; *vt* (capture) fassen

**collateral** [ku•LA•tu•rul] *n* Sicherheit F

**colleague** [KAH•leeg] *n* Kollege —in(f) M

**collect** [ku•LEKT] *vt vi* sammeln

**college** [KAH•lij] *n* Universität College (m) F

**collide** (with) [ku•LUYD] *vi* zusammenstoßen

**colloquial** [ku•LO•kwee•ul] *adj* umgangssprachlich

**colon** [KO•lun] *n* Dickdarm M

**colony** [KAH•lu•nee] *n* Kolonie F

**color 1** [KUH•lur] *n* Farbe F; *vi* anmalen

**color television** [KUH•lor TEL•i•VI•shn] *n* Farbfernsehen N

**color-blind** [KUH•lor•bluynd] *adj* farbenblind

**colorful** [KUH•lur•ful] *adj* farbenfreudig

**colossal** [ku•LAH•sul] *adj* spitze

**colt** [kolt] *n* Neuling M

**column** [KAH•luhm] *n* Säule F

**coma** [KO•mu] *n* Koma N

comb [kom] *n* Kamm M; *vt*
kämmen M

combat [CAHM•bat] *n* Kampf
M; vt/vt kämpfen M

combination
[KAHM•bi•NAI•shn] *n*
Zusammensetzung F

combine [kum•BUYN] *vt*
zusammensetzen

come [kuhm] *vi* kommen

come about (happen) *vi*
passieren

come across *vi* herüberkommen

come along (accompany) *vi*
mitkommen

come away *vi* abkommen

comeback [KUHM•bak] *vi*
zurückkommen

come in *vi* herinkommen

come on *vi* (follow)
nachkommen; *excl* komm!

come up against *vi* stoßen auf

come up with (plan) *vi* sich
ausdenken

comedian [ku•MEE•dee•un] *n*
Komiker M

comedy [KAH•mi•dee] *n*
Komödie F

comet [KAH•mit] *n* Komet M

comfort [KUHM•furt] *n*
Beruhigung F; *vt* beruhigen;
trösten

comfortable [KUHMF•tur•bl]
*adj* bequem; angenehm

comics (comic strip)
[KAH•miks] *npl* Comicstrips

coming [KUH•ming] *adj*
Ankunft F

comma [KAH•mu] *n*
Komma M

command [ku•MAND] *n*
Befehl M

commander [ku•MAN•dur] *n*
Kommandant M

commence [ku•MENS] *vt vi*
anfangen

commend [ku•MEND] *vt*
empfehlen

comment [KAH•ment] *n*
Kommentar M; *vi*
kommentieren

commerce [KAH•murs] *n*
Handel M

commercial [ku•MUR•shl] *n*
Sendung F

commission [ku•MI•shn] *n*
Auftrag M

commissioner [ku•MI•shu•nur]
*n* Kommisar M

commit [ku•MIT] *vt*
anvertrauen

committee [ku•MI•tee] *n*
Kommission F

committment [ku•MIT•munt] *n*
Verpflichtung F

commodity [ku•MAH•di•tee] *n*
Ware F

common [KAH•mun] *adj*
gemeinsam

common sense
[KAH•mun SENS] *n*
Menschenverstand M

commonly [KAH•mun•lee] *adv*
im allgemeinen

commonplace
[KAH•mun•PLAIS] *adj*
alltäglich

commotion [ku•MO•shn] *n*
Aufregung F

communicate
[ku•MYOO•ni•KAIT] *vt vi*
übertragen auf

**communion** [ku•MYOO•nyun] *n* Kommunion F

**communism** [KAH•myu•NI•zm] *n* Kommunismus M

**communist** [KAH•myu•nist] *adj n* Kommunist M

**community** [ku•MYOO•nu•tee] *n* Gemeinschaft F

**commute** [ku•MYOOT] *vt vi* umfahren

**compact** [kahm•PAKT] *adj* kompakt

**compact disc** [KAM•pakt DISK] *n* CD

**companion** [kum•PA•nyun] *n* Begleiter -in M

**company** [KUHM•pu•nee] *n* Firme; Gesellschaft F

**compare** [kum•PAIR] *vt* vergleichen

**comparison** [kum•PA•ri•sn] *n* Vergleich M

**compartment division** [kum•PAHRT•munt] *n* Abteilung F

**compass** [KAHM•pus] *n* Kompaß M

**compassion** [kum•PA•shn] *n* Mitleid N

**compassionate** [kum•PA•shu•nit] *adj* mitleidsvoll

**compatible** [kum•PA•ti•bl] *adj* vereinbar

**compel** [kum•PEL] *vt* zwingen

**compelling** [kum•PE•ling] *adj* zwingend

**compensate** [KAHM•pun•SAIT] *vt* vergütern

**compensation** [KAHM•pun•SAI•shn] *n* Vergütung F

**compete** [kum•PEET] *vi* konkurrieren

**competence** [KAHM•pi•tuns] *n* Fähigkeit F

**competent** [KAHM•pi•tunt] *adj* fähig

**competition** [KAHM•pu•TI•shn] *n* Wettbewerb M

**competitive** [kum•PE•tu•tiv] *adj* konkurrierend

**complacent** [kum•PLAI•sunt] *adj* gleichgültig

**complain** [kum•PLAIN] *vi* beklagen

**complaint** [kuhm•PLAINT] *n* Klage F

**complement** [KAHM•pli•munt] *vt* Vervollständigung F

**complete** [kum•PLEET] *adj* ganz; *vt* ergänzen

**comletely** [kum•PLEET•lee] *adv* völlig; volkommen

**complex** [kahm•PLEKS] *adj* kompliziert

**complexion** [kum•PLEK•shn] *n* Gesichtsfarbe F

**complicate** [KAHM•pli•KAIT] *vt* komplizieren

**complicated** [KAHM•pli•KAI•tid] *adj* kompliziert

**compliment** [KAHM•pli•ment] *n vt* Kompliment M

**comply** [kum•PLUY] *vi* entsprechen

**component** [kum•PO•nunt] *n* Teil M

**compose** [kum•POZ] *vt*
komponieren

**composer** [kum•PO•zur] *n*
Komponist M

**composition**
[KAHM•pu•ZI•shn] *n*
Abfassung F

**composure** [kum•PO•zhur] *n*
Gelassenheit F

**compound** [KAHM•pound] *adj*
zusammengesetzt

**comprehend**
[KAHM•pree•HEND] *vt*
verstehen

**comprehension**
[KAHM•pree•HEN•shn] *vt*
Verstand M

**comprehensive**
[KAHM•pree•HEN•siv] *adj*
umfassend

**compress** [kum•PRES] *vt*
drücken

**comprise** [kum•PRUYZ] *vt*
enthalten

**compromise**
[KAHM•pru•MUYZ] *n*
Kompromiß M; *vi*
Kompormisse schließen

**compulsive** [kum•PUHL•siv]
*adj* zwingend

**computer** [kum•PYOO•tur] *n*
Computer M

**computerize**
[kum•PYOO•tu•RUYZ] *vt* auf
Computer umstellen

**comrade** [KAHM•rad] *n*
Kamerad M

**conceal** [kun•SEEL] *vt*
verdecken

**concede** [kun•SEED] *vt vi*
zugestehen

**conceit** [kun•SEET] *n*
Eitelkeit F

**conceited** [kun•SEE•tid] *adj*
eitel

**conceive** [kun•SEEV] *vt vi*
empfangen

**concentrate**
[KAHN•sun•TRAIT] *vt vi*
konzentrieren; *n* Konzentrat N

**concept** [KAHN•sept] *n*
Begriff M

**concern** [kun•SURN] *n*
Angelegenheit F

**concerning** [kun•SUR•ning]
*prep* betreffend

**concert** [KAHN•surt] *n*
Konzert N

**concession** [kun•SE•shn] *n*
Zugeständnis N

**concise** [kun•SUYS] *adj* kurz;
knapp

**conclude** [kun•KLOOD] *vt vi*
beenden schließen

**concrete 1** [KAHN•kreet] *n*
Beton M

**concrete 2** [kahn•KREET] *adj*
konkrett

**condemn** [kun•DEM] *vt*
verdammen

**condense** [kun•DENS] *vt vi*
verdichten

**condescending**
[KAHN•di•SEN•ding] *adj*
herablassend

**condition** [kun•DI•shn] *n*
Bedingung F; *vt* bedingen

**condolences** [kun•DO•lun•ciz]
*npl* Beileid N

**condone** [kun•DON] *vt*
verzeihen

**conduct** [n KAHN•duhkt v kun•DUHKT] n Leitung F

**conductor** [kun•DUHK•tur] n Leiter M

**cone** [kon] n Kegel M

**confectionery** [kun•FEK•shu•NE•ree] s Konditorwaren

**confederation** [kun•FE•du•RAI•shn] n Bund M

**confer** [kun•FUR] vt/vi zuteilen

**conference** [KAHN•fu•runs] n Konferenz M

**confess** [kun•FES] vt vi eingestehen

**confession** [kun•FE•shn] n Zugeständnis N

**confidant** [KAHN•fi•DAHNT] n Vertraute F

**confide** [kun•FUYD] vt vi sich anvertrauen

**confidence** [KAHN•fi•duns] n Vertrauen N

**confident** [KAHN•fi•dunt] adj selbstsicher

**confidential** [KAHN•fi•DEN•shl] adj vertraulich

**confine** [kun•FUYN] vt einschränken

**confirm** [kun•FURM] vt bestätigen

**confirmation** [KAHN•fur•MAI•shn] n Bestätigung F

**confiscate** [KAHN•fi•SKAIT] vt einziehen

**conflict** [n. KAHN•flikt v. kun•FLIKT] n vi Konflikt M

**conform** [kun•FAURM] vt vi anpassen

**conformist** [kun•FAUR•mist] adj n Anhänger M

**confound** [kun•FOUND] vt verwechseln

**confront** [kun•FRUHNT] vt konfrontieren

**confuse** [kun•FYOOZ] vt verwirren

**confusing** [kun•FYOO•zing] adj verwirrt

**confusion** [kun•FYOO•zhn] n Verwirrung F

**congestion** [kun•JES•chn] n Stauung F

**congratulate** [kung•GRA•chu•LAIT] vt gratulieren

**congregate** [KAHNG•gri•GAIT] vi versammeln

**congregation** [KAHNG•gri•GAI•shn] n Versammlung F

**conjugation** [KAHN•joo•GAI•shn] n Konjugation F

**conjunction** [kun•JUHNK•shn] n Verbindung F

**connect** [ku•NEKT] vt verbinden

**conquer** [KAHGN•kur] vt erobern

**conqueror** [KAHNG•ku•rur] n Eroberer M

**conquest** [KAHNG•kwest] n Eroberung F

**conscience** [KAHN•shuns] n Gewissen N

**conscientious**
[KAHN•shee•EN•shus] *adj*
gewissenhaft

**conscious** [KAHN•shus] *adj*
bewußt

**consecrate** [KAHN•se•KRAIT]
*vt* weihen

**consecutive** [kun•SE•cyu•tiv]
*adj* aufeinanderfolgend

**consent** [kun•SENT] *n*
Zustimmung F; *vi* zustimmen

**consequence**
[KAHN•si•KWENS] *n*
Konsequenz F

**conservation**
[KAHN•sur•VAI•shn] *n*
Erhaltung; Bewahrung F

**conservative** [kun•SUR•vu•tiv]
*adj* konservativ

**consider** [kun•SI•dr] *vt*
überlegen M

**considerable** [kun•SI•du•ru•bl]
*adj* erheblich

**considerate** [kun•SI•du•rit] *adj*
rücksichtsvoll

**considering** [kun•SI•du•ring]
*prep* in Anbetracht

**consist** [kun•SIST] *vi* bestehen

**consistency** [kun•SI•stun•see] *n*
Festigkeit F

**consistent** [kun•SIS•tunt] *adj*
logisch

**consolation**
[KAHN•su•LAI•shn] *n*
Tröstung F

**console 1** [kun•SOL] *vt* trösten

**console 2** (control panel)
[KAHN•sol] *n* Kontrollpult N;
(cabinet) *n* Schrank M

**consolidate**
[kun•SAH•lu•DAIT] *vt*
vereinigen

**consonant** [KAHN•su•nunt] *n*
Konsonant M

**conspicuous** [kun•SPI•kyoo•us]
*adj* deutlich

**conspiracy** [kun•SPI•ru•see] *n*
Verschwörung F

**constant** [KAHN•stunt] *n/adj*
ständig

**constellation**
[KAHN•stu•LAI•shn] *n*
Sternbild N

**constituent** [kun•STI•choo•int]
*n* Wählerschaft F

**constitution**
[KAHN•sti•TOO•shn] *n*
Gründung F

**constraint** [kun•STRAINT] *n*
Zwang M

**construct** [kun•STRUHKT] *vt*
konstruieren; bauen

**construe** [kun•STROO] *vt*
konstruieren

**consulate** [KAHN•su•lit] *n*
Konsulat N

**consult** [kun•SUHLT] *vt vi*
konsultieren

**consume** [kun•SOOM] *vt*
aufessen

**consumer** [kun•SOOM•ur] *n*
Verbrauchsgüter M

**consummate**
[KAHN•su•MAIT] *vt*
vollenden

**consumption**
[kun•SUHMP•shn] *n*
Verbrauch M

**contact** [KAHN•takt] *n* Kontakt
M; *vt* sich in Verbindung
setzen

**contagious** [kun•TAI•jus] *adj*
ansteckend

**contain** [kun•TAIN] *vt*
enthalten

**container** [kun•TAI•nur] *n*
Behälter M

**contaminate**
[kun•TA•mi•NAIT] *vt*
verunreinigen

**contemplate**
[KAHN•tum•PLAIT] *vt vi*
nachdenken betrachten

**contemporary**
[kun•TEM•pu•RE•ree] *adj/n*
zeitgenössisch

**contempt** [kun•TEMPT] *n*
Verachtung F

**contemptible**
[kun•TEMP•tu•bl] *adj*
verächtlich

**contend** [kun•TEND] *v*
kämpfen

**content** [kun•TENT] *adj*
zufrieden M

**contents** [KAHN•tents] *npl*
Inhalt M

**contest** [n. KAHN•test v.
kun•TEST] *n* Wettkampt M;
*vt* kämpfen um

**context** [KAHN•tekst] *n*
Zusammenhang M

**continent** [KAHN•ti•nunt] *n*
Kontinent M

**contingency** [kun•TIN•jun•see]
*n* Möglichkeit F

**continual** [kun•TI•nyoo•ul] *adj*
dauernd

**continually** [kun•TI•nyoo•u•lee]
*adv* immer; wieder

**continuation**
[kun•TI•nyoo•AI•shn] *n*
Fortsetzung F

**continue** [kun•TI•nyoo] *v*
weitergehen

**contract** [n. KAHN•trakt v.
kun•TRAKT] *n* Vertrag M;
make a ~ *vi\* einen Vertrag
schließen

**contraction** [kun•TRAK•shn] *n*
Zusammenziehung F

**contradict** [KAHN•tru•DIKT]
*vt* widersprechen

**contradiction**
[KAHN•tru•DIK•shn] *n*
Widerspruch M

**contrary** [KAHN•TRE•ree]
*adj/n* entgegengesetzt

**contrast** [n. KAHN•trast v.
kun•TRAST] *n* Kontrast M

**contribute** [kun•TRI•byoot] *vt
vi* beitragen

**contribution**
[KAHN•tri•BYOO•shn] *n*
Beitragen N

**contrive** [kun•TRUYV] *vi*
erfinden

**control** [kun•TROL] *vt*
kontrollieren

**controller** [kun•TRO•lur] *n*
Aufseher M

**controversy**
[KAHN•tru•VUR•see] *n*
Kontroverse F

**convalescence**
[KAHN•vu•LE•suns] *n*
Genesung F

**convalescent**
[KAHN•vu•LE•sunt] *adj/n*
genesend

**convene** [kun•VEEN]
zusammenkommen

**convenience** [kun•VEE•nyuns]
*n* Annehmlichkeit F

**convenient** [kun•VEE•nyunt]
*adj* günstig
**convent** [KAHN•vent] *n*
Kloster N
**convention** [kun•VEN•shn] *n*
Tagung F
**converge** [kun•VURJ] *vi*
zusammenlaufen
**conversant** [kun•VUR•sunt] *adj*
bekannt
**conversation**
[KAHN•vur•SAI•shn] *n*
Unterhaltung F
**converse 1** [kun•VURS] *vi* sich
unterhalten; sprechen
**converse 2** [KAHN•vurs] *n*
Gegensatz M
**conversion** [kun•VUR•zhn] *n*
Verwandlung F
**convert** [n. KAHN•vurt v.
kun•VURT] *n* Bekehrte M
**convex** [kahn•VEKS] *adj*
konvex
**convey** [kun•VAI] *vt*
übermitteln
**conveyer belt** [kun•VAI•ur ~ ]
*n* laufendes Band N
**convict** [KAHN•vikt ] *n*
Sträfling M; *vt* [kun•VIKT]
vereuteilen
**convince** [kun•VINS] *vt*
überzeugen
**convincing** [kun•VIN•sing] *adj*
überzeugend
**convoy** [KAHN•voi] *n*
Begleitung F
**coo** [koo] *vi* gurren
**cook** [kuk] *n* Koch M; *vt*
kochen
**cookie** [KU•kee] *n* Keks M
**cooking** [KU•king] *s* Kochen N

**cool** [kool] *adj* kühl
**coolness** [KOOL•nis] *n*
Kühle F
**coop** [koop] *n* Hühnerkorb M
**cooperate** [ko•AH•pu•RAIT] *vi*
zusammenarbeiten
**cooperation**
[ko•AH•pu•RAI•shn] *n*
Zusammenarbeit F
**coordinate 1**
[ko•AUR•di•NAIT] *v*
koordinieren
**coordinate 2** [ko•AUR•di•nit ]
(math) *n* Koordinate F
**coordination**
[ko•AUR•di•NAI•shn] *n*
Beiordnung F
**cop** [kahp] *n* slang Polizist M
**cope** [kop] *vi* meistern
**copious** [KO•pee•us] *adj*
reichlich
**copper** [KAH•pur] *n* Kupfer N
**copy** [KAH•pee] *n* Kopie F
**copyright** [KAH•pee•RUYT] *n*
Urheberrecht N
**coral** [KAU•rul] *n* Koralle F
**cord** [kaurd] *n* Schnur F
**corduroy** [KAUR•du•ROI] *s*
Kord M
**cork** [kaurk] *n* Kork M
**corksrew** [KAURK•skroo] *n*
Korkenzieher M
**corn** [kaurn] *n* Korn N
**corner** [KAUR•nur] *n* Ecke F
**cornice** [KAUR•nis] *n*
Gesims N
**coronation** [KAU•ru•NAI•shn]
*n* Krönung F
**coroner** [KAU•ru•NUR] *n*
Leichenbeschauer M

**corporal** [KAUR•pu•rul] *adj*
körperlich

**corporation**
[KAUR•pu•RAI•shn] *n*
Korporation F

**corpse** [kaurps] *n* Leich M

**correct** [ku•REKT] *adj* richtig;
*vt* korrigieren

**correction** [ku•REK•shn] *n*
Verbesserung F

**correctly** [ku•REKT•lee] *adv*
richtig

**correspond** [KAU•ri•SPAHND]
*vi* entsprechen

**correspondence**
[KAU•ri•SPAHN•duns] *n*
Briefwechsel M

**correspondent**
[KAU•ri•SPAHN•dunt] *n*
Korrespondent -in M

**corresponding**
[KAU•re•SPAHN•ding] *adv*
entsprechend

**corridor** [KAU•ri•daur] *n*
Gang M

**corrode** [ku•ROD] *vt* wegätzen

**corrosion** [ku•RO•zhn] *n*
Rostfraß M

**corrupt** [ku•RUHPT] *adj*
unehrlich korrupt

**corruption** [ku•RUHP•shn] *n*
Verdorbenheit; Korruption F

**Corsica** [KAUR•si•ku] *n*
Korsika

**cosmetic** [kahz•ME•tik] *n*
Schönheitsmittel N

**cosmopolitan**
[KAHZ•mu•PAH•li•tn] *adj*
weltoffen; *n* Weltbürger M

**cost** [kaust] *n* Preis M

**costly** [KAUST•lee] *adj* teuer

**costume** [KAH•styoom] *n*
Kostüm M

**cot** [kaht] *n* Kinderbettchen N

**cottage** [KAH•tij] *n*
Sommerhaus N

**cotton** [KAH•tn] *n*
Baumwolle F

**couch** [kouch] *n* Sofa N

**cough** [kauf] *n* Husten M

**council** [KOUN•sl] *n* Rat M

**counsel** [KOUN•sl] *n*
Beratung F

**counselor** [KOUN•su•lur] *n*
Ratgeber M

**count** [kount] *vt vi* zählen

**count on** *vi prep* rechnen mit

**count up** *vt* zusammenzählen

**counter** [KOUN•tur] *n* Theke F

**counteract** [KOUN•tur•AKT]
*vt* entgegenwirken

**counterfeit** [KOUN•tur•FIT]
*adj* nachgemacht

**counterpart**
[KOUN•tur•PAHRT] *n*
Duplikat N

**countess** [KOUN•tis] *n*
Gräfin F

**countless** [KOUNT•lis] *adj*
zahllos

**country** [KUHN•tree] *n* Land N

**countryman** [KUHN•tree•mun]
*n* Landmann M

**county** [KOUN•tee] *n* Kreis M

**coup** [koo] *n* Coup M

**couple** [KUH•pl] *n* Paar N

**coupon** [KOO•pahn] *n*
Kupon M

**courage** [KU•rij] *n* Mut M

**courageous** [ku•RAI•jus] *adj*
tapfer

**courier** [KU•ree•ur] *n* Kurier M

**course** [kaurs] *n* Lauf M; of ~\
*excl* natürlich

**court** [kaurt] *n* Gericht N

**courteous** [KUR•tee•us] *adj*
höflich

**courtesy** [KUR•ti•see] *n*
Höflichkeit F

**courtyard** [KAURT•yahrd] *n*
Hof M

**cousin** [KUH•zin] *n* Vetter F;
Kusine F

**cove** [kov] *n* Bucht F

**covenant** [KUH•vu•nunt] *n*
Vertrag M

**cover** [KUH•vur] *vt* bedecken

**cover-up (scandal etc)** *n*
Skandal N

**coverage** [KUH•vu•rij] *n*
Erfassung F

**covering** [KUH•vu•ring] *n*
Bedekkung F

**covert** [KO•vurt] *adj* heimlich

**covet** [KUH•vit] *vt* begehren

**cow** [kou] *n* Kuh M

**coward** [KOU•urd] *n*
Feigling M

**cowardice** [KOU•ur•dis] *n*
Feigheit F

**cowardly** [KOU•urd•lee] *adj*
feig

**cowboy** [KOU•boi] *n*
Cowboy M

**cower** [KOU•ur] *vi* hocken

**coy** [koi] *adj* schüchtern

**cozy** [KO•zee] *adj* behaglich

**crab** [krab] *n* Krebs M

**crack** [krak] *n* Krach M

**cracker** [KRA•kur] *n* Keks M

**cradle** [KRAI•dl] *n* Wiege F

**craft** [kraft] *n* Geschicklichkeit;
Kunst; (boat) *n* Boot N

**crafty** [KRAF•tee] *adj* listig

**cram** [kram] *vt* vollstopfen

**cramp** [kramp] *n* Krampe F

**cranberry** [KRAN•BE•ree] *n*
Preiselbeere F

**crane** [krain] *n* Kranich M

**crank** [krank] *n* Schwengel M

**cranky** [KRANG•kee] *adj*
verschroben

**crape** [kraip] *n* Krepp M

**crash** [krash] *n*
Zusammenstoß M

**crate** [krait] *n* Packkorb M

**crater** [KRAI•tur] *n* Krater M

**crave** [kraiv] *vt* sich sehnen
nach

**crawl** [kraul] *vi* kriechen

**crayfish** [KRAI•fish] *n*
Flußkrebs M

**crayon** [KRAI•un] *n*
Pastellstift M

**craze** [kraiz] *n* Manie F

**crazy** [KRAI•zee] *adj* verrückt

**creak** [kreek] *vi* kreischen

**cream** [kreem] *n* Rahm M;
Sähne F; whipped~ *n*\ Schlag
F; *vt* (cosmetics) eincremen

**creamy** [KREE•mee] *adj* sahnig

**create** [kree•AIT] *vt* erschaffen

**creation** [kree•AI•shn] *n*
Erschaffung F

**creative** [kree•AI•tiv] *adj*
schöpferisch

**creator** [kree•AI•tur] *n*
Schöpfer M

**creature** [KREE•chur] *n*
Geschöpf N

**credible** [KRE•di•bl]] *adj*
glaubwürdig

**credit** [KRE•dit] *n* Ansehen N

**credit card** [KRE•dit KARD] *n*
Kreditkarte F
**creed** [kreed] *n* Glaube M
**creek** [kreek] *n* Flüßchen N
**creep** [kreep] *vi* schleichen
**crescent** [KRE•snt] *n*
Halbmond M
**crest** [krest] *n* Helm M
**crevice** [KRE•vis] *n* Spalte F
**crew** [kroo] *n* Mannschaft F
**crib** [krib] *n* Krippe F
**cricket** [KRI•kit] *n* Grille F
**crime** [kruym] *n* Verbrechen N
**criminal** [KRI•me•nul]
adjverbrecherisch; *n*
Kriminal M
**crimson** [KRIM•sun] *adj*
ochrot N
**cringe** [krinj] *vi* sich ducken
**cripple** [KRI•pl] *n* Krüppel M
**crisis** [KRUY•sis] *n* Krise F
**crisp** [krisp] *adj* knusprig
**criterion** [kruy•TEER•ree•un] *n*
Maßstab M
**critic** [KRI•tik] *n* Kritiker M
**criticism** [KRI•ti•SI•zm] *n*
Kritik F
**criticize** [KRI•ti•SUYZ] *vt vi*
kritisieren
**croak** [krok] *vi* krächzen
**crochet** [kro•SHAI] *n* Häkelei F
**crocodile** [KRAH•ku•DUYL] *n*
Krokodil N
**crook** [kruk] *n* Gauner M
**crooked** [KRU•kid] *adj* krumm
**crop** [krahp] *n* Feldfrucht F
**cross** [kraus] *n* Kreuz N
**cross-country**
[KRAUS•KUN•tree] *adj*
querfeldein

**crossfire** [KRAUS•fuyr] *n*
Kreuzfeuer N
**crossroads** [KRAUS•rodz] *n*
Querstraße F
**crossword (puzzle)**
[KRAUS•wurd] *n*
Kreuzworträtsel N
**crow** [kro] *n* Krähe F
**crowbar** [KRO•bahr] *n*
Stemmeisen N
**crowd** [kroud] *n* Menge F
**crown** [kroun] *n* Krone F
**crucial** [KROO•shl] *adj* kritisch
**crucifix** [KROO•si•FIKS] *n*
Kruzifix
**crude** [krood] *adj* grob
**cruel** [krooul] *adj* gemein
**cruise** [krooz] *n* Schiffahrt F
**crumb** [kruhm] *n* Krume F
**crumble** [KRUHM•bl] *vt*
zerbrökeln
**crunch** [kruhnch] *vt* knirschen
**crusade** [kroo•SAID] *n*
Kreuzzug M
**crush** [kruhsh] *n*
Versanstaltung F
**crust** [kruhst] *n* Kruste F
**crutch** [kruhch] *n* Krücke F
**cry** [kruy] *n* Schrei M
**cry out** *vi* aufschreiren
**crying** [KRUY•ing] *adj*
schreiend
**crystal** [KRI•stl] *n* Kristall M
**Cuba** [KYOO•bu] *n* Kuba
**Cuban** [KYOO•bun] *adj*
kubanisch
**cube** [kyoob] *n* Würfel M
**cubic** [KYOO•bik] *adj* kubisch
**cucumber** [KYOO•kuhm•bur] *n*
Gurke F
**cuddle** [KUH•dl] *vt* umarmen

**cue** [kyoo] *n* Wink M
**cuff** [kuhf] *n* Stulpe F
**culminate** [KUHL•mi•NAIT] *vi*
den Höhepunkt erreichen
**culprit** [KUHL•prit] *n* Schuldige
-r F/M
**cult** [kuhlt] *n* Kult M
**cultivate** (grow; raise)
[KUHL•ti•VAIT] *vt* anbauen
**cultural** [KUHL•chu•rul] *adj*
kulturell
**culture** [KUHL•chur] *n*
Kulture F
**cumulative** [KYOO•myu•lu•tiv]
*adj* steigernd
**cunning** [KUH•ning] *adj* schlau
**cup** [kuhp] *n* Tasse F
**cupboard** [KUH•burd] *n*
Schrank M
**curate** [KYOO•rit] *n*
Hilfsgeistlicher M
**curb** [kurb] *n* Zaum M
**curdle** [KUR•dl] *vt* gerinnen
lassen
**cure** [kyoour] *n* Heilmittel N
**curfew** [KUR•fyoo] *n*
Sperrstunde F
**curiosity**
[KYOOUR•ree•AH•si•tee] *n*
Neugier F
**curious** [KYOOUR•ree•us] *adj*
neugierig
**curl** [kurl] *n* Haarlocke F
**curly** [KUR•lee] *adj* lockig
**currant** [KUH•runt] *n*
Johannisbeere F
**currency** [KU•run•see] *n*
Devisen N

**current** [KU•runt] *adj*
gegenwärtig
**curry** [KU•ree] *n* Curry N
**curse** [kurs] *n* Fluch M
**curtail** [kur•TAIL] *vt*
beschneiden
**curtain** [KUR•tn] *n* Vorhang M
**curve** [kurv] *n* Kurve F
**cushion** [KU•shn] *n* Kissen N
**custard** [KUH•sturd] *n*
Vanillasoße F
**custodian** [KUH•STO•dyun] *n*
Hüter M
**custody** [KUH•stu•dee] *n*
Schutz M
**custom** [KUH•stum] *n*
Brauch M
**customer** [KUH•stu•mur] *n*
Kunde M
**cut** [kuht] *n* Schnitt M; *v*
shneiden
**cute** [kyoot] *adj* reizend
**cutlery** [KUHT•lu•ree] *n*
Messerwaren
**cutlet** [KUHT•lit] *n* Schnitzel
**cycle** [SUY•kl] *n* Zyklus M
**cyclone** [SUY•klon] *n* Zykon M
**cylinder** [SI•lin•dur] *n*
Zylinder M
**cynic** [SI•nik] *s* Zyniker M
**cynical** [SI•ni•kl] *adj* zynisch
**cypress** [SUY•pris] *n*
Zypresse F
**cyst** [sist] *n* Sackgeschwulst F
**czar** [zahr] *n* Zar M
**Czech** [chek] *adj* Tscheche;
tschechisch M
**Czechoslovakia**
[che•KO•slo•VAH•kee•uh] *n*
Tschechoslowakei F

# D

**dachsund** [DAHK•sund] *n*
Dachshund M

**dad** [dad] *n* Vater M

**daffodil** [DA•fu•DIL] *n*
Narzisse F

**daily** [DAI•lee] *adj* täglich

**dairy** [DAI•ree] *adj* Molkerei F

**daisy** [DAI•zee] *n*
Gänseblümchen N

**dam** [dam] *n* Damm M

**damage** [DA•mij] *n* Schaden M

**damp** [damp] *adj* feucht

**dampen** [DAM•pun] *vt*
befeuchten

**dance** [dans] *n* Tanz tanzen M

**dancer** [DAN•sur] *n* Tänzer
-in M

**dandelion** [DAN•di•LUY•un] *n*
Löwenzahn M

**dandruff** [DAN•druhf] *n*
Schuppen

**danger** [DAIN•jur] *n* Gefahr F

**dangerous** [DAIN•ju•rus] *adj*
gefährlich

**dangle** [DANG•gl] *vt*
herabhängen

**dare** [dair] *n* wagen

**daredevil** [DAIR•DE•vl] *n*
Teufelskerl M

**daring** [DAI•ring] *adj* kühn

**dark 1** [dahrk] *adj* dunkel; it's
getting ~\ es wird dunkel

**dark 2** [dahrk] *adj* (sinister,
evil) finster

**darken** [DAHR•kn] *vt*
verdunkeln

**darkness** [DAHRK•nis] *n*
Dunkelheit F

**darling** [DAHR•ling] *adj*
lieblings; *n* Liebling M

**darn** [dahrn] *vt* stopfen

**dart** [dahrt] *n* Wurfspeer M

**dash** [dash] *n* Stich M

**dashboard** [DASH•baurd] *n*
Spritzbrett M

**data** [DAI•tu] *n* Tatsachen

**date** [dait] *n* Datum M

**daughter** [DAU•tur] *n*
Tochter F

**daughter-in-law**
[DAU•tur•in•LAU] *s*
Schwiegertochter F

**daunt** [daunt] *vt* erschrecken

**dawdle** [DAU•tur] *vi* bummeln

**dawn** [daun] *n*
Morgendämmerung F

**day** [dai] *n* Tag M; these ~s\
heute; heutzutage

**daybreak** [DAI•braik] *n*
Tagesbruch M

**daydream** [DAI•dreem] *vi*
Träumerei F

**daze** [daiz] *n* Betäubung F

**dazzle** [DA•zl] *vt* verblüffen

**deadline** [DED•luyn] *n*
Termin M

**dead** [ded] *adj* tot

**deaden** [DED•en] *vt* dämpfen

**deadly** [DED•lee] *adj* tödlich

**deaf** [def] *adj* taub

**deafen** [DE•fn] *vt* taub machen

**deafening** [DE•fu•ning] *adj*
ohrenbetäubend

**deal 1** [deel] *n* (many) a good
~ \ viel

**deal 2** [deel] *æ* (business) *n*
Behandlung F; Geschäft

**dealer** [DEE•lur] *s* Händler M

**dealings** [DEE•lingz] *npl*
Verkehr N

**dean** [deen] *n* Fakultät F

**dear** [deer] *adj* lieb

**death** [deth] *n* Tod M

**debacle** [du•BAH•kl] *n*
Debakel N

**debase** [di•BAIS] *vt* verderben

**debate** [di•BAIT] *n* Debatte F

**debauchery** [di•BAU•chu•ree]
*n* Liederlichkeit F

**debit** [DE•bit] *n* Belastung F

**debt** [det] *n* Schuld F

**debtor** [DE•tur] *n* Debitor M

**debut** [DAI•byoo] *n* Debüt N

**decade** [DE•kaid] *n*
Jahrzehnt N

**decadence** [DE•ku•duns] *n*
Niedergang M

**decadent** [DE•ku•dunt] *adj*
verfallend

**decanter** [di•KAN•tur] *n*
Karaffe F

**decay** [di•KAY] *n* Rückgang M

**deceased** [di•SEEST] *adj*
verstorben

**deceit** [di•SEET] *n* Betrug M

**deceitful** [di•SEET•ful] *adj*
betrügerisch

**deceive** [di•SEEV] *vt vi*
täuschen

**December** [di•SEM•bur] *n*
. Dezember M

**decency** [DEE•sn•see] *n*
Anstand M

**decent** [DEE•sunt] *adj*
anständig

**deception** [di•SEP•shn] *n*
Täuschung F

**decide** [di•SUYD] *vt* sich
entscheiden

**decimal** [DE•si•ml] *n*
Dezimalzahl F

**decimate** [DE•si•MAIT] *vt*
vernichten

**decipher** [di•SUY•fur] *vt*
entziffern

**decision** [di•SI•zhn] *n*
Entscheidung F

**decisive** [di•SUY•siv] *adj*
entscheidend

**deck** [dek] *n* Deck N

**declare** [di•KLAIR] *vt* aussagen

**decline** [di•KLUYN] *n*
Niedergang M

**decode** [dee•KOD] *vt*
übersetzen

**decompose** [DEE•kum•POZ] *vi*
zersetzen

**decorate** [DE•ku•RAIT] *vt*
schmucken

**decoration** [DE•ku•RAI•shn] *n*
Schmuck M

**decorum** [di•KAU•rum] *n*
Anstand M

**decoy** [DEE•coi] *n*
Lockspeise F

**decrease** [dee•CREES] *n*
Abnahme F

**decree** [di•KREE] *n* Erlaß M

**decrepit** [di•KRE•pit] *adj*
verbraucht

**dedicate** [de•di•KAIT] *vt*
weihen

**dedication** [DE•di•KAI•shn] *n*
Weihung F

**deduct** [di•DUHKT] *vt*
abziehen

**deduction** [di•DUHK•shn] *n*
Abzug M

**deed** [deed] *n* Tat M

**deem** [deem] *vt* halten

**deep** [deep] *adj* tief

**deepen** [DEEP•n] *vt* vertiefen

**deer** [deer] *n* Reh M

**deface** [di•FAIS] *vt* beschädigen

**defamation** [DE•fu•MAI•shn]
*n* Verleumdung F

**defame** [di•FAIM] *vt*
verleumden

**default** [di•FAULT] *n*
Unterlassung F

**defeat** [di•FEET] *n*
Besiegung F

**defect 1** [DEE•fekt ] *n* Defekt;
Schaler M

**defect 2** [di•FEKT] *vi* sich
absetzen

**defend** [di•FEND] *vt*
verteidigen

**defendant** [di•FEN•dunt] *n*
Angeklagter M

**defense** [di•FENS] *n*
Verteidigung F

**defensive** [di•FEN•siv] *adj*
defensiv

**defer** [di•FUR] *vt* nachgeben

**defiance** [di•FUY•uns] *n*
Trotz M

**deficiency** [di•FI•shun•see] *n*
Mangel M

**deficient** [di•FI•shunt] *adj*
mangelhaft

**deficit** [DE•fi•sit] *n*
Unterbilanz F

**defile** [di•FUYL] *vt* bescmutzen

**define** [di•FUYN] *vt* bezeichnen

**definite** [DE•fi•nit] *adj*
bestimmt

**definitely** [DE•fi•nit•lee] *adv*
zweifellos

**definition** [DE•fi•NI•shn] *n*
Definition F

**deflate** [di•FLAIT] *vt* entleeren

**deflect** [di•FLEKT] (turn away,
aside or off) *vt* ablenken

**deformed** [di•FAURMD] *adj*
mißgestaltet

**defraud** [di•FRAUD] *vt*
betrügen

**defrost** [di•FRAUST] *vt*
entfrosten

**deft** [deft] *adj* geschickt

**defy** [di•FUY] *vt* trotzen

**degenerate 1** [di•JE•nu•rit] *adj*
verderbt

**degenerate 2** [di•JE•nu•RAIT]
*vi* degenerieren

**degrading** [di•GRAI•ding] *adj*
erniedrigend

**degree** [di•GREE] *n* Stufe M;
Grad F

**dehydrate** [di•HUY•drait] *vt*
trocknen

**deity** [DAI•i•tee] *n* gottheit F

**dejected** [di•JEK•tid] *adj*
deprimiert

**delay 1** [di•LAI] *n*
Verspätung F

**delay 2** [di•LAI] (halt, stop,
keep open) *vt* aufhalten

**delegate** [*n*. DE•li•gut *v*.
DE•li•GAIT] *n* Vertreter M

**delegation** [DE•li•GAI•shn] *n*
Abordnung F

**delete** [di•LEET] *vt* streichen

**deliberate** [*adj.* di•LI•brut *v.*
du•LI•bu•RAIT] *adj*
absichtlich

**delicacy** [DE•li•ku•see] *n*
Feinheit F

**delicate** [DE•li•kut] *adj* zart

**delicatessen** [DE•li•ku•TE•sun]
*n* Feinkost F

**delicious** [di•LI•shus] *adj*
köstlich

**delight** [di•LUYT] *n* Freude

**delighted** [di•LUY•tid] *adj*
entzückt

**delightful** [di•LUYT•ful] *adj*
entzückend

**delinquent** [di•LING•kwunt] *n*
Straftäter M; *adj* kriminell

**delirious** [di•LI•ree•us] *adj*
irreredend

**deliver** [di•LI•vur] *vt* liefern

**delivery** [di•LI•vu•ree] *n*
Lieferung F

**deluge** [DE•lyooj] *n*
Überschwemmung F

**delusion** [di•LOO•zhn] *n*
Täuschung F

**demagogue** [DE•mu•GAHG] *n*
Demagoge M

**demand** [di•MAND] *n*
Verlangen N

**demanding** [di•MAN•ding] *adj*
anspruchsvoll

**demeanor** [di•MEE•nur] *n*
Benehmen N

**demented** [di•MEN•tid] *adj*
wahnsinnig

**demerit** [di•ME•rit] *n* Schuld F

**demobilize** [di•MO•bi•LUYZ]
*vt* abrüsten

**democracy** [di•MAH•kru•see] *n*
Demokratie F

**democrat** [DE•mu•KRAT] *n*
Demokrat M

**democratic** [DE•mu•KRA•tik]
*adj* demokratisch

**demolish** [di•MAH•lish] *vt*
vernichten

**demonstrate**
[DE•mun•STRAIT] *vt*
darlegen

**demonstration**
[DE•mun•STRAI•shn] *n*
Darlegung F

**demonstrative**
[di•MAHN•stru•tiv] *adj*
ausdrucksvoll

**demoralize**
[di•MAU•ru•LUYZ] *vt*
verderben

**demure** [di•MYOOR] *adj*
zurückhaltend

**den** [den] *n* Höhle F

**denial** [di•NUYL] *n*
Ablehnung F

**Denmark** [DEN•mahrk] *n*
Dänemark

**denounce** [di•NOUNS] *vt*
verurteilen

**dense** [dens] *adj* dicht

**density** [DEN•si•tee] *n* Dichte F

**dent** [dent] *n* Beule F

**dental** [DEN•tl] *adj*
zahnärztlich

**dentist** [DEN•tist] *n*
Zahnartzt M

**deny** [di•NUY] *vt* leugnen

**depart** [di•PAHRT] *vi* abfahren

**department** [di•PAHRT•mint]
*n* Abteilung F

**department store**
[dee•PART•mint STOR] *n*
Kaufhaus N

**departure** [di•PAHR•chur] *s*
Abfahrt F

depend [di•PEND] vi abhängen von

dependable [di•PEND•u•bl] adj verlässig

depict [di•PIKT] vt darstellen

deplete [di•PLEET] vt erschöpfen

deplorable [di•PLAU•ru•bl] adj beklagenswert

deplore [di•PLAUR] vt bedauern

deport [di•PAURT] vt deportieren

depose [di•POZ] vt absetzen

deposit [di•PAH•zit] n Einzahlung F

depot [DEE•po] n Lagerhaus N

depreciate [di•PREE•shee•AIT] vi geringschätzen

depress [di•PRES] vt deprimieren

depressed [di•PREST] adj deprimiert

depressing [di•PRE•sing] adj erbärmlich

depression [di•PRE•shn] s Depression F

deprive [di•PRUYV] vt berauben

depth [depth] n Tiefe F

deputy [DE•pyu•tee] n Abgeordneter M

derail [di•RAIL] vi entgleisen

deranged [di•RAINJD] adj gestört

deride [di•RUYD] vt verspotten

derive [di•RUYV] vt erlangen

descend [di•SEND] vt vi heruntersteigen

descendant [di•SEN•dunt] n Nachkomme M

descent [di•SENT] n Absteig M

describe [di•SKRUYB] vt beschreiben

description [di•SKRIP•shn] n Beschreibung F

desert [n. DE•zurt v. di•ZURT] n Wüste F

deserter [di•ZUR•tur] n Deserteur M

deserve [di•ZURV] vt verdienen

deserving [di•ZUR•ving] adj verdienstvoll

design [di•ZUYN] n Entwurf M

designate [DE•zig•NAIT] vt bezeichnen

designer [di•ZUY•nur] n Modezeichner M

desirable [di•ZUY•ru•bl] adj erwünscht

desire [di•ZUYUR] n Wunsch M

desist [di•SIST] vi abstehen

desk [desk] n Schreibtisch M; information ~ n\ Informationsschalter M

desolate [DE•su•lut] adj wüst

despair [di•SPAIUR] n Verzweiflung F

desperate [DE•sprut] adj verzweifelt

desperation [DE•spu•RAI•shn] n Hoffnungslosigkeit F

despicable [di•SPI•ku•bl] adj verächtlich

despise [di•SPUYZ] vt verachten

despite [di•SPUYT] prep trotz

despondent [di•SPAHN•dunt] adj mutlos

despot [DE•sput] n Tyrann M

dessert [di•ZURT] n
Nachtisch M

destination [DE•sti•NAI•shn] n
Reiseziel N

destiny [DE•sti•nee] n
Schicksal N

destitute [DE•sti•TOOT] adj
verarmt

destroy [di•STROI] vt zerstören

destruction [di•STRUHK•shn]
n Zerstörung F

destructive [di•STRUHK•tiv]
adj zerstörend

detach [di•TACH] vt losmachen

detail [DEE•tail] n Einzelheit F

detain [di•TAIN] vt aufhalten

detect [di•TEKT] vt entdecken

detection [di•TEK•shn] n
Aufdeckung F

detention [di•TEN•shn] n
Festnahme F

deter [di•TUR] vt abhalten

detergent [di•TUR•junt] n
Waschmittel N

deteriorate
[di•TEER•ee•u•RAIT] vi sich
verschlectern

determination
[di•TUR•mi•NAI•shn] n
Festsetzung F

determine [di•TUR•min] vt
bestimmen

detest [di•TEST] vt
verabscheuern

detonate [DE•tu•NAIT] vt
explodieren

detour [DEE•toor] n
Umleitung F

detract [di•TRAKT] vt
herabsetzen

detrimental [DE•tri•MEN•tl]
adj schädlich

devastate [DE•vu•STAIT] vt
vernichten

devastating [DE•vu•STAI•ting]
adj vernichtend

develop [di•VE•lup] vt
entwickeln

development [di•VE•lup•munt]
n Entwicklung F

deviate [DEE•vee•AIT] vi
abgehen

device [di•VUYS] n Gerät N

devil [DE•vl] n Teufel M

devious [DEE•vee•us] adj irrig

devise [di•VUYZ] vt erfinden

devoid [di•VOID] adj leer an

devote [di•VOT] vt widmen

devoted [di•VO•tud] adj
liebevoll

devotion [di•VO•shn] n
Widmung F

devour [di•VOUUR] vt fressen

devout [di•VOUT] adj fromm

dew [doo] n Tau M

diabetes [DUY•u•BEE•teez] n
Zuckerkrankheit F

diabetic [DUY•u•BE•tik] adj n
Diabetiker M

diagnose [DUY•ug•NOS] vt
feststellen

diagnosis [DUY•ug•NO•sis] adj
n Beurteilung F

diagonal [duy•AG•nl] adj
schräg

diagram [DUY•u•GRAM] n
Schema M

dial [duyul] n Zifferblatt N

dialect [DUY•u•LEKT] n
Dialekt M

**dialog** [DUY•u•LAHG] *n*
Dialog M
**diameter** [duy•A•mi•tur] *s*
Durchmesser M
**diamond** [DUY•mund] *n*
Diamant M
**diamond-shaped** [-SHAIPT]
*adj* rautenförmig
**diary** [DUY•u•ree] *n*
Tagebuch N
**dice** [duys] (sing: die) *npl*
Würfel
**dictate** [DIK•tait] *vt* diktieren
**dictation** [dik•TAI•shn] *n*
Diktat
**dictator** [DIK•TAI•tur] *n*
Diktator M
**dictatorship**
[dik•TAI•tur•SHIP] *n*
Diktatur F
**dictionary** [DIK•shu•NE•ree] *n*
Wörterbuch
**did** [did] *pt k do* tat
**die 1** [duy] *vi* sterben; ~ down
*vi\* nachlassen; ~ out *vi\*
aussterben
**die 2** [duy] *npl* Würfel
**diet** [DUY•ut] *n* Diät F
**differ** [DI•fur] *vi* sich
unterscheiden
**difference** [DI•fruns] *n*
Unterschied M
**different** [DI•frunt] *adj*
verschieden
**differentiate**
[DI•fu•REN•shee•ait] *vt* einen
Unterschied machen
**difficult** [DI•fi•kult] *adj* schwer
schwierig
**difficulty** [DI•fi•kul•tee] *n*
Schwierigkeit F

**diffuse** [di•FYOOZ] *vt*
zerstreuen
**dig** [dig] *vt* graben; ~ out/up *vi\*
ausgraben
**digest** [n. DUY•jest v.
duy•JEST] *vt vi* verdauen
**digestion** [duy•JES•chn] *n*
Verdauung F
**digit** [DI•jit] *n* Zehe; Ziffer F
**digital** [DI•jit•ul] *adh* digital
**dignified** [DIG•ni•FUYD] *adj*
würdig
**dignify** [DIG•ni•FUY] *vt* ehren
**dignity** [DIG•ni•tee] *n* Hoheit F
**digress** [duy•GRES] *vt*
abschweifen
**dilate** [DUY•lait] *vt* ausdehnen
**dilemma** [di•LE•mu] *n*
Dilemma N
**diligence** [DI•li•juns] *n* Fleiß M
**diligent** [DI•li•junt] *adj* fleißig
**dilute** [duy•LOOT] *vt*
verdünnen
**dim** [dim] *adj* düster
**dimension** [di•MEN•shn] *n*
Maß
**diminish** [di•MI•nish] *vt vi*
vermindern
**dimple** [DIM•pl] *n* Vertiefung F
**din** [din] *n* Getöse N
**dine** [duyn] *vi* speisen
**diner** [DUY•nur] *n* Tischgast M
**dinghy** [DING•gee] *n* Beiboot
**dingy** [DIN•jee] *adj* schmutzig
**dining room** [DUY•ning ~ ] *n*
Eßzimmer
**dinner** [DI•nur] *n*
Abendessen N
**dinosaur** [DUY•nu•SAUR] *n*
Dinosaurier M

**diocese** [DUY•u•seez] *n*
Diözese F

**dip 1** [dip] *vt* ~into\ tauchen

**dip 2** [dip] *n* Eintauchen N

**diploma** [di•PLO•mu] *n* Diplom
N; go for a ~\ kurz
schwimmen gehen

**diplomacy** [di•PLO•mu•see] *n*
Diplomatie F

**diplomat** [DI•plu•MAT] *n*
Diplomat M

**diplomatic** [DI•plu•MA•tik] *adj*
diplomatisch

**dire** [duyr] *adj* schrecklich

**direct** [di•REKT] *adj* direkt

**direction** [di•REK•shn] *n*
Richtung F

**directly** [di•REKT•lee] *adv*
gerade

**director** [di•REK•tur] *n*
Direktor M

**directory** [di•REK•tu•ree] *n*
Adreßbuch N

**dirt** [durt] *n* Schmutz; Dreck M

**dirty** [DUR•tee] *adj* schmutzig

**disabled** [di•SAI•bld] *adj*
körperbehindert

**disadvantage**
[DI•sud•VAN•tij] *n*
Nachteil M

**disagree** [DI•su•GREE] *vi*
widersprechen

**disagreement**
[DI•su•GREE•munt] *n*
Widerspruch M

**disappear** [DI•su•PEEUR] *vi*
verschwinden

**disappoint** [DI•su•POINT] *vt*
enttäuschen

**disappointing**
[DI•su•POIN•ting] *adj*
enttäuschend

**disappointment**
[DI•su•POINT•munt] *n*
Enttäuschung F

**disapproval** [DI•su•PROO•vl]
*n* Mißbilligung F

**disapprove** [DI•su•PROOV] *vi*
mißbilligen

**disarm** [di•SAHRM] *vt vi*
abrüsten

**disarray** [DI•su•RAI] *n*
Verwirrung F

**disaster** [di•ZA•stur] *n*
Unglück N

**disastrous** [di•ZA•strus] *adj*
katastrophal

**disavow** [DI•su•VOU] *vt* in
Abrede stellen

**discard** (release) [di•SKAHRD]
*vt* abwerfen

**discern** [di•SURN] *vt* erkennen

**discharge** [*n.* DIS•charj *v.*
dis•CHARJ] *n* Ausladung F; *v*
abschießen

**disciple** [di•SUY•pl] *n*
Jünger M

**discipline** [DI•si•plin] *n*
Schulung F

**disclose** [di•SKLOZ] *vt*
bekanntgeben

**disclosure** [dis•KLO•zhur] *n*
Offenbarung F

**discomfort** [di•SKUHM•furt] *n*
Unbehagen N

**disconnect** [DI•sku•NEKT] *vt*
trennen

**discord** [DI•skaurd] *n* Streit M

**discount** [DI•skount] *n*
Ermäßigung F

**discourage** [di•SKU•rij] *vt*
entmutigen

**discourse** [di•SKAURS] *n*
Rede F

**discover** [di•SKUH•vur] *vt*
entdecken

**discovery** [di•SKUH•vu•ree] *n*
Entdeckung F

**discredit** [dis•KRE•dit] *n*
Verruf M

**discreet** [di•SKREET] *adj*
diskret

**discrepancy** [di•SKRE•pun•see]
*n* Verschiedenheit F

**discretion** [di•SKRE•shn] *n*
Besonnenheit F

**discriminate**
[di•SKRI•mi•NAIT] *vi*
unterscheiden

**discuss** [di•SKUHS] *vt*
diskutieren

**discussion** [di•SKUH•shn] *n*
Besprechung F

**disdain** [dis•DAIN] *n*
Verachtung F

**disease** [di•ZEEZ] *n*
Krankheit F

**disengage** [DI•sin•GAIJ] *vt*
befreien

**disfigure** [dis•FI•gyur] *vt*
entstellen

**disgrace** [dis•GRAIS] *n*
Schande F

**disgraceful** [dis•GRAIS•ful] *adj*
schändlich

**disgruntled** [dis•GRUHN•tld]
*adj* verärgert

**disguise** [dis•GÜYZ] *n*
Maske F

**disgust** [dis•GUHST] *n* Eikel M

**disgusting** [dis•GUH•sting] *adj*
eikel

**dish** [dish] *n* Schüssel F; do the
~es\ abwaschen

**dish out** *vt* austeilen

**dish up** *vt* auftischen

**dishearten** [dis•HAHR•tn] *vt*
entmutigen

**dishevelled** [di•SHE•vld] *adj*
ungepflegt

**dishonest** [dis•AH•nist] *adj*
unehrlich

**dishonor** [dis•AH•nur] *n*
Unehre F

**dishwasher** [DISH•WAH•shur]
*n* Geschirrspülmaschine F

**disillusion** [DIS•i•LOO•zhn] *n*
Ernüchterung F

**disinfect** [DI•sin•FEKT] *vt*
keimfrei machen

**disinfectant** [DI•sin•FEK•tunt]
*n* Desinfektionsmittel N

**disintegrate**
[di•SIN•tu•GRAIT] *vi*
auflösen

**disinterested** [dis•IN•tru•stid]
*adj* uninteresiert

**disk** [disk] *n* Scheibe F

**dislike** [di•SLUYK] *n*
Abneigung F

**dislocate** [DIS•lo•KAIT] *vt*
verrücken

**disloyal** [dis•LOI•ul] *adj* untreu

**dismal** [DI•zml] *adj* trübe

**dismay** [di•SMAI] *n* Schreck M

**dismiss** [dis•MIS] *vt* entlassen;
ablohnen

**dismissal** [dis•MI•sl] *n*
Entlassung F

**dismount** [dis•MOUNT] *vi*
absteigen

**disobedient**
[DI•so•BEE•dee•unt] *adj*
ungehorsam

**disobey** [DI•so•BAI] *vt* nicht
gehorchen

**disorder** [di•SAUR•dur] *n*
Unordnung F

**disorganized**
[di•SAUR•gu•NUYZD] *adj* in
Unordnung

**disoriented**
[di•SAU•ree•EN•tud] *adj* labil

**disown** [dis•ON] *vt* nicht
anerkennen

**disparaging** [di•SPA•ru•jing]
*adj* verächtlich

**dispassionate** [di•SPA•shu•nit]
*adj* leidenschaftslos

**dispel** [di•SPEL] *vt* vertreiben

**dispense** [di•SPENS] *vt*
spenden

**dispenser** [di•SPEN•sur] *n*
Spender M

**disperse** [di•SPURS] *vt*
zerstreuen

**displace** [dis•PLAIS] *vt*
versetzen

**display** [di•SPLAI] *n*
Ausstellung F

**displease** [dis•PLEEZ] *vt*
ärgern

**displeased** [dis•PLEEZD] *adj*
unzufrieden

**disposal** [di•SPO•zl] *n*
Anordnung F

**dispose** [di•SPOZ] *vt*
zurechtlegen

**disposed** [di•SPOZD] *adj*
gelaunt

**disposition** [DI•spu•ZI•shn] *n*
Aufstellung F

**disprove** [dis•PROOV] *vt*
widerlegen

**dispute** [di•SPYOOT] *n*
Wortstreit M

**disqualify** [dis•KWAH•li•FUY]
*vt* disqualifizieren

**disregard** [DIS•ree•GAHRD] *n*
Vernachlässigung F

**disreputable**
[dis•RE•pyu•tu•bl] *adj*
schändlich

**disrespect** [DIS•ru•SPEKT] *n*
Mißachtung F

**disrupt** [dis•RUHPT] *vt*
zerbrechen

**dissatisfy** [di•SAT•is•FUY] *vt*
nicht befriedigen

**dissect** [duy•SEKT] *vt* zerlegen

**dissemble** [di•SEM•bl] *vt vi*
sich verstellen

**disseminate** [di•SE•mi•NAIT]
*vt* ausstreuen

**dissent** [di•SENT] *n*
Abweichen N

**dissimulate** [di•SI•myu•LAIT]
*vt vi* dissimulieren

**dissipate** [DI•si•PAIT] *vt*
verschwenden

**dissociate** [di•SO•shee•AIT] *vt*
absondern

**dissolute** [DI•su•LOOT] *adj*
ausschweifend

**dissolve** [di•ZAHLV] *vt*
auflösen

**dissuade** [di•SWAID] *vt*
abraten

**distance** [DI•stuns] *n* Ferne F

**distant** [DI•stunt] *adj* entfernt

**distaste** [dis•TAIST] *n*
Abscheu M

**distill** [dis•TIL] *vt vi* destillieren

**distillery** [dis•TI•lu•ree] *n*
Brennerei F

**distinct** [dis•TINGKT] *adj*
selbständig

**distinguish** [di•STING•gwish]
*vt* unterscheiden

**distort** [di•STAURT] *vt*
verdrehen

**distract** [di•STRAKT] *vt*
verwirren

**distraught** [di•STRAUT] *adj*
durcheinander

**distress** [di•STRES] *n* Qual F

**distribute** [di•STRI•byoot] *vt*
austeilen

**distribution**
[DI•stri•BYOO•shn] *n*
Austeilung F

**district** [DI•strikt] s Bezirk M

**distrust** [dis•TRUST] *n*
Mißtrauen M

**distrustful** [dis•TRUST•ful] *adj*
mißtrauisch

**disturb** [di•STURB] *vt* stören

**disturbance** [di•STUR•buns] *n*
Störung F

**disturbing** [di•STUR•bing] *adj*
beunruhigend

**ditch** [dich] *n* Graben M

**ditto** [DI•to] *adv* ebenfalls

**dive** [duyv] *n* Tauchen N

**diverge** [di•VURJ] *vi*
abzweigen

**diverse** [di•VURS] *adj*
verschieden

**diversify** [di•VUR•si•FUY] *vt*
verändern

**diversity** [di•VUR•si•tee] *n*
Verscheidenheit F

**divert** [di•VURT] *vt* (avert
one's eyes) abwenden;
(traffic) umleiten (attention)
ablenken

**divide** [di•VUYD] *vt* einteilen

**divine** [di•VUYN] *adj* göttlich

**divinity** [di•VI•ni•tee] *n*
Göttlichkeit F

**division** [di•VI•zhn] *n*
Einteilung F

**divorce** [di•VAURS] *n*
Entscheidung F

**divulge** [di•VUHLJ] *vt*
bekanntmachen

**dizzy** [DI•zee] *adj* schwindelnd

**do** [doo] *vt* tun; machen;

**do away with** *vi* (law)
asbschaffen; (building)
abreißen

**do in** (kill) um die Ecke bringen
(exhausted done in) fertig
sein

**do without** *vi* auskommen
ohne

**docile** [DAH•sul] *adj* fügsam

**dock** [dahk] *n* Kaigebühr F

**doctor** [DAHK•tur] *n* Arzt;
Ärztin M

**doctorate** [DAHK•tu•rut] *n*
Doktorat N

**doctrine** [DAHK•trin] *n*
Lehre F

**document** [DAH•kyu•munt] *n*
Dokument N

**dodge** [dahj] *vt* vermeiden

**doe** [do] *n* Damhirschkuh M

**dog** [daug] *n* Hund M

**dogma** [DAUG•mu] *n*
Lehrsatz M

**doings** [DOO•ings] *npl* Tun N

**doll** [dahl] *n* Puppe F

**dollar** [DAH•lur] *n* Dollar M

**dolphin** [DAHL•fin] *n*
Delphin M

**domain** [do•MAIN] *n*
Staatsgut N

**dome** [dom] *n* Kuppel F

**domestic** [du•ME•stik] *adj*
häuslich

**dominant** [DAH•mi•nunt] *adj*
herrschend

**dominate** [DAH•mi•NAIT] *vt*
beherrschen

**domineering**
[DAH•mi•NEEU•ring] *adj*
tyrannisch

**donate** [DO•nait] *vt* schenken

**donation** [do•NAI•shn] *n*
Stiftung F

**donkey** [DAHNG•kee] *n*
Esel M

**donor** [DO•nur] *n* Geber M

**doodle** [DOO•dl] *vi* zeichnen

**doom** [doom] *n* Schicksal N

**doomed** [doomd] *adj* verdammt

**doomsday** [DOOMZ•dai] *n* das
Jüngste Gericht

**door** [daur] *n* Tür F

**doorbell** [DAUR•bel] *n*
Türklingel F

**doormat** [DAUR•mat] *n*
Türmatte F

**doorstep** [DAUR•step] *n*
Türstufe F

**dope** [dop] *n* Drogen; Stoff M

**dormitory**
[DAUR•mi•TAU•ree] *n*
Studentenwohnheim N

**dose** [dos] *n* Portion F

**dot** [daht] *n* Punkt M

**double** [DUH•bl] *adj* doppel; *n*
das Doppelte; *vt* verdoppeln

**double vision** [DUH•bl VI•shn]
*n* Doppelblick M

**double-breasted** [-BRE•stid]
*adj* zweireihig

**doubly** [DUH•blee] *adv* doppelt

**doubt** [dout] *n* Zweifel M; *vt*
bezweifeln

**doubtful** [DOUT•ful] *adj*
zweifelnd

**dough** [do] *n* Teig M

**douse** [dous] *vt* ins Wasser
tauchen

**dove** [duhv] *n* Taube F

**down** [doun] *adv* hinunter;
hinab

**down payment** [DOUN
PAI•mint] *n* Lohn M

**downcast** [DOUN•kast] *adj*
deprimiert

**downpour** [DOUN•paur] *n*
Regenguß M

**downstairs** [DOUN•STAIURZ]
*adj* die Treppe hinunter

**downward** [DOUN•wurd] *adj*
abwärts

**dowry** [DOU•ree] *n* Gabe F

**doze** [doz] *vi* schlummern

**dozen** [DUH•zn] *n* Dutzend N

**draft** [draft] *n* Entwurf M

**drag** [drag] *vt vi* schleppen

**dragon** [DRA•gn] *n* Drache M

**dragonfly** [DRA•gn•FLUY] *n*
Dracheflieger M

**drain** [drain] *n* Abfluß M

**drama** [DRAH•mu] *n*
Schauspiel N

**dramatic** [dru•MA•tik] *adj*
dramatisch

**dramatist** [DRAH•mu•tist] *n*
Dramatiker M

**dramatize** [DRAH•mu•TUYZ]
*vt* dramatisieren

**drape** [draip] *vt* behängen

**drapes** [draips] *npl* Vorhang M

**drastic** [DRA•stik] *adj*
durchgreifend

**draw** [drau] *n* Ziehen N

**drawer** [draur] *n* Schublade F

**drawing** [DRAU•ing] *n*
Zeichnen N

**dread** [dred] *n* Angst F

**dreadful** [DRED•ful] *adj*
fürchterlich

**dream** [dreem] *n* Traum M

**dreamy** [DREE•mee] *adj*
träumerisch

**dreary** [DREEU•ree] *adj* düster

**drench** [drench] *vt* durchnässen

**dress** [dres] *n* Kleid N; *vi* sich
anziehen; sich kleiden

**dress up** *vi* sich feinmachen;
(disguise) verkleiden

**dresser** [DRE•sur] *n* Anrichte F

**dressing** [DRE•sing] *n*
Ankleiden N

**dried** [druyd] *adj* getrocknet

**drift** [drift] *n* Abwanderung F;
*vi* treiben

**drill 1** [dril] *n* Bohrer M; *vt vi*
bohre

**drill 2** *vi* gedrilt werden

**drink** [dringk] *n* Getränk N; *vt
vi* trinken

**drip** [drip] *n* Tröpfeln N; *vi*
tropfen

**drive** [druyv] *n* Fahrt F; *vt*
fahren; ~ away *vi\* wegfahren

**drivel** [DRI•vl] *n* Unsinn;
Blödsin M

**driver** [DRUY•vur] *n* Fahrer M;
—in F

**drizzle** [DRI•zl] *n* Sprühregen M

**droop** [droop] *vi* herabhängen

**drop** [drahp] *n* Tropfen M;

**drop by** *vi* vorbeikommen

**drop out** (quit; leave) *vi*
auscheiden aus

**drought** [drout] *n* Dürre F

**drove** [drov] *n* Herde F

**drown** [droun] *vt* ertrinken

**drowsy** [DROU•zee] *adj*
schläfrig

**drug** [druhg] *n* Droge F

**drug addict** [DRUHG A•dikt] *n*
Süchtiger M

**druggist** [DRUH•gist] *n*
Apotheker M

**drum** [druhm] *n* Trommel F

**drummer** [DRUH•mur] *n*
Trommler M

**drunk** [druhngk] *adj* besoffen;
betrunken

**drunkenness**
[DRUHNG•kn•nis] *n*
Besoffenheit F

**dry** [druy] *adj* trocken

**dryer** [DRUY•ur] *n* Trockner M

**dual** [dooul] *adj* doppelt

**dubbed** [duhbd] *adj*
synchronisiert

**dubious** [DOO•byus] *adj*
zweifelhaft

**Dublin** [DUH•blin] *n* Dublin

**duchess** [DUH•chis] *n*
Herzogin F

**duck 1** [duhk] *n* Ente F

**duck 2** *vi* sich ducken

**duct** [duhkt] *n* Röhre F

**due** [doo] *adj* fällig; ~ to\
aufgrund

**duel** [dooul] *n* Zweikampf M

**dues** [dooz] *npl* Gebühr

**duet** [doo•ET] *n* Duett N

**duke** [dook] *n* Herzog M

**dull** [duhl] *adj* langweilig

**dumb** [duhm] *adj* dumm
**dumbfound** [DUHM•found] *vt*
  verblüffen
**dummy** [DUH•mee] *n*
  Dummkopf M
**dump** [duhmp] *v* abladen
**dunce** [duns] *n* Narrenkappe F
**dune** [doon] *n* Düne F
**dung** [duhng] *n* Mist M
**dungeon** [DUHN•jun] *n*
  Kerker M
**duplicate** [*adj. n.* DOO•pli•kut
  *v.* DOO•pli•KAIT] *adj*
  doppelt
**duplicity** [doo•PLI•si•tee] *n*
  Doppelzüngigkeit F
**durable** [DOOU•ru•bl] *adj*
  haltbar
**duration** [du•RAI•shn] *n*
  Dauer F
**dusk** [duhsk] *n* Dämmerung F

**dust** [duhst] *n* Staub M
**dustpan** [DUHST•pan] *n*
  Müllschaufel F
**Dutch** [duhch] *adj* holländisch
**duty** [DOO•tee] *n* Pflicht F
**duty-free** [DOO•tee FREE] *adj*
  zollfrei
**dwarf** [dwaurf] *n* Zwerg M
**dwell** [dwel] *vi* wohnen
**dwelling** [DWE•ling] *n*
  Wohnung F
**dwindle** [DWIN•dl] *vi*
  schwinden
**dye** [duy] *n* Farbstoff M
**dying** [DUY•ing] *adj* sterbend
**dynamic** [duy•NA•mik] *adj n*
  dynamisch
**dynamite** [DUY•nu•MUYT] *n*
  Dynamit N
**dynasty** [DUY•nu•stee] *n*
  Dynastie F

# E

**each** [eech] *adj* jeder; jede;
  jedes
**eager** [EE•gur] *adj* eifrig
**eagle** [EE•gl] *n* Adler M
**ear 1** [eeur] *n* Ohr N
**ear 2** (of grain) *n* Ähre F
**early** [UR•lee] *adj adv* früh
**earn** [urn] *vt* verdienen
**earnest** [UR•nist] *adj* ernst; in
  ~\ erntshaft
**earring** [EEU•ring] *n*
  Ohrring M
**earth** [urth] *n* Erde F

**earthquake** [URTH•kwaik] *n*
  Erdbeben N
**ease** [eez] *n* Bequemlichkeit F;
  Behagen N; *vt* (of pain)
  lindern; (situation) nachlassen
**easily** [EE•zi•lee] *adv* leicht
**east** [eest] *adj* ost; *n* Osten M
**Easter** [EE•stur] *n* Ostern N
**eastern** [EE•sturn] *adj* östlich
**eastward** [EEST•wurd] *adv*
  ostwärts
**easy** [EE•zee] *adj* leicht
**eat** [eet] *vt vi* essen

**eat out** *vi* essen gehen

**eat up** *vt vi* ausfessen

**ebb** [eb] *n* Ebbe F

**ebony** [E•bu•nee] *adj* Ebenholz N

**eccentric** [ek•SEN•trik] *adj* exzentrisch; *n* Exzenter M

**ecclesiastic** [ee•KLEE•zee•A•stik] *adj* kirchlich

**echo** [E•ko] *n* Echo N

**eclipse** [ee•KLIPS] *n* Verfinsterung F

**ecology** [ee•KAH•lu•jee] *n* Ökologie F

**economic** [E•ku•NAH•mik] *adj* wirtschaftlich

**economical** [E•ku•NAH•mi•kl] *adj* wirtschaflich

**economics** [E•ku•NAH•miks] *n* Wirtschaft F

**economy** [ee•KAH•nu•mee] *n* Ökonomie F

**ecstasy** [EK•stu•see] *n* Verzückung F

**ecstatic** [ek•STA•tik] *adj* begeistert

**edge** [ej] *n* Schärfe F

**edible** [E•di•bl] *adj* genießbar

**edit** [E•dit] *vt* bearbeiten

**edition** [e•DI•shn] *n* Ausgabe F

**editor** [E•di•tur] *n* Herausgeber M

**editorial** [E•di•TAU•ree•ul] *adj* redaktionell; *n* Leitartikel M

**educate** [E•ju•KAIT] *vt* unterrichten

**education** [E•ju•KAI•shn] *n* Ausbildung F

**educational** [E•ju•KAI•shu•nl] *adj* belehrend

**eel** [eeul] *n* Aal M

**effect** [i•FEKT] *n* Wirkung F; *vt* bewirken

**effective** [i•FEK•tiv] *adj* wirksam

**efficiency** [i•FI•shun•see] *n* Tüchtigkeit F

**efficient** [i•FI•shunt] *adj* tüchtig

**effort** [E•furt] *n* Mühe F

**egg** [eg] *n* Ei N

**eggplant** [EG•plant] *n* Eierfrucht F

**ego** [EE•go] *n* Ich N

**egotist** [EE•go•tist] *n* Egotist M

**Egypt** [EE•jipt] *n* Ägyptien

**Egyptian** [ee•JIP•shn] *adj* ägyptisch

**eight** [ait] *num* acht

**eighteen** [ai•TEEN] *num* achtzehn

**eighteenth** [ai•TEENTH] *num* achtzehnte

**eighth** [aith] *num* achte

**eighty** [AI•tee] *num* achtzig

**either** [EE•thur] *adj* jeder; *adj pron* einer; *adv; conj* (after negative) auch nicht; ~ or\ entweder . . . oder

**eject** [ee•JEKT] *vt* hinauswerfen

**elaborate** [adj. i•LA•brit ] *adj* ausgearbeitet; [*v.* i•LA•bu•RAIT] *vt* (explain) ausfürhen

**elastic** [i•LA•stik] *adj* elastisch; *n* Gummiband N

**elated** [i•LAI•tid] *adj* erregt

**elbow** [EL•bo] *n* Ellbogen M

**elder** [EL•dur] *adj* älter; *n* Ältere M

**elderly** [EL•dur•lee] *adj* ältlich

**elect** [i•LEKT] *vt* wählen

**election** [i•LEK•shn] *n* Wahl F

**electric** [i•LEK•trik] *adj*
elektrisch

**electricity** [i•LEK•TRI•si•tee] *n*
Elektrizität F

**electrocute**
[i•LEK•tru•KYOOT] *vt* auf
dem elektrischen Stuhl
hinrichten

**electronic** [i•LEK•TRAH•nik]
*adj* elektronisch

**elegance** [E•li•guns] *n*
Eleganz F

**elegant** [E•li•gunt] *adj* elegant

**element** [E•li•munt] *n*
Element N

**elementary** [E•li•MEN•tu•ree]
*adj* elementar

**elephant** [E•lu•fint] *n*
Elefant M

**elevate** [E•lu•VAIT] *vt*
emporheben

**elevator** [E•li•VAI•tur] *n*
Aufzug M

**eleven** [i•LE•vn] *num* elf

**eleventh** [i•LE•vnth] *num* elfte

**elicit** [i•LI•sit] *vt* herauslocken

**eligible** [E•li•ju•bl] *adj*
akzeptabel

**eliminate** [i•LI•mi•NAIT] *vt*
tilgen

**elite** [i•LEET] *adj* Elite F

**elitist** [i•LEE•tist] *adj n* elitär

**elk** [elk] *n* Elen M

**elm** [elm] *n* Ülme F

**elope** [i•LOP] *vi* entlaufen

**eloquence** [E•lu•kwens] *n*
Beredsamkeit F

**eloquent** [E•lu•kwent] *adj*
beredt

**else** [els] *adv* sonst

**elsewhere** [ELS•waiur] *adv*
anderswo

**elude** [i•LOOD] *vt* ausweichen

**emaciated** [i•MAI•shee•AI•tid]
*adj* abgemagert

**emanate** [E•mu•NAIT] *vi*
ausströmen

**emancipation**
[i•MAN•si•PAI•shn] *n*
Befreiung F

**embankment**
[em•BANGK•munt] *n*
Deich M

**embargo** [im•BAHR•go] *n*
Embargo N

**embarrass** [im•BA•rus] *vt* in
Verlegenheit bringen

**embarrassed** [im•BA•rust] *adj*
verlegen

**embarrassing** [im•BA•ru•sing]
*adj* unangenehm

**embarrassment**
[im•BA•rus•munt] *n*
Verlegenheit F

**embassy** [EM•bu•see] *n*
Botschaft F

**embellish** [im•BE•lish] *vt*
verschönen

**embers** [EM•burz] *npl* Funken

**embezzle** [em•BE•zl] *vt*
veruntreuen

**emblem** [EM•blum] *n*
Abzeichen N

**embody** [em•BAH•dee] *vt*
verkörpern

**embrace** [em•BRAIS] *n*
Umarmung F

**embroidery** [em•BROI•du•ree]
*n* Stickerei F

**embryo** [EM•bree•O] *n*
Embryo M

**emerald** [E•mu•ruld] *adj n* Smaragd M

**emerge** [i•MURJ] *vi* auftauchen

**emergency** [i•MUR•jun•see] *adj* Notfall M

**emergency exit** [ee•MUR•gin•cee EG•sit] *n* Notausgang M

**emigrant** [E•mi•grunt] *n* Auswanderer M

**emigrate** [E•mi•GRAIT] *vi* auswandern

**eminence** [E•mi•nuns] *n* Erhöhung F

**eminent** [E•mi•nunt] *adj* hervorragend

**emissary** [E•mi•SE•ree] *n* Bote M

**emission** [i•MI•shn] *n* Ausfluß M

**emit** [i•MIT] *vt* ausstrahlen

**emperor** [EM•pu•rur] *n* Kaiser M

**emphasis** [EM•fu•sis] *n* Betonung F

**emphasize** [EM•fu•SUYZ] *vt* unterstreichen

**empire** [EM•puyur] *n* Reich N

**employ** [em•PLOI] *vt* anstellen

**employee** [em•PLOI•YEE] *n* Angestellte M

**employer** [em•PLOI•yur] *n* Arbeitgeber M

**employment** [em•PLOI•ment] *n* Arbeit F

**empress** [EM•pris] *n* Kaiserin F

**empty** [EMP•tee] *adj* leer

**emulate** [E•myu•LAIT] *vt* nachahmen

**enable** [e•NAI•bl] *vt* befähigen

**enact** [e•NAKT] *vt* verfügen

**enamel** [i•NA•ml] *n* Emaille F

**enamored** [i•NA•murd] *adj* verliebt

**encampment** [en•KAMP•munt] *n* Lager N

**enchant** [en•CHANT] *vt* verzaubern

**enclose** [en•CLOZ] *vt* einschließen

**encompass** [en•KAHM•pus] *vt* umfassen

**encore** [AHN•kaur] *n* Zugabe F

**encounter** [en•KOUN•tur] *n* Begegnung F

**encourage** [en•KU•rij] *vt* ermutigen

**encouragement** [en•KU•rij•ment] *n* Ermutigung F

**encroach** [en•KROCH] *vi* eindringen

**encyclopedia** [en•SUY•klo•PEE•dee•u] *n* Enzyklopädie F

**end** [end] *n* Ende N; *vt* beenden; *vi* enden

**endanger** [en•DAIN•jur] *vt* gefährden

**endearing** [en•DEEU•ring] *adj* zärtlich

**endeavor** [en•DE•vur] *n* Bemühung F; *vt* sich bemühen

**ending** [EN•ding] *n* Schluß M

**endless** [END•lis] *adj* endlos

**endorse** [en•DAURS] *vt* überweisen

**endurance** [en•DU•runs] *n* Ausdauer F

**enemy** [E•nu•mee] *n* Feind M

**energetic** [E•nur•JE•tik] *adj* energisch

**energy** [E•nur•jee] *n* Energie F

**enforce** [en•FAURS] *vt*
auferlegen

**engage** [en•GAIJ] *vt* binden

**engaged** [en•GAIJD] *adj*
verlobt

**engagement** [en•GAIJ•munt] *n*
Verlobung F

**engaging** [en•GAI•jing] *adj*
reizend

**engine** [EN•jin] *n* Werkzeug N

**engineer** [EN•ji•NEEUR] *n*
Ingenieur M

**engineering** [EN•ji•NEE•ring]
*n* Technik F

**England** [ING•glund] *n* England

**English** [ING•glish] *adj* englisch

**engrave** [en•GRAIV] *vt*
einschneiden

**engraving** [en•GRAI•ving] *n*
Gravieren N

**engulf** [en•GUHLF] *vt*
verschlingen

**enhance** [en•HANS] *vt*
vergrößern

**enigma** [i•NIG•mu] *n* Rätsel N

**enjoy** [en•JOI] *vt* genießen; ~
oneself\ sich amüsieren; ~
yourself!\ *excl* viel Spaß

**enjoyable** [en•JOI•u•bl] *adj*
genießbar

**enlarge** [en•LAHRJ] *vt*
ausdehnen

**enlighten** [en•LUY•tn] *vt*
aufklären

**Enlightenment**
[en•LUY•tn•munt] *n*
Aufklärung F

**enlist** [en•LIST] *vt* sich
anwerben lassen

**enormous** [i•NAUR•mus] *adj*
enorm

**enough** [i•NUHF] *adj* genug;
*adv* genug; genügend

**enrage** [en•RAIJ] *vt* wütend
machen

**enrich** [en•RICH] *vt* bereichern

**enroll** [en•ROL] *vt* einschreiben

**enslave** [en•SLAIV] *vt*
versklaven

**ensuing** [en•SOO•ing] *adj*
folgend

**ensure** [en•SHOOUR] *vt*
versichern

**entail** [en•TAIL] *vt* auferlegen

**enter** [EN•tur] *vt* eintreten

**enterprise** [EN•tur•PRUYZ] *n*
Unternehmen N

**enterprising**
[EN•tur•PRUY•zing] *adj*
unternehmend

**entertain** [EN•tur•TAIN] *vt*
amüsieren

**entertaining**
[EN•tur•TAI•ning] *adj*
amüsant

**entertainment**
[EN•tur•TAIN•munt] *n*
Unterhaltung F

**enthusiasm**
[en•THOO•zee•A•zm] *n*
Enthusiasmus M

**enthusiastic**
[en•THOO•zee•A•stik] *adj*
begeistert

**enticing** [en•TUY•sing] *adj*
verlockend

**entire** [en•TUYUR] *adj* ganz

**entirely** [en•TUYUR•lee] *adv*
völlig N

**entirety** [en•TUYUR•tee] *n*
Ganze N

**entitled** [en•TUY•tl] *adj*
berechtigt

**entity** [EN•ti•tee] *n* Dasein N

**entrance 1** [EN•truns] *n*
Zutritt M

**entrance 2** [en•TRANS] *vt* in
Entzüchen versetzen

**entry** [EN•tree] *n* Zugang M

**enumerate** [i•NOO•mu•RAIT]
*vt* aufzählen

**envelop** [en•VE•luhp] *vt*
einschlagen

**envelope** [EN•vu•LOP] *n*
Umschlag M

**envious** [EN•vee•us] *adj*
neidisch

**environment**
[en•VUY•run•munt] *n*
Umgebung F

**envoy** [EN•voi] *n* Gesandter M

**envy** [EN•vee] *n* Neid M

**epic** [E•pik] *adj* episch

**epidemic** [E•pi•DE•mik] *n*
Seuche F

**episode** [E•pi•SOD] *n*
Vorfall M

**epistle** [i•PI•sl] *n*
Sendschreiben N

**epitaph** [E•pi•TAF] *n*
Grabschrift F

**epitome** [e•PI•to•mee] *n*
Abriß M

**epoch** [E•puk] *n* Epoche F

**equal** [EE•kwul] *adj* gleich

**equality** [ee•KWAH•li•tee] *n*
Gleichheit F

**equally** [EE•kwu•lee] *adv*
ebenso

**equation** [ee•KWAI•zhn] *n*
Ausgleich M

**equator** [ee•KWAI•tur] *n*
Äquator M

**equip** [i•KWIP] *vt* ausrüsten

**equipment** [i•KWIP•munt] *n*
Ausrüstung F

**equivalent** [i•KWI•vu•lunt] *adj*
entsprechend; *n* Gegenwert M

**era** [E•ru] *n* Zeitalter N

**eradicate** [i•RA•di•KAIT] *vt*
entwurzeln

**erase** [i•RAIS] *vt* erwischen

**eraser** [i•RAI•sur] *n* Wischer M

**erect** [i•REKT] *adj* aufrecht

**erection** [i•REK•shn] *n*
Erektion F

**erode** [i•ROD] *vt* erordieren

**erosion** [i•RO•zhn] *n*
Zerfressen N

**err** [er] *vi* sich irren

**errand** [E•rund] *n* Besorgung F

**error** [E•rur] *n* Fehler F

**erudite** [ER•yu•DUYT] *adj*
belesen

**erupt** [i•RUHPT] *vi* ausbrechen

**eruption** [i•RUHP•shn] *n*
Ausbruch M

**escalate** [E•sku•LAIT] *vt*
eskalieren

**escalator** [E•sku•LAI•tur] *n*
Rolltreppe F

**escape** [e•SKAIP] (from
pursuers) *vi* entkommen;
(avoid) *vt* entgehen; *n*
Flucht F

**escort** [*n.* E•skaurt *v.*
e•SKAURT] *n* Begleiter M

**especially** [e•SPE•shu•lee] *adv*
besonders

**espionage** [E•spee•u•NAHZH]
*n* Spionage F

**essay** [E•sai] *n* Aufsatz M

**essence** [E•suns] *n* Wesen N;
Essenz F

**essential** [e•SEN•shl] *adj* (most
important) wesentlich;
(necessary) erforderlich

**essentially** [e•SEN•shu•lee] *adv*
eigentlich

**establish** [e•STA•blish] *vt* (set
up) gründen; (prove) unter
Beweis stellen

**establishment**
[e•STA•blish•munt] *n*
Unternehmen N

**estate** [e•STAIT] *n* Besitz M

**esteem** [e•STEEM] *n*
Wertschätzung F

**estimate** [*n.* E•sti•mut *v.*
E•sti•MAIT] *n* Schätzung F

**estranged** [e•STRAINJD] *adj*
getrennt

**eternal** [ee•TUR•nl] *adj* ewig

**eternity** [ee•TUR•ni•tee] *n*
Ewigkeit F

**ethic** [E•thik] *n* Ethik F

**ethical** [E•thi•kl] *adj* ethisch

**Ethiopia** [EE•thee•O•pee•u] *n*
Äthiopien

**ethnic** [ETH•nik] *adj* ethnisch

**etiquette** [E•ti•kut] *n* Etikette F

**eulogy** [YOO•lu•jee] *n*
Lobrede F

**euphemism** [YOO•fu•MI•zm] *n*
Ausdruck M

**Europe** [YUH•rup] *n* Europa

**European** [YUH•ru•PEE•un]
*adj* europäisch

**European Community**
[YUH•ru•PEE•un
kuh•MYOO•ni•tee] *n*
Europäische Gemeinschaft F

**euthanasia**
[YOO•thu•NAI•zhu] *n* leichter
Tod

**evacuate** [i•VA•kyoo•AIT] *vt*
ausleeren

**evade** [i•VAID] *vt* vermeiden

**evaluate** [i•VAL•yoo•AIT] *vt*
abschätzen

**evaporate** [i•VA•pu•RAIT] *vt*
verdampfen

**evasive** [i•VAI•siv] *adj*
ausweichen

**eve** [eev] *n* Vorabend M

**even** [EE•vn] *adj* eben

**evening** [EEV•ning] *n*
Abend M

**evening gown** [EEV•ning
GOUN] *n* Frack M

**event** [i•VENT] *n* Ereignis N

**eventual** [i•VEN•choo•ul] *adj*
schließlich

**eventually** [i•VEN•choo•u•lee]
*adv* endlich

**ever** [E•vur] *adv* immer

**evergreen** [E•vur•GREEN] *n*
Immergrün N

**every** [E•vree] *adj* jede

**everybody** [E•vree•BUH•dee]
*pron* jedermann

**everyday** [E•vree•DAI] *adj*
jeden Tag

**everything** [E•vree•THING]
*pron* alles

**everywhere** [E•vree•WAIUR]
*adv* überall

**evict** [ee•VIKT] *vt* vertreiben

**evidence** [E•vi•duns] *n*
Beweis M

**evident** [E•vi•dunt] *adj*
offensichtlich

**evil** [EE•vl] *adj* übbel

**evoke** [ee•VOK] *vt* beschwören

**evolution** [E•vu•LOO•shn] *n*
Entwicklung F

**evolve** [ee•VAHLV] *vi* entfalten

**ewe** [yoo] *n* Mutterschaf N

**exact** [eg•ZAKT] *adj* genau

**exaggerate** [eg•ZA•ju•RAIT]
*vt vi* übertreiben

**exaggeration**
[eg•ZA•ju•RAI•shn] *n*
Übertreibung F

**exalt** [eg•ZAULT] *vt* erheben

**exam** [eg•ZAM] *n* Prüfung F

**examine** [eg•ZA•min] *vt* prüfen

**example** [eg•ZAM•pl] *n*
Beispiel N

**exasperate** [eg•ZA•spu•RAIT]
*vt* erbittern

**excavate** [EK•sku•VAIT] *vt*
ausgraben

**exceed** [ek•SEED] *vt*
überschreiten

**excel** [ek•SEL] *vi* hervorragen

**excellence** [EK•su•luns] *n*
Leistung

**excellent** [EK•su•lunt] *adj*
ausgezeichnet

**except** [ek•SEPT] *prep conj*
außer

**exception** [ek•SEP•shn] *n*
Ausnahme F

**exceptional** [ek•SEP•shu•nl]
*adj* ungewöhnlich

**excerpt** [EK•surpt] *n* Exzerpt N

**excess** [EK•ses] *adj* übermäßig

**exchange** [eks•CHAINJ] *n*
Tausch M; *vt* umtauschen

**excite** [ek•SUYT] *vt* aufregen

**excited** [ek•SUY•tid] *adj*
aufgeregt

**exciting** [ek•SUY•ting] *adj*
aufregend

**exclaim** [ek•SKLAIM] *vi*
aufschreien

**exclamation point**
[EK•sklu•MAI•shn ~ ] *n*
Ausrufungszeichen N

**exclude** [ek•SKLOOD] *vt*
ausweisen

**excrement** [EK•skri•munt] *n*
Auswurf M

**excursion** [ek•SKUR•zhn] *n*
Ausflug M

**excuse** [n. ek•SKYOOS v.
ek•SKYOOZ] *n* Ausrede F

**execute** [EK•si•KYOOT] *vt*
durchführen

**execution** [EK•si•KYOO•shn] *n*
Verrichtung F

**executioner**
[EK•si•KYOO•shu•nur] *n*
Scharfrichter M

**executive** [eg•ZE•kyu•tiv] *adj*
exekutiv

**exemplary** [eg•ZEM•plu•ree]
*adj* vorbildlich

**exemplify** [eg•ZEM•pli•FUY]
*vt* veranschaulichen

**exempt** [eg•ZEMPT] *adj*
ausgenommen

**exercise** [EK•sur•SUYZ] *n*
Ausübung F

**exert** [eg•ZURT] *vt* anwenden

**exhale** [eks•HAIL] *vt* ausatem

**exhaust** [eg•ZAUST] *n*
Auspuff M

**exhausted** [eg•ZAU•stid] *adj*
erschöpft

**exhaustion** [eg•ZAUS•chn] *n*
Erschöpfung F

**exhibit** [eg•ZI•bit] *n*
Ausstellung F

**exhilarating**
[eg•ZI•lu•RAI•ting] *adj*
erheiternd

**exile** [EG•zuyl] *n* Verbannung F

**exist** [EG•zist] *vi* existieren

**existence** [eg•ZI•stuns] *n*
Leben N

**exit** [EG•zit] *n* Ausgang M; *vt*
(from stage, etc.) *vt* abgehen

**exodus** [EK•su•dus] *n*
Massenflucht F

**exonerate** [eg•ZAH•nu•RAIT]
*vt* entlasten

**exotic** [eg•ZAH•tik] *adj*
exotisch

**expand** [ek•SPAND] *vt*
ausbreiten

**expansion** [ek•SPAN•shn] *n*
Ausbreitung F

**expect** [ek•SPEKT] (await) *vt*
erwarten; (supose) annehmen

**expectation**
[EK•SPEK•TAI•shn] *n*
Erwartung F

**expecting** [ek•SPEK•ting] *adj*
erwartet

**expedition** [EK•spu•DI•shn] *n*
Expedition F

**expel** [ek•SPEL] *vt*
hinauswerfen

**expend** [ek•SPEND] *vt*
ausgeben

**expenditure** [ek•SPEN•di•chur]
*n* Ausgabe F

**expense** [ek•SPENS] *n* Kosten;
Spensen N; ~ account *n*\
Spensenkonto N

**expensive** [ek•SPEN•siv] *adj*
teuer

**experience**
[ek•SPEEU•ree•uns] *n*
Erfahrung F; *vt* erleben; (feel)
empfinden

**experienced**
[ek•SPEEU•ree•unst] *adj*
erfahren

**experiment** [ek•SPE•ri•munt] *n*
Probe F

**expert** [EK•spurt] *adj n*
Fachmann M

**expire** [ek•SPUYUR] *vi*
ablaufen

**explain** [ek•SPLAIN] *vt*
erklären

**explanation**
[EK•splu•NAI•shn] *n*
Erklärung F

**explode** [ek•SPLOD] *vt*
explodieren

**exploit** [*n.* EK•sploit *v.*
es•SPLOIT] *n* Ausnutzung F;
(workers) *vt* ausbeuten;
(friends/people) nutzen

**exploration** [EK•splu•RAI•shn]
*n* Erforschung F

**explore** [ek•SPLAUR] *vt vi*
erforschen

**explorer** [ek•SPLAU•rur] *n*
Forscher M

**export** [EK•spaurt] *n* Export M

**expose** [ek•SPOZ] *vt* aussetzen

**exposure** [ek•SPO•zhur] *n*
Entblößung F

**express** [ek•SPRES] *adj*
bestimmt

**expression** [ek•SPRE•shn] *n*
Ausdruck M

**expressive** [ek•SPRE•siv] *adj*
ausdrücklich

**exquisite** [ek•SKWI•zit] *adj*
köstlich

**extend** [ek•STEND] *vt*
ausdehnen

**extension** [ek•STEN•shn] *n*
Ausdehnung F

**extensive** [ek•STEN•siv] *adj*
umfassend

**extent** [ek•STENT] *n* Strecke F

**exterior** [ek•STEEU•ree•ur] *adj*
äußer; *n* Äußere N

**exterminate**
[ek•STUR•mi•NAIT] *vt*
vertilgen

**external** [ek•STUR•nl] *adj*
äußer

**extinct** [ek•STINGKT] *adj*
ausgestorben

**extinguish** [ek•STING•gwish]
*vt* auslöschen

**extort** [ek•STAURT] *vt*
erpressen

**extra** [EK•stru] *adj* zusätzlich

**extract** [*n.* EK•strakt *v.*
ek•STRAKT ] *n* Extrakt M; *vt*
herausziehen

**extradite** [EK•stru•DUYT] *vt*
ausliefern

**extraordinary**
[ek•STRAU•di•NE•ree] *adj*
außerordentlich

**extravagance**
[ek•STRA•vu•guns] *n*
Verschwendung F

**extravagant**
[ek•STRA•vu•gunt] *adj*
verschwenderisch

**extreme** [ek•STREEM] *adj*
äußerst; *n* Äußerste N

**extremist** [ek•STREE•mist] *n*
Fanatiker M; *adj* fanatiker

**extrovert** [EK•stru•VURT] *adj*
*n* Extravertierter M

**exuberant** [eg•ZOO•bu•runt]
*adj* üppig

**exult** [eg•ZUHLT] *vi* jubeln

**eye** [uy] *n* Auge N

**eyewitness** [uy•WIT•nis] *n*
Zeugnis N

**eyeball** [UY•baul] *n*
Augapfel M

**eyebrow** [UY•brou] *n*
Augenbraue F

**eyelash** [UY•lash] *n*
Augenwimper F

**eyelid** [UY•lid] *n* Augenlid N

**eyesight** [UY•suyt] *n*
Sehkraft F

# F

**fable** [FAI•bl] *n* Fabel F

**fabric** [FA•brik] *n* Stoff M

**fabricate** [FA•bri•KAIT] *vt*
fabrizieren

**fabulous** [FA•byu•lus] *adj*
fabelhaft

**facade** [fu•SAHD] *n*
Fassade F

face [fais] n Gesicht N; vt
(opposite) gegenübersein;
(situation) vi liegen

facet [FA•sit] n Seite F

facetious [fu•SEE•shus] adj
witzig

facilities [fu•SI•li•tees] npl
Gefälligkeit F

facing [FAI•sing] prep
Schwenkung F

fact [fakt] n Tatsache F

factor [FAK•tur] n Faktor M

factory [FAK•tu•ree] n Fabrik F

faculty [FA•kul•tee] n
Fakultät F

fad [fad] n Marotte F

fade [faid] vt verblassen

fail [fail] vt durchfallen; vi
keinen Erflog habven

failure [FAIL•yur] n
Unterlassung F

faint [faint] adj schwach

fair 1 [faiur] adj gerecht; fair

fair 2 n Volksfest M;
Rummel M

fairly [FAIUR•lee] adv gerecht

fairy [FAIU•ree] n Fee F

fairy tale [FAIR•ee TAIL] n
Märchen N

faith [faith] n Glaube N

faithful [FAITH•ful] adj treu

fake [faik] falsch

falcon [FAL•kn] n Falke M

fall [faul] n Fall; Sturz M; vi (as
temperature) fallen

fall apart vi auseinanderfallen

fall back vi zurückgreifen auf

fall behind vi in Rückstand
geraten

fall down vi hinfallen

fall for vi sich verknallen in

fall off vi herunterfallen

fall through vi ins Wasser
fallen

false [fauls] adj falsch

falsify [FAUL•si•fuy] vt
fälschen

falter [FAUL•tur] vi schwanken

fame [faim] n Ruhm M

famed [faimd] adj beruhmt

familiar [fu•MI•lyur] adj
bekannt; vertraut

familiarize [fu•MI•lyu•RUYZ]
vt bekannt machen

family [FA•mu•lee] n Familie F

famine [FA•min] n
Hungersnot F

famished [FA•misht] adj
ausgehungert

famous [FAI•mus] adj beruhmt

fan [fan] n Lüfter M

fancy [FAN•see] adj luxus

fang [fang] n Fangzahn M

fantastic [fan•TA•stik] adj
fantastisch

fantasy [FAN•tu•see] n
Phantasie F

far [fahr] adv weit; adj fern

farce [fahrs] n Schwank M

fare [faiur] n Fahrpreis M

farewell [faiur•WEL] n
Lebewohl N

farm [fahrm] n Bauernhof M

farmer [FAHR•mur] n Bauer M

farming [FAHR•ming] n
Landwirtschaft F

farther [FAHR•thur] adj weiter

farthest [FAHR•thist] adj adv
am weitesten

fascinate [FA•si•NAIT] vt
faszinieren

**fascinating** [FA•si•NAI•ting] *adj* faszinierend

**fascination** [FA•si•NAI•shn] *n* Zauber M

**fascism** [FA•shi•zm] *n* Faschismus M

**fashion** [FA•shn] *n* Mode F

**fashionable** [FA•shu•nu•bl] *adj* modern

**fast** [fast] *adj* schnell

**fasten** [FA•sun] *vt* befestigen

**fastidious** [fa•STI•dee•us] *adj* heikel

**fat** [fat] *adj* dick

**fatal** [FAI•tl] *adj* tödlich

**fate** [fait] *n* Schicksal N

**fateful** [FAIT•ful] *adj* schicksalhaft

**father** [FAH•thur] *n* Vater M

**father-in-law** [FA•thur•in•LAU] *n* Schwiegervater M

**fatherland** [FAH•thur•LAND] *n* Vaterland N

**fatherly** [FAH•thur•lee] *adj* väterlich

**fathom** [FA•thum] *n* Faden M

**fatigue** [fu•TEEG] *n* Ermüdung F

**fatten** [FA•tun] *vt* dick machen

**fatuous** [FA•chu•us] *adj* sinnlos

**faucet** [FAU•sit] *n* Zapfern M

**fault** [fault] *n* Schuld F

**faulty** [FAUL•tee] *adj* schadhaft

**fauna** [FAU•nu] *n* Fauna F

**favor** [FAI•vur] *n* Gefallen M

**favorable** [FAI•vru•bl] *adj* günstig

**favorite** [FAI•vrit] *adj n* lieblings

**fawn** [faun] *n* Rehkalb N

**fear** [feeur] *n* Furcht; Angst; *vt* fürchten

**fearful** [FEEUR•ful] *adj* schrekhaft; fruchtbar

**fearless** [FEEUR•lis] *adj* furchtlos

**feasible** [FEE•zu•bl] *adj* möglich

**feast** [feest] *n* Festmahl M

**feat** [feet] *n* Großtat F

**feather** [FE•thur] *n* Feder F

**feature** [FEE•chur] *n* Hauptpunkt M; *vt* bringen

**February** [FE•broo•U•ree] *n* Februar M

**federal** [FE•du•rul] *adj* Bundes

**federation** [FE•du•RAI•shn] *n* Bundesrat M

**fee** [fee] *n* Beitrag M

**feeble** [FEE•bl] *adj* schwach

**feed** [feed] *n* Futter N; *vt* füttern; (insert) führen

**feel** [feeul] *v* fühlen; ~ like\ Lust haben

**feeling** [FEEU•ling] *n* Gefühl N

**feign** [fain] *vt* vortäuschen

**fellow** [FE•lo] *n* Genosse M

**fellowship** [FE•lo•SHIP] *n* Kameradschaft F

**felon** [FE•lun] *n* Verbrecher M

**felt** [felt] *n* Filz M

**female** [FEE•mail] *adj* weiblich

**feminine** [FE•mi•nin] *adj* weiblich

**fence** [fens] *n* Zaun M; *vt* (land) einzäuen

**fencing** [FEN•sing] *n* Fechten N

**fend** [fend] *vi* sich wehren

**fender** [FEN•dur] *n* Schutzblech N

**ferment** [*n.* FUR•ment *v.* fur•MENT] *v* gären; *n* Unruhe F

**fern** [furn] *n* Farn M

**ferocious** [fu•RO•shus] *adj* grausam

**ferret** [FE•rit] *n* Frettchen N

**ferry** [FE•ree] *n* Fähre F

**fertile** [FUR•tl] *adj* fruchtbar

**fertility** [fur•TI•li•tee] *n* Fruchtbarkeit F

**fertilize** [FUR•ti•LUYZ] *vt* befruchten

**fertilizer** [FUR•ti•LUY•zur] *n* Dünger M

**fervent** [FUR•vunt] *adj* glühend

**festival** [FE•sti•vl] *n* Fest N

**festive** [FE•stiv] *adj* festlich

**fetch** [fech] *vt* abholen

**fetus** [FEE•tus] *n* Fötus M

**feud** [fyood] *n* Fehde F

**feudal** [FYOO•dl] *adj* feudal

**fever** [FEE•vur] *n* Fieber N

**feverish** [FEE•vu•rish] *adj* fieberisch

**few** [fyoo] *adj* wenig

**fiancé** [fee•ahn•SAI] *n* Verlobter M

**fiancée** [fee•ahn•SAI] *n* Verlobte F

**fib** [fib] *n* Lüge F

**fiber** [FUY•bur] *n* Textur F

**fickle** [FI•kl] *adj* launenhaft

**fiction** [FIK•shn] *n* Dichtung F

**fiddle** [FI•dl] *n* Fiedel F

**fidelity** [fi•DE•li•tee] *n* Treue F

**fidget** [FI•jit] *vi* unruhig sein

**field** [feeuld] *n* Feld N; (sport) *n* Platz M

**fiend** [feend] *n* Teufel M

**fiendish** [FEEN•dish] *adj* teuflisch

**fierce** [feeurs] *adj* grimmig

**fiery** [FUY•u•ree] *adj* brennend

**fifteen** [fif•TEEN] *num* fünfzehn

**fifteenth** [fif•TEENTH] *num* fünfzehnte

**fifth** [fifth] *num* fünfte

**fiftieth** [FIF•tee•ith] *num* fünfzigste

**fifty** [FIF•tee] *num* fünfzig

**fig** [fig] *n* Feige F

**fight** [fuyt] *n* Streit M

**figurative** [FI•gyu•ru•tiv] *adj* bildlich

**figure** [FI•gyur] *n* Figur F

**figure out** *vt* schlau werden aus

**file** [fuyul] *n* Feile F

**fill** [fil] *vt* füllen

**fillet** [fi•LAI] *n* Roulade F

**filling** [FI•ling] *n* Füllung F

**film** [film] *n* Film M; *vt* filmen

**filter** [FIL•tur] *n* Filter M

**filth** [filth] *n* Schmutz M

**filthy** [FIL•thee] *adj* schmutzig

**fin** [fin] *n* Flosse F

**final** [FUY•nl] *adj* letzt

**finally** [FUY•nu•lee] *adv* endlich

**finance** [fuy•NANS] *n* Finanz F

**financial** [fuy•NAN•shl] *adj* finanziell

**finch** [finch] *n* Fink M

**find** [fuynd] *n* Fund M

**fine 1** [fuyn] *adj* schön

**fine 2** *n* Geldstrafe F

**finger** [FING•gur] *n* Finger M

**fingerprint** [FING•gur•PRINT] *n* Fingerabdruck M

**fingertip** [FING•gur•TIP] *n*
Fingerspitze F

**finish** [FI•nish] *n* Ende·N; *vt*
beenden; *vi* zu Ende sein

**Finland** [FIN•lund] *n* Finnland

**Finn** [fin] *n* Finner

**Finnish** [FI•nish] *adj* finnisch

**fir** [fur] *n* Tanne F

**fire** [fuyur] *n* Feuer N; *vt* (gun)
abschießen

**fire station** [FUYUR
STAI•shn] *n*
Feuerwehrwache F

**fireman** [FUYUR•man] *n*
Feuerwehrmann M

**fireplace** [FUYUR•plais] *n*
Kamin M

**firewood** [FUYUR•wud] *n*
Brennholz N

**fireworks** [FUYUR•wurks] *npl*
Feuerwerk N

**firm 1** [furm] *adj* fest

**firm 2** *n* Firma F

**first** [furst] *adj* erst

**first aid** [FURST AID] *n*
Verbandskasten F

**first name** [FURST NAIM] *n*
Vorname M

**first-class** [FURST•KLAS] *adj*
erster Klasse

**firsthand** [FURST•HAND] *adj*
*adv* direkt

**fiscal** [FI•skl] *adj* fiskalisch

**fish** [fish] *n* Fisch M

**fisherman** [FI•shur•mun] *n*
Fischer M

**fishing** [FI•shing] *n* Fischen N

**fission** [FI•shn] *n* Spaltung F

**fissure** [FI•shur] *n* Spalte F

**fist** [fist] *n* Faust F

**fit 1** [fit] *adj* passend

**fit 2** *n* Anfall M

**fitting room** [FI•ting ~ ] *n*
Probierzimmer N

**five** [fuyv] *num* fünf

**fix** [fiks] *vt* einsetzen

**fixation** [fik•SAI•shn] *n*
Fixierung F

**fixed** [fikst] *adj* befestigt

**fizz** [fiz] *n* Sodawasser N

**flag 1** [flag] *n* Fahne F

**flag 2** *vi* (grow weaker)
nachlassen

**flagpole** [FLAG•pol] *n*
Fahnenstock M

**flagrant** [FLAI•grunt] *adj*
schamlos

**flair** [flaiur] *n* Instinkt M

**flake** [flaik] *n* Flocke F

**flame** [flaim] *n* Flamme F

**flamingo** [flu•MING•go] *n*
Flamingo M

**flammable** [FLA•mu•bl] *adj*
brennbar

**flank** [flangk] *n* Weiche F

**flannel** [FLA•nl] *n* Flanell M

**flap** [flap] *n* Klappe F

**flare** [flaiur] *n* Leuchtsignal N

**flash** [flash] *n* Blitz M

**flashback** [FLASH•bak] *n*
Rückblick M

**flashlight** [FLASH•luyt] *n*
Blitzlicht N

**flashy** [FLA•shee] *adj* glänzend

**flask** [flask] *n* Flasche F

**flat** [flat] *adj* flach

**flatten** [FLA•tn] *vt* abflachen

**flatter** [FLA•tur] *vt* schmeicheln

**flattering** [FLA•tu•ring] *adj*
schmeichelhaft

**flattery** [FLA•tu•ree] *n*
Schmeichelei F

**flaunt** [flaunt] *vt* stolzieren

**flavor** [FLAI•vur] *n*
Geschmack M

**flaw** [flau] *n* Fehler M

**flax** [flaks] *n* Lein M

**flea** [flee] *n* Floh M

**fleck** [flek] *n* Lichtfleck M

**flee** [flee] *vt vi* fliehen

**fleece** [flees] *n* Schaffel N

**fleet** [fleet] *n* Flotte F

**flesh** [flesh] *n* Fleisch N

**fleshy** [FLE•shee] *adj* fleischig

**flex** [fleks] *vt vi* beugen

**flexible** [FLEK•si•bl] *adj*
flexibel

**flicker** [FLI•kur] *vi* Flattern N;
*vi* flackern

**flight** [fluyt] *n* Flug M

**flimsy** [FLIM•zee] *adj*
hauchdünn

**flinch** [flinch] *vi* zurückzucken

**fling** [fling] *vt* wegwerfen

**flint** [flint] *n* Flint M

**flip** [flip] *n* Klaps M

**flippant** [FLI•punt] *adj* keck

**flirt** [flurt] *n* Flirt M

**float** [flot] *vt* überschwemmen

**flock** [flahk] *s* Herde F

**flog** [flahg] *vt* peitschen

**flogging** [FLAH•ging] *n*
Prügel F

**flood** [fluhd] *n* Flut F; *vt*
überschwemmen

**floodlight** [FLUHD•luyt] *n*
Scheinwerfer N

**floor** [flaur] *n* Boden M

**flora** [FLAU•ru] *n* Flora F

**florist** [FLAU•rist] *n*
Blumenhändler M

**floss** [flaus] *n* Flaum M

**flounder** [FLOUN•dur] *n*
Flunder M

**flour** [flouur] *n* Mehl M

**flourish** [FLU•rish] *vi* blühen

**flout** [flout] *vt* spotten

**flow** [flo] *n* Flut F; *vi* fleißen

**flower** [flouur] *n* Blume F

**flown** [flon] (past of fly)
geflogen

**flu** [floo] *n* Grippe F

**fluctuate** [FLUHK•chu•AIT] *vi*
schwanken

**flue** [floo] *n* Rauchfang M

**fluency** [FLOO•un•see] *n*
Fluß M

**fluent** [FLOO•unt] *adj* fließend

**fluff** [fluf] *n* Federflocke F

**fluid** [FLOO•id] *adj* flüssig; *n*
Flüssigkeit F

**fluke** [flook] *n* Zufall M

**fluorescent** [flau•RE•sunt] *adj*
fluoreszierend

**fluoride** [FLAU•ruyd] *n*
Fluorid N

**flurry** [FLU•ree] *n* Windstoß M

**flush** [fluhsh] *vt* spülen

**fluster** [FLUH•stur] *vt*
durcheinanderbringen

**flute** [floot] *n* Flöte F

**flutter** [FLUH•tur] *vi* flattern

**fly** [fluy] *n* Fliegen N

**flying saucer** [FLUY•ing ~ ] *n*
fliegende Untertasse F

**foam** [fom] *n* Schaum M

**focal** [FO•kl] *adj* fokal

**focus** [FO•kus] *n* Fokus M

**fodder** [FAH•dur] *n* Futter N

**foe** [fo] *n* Gegner M

**fog** [fahg] *n* Nebel M

**foil** [foiul] *n* Folie F

**fold** [fold] *n* Falte F; *vt* folden

**folder** [FOLD•er] *n*
Aketenmappe F

**foliage** [FO•lee•ij] *n* Blätter

**folk** [fok] *adj* Volk N

**follow** [FAH•lo] *vt vi* folgen

**follower** [FAH•lo•ur] *n*
Verfolger M

**following** [FAH•lo•ing] *adj*
folgend

**folly** [FAH•lee] *n* Torheit F

**foment** [FO•ment] *vt* bähen

**fond** [fahnd] *adj* liebevoll

**fondle** [FAHN•dl] *vt* liebkosen

**food** [food] *s* Essen N

**fool** [fooul] *n* Narr;
Dummkopf M

**foolish** [FOOU•lish] *adj* albern

**foolproof** [FOOUL•proof] *adj*
narrensicher

**foot** [fut] *n* Fuß M; *vt* (~ the
bill) bezahlen

**football** [FUT•baul] *n*
Fußball M

**footnote** [FUT•not] *n*
Endnote F

**footpath** [FUT•path] *n*
Fußweg M

**footprint** [FUT•print] *n*
Fußspur F

**footstep** [FUT•step] *n* Tritt M

**for** [faur] *prep* für

**forage** [FAU•rij] *n* Futter N; *vi*
nach Futter suchen

**forbid** [faur•BID] *vt* verbieten

**force** [faurs] *n* Kraft F; *vt*
zwingen; (break open) *vt\*
aufbrechen

**forceful** [FAURS•ful] *adj*
kräftig

**forceps** [FAUR•seps] *npl*
Pinzette F

**ford** [faurd] *n* Furt F

**forearm** [FAUR•ahrm] *n*
Unterarm M

**forecast** [FAUR•kast] *n*
Voraussage F

**forefather** [FAUR•fah•thur] *s*
Vorfahren N

**forego** [faur•GO] *vt* vorangehen

**foreground** [FAUR•ground] *n*
Vorgrund M

**forehead** [FAUR•hed] *n*
Stirn M

**foreign** [FAU•run] *adj* fremd;
ausländisch

**foreigner** [FAU•ru•nur] *n*
Ausländer M

**foreman** [FAUR•mun] *n*
Obmann M

**foremost** [FAUR•most] *adj*
vorderst

**forerunner** [FAUU•ruh•nur] *n*
Vorläufer M

**foresee** [faur•SEE] *vt*
voraussehen

**foreshadow** [faur•SHA•do] *vt*
Vorahnung F

**foresight** [FAUR•suyt] *n*
Vorbedacht M

**forest** [FAU•rist] *n* Wald M

**foretell** [faur•TEL] *vt*
voraussagen

**forever** [fu•RE•vur] *adv* ewig

**foreword** [FAUR•wurd] *n*
Vorwort N

**forfeit** [FAUR•fit] *vt* verlieren

**forge** [faurj] *n* Schmiede F; *vt*
schmieden

**forget** [faur•GET] *vt vi*
vergessen

**forgetful** [faur•GET•fuhl] *adj*
vergeßlich

**forgive** [faur•GIV] *vt* vergeben

**forgo** [faur•GO] *vt* aufgeben

**fork** [faurk] *n* Gabel F

**forlorn** [faur•LAURN] *adj* verzweifelt

**form** [faurm] *n* Form F; *vt* bilden

**formal** [FAUR•ml] *adj* formell

**formality** [faur•MA•li•tee] *n* Formalität; F

**former** [FAUR•mur] *adj* ehemalig

**formidable** [FAUR•mi•du•bl] *adj* furchtbar

**formula** [FAUR•myu•lu] *n* Formel F

**forsake** [faur•SAIK] *vt* im Stich lassen

**forsaken** [faur•SAI•kn] *adj* verlassen

**fort** [faurt] *n* Feste F

**forth** [faurth] *adv* weiter

**forthcoming** [faurth•CUH•ming] *adj* bevorstehend

**fortification** [FAUR•ti•fi•KAI•shn] *n* Festigung F

**fortify** [FAUR•ti•FUY] *vt* stärken

**fortitude** [FAUR•ti•TOOD] *n* Fassung F

**fortnight** [FAURT•nuyt] *n* heute in 1 4 Tage

**fortress** [FAUR•tris] *n* Burg F

**fortuitous** [faur•TOO•i•tus] *adj* zufällig

**fortunate** [FAUR•chu•nut] *adj* glücklich

**fortunately** [FAUR•chu•nut•lee] *adv* glücklicherweise

**fortune** [FAUR•chun] *n* Glück N

**forty** [FAUR•tee] *num* vierzig

**forward** [FAUR•wurd] (ahead) *adj* vorwärts; (in place) vordere

**fossil** [FAH•sl] *n* Fossil N

**foul** [foul] *adj* verdorben

**found** [found] gefunden

**foundation** [foun•DAI•shn] *n* Unterbau M

**founder** [FOUN•dur] *n* Gründer M

**fountain** [FOUN•tun] *n* Quelle F

**four** [faur] *num* vier

**fourteen** [faur•TEEN] *num* vierzehn

**fourth** [faurth] *num* vierte

**fowl** [foul] *n* Geflügel N

**fox** [fahks] *n* Fuchs M

**fraction** [FRAK•shn] *n* Fragment N

**fracture** [FRAK•chur] *n* Fraktur F

**fragile** [FRA•jul] *adj* zerbrechlich

**fragment** [FRAG•munt] *n* Fragment N

**fragrance** [FRAI•gruns] *n* Duft M

**fragrant** [FRAI•grunt] *adj* duftend

**frame** [fraim] *n* Rahmen M; *vt* rahmen

**franc** [frangk] *n* Franc M

**France** [frans] *n* Frankreich N

**franchise** [FRAN•chuyz] *n* Bürgerrecht N

**frank** [frangk] *adj* offen

**frantic** [FRAN•tik] *adj* außer sich

**fraternal** [fru•TUR•nl] *adj* brüderlich

**fraternity** [fru•TUR•ni•tee] *n* Orden N

**fraud** [fraud] *n* Betrug M

**fraudulent** [FRAU•dyu•lunt] *adj* betrügerisch

**frayed** [fraid] *adj* durchgescheuert

**freak** [freek] *adj* Laune F

**free** [free] *adj* frei; (costing nothing) kostenlos

**free speech** [free speech] *n* Redefreiheit F

**free trade** [free traid] *n* Freihandel M

**free will** [free wil] *n* freier Wille M

**freedom** [FREE•dum] *n* Freiheit F

**freeze** [freez] *vt* frieren

**freezer** [FREE•zur] *n* Gefrierkammer M

**freight** [frait] *n* Fracht F

**French** [french] *adj* französisch

**french fries** [ ~ fruyz] *npl* pommes frites

**frenzy** [FREN•zee] *n* Wahnsinn M

**frequency** [FREE•kwun•see] *n* Häufigkeit M

**frequent** [adj. FREE•kwunt v. free•KWENT] *adj* häufig

**fresh** [fresh] *adj* frisch

**freshen** [FRE•shn] *vt* erfrischen

**freshman** [FRESH•mun] *n* Student M

**freshness** [FRESH•nus] *n* Frische F

**freshwater** [FRESH•WAU•tur] *adj* Süßwasser N

**fret** [fret] *vi* aufreiben

**friar** [fruyur] *n* Mönch M

**friction** [FRIK•shn] *n* Reibung F

**Friday** [FRUY•dai] *s* Freitag M

**friend** [frend] *n* Freund in M

**friendly** [FREND•lee] *adj* freundlich

**friendship** [FREND•ship] *n* Freundschaft F

**fright** [fruyt] *n* Schreck M

**frighten** [FRUY•tn] *vt* erschrecken

**frightening** [FRUY•tu•ning] *adj* entsetzlich

**frigid** [FRI•jid] *adj* eisig

**fringe** [frinj] *n* Einfassung F

**frisk** [frisk] *vt* herumtanzen

**frisky** [FRI•skee] *adj* munter

**frivolous** [FRI•vu•lus] *adj* leichtfertig

**frog** [frahg] *n* Frosch M

**frolic** [FRAH•lik] *vi* spaßen

**from** [fruhm] *prep* von (place of origin) aus; different ~\ ganz anders (indicating lowest amount) ab +

**front** [fruhnt] *adj* vorne; *n* Vorderseite F

**front door** [frunt dor] *n* Vordertür MF

**frontier** [fruhn•TEER] *n* Grenzgebiet N

**frost** [fraust] *n* Frost M

**frostbite** [FRAUST•buyt] *n* Erfrierung F

**froth** [frauth] *n* Schaum M

**frown** [froun] *n* Stirnrunzeln N

**frugal** [FROO•gl] *adj* sparsam

**fruit** [froot] *n* Frucht F; Obst N

**fruitless** [FROOT•lis] *adj*
vergeblich

**frustrate** [FRUH•strait] *vt*
frustrieren

**frustration** [fruh•STRAI•shn] *n*
Behinderung F

**fry** [fruy] *vt vi* braten

**fudge** [fuj] *n* Karamel M; *excl*
Quatsch!

**fuel** [fyooul] *n* Brennstoff M

**fugitive** [FYOO•ju•tiv] *n*
Flüchtling M

**fulfill** [ful•FIL] *vt* erfüllen

**fulfillment** [ful•FIL•munt] *n*
Erfüllung F

**full** [ful] *adj* voll; in ~\ vollst
ändig

**full moon** [FUL MOON] *n*
Vollmond M

**full-time** [ful•TUYM] *adj adv*
hauptberuflich

**fully** [FU•lee] *adv* völlig

**fumble** [FUHM•bl] *vt* sich
ungeschikt anstellen

**fumes** [fyoomz] *npl* Dampf M

**fumigate** [FYOO•mi•GAIT] *vt*
ausräuchern

**fun** [fuhn] *adj* Spaß M

**function** [FUNGK•shn] *n*
Tätigkeit F; *vi* funktionieren

**fund** [fuhnd] *n* Kapital N;
Fonds M

**fundamental** [FUHN•du•
MEN•tl] *adj* grundlegend

**funeral** [FYOO•nu•rul] *n*
Begräbnis N

**fungus** [FUNG•gus] *n*
Schwamm M

**funnel** [FUH•nl] *n*
Rauchabzug M

**funny** [FUH•nee] *adj* komisch

**fur** [fur] *n* Pelz M

**furious** [FYOOU•ree•us] *adj*
wütend

**furnace** [FUR•nis] *n*
Brennofen M

**furnish** [FUR•nish] *vt* ausstatten

**furniture** [FUR•ni•chur] *n*
Möbel F

**furry** [FU•ree] *adj* pelzartig

**further** [FUR•thur] *adj* weiter

**furthermore**
[FUR•thur•MAUR] *adv*
außerdem

**furthest** [FUR•thist] *adj adv* am
weitesten

**furtive** [FUR•tiv] *adj* heimlich

**fury** [FYU•ree] *n* Zorn M

**fuse** [fyooz] *n* Zünder M

**fusion** [FYOO•zhn] *n*
Schmelzen N

**fuss** [fuhs] *n* Aufregung F

**futile** [FYOO•tl] *adj* zwecklos

**future** [FYOO•chur] *adj*
zukünftig

**fuzzy** [FUH•zee] *adj* undeutlich

# G

**gable** [GAI•bl] *n* Giebel M

**gadget** [GA•jit] *n* Apparat M

**Gaelic** [GAIU•lik] *adj n*
Gälisch M

**gag** [gag] *n* Knebel M; *vt* gebeln

**gauge** [gaij] *n* Meßgerät N

**gain** [gain] *n* Steigerung F

**gait** [gait] *n* Gang M

**gale** [gaiul] *n* Sturm M

**gall** [gaul] *n* Galle F

**gallant** [GA•lunt] *adj* ritterlich

**gallery** [GA•lu•ree] *n* Gallerie F

**galley** [GA•lee] *n* Langboot N

**gallon** [GA•ln] *n* Galon M

**gallop** [GA•lup] *n* Galopp M

**gallows** [GA•loz] *npl* Galgen M

**gamble** [GAM•bl] *n* aufs Spiel setzen

**game** [gaim] *n* Spiel N; *adj* (brave) mutig

**gang** [gang] *n* Gruppe F

**gangster** [GANG•stur] *n* Gangster M

**gangway** [GANG•wai] *n* Durchgang M

**gap** [gap] *n* Lücke F

**gape** [gaip] *vi* staunen

**gaping** [GAI•ping] *adj* weit offen

**garage** [gu•RAHZH] *n* Garage F

**garbage** [GAHR•bij] *n* Müll M

**garbage can** [GAHR•bij KAN] *n* Mülleimer M

**garden** [GAHR•dn] *n* Garten M

**gargle** [GAHR•gl] *vi* ausspülen

**gargoyle** [GAHR•goil] *n* Wasserspeier M

**garland** [GAHR•lund] *n* Girlande F

**garlic** [GAHR•lik] *n* Knoblauch M

**garment** [GAHR•munt] *n* Kleidungsstück N

**garnish** [GAHR•nish] *v* schmücken; garnieren

**garrison** [GA•ri•sn] *n* Besatzung F

**garter** [GAHR•tr] *n* Strumpfband N

**gas** [gas] *n* Gas N

**gaseous** [GA•shs] *adj* gasartig

**gasket** [GA•skit] *n* Dichtungsmanschette F

**gasoline** [GA•su•LEEN] *n* Benzin M

**gasp** [gasp] *vi* nach Luft schnappen

**gate** [gait] *n* Tor N

**gather** [GA•thur] *vi* versammeln

**gathering** [GA•thu•ring] *n* Versammlung F

**gaudy** [GAU•dee] *adj* schmacklos

**gaunt** [gaunt] *adj* hager

**gauntlet** [GAUNT•lit] *n* Fehdehandschuh M

**gauze** [gauz] *n* Gaze F

**gay** [gai] *adj* lustig

**gaze** [gaiz] *vt* starren

**gazette** [gu•ZET] *n* Zeitung F

**gear** [geeur] *n* Triebwerk N

**gelatin** [JE•lu•tin] *n* Gelatine F

**gem** [jem] *n* Edelstein M

**gender** [JEN•dur] *n* Geschlecht N

**gene** [jeen] *n* Erbeinheit F

**general** [JE•nu•rl] *adj n* allgemein

**generalization** [JEN•ru•li•ZAI•shn] *n* Verallgemeinerung F

**generalize** [JE•nu•ru•LUYZ] *vt*
   verallgemeinern

**generally** [JE•nu•ru•lee] *adv* im
   allgemeinen

**generate** [JE•nu•RAIT] *vt*
   erzeugen

**generation** [JE•nu•RAI•shn] *n*
   Generation F

**generator** [JE•nu•RAI•tur] *n*
   Gaserzeuger M

**generosity** [JE•nu•RAH•si•tee]
   *n* Großzügigkeit F

**generous** [JE•nu•rus] *adj*
   großzügig

**genetic** [ji•NE•tik] *adj*
   genetisch

**genial** [JEE•nyul] *adj* freundlich

**genital** [JE•ni•tl] *adj*
   Geschlechts

**genius** [JEE•nyus] *n* Genie F

**gentle** [JEN•tl] *adj* sanft

**gentleman** [JEN•tl•mun] *n*
   Ehrenmann

**gently** [JENT•lee] *adv* zart

**gentry** [JEN•tree] *n* Adel M

**genuine** [JE•nyoo•in] *adj* echt

**geography** [jee•AH•gru•fee] *n*
   Geographie F

**geology** [jee•AH•lu•jee] *n*
   Geologie F

**geometric** [JEE•u•ME•trik] *adj*
   geometrisch

**geometry** [jee•AH•mu•tree] *n*
   Geometrie F

**germ** [jerm] *n* Keim M

**German** [JER•mun] *adj* deutsch

**Germany** [JER•mu•nee] *n*
   Deutschland

**germinate** [JER•mi•NAIT] *vi*
   keimen

**gesticulate** [je•STI•kyu•LAIT]
   *vi* gestikulieren

**gesture** [JES•chur] *n* Geste F;
   *vi* gestickulieren

**get** [get] *vt* bekommen; kriegen;
   (obtain) sich besorgen; (fetch)
   holen; (prepare) machen;
   (understand) kapieren

**ghastly** [GAST•lee] *adj*
   entsetzlich

**ghost** [gost] *n* Geist M

**giant** [JUY•unt] *adj n* Riese M

**gibberish** [JI•bu•rish] *n*
   Geschwafel N

**giddy** [GI•dee] *adj* schwindlig

**gift** [gift] *n* Geschenk N

**gifted** [GIF•tid] *adj* begabt

**gigantic** [juy•GAN•tik] *adj*
   gigantisch

**giggle** [GI•gl] *vi* kichern

**gilded** [GIL•did] *adj* vergoldet

**ginger** [JIN•jur] *n* Ingwer M

**gingerbread** [JIN•jur•BRED] *n*
   Pfefferkuchen M

**gingerly** [JIN•jur•lee] *adv*
   behutsam

**gipsy** [JIP•see] *n* Zigeuner in M

**giraffe** [ji•RAF] *n* Giraffe F

**girder** [GUR•dur] *n* Träger M

**girdle** [GUR•dl] *n* Gurt M

**girl** [gurl] *n* Mädchen N;
   Tochter F

**girlfriend** [GURL•frend] *n*
   Freundin F

**girth** [gurth] *n* Umfang M

**gist** [jist] *n* Wesentliche N

**give** [giv] *vt* geben; *vi* (spend)
   spenden

**give in** (surrender) sich
   ergeben

**give up** *vi* aufgeben

**given** [GI•vn] *prep* gegeben

**glacier** [GLAI•shur] *n*
Gletscher M

**glad** [glad] *adj* froh

**gladly** [GLAD•lee] *adv* gerne

**glamor** [GLA•mur] *n* Glanz M

**glamorous** [GLA•mu•rus] *adj*
schön

**glance** [glans] *n* Blick M

**gland** [gland] *n* Drüse F

**glare** [glaiur] *n* Glanz M; *vi*
grell scheinen

**glaring** [GLAIU•ring] *adj* grell

**glass** [glas] *n* Glas N

**glasses** [GLA•siz] *npl* Brille F

**glassy** [GLA•see] *adj* glasartig

**glaze** [glaiz] *n* Glasur F

**gleam** [gleem] *n* Schimmer M

**glean** [gleen] *vt* auflesen

**glee** [glee] *n* Fröhlichkeit F

**glib** [glib] *adj* leichtfertig

**glide** [gluyd] *vi* gleiten

**glimmer** [GLI•mur] *n*
Schimmer M

**glimpse** [glimps] *n* Anblick M

**glisten** [GLI•sn] *vi* glitzern

**glitter** [GLI•tur] *v* funkeln

**gloat** [glot] *vi* sich weiden an

**global** [GLO•bl] *adj*
weltumfassend

**globe** [glob] *n* Erdkugel F

**gloom** [gloom] *n* Düsterkeit F

**gloomy** [GLOO•mee] *n* düster

**glorify** [GLAU•ri•FUY] *vt*
preisen

**glorious** [GLAU•ree•us] *adj*
herrlich

**glory** [GLAU•ree] *n* Ruhm M

**gloss** [glaus] *n* Glanz M

**glossary** [GLAU•su•ree] *n*
Glossar N

**glossy** [GLAU•see] *adj* glatt

**glove** [gluhv] *n* Handschuh M

**glow** [glo] *n* Glühen N

**glowing** [GLO•wing] *adj*
glühend

**glucose** [GLOO•kos] *n*
Traubenzucker M

**glue** [gloo] *n* Klebstoff M

**glum** [gluhm] *adj* finster

**glut** [gluht] *n* Überfluß M

**glutton** [GLUH•tn] *n*
Vielfraß M

**gluttonous** [GLUH•tu•nus] *adj*
gierig

**gluttony** [GLUH•tu•nee] *n*
Eßlust F

**gnarled** [nahrld] *adj* knorrig

**gnash** [nash] *vt* knirschen

**gnat** [nat] *n* Steckmücke F

**gnaw** [nau] *vt* nagen an

**go** o *vi* gehen; (disappear)
weggehen

**go-between**
[GO•buh•TWEEN] *s*
vermitteln zwischen

**goal** [goul] *n* Ziel N

**goat** [got] *n* Ziege F

**gobble** [GAH•bl] *vt* kollern

**goblin** [GAH•blin] *n* Elf M

**God·** [gahd] *n* Gott M

**goddaughter**
[GAHD•DAU•tur] *n*
Patentochter F

**goddess** [GAH•dis] *n* Göttin F

**godfather** [GAHD•FAH•thur] *n*
Pate M

**godless** [GAHD•lis] *adj* gottlos

**godmother**
[GAHD•MUH•thur] *n* Patin F

**godsend** [GAHD•send] *n*
Glücksfall M

goggles [GAH•glz] npl
Schwimmbrille F

gold [gould] n Gold M

gold-plated [GOLD•PLAI•tid]
adj vergoldet

golden [GOL•dn] adj golden

goldfish [GOLD•fish] n
Goldfisch M

golf [gahlf] n Golf M

gong [gahng] n Gong M

good [gud] adj gut

good-looking [GUD•LU•king]
adj gutaussehend

goose [goos] n Gans F

gore [gaur] vt durchbohren

gorge [gaurj] n Hohlkehle F

gorgeous [GAUR•jus] adj
prachtvoll

gorilla [gu•RI•lu] n Gorilla M

gory [GAU•ree] adj mörderisch

gospel [GAH•spl] n
Evangelium N

gossip [GAH•sip] n Klatsch M

gothic [GAH•thik] adj gotisch

gourd [gaurd] n Kürbis M

gout [gout] n Gicht F

govern [GUH•vurn] vt vi
verwalten

governess [GUH•vur•nis] n
Hauslehrerin F

government [GUH•vurn•munt]
n Regierung F

governor [GUH•vur•nur] n
Gouverneur M

gown [goun] n Damenkleid N

grab [grab] vt greifen

grace [grais] n Gnade F

graceful [GRAIS•ful] adj
anmutig

gracious [GRAI•shus] adj
barmherzig

grade [graid] n Stufe F

grade school [GRAID skool] n
Grundschule F

gradual [GRA•joo•ul] adj
stufenweise

graduate [n. GRA•joo•it v.
GRA•joo•AIT] v matrikulieren

graft [graft] n Pfropfen N

grain [grain] n Getreide N

gram [gram] n Gramm M

grammar [GRA•mur] n
Grammatik F

grammatical [gru•MA•ti•kl]
adj grammatisch

granary [GRAI•nu•ree] n
Kornkammer F

grand [grand] adj großartig

granddaughter
[GRAN•DAU•tur] n
Enkelkind N

grandeur [GRAN•jur] n
Hoheit F

grandfather
[GRAND•FAH•thur] n
Großvater M

grandiose [GRAN•dee•OS] adj
prunkvoll

grandma [GRAND•mah] n
Oma F

grandmother
[GRAND•MUH•thur] n
Großmutter F

grandpa [GRAND•pah] n
Opa M

grandparents
[GRAND•PA•runts] npl
Großeltern M

grandson [GRAND•suhn] n
Enkelkind N

granite [GRA•nit] n Granit M

grant [grant] n Gewährung F

**granule** [GRA•nyoo•ul] *n*
Körnchen N

**grape** [graip] *n* Traube F

**grapefruit** [GRAIP•froot] *n*
Pampelmuse F

**graph** [graf] *n* Schaubild N

**graphic** [GRA•fik] *adj*
graphisch

**grapple** [GRA•pl] *vi*
verklammern

**grasp** [grasp] *vt* ergreifen; *n*
Griff M

**grass** [gras] *n* Gras N

**grasshopper** [GRAS•HAH•pur]
*n* Grashüpfer M

**grassy** [GRA•see] *adj*
grasbedeckt

**grate** [grait] *n* Gitter N

**grateful** [GRAIT•ful] *adj*
dankbar

**grater** [GRAI•tur] *n* Reibe F

**gratification**
[GRA•ti•fi•KAI•shn] *n*
Befriedigung F

**grating** [GRAI•ting] *adj*
kratzend

**gratitude** [GRA•ti•TOOD] *n*
Dankbarkeit F

**gratuity** [gru•TOO•i•tee] *n*
Trinkgeld N

**grave** [graiv] *adj* feierlich

**gravel** [GRA•vl] *n* Kies M

**gravity** [GRA•vi•tee] *n*
Schwerkraft F

**gravy** [GRAI•vee] *n*
Bratensaft F

**gray** [grai] *adj* grau; *n* Graue N

**graze** [graiz] *vt* abgrasen

**grease** [grees] *n* Schmalz N

**great** [grait] *adj* groß;
(excellent) Klasse

**Great Britain** [ ~ BRI•tn] *n*
Groß Britanien

**great-granddaughter**
[GRAIT•GRAN•DAW•tur] *n*
Urenkelin F

**great-grandfather**
[GRAIT•GRAND•FA•thur] *n*
Urgroßvater M

**great-grandmother**
[GRAIT•GRAND•MU•thur] *n*
Urgroßmutter F

**great-grandparents**
[GRAIT•GRAND•PAI•rintz]
*npl* Urgroßeltern

**great-grandson**
[GRAIT•GRAND•son] *n*
Urgroßenkel M

**greatness** [GRAIT•nis] *n*
Größe F

**Greece** [grees] *n*
Griechenland N

**greed** [greed] *n* Gier F

**greedy** [GREE•dee] *adj* gierig

**Greek** [greek] *adj* griechisch

**green** [green] *adj* grün; *n*
Grüne N

**greenhouse** [GREEN•hous] *n*
Gewächshaus N

**Greenland** [GREEN•lund] *n*
Grünland

**greet** [greet] *vt* begrüßen

**greeting** [GREE•ting] *n*
Begrüßung F

**grenade** [gru•NAID] *n*
Handgranate M

**grid** [grid] *n* Bleiplatte F

**grief** [greef] *n* Kummer M

**grievance** [GREE•vuns] *n*
Beschwerde F

**grieve** [greev] *vt* bekümmern

**grievous** [GREE•vus] *adj*
schmerzlich

**grill** [gril] *n* Rost M

**grille** [gril] *n* Gitterfenster N

**grim** [grim] *adj* erbarmungslos

**grimace** [gri•mus] *n* Grimasse F

**grime** [gruym] *n* Schmutz M

**grimy** [GRUY•mee] *adj*
schmutzig

**grin** [grin] *n* Grinsen N

**grind** [gruynd] *vt* mahlen

**grinder** [GRUYN•dur] *n*
Mahlwerk N

**grip** [grip] *n* Griff M

**gripe** [gruyp] *n* Leibweh N

**grisly** [GRIZ•lee] *adj* gräßlich

**gristle** [GRI•sl] *n* Knorpel M

**grit** [grit] *n* Kies M

**groan** [gron] *n* Stöhnen N

**groceries** [GROS•reez] *npl*
Lebensmittel N

**grocery** [GROS•ree] *n*
Lebensmittelgeschäft N

**groin** [groin] *n* Leiste F

**groom** [groom] *n* Bräutigam M;
*vt* (horse) striegen; well ~ed\
*adj* gepflegt

**groove** [groov] *n* Rinne F

**grope** [grop] *vi* herumsuchen

**gross 1** [gros] *n* Gros N

**gross 2** *adj* fett; feist

**grotesque** [gro•TESK] *adj*
grotesk

**grouch** [grouch] *n*
Miesepeter M

**ground** [ground] *n* Boden M;
(reason) *n* Grund M

**ground floor** [GROUND
·FLOR] *s* Erdgeschoß N

**groundless** [GROUND•lis] *adj*
grundlos

**group** [groop] *n* Gruppe F

**grove** [grov] *n* Hain M

**grovel** [GRAH•vl] *vi* am Boden
kriechen

**grow** [gro] *vt* wachsen

**growl** [grouul] *n* Brummen N

**growth** [groth] *n* Wachsen N

**grub** [gruhb] *n* Larve F

**grubby** [GRUH•bee] *adj*
schlampig

**grudge** [gruhj] *n* Mißgunst F

**grueling** [GROOU•ling] *adj*
tödlich

**gruff** [gruhf] *adj* schroff

**grumble** [GRUHM•bl] *vi*
murren

**grumpy** [GRUHM•pee] *adj*
verdrießlich

**grunt** [gruhnt] *n* Grunzen N

**guarantee** [GA•run•TEE] *n*
Garantie F

**guard** [gahrd] *n* Bahnwärter M

**guardien** [GAHR•dee•un] *n*
Hüter M

**guerrilla** [gu•RI•lu] *n* Partisan M

**guess** [ges] *n* Schätzung F

**guest** [gest] *n* Gast M

**guestroom** [GEST•ROOM] *n*
Gästezimmer N

**guffaw** [guh•FAU] *vi*
Gelächter N

**guidance** [GUY•duns] *n*
Leitung F

**guide** [guyd] *vt* führen

**guild** [gild] *n* Vereinigung F

**guile** [guyul] *n* List F

**guillotine** [GI•lu•TEEN] *n*
Guillotine F

**guilt** [gilt] *n* Schuld F

**guilty** [GIL•tee] *adj* schuldig

**guinea pig** [GI•nee ~ ] *n*
Meerschweinchen N
**guise** [guyz] *n* Gestalt F
**guitar** [gi•TAHR] *n* Guitarre F
**gulf** [guhlf] *n* Golf M
**gullet** [GUH•lit] *n*
Speiseröhre F
**gullible** [GUH•li•bl] *adj* naiv
**gully** [GUH•lee] *n*
Wasserrinne F
**gulp** [guhlp] *n* Schluck M
**gum** [guhm] *n* Gummi N
**gun** [guhn] *n* Pistole F
**gunfire** [GUHN•fuyur] *n*
Geschützfeuer N
**gunpowder** [GUHN•pow•dur]
*n* Schießpulver N
**gunshot** [GUHN•shaht] *n*
Schuß M

**gurgle** [GUR•gl] *vi* gurgeln
**gush** [guhsh] *n* Guß M
**gusset** [GUH•sit] *n* Zwickel M
**gust** [guhst] *n* Windstoß M
**gut** [guht] *n* Darm M
**gutter** [GUH•tur] *n*
Dachrinne F
**guy** [guy] *n* Kerl M
**guzzle** [GUH•zl] *vt* saufen
**gym** [jim] *n* Turnhalle F
**gymnasium** [jim•NAI•zee•um]
*n* Turnhalle F
**gymnast** [JIM•nust] *n*
Turner-in M
**gymnastics** [jim•NA•stiks] *npl*
turnerisch
**gypsy** [JIP•see] *n* Zigeuner F
**gyrate** [JUY•rait] *vi* wirbeln

# H

**habit** [HA•bit] *n* Gewohnheit F
**habitual** [hu•BI•choo•ul] *adj*
üblich
**hack** [hak] *vt* hacken
**hackneyed** [HAK•need] *adj*
abgenutzt
**hacksaw** [HAK•sau] *n*
Bügelsäge F
**haggard** [HA•gurd] *adj* hager
**haggle** [HA•gl] *vi* handeln um
**hail** [haiul] *n* Hagel M
**hailstone** [HAIUL•ston] *n*
Hagelstein M
**hair** [haiur] *n* Haar N
**hairbrush** [HAIUR•bruhsh] *n*
Haarbürste F

**haircut** [HAIUR•kuht] *n*
Haarschnitt M
**hairdresser** [HAIUR•DRE•sur]
*n* Friseur-in M
**hairless** [HAIUR•lis] *adj* kahl
**hairpin** [HAIUR•pin] *n*
Haarnadel F
**hairspry** [HAIUR•sprai] *n*
Spritz M
**hairstyle** [HAIUR•stuyul] *n*
Haarschnitt M
**hairy** [HAIUR•ee] *adj* haarig
**Haiti** [HAI•tee] *n* Haiti
**half** [haf] *adj* halb
**half-hearted** [-HAR•tid] *adj*
mit halbem Herzen

**half hour** [HAF OUR] *n* halbe
Stunde F

**half-mast** [HAF•MAST] *adj*
Halbmast M

**half-price** [HAF•PRUYS] *adj*
zum halben Preis

**halfway** [HAF•WAI] *adj adv*
auf halbem Weg

**halibut** [HA•li•but] *n*
Heilbutt M

**hall** [haul] *n* Saal M

**hallowed** [HA•lod] *adj* heiligt

**Halloween** [HAH•lo•WEEN] *n*
Allerheiligen

**hallucination**
[hu•LOO•si•NAI•shn] *n*
Wahnvorstellung F

**hallway** [HAUL•wai] *n* Diele F

**halo** [HAI•lo] *n* Halo M

**halt** [hault] *n* Halt M

**halter** [HAUL•tur] *n* Strick M

**halve** [hav] *vt* halbieren

**ham** [ham] *n* Schinken N

**hamburger** [HAM•BUR•gur] *n*
Frikadelle F

**hamlet** [HAM•lit] *n* Weiler M

**hammer** [HA•mur] *n*
Hammer M

**hammock** [HA•muk] *n*
Hängematte F

**hamper** [HAM•pur] *n* Korb M

**hand** [hand] *n* Hand F; *vt*
reichen; geben

**handbag** [HAND•bag] *n*
Tasche F

**handcuff** [HAND•kuhf] *n*
Handschellen

**handful** [HAND•ful] *n*
Handvoll F

**handicap** [HAN•dee•KAP] *n*
Behinderung F

**handicapped**
[HAN•dee•KAPT] *adj*
behindert

**handkerchief** [HANG•kur•chif]
*n* Handtuch N

**handle** [HAN•dl] *n* Griff M; *vt*
anfassen; (deal with)
anpacken

**handmade** [HAND•MAID] *adj*
von Hand gemacht

**handshake** [HAND•shaik] *n*
Händedruck M

**handwriting**
[HAND•WRUY•ting] *n*
Handschrift F

**handy** [HAN•dee] *adj* greifbar

**hang** [hang] *vt* hängen

**hangar** [HANG•ur] *n*
Flugzeughalle F

**hanger** [HANG•ur] *n*
Kleiderbügel M

**hangover** [HANG•O•vur] *n*
Katzenjammer M

**haphazard** [hap•HA•zurd] *adj*
zufällig

**hapless** [HAP•lis] *adj*
unglücklich

**happen** [HA•pn] *vi* passieren

**happening** [HA•pu•ning] *n*
Ereignis N

**happily** [HA•pi•lee] *adv*
glücklich

**happiness** [HA•pee•nis] *n*
Glücklichkeit F

**happy** [HA•pee] *adj* glücklich;
froh

**harass** [hu•RAS] *vt* belästigen

**harassment** [hu•RAS•munt] *n*
Störung F

**harbor** [HAHR•bur] *n* Hafen M

**hard** [hahrd] *adj* hart

**harden** [HAHR•din] *vt* härten

**hardly** [HAHRD•lee] *adv* kaum

**hardship** [HAHRD•ship] *n*
Not F

**hardware** [HAHRD•waiur] *n*
Eisenwaren

**hardworking**
[HAHRD•WUR•king] *adj*
fleißig

**hardy** [HAHR•dee] *adj* kräftig

**hare** [haiur] *n* Hase M

**harm** [hahrm] *n* Schaden M

**harmful** [HAHRM•ful] *adj*
schädlich

**harmless** [HAHRM•lis] *adj*
harmlos

**harmonica** [hahr•MAH•ni•ku] *n*
Glasharmonika F

**harmonious** [hahr•MO•nee•us]
*adj* harmonisch

**harmonize** [HAHR•mu•NUYZ]
*vt* harmonieren

**harmony** [HAHR•mu•nee] *n*
Harmonie F

**harness** [HAHR•nis] *n*
Geschirr N

**harp** [hahrp] *n* Harfe F

**harpoon** [hahr•POON] *n*
Harpune F

**harpsichord**
[HARP•si•KAURD] *n*
Cembalo N

**harsh** [hahrsh] *adj* rauh

**harvest** [HAHR•vist] *n* Ernte F

**haste** [haist] *n* Eile F

**hasten** [HAI•sn] *vt* sich beeilen

**hastily** [HAI•sti•lee] *adv* eilig

**hat** [hat] *n* Hut M

**hatch** [hach] *vt* ausbrüten

**hatchet** [HA•chit] *n* Beil N

**hate** [hait] *n* Haß M

**hateful** [HAIT•ful] *adj* verhaßt

**hatred** [HAI•trid] *n* Haß M

**haughty** [HAU•tee] *adj*
hochmütig

**haul** [haul] *vt* schleppen

**haunt** [haunt] *vt* quälen

**have** [hav] *aux verb* haben;
*modal aux* I ~ to\ ich muß

**haven** [HAI•vn] *n*
Zufluchtsort M

**havoc** [HA•vuk] *n* Zerstörung F

**hawk** [hauk] *n* Falke M

**hay** [hai] *n* Heu N

**haystack** [HAI•stak] *n*
Heuschober M

**hazard** [HA•zurd] *n* Gefahr F

**hazardous** [HA•zur•dus] *adj*
gefährlich

**haze** [haiz] *n* Dunst M

**hazelnut** [HAI•zl•NUHT] *n*
Haselnuß F

**hazy** [HAI•zee] *adj* dunstig

**he** [hee] *pers pron* er

**head** [hed] *n* Kopf M

**headache** [HE•daik] *n*
Kopfschmerz M

**heading** [HE•ding] *n* Titel M

**headlight** [HED•luyt] *n*
Scheinwerfer M

**headline** [HED•luyn] *n*
Schlagzeile F

**headphones** [HED•fonz] *npl*
Kopfhörer M

**headquarters**
[HED•KAUR•turz] *npl*
Hauptquartier N

**headrest** [HED•rest] *n*
Kopflehne F

**headstrong** [HED•straung] *adj*
eigensinnig

**headway** [HED•wai] *n*
Fortschritt M

**heal** [heeul] *vt* heilen

**health** [helth] *n* Gesundheit F

**healthy** [HEL•thee] *adj* gesund

**heap** [heep] *n* Haufen M

**hear** [heeur] *vt* hören

**hearing** [HEEU•ring] *n*
Hören N

**hearsay** [HEEUR•sai] *n*
Gerücht M

**hearse** [hurs] *n* Leichenwagen M

**heart** [hahrt] *n* Herz N

**heart attack** [HART A•tak] *n*
Herzanfall M

**heartbeat** [HAHRT•beet] *n*
Herzschlag

**heartbroken** [hahrt•BRO•kn]
*adj* untröstlich

**hearth** [hahrth] *n* Kamin M

**heartless** [HAHRT•lis] *adj*
herzlos

**heartwarming**
[HAHRT•WAR•ming] *adj*
herzlich

**hearty** [HAHR•tee] *adj* warm

**heat** [heet] *n* Hitze F

**heater** [HEE•tur] *n*
Heizgerät N

**heather** [HE•thur] *n*
Heidekraut N

**heating** [HEE•ting] *n*
Heizung F

**heat wave** [HEET WAIV] *n*
Hitzewelle F

**heave** [heev] *vt* hochheben

**heaven** [HE•vn] *n* Himmel M

**heavenly** [HE•vn•lee] *adj*
himmlich

**heavily** [HE•vu•lee] *adv* schwer

**heavy** [HE•vee] *adj* schwer

**heckle** [HE•kl] *vt* durch
Zwischenfragen belästigen

**hectic** [HEK•tik] *adj* hiktisch

**hedge** [hej] *n* Hecke F

**hedgehog** [HEJ•hahg] *n*
Igel M

**heed** [heed] *vt* beachten

**height** [huyt] *n* Höhe F

**heighten** [HUY•tn] *vt* erhöhen

**heir** [aiur] *n* Erbe M

**heiress** [AIU•ress] *n* Erbin F

**heirloom** [AIUR•loom] *n*
Erbstück N

**helicopter** [HE•li•KAHP•tur] *n*
Hubschrauber M

**hell** [hel] *n* Hölle F

**hellish** [HE•lish] *adj* höllisch

**hello** [hu•LO] *excl* Hallo

**helm** [helm] *n* Ruder N

**helmet** [HEL•mit] *n* Helm M

**help** [help] *n* Hilfe F; *vt vi*
helfen

**helper** [HEL•pur] *n* Helfer
-in M

**helping** [HEL•ping] *adj*
hilfreich

**helpless** [HELP•lis] *adj* hilflos

**hem** [hem] *n* Saum M

**hemisphere** [HE•mis•FEEUR]
*n* Hemisphäre F

**hemorrhage** [HE•mu•rij] *s*
Blütung F

**hemorrhoids** [HE•mu•roidz]
*npl* Hämorrhoiden

**hen** [hen] *n* Henne F

**hen-house** [HEN•hous] *n*
Hühnerstall M

**hence** [hens] *adv* von hier

**henceforth** [HENS•faurth] *adv*
fortan

**her** [hur] *pers pron* ihr; sie

**herald** [HE•ruld] *n* Herold M
**heraldry** [HE•rul•dree] *n* Wappenkunde F
**herb** [urb] *n* Kraut N
**herbal** [UR•bl] *adj* kräuter
**herd** [hurd] *n* Herde F
**here** [heeur] *adv* hier
**hereby** [heer•BUY] hiermit
**hereditary** [he•RE•di•TE•ree] *adj* vererbt
**heredity** [he•RE•di•tee] *n* Vererbung F
**herein** [heer•IN] hierin
**heresy** [HE•ru•see] *n* Irrlehre F
**herewith** [heeur•WITH] *adv* hiermit
**heritage** [HE•ri•tij] *n* Erbschaft F
**hermit** [HUR•mit] *n* Einsiedler M
**hernia** [HUR•nee•u] *n* Hernie F
**hero** [HEEU•ro] *n* Held M
**heroic** [hu•RO•ik] *adj* heroisch
**heroin** [HE•ro•in] *n* Heroin N
**heroine** [HE•ro•in] *n* Heldin F
**heroism** [HE•ro•I•zm] *n* Heldentum N
**heron** [HE•run] *n* Reiher M
**herring** [HE•ring] *n* Hering M
**hers** [hurz] *poss pron* ihrer e es
**herself** [hur•SELF] *pron* sich
**hesitant** [HE•zi•tunt] *adj* zögernd
**hesitate** [HE•zi•TAIT] *vi* zögern
**hesitation** [HE•zi•TAI•shn] *n* Zögern N
**heterosexual** [HE•tu•ro•SEK•shoo•ul] *adj n* heterosexuell

**hexagon** [HEK•su•GAHN] *n* Sechseck N
**hey** [hai] *excl* hei!
**heyday** [HAI•dai] *n* Höhepunkt M
**hibernate** [HUY•bur•NAIT] *vi* überwintern
**hibernation** [HUY•bur•NAI•shn] *n* Winterschlaf M
**hiccup** [HI•kuhp] *n* Schluckauf M
**hidden** [HI•dn] *adj* verborgen
**hide** [huyd] *vt* verstecken
**hideous** [HI•dee•us] *adj* abscheulich
**hiding** [HUY•ding] *n* Versteck N
**hiding place** [HUY•ding PLAIS] *n* Versteckplatz M
**hierarchy** [HUYU•RAHR•kee] *n* Hierarchie F
**high** [huy] *adj* hoch
**high school** [HUY skool] *n* Hochschule F
**highlight** [HUY•luyt] *n* Schlaglicht N
**highly** [HUY•lee] *adj* höchst
**highness** [HUY•nis] *n* Hoheit F
**highway** [HUY•wai] *n* Straße Autobahn F
**hike** [huyk] *vt* wandern
**hilarious** [hi•LAU•ree•us] *adj* lustig
**hill** [hil] *s* Hügel M
**hillside** [HIL•suyd] *n* Hang M
**hilltop** [HIL•tahp] *n* Bergspitze F
**hilly** [HI•lee] *adj* hügelig
**hilt** [hilt] *n* Heft N
**him** [him] *pers pron* ihn; ihm

**himself** [him•SELF] *pron* sich
**hind** [huynd] *adj* hinter
**hinder** [HIN•dur] *vt* verhindern
**hindrance** [HIN•druns] *n*
Hindernis N
**Hindu** [HIN•doo] *adj*
Hindu M
**hinge** [hinj] *n* Gelenk N
**hint** [hint] *n* Wink M
**hip** [hip] *n* Hüfte F
**hippopotamus**
[HI•pu•PAH•tu•mus] *n*
Nilpferd N
**hire** [huyur] *vt* anstellen
**his** [huiz] *poss adj* sein
**Hispanic** [hi•SPAN•ik] spanisch
**hiss** [his] *vi* zischen
**historian** [hi•STAU•ree•un] *n*
Historiker M
**historic** [hi•STAU•rik] *adj*
historisch
**history** [HI•stu•ree] *n*
Geschichte F
**hit** [hit] *n* Schlag M; *vt* schlagen
**hitch** [hich] *vt* Ruck M
**hitchhike** [HICH•huyk] *vi* per
Autostopp
**hitchhiker** [HICH•HUY•kur] *n*
Tramper M
**hitherto** [HI•thur•TOO] *adv*
bisher
**hive** [huyv] *n* Bienenkorb M
**hoard** [haurd] *n* Hort M
**hoarse** [haurs] *adj* heiser
**hoax** [hoks] *n* Falschmeldung F
**hobble** [HAH•bl] *vi* humpeln
**hobby** [HAH•bee] *n*
Steckenpferd N
**hobo** [HO•bo] *n*
Wanderarbeiter M
**hockey** [HAH•kee] *n* Hockey N

**hocus-pocus** [HO•kus•PO•kus]
*n* Hokuspokus M
**hog** [hahg] *n* Schwein N
**hoist** [hoist] *vt* hochziehen; *n*
Hebervorichtung F
**hold** [hold] *n* Halt; Grif M; *vt*
halten; (contain) enhalten;
(possess) haben
**holder** [HOL•dur] *n* Halter M
**holding** [HOL•ding] *n* Pacht F
**holdup** [HOLD•uhp] *n*
Stockung F
**hole** [hol] *n* Loch N
**holiday** [HAH•li•DAI] *n*
Feiertag M
**holiness** [HO•lee•nis] *n*
Heiligkeit F
**Holland** [HAH•lund] *n*
Niederlände
**hollow** [HAH•lo] *adj* hohl; *n*
Höhle
**holly** [HAH•lee] *n* Stechpalme F
**holocaust** [HAH•lu•KAUST] *n*
Massenvernichtung F
**holster** [HOL•stur] *n*
Pistolenhalfter F
**holy** [HO•lee] *adj* heilig
**home** [hom] *n* Heim M;
Haus N
**homeland** [HOM•land] *n*
Heimatland N
**homeless** [HOM•lis] *adj*
heimatlos
**homely** [HOM•lee] *adj* schlicht
**homemade** [HOM•MAID] *adj*
selbstgemacht
**homesick** [HOM•sik] *n*
Heimweh M
**homeward** [HOM•wurd] *adv*
heimwärts

**homework** [HOM•wurk] *n*
Hausaufgabe F

**homicide** [HAH•mi•SUYD] *n*
Mord M

**homosexual**
[HO•mo•SEK•shoo•ul] *adj n*
homosexuell

**honest** [AH•nist] *adj* ehrlich

**honesty** [AH•ni•stee] *n*
Ehrlichkeit F

**honey** [HU•nee] *n* Honig M

**honeymoon**
[HUH•nee•MOON] *n*
Hochzeitsreise F

**honk** [hahngk] *vi* hupen

**honor** [AH•nur] *n* Ehre F; *vt*
ehren

**honorable** [AH•nu•ru•bl] *adj*
ehrenwert

**hood** [hud] *n* Kapuze F

**hoodlum** [HUD•lum] *n*
Strolch M

**hoodwink** [HUD•wingk] *vt*
täuschen

**hoof** [huf] *n* Huf M

**hook** [huk] *n* Haken M

**hooky** [HU•kee] *n* schwänzen

**hoop** [hoop] *n* Ring M

**hoot** [hoot] *n* Schrei M

**hop** [hahp] *vt* hüpfen

**hope** [hop] *n* Hoffnung F

**hopeful** [HOP•ful] *adj*
hoffnungsvoll

**hopeless** [HOP•lis] *adj*
hoffnungslos

**horizon** [hu•RUY•zn] *n*
Horizont M

**horizontal** [HAU•ri•ZAHN•tl]
*adj* waagerecht

**hormone** [HAUR•mon] *n*
Hormon N

**horn** [haurn] *n* Horn N

**hornet** [HAUR•nit] *n*
Hornisse F

**horoscope** [HAU•ru•SKOP] *n*
Horoskop N

**horrible** [HAU•ri•bl] *adj*
schrecklich

**horrid** [HAU•rid] *adj* scheußlich

**horrify** [HAU•ri•FUY] *vt*
erschrecken

**horror** [HAU•rur] *n* Grau M

**horse** [haurs] *n* Pferd N

**horseback** [HAURS•bak] *adj*
*adv* zu Pferd

**horsepower**
[HAURS•POU•wur] *n*
Pfederstärke F

**horseradish** [HAURS•RA•dish]
*n* Meerrettich M

**horseshoe** [HAURS•shoo] *n*
Hufeisen M

**hose** [hoz] *n* Schlauch M

**hosiery** [HO•zhu•ree] *n*
Strumpfwaren

**hospitable** [hah•SPI•tu•bl] *adj*
empfänglich

**hospital** [HAH•spi•tl] *n*
Krankenhaus N

**hospitality**
[HAH•spi•TA•li•tee] *n*
Gastlichkeit F

**host** [host] *n* Gastgeber M

**hostage** [HAH•stij] *n* Geisel
M

**hostess** [HO•stis] *n*
Gastgeberin F

**hostile** [HAH•stul] *adj*
freindlich

**hostility** [hah•STI•li•tee] *n*
Feindschaft F

hot [haht] *adj* heiß

hot dog [HAHT daug] *n* Hot Dog

hot plate [HAHT plait] *n* Heizplatte F

hot-tempered [HOT•TEM•purd] *adj* ärgerlich

hotel [ho•TEL] *n* Hotel N

hound [hound] *n* Hund M

hour [ouur] *n* Stunde F

hourglass [OUUR•glas] *n* Stundenglas N

hourly [OUUR•lee] *adj adv* stündlich

house [n. hous v. houz] *n* Haus N

housekeeper [HOUS•KEE•pur] *n* Wirtschafterin F

housekeeping [HOUS•KEE•ping] *n* Hauswirtschaft F

housewife [HOUS•wuyf] *n* Hausfrau F

housework [HOUS•wurk] *n* Hausarbeit F

housing [HOU•zing] *n* Wohnung F

hovel [HUH•vl] *n* Schuppen M

hover [HUH•vur] *vi* schweben

how [hou] *adv* wie

however [hou•E•vur] *conj* jedoch; aber

howl [houul] *n* heulen

hub pivot [huhb] *n* Angelpunkt M

huddle [HUH•dl] *vi* zusammendrängen

hue [hyoo] *n* Farbe F

huff [huhf] *n* Ärger M

hug [huhg] *n* Umarmung F

huge [hyooj] *adj* riesig

hull [huhl] *n* Rumpf M

hum [huhm] *vt* summen

human [HYOO•mun] *adj* menschlich; *n* Mensch M

human being [HYOO•min BEE•ing] *n* Mensch M

human rights [HYOO•min RUYTS] *npl* Menschenrecht N

humane [hyoo•MAIN] *adj* menschlich

humanitarian [hyoo•MA•ni•TA•ree•un] *adj* humanitär

humanity [hyoo•MA•ni•TEE] *n* Menschheit F

humble [HUHM•bl] *adj* demütig

humid [HYOO•mid] *adj* feucht

humidity [hyoo•MI•di•tee] *n* Feuchtigkeit F

humiliate [hyoo•MI•lee•AIT] *v* demütigen

humiliation [hyoo•MI•lee•AI•shn] *n* Demütigung F

humility [hyoo•MI•li•tee] *n* Demut F

hummingbird [HUH•ming BURD] *n* Kolibri M

humor [HYOO•mur] *n* Humor M

humorous [HYOO•mu•rus] *adj* humorvoll

hump [huhmp] *n* Buckel M

hunch [huhnch] *n* Idee F

**hunchback** [HUHNCH•bak] *n*
Höcker M

**hunched** [huhnchd] *adj* bucklig

**hundred** [HUHN•drud] *num*
Hundert N

**hundredth** [HUHN•druth] *num*
hundertst

**Hungarian**
[HUNG•GAU•ree•un] *adj*
ungarisch

**Hungary** [HUNG•gu•ree] *n*
Ungarn

**hunger** [HUNG•gur] *n*
Hunger M

**hungry** [HUNG•gree] *adj*
hungrig

**hunt** [huhnt] *n* Jagd F; *vi* jagen

**hunter** [HUHN•tur] *n*
Jäger M

**hurdle** [HUR•dl] *n* Hürde F

**hurl** [hurl] *vt* werfen

**hurricane** [HU•ri•KAIN] *n*
Hurrikan M

**hurried** [HU•reed] *adj* eilig

**hurriedly** [HU•red•lee] *adv*
hastig

**hurry** [HU•ree] *n* Eile F; *vi* sich
beeilen; *vt* (work, etc)
schneller machen

**hurt** [hurt] *vt* Verletzung F

**hurtful** [HURT•ful] *adj*
schädlich

**husband** [HUHZ•bund] *n*
Mann M

**hush** [huhsh] *n* Stille F

**husk** [huhsk] *n* Hülse F

**husky** [HUH•skee] *adj* hülsig

**hustle** [HUH•sl] *n*
Gehetze F

**hut** [huht] *n* Hütte F

**hutch** [huhch] *n* Kiste F

**hyacinth** [HUY•u•SINTH] *n*
Hyazinth M

**hybrid** [HUY•brid] *adj n*
Kreuzung F

**hydrant** [HUY•drunt] *n*
Hydrant M

**hydraulic** [huy•DRAU•lik] *adj*
hydraulisch

**hydrogen** [HUY•dru•jun] *n*
Wasserstoff M

**hyena** [huy•EE•nu] *n* Hyäne F

**hygiene** [HUY•jeen] *n*
Hygiene F

**hymn** [him] *n* Hymne F

**hyperactive** [HUY•pur•AK•tiv]
*adj* übermäßig

**hyphen** [HUY•fn] *n*
Bindestrich M

**hypnosis** [hip•NO•sis] *n*
Hypnose F

**hypnotic** [hip•NAH•tik] *adj*
hypnotisch

**hypnotize** [HIP•nu•TUYZ] *vt*
hypnotisieren

**hypocrisy** [hi•PAH•kri•see] *n*
Heuchelei F

**hypocrite** [HI•pu•KRIT] *n*
Heuchler M

**hypocritical** [HI•pu•KRI•ti•kl]
*adj* heuchlerisch

**hypothesis** [huy•PAH•thi•sis] *n*
Hypothese F

**hypothetical**
[HUY•pu•THE•ti•kl] *adj*
angenommen

**hysterical** [hi•STE•ri•kl] *adj*
hysterisch

**hysterics** [hi•STE•riks] *npl*
Hysterie F

I

I [uy] pers *pron* ich
ice [uys] *n* Eis N
ice cube [UYS KYUB] *n*
  Eiswurfel M
ice skating [UYS SKAI•ting] *n*
  Schlittschuhlaufen N
ice-cream [uys•KREEM] *n*
  Eis N
ice-skate [UY•skait] *vi*
  Schlittschuh laufen
iceberg [UYS•burg] *n* Eisberg M
Iceland [UYS•lund] *n* Island
icing [UY•sing] *n* Glasur F
icy [UY•see] *adj* eisig
idea [uy•DEE•u] *n* Idee F
ideal [uy•DEEUL] *adj* ideal; *n*
  Ideal N
idealism [i•DEEUL•izm] *n*
  Idealismus M
idealistic [uy•DEEU•LI•stik]
  *adj* idealistisch
identical [uy•DEN•ti•kl] *adj*
  genau; gleich
identification
  [uy•DEN•ti•fi•KAI•shn] *n*
  Identifizierung F
identify [uy•DEN•ti•FUY] *vt*
  identifizieren
identity [uy•DEN•ti•tee] *n*
  Identität F
ideology [UY•dee•AH•lu•jee] *n*
  Ideologie F
idiot [I•dee•ut] *n* Idiot;
  Dummkopf M
idiotic [I•dee•AH•tik] *adj*
  idiotisch

idle [UY•dl] *adj* untätig; *vt*
  (engine) leerlaufen
idol [UY•dl] *n* Abgott M
idolize [UY•du•LUYZ] *vt*
  vergöttern
if [if] *conj* ob wenn
ignite [ig•NUYT] *vt* anzünden
ignition [ig•NI•shn] *n*
  Anzünden N
ignorance [IG•nu•runs] s
  Unwissenheit F
ignorant [IG•nu•runt] *adj*
  unkundig
ignore [ig•NAUR] *vt* ignorieren
ill [il] *adj* krank
ill at ease [IL at EEZ] *adj*
  unbequem
ill will *n* schlechte Laune F
illegal [i•LEE•gl] *adj* illegal
illegitimate [I•li•JI•ti•mut] *adj*
  unehelich
illicit [i•LI•sit] *adj* unerlaubt
illiteracy [i•LI•tu•ru•see] *n*
  Analphabetentum N.
illiterate [i•LI•tu•rut] *adj*
  analphabetisch
illness [IL•nis] *n* Krankheit F
illogical [i•LAH•ji•kl] *adj*
  unlogisch
illuminate [i•LOO•mi•NAIT] *vt*
  beleuchten
illusion [i•LOO•zhn] *n*
  Illusion F
illustrate [I•lu•STRAIT] *vt*
  erläutern
illustration [I•lu•STRAI•shn] *n*
  Erläuterung F

**illustrious** [i•LUH•stree•us] *adj*
berühmt

**image** [I•mij] *n* Standbild N

**imagery** [I•mu•jree] *n*
Bildwerk N

**imaginary** [i•MA•ji•NE•ree] *adj*
scheinbar

**imagination** [i•MA•ji•NAI•shn]
*n* Phantasie F

**imaginative** [i•MA•ji•nu•tiv]
*adj* erfinderisch

**imagine** [i•MA•jin] *vt* sich
vorstellen

**imbalance** [im•BA•luns] *n*
Unausgewogenheit F

**imbecile** [IM•bu•sil] *n* Narr;
Dummkopf M

**imitate** [I•mi•TAIT] *vt*
nachahmen

**imitation** [I•mi•TAI•shn] *n*
Nachahmung M

**immaculate** [i•MA•kyu•lut] *adj*
makellos

**immaterial** [I•mu•TEEU•ree•ul]
*adj* unwesentlich

**immature** [I•mu•CHOOUR] *adj*
unreif

**immediate** [i•MEE•dee•ut] *adj*
augenblicklich

**immediately**
[i•MEE•dee•ut•lee] *adv* sofort

**immense** [i•MENS] *adj*
ungeheuer

**immerse** [i•MURS] *vt*
eintauchen

**immigrant** [I•mi•grant] *n*
Einwanderer M

**immigration** [I•mi•GRAI•shn]
*n* Einwanderung F

**imminent** [I•mi•nunt] *adj*
bevorstehend

**immobile** [i•MO•bl] *adj*
unbeweglich

**immobilize** [i•MO•bi•LUYZ] *vt*
unbeweglich machen

**immoral** [i•MAU•rl] *adj*
unsittlich

**immorality** [I•mau•RA•li•tee] *n*
Sittenlosigkeit F

**immortal** [i•MAUR•tl] *adj*
unsterblich

**immortality**
[I•MAUR•TA•li•tee] *n*
Unsterblichkeit MF

**immune** [i•MYOON] *adj*
immun

**immunity** [i•MYOO•ni•tee] *n*
Immunität F

**immunize** [I•myu•NUYZ] *vt*
immun machen

**imp** [imp] *n* Teufelchen N;
Kobold M

**impact** [IM•pakt] *n* Auftreffen
N; (of moving objects)
Zusammenprall M

**impair** [im•PAIR] *vt* schädigen;
beeinträchtigen

**impart** [im•PAHRT]
(information) *vt* mitteilen;
(bestow) *vt* verleihen

**impartial** [im•PAHR•shl] *adj*
unvoreingenommen

**impassioned** [im•PASH•und]
leidenschaftlich

**impatience** [im•PAI•shns] *n*
Ungeduld F

**impatient** [im•PAI•shnt] *adj*
ungeduldig

**impeach** [im•PEECH] *vt*
beschuldigen

**impede** [im•PEED] *vt*
verhindern

**impediment** [im•PE•di•ment] *n*
Verhinderung F

**impel** [im•PEL] *vt* drängen

**imperative** [im•PE•ru•tiv] *adj*
befehlend

**imperfect** [im•PUR•fikt] *adj*
unvollständig

**imperial** [im•PEEU•ree•ul] *adj*
kaiserlich

**imperious** [im•PEEU•ree•us]
*adj* herrisch

**impersonal** [im•PUR•su•nl] *adj*
unpersönlich

**impersonate**
[im•PUR•so•NAIT] *vt*
verkörpern

**impertinent** [im•PUR•ti•nunt]
*adj* unverschämt

**impervious** [im•PUR•vee•us]
*adj* undurchdringlich

**impetuous** [im•PE•choo•us] *adj*
ungestüm

**impetus** [IM•pit•tus] *n*
Triebkraft F

**implant** [im•PLANT] *vt*
einimpfen

**implement** [*n.* IM•pli•munt *v.*
IM•pli•MENT] *n* Werkzeug
N; *vt* vollenden

**implicate** [IM•pli•KAIT] *vt*
hineinziehen

**implicit** [im•PLI•sit] *adj*
inbegriffen

**implore** [im•PLAUR] *vt*
dringend bitten

**imply** [im•PLUY] *vt* andeuten

**impolite** [IM•pu•LUYT] *adj*
unhöflich

**import** [*n.* IM•paurt *v.*
im•PAURT] *n* Import M;
[im•paurt] *vt* importieren

**importance** [im•PAUR•tuns] *n*
Wichtigkeit; Bedeutung F

**important** [im•PAUR•tunt] *adj*
wichtig; it's not ~\ das macht
nichts

**impose** [im•POZ] *vt* aufdrängen

**imposition** [IM•po•ZI•shn] *n*
Auflage F

**impossible** [im•PAH•si•bl] *adj*
unmöglich; *excl*
ausgeschlossen!

**impostor** [im•PAH•stur] *n*
Betrüger M

**impotent** [IM•pu•tunt] *adj*
impotent

**impress** [im•PRES] *vt*
beeindrucken

**impression** [im•PRE•shn] *n*
Beeindruck M

**impressive** [im•PRE•siv] *adj*
eindrucksvoll

**imprint** [IM•print] *n* Abdruck M

**imprison** [im•PRI•zn] *vt* ins
Gefängnis werfen; inhaftieren

**improbable** [im•PRAH•bu•bl]
*adj* unwahrscheinlich

**improper** [im•PRAH•pur] *adj*
unschicklich

**improve** [im•PROOV] *vt*
verfeinern

**improvement**
[im•PROOV•munt] *n*
Verbesserung F; (health)
Besserung F; (work) *npl*
Fortschritte

**improvise** [IM•pruh•VUYZ] *vt*
*vi* improvisieren

**imprudent** [im•PROO•dunt] *adj*
unklug

**impudent** [IM•pyu•dunt] *adj*
unverschämt

**impulsive** [im•PUHL•siv] *adj*
impulsiv

**impunity** [im•PYOO•ni•tee] *n*
Straflosigkeit F

**impure** [im•PYUR] *adj* unrein

**impurity** [im•PYU•ri•tee] *n*
Unreinheit F

**in** [in] *pre* in; (time) in; (within)
innerhalt von; *adv* da; (at
home) zu Hause

**in love** (with) *adj* verliebt

**in-laws** [IN•lauz] *npl* schwieger

**inability** [I•nu•BI•li•tee] *n*
Unfähigkeit F

**inaccurate** [in•A•kyu•rut] *adj*
ungenau

**inactive** [in•AK•tiv] *adj* untätig

**inadequate** [in•A•du•kwit] *adj*
ungenügend

**inadvertent** [IN•ud•VER•tunt]
*adj* unachtsam; ungewollt

**inane** [i•NAIN] *adj* albern

**inanimate** [in•AN•uh•muht] *adj*
leblos

**inappropriate**
[IN•u•PRO•pree•ut] *adj*
ungeeignet

**inauguration**
[i•NAU•gyu•RAI•shn] *n*
Einweihung F

**incapable** [in•KAI•pu•bl] *adj*
unfähig

**incense** [*n.* IN•sens *v.* in•SENS]
*n* Weihrauch M [ im•sens] v
beräuchern

**incentive** [in•SEN•tif] *n*
Antrieb M

**incessant** [in•SE•sunt] *adj*
unaufhörlich

**inch** [inch] *n* Zoll M

**incident** [IN•si•dunt] *n*
Vorfall M

**incidental** [IN•si•DEN•tl]
beiläufig

**incite** [in•SUYT] *vt* anregen

**incline** [in•KLUYN] *n*
Neigung F

**include** [in•KLOOD] *vt*
einrechnen

**including** [in•KLOO•ding] *prep*
einberechnet

**income** [IN•kuhm] *n*
Einkommen N

**income tax** [IN•kum TAKS] *n*
Steuer F

**incomparable**
[in•KAHM•pra•bl] nicht
vergleichbar

**incompatible**
[IN•kum•PA•ti•bl] *adj*
widersprechend

**incompetent**
[in•KAHM•pu•tunt] *adj*
unfähig

**incomplete** [IN•kum•PLEET]
*adj* unvollendet

**inconsiderate**
[IN•kun•SI•du•rut] *adj*
rücksichtslos

**inconsistent** [IN•kun•SIS•tnt]
*adj* gegensätzlich

**inconspicuous**
[IN•kun•SPI•kyoo•us] *adj*
unscheinbar

**inconvenient**
[IN•kun•VEE•nyunt] *adj* lästig

**incorporate**
[in•KAUR•pu•RAIT] *vt*
vereinigen

**incorrect** [IN•ku•REKT] *adj*
unrichtig

**increase** [IN•krees] *n*
Vermehrung F; [in•KREES] *v*
vermehren

**increasingly**
[in•KREE•sing•lee] *adv*
immer; mehr

**incredible** [in•KRE•di•bl] *adj*
unglaublich

**incredulous** [in•KRE•dyu•lus]
*adj* skeptisch

**incriminate** [in•KRI•mi•NAIT]
*vt* beschuldigen

**incur** [in•KUR] *vt* zuziehen

**incurable** [in•KYOOU•ru•bl]
*adj* unheilbar

**incursion** [in•KUR•zuhn] *n*
Einfall M

**indebted** [in•DE•tid] *adj*
verschuldet

**indecent** [in•DEE•sunt] *adj*
unanständig

**indeed** [in•DEED] *adv*
tatsächlich; wirklich

**indefinite** [in•DE•fi•nit] *adj*
unbestimmt

**indemnity** [in•DEM•ni•tee] *n*
Schadenersatz M

**indent** [in•DENT] *vt* einrücken

**independence**
[IN•du•PEN•duns] *n*
Unabhängigkeit F

**independent**
[IN•du•PEN•dunt] *adj*
unabhängig

**indestructible**
[IN•di•STRUHK•ti•bl] *adj*
unzerstörbar

**index** [in•DEKS] *n*
Inhaltverzeichnis N

**index finger** [IN•deks
FING•ur] *n* Zeigefinger M

**India** [IN•dee•u] *n* Indien

**Indian** [IN•dee•un] *adj* indisch

**indicate** [IN•di•KAIT] *vt*
anzeigen

**indicator** [IN•di•KAI•tur] *n*
Anzeiger M

**indict** [in•DUYT] *vt* anklagen

**indifferent** [in•DI•fu•runt] *adj*
gleichgültig

**indigenous** [in•DI•ji•nus] *adj*
einheimisch

**indigestion** [in•di•JES•chn] *n*
Verdauungsstörung F

**indignant** [in•DIG•nunt] *adj*
empört

**indigo** [IN•di•GO] *adj n*
Indigo M

**indirect** [IN•di•REKT] *adj*
indirekt

**indiscreet** [IN•di•SKREET] *adj*
unbedacht

**indispensable**
[IN•di•SPEN•su•bl] *adj*
unerläßlich

**indisposed** [IN•di•SPQSD]
indisponiert

**indistinct** [IN•di•STINKT] *adj*
undeutlich

**individual** [IN•di•VI•joo•ul] *adj*
einzeln

**indoctrinate**
[in•DAHK•tri•NAIT] *vt*
unterweisen

**Indonesia** [IN•do•NEE•zhu] *n*
Indonesien

**indoor** [IN•DAUR] *adj* zu
Hause

**induce** [in•DOOS] verursachen

**induct** [in•DUHKT] *vt*
einweihen

**indulge** [in•DUHLJ] sich einlassen auf

**industrial** [in•DUH•stree•ul] *adj* industriell

**industrious** [in•DUH•stree•us] *adj* fleißig

**industry** [IN•duh•stree] *n* Industrie F

**inebriated** [i•NEE•bree•AI•tid] *adj* betrunken

**ineffective** [IN•u•FEK•tiv] *adj* unwirksam

**inequality** [IN•ee•KWAH•li•tee] *n* Ungleichheit F

**inevitable** [i•NE•vi•tu•bl] *adj* unvermeidlich

**inexpensive** [IN•ek•SPEN•siv] *adj* billig

**inexperienced** [IN•ek•SPEEU•ree•unst] *adj* unerfahren

**infallible** [in•FA•li•bl] *adj* unfehlbar

**infamous** [IN•fu•mus] *adj* verrufen

**infancy** [IN•fan•see] *n* Säuglingsalter N

**infant** [IN•fant] *n* Säugling N

**infantry** [IN•fan•tree] *n* Infanterie F

**infect** [in•FEKT] *vt* infizieren

**infection** [in•FEK•shn] *n* Ansteckung F

**infectious** [in•FEK•shus] *adj* ansteckend

**infer** [in•FUR] *vt* ableiten

**inferior** [in•FEEU•ree•ur] *adj n* niedriger

**infidelity** [IN•fi•DE•li•tee] *n* Untreue F

**infinite** [IN•fi•nit] *adj* unendlich

**infinitive** [in•FI•ni•tiv] *n* Infinitiv M; *adj* infinitivisch

**infinity** [in•FI•ni•tee] *n* Unendlichkeit F

**infirmity** [in•FUR•mi•tee] *n* Gebrechlichkeit F

**inflame** [in•FLAIM] *vt* entzünden

**inflate** [in•FLAIT] *vt* aufblasen

**inflation** [in•FLAI•shn] *n* Inflation F

**inflection** [in•FLEK•shn] *n* Biegung F

**inflict** [in•FLIKT] *vt* zufügen

**influence** [IN•FLOO•uns] *n* Einfluß M; *vt* beeinflussen

**influenza** [IN•floo•EN•zu] *n* Grippe F

**influx** [IN•fluhks] *n* Einfließen N

**inform** [in•FAURM] *vt* benachrichtigen

**informal** [in•FAUR•ml] *adj* nicht förmlich

**information** [IN•fur•MAI•shn] *n* Nachricht F

**infringe** [in•FRINJ] *vt* verletzen

**infuriate** [in•FYU•ree•AIT] *vt* wütend machen

**ingenious** [in•JEE•nyus] *adj* genial

**ingratitude** [in•GRA•ti•TOOD] *n* Undankbarkeit F

**ingredient** [in•GREE•dee•unt] *n* Bestandteil M

**inhabit** [in•HA•bit] *vt* bewohnen

**inhale** [in•HAIUL] *vt* einatmen

**inherent** [in•HE•runt] *adj* angeboren

**inherit** [in•HE•rit] *vt* erben

**inheritance** [in•HE•ri•tuns] *n*
Erbschaft F

**inhibit** [in•HI•bit] *vt* hemmen

**inhuman** [in•HYOO•mun] *adj*
unmenschlich

**initial** [i•NI•shl] *adj* anfänglich

**initiate** [i•NI•shee•AIT] *vt*
beginnen

**inject** [in•JEKT] *vt* einspritzen

**injure** [IN•jur] *vt* verletzen

**injury** [IN•ju•ree] *n*
Verletzung F

**injustice** [in•JUH•stis] *n*
Unrecht N

**ink** [ingk] *n* Tinte F

**inmate** [IN•mait] *n* Insasse M

**inmost** [IN•most] innerst

**inn** [in] *n* Gasthaus -hof (m) N

**innate** [i•NAIT] *adj* angeboren

**inner** [I•nur] *adj* inner

**innkeeper** [IN•KEE•pur] *n*
Gastwirt M

**innocence** [I•nu•suns] *n*
Schuldlosigkeit F

**innocent** [I•nu•sunt] *adj*
unschuldig

**innovation** [I•nu•VAI•shn] *n*
Neuerung F

**innuendo hint indication**
[IN•yoo•EN•do] *n*
Andeutung F

**inoculate** [i•NAH•kyu•LAIT] *vt*
einimpfen

**inorganic** [IN•aur•GA•nik] *adj*
unorganisch

**inquire** [in•KWUY•ur] *vi* fragen
nach

**inquiry** [in•KWU•ree] *n*
Nachfrage F

**inquisition** [IN•kwi•ZI•shn] *n*
Untersuchung F

**inquisitive** [in•KWI•zi•tiv] *adj*
neugierig

**insane** [in•SAIN] *adj* verrückt

**insanity** [in•SA•ni•tee] *n*
Geisteskrankheit F

**insatiable** [in•SAI•shu•bl] *adj*
unersättlich

**inscription** [in•SKRIP•shn] *n*
Beschriftung F

**insect** [IN•sekt] *n* Insekt N

**insecticide** [in•SEK•ti•SUYD] *n*
Insektengift N

**insecure** [IN•su•CYUR] *adj*
unsicher

**insensitive** [in•SEN•si•tiv] *adj*
unempfindlich

**inseparable** [in•SE•pru•bl] *adj*
untrennbar

**insert** [in•SURT] *vt* einsetzen

**inside** [in•SUYD] *adj* inner; *n*
Inere N; *prep* (place) innen in

**insight** [IN•suyt] *n* Einblick M

**insignificant**
[IN•sig•NI•fi•kunt] *adj*
unwichtig

**insipid** [in•SI•pid] *adj* fade

**insist** [in•SIST] *vi* verlangen

**insistent** [in•SI•stunt] *adj*
beharrlich

**insolent** [IN•su•lunt] *adj*
unverschämt

**insomnia** [in•SAHM•nee•u] *n*
Schlaflosigkeit F

**inspect** [in•SPEKT] *vt*
untersuchen

**inspection** [in•SPEK•shn] *n*
Untersuchung F

**inspector** [in•SPEK•tur] *n*
Inspektor M

**inspiration** [IN•spu•RAI•shn] *n*
Erleuchtung F

**inspire** [in•SPUY•ur] *vt*
begeistern

**install** [in•STAUL] *vt* montieren

**installation** [IN•stu•LAI•shn] *n*
Einrichtung F

**instance** [IN•stuns] *n* Fall M

**instant** [IN•stunt] *adj*
augenblicklich; *n*
Augenblick M

**instead** [in•STED] *adv* statt;
*adv* statt dessen

**instigate** [IN•sti•GAIT] *vt*
anstiften

**instill** [in•STIL] *vt* einflößen

**instinct** [IN•stingkt] *n*
Instinkt M

**institute** [IN•sti•TOOT] *n*
Gesellschaft F

**instruct** [in•STRUHKT] *vt*
belehren

**instruction** [in•STRUHK•shn] *n*
Belehrung F

**instructor** [in•STRUHK•tor] *n*
Lehrer M

**instrument** [IN•stru•munt] *n*
Instrument N

**insufficient** [IN•su•FI•shunt]
*adj* unzureichend

**insulate** [IN•su•LAIT] *vt*
isolieren

**insulation** [IN•su•LAI•shn] *n*
Isolierung F

**insult** [*n.* IN•suhlt *v.* in•SUHLT]
*n* Beleidigung F

**insurance** [in•SHOOU•runs] *n*
Versicherung F

**insure** [in•SHOOUR] *vt*
versichern

**intact** [in•TAKT] *adj* unversehrt

**integral** [IN•tu•grul] *adj*
wesentlich

**integration** [IN•tu•GRAI•shn]
*n* Integration F

**integrity** [in•TE•gri•tee] *n*
Rechtschaffenheit F

**intellectual** [IN•tu•LEK•chu•ul]
*adj n* intellektuell

**intelligence** [in•TE•li•juns] *n*
Klugheit F

**intelligent** [in•TE•li•junt] *adj*
klug

**intend** [in•TEND] *vt*
beabsichtigen

**intense** [in•TENS] *adj* stark

**intensify** [in•TEN•si•FUY] *vt*
verstärken; *n* Heftigkeit F

**intensity** [in•TEN•si•tee] *n*
intensiv

**intensive** [in•TEN•siv] *adj*
heftig

**intent** [in•TENT] *adj* Absicht F

**intention** [in•TEN•shn] *n*
Vorhaben N

**intentional** [in•TEN•shu•nl] *adj*
absichtlich

**intercept** [IN•tur•SEPT] *vt*
auffangen

**interchange** [*n.* IN•tur•chainj
*v.* in•tur•CHAINJ] *n*
Austausch M

**intercom** [IN•tur•KAHM] *n*
Wechselsprechanlage F

**intercourse** [IN•tur•KAURS] *n*
Verkehr N

**interest** [IN•trust] *n* Interesse F

**interesting** [IN•tru•sting] *adj*
interessant

**interfere** [IN•tur•FEEUR] *vi*
sich einmischen

**interference**
[IN•tur•FEEU•runs] *n*
Einmischung F

**interim** [IN•tu•rim] *adj*
Zwischenzeit F

**interior** [in•TEEU•ree•ur] *adj n*
inner

**interlock** [IN•tur•LAHK] *vi*
schließen

**intermediate**
[IN•tur•MEE•dee•ut]] *adj*
dazwischenliegend

**interminable**
[in•TUR•mi•nu•bl] *adj*
grenzenlos

**intermission** [IN•tur•MI•shn] *n*
Pause F

**intern** [IN•turn] *n*
Pflichtassistent M

**internal** [in•TUR•nl] *adj*
inwendig

**international**
[IN•tur•NA•shu•nl] *adj*
international

**interpret** [in•TUR•prit] *vt*
verdometschen

**interpretation**
[in•TUR•pru•TAI•shn] *n*
Übersetzung F

**interpreter** [in•TUR•pri•tur] *n*
Dolmetscher M

**interrogate** [in•TE•ru•GAIT] *vt*
befragen

**interrogation**
[in•TE•ru•GAI•shn] *n*
Befragung F

**interrupt** [IN•tu•RUHPT] *vt vi*
unterbrechen

**interruption** [IN•tu•RUHP•shn]
*n* Unterbrechung F

**intersect** [IN•tur•SEKT] *vt*
kreuzen

**intersection** [IN•tur•SEK•shn]
*n* Kreuzung F

**intertwine** [IN•tur•TWUYN] *vt*
verschlingen

**interval** [IN•tur•vl] *n*
Zwischenraum M

**intervene** [IN•tur•VEEN] *vt*
dazwischen; kommen

**intervention** [IN•tur•VEN•shn]
*n* Vermittlung F

**interview** [IN•tur•VYOO] *n*
Interview N

**intestine** [in•TE•stin] *n*
Darm M

**intimacy** [IN•ti•mu•see] *n*
Vertrautheit F

**intimate** [*adj.* IN•ti•mit *v.*
IN•ti•MAIT] *adj* intim

**into** [IN•too] *prep* in

**intolerable** [in•TAH•lu•ru•bl]
*adj* unerträglich

**intolerance** [in•TAH•lu•runs] *n*
Intoleranz F

**intolerant** [in•TAH•lu•runt] *adj*
unduldsam

**intoxicated**
[in•TAHK•si•KAI•tid] *adj*
betrunken; berauscht

**intravenous** [IN•tru•VEE•nus]
*adj* intravenös

**intricate** [IN•tri•kut] *adj*
verwickelt

**intrigue** [in•TREEG] *n* Ränke
schmieden

**introduce** [IN•tru•DOOS] *vt*
sich vorstellen

**introduction**
[IN•tru•DUHK•shn] *n*
Vorstellung F

**introvert** [IN•tru•VURT] *n*
nach innen richten

**introverted** [IN•tru•VUR•tid]
*adj* nach innen

**intrude** [in•TROOD] *vi*
hineindrängen

**intruder** [in•TROO•dur] *n*
Eindringling M

**intrusion** [in•TROO•zhn] *n*
Belästigung F

**intuition** [IN•too•I•shn] *n*
Intuition F

**inundate** [I•nun•DAIT] *vt*
überschwemmen

**invade** [in•VAID] *vt* überfallen

**invalid** [*adj.* in•VA•lid *n.*
IN•vu•lid] *adj* ungültig

**invaluable** [in•VA•lyu•bl] *adj*
unschätzbar

**invariably** [in•VA•ryu•blee] *adv*
ausnahmslos

**invasion** [in•VAI•zhn] *n*
Einfall M

**invent** [in•VENT] *vt* erfinden

**invention** [in•VEN•shn] *n*
Erfindung F

**inventive** [in•VEN•tiv] *adj*
erfinderisch

**inventor** [in•VEN•tur] *n*
Erfinder M

**inventory** [IN•vun•TAU•ree] *n*
Lagerbestand M

**invest** [in•VEST] *vt vi*
investieren

**investigate** [in•VE•sti•GAIT]
*vt* untersuchen

**investigation**
[in•VE•sti•GAI•shn] *n*
Untersuchung F

**investment** [in•VEST•munt] *n*
Investierung F

**investor** [in•VE•stur] *n*
Kapitalanleger M

**invigorating**
[in•VI•gu•RAI•ting] *adj*
kräftigen

**invincible** [in•VIN•si•bl] *adj*
unbesiegbar

**invisible** [in•VI•zi•bl] *adj*
unsichtbar

**invitation** [IN•vi•TAI•shn] *n*
Einladung F

**invite** [in•VUYT] *vt* einladen

**inviting** [in•VUY•ting] *adj*
verlockend

**invoice** [IN•vois] *n* Fraktura F

**invoke** [in•VOK] *vt* flehen um

**involuntary**
[in•VAH•lun•TE•ree] *adj*
unfreiwillig

**involve** [in•VAHLV] *vt*
verwickeln

**inward** [IN•wurd] *adj adv* nach
innen gehend

**iodine** [UY•u•DUYN] *n* Jod N

**Iran** [i•RAN] *n* Iran

**Iranian** [i•RAI•nyun] *adj*
iranisch

**Iraq** [i•RAK] *n* Irak

**Iraqi** [i•RA•kee] *adj* irakisch

**Ireland** [UYUR•lund] *n* Irland

**iris** [UY•ris] *n* Iris F

**Irish** [UY•rish] *adj* irisch

**iron** [UY•urn] *n* Eisen N

**ironic** [uy•RAH•nik] *adj*
ironisch

**ironing** [UY•ur•ning] *n* bügeln

**irony** [UY•ru•nee] *n* Ironie F

**irrational** [i•RA•shu•nl] *adj*
unvernünftig

**irregular** [i•RE•gyu•lur] *adj*
unregelmäßig

irregularity
[i•RE•gyu•LA•ri•tee] *n*
Unregelmäßigkeit F

irrelavant [i•RE•lu•vunt] *adj*
unanwendbar

irreparable [i•RE•pru•bl] *adj*
unersetzlich

irreplaceable [i•ri•PLAI•su•bl]
*adj* unersetzbar

irresistible [I•ru•ZI•stu•bl] *adj*
unwiderstehlich

irresponsible
[I•ri•SPAHN•su•bl] *adj*
unverantwortlich

irrigate [I•ri•GAIT] *vt*
bewässern

irrigation [I•ri•GAI•shn] *n*
Bewässerung F

irritable [I•ri•tu•bl] *adj* reizbar

irritate [I•ri•TAIT] *vt* verärgern

irritating [I•ri•TAI•ting] *adj*
ärgerlich

Islam [iz•LAHM] *n* Islam M

island [UY•lund] *n* Insel F

isolate [UY•su•LAIT] *vt*
isolieren

isolation [UY•su•LAI•shn] *n*
Absonderung F

issue [I•shoo] *n* Sachverhalt M;
*vt* ausstellen; (question) *n*
Frage F

it *pron* er sie es

Italian [i•TAL•yun] *adj*
italienisch

italic [uy•TA•lik] *adj* italisch

itch [ich] *n* Jucken N

itchy [I•chee] *adj* juckend

item [UY•tum] *n* Gegenstand M

itemize [UY•tu•MUYZ] *vt*
verzeichnen

itinerary [uy•TI•nu•RE•ree] *n*
Reiseplan M

its [its] *poss pron* sein ihr
dessen deren

itself [it•SELF] *pron* sich
(selbts)

ivory [UY•vree] *n* Elfenbein N

ivy [UY•vee] *n* Efeu M

# J

jab [jab] *n* Stich M; *vt* stoßen

jack [jak] *n* Klinke F

jackal [JA•kl] *n* Schakal M

jacket [JA•kit] *n* Jacke F

jackpot [JAK•paht] *n* Jackpot M

jaded [JAI•did] *adj* ermattet

jagged [JA•gid] *adj* zerklüftet;
zackig

jail [jaiul] *n* Gefängnis N

jam [jam] *n* Marmelade F

janitor [JA•ni•tur] *n* Pförtner M

January [JA•nyoo•E•ree] *n*
Januar M

Japan [ju•PAN] *n* Japan

Japanese [JA•pu•NEEZ] *adj*
japanish

jar [jahr] *n* Topf M

jargon [JAHR•gun] *n* Jargon M

jaundice [JAUN•dis] *n*
Gelbsucht F

javelin [JA•vu•lin] *n*
Wurfspieß M

**jaw** [jau] *s* Kiefer M

**jazz** [jaz] *n* Jazzmusik F

**jealous** [JE•lus] *adj* eifersüchtig

**jealousy** [JE•lu•see] *n*
Eifersucht F

**jeans** [jeenz] *npl* Hose F

**jeer** [jeeur] *vi* spotten

**jelly** [JE•lee] *n* Gallerte F

**jellyfish** [JE•lee•FISH] *n*
Qualle F

**jeopardize** [JE•pur•DUYZ] *vt*
gefährden

**jerk** [jurk] *n* Stoß M

**jersey** [JUR•zee] *n* Unterjacke F

**jest** [jest] *n* Spaß M

**jet** [jet] *n* Jett M

**jetty** [JE•tee] *n* Hafendamm M

**Jew** [joo] *n* Jude M

**jewel** [jooul] *n* Juwel N

**jeweler** [JOOU•lur] *n*
Juwelier N

**jewelry** [JOOUL•ree] *n* Juwelen

**Jewish** [JOO•ish] *adj* judisch

**jig** [jig] *n* Gigue F

**jiggle** [JI•gl] *vt* rütteln

**jigsaw** (puzzle) [JIG•sau] *n*
Schweifsäge F

**jilt** [jilt] *vt* sitzen lassen

**jingle** [JING•gl] *n* Klingel N

**job** [jahb] *n* Arbeit F;
(employment) *n* Stelle F

**jockey** [JAH•kee] *n* Jockei M

**jog** [jahg] *vi* laufen; *n* Lauf M

**jogging** [JAH•ging] *n*
Jogging M

**join** [join] *vt* verbinden;
(become a member of) gehen
zu; (~ together) verbunden
sein

**joint** [joint] *adj* gemeinsam M

**joint account** [JOINT
a•KOUNT] *n*
Gemeinschaftskonto N

**joke** [jok] *n* Witz M; *vi* Witz
machen

**joker** [JO•kur] *n* Joker M

**jolly** [JAH•lee] *adj* lustig

**jolt** [jolt] *n* Stoß M

**jot** [jaht] *vt* schnell hinschreiben

**journal** [JUR•nl] *n* Tagebuch N

**journalism** [JUR•nu•LI•zm] *n*
Journalismus M

**journalist** [JUR•nu•list] *n*
Journalist M

**journey** [JUR•nee] *n* Reise F

**jovial** [JO•vyul] *adj* heiter

**joy** [joi] *n* Freude F

**joyful** [JOI•ful] *adj* erfreut

**jubilant** [JOO•bi•lunt] *adj*
jubelnd

**judge** [juhj] *n* Richter M; *vi*
Richeter sein

**judgment** [JUHJ•ment] *n* Urteil
N; (opinion) Ansichts F

**judicial** [joo•DI•shl] *adj*
gerichtlich

**judicious** [joo•DI•shus] *adj*
vernünftig

**jug** [juhg] *n* Krug M

**juggle** [JUH•gl] *vt* gaukeln

**juggler** [JUH•glur] *n*
Jongleur M

**juice** [joos] *n* Saft M

**juicy** [JOO•see] *adj* saftig

**jukebox** [JOOK•bahks] *n*
Jukebox F

**July** [ju•LUY] *n* Juli M

**jump** [juhmp] *n* Sprung M

**junction** [JUHNGK•shn] *n*
Verbindung F

**June** [joon] *n* Juni M

**jungle** [JUHNG•gl] *n*
   Dschungel M

**junior** [JOO•nyur] *adj* junior

**junk** [juhngk] *n* Altwaren

**jurisdiction**
   [JOOU•ris•DIK•shn] *n*
   Rechtsprechung F

**juror** [JOOU•rur] *n*
   Geschworener M

**jury** [JOOU•ree] *n*
   Geschworenen

**just 1** [juhst] (time) *adj* gerade;
   (barely) gerade nach;
   (exactly) genau; (simply) nur;
   bloß; ~ about in\ etwa

**just 2** *adj* gerecht

**justice** [JUH•stis] *n* Justiz M

**justify** [JUH•sti•FUY] *vt*
   rechtfertigen

**juvenile** [JOO•vu•NUYUL] *adj*
   jugendlich

**juxtapose** [JUHK•stu•POZ] *vt*
   nebeneinanderstellen

# K

**kaleidoscope**
   [ku•LUY•du•SKOP] *n*
   Kaleidoskop N

**kangaroo** [KANG•gu•ROO] *n*
   Känguruh N

**keen** [keen] *adj* scharf;
   (enthusiastic) begeistert

**keep** [keep] *vt* behalten;
   (maintain) halten; (put aside)
   aufheben

**keep away** *vi* wegbleiben

**keep back** *vi* zurückbleiven

**keep out** *vi* (of building)
   draußen bleiben

**keeper** [KEE•pur] *n* Wächter M

**keeping** [KEE•ping] *n* Pflege F

**keepsake** [KEEP•saik] *n*
   Andenken N

**keg** [keg] *n* Faß N

**kennel** [KE•nl] *n* Hundehütte F

**Kenya** [KE•nyu] *n* Kenya

**kernel** [KUR•nl] *n* Kern M

**kerosene** [KE•ru•SEEN] *n*
   Kerosin N

**ketchup** [KE•chup] *n*
   Ketchup M

**kettle** [KE•tl] *n* Kessel M

**key** [kee] *n* Schlüssel M

**key ring** [KEE ring] *n* -ring

**keyboard** [KEE•baurd] *n*
   Klaviatur F

**khaki** [KA•kee] *adj* Khaki N

**kick** [kik] *n* Tritt M

**kid 1** [kid] *n* Kind N

**kid 2** (young goat) *n* Kitz N

**kidnap** [KID•nap] *v* entführen

**kidnaping** [KID•na•ping] *n*
   Entführung F

**kidnapper** [KID•na•pur] *n*
   Entführer M

**kidney** [KID•nee] *n* Niere F

**kill** [kil] *vt* töten; umbringen

**killer** [KI•lur] *n* Mörder M

**kiln** [kiln] *n* Darrofen M

**kilogram** [KI•lu•GRAM] *n*
Kilogramm N

**kilometer** [ki•LAH•mi•tur] *n*
Kilometer M

**kilowatt** [KI•lu•WAHT] *n*
Kilowattstunde F

**kilt** [kilt] *n* Kilt M

**kin** [kin] *n* Verwandtschaft F

**kind** [kuynd] *adj* nett

**kindergarten**
[KIN•dur•GAHR•tn] *n*
Kindergarten M

**kindle** [KIN•dl] *vt* aufflammen

**kindly** [KUYND•lee] *adj*
freundlich

**kindness** [KUYND•nis] *n*
Freundlichkeit F

**king** [king] *n* König M

**kingdom** [KING•dum] *n*
Königreich N

**kinky** [KING•kee] *adj*
Kräuselung F

**kiss** [kis] *n* Kuß M

**kit** [kit] *n* Seesack M

**kitchen** [KI•chn] *n* Küche F

**kitchen sink** [KI•chin SINK] *n*
Spülstein M

**kite** [kuyt] *n* Papierdrachen M

**kitten** [KI•tn] *n* Kätzchen N

**knack** [nak] *n* Kunstgriff M

**knapsack** [NAP•sak] *n*
Rucksack M

**knead** [need] *vt* kneten

**knee** [nee] *n* Knie N

**kneecap** [NEE•kap] *n*
Kniescheibe F

**kneel** [neeul] *vi* knien

**knife** [nuyf] *n* Messer N

**knight** [nuyt] *n* Ritter M

**knit** [nit] *vt vi* stricken

**knitting** [NI•ting] *n* Stricken N

**knob** [nahb] *n* Knopf M

**knock** [nahk] *n* Schlag M

**knocker** [NAH•kur] *n*
Klopfer M

**knot** [naht] *n* Knoten M

**know** [no] *vt vi* wissen; (be
acquainted with) kennen;
(recognize) erkennen

**know-how** [NO•hou] *n*
Sachkenntnis F

**know-it-all** [NO•it•AL] *n*
Besserwisser M

**knowledge** [NAH•lij] *n*
Kenntnis F

**knuckle** [NUH•kl] *n*
Fingergelenk N

**Korea** [ku•REE•u] *n* Korea

**kosher** [KO•shur] *adj* koscher

**Kuwait** [ku•WAIT] *n* Kuwait

# L

**lab** [lab] *n* Labor N

**label** [LAI•bl] *n* Zettel M; *vt*
eitkettieren

**labor** [LAI•bur] *n* Arbeit F; *vi*
arbeiten

**Labor Party** [LAI•bor PAR•tee]
*n* Labour Party

**labor union** [LAI•borU•nyun] *n*
Gewerkschaftsbund M

**laboratory** [LA•bru•TAU•ree] *n*
Laboratorium N

**laborer** [LAI•bu•rur] *n*
Arbeiter M

**lace** [lais] *n* Spitze F

**lack** [lak] *n* Mangel M; *vi* fehlen

**lacquer** [LA•kur] *n* Lack M

**ladder** [LA•dur] *n* Leiter F

**ladle** [LAI•dl] *n* Suppenkelle F

**lady** [LAI•dee] *n* Dame F

**lag** [lag] *vi* zurückbleiben;
(time) *vi* langsam vergehen; *n*
Zeitdifferenz F

**lagoon** [lu•GOON] *n* Lagune F

**lair** [laiur] *n* Lager N

**lake** [laik] *n* See M

**lamb** [lam] *n* Lamm N

**lame** [laim] *adj* lahm

**lament** [lu•MENT] *vi* jammern

**laminate** [LA•mi•NAIT] *vt*
aufspalten

**lamp** [lamp] *n* Lampe F

**lamppost** [LAMP•post] *n*
Laternenpfahl M

**lampoon** [lam•POON] *n*
Schmähschrift F

**lance** [lans] *n* Speer M

**land** [land] *n* Land N; *vt* landen

**landing** [LAN•ding] *n*
Landung F

**landlady** [LAND•LAI•dee] *n*
Besitzerin F

**landlord** [LAND•laurd] *n*
Besitzer M

**landmark** [LAND•mahrk] *n*
Grenzstein M

**landowner** [LAND•O•nur] *n*
Grundbesitzer M

**landslide** [LAND•sluyd] *n*
Erdrutsch M

**lane** [lain] *n* Weg M

**language** [LANG•gwuj] *n*
Sprache F

**languid** [LANG•gwid] *adj* matt

**lantern** [LAN•turn] *n* Laterne F

**lap 1** [lap] *n* Schoß M

**lap 2** (sport) *n* Runde F

**lap 3** (lick) *vt* lecken

**lapel** [lu•PEL] *n* Revers N

**lapse** [laps] *n* Versehen N

**larceny** [LAHR•su•nee] *n*
Diebstahl M

**lard** [lahrd] *n* Schweinefett N

**large** [lahrj] *adj adv* groß

**largely** [LAHRJ•lee] *adv*
größenteils

**lark** [lahrk] *n* Lerche F

**lash** [lash] *n* Wimper F

**last 1** [last] *adj* letzte; *n* der die
das letzte

**last 2** *vi* (continue) dauern;
(remain intact) halten

**last name** [LAST NAIM] *n*
Familienname M

**lasting** [LA•sting] *adj* dauernd

**latch** [lach] *n* Klinke F;
Riegel M

**late** [lait] *adj* spät

**latent** [LAI•tunt] *adj* latent

**lather** [LA•thur] *n*
Seifenschaum M

**Latin** [LA•tin] *adj n* Latein
lateinisch

**Latin America** [LA•tin
u•ME•ri•ku] *n*
Lateinamerika N

**latitude** [LA•ti•TOOD] *n*
Breite F

**latter** [LA•tur] *adj* letzter

**lattice** [LA•tis] *n* Gitter N

**Latvia** [LAHT•vee•u] *n* Lettein

**laugh** [laf] *vi* lachen; *n*
Lachen N

**laughter** [LAF•tur] *n*
Gelächter N

**launch** [launch] *vt* abschießen;
*n* Barkasse F

**launch into (attack)** angreifen

**launder** [LAUN•dur] *vt*
waschen

**laundry** [LAUN•dree] *n*
Wäsche F

**laurel** [LAU•rl] *n* Lorbeer M

**lava** [LAH•vu] *n* Lava F

**lavatory** [LA•vu•TAU•ree] *n*
Waschraum M

**lavish** [LA•vish] *adj*
verschwenderisch

**law** [lau] *n* Gesetz N

**law school** [LAW skool] *n*
Rechtsakademie F

**law-abiding**
[LAW•a•BUY•ding] *adj*
gesetzestreu

**lawful** [LAU•ful] *adj* gesetzlich

**lawn** [laun] *n* Rasen M

**lawn mower** [LAWN
MO•wur] *s* Rasenmäher M

**lawsuit** [LAU•soot] *n* Prozeß M

**lawyer** [LAU•yur] *n*
Rechtsanwalt M

**lax** [laks] *adj* locker

**laxative** [LAK•su•tiv] *n*
Abführmittel N

**lay** [lai] *vt* legen; (~ bricks etc)
verlegen

**layer** [LAI•ur] *n* Schicht F

**layout** [LAI•out] *n* Planung F

**lazy** [LAI•zee] *adj* faul

**lead 1** [leed] *n* Leitung; *vt*
vorangehen

**lead 2** [lead] *n* Blei N

**leader** [LEE•dur] *n* Leiter M

**leadership** [LEE•dur•SHIP] *n*
Leitung F

**leading** [LEE•ding] *adj* leitend

**leaf** [leef] *n* Blatt N

**league** [leeg] *n* Liga F

**leak** [leek] *n* Loch N; undichte
Stelle; *vt* durchlassen; *vi*
lecken

**lean 1** [leen] *adj* mager

**lean 2** *vt* lehnen

**leap** [leep] *n* springen

**leap year** [LEEP YEER] *n*
Schaltjahr N

**learn** [lurn] *vt vi* erfahren;
lernen

**learning** [LUR•ning] *n*
Gelehrsamkeit F

**lease** [lees] *n* Miete F

**leash** [leesh] *n* Koppelleine F

**least** [leest] *adj* geringst

**leather** [LE•thur] *n* Leder N

**leave** [leev] *n* Abschied M

**Lebanon** [LE•bu•nahn] *n*
Lebanon

**lecherous** [LE•chu•rus] *adj* geil

**lecture** [LEK•chur] *n* Vortrag M

**ledge** [lej] *n* Riff N

**ledger** [LE•jur] *n* Hauptbuch N

**leech** [leech] *n* Blutegel M

**leek** [leek] *n* Lauch M

**leer** [leeur] *n* Seitenblick M

**left** [left] *n* links

**left-handed** [-HAN•did] *adj*
Linkshänder-in M

**left-overs** [LEFT•O•vurz] *npl*
Überbleibsel N

**left-wing** [LEFT•WING] *adj*
Links

**leftist** [LEF•tist] *adj n*
Linksradikale M

**leg** [leg] *n* Bein N

**legacy** [LE•gu•see] *n* Legat N

**legal** [LEE•gl] *adj* gesetzlich; legal

**legalize** [LEE•gu•LUYZ] *vt* legalisieren

**legend** [LE•jund] *n* Sage F

**legendary** [LE•jun•DE•ree] *adj* legendär

**legible** [LE•ji•bl] *adj* leserlich

**legislation** [LE•jis•LAI•shn] *n* Gesetzgebung F

**legislature** [LE•jis•LAI•chur] *n* Gesetzgebungs F

**legitimate** [lu•JI•ti•mit] *adj* legitim

**leisure** [LEE•zhur] *n* freie Zeit

**lemon** [LE•mun] *n* Zitrone F

**lemonade** [LE•mu•NAID] *n* Zitronenlimonade F

**lend** [lend] *vt* ausleihen

**length** [length] *n* Länge F

**lengthen** [LENG•thun] *vt* verlängern

**lens** [lenz] *n* Linse F

**Lent** [lent] *n* Fastenzeit F

**leopard** [LE•purd] *n* Leopard M

**leper** [LE•pur] *n* Aussätziger M

**leprosy** [LE•pru•see] *n* Lepra F

**lesbian** [LEZ•bee•un] *n* lesbisch

**less** [les] *adj* wenig; *prep* weniger

**lessen** [LE•sn] *vt* verringern

**lesser** [LE•sur] *adj* geringer

**lesson** [LE•sn] *n* Lektion F

**let** [let] *vt* lassen; (rent) zu vermieten

**lethal** [LEE•thl] *adj* tödlich

**lethargy** [LE•thur•jee] *n* Lethargie F

**letter** [LE•tur] *n* Brief M

**lettuce** [LE•tus] *n* Salat M

**level** [LE•vl] *n* Ebene F; *adj* eben; on the ~\ es ist reel; *vt* (ground, etc) einbenden

**lever** [LE•vur] *n* Anker M

**levy** [LE•vee] *n* Erhebung F

**lewd** [lood] *adj* unzüchtig

**liability** [LUY•u•BI•li•tee] *n* Schuld F

**liable** [LUY•u•bl] *adj* verantwortlich

**liaison** [LEE•ai•ZAUN] *n* Verhältnis N

**liar** [LUY•ur] *n* Lügner M

**libel** [LUY•bl] *n* Verleumdung F

**liberal** [LI•brul] *adj n* liberal

**liberate** [LI•bu•RAIT] *vt* befreien

**liberation** [LI•bu•RAI•shn] *n* Befreiung F

**liberty** [LI•bur•tee] *n* Freiheit F

**librarian** [luy•BRE•ree•un] *n* Bibliothekar -in M

**library** [LUY•BRE•ree] *n* Bibliothek F

**Libya** [LI•bee•u] *n* Libya

**license** [LUY•sns] *n* Schein M

**lick** [lik] *vt* lecken

**lid** [lid] *n* Deckel M

**lie** [luy] *n* Lüge F; *vt* lugen

**lieutenant** [loo•TE•nunt] *n* Leutnant M

**life** [luyf] *n* Leben N; (of object) Lebensdauer F

**life expectancy** [LUYF ek•SPEK•ten•cee] *n* Lebenserwartung F

**life jacket** [LUYF JA•ket] *n* Schwimmweste F

**life sentence** [LUYF SEN•tinz]
*n* lebenslängliche
Freiheitsstrafe F

**lifeboat** [LUYF•bot] *n*
Rettungsboot N

**lifeless** [LUYF•lis] *adj* leblos

**lifelike** [LUYF•luyk] *adj*
lebenswahr

**lifelong** [LUYF•laung] *adj*
lebenslänglich

**lifespan** [LUYF•span] *n*
Lebenslauf M

**lifestyle** [LUYF•stuyul] *n*
Lebensstil M

**lift** [lift] *n* Heben N; *vt*
hocheben

**ligament** [LI•gi•mint] *n*
Ligament N

**light** [luyt] *adj* hell

**lighten** [LUY•tn] *vt* erleichtern

**lighter** [LUY•tur] *n*
Freuerzeug N

**lighthouse** [LUYT•haus] *n*
Leuchtturm M

**lighting** [LUY•ting] *n*
Beleuchtung F

**lightly** [LUYT•lee] *adv* leicht

**lightness** [LUYT•lee] *n*
Leichtheit F

**lightning** [LUYT•ning] *n*
Blitz M

**likable** [LUY•ku•bl] *adj*
liebenswert

**like** [luyk] *adj* gleich

**likely** [LUYK•lee] *adj*
wahrscheinlich

**likeness** [LUYK•nis] *n*
Ähnlichkeit F

**likewise** [LUYK•wuyz] *adv*
gleichfalls

**liking** [LUY•king] *n*
Zuneigung F

**limb** [lim] *n* Glied N

**lime** [luym] *n* Limonelle F

**limelight** [LUYM•luyt] *n*
Öffentlichkeit F

**limit** [LI•mit] *n* Schranke F; *vt*
beschränken

**limitation** [LI•mi•TAI•shn] *n*
Beschränkung F

**limousine** [LI•mu•ZEEN] *n*
Limousine F

**limp** [limp] *adj* schlaff

**line** [luyn] *n* Linie F; (row)
Reihe F; air ~\ Linie F;
telephone ~\ Leitung F;
(written) Zeile F; *vt* ~ up\
sich aufstellen

**linen** [LI•nun] *n* Leinen N

**linger** [LING•gur] *vi* verweilen

**lingerie** [LAHN•zhu•RAI] *n*
Damenunterwäsche M

**lingo** [LING•go] *n* Jargon M

**linguistics** [ling•GWI•stiks] *n*
Sprachwissenschaft F

**lining** [LUY•ning] *n*
Auskleidung F

**link** [lingk] *n* Glied N

**lint** [lint] *n* Fussel F

**lion** [LUY•un] *n* Löwe M

**lioness** [LUY•u•nes] *n* Löwin F

**lip** [lip] *n* Lippe F

**lip-read** [LIP•reed] *vt* von den
Lippen ablesen

**lipstick** [lip] *n* Lipenstift M

**liquid** [LI•kwid] *n* Flüssigkeit F;
*adj* flüssig

**liquidate** [LI•kwi•DAIT] *vt*
tilgen

**liquor** [LI•kur] *n* Alkohol M

list [list] n Liste F; vt notieren

listen [LI•sn] vi hören

listener [LI•su•nur] n
Zuhörer M

literal [LI•tu•rl] adj
wortwörtlich

literary [LI•tu•RE•ree] adj
literarisch

literature [LI•tu•RU•chur] n
Literatur F

litigation [LI•ti•GAI•shn] n
Prozeß M

litter [LI•tur] n Streu F

little [LI•tl] adj klein; adv
wenig

live 1 [luyv] adj lebendig; vi
(reside) wohnen; vi leben

live 2 (alive) adj lebend

lively [LUYV•lee] adj lebendig

liven [LUY•vn] vt beleben

liver [LI•vur] n Leber F

livery [LI•vu•ree] n Livree F

livestock [LUYV•stahk] n
Vieh N

livid [LI•vid] adj bleich

living [LI•ving] adj lebend

lizard [LI•zurd] n Eidechse F

load [lod] n Last F

loaf [lof] n Laib M

loafer [LO•fur] n Bummler M

loan [lon] n Leihen N

loathe [loth] vt verabscheuen

loathsome [LOTH•sum] adj
widerlich

lobby [LAH•bee] n Vorhalle F

lobe [lob] n Lappen M

lobster [LAHB•stur] n
.Hummer M

local [LO•kl] adj örtlich

locality [lo•KA•li•tee] n Ort M

locate [LO•kait] vt ausfindig
machen

location [lo•KAI•shn] n Platz M

lock [lahk] n Schloß N

locomotive [LO•ku•MO•tiv] n
Lokomotive F

locust [LO•kust] n Robinie F

lodge [lahj] n Jagdhütte F

lodger [LAH•jur] n Mieter M

lodgings [LAH•jingz] n
Wohnen N

loft [lauft] n Speicher M

log [lahg] n Klotz M

logic [LAH•jik] n Logik F

logical [LAH•ji•kl] adj logisch

logo [LO•go] n Logo

loin [loin] n Lende F

loiter [LOI•tur] vi bummeln

lollipop [LAH•lee•PAHP] n
Lutschbonbon M

London [LUHN•dn] n London

lone [lon] adj einsam

loneliness [LON•lee•nis] n
Einsamkeit F

lonely [LON•lee] adj einsam

long 1 [laung] adj lang; adv
lang(e)

long 2 (~ for) vt sich sehen

longitude [LAUN•ji•TOOD] n
Länge F

look [luk] n Blick M; (air,
appearance) N Aussehen N; vi
(see, glance) glucken

look at vt anschauen

look for (seek) vi suchen

look into vi untersuchen

look up vi ausfehen

loom [loom] n Webmaschine F

loony [LOO•nee] adj verrückt

loop [loop] n Schlinge F

**loophole** [LOOP•houl] *n*
Sehschlitz M

**loose** [loos] *adj* locker

**loosely** [LOOS•lee] *adv* locker

**loosen** [LOO•sn] *vt* öffnen

**loot** [loot] *n* Beute F

**lord** [laurd] *n* Herr M

**lore** [laur] *n* Lehre F

**lose** [looz] *vt* verlieren

**loss** [laus] *n* Verlust M

**lost** [laust] *adj* verloren

**lot** [laht] *n* Los N

**lotion** [LO•shn] *n* Hautwasser N

**loud** [loud] *adj* laut

**loudspeaker**
[LOUD•SPEE•kur] *n*
Lautsprecher M

**lounge** [lounj] *n* Diele F

**louse** [lous] *n* Laus F

**lout** [lout] *n* Lümmel M

**lovable** [LUH•vu•bl] *adj*
liebenswürdig

**love** [luhv] *n* Liebe F

**love affair** [LUV a•FAIR] *n*
Liebesaffäre F

**lovely** [LUHV•lee] *adj* schön

**lover** [LUH•vur] *n* Liebhaber M

**low** [lo] *adj* niedrig

**lower** [LO•ur] *adj* niedriger

**lowly** [LO•lee] *adj* niedrig

**loyal** [LOI•ul] *adj* treu

**loyalty** [LOI•ul•tee] *n* Treue F

**lubricant** [LOO•bri•kunt] *n*
Schmiermittel N

**lubricate** [LOO•bri•KAIT] *vt*
schmieren

**lucid** [LOO•sid] *adj* klar

**luck** [luhk] *n* Glück N

**luckily** [LUH•ku•lee] *adv*
glücklicherwise

**lucky** [LUH•kee] *adj* glücklich

**ludicrous** [LOO•di•krus] *adj*
lächerlich

**lug** [luhg] *vt* schleppen

**luggage** [LUH•gij] *n* Gepäck N

**lukewarm** [LOOK•WAURM]
*adj* lauwarm

**lull** [luhl] *n* Pause F

**lullaby** [LUH•lu•BUY] *n*
Wiegenlied N

**lumber** [LUHM•bur] *n*
Bauholz N

**lumberjack** [LUHM•bur•JAK]
*n* Holzfäller M

**luminous** [LOO•mi•nus] *adj*
leuchtend

**lump** [luhmp] *n* Klumpen M

**lunar** [LOO•nur] *adj* Mond

**lunatic** [LOO•nu•TIK] *n*
Wahnsinniger M

**lunch** [luhnch] *n* Mittagessen N

**lunch hour** *n* Mittagspause F

**lung** [luhng] *n* Lunge F

**lunge** [luhnj] *vi* losstürzen

**lurch** [lurch] *n* Rollen N

**lure** [loour] *n* Lockung F

**lurid** [LU•rid] *adj* grell

**lurk** [lurk] *vi* verborgen liegen

**luscious** [LUH•shs] *adj* lecker

**lust** [luhst] *n* Gier F

**luster** [LUH•stur] *n* Glanz M

**luxurious** [luhg•ZHU•ree•us]
*adj* luxus

**luxury** [LUHK•shu•ree] *adj*
Luxus M

**lying** [LUY•ing] *adj* liegend

**lynch** [linch] *vt* lynchen

**lyric** [LEEU•rik] *adj* Lyrik F

**lyrical** [LEEU•ri•kl] *adj* lyrisch

**lyrics** [LEEU•riks] *npl* Lyrik F

# M

macaroni [MA•ku•RO•nee] *n*
Makkaroni

machine [mu•SHEEN] *n*
Maschine F

machine gun [ma•SHEEN
GUN] *n* Maschinengewehr N

machinery [mu•SHEE•nu•ree]
*n* Maschinerie F

mackerel [MA•krul] *n*
Makrele F

mad [mad] *adj* böse;
wahnsinnig; (enthusiastic) auf
(etw) verrückt sein

madam [MU•dam] *n* gnädige
Frau F

madden [MA•dn] *vt* rasend
machen

madly [MAD•lee] *adv*
wahnsinnig

madman [MAD•man] *n*
Verrückter M

madness [MAD•nis] *n*
Wahnsinn M

magazine [MA•gu•ZEEN] *n*
Zeitschrift F

magic [MA•jik] *adj* Magie F

magical [MA•ji•kl] *adj* magisch

magicien [ma•JI•shn] *n*
Magier M

magistrate [MA•ji•STRAIT] *n*
Beamter M

magnet [MAG•nit] *n* Magnet M

magnetic [mag•NE•tik] *adj*
magnetisch

magnificence [mag•NI•fi•suns]
*n* Großartigkeit F

magnificent [mag•NI•fi•sunt]
*adj* großartig

magnify [MAG•ni•FUY] *vt*
vergrößern

magnifying glass
[MAG•ni•FUY•ing ~ ] *n*
Vergrößerungsglas N

magnitude [MAG•ni•TOOD] *n*
Ausmaß N

mahogany [mu•HAH•gu•nee] *n*
Mahagonibaum M

maid [maid] *n* Magd N

maiden name [MAI•dn] *n*
Mädchenname M

mail [maiul] *n* Post F

mailbox [MAIUL•bahks] *n*
Briefkasten M

mailman [MAIUL•man] *n*
Briefträger M

maim [maim] *vt* verstümmeln

main [main] *adj* haupt

main course [MAIN KAURS]
*n* Hauptgericht N

mainland [MAIN•land] *n*
Festland N

maintain [main•TAIN] *vt*
aufhalten

maintenance [MAIN•tu•nuns]
*n* Wartung F

majestic [mu•JE•stik] *adj*
majestätisch

majesty [MA•ji•stee] *n*
Majestät M

major [MAI•jur] *adj*
bedeutend M

majority [mu•JAU•ri•tee] *n*
Mehrheit F

**make 1** [maik] *vt* machen;
(earn) verdienen; (reach)
schaffen

**make 2** (brand) *n* Marke F

**make-up** [MAI•kuhp] *n*
Schminke F

**male** [maiul] *adj* männlich

**malice** [MA•lis] *n* Bosheit F

**malicious** [mu•LI•shus] *adj*
boshaft

**malign** [mu•LUYN] *vt*
verleumden

**malignant** [mu•LIG•nunt] *adj*
böswillig

**mallet** [MA•lit] *n* Schlegel M

**malpractice** [MAL•PRAK•tis] *n*
Übeltat F

**mammal** [MA•ml] *n*
Säugetier N

**mammoth** [MA•muth] *adj*
Mammut N

**man** [man] *n* Mann M

**manage** [MA•nij] *vt* verwalten

**management** [MA•nij•munt] *n*
Verwaltung F

**manager** [MA•ni•jur] *n*
Verwalter M

**mandate** [MAN•dait] *n*
Mandat N

**mandatory**
[MAN•du•TAU•ree] *adj*
vorschreibend

**mane** [main] *n* Mähne F

**maneuver** [mu•NOO•vur] *n*
Manöver N

**manhood** [MAN•hud] *n*
Menschentum M

**mania** [MAI•nee•u] *n* Manie F

**manicure** [MA•ni•KYUR] *n*
Nagelpflege F

**manifest** [MA•ni•FEST] *adj*
offenbar

**manipulate** [mu•NI•pyu•LAIT]
*vt* mainpulieren

**mankind** [MAN•KUYND] *n*
Menschheit F

**manner** [MA•nur] *n* Art F

**manor** [MA•nur] *n* Schloß N

**manpower** [MAN•pouur] *n*
menschliche Arbeitskraft F

**mansion** [MAN•shn] *n* Villa F

**manslaughter**
[MAN•SLAU•tur] *n*
Totschlag M

**mantelpiece** [MAN•tl•PEES] *n*
Kamineinfassung F

**manual** [MA•nyoo•ul] *adj* mit
der Hand; *n* Handbuch N

**manufacture**
[MA•nyu•FAK•chur] *n*
Herstellung F

**manufacturer**
[MA•nyu•FAK•chu•rur] *n*
Erzeuger M

**manure** [MU•noour] *n* Dung M

**manuscript** [MA•nyu•SKRIPT]
*n* Manuskript N

**many** [ME•nee] *adj* viele

**map** [map] *n* Landkarte F

**maple** [MAI•pl] *n* Ahorn M

**mar** [mahr] *vt* beschädigen

**marathon** [MA•ru•THAHN] *n*
Marathonlauf M

**marble** [MAHR•bl] *n*
Marmor M

**March** [mahrch] *n* März M

**march** [mahrch] *vt* marschieren

**mare** [maiur] *n* Stute F

**margarine** [MAHR•ju•rin] *n*
Margarine F

**margin** [MAHR•jin] *n* Rand M

**marginal** [MAHR•ji•nl] *adj*
mindest

**marigold** [MA•ri•GOLD] *n*
Ringelblume F

**marijuana** [MA•ri•WAH•nu] *n*
Marihuanahanf M

**marinate** [MA•ri•NAIT] *vt*
marinieren

**marine** [mu•REEN] *adj* see; *n*
Marine F

**mark** [mahrk] *n* Markierung F

**marker** [MAHR•kur] *n*
Anzeiger M

**market** [MAHR•kit] *n* Markt M

**market value** [MAR•kit ~ ] *n*
Marktpreis M

**marmalade** [MAHR•mu•LAID]
*n* Marmelade F

**maroon** [mu•ROON] *adj*
kastanienbraun

**marriage** [MA•rij] *n* Ehe F

**married** [MA•reed] *adj*
verheiratet

**marry** [MA•ree] *vt* verheiraten

**Mars** [mahrz] *n* Mars M

**marsh** [mahrsh] *n* Sumpf M

**marshal** [MAHR•shl] *n*
Marschall M

**marshy** [MAHR•shee] *adj*
sumpfig

**martial** [MAHR•shl] *adj*
streitbar

**martyr** [MAHR•tur] *n*
Märtyrer M

**marvel** [MAHR•vl] *n*
Wunder N

**marvelous** [MAHR•vu•lus] *adj*
wunderbar

**mascara** [ma•SKA•ru] *n*
Wimperntusche F

**masculine** [MA•skyu•lin] *adj*
männlich

**mash** [mash] *vt* zerdrücken

**mask** [mask] *n* Maske F

**mason** [MAI•sn] *n* Maurer M

**masquerade** [MA•sku•RAID] *n*
Maskenball M

**mass** [mass] *n* Messe F

**massacre** [MA•su•kr] *n*
Massaker N

**massage** [mu•SAHZH] *n*
Massage F

**massive** [MA•siv] *adj* massiv

**mast** [mast] *n* Mast M

**master** [MA•stur] *adj n*
Meister M

**masterpiece** [MA•stur•PEES] *n*
Meisterstück N

**mat** [mat] *n* Matte F

**match** [mach] *n* Zünder M

**mate** [mait] *n* Partner M

**material** [mu•TEEU•ree•ul] *adj*
Stoff M

**materialist**
[mu•TEEU•ree•u•list] *n*
Materialist M

**materialistic**
[mu•TEEU•ree•u•LI•stik] *adj*
materialistisch

**maternal** [mu•TUR•nl] *adj*
mütterlich

**mathematics**
[MA•thu•MA•tiks] *n*
Matematik F

**matriculation**
[mu•TRI•kyu•LAI•shn] *n*
Immatrikulation F

**matrimony** [MA•tri•MO•nee] *n*
Ehe F

**matrix** [MAI•triks] *n* Matrix F

**matter** [MA•tur] *n* Substanz F;
*vi* it doesn't ~\ macht nichts

**mattress** [MA•tris] *n*
Matratze F

**mature** [mu•CHOOUR] *adj* reif

**maturity** [mu•CHOOU•ri•tee] *n*
Reife F

**maximum** [MAK•si•mum] *n*
Maximum N; *adj* maximum

**may** [mai] *modal v* dürfen

**May** [mai] *n* Mai M

**mayonnaise** [MAI•u•NAIZ] *n*
Mayonnaise F

**mayor** [MAI•yur] *n*
Bürgermeister M

**maze** [maiz] *n* Labyrinth N

**me** [mee] *pers pron* mir mich

**meadow** [ME•do] *n* Wiese F

**meager** [MEE•gr] *adj* mager

**meal** [meeul] *n* Mahlzeit F

**mean 1** [meen] *adj* gemein;
(miserly) geizig

**mean 2** pp mean *vt* bedeuten

**meaning** [MEE•ning] *n*
Bedeutung F

**means** [meenz] *npl* Mittel N

**meantime** [MEEN•tuym] *adv*
Zwischenzeit F

**meanwhile** [MEEN•wuyul] *adv*
unterdessen

**measles** [MEE•zlz] *n* Maśern

**measure** [ME•zhur] *n* Maß N;
*vt* messen

**measurement** [ME•zhur•munt]
*n* Messung F

**meat** [meet] *n* Fleisch N

**meatball** [MEET•baul] *n*
Fleischklößchen N

**mechanic** [mu•KA•nik] *n*
Mechaniker M

**mechanical** [mu•KA•ni•kl] *adj*
mechanisch

**mechanism** [ME•ku•NI•zm] *n*
Mechanismus M

**medal** [ME•dl] *n* Medaille F

**medallion** [mu•DAHL•yun] *n*
Madaillon N

**meddle** [ME•dl] *vi* sich
einmischen

**media** [MEE•dee•u] *npl*
Media F

**mediate** [MEE•dee•AIT] *vt*
vermitteln

**mediator** [MEE•dee•AI•tur] *n*
Vermittler M

**medical** [ME•di•kl] *adj*
medizinisch

**medicate** [ME•di•KAIT] *vt*
medizinisch behandeln

**medicine** [ME•di•sin] *n*
Medizin F

**medieval** [mi•DEE•vl] *adj*
mittelalterlich

**mediocre** [MEE•dee•O•kr] *adj*
mittelmäßig

**meditate** [ME•di•TAIT ]*vi*
nachsinnen

**medium** [MEE•dee•um] *adj*
mitte

**meek** [meek] *adj* mild

**meet** [meet] *vt* begegnen

**meeting** [MEE•ting] *n*
Begegnung F

**megaphone** [ME•gu•FON] *n*
Megaphon N

**melancholy** [ME•lun•KAH•lee]
*adj* Melancholie F

**mellow** [ME•lo] *adj* mürbe

**melody** [ME•lu•dee] *n*
Melodie F

**melon** [ME•lun] *n* Melone F

**melt** [melt] *vt* schmelzen

**member** [MEM•bur] *n*
Mitglied N

**membership** [MEM•bur•SHIP]
*n* Zugehörigkeit F

**memo** [ME•mo] *n* Notiz F

**memoirs** [MEM•wahrz] *npl*
Denkschrift F

**memorial** [me•MAU•ree•ul] *adj*
Denkmal N

**memorize** [ME•mu•RUYZ] *vt*
auswendig lernen

**memory** [ME•mu•ree] *n*
Gedächtnis N

**menace** [ME•nus] *n* Gefahr F

**menacing** [ME•nu•sing] *adj*
bedrohend

**mend** [mend] *vt* reparieren

**menial** [MEEN•yul] *adj*
unterwürfig

**menopause** [ME•nu•PAUZ] *n*
Wechseljahre F

**menstruation**
[MEN•stroo•AI•shn] *n*
Regel F

**mental** [MEN•tl] *adj* geistig

**mentality** [men•TA•li•tee] *n*
Mentalität F

**mention** [MEN•chn] *vt*
erwähnen

**menu** [ME•nyoo] *n*
Speisekarte F

**mercenary** [MUR•su•NE•ree]
*adj n* käuflich

**merchandise**
[MUR•chun•DUYS] *n*
Waren F

**merchant** [MUR•chunt] *n*
Kaufmann M

**merciful** [MUR•si•ful] *adj*
barmherzig

**merciless** [MUR•si•lis] *adj*
erbarmungslos

**mercury** [MUR•kyu•ree] *n*
Merkur M

**mercy** [MUR•see] *n*
Barmherzigkeit F

**mere** [meeur] *adj* bloß

**merely** [MEEUR•lee] *adv* bloß

**merge** [murj] *vt* verschmelzen

**merger** [MUR•jur] *n*
Zusammenlegung F

**merit** [ME•rit] *n*
Verdienstlichkeit F

**mermaid** [MUR•maid] *n*
Meerweib N

**merry** [ME•ree] *adj* lustig

**merry-go-round**
[MAI•ree•go•ROUND] *n*
Karusell N

**mesh** [mesh] *n* Masche F

**mesmerize** [MEZ•mu•RUYZ]
*vt* faszinieren

**mess** [mes] *n* Mischmasch M

**message** [ME•sij] *n* Botschaft F

**messenger** [ME•sin•jur] *n*
Bote M

**messy** [ME•see] *adj*
unordentlich

**metal** [ME•tl] *n* Metall N

**metallic** [mu•TA•lik] *adj*
metallen

**metaphor** [ME•tu•FAUR] *n*
Metapher F

**meteor** [MEE•tee•ur] *n*
Meteor M

**meteorology**
[MEE•tee•u•RAH•lu•jee] *n*
Witterungskunde F

**meter** [MEE•tur] *n* Zähler M

**method** [ME•thud] *n*
Methode F

**meticulous** [mu•TI•kyu•lus] *adj*
peinlich genau

**metric** [ME•trik] *adj* metrisch

**metropolitan**
[ME•tru•PAH•li•tun] *adj*
hauptstätdtisch

**Mexican** [MEK•si•kun] *adj*
mexicanisch

**Mexico** [MEK•si•KO] *n* Mexico

**mice** [muys] *npl* Mäuser

**microchip** [MUY•cro•CHIP] *n*
Mikrochip M

**microphone** [MUY•kru•FON]
*n* Mikrophon N

**microscope** [MUY•kru•SKOP]
*n* Mikroskop N

**microscopic**
[MUY•kru•SKO•pik] *adj*
mikroskopisch

**microwave** [MUY•kru•WAIV]
*n* Mikrowelle F

**mid** [mid] *adj* mitte

**middle** [MI•dl] *n* Mitte F

**Middle Ages** [MI•dl A•jis] *npl*
Mittelalter N

**middle class** [MI•dl KLAS] *n*
Mittelstand M

**Middle East** [MI•dl EEST] *n*
Mittlere Osten

**midnight** [MID•nuyt] *n*
Mitternacht F

**midst** [midst] *n* Mitte F

**midwife** [MID•wuyf] *n*
Hebamme F

**might 1** [muyt] *modal v* mögen

**might 2** [muyt] *n* Kraft F

**mighty** [MUY•tee] *adj* kräftig

**migraine** [MUY•grain] *n*
Migräne F

**migrant** [MUY•grunt] *n*
Umsiedler M

**migrate** [MUY•grait] *vi*
umsiedeln

**mild** [muyld] *adj* sanft

**mildew** [MIL•doo] *n*
Mehltaupilz M

**mile** [muyl] *n* Meile F

**militant** [MI•li•tunt] *adj n*
militant

**military** [MI•li•TE•ree] *adj*
militarisch

**militia** [mi•LI•shu] *n* Miliz F

**milk** [milk] *n* Milch F

**mill** [mil] *n* Mühle F

**millenium** [mi•LE•nee•um] *n*
Jahrtausend

**million** [MIL•yun] *num*
Million F

**millionaire** [MIL•yu•NAIUR] *n*
Millionär M

**mimic** [MI•mik] *n*
Nachahmer M

**mince** [mins] *vt* zerhacken

**mind** [muynd] *n* Sinn M

**mindful** [MUYND•ful] *adj*
aufmerksam

**mine** [muyn] *n* mein

**mineral** [MI•nu•rul] *adj n*
Mineral N

**mingle** [MING•gl] *vi* sich
vermischen

**miniature** [MI•nu•CHUR] *adj n*
Miniatur N

**minimize** [MI•ni•MUYZ] *vt*
bagatellisieren

**minimum** [MI•ni•mum] *adj n*
Minimum N

**mining** [MUY•ning] *n*
Bergbau M

**minister** [MI•ni•stur] *n*
Pfarrer M

**ministry** [MI•ni•stree] *n*
Ministerium N

**mink** [mingk] *n* Nerz M

**minor** [MUY•nur] *adj* klein; *n*
Minderjähriger M

**minority** [muy•NAU•ri•tee] *n*
Minderheit F

**mint** [mint] *n* Minze F

**minus** [MUY•nus] *prep* minus

**minute** [adj. muy•NYOOT] *adj*
Minute F

**miracle** [MI•ru•kl] *n* Wunder N

**miraclulous** [mi•RA•kyu•lus]
*adj* wunderlich

**mirage** [mi•RAHZH] *n*
Luftspiegelung F

**mirror** [MI•rur] *n* Spiegel M

**misanthrope** [MI•san•THROP]
*n* Menschenhaß M

**misappropriation**
[mis•U•PRO•pree•AI•shn] *n*
Unterschlagung F

**misbehave** [MIS•bee•HAIV] *vi*
sich schlecht benehmen

**miscarriage** [MIS•KA•rij] *n*
Fehlschlag M

**miscellaneous**
[MI•su•LAI•nee•us] *adj*
vielseitig

**mischief** [MIS•chif] *n* Unheil N

**mischievous** [MIS•chi•vus] *adj*
verderblich

**misconception**
[MIS•kun•SEP•shn] *vt*
Mißverständnis N

**misconduct** [mis•KAHN•duhkt]
*n* Ungebühr F

**misconstrue**
[MIS•kun•STROO] *vt* falsch
auslegen

**miscount** [mis•KOUNT] *vt vi*
falsch zählen

**misdeed** [mis•DEED] *n*
Missetat F

**misdemeanor**
[MIS•du•MEE•nur] *n*
Straffälliger M

**miser** [MUY•zur] *n* Geizhals

**miserable** [MIZ•ru•bl] *adj*
elend

**miserly** [MUY•zur•lee] *adj*
geizig

**misery** [MI•zu•ree] *n* Elend N

**misfire** [mis•FUYUR] *vi*
versagen

**misfit** [MIS•fit] *n*
Eigenbrötler M

**misfortune** [MIS•FAUR•chun]
*n* Mißgeschick N

**misgivings** [MIS•GI•vingz] *npl*
Zweifel M

**mishap** [MIS•hap] *n* Unfall M

**misinform** [MIS•in•FAURM] *vt*
falsch berichtigen

**misjudge** [mis•JUHJ] *vt* falsh
urteilen

**misleading** [MIS•LEE•ding]
*adj* irreführend

**misplace** [mis•PLAIS] *vt*
verlegen

**misprint** [MIS•print] *n*
Druckfehler M

**Miss** [mis] *n* Fräulein N

**miss** [mis] *vt* verpassen

**missile** [MI•sul] *n* Geschoß N

**missing** [MI•sing] *adj* fehlend

**mission** [MI•shn] *n* Mission F

**missionary** [MI•shu•NE•ree] *n*
Missionar M

**misspell** [mis•SPEL] *vt* falsh
buchstabieren

**mist** [mist] *n* Nebel M

**mistake** [mi•STAIK] *n*
Fehler M

**mistaken** [mi•STAI•kn] *adj*
falsch

**mister** [MI•stur] *n* Herr M

**mistreat** [mis•TREET] *vt*
mißhandeln

**mistress** [MI•strus] *n* Herrin F

**mistrust** [mis•TRUHST] *n*
Mißtrauen N

**misty** [MI•stee] *adj* dunstig

**misunderstand**
[mis•UHN•dur•STAND] *vt*
mißverstehen

**misunderstanding**
[mis•UHN•dur•STAN•ding] *n*
Mißverständnis N

**misuse** [*n.* mis•YOOS *v.*
mis•YOOZ] *n* Mißbrauch M

**mitigating** [MI•ti•GAI•ting] *adj*
strafmildernde

**mitten** [MI•tn] *n* Handschuh M

**mix** [miks] *vt* mischen

**mixture** [MIKS•chur] *n*
Mischung F

**moan** [mon] *n* Ächzen N

**moat** [mot] *n* Burggraben M

**mob** [mahb] *n* Bande F

**mobile** [MO•bl] *adj* beweglich

**mobilize** [MO•bu•LUYZ] *vt*
mobilisieren

**mock** [mahk] *vt* verspotten

**mockery** [MAH•ku•ree] *n*
Spott M

**mode** [mod] *n* Weise F

**model** [MAH•dl] *adj* Mode F

**moderate** [*adj. n.* MAH•du•rit
*v.* MAH•du•RAIT] *adj*
gemäßigt; *n* Gemäßigte F

**moderation**
[MAH•du•RAI•shn] *n*
Mäßigung F

**modern** [MAH•durn] *adj*
modern

**modernize** [MAH•dur•NUYZ]
*vt* modernisieren

**modest** [MAH•dist] *adj*
anständig

**modesty** [MAH•di•stee] *n*
Einfachheit F

**modify** [MAH•di•FUY] *vt*
modifizieren

**moist** [moist] *adj* feucht

**moisten** [MOI•sn] *vt* befeuchten

**moisture** [MOIS•chur] *n*
Feuchtigkeit F

**molar** [MO•lur] *n* Molen

**molasses** [mu•LA•sis] *n*
Melasse F

**mold** [mold] *n* Schimmelpilz M

**mole** [mol] *n* Maulwurf M

**molest** [MU•lest] *vt* belästigen

**mollusk** [MAH•lusk] *n*
Molluske F

**molten** [MOL•tn] *adj*
geschmolzen

**moment** [MO•munt] *n*
Moment M

**momentary** [MO•mun•TE•ree]
*adj* momentan

**momentous** [mo•MEN•tus] *adj*
bedeutsam

**monarch** [MAH•nahrk] *n*
Monarch M

**monarchy** [MAH•nahr•kee] *n*
Monarchie F

**monastery** [MAH•nu•STE•ree]
*n* Kloster N

**Monday** [MUHN•dai] *n*
Montag M

**monetary** [MAH•nu•TE•ree]
*adj* geldlich
**money** [MUH•nee] *n* Geld N
**mongrel** [MAHN•grul] *n*
Mischling M
**monk** [muhngk] *n* Mönch M
**monkey** [MUHNG•kee] *n*
Affe M
**monologue** [MAH•nu•LAHG]
*n* Monolog M
**monopolize**
[mu•NAH•pu•LUYZ] *vt*
monopolisieren
**monopoly** [mu•NAH•pu•lee] *n*
Monopol M
**monotone** [MAH•nu•TON] *n*
Monotonie F
**monotonous** [mu•NAH•tu•nus]
*adj* eintönig
**monotony** [mu•NAH•tu•nee] *n*
Eintönigkeit F
**monsoon** [mahn•SOON] *n*
Monsun M
**monster** [MAHN•stur] *n*
Ungeheur N
**monstrosity**
[mahn•STRAH•si•tee] *n*
Ungeheuererlichkeit N
**monstrous** [MAHN•strus] *adj*
riesig
**month** [muhnth] *n* Monat M
**monthly** [MUHNTH•lee] *adj n*
monatlich
**monument** [MAH•nyu•munt] *n*
Denkmal N
**monumental**
[MAH•nyu•MEN•tl] *adj*
gewaltig
**moo** [moo] *n* Muhen N
**mood** [mood] *n* Stimmung F
**moody** [MOO•dee] *adj* launisch

**moon** [moon] *n* Mond M
**moonlight** [MOON•luyt] *n*
Mondlicht N
**moor** [moour] *n* Heideland N
**Moor** [moour] *n* Maure M
**mop** [mahp] *n* Schrubber M
**mope** [mop] *vi* Trübsinn M
**moral** [MAU•rul] *adj* moralisch
**morale** [mau•RAL] *n* Moral F
**morality** [mu•RA•li•tee] *n*
Moral F
**morbid** [MAUR•bid] *adj*
morbid
**more** [maur] *adj* mehr
**moreover** [mau•RO•vur] *adv*
außerdem
**morgue** [maurg] *n*
Leichenschauhaus N
**morning** [MAUR•ning] *n*
Morgen M
**Morocco** [mu•RAH•ko] *n*
Morokko
**moron** [MAU•rahn] *n*
Schwachsinniger M
**morsel** [MAUR•sl] *n*
Stückchen N
**mortal** [MAUR•tl] *adj* sterblich;
*n* Sterblicher M
**mortality** [maur•TA•li•tee] *n*
Sterblichkeit F
**mortar** [MAUR•tur] *n*
Mörser M
**mortgage** [MAUR•gij] *n*
Pfandgut N
**mortify** [MAUR•ti•FUY] *vt*
demütigen
**mosaic** [mo•ZAI•ik] *n*
Mosaik N
**Moscow** [MAH•skou] *n*
Moskow
**mosque** [mahsk] *n* Moschee F

**mosquito** [mu•SKEE•to] *n*
Mücke F

**moss** [maus] *n* Moos N

**most** [most] *adj* meist

**mostly** [MOST•lee] *adv*
größtenteils

**moth** [mauth] *n* Motte F

**mother** [MUH•thur] *n* Mutter F

**mother-in-law**
[MUH•thur•in•LAU] *n*
Schwiegermutter F

**motherhood** [MUH•thur•HUD]
*n* Mutterschaft F

**motherly** [MUH•thur•lee] *adj*
mütterlich

**motif** [mo•TEEF] *n* Vorwurf M

**motion** [MO•shn] *n*
Bewegung F

**motivate** [MO•ti•VAIT] *vt*
motivieren

**motivation** [MO•ti•VAI•shn] *n*
Motivierung F

**motive** [MO•tiv] *n* Motiv N

**motor** [MO•tur] *n* Motor M

**motorboat** [MO•tur•BOT] *n*
Motorboot N

**motorcycle** [MO•tur•SUY•kl] *n*
Motorrad N

**motto** [MAH•to] *n* Motto N

**mound** [mound] *n* Erdwall M

**mount** [mount] *n* Berg M

**mountaineer**
[MOUN•tu•NEEUR] *n*
Bersteiger M

**mountainous** [MOUN•tu•nus]
*adj* bergig

**mourn** [maurn] *vt* trauern

**mourning** [MAUR•ning] *n*
Trauer F

**mouse** [mous] *n* Maus F

**moustache** [MUH•stash] *n*
Schnurrbart M

**mouth** [mouth] *n* Mund M

**mouthful** [MOUTH•ful] *n*
Mundvoll M

**mouthwash** [MOUTH•wahsh]
*n* Mundwasser N

**movable** [MOO•vu•bl] *adj*
beweglich

**move** [moov] *n* Bewegung; (in
game) *n* Zug M; (of house) N
Umzug M; *vt* bewegen;
(change location) *vt* verlegen;
*vi* sich bewegen

**movement** [MOOV•munt] *n*
Bewegung

**movie** [MOO•vee] *n* Film M

**moving** [MOO•ving] *adj*
bewegend

**mow** [mo] *vt* mähen

**much** [muhch] *adj* viel

**mucous** [MYOO•kus] *n*
Schleim M

**mud** [muhd] *n* Schlamm M

**muddle** [MUH•dl] *n*
Durcheinander N

**muddy** [MUH•dee] *adj*
schlammig

**muffin** [MUH•fin] *n* Semmel F

**muffle** [MUH•fl] *vt* umwickeln

**mug** [muhg] *n* Krug M

**mule** [myooul] *n* Maultier N

**multiple** [MUHL•ti•pl] *adj n*
mehrfach

**multiplication**
[MUHL•ti•pli•KAI•shn] *n*
Vermehrung F

**multiply** [MUHL•ti•PLUY] *vt*
vermehren

**multitude** [MUHL•ti•TOOD] *n*
Menge F

mumble [MUHM•bl] *vt vi*
murmeln

mummy [MUH•mee] *n*
Mumie F

mumps [muhmps] *n*
Ziegenpeter M

munch [muhnch] *vt vi* kauen

mundane [muhn•DAIN] *adj*
irdisch

municipal [myoo•NI•si•pl] *adj*
städtisch

municipality
[myoo•NI•si•PA•li•tee] *n*
Stadt F    •

mural [MYOOU•rul] *n*
Wandgemälde N

murder [MUR•dur] *n* Mord M

murderer [MUR•du•rur] *n*
Mörder M

murderous [MUR•du•rus] *adj*
mörderlich

murky [MUR•kee] *adj* dunkel

murmur [MUR•mur] *n*
Murmeln N

muscle [MUH•sl] *n*
Muskel M

muscular [MUH•skyu•lur] *adj*
muskulös

muse [myooz] *n* Muse F

museum [myoo•ZEE•um] *n*
Museum N

mushroom [MUHSH•rum] *n*
Pilz M

music [MYOO•zik] *n* Musik F

musical [MYOO•zi•kl] *adj*
musikalisch

musician [myoo•ZI•shn] *n*
Musike M

Muslim [MUHZ•lim] *adj*
moslem

mussel [MUH•sl] *n*
Muschel F

must [muhst] *modal v* müssen;
(have to) muß

mustache [MUH•stash] *n*
Bart M

mustard [MUH•sturd] *n*
Senf M

muster [MUH•stur] *vt*
auftreiben

musty [MUH•stee] *adj*
verstaubt

mute [myoot] *adj n* stumm
Stummer M

mutilate [MYOO•ti•LAIT] *vt*
verstümmeln

mutiny [MYOO•ti•nee] *n*
Auflehnung F

mutter [MUH•tur] *vt vi*
murmeln

mutton [MUH•tn] *s*
Hammelfleisch N

mutual [MYOO•choo•ul] *adj*
gemeinsam

muzzle [MUH•zl] *n* Maul N

my [muy] *poss adj* mein; meine

myself [muy•SELF] *pron* mir;
mich; ich; selbst

mysterious [mi•STEEU•ree•us]
*adj* geheimnisvoll

mystery [MI•stu•ree] *n*
Geheimnis N

mystic [MI•stik] *n* Mysticker M

mystical [MI•sti•kl] *adj*
mystisch

myth [mith] *n* Sage F

mythical [MI•thi•kl] *adj*
sagenhaft

mythology [mi•THAH•lu•jee]
*n* Mythologe M

# N

**nab** [nab] *vt* schnappen

**nag** [nag] *vt* nörgeln

**nail** [naiul] *n* Nagel M

**naive** [nuy•EEV] *adj* naiv

**naked** [NAI•kid] *adj* nackt

**nakedness** [NAI•kid•nis] *n* Nacktheit F

**name** [naim] *n* Name M

**namely** [NAIM•lee] *adv* nämlich

**nap** [nap] *n* Schläfchen N

**napkin** [NAP•kin] *n* Serviette F

**narcotic** [nahr•KAH•tik] *adj n* narkotisch

**narrate** [NA•rait] *vt* erzählen

**narration** [na•RAI•shn] *n* Erzählung F

**narrative** [NA•ru•tiv] *adj* erzählungs

**narrator** [na•RAI•tur] *n* Erzähler M

**narrow** [NA•ro] *adj* eng

**narrow-minded** [NAI•row•MUYN•did] *adj* Engstirnigkeit F

**nasal** [NAI•zl] *adj* Nasen

**nasturtium** [nu•STUR•shum] *n* Kapuzinerkresse F

**nasty** [NA•stee] *adj* ekelhaft

**nation** [NAI•shn] *n* Nation F

**national** [NA•shu•nl] *adj* national

**nationality** [NA•shu•NA•li•tee] *n* Nationalität F

**nationalize** [NA•shu•nu•LUYZ] *vt* verstaatlichen

**native** [NAI•tiv] *adj* einheimisch; ~ town\ Heimat-; ~ language\ Mutter-; *n* Einheimische(r)

**Nativity** [nu•TI•vi•tee] *n* Geburt Christi F

**natural** [NA•chrul] *adj* natürlich

**naturalize** [NA•chru•LUYZ] *vt* einbürgen

**naturally** [NA•chru•lee] *adv* von Natur F

**nature** [NA•chur] *n* Natur F

**naughty** [NAU•tee] *adj* unartig

**nausea** [NAU•zee•u] *n* Übelkeit F

**nauseate** [NAU•zee•AIT] *vt* sich ekeln

**nauseous** [NAU•shus] *adj* ekelerregend

**naval** [NAI•vl] *adj* see

**navel** [NAI•vl] *n* Nabel M

**navigate** [NA•vi•GAIT] *vt* schiffen

**navigation** [NA•vi•GAI•shn] *n* Nautik F

**navigator** [NA•vi•GAI•tur] *n* Seefahrer M

**navy** [NAI•vee] *adj* Kriegsmarine F

**near** [neeur] *adj prep* nahe; (accurately) genau

**near-sighted** [NEEUR•suy•tid] *adj* kurzsichtig

**nearby** [NEEUR•buy] *adj* in der Nähe

**nearly** [NEEUR•lee] *adv* beinahe

**neat** [neet] *adj* sauber

**necessary** [NE•su•SE•ree] *adj* notwendig

**necessity** [nu•SE•si•tee] *n* Notwendigkeit F

**neck** [nek] *n* Hals M

**need** [need] *n* Bedarf M; Notwendigkeit F; (requirement) Bedfürtis; *vt* brauchen; (have to) mussen

**needle** [NEE•dl] *n* Nadel F

**needless** [NEED•lis] *adj* unnötig

**needy** [NEE•dee] *adj* arm

**negative** [NE•gu•tiv] *adj* negativ

**neglect** [ni•GLEKT] *n* Vernachlässigung F

**negligence** [NE•gli•juns] *n* Nachlässigkeit F

**negligent** [NE•gli•junt] *adj* nachlässig

**negotiate** [ni•GO•shee•AIT] *vt vi* verhandeln

**negotiation** [ni•GO•shee•AI•shn] *n* Verhandlung F

**Negro** [NEE•gro] *adj n* Neger M

**neigh** [nai] *vi* wiehern

**neighbor** [NAI•bur] *n* Nachbar M

**neighborhood** [NAI•bur•HUD] *n* Nachbarschaft F

**neither** [NEE•thur] *adj* weder

**nephew** [NE•fyoo] *n* Neffe M

**Neptune** [NEP•toon] *n* Neptun M

**nerve** [nurv] *n* Nerv M

**nervous** [NUR•vus] *adj* nervös

**nest** [nest] *n* Nest N

**net** [net] *adj* Netz N

**Netherlands** [NE•thur•lundz] *npl* Niederlande

**nettle** [NE•tl] *n* Nessel F

**network** [NET•wurk] *n* Netzwerk N

**neurosis** [nu•RO•sis] *n* Neurose F

**neurotic** [nu•RAH•tik] *adj n* neurotisch

**neuter** [NOO•tur] *adj* sächlich

**neutral** [NOO•trul] *adj* neutral

**neutrality** [noo•TRA•li•tee] *n* Neutralität F

**neutralize** [NOO•tru•LUYZ] *vt* neutralisieren

**never** [NE•vr] *adv* nie

**nevertheless** [NE•vur•thu•LES] *adv* trotzdem

**new** [noo] *adj* neu

**New Year** [NOO yeer] *n* Neujahr N

**newly** [NOO•lee] *adv* neulich

**news** [nooz] *n* Nachrichten

**newscast** [NOOZ•kast] *n* Nachrichtensendung F

**newsletter** [NOOZ•le•tur] *n* Rundschreiben N

**newspaper** [NOOZ•pai•pur] *n* Zeitung F

**next** [nekst] *adj* nächst

**next-door** [NEXT•DOR] *adj* nebenan

**nibble** [NI•bl] *vt* benagen

**nice** [nuys] *adj* nett

**nicely** [NUYS•lee] *adv* net

**niche** [nich] *n* Nische F

**nick** [nik] *n* Kerbe F

**nickname** [NIK•naim] *n* Spitzname M

**nicotine** [NI•ku•TEEN] *n*
Nikotin N

**niece** [nees] *n* Nichte F

**night** [nuyt] *n* Nacht F

**nightclub** [NUYT•kluhb] *n*
Klub M

**nightfall** [NUYT•faul] *n*
Einbruch der Nacht

**nightingale**
[NUY•ting•GAIUL] *n*
Nachtigall F

**nightly** [NUYT•lee] *adj*
nächtlich

**nightmare** [NUYT•maiur] *n*
Alp M

**nimble** [NIM•bl] *adj* flink

**nine** [nuyn] *num* neun

**nineteen** [nuyn•TEEN] *num*
neunzehn

**ninety** [NUYN•tee] *num*
neunzig

**ninth** [nuynth] *num* neunte

**nipple** [NI•pl] *n* Brustwarze F

**nitrogen** [NUY•tru•jun] *n*
Stickstoff M

**no** [no] *adv* nein; *adj* kein

**nobility** [no•BI•li•tee] *n* Adel M

**noble** [NO•bl] *adj* adlig

**nobody** [NO•bu•dee] *pron*
niemand

**nocturnal** [nahk•TUR•nl] *adj*
nächtlich

**nod** [nahd] *n* Nicken N; *vi*
nicken

**noise** [noiz] *n* Lärm M

**noisy** [NOI•zee] *adj* laut

**nominal** [NAH•mi•nul] *adj*
nominell

**nominate** [NAH•mi•NAIT] *vt*
ernennen

**nomination**
[NAH•mi•NAI•shn] *n*
Ernennung F

**nonchalant**
[NAHN•shu•LAHNT] *adj*
gleichgültig

**nonconformist**
[NAHN•kun•FAUR•mist] *adj*
*n* Dissident M

**none** [nuhn] *pron adj* kein;
keine

**nonentity** [NAHN•EN•ti•tee] *n*
Nichtdasein N

**nonetheless** [NUHN•thu•LES]
*adv* nichtsdestoweniger

**nonfiction** [nahn•FIK•shn] *s*
Sachbücher

**nonsense** [NAHN•sens] *n*
Unsinn M

**nonsmoker** [NAHN•SMO•kur]
*n* Nichtraucher M

**nonstop** [NAHN•STAHP] *adj*
durchgehend

**noodles** [NOO•dlz] *npl* Nudel F

**noon** [noon] *n* Mittag M

**noose** [noos] *n* Schlinge F

**nor** [naur] *conj* noch

**norm** [naurm] *n* Norm F

**normal** [NAUR•ml] *adj* normal

**normally** [NAUR•mu•lee] *adv*
gewöhnlich

**north** [naurth] *adj* Nord M

**North America** [NAURTH
u•ME•ri•ku] *n* Nord Amerika

**North Pole** [NAURTH POL] *n*
Nordpol M

**northern** [NAUR•thurn] *adj*
nördlich

**Northern Ireland**
[NAUR•thurn UYUR•lend] *n*
Nordirland N

**northward(s)**
[NAURTH•wurd(z)] *adv*
nordwärts

**Norwegian** [naur•WEE•jun] *adj*
norwegisch

**Norway** [NAUR•wai] *n*
Norwegen

**nose** [noz] *n* Nase F

**nostalgia** [nah•STAL•ju] *n*
Sehnsucht F

**nostril** [NAH•stril] *n*
Nasenloch N

**nosy** [NO•zee] *adj* neugierig

**not** [ʀaht] *adv* nicht

**notable** [NO•tu•bl] *adj*
bemerkenswert

**notably** [NO•tu•blee] *adv*
denkwürdig

**notary** [NO•tu•ree] *n* Notar M

**notch** [nahch] *n* Kerbe F

**note**
*n* Zeichen N

**notebook** [NOT•buk] *n* Heft N

**noteworthy** [NOT•wur•thee]
*adj* bemerkenswert

**nothing** [NUH•thing] *pron*
nichts

**notice** [NO•tis] *n* Notiz F

**noticeable** [NO•ti•su•bl] *adj*
merklich

**notify** [NO•ti•FUY] *vt*
bekanntgeben

**notion** [NO•shn] *n* Begriff M

**notoriety** [NO•tu•RUY•u•tee] *n*
Allbekanntheit F

**notorious** [no•TAU•ree•us] *adj*
notorisch

**notwithstanding**
[NAHT•with•STAN•ding] *adv*
trotz

**noun** [noun] *n* Substantiv N

**nourish** [NU•rish] *vt* ernähren

**nourishing** [NU•ri•shing] *adj*
nahrhaft

**nourishment** [NU•rish•munt] *n*
Nahrung F

**novel** [NAH•vl] *n* Roman M

**novelist** [NAH•vu•list] *n*
Schriftsteller M

**novelty** [NAH•vul•tee] *n*
Neuheit F

**November** [no•VEM•bur] *n*
November M

**novice** [NAH•vis] *n* Neuling M

**now** [nau] *adv* jetzt

**nowhere** [NO•waiur] *adv*
nirgendwo

**noxious** [nahk•shus] *adj*
schädlich

**nozzle** [NAH•zl] *n* Schnauze F

**nuance** [NOO•ahns] *n*
Nuance F

**nuclear** [NOO•klee•ur] *adj*
kernförmig

**nucleus** [NOO•klee•us] *n*
Kern M

**nude** [nood] *adj* nackt; *n*
Nacktheit F

**nudge** [nuhj] *n* Rippenstoß M

**nudist** [NOO•dist] *n*
Nacktkultur F

**nudity** [NOO•di•tee] *n*
Nacktheit F

**nuisance** [NOO•suns] *n*
Ärgernis N

**null** [nuhl] *adj* nichtig

**nullify** [NUH•li•FUY] *vt*
vernichten

**numb** [nuhm] *adj* starr

**number** [NUHM•bur] *n*
Nummer F; (math) *n* Zahl F;
Zimmer F; *vt* numerieren

**numeral** [NOO•mu•rul] *n*
Zahlzeichen N
**numerous** [NOO•mu•rus] *adj*
zahlreich
**nuptial** [NUHP•shl] *adj*
hochzeitlich
**nurse** [nurs] *n*
Krankenschwester F
**nursery** [NUR•su•ree] *n*
Kinderzimmer N
**nursery rhyme** [NUR•shree
RUYM] *n* Kinderlied N

**nurture** [NUR•chur] *vt* ernähren
**nut** [nuht] s Nuß F
**nutcrackers** [NUHT•kra•kurz]
*npl* Nußknacker M
**nutrition** [noo•TRI•shn] *n*
Nahrung F
**nutritious** [noo•TRI•shus] *adj*
nahrhaft
**nylon** [NUY•lahn] *n* Nylon N
**nymph** [nimf] *n* Nymphe F

# O

**o'clock** [u•KLAHK] *adv* Uhr F
**oak** [ok] *n* Eiche F
**oar** [aur] *n* Ruder N
**oasis** [o•AI•sis] *n* Oase F
**oath** [oth] *n* Eid M
**oatmeal** [OT•meeul] *n*
Hafermehl N
**oats** [ots] *npl* Hafer M
**obedience** [o•BEE•dee•uns] *n*
Gehorsam M
**obedient** [o•BEE•dee•unt] *adj*
gehorsam
**obese** [o•BEES] *adj* fettleibig
**obey** [o•BAI] *vt* gehorchen
**obituary** [o•BI•choo•E•ree] *n*
Nachruf M
**object 1** [AHB•jekt] thing *n*
Gegenstand M; Objekt,
Ding N
**object 2** [ub•JEKT] *vi* dragen
sein; protestieren; *vt*
einwenden

**objection** [ub•JEK•shn] *n*
Einspruch M; Einwand M
**objective** [ub•JEK•tiv] *adj n*
Objektiv M
**obligation** [AH•bli•GAI•shn] *n*
Verpflichten N
**obligatory** [u•BLI•gu•TAU•ree]
*adj* verplifchtend
**oblige** [u•BLUYJ] *vt*
verpflichten; (compel)
zwingen
**obliging** [u•BLUY•jing] *adj*
verbindlich
**oblique** [o•BLEEK] *adj* schief
**obliterate** [u•BLI•tu•RAIT] *vt*
auslöschen
**oblivion** [u•BLI•vee•un] *n*
Vergessenheit F
**oblivious** [u•BLI•vee•us] *adj*
vergeBlich
**obnoxious** [ub•NAHK•shus]
*adj* anstößig F

obscene [ub•SEEN] *adj*
unzüchtig

obscenity [ub•SE•ni•tee] *n*
Unanständigkeit F

obscure [ub•SKYOOUR] *adj*
düster; unklar; *vt* (hide)
verdecken

obscurity [ub•SKYU•ri•tee] *n*
Dunkelheit F

observance [ub•ZUR•vuns] *n*
Beobachtung F

observant [ub•ZUR•vunt] *adj*
beobachtend

observation
[AHB•sur•VAI•shn] *n*
Beobachtung F

observatory
[ob•SUR•vuh•TAUR•ee] *n*
Observatorium N

observe [ub•ZURV] *vt*
beobachten

observer [ub•ZUR•vur] *adj*
Beobachter M

obsess [ub•SES] *vt* verfolgen

obsession [ub•SE•shn] *n*
Besessenheit

obsessive [ub•SE•siv] *adj*
besessen

obsolete [AHB•su•LEET] *adj*
veraltet

obstacle [AHB•sti•kl] *n*
Hindernis N

obstinacy [AHB•sti•ni•cee] *n*
Eigensinn M

obstinate [AHB•sti•nit] *adj*
hartnäckig

obstruct [ub•STRUHKT] *vt*
versperren

obstruction [ub•STRUHK•shn]
*n* Behinderung F

obtain [ub•TAIN] *vt* bekommen

obtuse [ub•TOOS] *adj* stumpf

obvious [AHB•vee•us] *adj*
offensichtlich

obviously [AHB•vee•us•lee] *adj*
offensichtlich

occasion [u•KAI•zhn] *n*
Gelegenheit F

occasional [u•KAI•zhu•nl] *adj*
gelegentlich

occasionally
[u•KAI•zhu•nu•lee] *adv*
gelegentlich

occult [u•KUHLT] *adj* okkult

occupant [AH•kyu•punt] *n*
Inhaber M

occupation [AH•kyu•PAI•shn]
*n* Beruf M

occupy [AH•kyu•PUY] *vt*
besitzen; (house) bewohnen;
(be busy) beschäftigen

occur [u•KUR] *vi* vorkommen

occurence [u•KU•runs] *n*
Vorkommen N

ocean [O•shn] *n* Meer N

octagon [AHK•tu•GAHN] *n*
Achteck N

October [ahk•TO•bur] *n*
Oktober M

octupus [AHK•tu•pus] *n*
Krake M

odd [ahd] *adj* sonderbar;
merkwürdig

oddity [AH•di•tee] *n*
Seltsamkeit F

odious [O•dee•us] *adj* verhaßt

odor [O•dur] *n* Geruch M

of [uhv] *prep* von; made ~\ aus

off [auf] *adj* weg; be ~\ gehen;
(of lights, etc) aus; (motion,
removal, etc) von

offend [u•FEND] *vt* beleidigen

**offense** [u•FENS] *n* Verstoß M

**offensive** [u•FEN•siv] *adj* angreifend

**offer** [AU•fur] *n* anbieten

**offering** [AU•fu•ring] *n* Opfer N

**offhand** [AUF•HAND] *adj* ohneweiteres

**office** [AU•fis] *n* Büro N

**officer** [AU•fi•sur] *n* Offizier M

**official** [u•FI•shl] *adj* offiziell

**offspring** [AUF•spring] *n* Nachkommen N

**offstage** [AUF•STAIJ] *adj adv* hinter den Kulissen

**often** [AU•fn] *adv* oft

**oil** [oiul] *n* Öl N

**oily** [OIU•lee] *adj* ölig

**ointment** [OINT•munt] *n* Salbe F

**old** [old] *adj* alt

**old age** [OLD AIJ] *n* Alter N

**old-fashioned** [OLD•FA•shund] *adj* altmodisch

**olive** [AH•liv] *adj n* Olive F

**omelet** [AHM•lit] *n* Omelett N

**omen** [O•mn] *n* Omen N

**ominous** [AH•mi•nus] *adj* drohend

**omission** [o•MI•shn] *n* Weglassung F

**omit** [o•MIT] *vt* weglassen

**omnipotent** [ahm•NI•pu•tunt] *adj* allmächtig

**omniscience** [ahm•NI•shent] *adj* allwissend

**on** [ahn] *prep* auf; ~ fott zu fuß; (about; concerning; etc) über; (lights; etc) angezogen

**once** [wuhns] *adv* einmal

**one** [wuhn] *num* eins; *pron* eine(r); *impers pron* man

**one-sided** [WUHN•SUY•did] *adj* einseitig

**one-way** [WUHN•WAI] *adj* einbahn

**oneself** [wuhn•SELF] *pron* sich; selbst

**onion** [UH•nyun] *n* Zwiebel F

**onlooker** [AHN•lu•kur] *n* Zuschauer M

**only** [ON•lee] *adj* einzig

**onslaught** [AHN•slaut] *n* Angriff M

**onward** [AHN•wurd] *adv* vorwärts

**ooze** [ooz] *vi* durchsickern

**opal** [O•pl] *n* Opal M

**opaque** [o•PAIK] *adj* undurchsichtig

**open** [O•pn] *adj* offen; *vt* aufmachen; *vi* aufgeben

**open-minded** [O•pn•MUYN•did] *adj* aufgeschlossen

**opening** [O•pu•ning] *adj* Eröffnung F

**openly** [O•pn•lee] *adv* offen

**opera** [AH•pru] *n* Oper F

**operate** [AH•pu•RAIT] *vt* funktionieren; *vi* opeerieren; (business) fürhen

**operation** [AH•pu•RAI•shn] *n* Wirkung F

**operator** [AH•pu•RAI•tur] *n* Maschinist M

**opinion** [u•PI•nyun] *n* Meinung F

**opinionated** [u•PI•nyu•NAI•tid] *adj* eigensinnig

**opponent** [u•PO•nunt] *n*
Gegner

**opportune** [AH•pur•TOON]
*adj* günstig

**opportunist**
[AH•pur•TOO•nist] *n*
Opportunist M

**opportunity**
[AH•pur•TOON•ah•tee] *n*
Gelegenheit

**oppose** [u•POZ] *vt*
entgegensetzen

**opposed** [u•POZD] *adj*
dagegen

**opposing** [u•PO•zing] *adj*
gegenüberliegend

**opposite** [AH•pu•sit] *n*
Gegenteil M; *adj* (facing)
gegenüberliegend

**opposition** [AH•pu•ZI•shn] *n*
Gegenüberstellung F

**oppress** [u•PRES] *vt* bedrücken

**oppression** [u•PRE•shn] *n*
Unterdrückung F

**oppressive** [u•PRE•siv] *adj*
gewaltsam

**opt** [ahpt] *vi* wählen

**optical** [AHP•ti•kl] *adj* optisch

**optician** [ahp•TI•shn] *n*
Optiker M

**optimism** [AHP•ti•MI•zm] *n*
Optimismus M

**optimist** [AHP•ti•mist] *n*
Optimist M

**optimistic** [AHP•ti•MI•stik] *adj*
optimistisch

**option** [AHP•shn] *n*
Entscheidung; Wahl F

**optional** [AHP•shu•nl] *adj*
freigestellt

**opulence** [AH•pyu•luns] *n*
Reichtum M

**opulent** [AH•pyu•lunt] *adj*
üppig

**or** [aur] *conj* oder; (with neg.)
noch

**oracle** [AU•ru•kl] *n* Orakel N

**orange** [AU•runj] *adj* orange

**orator** [AU•rai•tur] *n* Redner M

**oratory** [AU•ru•TAU•ree] *n*
Rhetorik F

**orbit** [AUR•bit] *n*
Himmelskörper M

**orchard** [AUR•churd] *n*
Obstgarten M

**orchestra** [AUR•ku•stru] *n*
Orchester N

**orchestral** [aur•KE•strul] *adj*
orchestral

**orchid** [AUR•kid] *n* Orchidee F

**order** [AUR•dur] *n* Ordnung F;
(condition) *n* Zustand M;
(command) *n* Befehl M; *vt*
befehlen; anorden

**orderly** [AUR•dur•lee] *adj*
ordentlich

**ordinarily** [AUR•di•NE•ri•lee]
*adv* normalerweise

**ordinary** [AUR•di•NE•ree] *adj*
gewöhnlich

**ore** [aur] *n* Erz N

**oregano** [au•RE•gu•NO] *n*
Oregano M

**organ** [AUR•gn] *n* Organ N

**organic** [aur•GA•nik] *adj*
organisch

**organism** [AUR•gu•NI•zm] *n*
Organismus M

**organization**
[AUR•gu•ni•ZAI•shn] *n*
Gliederung F

**organize** [AUR•gu•NUYZ] *vt*
organisieren

**orgasm** [AUR•ga•zm] *n*
Orgasmus M

**orgy** [AUR•gee] *n* Orgie F

**oriental** [AU•ree•EN•tl] *n*
östlich; morgenländisch

**orientate** [AU•ree•un•TAIT] *vt*
orientieren

**orientation**
[AU•ree•un•TAI•shn] *n*
Orientierung F

**orifice** [AU•ri•fis] *n* Öffnung F

**origin** [AU•ri•jin] *n* Ursprung M

**original** [u•RI•ji•nl] *adj*
original; *n* Original N

**originality** [u•RI•ji•NA•li•tee] *n*
Echtheit F

**originally** [u•RI•ji•nu•lee] *adv*
ursprunglich

**originate** [u•RI•ji•NAIT] *vt*
entstehen

**ornament** [AUR•nu•munt] *n*
Schmuck M

**ornamental** [AUR•nu•MEN•tl]
*adj* dekorativ

**ornate** [aur•NAIT] *adj* reich;
verziert

**orphan** [AUR•fn] *n* Waise F

**orphanage** [AUR•fu•nij] *n*
Waisenhaus N

**orthodox** [AUR•thu•DAHKS]
*adj* orthodox

**oscillate** [AH•si•LAIT] *vi*
schwingen

**ostensible** [ah•STEN•si•bl] *adj*
scheinbar

**ostentatious**
[AH•stun•TAI•shus] *adj*
prahlend

**ostrich** [AHS•trich] *n* Strauß M

**other** [UH•thur] *adj* ander

**otherwise** [UH•thur•WUYZ]
*adv* sonst; anders; *conj* sonst

**otter** [AH•tur] *n* Otter M

**ought** [aut] *aux v* sollen

**ounce** [ouns] *n* Unze F

**our** [ouur] *poss adj* unser

**ours** [ouurz] *poss pron* unser

**ourselves** [ouur•SELVZ] *pron*
*pl* uns

**oust** [oust] *vt* vertreiben

**out** [out] *adv* hinaus; (not in sth)
außen; (light, fire, etc) aus

**outbreak** [OUT•braik] *n*
Ausbruch M

**outburst** [OUT•burst] *n*
Ausbruch M

**outcast** [OUT•kast] *n*
Ausgestoßener M

**outcome** [OUT•kuhm] *n*
Ergebnis N

**outcry** [OUT•cruy] *n* Schrei M

**outdated** [out•DAI•tid] *adj*
veraltet

**outdoor** [OUT•dauur] *adj*
draußen

**outdoors** [out•DAUURZ] *adv*
draußen

**outer** [OU•tur] *adj* außer

**outfit** [OUT•fit] *n* Anzug M

**outgoing** [OUT•go•ing] *adj*
ausgeschlossen

**outhouse** [OUT•hous] *n*
Außenabort M

**outing** [OU•ting] *n* Ausflug M

**outlaw** [OUT•lau] *vt* verbieten;
*n* Verbrecher M

**outlet** [OUT•let] *n*
Stromverbraucher M

**outline** [OUT•luyn] *n* Skizze F

**outlive** [out•LIV] *vt* überleben

**outlook** [OUT•luk] *n*
Aussicht F

**outmoded** [out•MO•did] *adj*
altmodisch

**outnumber** [out•NUHM•bur] *vt*
an Zahl übertreffen

**output** [OUT•put] *n* Ertrag M

**outrage** [OUT•raij] *n* Frevel M

**outrageous** [out•RAI•jus] *adj*
abscheulich

**outright** [out•RUYT] *adj* total

**outset** [OUT•set] *n* Anfang M

**outside** [out•SUYD] *adj*
Außenseite F; *adj* Außen;
*prep* außerhalb

**outsider** [out•SUY•dur] *n*
Außenseiter M

**outskirts** [OUT•skurts] *npl*
Umgebung F

**outspoken** [out•SPO•kn] *adj*
freimütig

**outstanding** [out•STAN•ding]
*adj* hervorragend

**outward** [OUT•wurd] *adj*
äußerlich

**outwardly** [OUT•wurd•lee] *adv*
auswärts

**outweigh** [out•WAI] *vt*
überwiegen

**oval** [O•vl] *adj n* oval Oval N

**ovary** [O•vu•ree] *n* Eierstock M

**ovation** [o•VAI•shn] *n*
Ovation F

**oven** [UH•vn] *n* Ofen M

**over** [O•vr] *adj* über; (during)
wärhend; *ad* hinüber; (ended)
zu Ende

**overall** [O•vur•AUL] *adj* überall

**overalls** [O•vur•aulz] *npl*
Hose F

**overbearing**
[O•vur•BAIU•ring] *adj*
arrogant

**overboard** [O•vur•BAURD]
*adv* über Bord

**overbook** [O•vur•BUK] *vt*
überbuchen

**overcast** [O•vur•kast] *adj*
bewölkt

**overcharge** [O•vur•CHAHRJ]
*vt* überteuern

**overcoat** [O•vur•KOT] *n*
Mantel M

**overcome** [O•vur•KUHM] *vt*
überwinden

**overdo** [O•vur•DOO] *vt*
übertreiben

**overdraw** [O•vur•DRAU] *vt*
überziehen

**overdrawn** [O•vur•DRAUN]
*adj* übergespannt

**overflow** [O•vur•FLO] *n*
Überschwemmung F

**overgrown** [O•vur•GRON] *adj*
überwachsen

**overhaul** [O•vur•HAUL] *vt*
überholen

**overhear** [O•vur•HEEUR] *vt*
überhören

**overjoyed** [O•vur•JOID] *adj*
außer sich vor Freude

**overlap** [O•vur•LAP] *vt*
übergreifen auf

**overlook** [O•vur•LUK] *vt*
übersehen

**overnight** [O•vur•NUYT] *adj*
übernacht

**overpower** [O•vur•POU•ur] *vt*
überwältigen

**overrun** [O•vur•RUHN] *adj*
überfluten

**overseas** [O•vur•SEEZ] *adj adv*
übersee

**oversee** [O•vur•SEE] *vt*
übersehen

**overseer** [O•vur•SEE•ur] *n*
Aufseher M

**overshadow** [O•vur•SHA•do]
*vt* in den Schatten stellen

**overstep** [O•vur•STEP] *vt*
überschreiten

**overtake** [O•vur•TAIK] *vt*
einholen

**overthrow** [O•vur•THRO] *vt*
besiegen

**overtime** [O•vur•tuym] *n*
Überstundenlohn M

**overture** [O•vur•chur] *n*
Einleitung F

**overweight** [O•vur•WAIT] *adj*
Übergewicht N

**overwhelm** [O•vur•WELM] *vt*
übermannen

**overwhelming**
[O•vur•WEL•ming] *adj*
überwältigend

**overwork** [O•vur•WURK] *vt*
überlasten

**owe** [o] *vt* schulden

**owl** [ouul] *n* Eule F

**own 1** [on] *vt* besitzen

**own 2** [on] *adj* eigen

**owner** [O•nur] *n* Besitzer M

**ownership** [O•nur•SHIP] *n*
Eigentum N

**ox** [ahks] *n* Ochse M

**oxygen** [AHK•si•jun] *n*
Sauerstoff M

**oyster** [OI•stur] *n* Auster F

# P

**pace** [pais] *n* Schritt M; *vi* (~
up and down) auf und ab
gehen

**Pacific** [pu•SI•fik] *adj* pazifisch

**pacify** [PA•si•FUY] *vt* befrieden

**pack** [pak] *n* Pack M; *vt*
vollpacken; packen; *vi* passen;
einpacken

**package** [PA•kij] *n* Paket N

**packet** [PA•kit] *n* Päckchen N

**packing** [PA•king] *n*
Verpacken N

**pact** [pakt] *n* Vertrag M

**pad** [pad] *n* Polster N; *vt*
polstern

**padding** [PA•ding] *n*
Wattierung F

**paddle** [PA•dl] *n* Paddelruder N

**padlock** [PAD•lahk] *n*
Vorlegeschloß N

**pagan** [PAI•gn] *adj n* Heide M

**page** [paij] *n* Seite F

**pail** [paiul] *n* Eimer M

**pain** [pain] *n* Schmerz M

**painful** [PAIN•ful] *adj*
schmerzend

**painless** [PAIN•lis] *adj*
schmerzlos

**painstaking** [PAIN•STAI•king]
*adj* sorgfältig

**paint** [paint] *n* Lack M

**paintbrush** [PAINT•bruhsh] *n* Pinsel M

**painter** [PAIN•tur] *n* Maler M

**painting** [PAIN•ting] *n* Gemälde N

**pair** [paiur] *n* Paar N

**pajamas** [pu•JA•muz] *npl* Pyjama M

**Pakistan** [PA•ki•STAN] *n* Pakistan

**pal** [pal] *n* Freund M

**palace** [PA•lis] *n* Schloß N

**palatable** [PA•li•tu•bl] *adj* schmackhaft

**palate** [PA•lit] *n* Gaumen M

**pale** [paiul] *adj* blaß

**Palestine** [PA•li•STUYN] *n* Palastina

**palette** [PA•lit] *n* Palette F

**palm** [pahm] *n* Handfläche F

**Palm Sunday** [PALM SUN•dai] *n* Palmsonntag M

**palpable** [PAL•pu•bl] *adj* handgreiflich

**paltry** [PAUL•tree] *adj* armselig

**pamper** [PAM•pur] *vt* verwöhnen

**pamphlet** [PAM•flit] *n* Broschüre F

**pan** [pan] *n* Pfanne F

**panacea** [PA•nu•SEE•u] *n* Wundermittel N

**Panama** [PA•nu•MAH] *n* Panama

**pancake** [PAN•kaik] *n* Pfannkuchen M

**panda** [PAN•du] *n* Panda M

**pane** [pain] *n* Scheibe F

**panel** [PA•nl] *n* Tafel F

**pang** [pang] *n* Weh N

**panic** [PA•nik] *n* Panik F; *vi* Panik geraten; don't ~\ nur keine Panik

**pansy** [PAN•zee] *n* Stiefmütterchen N

**pant** [pant] *vi* keuchen

**panther** [PAN•thur] *n* Panther M

**panties** [PAN•teez] *npl* Unterhose F

**pantihose** [PAN•tee•HOZ] *n* Strumpfhose F

**pantry** [PAN•tree] *n* Speiseschrank M

**pants** [pants] *npl* Hose F

**papa** [PAH•pu] *n* Papa M

**papal** [PAI•pl] *adj* päpstlich

**paper** [PAI•pur] *adj* Papier N; (newspaper) Zeitung F; (school paper) Arbeit F

**paperback** [PAI•pur•BAK] *n* Buch N

**par** [pahr] *n* Pari N

**parable** [PA•ru•bl] *n* Parabel F

**parachute** [PA•ru•SHOOT] *n* Fallschirm M

**parade** [pu•RAID] *n* Umzug M

**paradise** [PA•ru•DUYS] *n* Paradies N

**paradox** [PA•ru•DAHKS] *n* Paradox N

**paragraph** (break; pause) [PA•ru•GRAF] *n* Absatz M

**Paraguay** [PA•ru•GWAI] *n* Paraguay

**parakeet** [PA•ru•KEET] *n* Sittich M

**parallel** [PA•ru•LEL] *adj* parallel

**paralysis** [pu•RA•lu•sis] *n* Lähmung F

**paralyze** [PA•ru•LUYZ] *vt*
lähmen

**paranoid** [PA•ru•NOID] *adj*
paranoid

**paraphernalia**
[PA•ru•fu•NAIU•lyu] *n*
Zubehör N

**parasite** [PA•ru•SUYT] *n*
Schmarotzer M

**parasol** [PA•ru•SAUL] *n*
Sonnenschirm M

**parcel** [PAHR•sl] *n* Paket N

**parched** [pahrchd] *adj* durstig

**parchment** [PAHRCH•munt] *n*
Pergament N

**pardon** [PAHR•dn] *n*
Verzeihung F

**parent** [PA•runt] *n* Eltern

**parenthesis** [pu•REN•thu•sis] *n*
Klammern

**parish** [PA•rish] *adj*
Pfarrbezirk N

**park** [pahrk] *n* Park M; *vi*
parken

**parking** [PAHR•king] *n*
Parkplatz M

**parking lot** [PAR•king LOT] *n*
Parkplatz M

**parlance** [PAHR•luns] *n*
Sprache F

**parliament** [PAHR•lu•munt] *n*
Parlament N

**parliamentary**
[PAHR•lu•MEN•tu•ree] *adj*
parlamentarisch

**parlor** [PAHR•lur] *n* Salon M

**parochial** [pu•RO•kee•ul] *adj*
parochial

**parody** [PA•ru•dee] *n* Parodie F

**parole** [pu•ROUL] *n* bedingte
Haftenlasung F

**parrot** [PA•rut] *n* Papagei M

**parsley** [PAHR•slee] *n*
Petersilie F

**parsnip** [PAR•snip] *n*
Pastinak M

**parson** [PAHR•sn] *n* Pfarrer M

**part** [pahrt] *n* Teil M; *adv* teils,
tilweise; *vt* teilen; trenen; *vi*
sich treilen; sich trenen

**part-time** [PAHRT•TUYM] *adj*
*adv* teilzeitig

**partial** [PAHR•shl] *adj* teilweise

**partiality** [PAHR•shee•A•li•tee]
*n* Vorliebe F

**partially** [PAHR•shu•lee] *adv*
teilweise

**participant** [pahr•TI•si•punt] *n*
Teilnehmer M

**participate** [pahr•TI•si•PAIT] *vi*
teilnehmen

**participation**
[pahr•TI•si•PAI•shn] *n*
Teilnahme F

**particle** [PAHR•ti•kl] *n*
Teilchen N

**particular** [pur•TI•kyu•lur] *adj*
besonder

**particularly**
[pur•TI•kyu•lur•lee] *adv*
besonders

**parting** [PAHR•ting] *n* Scheide

**partisan** [PAHR•ti•sun] *adj n*
Parteigänger M

**partition** [pahr•TI•shn] *n*
Aufteilung F

**partly** [PAHRT•lee] *adv* zum
Teil

**partner** [PAHRT•nur] *n*
Partner M

**partnership**
[PAHRT•nur•SHIP] *n*
Partnerschaft F

**partridge** [PAHR•trij] *n*
Rebhuhn N

**party** [PAHR•tee] *n* Partei F;
Fest N

**pass** [pas] *n* Paß; Ausweis M; *vt*
vorbeigehen an; vorbeifahren;
(time) vergehen; (exam)
bestehen

**passage** [PA•sij] *n*
Durchgang M

**passenger** [PA•sin•jur] *n*
Passagier M

**passerby** [PA•sur•BUY] *n*
Passant M

**passion** [PA•shn] *n*
Leidenschaft F

**passionate** [PA•shu•nit] *adj*
leidenschaftlich

**passive** [PA•siv] *adj* passiv

**passport** [PAS•paurt] *n* Paß M

**password** [PAS•wurd] *n*
Kennwort N

**past** [past] *adj* vergangen

**pasta** [PAH•stu] *n* Pasta N

**paste** [paist] *n* Klebstoff M

**pastel** [pa•STEL] *adj n*
Waidblau N

**pasteurize** [PAS•chu•RUYZ] *vt*
pasteurisieren

**pastime** [PAS•tuym] *n*
Freizeit F

**pastor** [PA•stur] *n* Pfarrer M

**pastry** [PAI•stree] *n*
Konditorware F

**pastry shop** [PAI•stree SHOP]
*n* Konditorei F

**pasture** [PAS•chur] *n* Weide F

**pat** [pat] *n* Schlag M

**patch** [pach] *n* Lappen M

**pâté** [pa•TAI] *n* Pastete F

**patent** [PA•tunt] *adj* Patent

**patent leather** [PA•tint
LE•thur] *n* Patentleder F

**paternal** [pu•TUR•nl] *adj*
väterlich

**paternity** [pu•TUR•ni•tee] *n*
Vaterschaft F

**path** [path] *n* Weg M

**pathetic** [pu•THE•tik] *adj*
ergreifend

**pathology** [pa•THAH•lu•jee] *n*
Pathologie F

**pathway** [PATH•wai] *n* Bahn F

**patience** [PAI•shns] *n* Geduld F

**patient** [PAI•shnt] *adj* geduldig;
*n* Patient M

**patriot** [PAI•tree•ut] *n* Patriot M

**patriotic** [PAI•tree•AH•tik] *adj*
patriotisch

**patriotism** [PAI•tree•u•TI•zm]
*n* Patriotismus M

**patrol** [pu•TROUL] *n* Runde F

**patron** [PAI•trun] *n* Patron M

**patronize** [PAI•tru•NUYZ] *vt*
begünstigen

**patronizing**
[PAI•tru•NUY•zing] *adj*
gönnerhaft

**patter** [PA•tur] *n* Geplapper N

**pattern** [PA•turn] *n* Muster N

**pause** [pauz] *n* Pause F

**pave** [paiv] *vt* pflastern

**pavement** [PAIV•ment] *n*
Bürgersteig M

**pavilion** [pu•VIL•yun] *n* Zelt N

**paw** [pau] *n* Pfote F

**pawn** [paun] *n* Bauer M

**pawnshop** [PAUN•shahp] *n*
Pfandhaus N

**pay** [pai] *n* Zahl F; *vt vi* zahlen

**pay off** *vt* ablohnen

**pay phone** [PAI fon] *n*
Telefonzelle F

**payable** [PAI•yu•bl] *adj* zahlbar

**paycheck** [PAI•chek] *n*
Lohnscheck M

**payment** [PAI•munt] *n*
Zahlung F

**payroll** [PAI•roul] *n* Lohnliste F

**pea** [pee] *n* Erbse F

**peace** [pees] *n* Frieden M

**peaceful** [PEES•ful] *adj*
friedlich

**peach** [peech] *n* Pfirsich M

**peacock** [PEE•cahk] *n* Pfau M

**peak** [peek] *n* Spitze F

**peal** [peeul] *vt* erschallen

**peanut** [PEE•nuht] *n* Erdnuß F

**peanut butter** [PEE•nut
BUH•tur] *n* Erdnußbutter F

**pear** [paiur] *n* Birne F

**pearl** [purl] *n* Perle F

**peasant** [PE•znt] *n* Bauer M

**peat** [peet] *n* Torf M

**pebble** [PE•bl] *n* Kieselstein M

**peck** [pek] *n* Viertelscheffel M

**peculiar** [pi•KYOOU•lyur] *adj*
eigen

**pedal** [PE•dl] *n* Pedal N

**pedant** [PE•dunt] *n* Pedant M

**pedantic** [pi•DAN•tik] *adj*
pedantisch

**peddle** [PE•dl] *vt* hausieren
gehen

**pedestal** [PE•du•stl] *n* Podest N

**pedestrian** [pi•de•stree•un] *n*
Fußgänger M

**pedigree** [PE•di•GREE] *adj*
Stammbaum M

**peek** [peek] *vi* gucken

**peel** [peeul] *n* Schale F; *vt*
vischälen

**peep** [peep] *vi* piepsen

**peephole** [PEEP•houl] *n*
Guckloch N

**peer** [peeur] *n* Kollege M

**peg** [peg] *n* Nagel M

**pellet** [PE•lit] *n* Kügelchen N

**pelt** [pelt] *n* Wurf M

**pen 1** [pen] *n* Kugelschreiber M

**pen 2** (for cattle) *n* Pferch M

**penal** [PEE•nl] *adj* strafrechtlich

**penalty** [PE•nl•tee] *n* Strafe F

**penance** [PE•nuns] *n* Buße F

**penchant** [PEN•chnt] *n*
Neigung F

**pencil** [PEN•sl] *n* Bleistift M

**pencil sharpener** [PEN•sil
SHAR•pin•ur] *n*
Bleistiftspitzer M

**pendant** [PEN•dnt] *n*
Pendant N

**pending** [PEN•ding] *adj*
hängend

**pendulum** [PEN•dyu•lum] *n*
Pendel N

**penetrate** [PE•nu•TRAIT] *vt*
durchdringen

**penguin** [PENG•gwin] *n*
Pinguin M

**penicillin** [PE•ni•SI•lin] *n*
Penicillin N

**peninsula** [pu•NIN•su•lu] *n*
Halbinsel F

**penis** [PEE•nis] *n* Penis M

**pennant** [PE•nunt] *n*
Fähnchen N

**penniless** [PE•nee•lis] *adj*
mittellos

**penny** [PE•nee] *n* Pfennig M

**pension** [PEN•shn] *n* Pension F

**pensive** [PEN•siv] *adj*
nachdenklich

**penthouse** [PENT•haus] *n*
Schirmdach N
**people** [PEE•pl] *npl* Leute F
**pepper** [PE•pur] *n* Pfeffer M
**peppermint** [PE•pur•mint] *n*
Pfefferminze F
**per** [pur] *prep* per
**perceive** [pur•SEEV] *vt*
wahrnehmen
**percent** [pur•SENT] *adv*
Prozent M
**percentage** [pur•SEN•tij] *n*
Prozentgehalt M
**perception** [pur•SEP•shn] *n*
Wahrnehmung F
**perch** [purch] *n* Sitzstange F
**perennial** [pu•RE•nee•ul] *adj*
winterhart
**perfect** [PUR•fikt] *adj*
vollkommen
**perfection** [pur•FEK•shn] *n*
Vollkommenheit F
**perfectionist**
[pur•FEK•shu•nist] *n*
Perfektionist M
**perfectly** [PUR•fikt•lee] *adv*
völlig
**perforate** [PUR•fu•RAIT] *vt*
durchbohren
**perform** [pur•FAURM] *vi*
ausführen
**performance** [pur•FAUR•mns]
*n* Ausführung F
**perfume** [PUR•fyoom] *n*
Duft M
**perhaps** [pur•HAPS] *adv*
vielleicht
**peril** [PE•ril] *n* Risiko N
**perimeter** [pu•RI•mi•tur] *n*
Umkreis M

**period** [PEEU•ree•ud] *n*
Zeitdauer F
**periodic** [PI•ree•AH•dik] *adj*
periodisch
**periodical** [PI•ree•AH•di•kl] *n*
Zeitschrift F
**perish** [PE•rish] *vi* umkommen
**perjury** [PUR•ju•ree] *n*
Meineid M
**perm** [purm] *n* Dauerwelle F
**permanent** [PUR•mi•nunt] *adj*
ständig
**permeate** [PUR•mee•AIT] *vt*
durchdringen
**permission** [pur•MI•shn] *n*
Erlaubnis N
**permit** [PUR•mit] *n*
Genehmigung F; [pur•MIT]*vt*
erlauben; getatten
**perpendicular**
[PUR•pn•DI•kyu•lur] *adj n*
senkrecht; Senkrechte F
**perpetrate** [PUR•pu•TRAIT] *vt*
verüben
**perpetual** [pur•PE•choo•ul] *adj*
immerwährend
**perplex** [pur•PLEKS] *vt*
verwirren
**perplexed** [pur•PLEKST] *adj*
verwirrt
**persecute** [PUR•si•KYOOT] *vt*
belästigen
**perseverance**
[PUR•si•VEEU•rns] *n*
Beharrlichkeit F
**persevere** [PUR•si•VEEUR] *vi*
beharren
**Persian Gulf** [PUR•zhn ~ ] *n*
Persischer Golf M
**persist** [pur•SIST] *vi*
ausverharren

**persistence** [pur•SI•stns] *n*
Beharrlichkeit F

**persistent** [pur•SI•stnt] *adj*
hartnäckig

**person** [PUR•sn] *n* Person F

**personal** [PUR•su•nl] *adj*
persönlich

**personality** [PUR•su•NA•li•tee]
*n* Persönlichkeit

**personnel** [PUR•su•NEL] *n*
Personal N

**perspective** [pur•SPEK•tiv] *n*
Perspektiv M

**perspiration**
[PUR•spu•RAI•shn] *n*
Schwitzen N

**perspire** [pur•SPUYUR] *vi*
schwitzen

**persuade** [pur•SWAID] *vt*
überreden

**persuasion** [pur•SWAI•zhn] *n*
Überzeugung F

**persuasive** [pur•SWAI•siv] *adj*
überzeugend

**pertain** [pur•TAIN] *vi* gehören

**pertinent** [PUR•ti•nunt] *adj*
angemessen

**perturb** [pur•TURB] *vt*
beunruhigen

**perverse** [pur•VURS] *adj*
verkehrt

**pervert** [PUR•vurt] *n* Verdreher
M; [pur•VURT] *vt* verkehren

**pessimism** [PE•si•MI•zm] *n*
Pessimismus M

**pessimist** [PE•si•mist] *n*
Pessimist M

**pessimistic** [PE•si•MI•stik] *adj*
pessimistisch

**pest** [pest] *n* Pest F

**pester** [PE•stur] *vt* quälen

**pet** [pet] *n* Haustier N

**petal** [PE•tl] *n* Blumenblatt N

**petition** [pu•TI•shn] *n*
Antrag M

**petrified** [PE•tri•FUYD] *adj*
versteinert

**petroleum** [pu•TRO•lee•um] *n*
Benzin M

**petty** [PE•tee] *adj* unbedeutend

**pew** [pyoo] *n* Kirchenstuhl M

**phantom** [FAN•tum] *n*
Phantom M

**pharmacist** [FAHR•mu•sist] *n*
Apotheker M

**pharmacy** [FAHR•mu•see] *n*
Apotheke F

**phase** [faiz] *n* Phase F; *vt*
schrittweise

**phenomenon**
[fu•NAH•mu•nahn] *n*
Phänomen N

**philosopher** [fi•LAH•su•fur] *n*
Philosoph M

**philosophical** [FI•lu•SAH•fi•kl]
*adj* philosophisch

**philosophy** [fi•LAH•su•fee] *n*
Philosophie F

**phone** [fon] *n* Telefon N; *vi*
anrufen; telefonieren

**phone booth** [FON BOOTH] *n*
Telefonzelle F

**phone call** [FON KAL] *n*
Anruf M

**phonetics** [fu•NE•tiks] *n*
Phonetik F

**phony** [FO•nee] *adj* falsch

**photo** [FO•to] *n* Foto N

**photograph** [FO•tu•graf] *n*
Aufnahme F

**photographer**
[fu•TAH•gru•fur] *n*
Photograph (in) M

**photography** [fu•TAH•gru•fee] *n* Photographie F

**phrase** [fraiz] *n* Redewendung F

**physical** [FI•zi•kl] *adj* körperlich

**physician** [fi•ZI•shn] *n* Arzt M

**physicist** [FI•zi•sist] *n* Physiker M

**physics** [FI•ziks] *n* Physik F

**physique** [fi•ZĘEK] *n* Figur F

**pianist** [pee•U•nist] *n* Klavierspieler (in) M

**piano** [pee•A•no] *n* Klavier N

**pick** [pik] *n* Picke M; *vt* wählen

**picket** [PI•kit] *n* Pfahl M

**pickle** [PI•kl] *n* Gewürzgurke F

**pickpocket** [PIK•PAH•kit] *n* Taschendieb M

**picnic** [PIK•nik] *n* Picknick N

**picture** [PIK•chur] *n* Bild N; *vt* (imagine) sich vorstellen

**picturesque** [PIK•chu•RESK] *adj* malerisch

**pie** [puy] *n* Pastete F

**piece** [pees] *n* Stück N

**pier** [peeur] *n* Piet M

**pierce** [peeurs] *vt* durchbohren

**pig** [pig] *n* Schwein N

**pig-headed** [PIG•HE•did] *adj* dickköpfig

**pigeon** [PI•jn] *n* Taube F

**pigment** [PIG•munt] *n* Pigment N

**pigsty** [PIG•stuy] *n* Schlamperei F

**pile** [puyul] *n* Haufen M

**pilgrim** [PIL•grim] *n* Pilger M

**pilgrimage** [PIL•gri•mij] *n* Wallfahrt F

**pill** [pil] *n* Pille F

**pillar** [PI•lur] *n* Pfeiler M

**pillow** [PI•lo] *n* Kissen N

**pillowcase** [PI•lo•KAIS] s Kissenbezug M

**pilot** [PUY•lut] *n* Pilot M; *vt* (plane) fliegen; (boat) lotsen

**pimp** [pimp] *n* Strichjunge M

**pimple** [PIM•pl] *n* Pickel M

**pin** [pin] *n* Nadel F; *vt* stecken

**pinch** [pinch] *n* Zwicken N

**pine** [puyn] *n* Kiefer F

**pineapple** [PY•NA•pul] *n* Ananas

**pink** [pingk] *adk n* rosa; Rosa N

**pinnacle** [PI•nu•kl] *n* Spitze F

**pint** [puynt] *n* halbes Liter

**pioneer** [PUY•u•NEEUR] *n* Pionier M

**pious** [PUY•us] *adj* fromm

**pipe** [puyp] *n* Rohr N

**pique** [peek] *n* Gereizheit F

**pirate** [PUY•rit] *adj* Seeräuber M

**pistol** [PI•stl] *n* Pistole F

**piston** [PI•stn] *n* Kolben M

**pitch** [pich] *n* Gefälle F

**pitcher** [PI•chur] *n* Werfer M

**pitchfork** [PICH•faurk] *n* Heugabel F

**piteous** [PI•tee•us] *adj* kläglich

**pitiful** [PI•ti•ful] *adj* mitfühlend

**pitiless** [PI•tee•lis] *adj* unbarmherzig

**pity** [PI•tee] *n* Schade F

**pivot** [PI•vut] *n* Drehpunkt M

**placard** [PLA•kurd] *n* Plakat N

**placate** [PLAI•kait] *vt* beswichtigen

**place** [plais] *n* Platz M; *vt* setzen

**placid** [PLA•sid] *adj* ruhig

**plague** [plaig] *n* Seuche F

**plaid** [plad] *n* Plaid N; *adj*
schottisches

**plain** [plain] *adj* einfach

**plainly** [PLAIN•lee] *adv* einfach

**plaintiff** [PLAIN•tif] *n*
Kläger M

**plan** [plan] *n* Plan M; *vt* planen

**plane 1** [plain] *adj* Flugzeug N;
(tool) Höbel

**plane 2** (geog) *n* Platane F

**planet** [PLA•nit] *n* Planet M

**plank** [plangk] *n* Planke F

**planning** [PLA•ning] *n*
Planung F

**plant** [plant] *n* Pflanze F; *vt*
pflanzen; setzen; (factory) *n*
Werk N

**plantation** [plan•TAI•shn] *n*
Plantage F

**plaque** [plak] *n* Platte F

**plaster** [PLA•stur] *n* Pflaster N

**plastic** [PLA•stik] *adj* plastisch;
*n* Plastik N

**plate** [plait] *n* Teller M

**plateau** [pla•TO] *n*
Hochebene F

**plated** [PLAI•tid] *adj* plattiert

**platform** [PLAT•faurm] *n*
Bühne F

**platinum** [PLAT•num] *n*
Platin N

**platter** [PLA•tur] *n*
Servierplatte F

**play** [plai] *n* Spiel spielen N

**playboy** [PLAI•boi] *n*
Playboy M

**player** [PLAI•ur] *n* Spieler M

**playful** [PLAI•ful] *adj*
spielerisch

**playground** [PLAI•ground] *n*
Tummelplatz M

**plaything** [PLAI•thing] *n*
Spielzeug N

**playwright** [PLAI•ruyt] *n*
Dramatiker M

**plea** [plee] *n* Ausrede F

**plead** [pleed] *vt* plädieren

**pleasant** [PLE•znt] *adj*
angenehm

**please** [pleez] *vt* gefallen; *interj*
bitte

**pleased** [pleezd] *adj* bitte

**pleasing** [PLEE•zing] *adj*
gefällig

**pleasure** [PLE•zhur] *n*
Vergnügen N

**pleat** [pleet] *n* Falte F

**pledge** [plej] *n* Pfand N

**plentiful** [PLEN•ti•ful] *adj* im
Überfluß M

**plenty** [PLEN•tee] *adj* genug

**pliable** [PLUY•u•bl] *adj*
geschmiedig

**pliers** [PLUY•urz] *npl*
Drahtzange F

**plight** [pluyt] *n* Notlage F

**plod** [plahd] *vi* mühsam gehen

**plot** [plaht] *n* (of story)
Handlung F; (of land) Stück;
*vt* planen

**plow** [plou] *n* Pflug M

**ploy** [ploi] *n* List F

**pluck** [pluhk] *vt* zupfen N

**plug** [pluhg] *n* Stöpsel M

**plum** [pluhm] *n* Pflaume F

**plumber** [PLUH•mur] *n*
Klempner M

**plumbing** [PLUH•ming] *n*
Klempner

**plume** [ploom] *n* Feder

**plump** [pluhmp] *adj* rundlich;
pummelig

**plunder** [PLUHN•dur] *vt*
plündern

**plunge** [pluhnj] *n*
Untertauchen N

**plunger** [PLUHN•jur] *n*
Taucher M

**plural** [PLOOU•rl] *adj*
mehrfach; *n* Mehrzahl F

**plus** [pluhs] *n* Plus N

**plush** [pluhsh] *n* vornehm

**ply** [pluy] *vt* Schicht F

**plywood** [PLUY•wud] *n*
Furnierholz N

**pneumonia** [noo•MO•nyu] *n*
Lungenentzündung F

**poach** [poch] *vt* pochieren

**pocket** [PAH•kit] *n* Tasche F

**pocketbook** [PAH•kit•BUK] *n*
Tasche F

**pocketknife** [PAH•kit•NUYF]
*n* Taschenmesser N

**pod** [pahd] *n* Hülse F

**poem** [pom] *n* Gedicht N

**poet** [PO•it] *n* Dichter M

**poetic** [po•E•tik] *adj* poetisch

**poetry** [PO•e•tree] *n* Poesie F

**point** [point] *n* Punkt M; *vt*
richen; *vi* zeigen; deuten

**point of view** [POINT uhv
VYU] *n* Gesichtspunkt M

**pointed** [POIN•tid] *adj* spitzig

**pointer** [POIN•tur] *n* Zeiger M

**pointless** [POINT•lis] *adj*
punktlos

**poise** [poiz] *n* Schwebe F

**poison** [POI•zn] *n* Gift N

**poisoning** [POI•zu•ning] *n*
Vergiftung F

**poisonous** [POI•zu•nus] *adj*
giftig

**poke** [pok] *vt* stoßen

**poker** [PO•kur] *n* Pokerspiel N

**Poland** [PO•lund] *n* Polen

**polar** [PO•lur] *adj* polar

**pole** [poul] *n* Pfosten M

**Pole** [poul] *n* Pole; Polin M

**police** [pu•LEES] *npl* Polizei F

**police officer** [po•LEES
AW•fi•sir] *n* Polizist M

**police station** [po•LEES
STAI•shn] *n* Polizeiwache

**policeman** [pu•LEES•man] *n*
Polizist M

**policewoman**
[pu•LEES•WU•mun] *n*
Polizistin F

**policy** [PAH•li•see] *n*
Verfahrensweise F

**Polish** [PO•lish] *adj* polisch

**polish** [PAH•lish] *n* (furnitur)
Politur F; (floor ~)
Bohnerwachs N; (shoe ~ )
Creme F; (shine) Glanz M; *vt*
polieren

**polite** [pu•LUYT] *adj* höflich

**politeness** [pu•LUYT•nis] *n*
Höflichkeit

**political** [pu•LI•ti•kl] *adj*
politisch

**politician** [PAH•li•TI•shn] *n*
Politiker M

**politics** [PAH•li•TIKS] *n*
Politik F

**poll** [poul] *n* Stimmenzählung F

**pollen** [PAH•ln] *n* Pollen M

**pollute** [pu•LOOT] *vt*
beschmutzen

**pollution** [pu•LOO•shn] *n*
Pollution F

**polo** [PO•lo] *n* Polo N

**Polynesia** [PAH•li•NEE•zhu] *n*
Polinesien

**pomp** [pahmp] *n* Prunk M

**pompous** [PAHM•pus] *adj*
prunkvoll

**pond** [pahnd] *n* Teich M

**ponder** [PAHN•dur] *vt*
nachdenken

**pony** [PO•nee] *n* Pferdchen N

**ponytail** [PO•nee•TAIUL] *n*
Pferdesschwanz M

**poodle** [POO•dl] *n* Pudel M

**pool 1** [pooul] *n*
Schwimmbad N

**pool 2 (common fund)** *n*
Kasser F; *vt* zusammenlegen

**poor** [poour] *adj* arm

**pop 1** [pahp] *n* Limonade F

**pop 2 (music)** *n* Popmusik F;
Pop m

**pop 3 (sound)** *n* Knall M

**pope** [pop] *n* Papst M

**poplar** [PAHP•lur] *n* Pappel F

**poppy** [PAH•pee] *n* Mohn M

**populace** [PAH•pyu•lus] *n*
Volk N

**popular** [PAH•pyu•lur] *adj*
populär

**popularity**
[PAH•pyu•LA•ri•tee] *n*
Beliebtheit

**popularize**
[PAH•pyu•lu•RUYZ] *vt*
populär machen

**populate** [PAH•pyu•LAIT] *vt*
bevölkern

**population**
[PAH•pyu•LAI•shn] *n*
Bevölkerung F

**porcelain** [PAURS•lun] *n*
Porzellan N

**porch** [paurch] *n* Vorhalle F

**porcupine** [PAUR•kyu•PUYN]
*n* Stachelschwein N

**pore** [paur] *n* Pore F

**pork** [paurk] *n*
Schweinefleisch N

**pornagraphy**
[paur•NAH•gru•fee] *n*
Pornographie F

**porous** [PAU•rus] *adj* porig

**porpoise** [PAUR•pus] *n*
Tümmler M

**porridge** [PAU•rij] *n*
Haferbrei M

**port** [paurt] *n* Hafen M

**port 2 (naut)** *n* Backbord M;
*adj* backbord

**port 3 (wine)** *n* Portwein M

**portable** [PAUR•tu•bl] *adj*
tragbar

**porter** [PAUR•tur] *n* Portier M

**portfolio** [paurt•FO•lee•O] *n*
Aktentasche F

**porthole** [PAURT•houl] *n* Luke

**portion** [PAUR•shn] *n* Teil M

**portly** [PAURT•lee] *adj* stattlich

**portrait** [PAUR•trit] *n*
Bildnis N

**portray** [paur•TRAI] *vt*
darstellen

**portrayal** [paur•TRAI•ul] *n*
Darstellung

**Portugal** [PAUR•chu•gl] *n*
Portugal

**Portuguese** [PAUR•chu•geez]
*adj* portugiese

**pose** [poz] *v* sich in Positur
setzen

**position** [pu•ZI•shn] *n* Lage F;
Platz M; *vt* ausfellen;
postieren

**positive** [PAH•zi•tiv] *adj*
positiv

**possess** [pu•ZES] *vt* besitzen

**possession** [pu•ZE•shn] *n*
Besitz M

**possibility** [PAH•si•BI•li•tee] *n*
Möglichkeit

**possible** [PAH•si•bl] *adj*
möglich

**possibly** [PAH•si•blee] *adv*
möglicherweise

**post** [post] *n* Post F

**post office** [POST AW•fis] *n*
Postamt N

**postage** [PO•stij] *n*
Postgebühr F

**postal** [PO•stl] *adj* postalisch

**postcard** [POST•kard] *n*
Ansichtskarte F

**postdate** [post•DAIT] *vt*
nachdatieren

**poster** [PO•stur] *n* Plakat M

**posterior** [pah•STEE•ree•ur]
*adj n* Hinterteil N

**posthumous** [PAH•styu•mus]
*adj* postum

**postman** [POST•man] *n*
Briefträger M

**postpone** [post•PON] *vt*
verschieben

**posture** [PAHS•chur] *vt*
Positur F

**pot** [paht] *n* Topf M

**potassium** [pu•TA•see•um] *n*
Kalium N

**potato** [pu•TAI•to] *n*
Kartoffel F

**potent** [PO•tunt] *adj* stark

**potential** [pu•TEN•shl] *adj n*
eventuell

**potentially** [pu•TEN•shu•lee]
*adv* möglicherweise

**pothole** [PAHT•houl] *n*
Schlagloch N

**potion** [PO•shn] *n* Trank M

**pottery** [PAH•tu•ree] *n*
Töpferei F

**pouch** [pouch] *n* Beutel F

**poultry** [POUL•tree] *n*
Geflügel N

**pounce** [pouns] *vi* herabstoßen

**pound 1** [pound] *n* Pfund M

**pound 2** *vt* hämmern (meat)
klopfen; (dough) kneten

**pour** [paur] *vt* gießen

**pout** [pout] *vi* schmollen

**poverty** [PAH•vur•tee] *n*
Armut F

**powder** [POU•dur] *n* Pulver N

**powdered** [POU•durd] *adj*
puder

**power** [POU•ur] *n* Kraft F; *vt*
(engine) antreiben; (fuel)
betreiben

**powerful** [POU•ur•ful] *adj*
kräftig

**powerless** [POU•ur•lis] *adj*
kraftlos

**practical** [PRAK•ti•kl] *adj*
praktisch

**practical joke** [PRAK•ti•kul
JOK] *n* Witz M

**practice** [PRAK•tis] *n* Übung F

**practicing** [PRAK•ti•sing] *adj*
übender

**prairie** [PRAIU•ree] *n* Wiese F

**praise** [praiz] *n* Lob M; *vt* loben

**prance** [prans] *vi* tänzeln

**prank** [prangk] *n* Streich M

**pray** [prai] *vi* beten

**prayer** [praiur] *n* Gebet N

**preach** [preech] *vt vi* predigen
**preacher** [PREE•chur] *n*
　Prediger M
**precarious** [pri•KA•ree•us] *adj*
　unsicher
**precaution** [pree•KAU•shn] *n*
　Vorsichtsmaßregel F
**precede** [pri•SEED] *vt*
　vorangehen
**precedence** [PRE•si•duns] *n*
　Vorhergehen N
**precedent** [PRE•si•dunt] *n*
　Präzedenzfall M
**precious** [PRE•shus] *adj* edel
**precipitate** [pri•SI•pi•TAIT] *vt*
　niederschlagen
**precipitation**
　[pri•SI•pi•TAI•shn] *n*
　Niederschlag M
**precise** [pri•SUYS] *adj* präzis
**precisely** [pree•SUYS•lee] *adv*
　gerade
**precision** [pri•SI•zhn] *n*
　Genauigkeit F
**preclude** [pri•KLOOD] *vt*
　ausschließen
**precocious** [pri•KO•shus] *adj*
　frühreif
**predator** [PRE•du•tur] *n*
　Raubtier N
**predecessor** [PRE•di•SE•sur] *n*
　Vorgänger
**predestined** [pree•DES•tind]
　*adj* prädestiniert
**predicament** [pri•DI•ku•munt]
　*n* mißliche Lage F
**predicate** [PRE•di•kit] *adj n*
　Prädikat N
**predict** [pri•DIKT] *vt*
　voraussagen

**predictable** [pri•DIK•tu•bl] *adj*
　voraussagbar
**prediction** [pri•DIK•shn] *n*
　Voraussagung F
**predisposed** [PREE•dis•POZD]
　*adj* empfänglich
**predominant**
　[pri•DAH•mi•nunt] *adj*
　vorherrschend
**preface** [PRE•fus] *n* Vorrede F
**prefer** [pri•FUR] *vt* vorziehen
**preferable** [PRE•fru•bl] *adj*
　vorzüglicher
**preferably** [PRE•fru•blee] *adv*
　lieber
**preference** [PRE•fruns] *n*
　Bevorzugung F
**preferential** [PRE•fu•REN•shl]
　*adj* bevorzugt
**prefix** [PREE•fiks] *n* Vorsilbe F
**pregnancy** [PREG•nun•see] *n*
　Schwangershaft F
**pregnant** [PREG•nunt] *adj*
　schwanger
**prejudice** [PRE•ju•dis] *n*
　Vorurteil N
**prejudiced** [PRE•ju•dist] *adj*
　nachteilig
**preliminary** [pri•LI•mi•NE•ree]
　*adj* einleitend
**prelude** [PRAI•lood] *n*
　Vorspiel N
**premarital** [pree•MA•ri•tl] *adj*
　vorehelich
**premature**
　[PREE•mu•CHOOUR] *adj*
　vorzeitig
**premier** [pre•MEEUR] *adj* erst
**premiere** [pri•MEEUR] *n*
　Premiere F

**premise** [PRE•mis] *n*
Voraussetzung F

**premium** [PREE•mee•um] *n*
Prämie F

**premonition** [PRE•mu•NI•shn]
*n* Warnung F

**preoccupied**
[pree•AH•kyu•PUYD] *adj*
vertieft

**prepaid** [pree•PAID] *adj*
vorausbezahlt

**preparation** [PRE•pu•RAI•shn]
*n* Vorbereitung F

**prepare** [pri•PAIUR] *vt*
vorbereiten

**preposition** [PRE•pu•ZI•shn] *n*
Präposition F

**preposterous** [pri•PAH•stu•rus]
*adj* absurd

**prerequisite** [pri•RE•kwi•zit] *n*
Vorbedingung F

**prerogative** [pru•RAH•gu•tuv]
*n* Privilegium N

**prescribe** [pri•SKRUYB] *vt*
vorschreiben

**prescription** [pri•SKRIP•shn] *n*
Vorschrift F

**presence** [PRE•zns] *n*
Anwesenheit F

**present 1** [PRE•znt] *adj*
anwesend; at ~\ zur Zeit; im
Moment

**present 2** [PRE•znt] *n*
Geschenk N; *vt* [pre•ZENT]
schenken

**presentable** [pri•ZEN•tu•bl]
*adj* darstellbar

**presentation**
[PRE•zn•TAI•shn] *n*
Vorstellung F

**presently** [PRE•znt•lee] *adv*
alsbald

**preserve** [pri•ZURV] *vt*
bewahren

**preserve** (keep; maintain)
[pree•ZURV] *vi* aufbewahren

**president** [PRE•zi•dunt] *n*
Präsident M

**press 1** [pres] *n* Druck M; *vt*
drücken; treten; presen

**press 2** [pres] *n* Presse F

**pressing** [PRE•sing] *adj*
dringend

**pressure** [PRE•shur] *n* Druck M

**prestige** [pre•steezh] *n*
Prestige N

**presumably** [pri•ZOO•mu•blee]
*adj* vermutlich

**presume** [pri•ZOOM] *vt*
vermuten

**presumption** [pri•ZUMP•shn]
*n* Vermutung F

**pretend** [pri•TEND] *vi*
vorgeben

**pretension** [pri•TEN•shn] *n*
Einbildung F

**pretentious** [pri•TEN•shus] *adj*
eingebildet

**pretext** [PREE•tekst] *n*
Vorwand M

**pretty** [PRI•tee] *adj* schön

**prevail** [pri•VAIUL] *vi* die
Oberhand gewinnen

**prevailing** [pree•VAIU•ling]
*adj* vorherrschend

**prevalent** [PRE•vu•lunt] *adj*
überwiegend

**prevent** [pri•VENT] *vt*
verhindern

**preventive** [pri•VEN•tiv] *adj*
vorbeugend

**preview** [PREE•vyoo] *n*
Vorschau F

**previous** [PREE•vee•us] *adj*
vorher

**prey** [prai] *n* Raub M

**price** [pruys] *n* Preis M

**priceless** [PRUYS•lis] *adj*
unschätzbar

**prick** [prik] *vt* stechen

**pride** [pruyd] *n* Stolz M

**priest** [preest] *n* Priester M

**priesthood** [PREEST•hud] *n*
Priestershaft F

**prim** [prim] *adj* steif

**primarily** [pruy•ME•ri•lee] *adv*
hauptsächlich

**primary** [PRUY•me•ree] *adj*
haupt

**primate** [PRUY•mait] *n*
Primaten

**prime** [pruym] *adj* wesentlichst

**primer** [PRUY•mur] *n*
Zünddraht M

**primitive** [PRI•mi•tiv] *adj*
primitiv

**primrose** [PRIM•roz] *n*
Primel F

**prince** [prins] *n* Prinz M

**princess** [PRIN•ses] *n*
Prinzessin F

**principal** [PRIN•si•pl] *adj*
hauptsächlich

**principle** [PRIN•si•pl] *n*
Prinzip N

**print** [print] *n* Druck M; *vt*
drucken; (typeface) *n*
Schrift F

**printer** [PRIN•tur] *n* Drucker M

**printing** [PRIN•ting] *n*
Drucken N

**prior** [PRUY•ur] *adj* früher

**priority** [pruy•AU•ri•tee] *n*
Priorität F

**prism** [pri•zm] *n* Prisma N

**prison** [PRI•zn] *n* Gefängnis N

**prisoner** [PRI•zu•nur] *n*
Gefangene M

**privacy** [PRUY•vu•see] *n*
Alleinsein N

**private** [PRUY•vit] *adj* privat

**privation** [pruy•VAI•shn] *n*
Wegnahme F

**privilege** [PRIV•lij] *n*
Privileg N

**prize** [pruyz] *adj* Preis M

**pro** [pro] *n* Profi M

**probability**
[PRAH•bu•BI•li•tee] *n*
Wahrscheinlichkeit

**probable** [PRAH•bu•bl] *adj*
wahrscheinlich

**probably** [PRAH•bu•blee] *adv*
wahrscheinlich

**probation** [pro•BAI•shn] *n*
Probezeit F

**probe** [prob] *n* Untersuchung F

**problem** [PRAH•blum] *n*
Problem N

**procedure** [pru•SEE•jur] *n*
Prozeß M

**proceed** [pru•SEED] *vi*
weitergegen

**proceeding** [pru•SEE•ding] *adj*
Verfahren N

**proceeds** [PRO•seedz] *npl*
Erlös M

**process** [PRAH•ses] *s* Prozeß M

**procession** [pru•SE•shn] *n*
Umzug M

**proclaim** [pru•CLAIM] *vt*
verkündigen

**procrastinate**
[pru•KRA•sti•NAIT] *vi* zögern
**procure** [pru•KYOOUR] *vt*
verschaffen
**prod** [prahd] *vt* stechen
**prodigal** [PRAH•di•gl] *adj*
verlorene
**prodigy** [PRAH•di•jee] *n*
Wunder N
**produce** [PRO•doos] *n* (aggr)
Produkt N; *vt* [pru•DOOS]
produzieren
**producer** [pru•DOO•sur] *n*
Hersteller M
**product** [PRAH•duhkt] *n*
Produkt M
**production** [pru•DUHK•shn] *n*
Herstellung F
**productive** [pru•DUHK•tiv] *adj*
erzeugend
**profane** [pru•FAIN] *adj* profan
**profession** [pru•FE•shn] *n*
Beruf M
**professional** [pru•FE•shu•nl]
*adj* beruflich; *n* Fach M
**professor** [pru•FE•sur] *n*
Professor M
**proficiency** [pru•FI•shn•see] *n*
Können N
**profile** [PRO•fuyul] *n* Profil N
**profit** [PRAH•fit] *n* Gewinn M
**profitable** [PRAH•fi•tu•bl] *adj*
gewinnbringend
**profound** [pru•FOUND] *adj*
tief
**profuse** [pru•FYOOS] *adj*
üppig
**program** [PRO•gram] *n*
Programm N; *vt* (computer)
programmieren

**progress** [PRAH•gres] *n*
Fortschritt M; [pru•gres] *vi*
sich vörwarts bewegen
**progressive** [pru•GRE•siv] *adj*
fortschrittlich
**prohibit** [pru•HI•bit] *vt*
verbieten
**prohibition** [PRO•hi•BI•shn] *n*
Verbot N
**project** [*n.* PRAH•jekt *v.*
pru•JEKT] *n* Projekt N
**projection** [pru•JEK•shn] *n*
Vorsprung M
**proletariat** [PRO•lu•TA•ree•ut]
*n* Proletariat N
**prolong** [pro•LAUNG] *vt*
verlängern
**promenade**
[PRAH•mu•NAHD] *n*
Spaziergang M
**prominent** [PRAH•mi•nunt] *adj*
vorstehend
**promiscuous**
[pru•MI•skyoo•us] *adj*
verworren
**promise** [PRAH•mis] *n*
Versprechen N
**promising** [PRAH•mi•sing] *adj*
hoffnungsvoll
**promote** [pru•MOT] *vt* fördern
**promoter** [pru•MO•tur] *n*
Veranstalter M
**promotion** [pru•MO•shn] *n*
Beförderung F
**prompt** [prahmpt] *adj* sofortig
**promptly** [PRAHMPT•lee] *adv*
sofort
**prone** [pron] *adj* geneigt
**prong** [prahng] *n* Zacke F
**pronoun** [PRO•noun] *n*
Pronomen N

**pronounce** [pru•NOUNS] *vt*
erklären

**pronounced** [pru•NOUNST]
*adj* ausgesprochen

**pronunciation**
[pru•NUHN•see•AI•shn] *n*
Aussprache F

**proof** [proof] *n* Beweis M

**prop** [prahp] *n* Stütze F

**propaganda**
[PRAH•pu•GAN•du] *n*
Propaganda F

**propel** [pru•PEL] *vt* antreiben

**propeller** [pru•PE•lur] *n*
Propeller M

**proper** [PRAH•pur] *adj*
geeignet; richtig

**properly** [PRAH•pur•lee] *adv*
richtig

**property** [PRAH•pur•tee] *n*
Eigentum N

**prophecy** [PRAH•fi•see] *n*
Weissagung F

**prophesy** [PRAH•fi•SUY] *vt*
weisaussagen

**prophet** [PRAH•fit] *n*
Prophet M

**proportion** [pru•PAUR•shn] *n*
Ebenmaß N

**proposal** [pru•PO•zl] *n*
Vorschlag M

**propose** [pru•POZ] *vt*
vorschlagen

**proposition** [PRAH•pu•ZI•shn]
*n* Vorschlag M

**proprietor** [pru•PRUY•u•tur] *n*
Eigentümer M

**prose** [proz] *n* Prosa F

**prosecute** [PRAH•si•KYOOT]
*vt* weiterführen

**prosecution**
[PRAH•si•KYOO•shun] *n*
Verfolgung F

**prosecutor**
[PRAH•si•KYOO•tur] *n*
Kläger M

**prospect** [PRAH•spekt] *n*
Aussicht F

**prospective** [pro•SPEK•tiv] *adj*
voraussichtlich

**prosper** [PRAH•spur] *vi* Erfolg
haben

**prosperity** [prah•SPAR•itee] *n*
Wohlstand M

**prosperous** [PRAH•spur•us]
*adj* erfolgreich

**prostitute** [PRAH•sti•TOOT] *n*
Prostituierte F

**prostrate** [PRAH•strat] *adj*
hingestreckt

**protect** [pro•TEKT] *vt* schützen

**protection** [pro•TEK•shun] *n*
Schutz M

**protective** [pro•TEK•tiv] *adj*
beschützend

**protector** [pro•TEK•tor] *n*
Beschützer M

**protein** [PRO•teen] *n* Eiweiß N

**protest** [PRO•test] *vt*
protestieren

**Protestant** [PRAH•tes•tant] *n*
Protestant M

**protoplasm** [PRO•to•PLA•zm]
*n* protoplasma N

**protract** [pro•TRAKT] *vi*
hinziehen

**protrude** [pro•TROOD] *vi*
herausstehen

**protuberance**
[pro•TROO•ber•ans] *n*
Auswuchs M

**proud** [prod] *adj* stoltz

**prove** [proov] *vt* beweisen; *vr*
sich bewähren

**proverb** [PRAH•verb] *n*
Sprichwort N

**provide** [pro•VUYD] *vt*
versorgen

**providence** [PRAH•vi•dens] ] *n*
Vorsorge F

**provider** [pro•VUY•dr] *n*
Versorger M

**province** [PRAH•vins] *n*
Provinz F

**provincial** [pro•VIN•shul] *adj*
provinziell

**provision** [pro•VI•shun] *n*
Maßnahme F

**proviso** [pro•VEE•zo] *n*
Vorbehalt M

**provoke** [pro•VOK] *vt* erzürnen

**provost** [PRO•vost] *n*
Vorsteher M

**prow** [prou] *n* Schiffsschnabel M

**prowess** [PROU•ess] *n*
Tapferkeit F

**prowl** [proul] *vt* durchstreifen

**proximity** [prahk•ZIM•i•tee] *n*
Nähe F

**proxy** [PRAHK•zee] *n*
Stellvertretung F

**prude** [prood] *n* Prüde F

**prudence** [PROO•dens] *n*
Klugheit F

**prudent** [PROO•dent] *adj* klug

**prune** [proon] *n* Pflaume F

**pry** [pruy] die Nase stecken

**psalm** [salm] *n* Psalm M

**pseudonym** [SOO•do•NIM] *n*
Pseudonym N

**psychiatrist** [suy•KUY•a•trist]
*n* Psychiater M

**psychiatry** [suy•KUY•a•tree] *n*
Psychiatrie F

**psychological**
[SUY•ko•LA•ji•kl] *adj*
psychologisch

**psychologist** [suy•KA•lo•jist]
Psychologe M

**psychology** [suy•KA•lo•jee] *n*
Psychologie F

**public** [PUH•blik] *n* Publikum N

**publication** [PUH•bli•KAI•shn]
*n* Bekanntmachung F

**publicize** [PUH•bli•SUYZ] *vt*
bekanntmachen

**publisher** [PUH•bli•shur] *n*
Herausgeber M

**pucker** [PUH•kur] *vt* runzeln

**pudding** [PU•ding] *n*
Pudding M

**puddle** [PUH•dl] *n* Pfütze F

**puff** [puhf] *n* Hauch M

**pug** [puhg] *n* Boxer M

**pull** [puhl] *vt* ziehen; *n*
Ziehen N

**pulley** [PUHL•ee] *n* Seilrolle F

**pulp** [puhlp] *n* Fruchtfleisch N

**pulpit** [PUHL•pit] *n* Kanzel F

**pulsate** [PUHL•sait] *vt*
pulsieren

**pulsation** [puhl•SAI•shn] *n*
Pochen N

**pulse** [puhlz] *n* Pulsschlag M

**pulverize** [PUHL•vur•UYZ] *vt*
zermahlen

**pumice** [PUH•mis] *n*
Birnstein M

**pump** [puhmp] *n* Pumpe F

**pumpkin** [PUHMP•kin] *n*
Kürbis M

**pun** [puhn] *n* Wortspiel N

**punch** [puhnch] *vt* schlagen

**punctual** [PUHNK•tyu•ul] *adj*
pünktlich
**punctuation**
[PUHNK•tyu•AI•shn] *n*
Zeichenstetzung F
**puncture** [PUHNK•tyur] *vt*
durchstechen
**punish** [PUH•nish] *vt* strafen
**punishment** [PUH•nish•mint] *n*
Strafe F
**pup** [puhp] *n* junger Hund M
**pupil** [PYU•pil] *n* Schüler M
**puppet** [PUH•pit] *n*
Marionette F
**purchase** [PUR•chis] *n* Kauf M
**pure** [pyur] *adj* rein
**purgatory** [PUR•gi•TOR•ee] *n*
Fegefeuer
**purge** [purj] *vt* klären
**purify** [PYUR•i•FUY] *vt*
reinigen
**purity** [PYUR•i•tee] *n*
Reinheit F

**purple** [PUR•pl] purpurn
**purport** [pur•PORT] *vt*
behaupten
**purpose** [PUR•pus] *n* Zweck M
**purr** [pur] *vt* schnurren
**purse** [purs] *n* Tasche F
**pursue** [pur•SOO] *vt* verfolgen
**pursuit** [pur•SOOT] *n*
Verfolgung F
**push** [push] *n* Schubs M; *vt*
schieben; stoßen
**put** [put] *vt* (place) tun; stellen;
(place, thrust, etc) stecken;
(express) sagen
**putrefy** [PYU•tri•FUY] *vt*
verfaulen
**putrid** [PYU•trid] *adj* verfault
**putter** [PUH•tir] *n* Putter M
**putty** [PUH•tee] *n* Kitt M
**puzzle** [PUH•zl] *n* Rätsel N
**pylon** [PUY•lon] *n* Mast M
**pyramid** [PEER•uh•MID] *n*
Pyramide F

# Q

**quack** [kwak] *vt* quaken
**quadrant** [kwa•drant] *n*
Quadrant M
**quadrilateral**
[KWAH•dri•LA•tu•rl] *adj*
vierseitig
**quagmire** [KWAG•muyr] *n*
Moorboden M
**quail** [kwail] *n* Wachtel F
**quaint** [kwaint] *adj* wunderlich
**quake** [kwaik] *vi* zittern

**qualification**
[KWA•li•fi•KAI•shn] *n*
Qualifikation F
**qualify** [KWA•li•FUY] *vi*
qualifizieren
**qualitative** [kwa•li•TAI•tif] *adj*
qualitativ
**quality** [KWA•li•tee] *n*
Qualität F
**qualm** [kwalm] *n*
Zweifel M

**quantitative**
[KWAHN•ti•TAI•tif] *n*
Maßanalyse F

**quantity** [KWAHN•ti•tee] *n*
Quantität F

**quarantine**
[KWAHR•in•TEEN] *n*
Quarantäne F

**quarrel** [KWAH•rl] *n* Streit M;
*vi* sich streiten

**quarry 1** [KWAH•ree] *n*
Fundgrube F

**quarry 2** (hunt) *n* Beute F

**quart** [kwart] *n* Quart N

**quarter** [KWAH•tur] *n* Viertel
N; *adj* viertel; ~ past (hour)
vierteil nach (uhr); *vt* vierteln

**quarterly** [KWAHR•tur•lee] *adj*
vierteljährlich

**quartet** [kwar•TET] *n*
Quartett N

**quartz** [kwartz] *n* Quarz M

**quaver** [KWAI•vur] *vi* zittern

**quay** [kway] *n* Kaigeld N

**queen** [kween] *n* Königin F

**queer** [kweer] *adj* seltsam;
komisch

**quell** [kwell] *vt* bezwingen

**quench** [kwench] *vt* löschen

**query** [KWEER•ee] *n* Frage F

**quest** [kwest] *n* Suche F

**question** [KWEST•shn] *n*
Frage F

**question mark** [KWEST•shn
MARK] *n* Fragezeichen N

**questionable**
[KWEST•shn•uh•bl] *adj*
fraglich

**questionnaire**
[KWEST•shn•AIR] *n*
Fragebogen M

**quibble** [KWIH•bl] *vt*
herumreden

**quick** [kwik] *adv* schnell;
(short) kurz; klein

**quicken** [KWIK•in] *vt*
beschleunigen

**quickly** [KWIK•lee] *adv* schnell

**quickness** [KWIK•nis] *n*
Flinkheit

**quicksand** [KWIK•sand] *n*
Treibsand M

**quicksilver** [KWIK•SIL•vur] *n*
Quecksilber N

**quid** [kwid] *n* Pfund N

**quiescence** [kwee•EH•sinz] *n*
Stille F

**quiet** [KWUY•it] *adj* ruhig

**quietly** [KWUY•it•lee] *adj* leise

**quietness** [KWUY•it•nis] *n*
Ruhe F

**quill** [kwill] *n* Feder F

**quilt** [kwilt] *n* Steppdecke F

**quince** [kwinz] *n* Quitte F

**quinine** [KWUY•nyn] *n*
Chinin N

**quintet** [kwin•TET] *n*
Quintett N

**quintuplet** [kwin•TUH•plit] *n*
Fünflinge F

**quip** [kwip] *vt* witzeln

**quit** [kwit] *vt* verzichten auf

**quite** [kwuyt] *adv* ganz

**quitter** [KWIH•tur] *n*
Feigling M

**quiver** [KWIH•vur] *vt* beben

**quixotic** [kwihk•ZAH•tik] *adj*
phantastisch

**quiz** [kwiz] *n* Prüfung F

**quorum** [KWOR•uhm] *n*
beschlußfähige Anzahl F

**quota** (part; portion) [KWO•ta]
n Anteil N
**quotation** [kwo•TAI•shn] n
Zitat F

**quote** [kwot] vt zitieren
**quotient** [KWO•shnt] n
Quotient M

# R

**rabbi** [RA•buy] n Rabbiner M
**rabbit** [RA•bit] n Hase M
**rabble** [RA•bl] n Kratze F
**rabid** [RA•bid] adj wütend
**raccoon** [ra•KOON] n
Waschbär M
**race 1** [rayz] n Wettrennen N; vt
(sports) laufen; vi (compete)
laufen; fahren; schwimmen
etc.
**race 2** (ethnic group) n
Rasse F
**racer** [RAI•sur] n Läufer M
**rack 1** [rak] n Gestell N; vt
(with pain) quälen
**rack 2** n ~ and ruin\
herunterkommen
**racket** [RA•kit] n Schläger M
**racketeer** [RA•ki•TEER] n
Gangster M
**radiance** [RAI•dee•enz] n
Strahlen N
**radiant** [RAI•dee•ent] adj
strahlend
**radiation** [RAI•dee•AI•shn] n
Strahlung F
**radiator** [RAI•dee•AI•tur] n
Heizkörper M
**radical** [RA•di•kul] adj radikal
**radio** [RAI•dee•O] n Radio N
**radish** [RA•dish] n Rettich M

**radius** [RAI•dee•is] n Radius M
**raffle** [RA•fl] n Tombola F
**raft** n Floß N
**rafter** [RAF•tur] n Flößer M
**rag** n Lumpen M
**rage** [raij] n Wut F; vi toben
**ragged** [RA•gid] adj abgerissen
**raid** n Einfall M; vt überfallen;
police ~ n\ Razzia F;
**rail** n Bahn F
**railroad** [RAIL•rod] n
Eisenbahn F
**railroad station** [RAIL•rod
STAI•shn] n Bahnhof M
**railway** [RAIL•wai] n Bahn F
**rain** n Regen M; vt vi regen
**rainbow** [RAIN•bo] n
Regenbogen M
**raindrop** [RAIN•drahp] n
Regentropf M
**rainfall** n Regen M
**rainy** [RAI•nee] adj regnerisch
**raise** [raiz] vt heben; (increase)
anheben; (build) errichten; (as
question) werfen; (children,
animals) aufziehen; (in salary)
n Gehaltserhöhung
**raisin** [RAIZ•in] n Rosine F
**rally** [RA•lee] n Treffen N
**ram** n Widder M; vt stoßen
**ramble** [RAM•bl] vi bummeln

**rancid** [RAN•sid] *adj* widerlich

**rancor** [RAN•kor] *n* Erbitterung F

**random** [RAN•dom] *adj* zufällig

**rang** (*past tense* ring) klingelte

**range** [rainj] *n* Entfernung M; (scop) *n* Aktionsradius M; (extend from to) gehen von . . . bis

**rank 1** *n* Linie F; (clss) *n* Stand

**rank 2** (smell) *adj* übel

**ransack** [RAN•sak] *vt* plündern

**ransom** [RAN•som] *n* Loskauf M; *vt* Lösgeld

**rant** *vt* toben

**rap** *vt* klopfen

**rape** [raip] *n* Vergewaltigung F; *vt* vergewaltigen

**rapid** [RAP•id] *adj* schnell

**rapt** *adj* versunken

**rapture** [RAP•chur] *n* Verzückung F

**rare** [rair] *adj* rar

**rarity** [RAIR•i•tee] *n* Seltenheit F

**rascal** [RA•skul] *n* Schurke M

**rash** *adj* hastig

**rasp** *vt* krächzen

**raspberry** [RAZ•bur•ee] *n* Himbeere F

**rat** *n* Ratte F

**rate** [rait] *n* Geschwindigkeit F; *vt* (estimate) einschätzen

**rather** [RA•thur] *adv* lieber

**ratify** [RA•ti•FUY] *vt* bestätigen

**rating** [RAI•ting] *n* Schätzung F

**ratio** [RAI•she•O] *n* Verhältnis N

**rational** [RA•sha•nl] *adj* vernünftig

**rattle** [RAT•tl] *vt* klappern

**rattlesnake** [RAT•tl•SNAIK] *n* Klapperschlange F

**raucous** [RAW•kus] *adj* rauh

**ravage** [RA•vij] *vt* verwüsten

**rave** [raiv] *vi* irrereden

**raven** [RAI•vin] *n* Rabe M

**ravenous** [RA•vi•nis] *adj* hungrig

**ravine** [ruh•VEEN] *n* Schlucht M

**ravish** [RA•vish] *vt* entzücken

**raw** *adj* roh

**raw material** [RAW muh•TEE•ree•ul] *n* Rohstoff M

**ray** [rai] *n* Strahl M

**rayon** [RAI•on] *n* Kunstseide F

**raze** [raiz] *vt* tilgen

**razor** [RAI•zor] *n* Rasiermesser N

**re-enter** [REE•EN•tur] *vt* wiedereintreten

**re-establish** [REE•a•STA•blish] *vt* wiedereinführen

**reach** [reech] *vt* reichen

**react** [ree•AKT] *vi* reagieren

**reaction** [ree•AK•shn] *n* Reagierung F

**reactionary** [ree•AK•shn•AIR•ee] *adj* reaktionär

**read** [reed] *vt* lesen

**reader** [REE•dur] *n* Leser M

**readily** [RED•i•lee] *adv* sogleich

**readiness** [RED•i•nis] *n* Bereitschaft F

**reading** [REE•ding] *n* Lesung F

**readjust** [REE•uh•JUST] *vt* wieder anpassen

**ready** [REH•dee] *adj* bereit

**real** [reel] *adj* echt; wirklich; ~ estate\ *npl* Immobilien

**realism** [REEL•izm] *n* Realismus M

**realist** [REEL•ist] *n* Realist M

**realistic** [reel•IS•tik] *adj* realistisch

**reality** [ree•A•li•tee] *n* Realität F

**realization** [REEL•i•ZAI•shn] *n* Verwirklichung F

**realize** [REE•LUYZ] *vt* erkennen

**really** [REEL•lee] *adj* wirklich

**realm** [relm] *n* Reich N

**reap** [reep] *vt* ernten

**reappear** [REE•uh•PEER] *vt* wieder erscheinen

**rear 1** [reer] *n* Hinterseite F; Hintern M

**rear 2** (as animal) *vt* aufziehen; ~ up\ sich aufbäumen

**reason** [REE•zon] *n* Grund M; *npl* (common sense) Verstand M; *vi* vernünftig

**reasonable** [REE•zon•uh•bl] *adj* vernünftig

**reasonably** [REE•zon•uh•blee] *adj* ziemlich

**reasoning** [REE•zon•ing] *n* Denken N

**reassure** [REE•uh•SHUR] *vt* beruhigen

**rebate** [REE•bait] *n* Rebatte F

**rebel** [REH•bl] *n* Rebell M;

**rebellion** [ree•BEL•yin] *n* Aufstand M

**rebellious** [re•BEL•yis] *adj* aufständig

**rebirth** [REE•burth] *n* Wiedergeburt F

**rebound** [REE•bownd] *vi* zurückfallen

**rebuild** [ree•BILD] *vt* wiederaufbauen

**rebuke** [ree•BYOOK] *vi* zurechtweisen

**recall** [ree•KAL] *vi* zurückrufen

**recede** [re•SEED] *vt* verschwinden

**receipt** [re•SEET] *n* Quittung F

**receive** [re•SEEV] *vt* bekommen

**receiver** [re•SEE•vur] *n* Empfänger M

**receiver (telephone)** [re•SEE•vur] *n* Hörer M

**recent** [REE•sent] *adv* vor kurzem

**receptacle** [re•SEP•ti•kl] *n* Behälter M

**reception** [re•SEP•shn] *n* Empfang M

**recess** [REE•sess] *n* (break) Pause F; (of court) Ferien

**recipe** [RE•si•pee] *n* Rezept N

**recipient** [re•SI•pee•int] *n* Empfänger M

**reciprocal** [re•SI•pri•kl] *adj* gegenseitig

**reciprocate** [re•SI•pri•KAIT] *vt* erwidern

**recital** [ree•SUY•tl] *n* Vorlesung F

**recite** [ree•SUYT] *vt* rezitieren

**reckless** [REK•lis] *adj* fahrlässig

**recklessness** [REK•lis•nis] *n* Sorglosigkeit F

**reckon** [REK•kon] *vt* rechnen

**reckoning** [REK•kon•ning] *n* Rechnen N

**reclaim** [ree•KLAIM] *vt* reklamieren

**recline** [ree•KLUYN] *vi* sich lehnen

**recluse** [REH•kloos] *n* Einsiedler M

**recognition** [RE•kuh•NI•shn] *n* (identification) Erkennen N

**recognize** [RE•kug•NUYZ] *vt* erkennen

**recoil** [ree•KOIL] *vt* zurückprallen

**recollect** [RE•ko•LEKT] *vi* sich erinnern

**recollection** [RE•ko•LEK•shn] *n* Erinnerung F

**recommend** [RE•ko•MEND] *vt* empfehlen

**recommendation** [RE•ko•men•DAI•shn] *n* Empfehlung F

**recompense** [RE•kom•PENZ] *vt* belohnen

**reconcile** [RE•kon•SUYL] *vt* aussöhnen

**reconciliation** [RE•kon•SI•lee•AI•shn] *n* Aussöhnung F

**reconnaissance** [re•KON•nai•zanz] *n* Aufklärung F

**reconsider** [REE•kon•SI•dur] *vt* überlegen

**reconstruct** [REE•kon•STRUKT] *vt* wieder aufbauen

**record** [ri•KORD] *vt* (on tape, etc) aufnehmen; (writing) aufzeichnen; *n* (account) [RE•kord] Aufzeichnung F; (of history) Vorstrafen F; (music) Platte F; (sports) Rekord M

**recording** [ree•KOR•ding] *n* Aufnahme M ~in F

**recount** [ree•KOUNT] *vt* nachzählen

**recoup** [ree•KOOP] *vt* wiedereinbringen

**recourse** [REE•korz] *n* Zuflucht F

**recover** [ree•KUH•vur] *vt* wiedergewinnen; *vi* ( get better) sich erholen

**recovery** [ree•KUH•vree] *n* Erholung F

**recreation** [RE•kree•AI•shn] *n* Entspannung F

**recruit** [re•KROOT] *vt* einziehen; *n* Rekrut M

**rectangle** [REK•TAN•gl] *n* Rechteck N

**rectify** [REK•ti•FUY] *vt* berichtigen

**rector** [REK•tur] *n* Pfarrer M

**recuperate** [ree•KOO•pur•AIT] *vi* sich erholen

**recur** [ree•KUR] *vt* wiederkehren

**red** [red] *adj* rot

**redden** [RED•din] *vt* röten

**redeem** [ree•DEEM] *vt* ablösen

**redeemer** [ree•DEE•mur] *n* Erlöser M

**redemption** [ree•DEM•shn] *n* Ablösung F

**redness** [RED•nis] *n* Röte F

**redress** [ree•DRES] *vt*
beseitigen

**reduce** [ree•DOOS] *vt*
vermindern; ~ weight\
abnehmen

**reduction** [ree•DUK•shun] *n*
Reuzierung; Ferringerung F

**reed** [reed] *n* Riedgras N

**reef** *n* Riff N

**reek** *n* Gestank M

**reel** *n* Haspel F; *vi* taumeln;
torkeln

**refer** [ree•FUR] *vt* hinweisen; ~
to\ sprechen von

**referee** [RE•fur•EE] *n*
Richter M

**reference** [RE•fur•enz] *n*
Hinweis M

**refill** [REE•fill] *n* Ersatzfüllung F

**refine** [ree•FUYN] *vt* raffinieren

**refined** [ree•FUYND] *adj*
raffiniert

**refinement** [ree•FUYN•mint] *n*
Raffinierung F

**refinery** [ree•FUY•nur•ee] *n*
Raffinerie F

**reflect** [ree•FLEKT] *vt* (of
light) widerspiegeln; ~ upon\
widerspiegeln

**reflection** [ree•FLEK•shn] *n*
Spiegelung F

**reflexive** [ree•FLEK•ziv] *adj*
reflexiv

**reform** [ree•FAURM] *n*
Reform F

**refraction** [re•FRAK•shn] *n*
Refraktion F

**refrain** [ree•FRAIN] *vt* absehen
von

**refresh** [ree•FRESH] *vt*
erfrischen

**refreshing** [ree•FRESH•ing] *adj*
erfrischend

**refreshment** [ree•FRESH•mint]
*n* Erfrischung F

**refrigeration**
[re•FRI•jur•AI•shn] *n*
Kühlung F

**refuge** [RE•fyooj] *n* Zuflucht F

**refund** [REE•fund] *n*
Rückzahlung F; *vt*
zurückerstaten

**refusal** [ree•FYOO•sl] *n*
Verweigerung F

**refuse 1** [ree•FYOOZ] *v*
(decline; reject ) ablehnen

**refuse 2** [RE•fyoos] *n* Müll;
Abfall M

**refute** [ree•FYOOT] *vi*
widerlegen

**regain** [ree•GAIN] *vt*
wiedergewinnen

**regal** [REE•gul] *adj* königlich

**regalia** [ree•GAI•lee•uh] *n*
Amtsinsignien

**regard** [ree•GARD] *vt*
betrachten; *n* Rücksicht F

**regarding** [ree•GAR•ding] *adj*
hinsichtlich

**regime** [re•JEEM] *n* Regime N

**regiment** [RE•ji•mint] *n*
Regiment N

**region** [REE•jin] *n* Gegend F

**register** [RE•jis•tur] *vt*
eintragen; *n* Register N

**registration** [RE•jis•TRAI•shn]
*n* Eintragung F

**regret** [ree•GRET] *vt* bedauern

**regular** [RE•gyu•lur] *adj*
regelmäßig

**regularly** [RE•gyu•lur•lee]
regelmäßig

**regulate** [RE•gyu•LAIT] vt
ordnen

**regulation** [RE•gyu•LAI•shn] n
Regelung F

**rehearsal** [ree•HUR•sul] n
Probe F

**rehearse** [ree•HURZ] vt
wiederholen

**reign** [rain] vt vorherrschen

**reimburse** [REE•im•BURZ] vt
entschädigen

**rein** [rain] n Zügel M; ~ in\ vt
zügeln .

**reindeer** [RAIN•deer] n
Renntier N

**reinforce** [REE•in•FAURS] vt
verstärken

**reiterate** [ree•i•tur•AIT] vt
wiederholen

**reject** [ree•JEKT] vt ablehnen

**rejoice** [ree•JOIS] vi sich freuen

**rejoicing** [ree•JOI•sing] n
Freude F

**rejoin** [ree•JOIN] vt
wiedervereinigen

**rejuvenate** [ree•JOO•vi•NAIT]
vi verjüngen

**relapse** [ree•LAPS] vt
zurückfallen

**relate** [ree•LAIT] vt berichten;
(story) erzählen

**related** [ree•LAI•tid] adj
verwandt

**relation** [ree•LAI•shn] n
Verhältnis N

**relationship**
[ree•LAI•shn•SHIP] n
Beziehung F

**relative** [RE•luh•tiv] n
Verwandter M; adj relativ

**relax** [ree•LAKS] vt entspannen

**relaxation** [ree•LAK•SAI•shn]
n Entspannung F

**relay** [REE•lai] n Staffellauf M

**release** [ree•LEES] n
Entlassung F; vt entlassen

**relent** [ree•LENT] vi erweichen

**relentless** [ree•LENT•les] adj
schonungslos

**relevant** [RE•li•vint] adj
sachdienlich

**reliability**
[ree•LUY•uh•BI•li•tee] n
Zuverlässigkeit F

**reliable** [ree•LUY•uh•bl] adj
zuverlässig

**reliance** [ree•LUY•enz] n
Vertrauen N

**relief** [ree•LEEF] n
Erleichterung F;
(organization) Hilfs

**relieve** [ree•LEEV] vt
erleichtern

**religion** [re•LI•jin] n Religion F

**religious** [re•LI•jis] adj religiös

**relinquish** [re•LIN•kwish] vt
aufgeben

**relish** [RE•lish] vt gern essen

**reluctant** [ree•LUK•tant] adj
widerwillig

**reluctantly** [ree•LUK•tant•lee]
adv zögernd

**rely** [ree•LUY] vi sich verlassen

**remain** [ree•MAIN] vi bleiben

**remainder** [ree•MAIN•dur] n
Rest M

**remains** [ree•MAINZ] n
Übrigbleibsel N

**remark** [ree•MARK] *n*
Bemerkung

**remarkable** [ree•MAR•kuh•bl]
*adj* bemerkenswert

**remedy** [RE•mi•dee] *n*
Heilmittel N

**remember** [re•MEM•bur] *vi*
sich erinnern an

**remind** [ree•MUYND] *vt*
erinnern

**reminder** [ree•MUYN•der] *n*
Erinnerung

**reminiscence** [RE•mi•NI•senz]
*n* Erinnerung F

**remiss** [re•MIS] *adj* nachlässig

**remission** [re•MI•shn] *n*
Vergebung F

**remit** [ree•MIT] *vt* verschieben

**remnant** [REM•nent] *n*
Stoffrest M

**remodel** [ree•MO•dl] *vt*
umbauen

**remorse** [ree•MORZ] *n* Reue F

**remote** [ree•MOT] *adj* fern

**removal** [ree•MOO•vl] *n*
Abfuhr

**remove** [ree•MOOV] *vt*
entfernen

**removed** [ree•MOOVD] *adj*
entfernt

**renaissance** [RE•nai•SANZ] *n*
Renaissance F

**render** [REN•dur] *vt* vergelten

**renew** [re•NOO] *vt* erneuern

**renewal** [re•NOO•wl] *n*
Erneuerung F

**renovate** [RE•no•VAIT] *vt*
erneuern

**renown** [ree•NOWN] *n*
Ruhm M

**rent** *vt* vermieten

**rental** [REN•tl] *n* Mietbetrag M

**reopen** [ree•O•pin] *vt*
wiedereröffnen

**repair** [ree•PAIR] *vt* reparieren

**reparation** [RE•pur•AI•shn] *n*
Wiedergutmachung F

**repay** [ree•PAI] *vt*
wiederbezahlen

**repeal** [ree•peel] *vt* widerrufen

**repeat** [ree•PEET] *vt*
wiederholen

**repel** [re•PEL] *vt* abweisen

**repent** [re•PENT] *vt* bereuen

**repetition** [RE•pi•TI•shn] *n*
Wiederholung

**replace** [re•PLAIS] *vt* wieder
hinstellen

**replenish** [ree•PLE•nish] *vt*
auffüllen

**replica** [RE•pli•kuh] *n* Kopie F

**reply** [re•PLUY] *vi* antworten

**report** [re•PAURT] *n* Bericht
M; *vt* melden; *vi* sich melden

**reporter** [re•PAUR•tur] *n*
Berichterstatter M

**repose** [ree•POZ] *n* Ruhe F

**represent** [RE•pree•ZENT] *vt*
vertreten

**representation**
[RE•pree•ZEN•TAI•shn] *n*
Vertretung F

**representative**
[RE•pree•ZEN•te•tiv] *n*
Stellvertreter M

**repress** [re•PRES] *vt*
unterdrücken; (psych)
verdrängen

**reprimand** [RE•pri•MAND] *n*
Verweis M

**reproach** [re•PROCH] *n*
Vorwurf M

**reproduce** [REE•pro•DOOS] *vt*
wiedererzeugen; (biol) sich
vermehren

**reproduction**
[REE•pro•DUK•shn] *n*
Wiedererzeugung

**reproof** [re•PROOF] *n* Tadel M

**reprove** [re•PROOV] *vt* tadeln

**reptile** [REP•tuyl] *n* Reptil N

**republic** [ree•PUH•blik] *n*
Republik

**republican** [ree•PUH•bli•ken] *n*
Republikaner M

**repudiate** [re•PYOO•di•AIT] *vt*
nicht anerkennen

**repugnant** [ree•PUG•nent] *adj*
widerlich

**repulse** [ree•PULS] *vt* abweisen

**repulsive** [ree•PUL•siv] *adj*
widerwärtig

**reputable** [RE•PYOO•tuh•bl]
*adj* anständig

**reputation** [RE•pyu•TAI•shn] *n*
Ruf M

**repute** [re•PYOOT] *vi* gelten
als; *n* Ruf M

**request** [re•KWEST] *n* Bitte F

**require** [re•KWUYR] *vt*
erfordern; (need) brauchen

**required** [re•KWUYRD] *adj*
erforderlich

**requirement**
[re•KWUYR•mint] *n*
Bedingung F

**rescue** [RES•kyoo] *vt* retten

**research** [REE•surch] *n*
Forschung F

**resemblancé** [re•ZEM•blinz] *n*
Ähnlichkeit

**resemble** [re•ZEM•bl] *vt*
ähnlich sein

**resent** [re•ZENT] *vt* verübeln

**resentful** [re•ZENT•ful] *adj*
ärgerlich

**reservation** [RE•zur•VAI•shn]
*n* Vorbehalt M; *vt* make a ~\
ein Zimmer reserviert machen

**reserve** [re•ZURV] *vt*
reservieren

**reside** [re•ZUYD] *vi* wohnen

**residence** [RE•zi•denz] *n*
Wohnung F

**residue** [RE•zi•DOO] *n*
Nachlaß M

**resign** [ree•ZUYN] *vt* aufgeben

**resignation** [RE•zig•NAI•shn]
*n* Aufgabe F

**resist** [re•ZIST] *vt* widerstehen

**resistance** [re•ZI•stenz] *n*
Widerstand M

**resolute** [RE•zo•LOOT] *adj*
entschieden

**resolution** [RE•zo•LOO•shn] *n*
Entschlossenheit

**resolve** [re•ZOLV] *vt* auflösen

**resonance** [RE•zo•nenz] *n*
Resonanz

**resonant** [RE•zo•nent] *adj*
nachhallend

**resort** [ree•ZAURT] *n* Kurort M:

**resource** [REE•zaurs] *n*
Quelle F

**respect** [re•SPEKT] *n*
Rücksicht; *vt* respecktieren

**respectable** [re•SPEK•tuh•bl]
*adj* beachtlich

**respectful** [re•SPEKT•fl] *adj*
respektvoll

**respective** [re•SPEK•tiv] *adv*
jeweilig

**respite** [RE•spit] *n* Frist

**respond** [re•SPAHND] *vt*
beantworten

**response** [re•SPAHNS] *n*
Antwort

**responsibility**
[re•SPAHN•si•BI•li•tee] *n*
Verantwortlichkeit

**responsible** [re•SPAHN•si•bl] *n*
verantwortlich

**rest 1** [rest] *n* Rest M; Ruhe F;
*vi* sich ausruhen

**rest 2** (remainder) the ~\ der
Reste; das übrige

**restaurant** [RES•trahnt] *n*
Restaurant N

**restful** [REST•fl] *adj* erholt

**restitution** [RE•sti•TOO•shn] *n*
Rückerstattung F

**restless** [REST•les] *adj* unruhig

**restlessness** [REST•les•nes] *n*
Rastlosigkeit

**restoration** [RES•to•RAI•shn]
*n* Restaurierung

**restore** [re•STAUR] *vt*
wiederherstellen

**restrain** [re•STRAIN] *vt*
zurückhalten

**restrict** [re•STRIKT] *vt*
beschränken

**restriction** [re•STRIK•shn] *n*
Beschränkung F

**result** [re•ZUHLT] *n* Resultat F

**resume** [re•ZOOM] *vt*
wiederaufnehmen

**resuscitate** [re•SUS•si•TAIT] *vt*
wiedererwecken

**retail** [REE•tail] *n* Einzelhandel
M *vt* im Eizenelhandel
verkaufen

**retailer** [REE•tai•lur] *n*
Kleinhändler M

**retaliate** [ree•TA•lee•AIT] *vi*
vergelten

**retaliation** [ree•TA•lee•AI•shn]
*n* Vergeltung F

**retard** [ree•TARD] *vt* verzögern

**retinue** [RE•ti•NOO] *n*
Gefolge N

**retire** [ree•TUYR] ins Pension
gehen

**retirement** [ree•TUYR•mint] *n*
Pension N

**retort** [ree•TORT] *n*
Erwiderung

**retract** [ree•TRAKT] *vt*
zurücknehmen

**retreat** [ree•TREET] *n* Rückzug
M; Abzug M; *vt* zurückgehen

**retrieve** [ree•TREEV] *vt*
zurückholen

**retroactive** [RE•tro•AK•tiv] *adj*
rückwirkend

**return** [ree•TURN] *vi* (combe
back) zurückkehren; *vt* (give
back) zurückgeben; *n* (profit)
Einkommen N; Tax ~\
Steuererklärung F

**return address** [ree•TURN
a•DRES] *n* Adresse F

**returns** (election) [ree•TURNZ]
*vi* Wahlzählung F

**reunion** [ree•YOO•nyun] *n*
Wiedervereinigung F

**reunite** [REE•yoo•NUYT] *vt*
wiedervereinigen

**reveal** [ree•VEEL] *n* offenbaren

**revelation** [RE•vi•LAI•shn] *n*
Offenbarung

**revelry** [RE•vil•ree] *n*
Restlichkeit F

**revenge** [ree•VENJ] *n* Rache F

**revenue** [RE•vi•NOO] *n*
Einkommensquelle
**revere** [re•VEER] *vt* verehren
**reverence** [RE•vur•enz] *n*
Verehrung
**reverend** [RE•vur•end] *adj*
ehrwürdig
**reverent** [RE•vur•ent] *adj*
eherbietig
**reverse** [re•VERS] *n*
Gegenteil N
**revert** [re•VERT] *vt*
zurückkehren
**review** [re•VYOO] *vt*
Nachprüfung F
**revile** [re•VUYL] *vt* schmähen
**revise** [re•VUYZ] *vt* revidieren
**revision** [re•VI•shn] *n*
Durchsicht F
**revival** [re•VUY•vul] *n*
Erweckung F
**revoke** [re•VOK] *vt* widerrufen
**revolt** [re•VOLT] *n* Aufruhr M
**revolution** [RE•vo•LOO•shn] *n*
Revolution
**revolutionary**
[RE•vo•LOO•shn•AI•ree] *adj*
revolutionär
**revolve** [re•VAHLV] *vi* sich
drehen
**reward** [re•WAURD] *n*
Belohnung F
**rewrite** [re•RUYT] *vt vi*
umschreiben
**rhetoric** [RE•to•rik] *n*
Rhetorik F
**rheumatism** [ROO•muh•TI•zm]
*n* Rheumatismus M
**rhinoceros** [ruy•NAHS•rus] *n*
Rhinozeros N

**rhubarb** [ROO•barb] *n*
Rhabarber M
**rhyme** [ruym] *n* Reim M
**rhythm** [RI•thim] *n*
Rhythmus M
**rib** *n* Rippe F; *vt* (tease) necken;
foppen
**ribbon** [RI•bin] *n* Band M
**rice** [ruys] *n* Reis M
**rich** *adj* reich; *npl* the ~\
Reichen
**richness** [RICH•nes] *n*
Reichtum M
**rid** *vt* befreien
**riddle** [RI•dl] *n* Rätsel N
**ride** [ruyd] *n* Fahrt F; (on horse)
Reitt M; *vi* reiten
**ride** (bicycle) [ruyd
(buy•si•kul)] Rad fahren
**ride** (horseback) [ruyd] *vi* reiten
**rider** [RUY•dur] *n* Reiter M; -in
F
**ridge** [rij] *n* Kamm M
**ridicule** [RI•di•KYUL] *n*
Spott M
**ridiculous** [ri•DI•kyu•lus] *adj*
lächerlich
**rifle** [RUY•fl] *n* Gewehr N
**rig** *n* Rüstung F
**right** [ruyt] *adj* richtig;
(direction) rechts
**right away** [RUYT a•WAI] *adj*
sofort
**right-hand** [RUYT•hand] *adj*
rechtshändig
**righteous** [RUY•chus] *adj*
gerecht
**righteousness** [RUY•chus•nes]
*n* Rechtschaffenheit F
**rigid** [RI•jid] *adj* starr

**rigidity** [ri•JI•di•tee] *n*
Steifheit F

**rigor** [RI•gor] *n* Strenge F

**rim** *n* Rand M

**rind** [ruynd] *n* Rinde F

**ring 1** [ring] *n* Ring M; *vt*
(surround) umringen

**ring 2** (sound) N Klang M;
Läuten N; *vi* klingen; (bell)
läuten

**rink** *n* Eisbahn F

**rinse** *vt* ausspülen

**riot** [RUY•ut] *n* Aufruhr M; *vi*
randalieren

**rip** *n* Riß M; *vt* einen Riß
machen

**ripe** [ruyp] *adj* reif

**ripple** [RI•pul] *n* kleine
Welle F

**rise** [ruyse] *n* Anstieg M; *vi*
aufstehen; sich erheben

**risk** *n* Risiko N; *vt* riskieren

**rite** [ruyt] *n* Zeremonie F

**ritual** [RI•chu•ul] *n* Ritual N

**rival** [RUY•vl] *n* Rivale M

**rivalry** [RUY•vl•ree] *n*
Wettstreit M

**river** [RI•vur] *n* Fluß M

**road** [rod] *n* Straße F; on
the ~\ unterwegs sein; *n* (fig)
Weg M

**roam** [rom] *vi* wandern

**roar** [ror] *vi* brüllen

**roast** [rost] *vt* braten

**rob** [rahb] *vt* rauben

**robber** [RA•bur] *n* Räuber M

**robbery** [RA•bree] *n* Raub M

**robe** [rob] *n* Robe F

**robin** [RA•bin] *n* Rotkehlchen N

**robust** [ro•BUST] *adj* kräftig

**rock 1** [rahk] *n* Fels M;
(substance) Stein M

**rock 2** *vt vi* schaukeln; (as
baby) wiegen

**rocket** [RAH•kit] *n* Rakete F

**rocking chair** [RAH•king
CHAIR] *n* Schaukelstuhl M

**rocky** [RAH•kee] *adj* felsig

**rod** [rahd] *n* Rute F

**role** [rol] *n* Rolle F

**roll** [rol] *n* (of paper) Rolle F; *vi*
rollen

**Roman** [RO•man] *adj*
romanisch

**romance** [ro•MANS] *n*
Liebesroman M

**romantic** [ro•MAN•tik] *adj*
romantisch

**romanticism**
[ro•MAN•ti•SIZM] *n*
Romantik F

**romanticist** [ro•MAN•ti•sist] *n*
Romantiker M

**room** *n* Zimmer N; Raum M

**roommate** [ROOM•mait] *n*
Zimmerkollege M

**roomy** [ROO•mee] *adj*
geräumig

**roost** *n* Hühnerstange F

**root** *n* Wurzel F

**rope** [rop] *n* Seil N

**rosary** [RO•suh•ree] *n*
Rosenkranz M

**rose** [roz] *n* (flower) Rose F;
*adj* rosarot

**rosy** [RO•zee] *adj* rosenrot

**rot** [raht] *vt* verfaulen; *n*
Fäulnis F

**rotary** [RO•tuh•ree] *n*
Rotary-Club

**rotation** [ro•TAI•shn] *n*
Drehung F

**rote** [rot] *adj* mechanisch

**rotten** [RAH•tin] *adj* mürbe

**rough** [ruhf] *adj* rauh

**rough estimate** [RUHF
E•sti•MAIT] *n* Schätzung F

**roughen** [RUHF•in] *vi* rauh
werden

**roughly** [RUHF•lee] *adv*
ungefähr

**round** [round] *adj* rund; *vt*
make ~s\ runden

**round off (edges)** abrunden;
(series) voll machen

**round up** *vt* (people)
zusammentrommeln; (cattle)
zusammentreiben

**rouse** [rowz] *vt* aufwecken

**route** [root] *n* Route F; *vt* [rout]
legen

**routine** [roo•TEEN] *n*
Routinesache; *adj*
rountinemäßig

**row** [ro] *n* Reihe F

**rub-down** [RUHB•doun] *vt*
abreiben

**rubber** [RUH•bur] *n* Gummi N

**rubbish** [RUH•bish] *npl* Abfall;
Abfälle M

**rubble** [RUH•bl] *n* Schotter M

**ruby** [ROO•bee] *n* Rubin M

**rudder** [RUH•dur] *n* Ruder N

**rude** [rood] *adj* grob; unhöflich

**rueful** [ROO•ful] *adj*
jämmerlich

**ruffian** [RUH•fee•in] *n*
Rohling M

**ruffle** [RUH•fl] *n* Krause

**rug** [ruhg] *n* Teppich M

**rugged** [RUH•gid] *adj*
zerklüftet

**ruin** [ROO•in] *n* Ruine F

**rule** [rool] *n* Regel F; *vt*
beherrschen; *vi* (reign)
herrschen

**rum** *n* Rum M

**rumble** [RUHM•bl] *vi* rattern

**ruminate** [ROO•mi•NAIT] *vt*
wiederkäuen

**rumor** [roo•mur] *n* Gerücht N

**rump** [ruhmp] *n* Hinterteil N

**rumple** [RUHM•pl] *vt*
zerknittern

**run** [ruhn] *n* Lauf M; *vi* laufen,
rennen; *vt* (operate) betreiben

**run-down** [RUN•DOUN] *adj*
erschöpft

**runaway** [RUHN•uh•WAI] *n*
Flüchtlinge F; *vi* davonlaufen

**runner** [RUH•nur] *n* Läufer M;
-in F

**running** [RUH•ning] *n*
Laufen N

**runt** [ruhnt] *n* Zwergrind N

**rupture** [RUHP•chur] *n*
Bruch M

**rural** [RUR•uhl] *adj* ländlich

**ruse** [rooz] *n* Trick M

**rush** [ruhsh] *n* (of crowd)
Gedränge N; (of air) stroß M;
*vi* rasen; eilen; hetzen; (do
quickly) hastig machen

**rush hour** [RUSH OUR] *n*
Hauptverkehrszeit F

**russet** [RUH•sit] *adj* rostbraun

**Russia** [RUH•sha] *n* Rußland

**Russian** [RUH•shin] *adj*
russisch

**rust** [ruhst] *n* Rost M

**rustic** [RUH•stik] *adj* simpel
**rusty** [RUH•stee] *adj* rostig
**rut** [ruht] *n* Geleise F

**ruthless** [ROOTH•les] *adj*
mitleidlos
**rye** [ruy] *n* Roggen M

# S

**Sabbath** [SA•beth] *n* Sonntag M
**saber** [SAI•bur] *n* Säbel M
**sabotage** [SA•bo•TAJ] *n*
Sabotage F
**sack** [sak] *n* Sack M
**sacrament** [SA•kra•mint] *n*
Sakrament N
**sacred** [SAI•krid] *adj* heilig
**sacrifice** [SA•kri•FUYS] *n*
Opfer N
**sad** *adj* traurig
**sadden** [SA•din] *vt* betrüben
**saddle** [SAD•dl] *n* Sattel M
**sadistic** [sa•DIS•tik] *adj*
sadistisch
**sadness** [SAD•nes] *n*
Traurigkeit F
**safe 1** [saif] *n* Safe M
**safe 2** *adj* sicher
**safely** [SAIF•lee] *adv* sicher
**safety** [SAIF•tee] *n* Sicherheit F
**safety pin** [SAIF•tee PIN] *n*
Sicherheitsnadel F
**saffron** [SA•frahn] *n* Safran M
**sag** *vi* sich senken
**sagacious** [sa•GAI•shus] *adj*
scharfsinnig
**sagacity** [sa•GA•si•tee] *n*
Scharfsinn M
**sage** [saij] *n* Salbei M
**sail** *vi* segeln
**sailboat** [SAIL•bot] *n* Segel N

**sailing** [SAI•ling] *vi* segeln
**sailor** [SAI•lur] *n* Matrose M
**saint** *n* Heiliger M
**saintly** [SAINT•lee] *adj* heilig
**sake** [saik] *n* willen
**salad** [SA•lid] *n* Salat M
**sale** [saiul] *n* Verkauf M
**sale price** *n* Ausverkaufspreis M
**salesclerk** [SAIULZ•klerk] *n*
Verkaufer M; -in F
**saleswoman**
[SAIULZ•WU•man] *n*
Verkäuferein F
**saliva** [su•LUY•vu] *n*
Speichel M
**salmon** [SA•mun] *npl* Lachs M;
*adj* (color) lachs (farben)
**salon** [suh•LAHN] *n* Salon M
**salt** [sault] *n* Salz N
**saltwater** [SAULT•WAU•tur] *n*
Salzwasser N
**salty** [SAHL•tee] *adj* salzig
**salute** [su•LOOT] *n* Gruß M; *vt*
grüßen; (person) salutieren
vor
**salvage** [SAL•vij] *n*
Bergungsaktion F; ~ vessel *n*\
Bergungsschiff M
**salvation** [sal•VAI•shn] *n*
Rettung F
**same** [saim] *adj* der/die/das
gleiche; they are all the ~\

sie sind alle gleich; ~ time, ~
place\ gleicher Ort, gleiche
Zeit; in the ~ way\ gleich; it's
all the ~ to me\ es ist mir
egal; just the ~\ trotzdem; ~
to you\ gleichfalls

**sample** [SAM•pl] *n* Beispel N;
*vt* probieren; kosten

**sanction** [SANGK•shn] *n*
Zustimmung F; *vt*
sanktionieren

**sanctity** [SANG•ti•tee] *n* (of
place) Heiligkeit F; (of rights)
Unantastbarkeit
sanctuary[SANG•choo•E•ree]
*n* Heiligtum N; Altrum; to
seek ~\ Zuflucht suchen bei;
(for animals) Schutzgebiet N

**sand** [sand] *n* Sand M; *vt*
(smooth) schmirgen; (spread)
streuen

**sandal** [SAN•dl] *n* Sandale F

**sandwich n** [SAND•wich] *n*
belegtes Brot; Sandwich N

**sane** [sain] *adj* normal

**Santa Claus** [SAN•ta CLAUS]
*n* der Weihnactsmann

**sarcasm** [SAR•ka•zm] *n*
Sarkasmus M

**Satan** [SAI•tn] *n* Satan M

**satellite** [SA•tu•LUYT] *n*
Satellit M

**satisfaction** [SA•tis•FAK•shun]
*n* Befriedigung F; (of
conditions, contract)
Erfüllung F

**satisfactory**
[SA•tis•FAK•tor•ee] *adj*
befriedigend

**satisfy** [SA•tis•FUY] *vt*
befriedigen; *vr* to ~ oneself\
sich von etw überzeugen

**saturate** [SA•chur•AIT] *vt*
tränken

**Saturday** *n* Samstag

**save** [saiv] *vt* (rescue) retten;
(money) aufheben; aufsapren;
(avoid using up)'sparen; *vi*
(with money) sparen

**saving** [SAI•ving] *n npl* Rettung
F; Sparen N

**savior** [SAI•vyor] *n* Retter M;
-in F

**say** [sai] *vt vi* sagen; (text)
sprechen; *n* Mispracherect N

**saying** [SAI•ing] *n* Redensart F

**scale 1** [skail] *n* (of fish)
Schuppe F

**scale 2** *n* Skala F

**scale 3** *vt* (mountain, wall)
erklettern

**scale down** *vt* verkleinern

**scalp** [skalp] *n* Kopfhaut F

**scan** [skan] *vt* schwnken über; *n*
(med) Scan M

**scandal** [SKAN•dul] *n*
Skandal M

**Scandinavia**
[SKAN•di•NAI•vee•u] *n*
Skandinavien N

**Scandinavian** *adj*
skandinavisch

**scar** [skahr] *n* Narbe F

**scarab** [SKA•rub] *n*
Mistkäfer M

**scarce** [skairz] *adj* (short
supply) knapp; (rare) selten

**scare** [skair] *vt* erschrecken; *n*
Schreck M

**scarf** [skahrf] *n* Schal M

**scarlet** [SKAHR•let] *n*
Scharlach M

**scary** [SKAIR•ee] *adj*
erschreckend

**scathe** [skaith] *vt* versengen

**scatter** [SKA•tur] *vt* streuen

**scavenger** [SKA•ven•jur] *n*
Aasfresser M

**scenario** [suh•NAI•ree•o] *n*
Plan M

**scene** [seen] *n* Scahuplaz M;
(theatrical) Szene F;
(landscape) Landschaft F;
make a ~\ eine Szene machen

**scenery** [SEE•nur•ee] *n*
Landschaft F

**scepter** [SEP•tur] *n* Zepter N

**schedule** [SKE•dyul] *n* Schiff
N; *vt* planen

**scheme** [skeem] *n* Schema N;
(plot) Plan N; *vi* intrigieren

**schism** [SKI•zim] *n*
Kirchenspaltung F

**schist** *n* Schiefer M

**scholar** [SKAH•lur] *n*
Gelehrter M

**scholarly** [SKAH•lur•lee] *adj*
gelehrt

**scholarship** [SKAH•lur•ship] *n*
Stipendium N

**scholastic** [sko•LAS•tik] *adj*
akademisch

**school** [skool] *n* Schule F; *vt*
lehren

**school** (boarding) [skool]
(BOR•ding)] *n* Privatschule F

**schoolboy** [SKOOL•boi] *n*
Schüler M

**schoolmaster**
[SKOOL•MA•stur] *n*
Schulleiter M

**schoolteacher**
[SKOOL•TEE•chur] *n* Lehrer
in M

**schooner** [SKOO•nur] *n*
Schoner M

**science** [SUY•enz] *n*
Wissenschaft F

**scientific** [SUY•yen•TI•fik] *adj*
wissenschaftlich

**scientist** [SUY•yen•tist] *n*
Wissenschaftler M

**scissors** [SI•sorz] *n* Schere F

**scoff** [skoff] *n* Spott M

**scold** [skold] *vt* schelten

**scolding** [SKOL•ding] *n*
Schelten N

**sconce** [skahnz] *n* Leuchter M

**scone** [skoan] *n* Teegebäck N

**scoop** [skoop] *vt* schaufeln

**scope** [skoap] *n* Bereich M

**scorch** [skorch] *vt* verbrennen

**score** [skor] *n* (sports)
Spielergebnis N; (music)
Noten *pl;* (line, cut) Kerbe F;
(reason) Grund M; *vt* erzielen;
bekommen; *vi* einen Punkt
erzielen

**scorn** [skorn] *n* Verachtung F;
*vt* verachten

**scorpion** [SKOR•pee•in] *n*
Skorpion M

**Scot** [skot] *n* Schotte M

**Scotland** [SKOT•lind] *n*
Schottland M

**scoundrel** [SKOUN•drul] *n*
Schurke M

**scour** [skour] *vt* schrubben

**scourge** [skorj] *n* Peitsche F

**scout** [skout] *n* Kundschaften
M; *vi* erkunden

**scouting** [SKOUT•ting] *vt*
erkunden

**scowl** [skoul] *vt* finster
anblicken

**scramble** [SKRAM•bl] *vt*
verrühren

**scrap** [skrap] *n* Brocken M

**scrape** [skraip] *vt* kratzen;
schaben

**scraper** [SKRAI•pur] *n*
Kratzer M

**scratch** [skratch] *n* Kratzer M;
*vt* zerkratzen; *adj* (food from
~) improvisiert

**scrawl** [skraul] *vt* kritzeln

**scream** [skreem] *n* Schrei M; *vt*
*vi* schreien

**screech** [skreech] *n* Kreischen;
*vt* kreischen

**screen** [skreen] *n* Leinwand F

**screen** (movies) *n* Kino N

**screw** [skrew] *vt* schrauben

**screwdriver**
[SKREW•DRUY•vur] *n*
Schraubenzieher M

**scribble** [SKRIB•bl] *vt*
hinkritzeln

**scribe** [skruyb] *n* Schreiber M

**script** [skript] *n* Schrift F

**scripture** [SKRIP•chur] *n*
Heilige Schrift F

**scroll** [skroll] *n* Schriftrolle F

**scrub** [skrub] *vt* schrubben

**scruff** [skruff] *n* Genick N

**scruple** [SKROO•pl] *n*
Skrupel M

**scrupulous** [SKROO•pyu•lus]
voller Skrupel

**scrutinize** [SKROO•ti•NUYZ]
*vt* genau prüfen

**scrutiny** [SKROO•ti•nee] *n*
Untersuchung F

**sculptor** [SKULP•tur] *n*
Bildhauer M

**sculpture** [SKULP•tyur] *n*
Skulptur F

**scum** [skuhm] *n* Schaum M

**scurrilous** [SKUR•ri•les] *adj*
ordinärscherzhaft

**scurry** [SKUR•ree] *vi* hasten

**scythe** [suyth] *n* Sense F

**sea** [see] *n* See F; Meer N

**seal 1** [seel] *n* Seehund M

**seal 2** *n* Siegel N; (label)
Aufkleber; *vt* versiegeln;
(envelope, etc) zukleben

**seam** [seem] *n* Naht F

**seamstress** [SEEM•stres] *n*
Näherin F

**sear** [seer] *vt* versengen

**search** [surch] *n* Suche F; *vt*
suchen

**search warrant** [SURCH
WAHR•rent] *n*
Haussuchungsbefehl M

**seasick** [SEE•sik] *adj* seekrank

**season** [SEE•zon] *n* Jahreszeit
F; *vt* (food) würtzen

**season ticket** [SEE•zon
TIK•ket] *n* Zeitkarte F

**seasonable** [SEE•zon•uh•bl]
*adj* rechtzeitig

**seasoning** [SEE•zon•ning] *n*
Würze F

**seat** [seet] *n* Sitz M; (in theatre,
etc) Platz

**secede** [se•SEED] *vt* sich
trennen

**secession** [se•SES•shn] *n*
Abfall M

**seclude** [se•KLOOD] *vt*
absondern

**seclusion** [se•KLOO•shn] *n*
Zurückgezogenheit F

**second** [SE•kond] *adj* zweite

**second-hand** [SE•kond•HAND] *adj* gebraucht

**second-rate** [SE•kond•RAIT] *adj* zweitrangig

**secondary** [SE•kon•DAI•ree] *adj* sekundär

**secondly** [SE•kond•lee] *adv* zweitens

**secrecy** [SEE•kruh•see] *n* Verborgenheit F

**secret** [SEE•kret] *n* Geheimnis N

**secretary** [SE•kre•TAI•ree] *n* Sekretärin F

**secrete** [se•KREET] *vt* absondern

**secretion** [se•KREE•shn] *n* Sekretion F

**secretive** [SE•kreh•tiv] *adj* geheimnisvoll

**sect** [sekt] *n* Religionsgemeinschaft F

**sectarian** [sek•TAI•ree•in] *adj* sektiererisch

**section** [SEK•shun] *n* Schnitt M; (of book) Teil M

**sector** [SEK•tor] *n* Sektor M

**secular** [SE•kyu•lur] *adj* weltlich

**secularize** [SE•kyu•la•RUYZ] *vt* verweltlichen

**secure** [se•KYUR] *vt* sichern; *adj* sicher

**securely** *adv* (firmly) fest; (safely) sicher

**security** [se•KYU•ri•tee] *n* Sicherheit F

**sedan** [se•DAN] *n* Limousine F

**sedate** [se•DAIT] *adj* ruhig

**sedative** [SE•duh•tiv] *n* Beruhigungsmittel N

**sedentary** [SE•din•TAI•ree] *adj* sitzend

**sediment** [SE•di•mint] *n* Bodensatz M

**sedition** [se•DI•shn] *n* Volksverhetzung F

**seditious** [se•DI•shus] *adj* umstürzlerisch

**seduce** [se•DOOS] *vt* verführen

**seducer** [se•DOO•zur] *n* Verführer M

**seduction** [se•DUK•shn] *n* Verführung F

**seductive** [se•DUK•tiv] *adj* verführerisch

**see** *vi* sehen; (visit) besuchen; (meet with) sehen; (visualize) sich vorstellen

**seed** *n* Same M; *vt* besäen

**seek** *vt* suchen

**seem** *vi* scheinen

**seep** *vt* tropfen

**seer** [SEE•ur] *n* Seher M

**seesaw** [SEE•sau] *n* Wippen N

**seethe** *vt* sieden

**segment** [SEG•mint] *n* Teil M

**segregate** [SE•gruh•GAIT] *vt* trennen

**seize** [seez] *vt* ergreifen

**seizure** [SEE•shur] *n* Ergreifung F

**seldom** [SEL•dum] *adv* selten

**select** [se•LEKT] *vt* wählen

**selection** [se•LEK•shn] *n* Wahl F

**selective** [se•LEK•tiv] *adj* wählerisch

**self** *n* Ich; Selbst N

**self-centered** [SELF•SEN•turd] *adj* ichbezogen

**self-confident**
[SELF•KON•fi•dint] adj
selbstvertrauerisch

**self-conscious**
[SELF•KON•shus] adj
gehemmt

**self-control** [SELF•kon•TROL]
adj selbstbeherrscht

**self-defense** [SELF•dee•FENS]
n Selbstverteidigung F

**self-respect** [SELF•ree•SPEKT]
n Selbstachtung F

**self-starter** [SELF•STAR•tur] n
Anlasser M

**self-taught** [SELF•TAUT] adj
autodidaktisch

**selfish** [SEL•fish] adj
selbstsüchtig

**selfishness** [SEL•fish•nis] n.
Selbstsucht F

**sell** vt verkaufen

**semblance** [SEM•blens] n
Gestalt F

**semiannual** [SE•mee•AN•yul]
adj halbjährlich

**semicolon** [SE•mee•KO•lun] n
Strichpunkt M

**seminary** [SE•mi•NAI•ree] n
Pristerseminar N

**senate** [SE•nit] n Senat M

**senator** [SE•ni•tur] n Senator M

**send** vi schicken; (signal)
senden; (make go) schießen

**sender** [SEN•dur] n
Absender M

**senile** [SEE•nuyl] adj senil

**senility** [se•NI•li•tee] n
Senilität F

**senior** [SEE•nyur] n Älterer M;
adj älter; (in rank) vorgesetzt

**seniority** [se•NYAU•ri•tee] n
höheres Dienstalter N

**sensations** [sen•SAI•shns] n
Gefühl N

**sense** [senz] n Sinn M;
(feeling) Gefühl N; vt fühlen;
spüren

**sense** (common) n
Vernünftigkeit F

**senseless** [SENS•les] adj
besinnungslos

**sensibility** [SEN•si•BI•li•tee] n
Sensibilität F

**sensible** [SEN•si•bl] adj
vernünftig

**sensitive** [SEN•si•tiv] adj
sensibel

**sensitivity** [SEN•si•TI•vi•tee] n
Feingefühl N

**sensual** [SEN•shu•al] adj
wollüstig

**sentence** [SEN•tuhns] n Satz M

**sentence** (death) [SEN•tuhns] n
Todesurteil N

**sentiment** [SEN•ti•mint] n
Empfindung F

**sentimentality**
[SEN•ti•men•TA•li•tee] n
Rührseligkeit F

**sentinel** [SE•ti•nel] n
Wächter M

**separable** [SE•pruh•bl] adj
trennbar

**separate** [SE•pa•rit] adj
getrennt; [SE•pa•RAIT] vt
trennen; vi sich trennen

**separately** [SE•prit•lee] adv
trennend

**separation** [SE•puh•RAI•shn] n
Trennung F

**separatism** [SE•pruh•TI•zim] *n*
Separatismus M

**September** [sep•TEM•bur] *n*
September

**septic** [SEP•tik] *adj* septisch

**sepulcher** [SE•pul•kur] *n*
Grabstätte F

**sequel** [SEE•kwel] *n* Folge F

**sequence** [SEE•kwenz] *n*
Lauf M

**sequester** [see•KWES•tur] *vt*
absondern

**sequestration**
[SEE•kwes•TRAI•shn] *n*
Absonderung F

**serenade** [SAIR•uh•NAID] *n*
Nachtmusik F

**serene** [suh•REEN] *adj* heiter

**serenity** [suh•RE•ni•tee] *n*
Heiterkeit F

**sergeant** [SAR•jint] *n*
Feldwebel M

**serial** [SEE•ree•ul] *n*
Fortsetzungen

**series** [SEE•reez] *n* Serie F

**serious** [SEE•ree•uhs] *adj* ernst

**seriously** [SEE•ree•uhs•lee] im
Ernst

**seriousness** [SEE•ree•uhs•nes]
*n* Ernst M

**sermon** [SUR•min] *n* Predigt M

**serpent** [SUR•pint] *n*
Schlange F

**serum** [SEER•uhm] *n* Serum N

**servant** [SUR•vint] *n* Diener M

**servant** (civil) [SUR•vint] *n*
Beamte M

**serve** [surv] *vt* dienen; (in
restaurant, etc) servieren

**service** [SURV•is] *n* Dienst M;
*vt* (of car etc) warten

**serviceable** [SUR•vi•suh•bl]
*adj* verwendbar

**servile** [SUR•vuyl] *adj*
sklavisch

**servitude** [SUR•vi•TOOD] *n*
Knechtschaft F

**session** [SE•shun] *n* Sitzung F

**set** *n* Sortiment N; (group of
people) Kreis M; (TV; radio;
etc) Gerät n; apparat M; *adj*
(ready) fertig; bereit; *vt*
stellen; (mount) fassen; (med)
einrichten; (~ the table)
decken; (hair) legen;
eindrehen; *vi* (sun, etc)
untergehen

**setting** [SET•ting] *n* Service N

**settle** [SET•tl] *vi* sich ansiedeln

**settlement** [SET•tl•mint] *n*
Ansiedlung F

**seven** [SE•vin] *num* sieben

**seventeen** [SE•vin•TEEN] *num*
siebzehn

**seventeenth**
[SE•vin•TEENTH] *num*
siebzehnte

**seventh** [SE•vinth] *num* siebte

**seventieth** [SE•vin•tee•eth]
*num* siebzigste

**seventy** [SE•vin•tee] *num*
siebzig

**sever** [SE•vur] *vt* abtrennen

**several** [SE•vur•uhl] *adj* viele

**severe** [se•VEER] *adj* streng

**sew** [so] *vt* nähen

**sewer** [SOO•ur] *n*
Abwasserkanal M

**sewing** [so•ing] *n* Näharbeit F

**sewing machine** [SO•ing
muh•SHEEN] *n*
Nähmaschine F

**sewn** [son] *adj* genäht

**sex** *n* Geschlecht N

**sexton** [SEKS•tin] *n*
Totengräber M

**sexual** [SEK•shoo•uhl] *adj*
sexuell

**shabby** [SHA•bee] *adj* schäbig

**shack** [shak] *n* Hütte F

**shackle** [SHA•kl] *n* Lasche F

**shad** *n* Alse F

**shade** [shaid] *n* Schatten M; *vt*
abschirmen

**shadow** [SHA•do] *n* Schatten
M; *vt* (follow) beschatten

**shake** [shayk] *n* Schütteln; *vt*
schütteln; *vi* wacken

**shallow** [SHA•lo] *adj* flach

**shame** [shaim] *n* Scham F; *vt*
Schande machen; to feel ~ at\
sth\ sich für etw shämen

**shameless** [SHAIM•les] *adj.*
schamlos

**shampoo** [sham•POO] *n*
Shampoo; Schampon N

**shape** [shaip] *n* form F;
(unidientified figure) Gestalt F
*vt* berbeiten; *vi* sich
entwickeln

**shaped** [shaipd] *adj* geformt

**share** [shair] *n* portion) Anteil
M; *vt* (divide) teilen

**shareholder** [SHAIR•HOL•dur]
Aktionär M; -in F

**sharp** [sharp] *adj* scharf

**sharpen** [SHARP•un] *vt* (knife)
schleifen

**shatter** [SHAT•ur] *vt*
zertrümmer

**shave** [shayv] *n* Rasur F; *vt*
rasieren; *vi* (person) sich
rasieren

**shawl** [shawl] *n* Tuch N

**she** *pron* sie;n Sie F

**shed 1** *vt* ausziehen

**shed 2** *n* Schuppen M

**sheep** *npl* Schaf N

**sheer** (absolute) *adj* rein

**sheet** *n* (for bed) Bettuch N;
(of paper) Blatt N; (of water)
Fläche

**shelf** *n* Breet; Bord N

**shell** *n* Schae F; (frame)
Mauerwerk N; *vt* enthülsen

**shelter** [SHEL•tur] *n* Schutz M;
*vt* schützen

**shield** [sheeld] *n* Schild M; *vy*
schützen

**shift** *n* (change) Änderung; (in
idea) Wandel M; *vt* (move)
bewegen; *vi* (move) sich
bewegen

**shin** *n* Schienbein N

**shine** [shuyn] *n* Glanz M; *vi*
leuchten

**ship** *n* Schiff N

**ship out** *vt* versenden

**shipment** [SHIP•munt]
Sendung F

**shirt** [shurt] *n* Hemd N

**shiver** [SHI•vur] *vi* zittern

**shock** [shok] *n* Erschütterung F;
*vt* erschüttern

**shoddy** [SHAH•dee] *n*
Kitsch M

**shoe** [shoo] *n* Schuh M

**shoelace** [SHOO•lais] *n*
Schnürsenkel M

**shoemaker** [SHOO•MAI•kur] *n*
Schuhmacher M

**shoot** *vt* schießen

**shooter** [SHOO•tur] *n*
Schießer M

**shooting** [SHOO•ting] *n*
Schießen N

**shop** *n* Geschäft N; *v* einkaufen
gehen

**shopkeeper** [SHAHP•KEE•pur]
*n* Ladenbesitzer M

**shopper** [SHAH•pur] *n* Käufer
-in M

**shopping** [SHAH•ping] *n*
Einkaufen N

**shopping** *v* einkaufen
gehen

**shore** [shor] *n* Küste F

**short** *adj* kurz; *adv* to fall ~\ zu
kurz landen; ( abruptly)
abrupt; ~ of\ außer

**short circuit** Kurzschluß

**short story** [SHAURT
STAUR•ee] *n*
Kurzgeschichte F

**shortage** [SHAUR•tij] *n*
Mangel M

**shortcoming**
[SHAURT•kuh•ming] *n*
Fehlbetrag M

**shortcut** [SHAURT•kut] *n*
Abkürzung F

**shorten** [SHAUR•tin] *vt*
verkürzen

**shortening** [SHAURT•ning] *n*
Backfett N

**shorthand** [SHAURT•hand] *n*
Kurzschrift F

**shortly** [SHAURT•lee] *adv* im
kürzem

**shot** [shaht] *n* Schuß M

**shotgun** [SHAHT•gun] *n*
Schießgewehr N

**should** [shud] *aux* sollen

**shoulder** [SHOL•dur] *n*
Schulter M

**shout** *vi* rufen; *n* Ruf; Schrei M

**shove** [shuhv] *vt* schieben; *n*
Schubs; Stoß

**shovel** [SHUH•vl] *n* Schaufel F

**show** [sho] *n* (outward
appearance) Schau F;
(exhibit) Austelung; (theat)
Aufführung F; (TV) Show F;
*vt vi* zeigen; (be visible) zu
sehen sein; (prove) beweisen

**shower** [SHOU•ur] *n* Dusche F

**showy** [SHO•ee] *adj* prunkhaft

**shred** [shred] *n* Fetzen M; *vt*
zerfetzen

**shrew** [shroo] *n* Spitzmaus F

**shrewd** [shrood] *adj* schlau

**shrewish** [SHROO•ish] *adj*
boshaft

**shriek** [shreek] *n* Schrei M; *vt*
schriller

**shrike** [shruyk] *n* Würger M

**shrill** *adj* schrill

**shrimp** *n* Garnele F

**shrine** [shruyn] *n*
Heiligengrab N

**shrink** *vt* einschrumpfen

**shrinkage** [SHRINK•kij] *n*
Einschrumpfen N

**shrivel** [SHRI•vil] *vt*
schrumpeln

**shroud** *n* Leichentuch N

**shroud** *vt* hüllen

**Shrove Tuesday** [SHROV
TOOZ•dai] *n*
Fastnachtsdienstag M

**shrub 1** *n* Strauch M

**shrub 2** *n* Punsch M

**shrubbery** [SHRUB•bree] *n*
Gebüsch N

**shrunk** *adj* geschrumpft

**shrunken** [SHRUN•kin] *adj*
abgemagert

**shudder** [SHUH•dur] *vi*
schaudern

**shuffle** [SHUH•fl] *vi* schlurfen

**shun** *vt* vermeiden

**shunt** *vt* beiseite schieben

**shut** *vt* schließen; zumachen;
*adj* geschlossen

**shutter** [SHUH•dur] *n*
Rolladen M

**shuttle** [SHUH•tl] *v* pendeln

**shy** [shuy] *adj* scheu

**shyness** [SHUY•nis] *n* Scheu F

**sibyl** [SI•bil] *n* Sibylle F

**sick** [sik] *adj* krank; *vt* to be~\
brechen; spucken

**sicken** [SI•kin] *vi* erkranken

**sickening** [SIK•ning] *adj*
ekelhaft

**sickle** [SI•kil] *n* Sichel F

**sickly** [SIK•lee] *adj* kränklich

**sickness** [SIK•nis] *n*
Krankheit F

**side** [suyd] *n* Seite F; (edge)
Rand M; (opposing team)
Mannschaft; *adj* (on one ~)
Seiten-

**sideboard** [SUYD•baurd] *n*
Anrichtetisch M

**sidetrack** [SUYD•trak] *n*
Nebengleis N

**sidewalk** [SUYD•walk] *n*
Bürgersteig M

**sideways** [SUYD•waiz] *adj*
seitlich

**siding** [SUY•ding] *n*
Anschlußgleis N

**siege** [seej] *n* Belagerung F

**sieve** [siv] *n* Sieb N

**sift** *vt* durchsieben

**sigh** [suy] *vi* seufzen

**sight** [suyt] *n* Sicht F; (sth
seen) Anblick M (faculty)
Sehvermögen

**sightseeing** [SUYT•SEE•ing] *n*
Besichtigung F

**sign 1** [suyn] *n* Schild N

**sign 2** (street) *n* Zeichen N

**signal** [SIG•nuhl] *n* Signal N

**signalize** [SIG•nuh•LUYZ] *vi*
bemerkenswert machen

**signature** [SIG•nuh•CHUR] *n*
Unterschrift F

**signet** [SIG•nit] *n* Siegel N

**significance** [sig•NI•fi•kenz] *n*
Bedeutung F

**significant** [sig•NI•fi•kent] *adj*•
wichtig

**signify** [SIG•ni•FUY] *vt*
andeuten

**silence** [SUY•lenz] *n* Schweigen
N; *vt* zum Schweigen bringen

**silencer** [SUY•len•zur] *n*
Schalldämpfer M

**silently** [SUY•lent•lee] *adv*
schweigsam

**silhouette** [SIL•ho•WET] *n*
Schattenbild N

**silk** *n* Seide F

**silken** [SILK•in] *vt* seiden

**sill** *n* Fensterbrett N

**silly** [SIL•lee] *adj* blöd; albern

**silt** *n* Schlamm M

**silver** [SIL•vur] *n* Silber N

**silversmith** [SIL•vur•smith] *n*
Silberschmied M

**silverware** [SIL•vur•WAIR] *n*
Besteck N

**similar** [SI•mi•lur] *adj* ähnlich

**similarly** [SI•mi•lur•lee] ähnlich

**similitude** [si•MI•li•TOOD] *n*
Ähnlichkeit F

**simmer** [SIM•mur] *vt* brodeln

**simple** [SIM•pl] *adj* einfach

**simpleton** [SIM•pl•tin] *n*
Einfaltspinsel M

**simplicity** [sim•PLI•ci•tee] *n*
Einfalt F

**simplification**
[SIM•pli•fi•KAI•shn] *n*
Vereinfachung F

**simplify** [SIM•pli•FUY] *vt*
vereinfachen

**simulate** [SIM•yoo•LAIT] *vt*
vortäuschen

**simultaneous**
[SUY•muhl•TAI•nee•us] *adj*
gleichzeitig

**sin** *n* Sünde F

**since** [sinz] *adv* seitdem

**sincere** [sin•SEER] *adj* ehrlich

**sincerity** [sin•SAIR•i•tee] *n*
Ehrlichkeit F

**sinew** [SI•noo] *n* Flechse F

**sing** [sing] *vi* singen

**singe** [sinj] *vt* ansengen

**single** [SIN•gl] *adj* einzig

**single-handed**
[SIN•gl•HAN•did] *adj*
einhändig

**singular** [SIN•gyu•lur] einzeln

**sinister** [SI•ni•stur] *adj* böse

**sink 1** *vi* sinken; *n* Spülstein M

**sink 2** *n* Ausguß M

**sinker** [SINK•kur] *n* Abteufer M

**sinless** [SIN•les] *adj* sündenlos

**sinner** [SIN•nur] *n* Sünder M

**sinus** [SUY•nis] *n* Sinus M

**sinusitis** [SUY•nyu•SUY•tis] *n*
Nebenhöhlenentzündung F

**sip** *vt* nippen an

**siphon** [SUY•fuhn] *n*
Saugheber M

**sir** [sur] Herr

**sire** [suyr] *n* Eure Majestät F

**siren** [SUY•rin] *n* Sirene F

**sirloin** [SUR•loin] *n*
Lendenstück N

**sister** [SIS•tur] *n* Schwester F

**sister-in-law** [SIS•tur•in•LAU]
*n* Schwägerin F

**sit** *vi* sitzen; *vt* setzen

**site** [suyt] *n* Stelle F

**sitter** [SI•tur] *n* Sitzender M

**sitting** [SIT•ting] *n* Sitzen N

**sitting-room** *n* Wohnzimmer N

**situate** [SI•choo•WAIT] *vt*
aufstellen

**situation** [SI•choo•WAI•shn] *n*
Lage F

**six** [siks] *num* sechs

**sixteen** [siks•TEEN] *num*
sechszehn

**sixteenth** [siks•TEENTH] *num*
sechszehnte

**sixth** [sikths] *num* sechste

**sixtieth** [SIKS•tee•ith] *adj*
sechzigst

**sixty** [SIKS•tee] *num* sechzig

**size** [suyz] *n* Größe F

**sizzle** [SI•zul] *vi* zischen

**skate** [skait] *n* Schlittschuh
Rollschuh M

**skate (ice)** [skait] *vi*
Schlittschuh laufen

**skate (roller)** Rollschuh laufen

**skein** [skain] *n* Strang M

**skeleton** [SKEL•i•tin] *n*
Skelett N

**skeptic** [SKEP•tik] *adj*
skeptisch

**sketch** n Skizze F; n Abriß M; vt skizzieren
**skewer** [SKYOO•ur] n Fleischspieß M
**ski** [skee] n Schi M
**skid** vi rutschen; n Schleudern N
**skill** [skil] n Geschicklichkeit F
**skilled** [skild] adj geschickt
**skillet** [SKI•lit] n Bratpfanne F
**skillful** [SKIL•ful] adj geschickt
**skim** vt abschöpfen
**skin** n Haut F; vi (animal) häuten; (fruit) schälen
**skin-deep** adj oberflächlich
**skinflint** n Knicker M
**skinny** [SKI•nee] adj dünn
**skip 1** n Sprung M; vi hüpfen
**skip 2** (omit) schwänzen
**skipper** [SKIP•pur] n Schiffer M
**skirt** [skurt] n Rock M
**skit** n Satire F
**skittish** adj lebhaft
**skulk** vi lauern
**skull** n Schädel M
**skunk** n Stinktier N
**sky** [skuy] n Himmel M
**skylight** [SKUY•luyt] n Oberlicht N
**skyscraper** [SKUY•SKRAI•pur] n Wolkenkratzer M
**slab** n Tafel F; Platte F
**slack** [slak] adj schlaff; locker; (negligent) nachlässig
**slacken** [SLAK•kin] vt lockern vi sich lockern
**slacker** [SLAK•kur] n Faulpelz M
**slag** vi verschlacken
**slam** vt zuschlagen; zucknallen; n Zuschlagen N no pl

**slander** [SLAN•dur] n Verleumdung F; vt verleumden
**slang** [slang] n Umgangssprache F
**slant** n Schräge F
**slap** n Klaps M
**slash** vt zerfetzen
**slat** n Stab M
**slate** [slait] n Schiefer M
**slattern** [SLA•turn] n Schlampe F
**slaughter** [SLAU•tur] vt schlachten
**slave** [slaiv] n Sklave M; Sklavin F; vi sich abplagen; schuften
**slavish** [SLAI•vish] adj sklavisch
**slaw** [slau] n Krautsalat M
**slay** [slai] vi töten
**sledding** [SLED•ding] n Schlittenfahren N
**sledge** [slej] n Schmiedehammer M
**sleek** adj glatt
**sleep** n Schlaf; vi schlafen; go to ~\ einschlaffen
**sleeper** [SLEE•pur] n Schläfer M
**sleepiness** [SLEE•pee•nis] n Schläfrigkeit F
**sleeping** [SLEE•ping] adj schlafend
**sleepless** [SLEEP•les] adj schlaflos
**sleepy** [SLEE•pee] adj schläfrig
**sleet** n Schneeregen M
**sleeve** [sleev] n Ärmel M
**sleigh** [slai] n schlitten M
**sleight** [sluyt] n Kunstgriff M

**sleuth** [slooth] *n* Spürhund M

**slice** [sluys] *n* Scheibe F; *vt* schneiden

**slick** [slik] *adj* glatt; clever

**slicker** [SLI•kur] *n* Regenmantel M

**slide** [sluyd] *n* Rutschbahn F; (fall) Abfall M; (move smoothly) sich schieben lassen; *vi* gleiten

**slight** [sluyt] *adj* leicht; *n* (affront) Affront M; *vt* kränken

**slightly** [SLUYT•lee] *adj* etwas

**slim** *adj* schlank

**slime** [sluym] *n* Schleim M

**sling** [sling] *n* Schleuder F

**slink** *vi* schleichen

**slip** *n* Rutschen N; *vt* schieben; *vi* ausrutschen

**slipper** [SLIP•pur] *n* Hausschuh M

**slippery 1** [SLIP•pree] *adj* glitschig

**slippery 2** [slip•pree] *adj* glatt

**slit** *vt* aufschneiden

**slither** [SLI•thur] *vi* schlittern

**sliver** [SLI•vur] *n* Splitter M

**slobber** [SLAH•bur] *vi* sabbern

**slogan** [SLO•gen] *n* Schlagwort N

**sloop** *n* Schaluppe F

**slop** [slahp] *n* Klamotten

**slope** [slop] *n* Abhang M

**slow** [slo] *adj* langsam

**small** [smahl] *adj* klein

**smart** [smahrt] *adj* schick; *vi* brennen

**smash** [smash] *vt* zerschlagen; *vi* zerbrechn

**smell** *n* Grech M; *vt vi* riechen

**smile** *n* Lächeln N; *vi* lächeln

**smoke** [smok] *n* Rauch M; *vt* rauchen

**smooth** *adj* glatt; glätten

**smoothly** [SMOOTH•lee] *adv* weich

**smuggle** [SMUG•l] *vt vi* schmuggeln

**snack** [snak] *n* Kleinigkeit

**snag** *n* Haken M; Schweierigkeit F

**snap** *n* (sound) Schnappen

**snapshot** [SNAP•shaht] *n* Schnappschuß

**sneak** [sneek] *n* Schleicher M

**sneaky** [SNEEK•ee] *adj* raffiniert

**sneer** *n* spöttisches Lächeln

**sneeze** [sneez] *n* Nieser M; *vi* niesen

**snort** *vt* schnauben

**snout** *n* Schnauze F

**snow** [sno] *n* Schnee M

**snowball** [SNO•bahl] *n* Schneeball M

**snowdrift** *n* Schneewehe F

**snowfall** [SNO•fahl] *n* Schneefall M

**snowflake** [SNO•flaik] *n* Schneeflocken N

**snowplow** [SNO•plou] *n* Schneepflug M

**snub** [snuhb] *vi* verächtlich behandeln

**snuff** [snuhf] *n* Schnuppe F

**snuffle** [SNUHF•fl] *vi* schnuppern

**snug** [snuhg] *adj* behaglich

**so** *adv* so ~ much\ . . . so viel; (emphatic) sehr; (likewise) auch; *conj* (expressing purpose) damit; (therefore, questions, exclmations) also; ~ what\ und?

**soak** [sok] *vi* sich vollsaugen

**soap** [sop] *n* Seife F

**soar** [zor] *vi* aufsteigen

**sob** *vi* weinen

**sober** [SO•bur] *adj* nüchtern

**soberly** [SO•bur•lee] *adv* nüchternd

**sobriety** [so•BRUY•i•tee] *n* Nüchternheit F

**sociable** [SO•shuh•bl] *adj* gesellig

**social** [SO•shuhl] gesellig

**socialism** [SO•shuh•LIZM] *n* Sozialismus M

**socialist** [SO•shuh•list] *n* Sozialist M

**society** [so•SUY•i•tee] *n* Gesellschaft F

**sociology** [SO•shee•AH•lo•gee] *n* Soziologie F

**sock** [sahk] *n* Socke F

**socket** [SAH•kit] *n* Steckdose F

**sod** [sahd] *n* Grasnarbe F

**soda** [SO•duh] *n* Soda F

**sodium** [SO•dee•um] *n* Natrium N

**sofa** [SO•fuh] *n* Sofa N

**soft** *adj* weich

**soften** [SOF•fin] *vi* weich machen

**softness** [SOFT•nis] *n* Weichheit F

**soil** *n* Erdboden M

**sojourn** [SO•jurn] *n* Aufenthaltsort M

**solace** [SAH•les] *n* Trost M

**solar** [SO•lur] *adj* sonnen

**solder** [SAH•dur] *n* Lot N

**soldier** [SOL•jur] *n* Soldat M

**sole** [sol] *n* Sohle F

**solecism** [SAH•li•SI•zm] *n* Schnitzer M

**solemn** [SAH•lim] *adj* feierlich

**solemnity** [so•LEM•ni•tee] *n* Feierlichkeit F

**solemnize** [SAH•lem•NUYZ] *vi* feierlich begehn

**solicit** [so•LI•sit] *vt* bitten

**solicitation** [so•LI•ci•TAI•shn] *n* Bewerbung F

**solicitor; lawyer** [so•LI•ci•tur] *n* Anwalt M

**solicitous** [so•LI•si•tus] *adj* bekümmert

**solid** [SAH•lid] *adj* fest

**solidarity** [SAH•li•DAIR•i•tee] *n* Solidarität F

**solidify** [so•LI•di•FUY] *vi* fest werden lassen

**solidity** [so•LI•di•tee] *n* Festigkeit F

**soliloquy** [so•LI•lo•kwee] *n* Monolog M

**solitary** [SAH•li•TAI•ree] *adj* einsam

**solitude** [SAH•li•TOOD] *n* Einsamkeit F

**solo** [SO•lo] *adj* allein M

**solstice** [SOL•stis] *n* Sonnenwende F

**solution** [so•LOO•shn] *n* Lösung F

**solve** [solv] *vt* lösen

**solvent** [SOL•vint] *n* Lösungsmittel N

**somber** [SAHM•bur] *adj* düster

**some** [suhm] *adv* einige; (with singular nouns) etwas; (vauge) irgendein; (in

exclamations) vielleicht ein;
*adv* ungefähr; etwa; zirka

**somebody** [SUHM•bo•dee]
jemand

**somehow** [SUHM•how] *adv*
irgendwie

**someone** [SUHM•wuhn]
irgendjemand

**somersault** [SUHM•ur•SALT]
*n* Salto M

**something** [SUHM•thing] *pron*
etwas

**sometime** [SUHM•tuym]
irgendwann

**sometimes** [SUHM•tuyms]
manchmal

**somewhat** [SUHM•wuht] *adv*
etwa

**somewhere** [SUHM•wair]
irgendwo

**somnolent** [SAHM•nuh•lint]
*adj* schläfrig

**son** [suhn] *n* Sohn M

**son-in-law** [SUHN•in•LAU] *n*
Schwiegersohn M

**sonata** [so•NAH•tuh] *n*
Sonate F

**song** *n* Lied N

**song-bird** *n* Singvogel M

**sonnet** [SAH•nit] *n* Sonett N

**sonorous** [sah•NO•ruhs] *adj*
resonant

**soon** *adv* bald

**soot** [sut] *n* Ruß M

**soothe** [sooth] *vt* besänftigen

**soothsayer** [SOOTH•SAI•ur] *n*
Wahrsager M

**sooty** [SOOT•tee] *adj* rußig

**sop** *vt* eintunken

**sophisticated**
[so•FI•sti•KAI•tid] *adj*
erfahren

**sophistication**
[so•FI•sti•KAI•shn] *n*
Kultiviertheit F

**sophomore** [SAUF•maur] *n*
Student in M

**soporific** [SO•po•RI•fik] *adj*
einschläfernd

**soprano** [so•PRA•no] *n*
Sopran M

**sorcerer** [SAUR•sir•rur] *n*
Zauberer M

**sordid** [SAUR•did] *adj* schäbig

**sore** [sor] *adj* wund; weh; *n*
wunde Stelle

**sorrow** [SAH•ro] *n* Kummer M

**sorrowful** [SAH•ro•ful] *adj*
bekümmert

**sorry** [SAH•ree] *adj* betrübt

**sort** *n* (kind) Art F; *vt* sortieren;
*adv* ~ of\ irgendwie

**soul** [sol] *n* Seele F

**sound 1** *adj* (healthy) gesund;
(valid) solide; *adv* (~ asleep)
fest schlafen

**sound 2** *n* Laut M; (noise)
Geräusch N; *vi* erklingen;
ertönen

**soundless** [SOUND•les] *adj*
lautlos

**soundproof** *adj* schalldämpfig

**soup** [soop] *n* Suppe F

**sour** [SOU•ur] *adj* sauer

**source** [sorz] *n* Quelle F

**south** *adj* südlich

**South America** [SOUTH
u•ME•ri•ku] *n* Süd Amerika

**southeast** [south•EEST] *adj*
südöstlich

**southerner** [SUHTH•thur•nur]
*n* Südstaatler M

**southward** [SOUTH•wurd] *adv*
  südwärts

**southwest** *adv* südwestlich

**souvenir** [SOO•ven•NEER] *n*
  Andenken N

**sovereign** [SAHV•rin] *n*
  Souverän M

**Soviet** [SO•vee•it] Sovjet

**sow** [so] *n* Sau F

**space** [spais] *n* Raum M;
  (room) Platz; Raum M

**spacious** [SPAI•shus] *adj*
  räumig

**spade** [spaid] *n* Spaten M

**span** *n* Spanne F

**spangle** [SPANG•gl] *n*
  Flitter M

**Spaniard** [SPAN•yurd] *n*
  Spanier M; -in F

**spaniel** [SPAN•yuhl] *n*
  Wachtelhund M

**Spanish** [SPA•nish] *n* Spanisch

**spank** *vt* verhauen

**spanking** [SPANK•king] *n*
  Haue F

**spar** [spahr] *vi* sparren

**spare** [spair] *vt* verschonen; *n*
  Ersatz M

**spark** [spahrk] *n* Funken M

**spark plug** *n* Zünderkerze F

**sparkle** [SPAHR•kl] *vi* funkeln

**sparkling** [SPAHRK•kling] *adj*
  funkelnd

**sparrow** [SPAIR•ro] *n*
  Sperling M

**sparse** [spahrz] *adj* spärlich

**spasm** [SPA•zim] *n* Krampf M

**spatter** [SPA•tur] *vt* bespritzen

**spawn** *n* Laich M

**speak** [speek] *vi* sprechen

**speaker** [SPEE•kur] *n*
  Sprecher M

**spear** [speer] *n* Speer M

**special** [SPE•shul] *adj*
  besonders

**specialist** [SPE•shuh•list] *n*
  Fachmann M

**specialize** [SPE•shuh•LUYZ] *vi*
  sich spezialisieren

**species** [SPEE•sheez] *n* Art F

**specific** [spuh•SI•fik] *adj*
  spezifisch

**specify** [SPE•si•FUY] *vt*
  bestimmen

**specimen** [SPE•si•min] *n*
  Exemplar N

**specious** [SPEE•shus] *adj*
  bestechend

**speckle** [SPE•kl] *vt* flecken

**spectacle** [SPEK•ti•kl] *n*
  Schau F

**spectacular**
  [spek•TAK•kyu•lur] *adj*
  eindrucksvoll

**spectator** [SPEK•TAI•tur] *n*
  Zuschauer M

**specter** [SPEK•tur] *n*
  Gespenst N

**spectrum** [SPEK•trum] *n*
  Spektrum N

**speculate** [SPEK•kyu•LAIT] *vi*
  nachsinnen

**speculation**
  [SPEK•kyu•LAI•shn] *n*
  Betrachtung F

**speculative** [SPEK•kyu•luh•tiv]
  *adj* spekulativ

**speculator** [SPEK•kyu•LAI•tur]
  *n* Denker M

**speech** *n* Rede F

**speed** *n* Geschwindigkeit F

**speed limit** [SPEED LI•mit] *n* Geschwindigkeitsgrenze F

**speedily** [SPEED•di•lee] *adv* schnell

**speedway** [SPEED•wai] *n* Rennbahn F

**speedy** [SPEED•dee] *adv* schnell

**spell 1** *vi* buchstabieren; *vt* schreiben

**spell 2** *n* Zauber M

**spell 3** *n* (period) Weile F

**spellbound** *adj* fasziniert

**spelling** [SPEL•ling] *n* Rechtschreibung F

**spend** *vt* ausgeben

**spendthrift** *n* Verschwender M

**spew** [spyoo] *vi* sich erbrechen

**sphere** [sfeer] *n* Sphäre F

**spherical** [SFEER•i•kl] *adj* kugelförmig

**spice** [spuys] *n* Gewürz N

**spider** [SPUY•dur] *n* Spinne F

**spigot** [SPI•git] *n* Zapfen M

**spike** [spuyk] *n* Stift M

**spill** [spil] *vt* überlaufen lassen

**spin** *vt* spinnen; *n* Drehung F

**spinach** [SPI•nich] *n* Spinat

**spinal** [SPUY•nl] rückgrat

**spinal column** [SPUY•nl KAH•lim] *n* Wirbelsäule F

**spinal cord** [SPUY•nl KAURD] *n* Rückenmark N

**spinner** [SPI•nur] *n* Spinner M

**spinning-wheel** [SPIN•ning WEEL] *n* Spinnrad N

**spinster** [SPIN•stur] *n* älteres Fräulein N

**spiral** [SPUY•rl] *adj* gewunden

**spire** [spuyr] *n* Spirale F

**spirit** [SPI•rit] *n* Geist M

**spirited** [SPI•ri•tid] *adj* lebendig

**spiritual** [SPI•ri•chul] *adj* geistig

**spiritualism** [SPI•ri•chuh•LI•zm] *n* Geisterglaube M

**spirituality** [SPI•ri•choo•AL•i•tee] *n* Geistigkeit F

**spit** *vi* spucken

**spite** [spuyt] *n* Boshaftigkeit F

**splash** *vt* bespritzen

**spleen** *n* Milz F

**splendid** [SPLEN•did] *adj* glänzend

**splendor** [SPLEN•dor] *n* Pracht F

**splice** [spluys] *vt* splissen

**splint** *n* Splitter M

**splinter** [SPLIN•tur] Splitter M

**split** *vt* zerspalten

**spoil** *vt* verderben

**spoke** [spok] *n* Speiche F

**spokesperson** [SPOKS•PUR•sin] *n* Wortführer M

**sponge** [spuhnj] *n* Schwamm M

**sponge cake** [SPUHNJ caik] *n* Kuchen M

**sponger** [SPUHN•jur] *n* Schwammtaucher M

**sponsor** [SPAHN•sur] *n* Bürge M

**spontaneity** [SPAHN•tuh•NAI•i•tee] *n* Freiwilligkeit

**spontaneous** [spahn•TAI•nee•us] *adj* spontan

**spook** *vi* spuken

**spool** *n* Spule F

**spoon** *n* Löffel M
**spoonful Löffelvoll**
**sport** *n* Sport M
**sportsman** *n* Sportler M
**spot** |spaht| *n* Fleck; Tupfen;
Punkt M (place) Stelle F; *vt*
(notice) entdecken; sehen
**spotted** [SPAH•tid] *adj* befleckt
**spouse** [spous] *n* Gatte in M
**spout** *vt* ausspeien
**sprain** *n* Verstauchung F
**sprawl** *adj* ausgestreckt
**spray** |sprai| *n* Sprühregen; *vt*
zerstäuben; *vi* sprühhen;
spritzen
**sprayer** |SPRAI•ur| *n* Gischt F
**spread** |spred| *n* ( fo wings)
Spanweite F; (range)
Verteilung F; *vt* ausbreiten;
(spread news) verbreiten;
(extend) sich erstrecken
**spreadsheet** [SPRED•sheet] *n*
Arbeitsblatt N
**spree** *n* Jux M
**sprightly** |SPRUYT•lee| *adv*
munter
**spring** *n* Frühling M; (leap)
Sprung M; *vi* (leap) springen
**sprinkle** [SPRINK•kl] *vt*
sprenkeln
**sprint** *vi* rennen
**sprout** *n* Sproß M
**spruce** |sproos| *n* Fichte F
**spun pp gesponnen**
**spur** *n* Sporn M
**spurn** *vt* verschmähen
**spurt** *n* Ruck M
**spy** |spuy| *n* Spion M; *vi*
spionieren
**squabble** |SKWAH•bl| *vi*
kabbeln; *n* Zank M

**squadron** |SKWAH•druhn| *n*
Battaillon N
**squalid** [SKWAH•lid] *adj*
schmutzig
**squall** [skwahl] *n* Windstoß M
**squander** |SKWAHN•dur| *vt*
verschwenden
**square** |skwair| *n* Quadrat N;
*adj* quadratisch; *adv*
rechtwinklig; *vt* (make ~)
quadratisch machen
**squash** |skwahsh| *vt*
zerquetschen
**squat** |skwaht| *vi* hocken
**squawk** |skwahk| *vi* kreischen
**squeak** |skweek| *vi* piepsen
**squeal** |skweel| *vi* winseln
**squeamish** |SKWEE•mish| *adj*
zimperlich
**squeeze** |skweeze| *vt*
auspressen
**squelch** |skwelch| *vt* zermalmen
**squint** |skwint| *vi* schielen
**squire** |skwuyr| *n* Gutsherr M
**squirm** |skwirm| *vi* sich
krümmen
**squirrel** |skwirl| *n*
Eichhörnchen N
**squirt** |skwirt| *vi* spritzen
**stab** *vt* erstechen
**stability** |stuh•BI•li•tee| *n*
Stabilität F
**stabilize** |STAI•bi•LUYZ| *vt*
stabilisieren
**stable 1** [STAI•bl] *adj* stabil
**stable 2** *n* Stall M
**stack** |stak| *n* Schober M
**stadium** |STAI•dee•um| *n*
Stadion N
**staff** |staf| *n* Personal N;
Stock M

**stag** *n* Rothirsch M

**stage** [staij] *n* Bühne F

**stage door** [STAIJ DOR] *n*
Bühneneingang M

**stage fright** [STAIJ FRUYT] *n*
Lampenfieber N

**stage-struck** [STAIJ•struk] *adj*
bühnenbegeistert

**stagger** [STAG•gur] *vi* taumeln

**stagnant** [STAG•nint] *adj*
stockend

**staid** *adj* gesetzt

**stain** *n* Fleck M

**stainless** [STAIN•lis] *adj*
fleckenlos

**stair** *n* Treppe; Stiege F

**stake** [staik] *n* Pfosten M;
(financial interest) Anteil M;
*vt* ampflocken; ~ out\
abstecken

**stale** [stail] *adj* alt

**stalk 1** [stauk] *vi* pirschen

**stalk 2** *n* Stengel M

**stall** *n* Stand M

**stallion** [STAL•yun] *n* Hengst M

**stalwart** [STAL•wurt] *adj*
stramm

**stamina** [STA•mi•nuh] *n*
Zähigkeit F

**stammer** [STAM•mur] *vi*
stottern

**stamp** *n* Stempel M; *vt*
aufstampen; *vi* stampfen;
postage ~\ Briefmarke

**stampede** [stam•PEED] in
wilde Flucht jagen

**stanch** *vt* stillen

**stand** *n* Stillstand M; *vi* stehen;
*vt* stellen; ~ firm\ festblieben

**stand up** *vi* aufstehen

**standard** [STAN•dird] *n*
Standard M

**standardization**
[STAN•dir•di•ZAI•shn] *n*
Normung F

**standardize** [STAN•dir•DUYZ]
*vt* standardisieren

**standing** [STAN•ding] *n*
Stehen N

**stanza** [STAN•zuh] *n* Strophe F

**staple 1** [STAI•pl] *adj* haupt

**staple 2** *vt* klammern

**star** [stahr] *n* Sterne F

**starboard** [STAHR•baurd] *n*
Steuerbord N

**starch** *n* Wäschestärke F

**starchy** [STAHR•chee] *adj*
streif

**stark** [stahrk] *adj* steif

**start** [stahrt] *vi* anfangen
beginnen

**starting** [STAHR•ting] *n*
Anfang M

**starting point** [STAHR•ting
POINT] *n* Startpunkt M

**startle** [STAHR•tl] *vi*
erschrecken

**starvation** [stahr•VAI•shn] *n*
Hungern N

**starve** [stahrv] *vi* verhungern

**state 1** [stait] *n* Staat M

**state 2** (condition) *n*
Zustand M

**state 3** *vt* darlegen; vortragen

**stately** [STAIT•lee] *adj* stattlich

**statement** [STAIT•mint] *n*
Aussage F

**stateroom** [STAIT•room] *n*
Staatszimmer N

**statesman** [STAITZ•min] *n*
Staatsmann M

**static** [STA•tik] *adj* statisch
**station** [STAI•shin] *n*
Haltestelle F
**stationary** [STAI•shi•NAI•ree]
*adj* ortsfest
**stationery**
[STAI•shun•NAI•ree] *npl*
Schreibwaren
**statistics** [stuh•TI•stiks] *n*
Statistik F
**statue** [STA•choo] *n* Statue F
**status** [STA•tus] *n* Status M
**statute** [STA•choot] *n* Gesetz N
**staunch** *adj* zuverlässig
**stay** [stai] *vi* (remain) bleiben; *n*
Auftenhalt M; ~ the course\
durchalten
**stead** [sted] *n* Stelle F
**steadfast** [STED•fast] *adj* fest
**steadily** [STED•i•lee] *adj* stabil
**steadiness** [STE•dee•nes] *n*
Festigkeit F
**steady** [STE•dee] *adj* fest
**steak** [staik] *n* Kotelett N
**steal** [steel] *vt* stehlen
**stealth** [stelth] *n* Heimlichkeit F
**steam** [steem] *n* Dampf M
**steam engine** [STEEM EN•jin]
*n* Dampfer M
**steamboat** [STEEM•bot] *n*
Dampfschiff N
**steamer** [STEE•mur] *n*
Dampfer M
**steamship** [STEEM•ship]
Dampfschiff N
**steed** *n* Roß N
**steel** *n* Stahl M
**steep** *adj* steif
**steep** *vt* eintauchen
**steeple** [STEE•pl] *n*
Kirchturm M

**steer** *vt* steuern
**steer** *n* Schlachtvieh N
**stem** *n* Stamm M; Stiel M
**stench** *n* Gestank M
**stencil** [STEN•sul] *n*
Schablone F
**stenographer**
[ste•NAH•gruh•fur] *n*
Stenographin F
**step** *n* Stufe F; Schritt M; *vi*
gehen
**stepchild** [STEP•chuyld] *n*
Stiefkind N
**stepdaughter** [STEP•DAU•tur]
*n* Stieftochter F
**stepfather** [STEP•FA•thur] *n*
Stiefvater M
**stepladder** [STEP•LA•dur] *n*
Trittleiter F
**stepmother** [STEP•MUH•thur]
*n* Stiefmutter F
**stepson** [STEP•suhn] *n*
Stiefsohn M
**stereo** [STAIR•ree•O] *n*
Stereo N
**stereotype**
[STAIR•ree•o•TUYP] *n*
Stereotypie F
**sterile** [STAIR•ruyl] *adj*
keimfrei
**sterility** [stair•RI•li•tee] *n*
Sterilität F
**sterilize** [STAIR•ri•LUYZ] *vt*
sterilisieren
**sterling** [STUR•ling] *n*
Sterling M
**stern** [sturn] *adj* streng
**stethoscope**
[STETH•uh•SKOP] *n*
Stethoskop N

**stevedore** [STEE•vuh•dor] *n*
Stauer M

**stew** [stoo] *vt* langsam kochen;
*n* Eintopf M

**steward** [STOO•wurd] *n*
Verwalter M

**stewardess** [STOO•wur•des] *n*
Stewardeß F

**stick 1** [stik] *n* Stock M

**stick 2** *vt* kleben; tun

**stiff** *adj* steif

**stiffen** [STIF•fin] *vt* steifen

**stiffness** [STIF•nes] *n*
Steifheit F

**stifle** [STUY•fl] *vt* ersticken

**stigma** [STIG•muh] *n* Stigma N

**still 1** [stil] *adv* noch

**still 2** *adj* still

**stillness** [STIL•nis] *n* Stille F

**stilt** *n* Pfeiler M

**stimulant** [STIM•yoo•lint] *n*
Anregungsmittel N

**stimulate** [STIM•yoo•LAIT] *vt*
anregen

**stimulation**
[STIM•yoo•LAI•shn] *n*
Antrieb M

**stimulus** [STIM•yoo•lus] *n*
Reiz M

**sting** *vt* stechen; *n* Stachel M

**stinginess** [STIN•jee•nes] *n*
Geiz M

**stingy** [STIN•jee] *adj* geizig

**stink** *vi* stinken

**stint** *n* Beschränkung F

**stipend** [STUY•pend] *n*
Gehalt N

**stipulate** [STIP•yoo•LAIT] *vt*
festsetzen

**stir** [stur] *vt* rühren; *vi* sich
regen; ~ up\ erregen

**stirring** [STUR•ring] *n*
Rühren N

**stirrup** [STUR•rip] *n*
Steigbügel M

**stitch** *n* Stich M

**stock** [stok] *n* Gut N; (supply)
Vorrat M; *vt* führen

**Stock Exchange** [STAHK
ex•CHAINJ] *n* Börse F

**stock market** [STAHK
MAHR•kit] *n* Börsenkurse F

**stockade** [stah•KAID] *n*
Palisade F

**stockbroker**
[STAHK•BRO•kur] *n*
Broker M

**stockholder**
[STAHK•HOL•dur] *n*
Aktionär M

**stocking** [STAHK•king] *n*
Strümpfe F

**stockroom** [STAHK•room] *n*
Lagerraum M

**stocky** [STAHK•kee] *adj*
stämmig

**stockyards** [stahk•yardz] *n*
Viehhof M

**stoic** [STO•ik] *n* Stoiker M

**stoicism** [STO•i•SI•zm] *n*
Stoizismus M

**stoke** [stok] *vt* schüren

**stole** [stol] *n* Stola F

**stolid** [STAH•lid] *adj* stur

**stomach** [STUH•mik] *n* Bauch;
Magen M

**stomachache** [STUH•mik•AIK]
*n* Magenschmerz M

**stone** [ston] *n* Stein M

**stonework** [STON•wurk] *n*
Steinwerk N

**stony** [STO•nee] *adj* steinern

stool *n* Hocker M

stool pigeon [STOOL PI•jin] *n*
Lockvogel M

stoop *n* Vorhalle F

stop [stahp] *n* Halt m;*vt*
aufhören; halten; anhalten; (~
from continuing) ein Ende
machen; (cease) aufhören;
(suspend) stoppen (prevent)
verhindern

stoppage [STAH•pij] *n*
Stillstand M

stopper [STAH•pur] *n*
Stöpsel M

stopwatch [STAHP•wahtch] *n*
Stopuhr F

storage [STOR•aij] *n*
Lagerung F

store [stor] *n* Lager N; (stock)
Vorrat M; *vt* lagern

storekeeper [STOR•KEE•pur]
*n* Lagerverwalter M

stork *n* Storch M

storm [staurm] *n* Sturm M

stormy [STAUR•mee] *adj*
stürmisch

story 1 [STAU•ree] *n*
Geschichte F

story 2 (of house) *n* Stock M

stout *adj* dick

stove [stov] *n* Ofen M; Herd M

stow [sto] *vt* verstauen

straddle [STRAD•dl] die Beine
spreizen

straggle [STRAG•gl] *vt*
umherstreifen

straight [strait] *adj* gerade

straighten [STRAI•tin] v
gerade machen

straightforward
[STRAIT•FOR•wurd] *adj*
direkt

straightway [STRAIT•wai] *adv*
sofort

strain *n* Anstrengung F

strainer [STRAI•nur] *n* Filter M

strait *n* Meerenge F

strand 1 *n* Litze F

strand 2 *vi* scheitern lassen

strange [strainj] *adj*
merkwürdig

strangeness [STRAINJ•nes] *n*
Fremdheit F

stranger [STRAIN•jur] *n*
Fremder M

strangle [STRAN•gl] *vt*
erwürgen

strangulate untie
[STRAN•gyu•LAIT] *vt*
abbinden

strangulation
[STRAN•gyu•LAI•shn] *n*
Erdrosselung F

strap *n* Riemen M

strategic [struh•TEE•jik] *adj*
strategisch

strategy [STRA•ti•jee] *n*
Strategie F

stratosphere
[STRA•to•SFEER] *n*
Stratosphäre F

straw [strau] *n* (drinking)
Strohhalm M; (stalk) Stroh N

strawberry [STRAU•bair•ree] *n*
Erdbeere F

stray [strai] *vi* sich verlaufen

streak [streek] *n* Strich M

stream [streem] *n* Bach M

streamer [STREE•mur] *n*
Fahne F

streamlined
[STREEM•LUYND] *adj*
windschnittig

**street** *n* Straße F
**streetcar** [STREET•kahr] *n* Straßenbahn F
**strength** *n* Kraft F
**strengthen** [STRENGTH•en] *vi* stärken
**strenuous** [STREN•yoo•us] *adj* emsig
**stress** [stres] *n* Druck M; (accent) Betonung F; *vt* betonen
**stretch** [strech] *vt* ausstrecken
**stretcher** [STRECH•chur] *n* Krankentrage F
**strew** [stroo] *vt* ausstreuen
**strict** [strikt] *adj* streng
**stride** [struyd] *vi* schreiten
**strident** [STRUY•dint] *adj* durchdringend
**strife** [struyf] *n* Kampf M
**strike** [struyk] *n* Streik M; *vt* schlagen; (clock) anschlagen; *vi* (hit) treffen; (workers) streiken
**striker** [STRUY•kur] *n* Streiker M
**striking** [STRUY•king] *adj* bemerkenswert
**string** *n* Schnur F
**strip 1** *n* Streifen M
**strip 2** (clothes) *vt* ausziehen
**stripe** [struyp] *n* Streifen M
**strive** [struyv] *vi* sich bemühen
**stroke 1** [strok] *n* Hieb M
**stroke 2** (medical) *n* Anfall M
**stroll** [stol] *vi* schlendern
**strong** [straung] *adj* stark
**stronghold** [STRAUNG•hold] *n* Hochburg F
**strongly** [STRAUNG•lee] *adj* kräftig

**structural** [STRUK•chur•ul] *adj* strukturell
**structure** [STRUK•chur] *n* Struktur F; *vt* strukturieren
**struggle** [STRUH•gl] *vi* kämpfen
**strut** [struht] *n* Strebe F
**stub** [stuhb] *n* Stumpf M
**stubble** [STUHB•bl] *n* Stoppel F
**stubborn** [STUHB•born] *adj* eigensinnig
**stubbornness** [STUHB•born•nes] *n* Starrsinn M
**stucco** [STUH•ko] *n* Stuck M
**stuck-up** [STUH•KUHP] *adj* hochnäsig
**stud** [stuhd] *n* (wood etc) Knopf M; (animal)Zucht F
**student** [STOO•dent] *n* Student in M
**studio** [STOO•dee•o] *n* Atelier N
**study** [STUH•dee] *vi* studieren; *n* Studium; Lernen N
**stuff** [stuhf] *n* Material; Zeug N; *vt* vollstopfen
**stuffing** [STUHF•fing] *n* Füllung F
**stuffy** [STUH•fee] *adj* dumpf; (narrow-minded) spießig
**stumble** [STUHMB•bl] *vi* stolpern
**stump** [stuhmp] *n* Stummel M;
**stun** [stuhn] *vt* betäuben; benommen machen
**stunt 1** [stuhnt] *n* Schaunummer F
**stunt 2** *vt* verkrüppeln

**stupefy** [STOO•pi•FUY] *vt*
verdummen

**stupendous** [stoo•PEN•dus] *adj*
erstaunlich

**stupid** [STOO•pid] *adj* dumm

**stupidity** [stoo•PI•di•tee] *n*
Dummheit F

**stupor** [STOO•pur] *n*
Stumpfheit F

**sturdy** [STUR•dee] *adj* stabil

**sturgeon** [STUR•jun] *n* Stör M

**stutter** [STUH•tur] *vi* stottern

**sty 1** [stuy] *n* Schweinestall M

**sty 2** *n* (med) Gerstenkorn N

**style** [stuyl] *n* Stil M; (of
painting) Mastil M; (of
fashion) Mode F

**stylish** [STUY•lish] *adj* modisch

**subcommittee**
[SUB•ko•MI•tee] *n*
Unterausschuß M

**subconscious** [sub•KON•shus]
*adj* unterbewußt

**subdivision** [SUB•di•VI•shn] *n*
Unterteilung F

**subdue** [sub•DOO] *vt*
unterjochen

**subject** [SUB•jekt] *n* Gegestand
M (pol) Straatsbürger; *vt*
[sub•JEKT] unterwerfen

**subjection** [sub•JEK•shn] *n*
Unterwerfung F

**subjective** [sub•JEK•tiv] *adj*
subjektiv

**subjugate** [SUB•juh•GAIT] *vt*
unterwerfen

**subjunctive** [sub•JUNK•tiv] *adj*
konjunktiv

**sublet** [SUB•LET] *vt*
weitervermieten

**sublime** [sub•LUYM] *adj*
sublim

**submarine** [SUB•muh•REEN]
*n* Unterseeboot N

**submerge** [sub•MURJ] *vt*
untertauchen

**submission** [sub•MI•shn] *n*
Unterwerfung F

**submit** [sub•MIT] *vt* aussetzen

**subordinate**
[suhb•BAUR•di•nait] *adj*
untergeordnet

**subpoena** [suh•PEE•nuh] *n*
Ladung F

**subscribe** [suhb•SKRUYB] *vt*
unterzeichnen

**subscriber** [suhb•SKRUY•bur]
*n* Unterzeichner M

**subscription** [sub•SKRIP•shn]
*n* Unterzeichnung F

**subsequent** [SUB•se•kwent]
*adj* nachfolgend

**subservient** [sub•SUR•vee•ent]
*adj* dienstbar

**subside** [suhb•SUYD] *vi* sich
senken

**subsidize** [SUHB•si•DUYZ] *vt*
unterstützen

**subsist** [SUHB•sist] *vt* bestehen

**substance** [SUHB•stenz] *n*
Substanz F

**substantial** [stuhb•STAN•shul]
*adj* wesentlich

**substantive** [SUHB•stan•tiv]
*adj* wirklich

**subterranean**
[SUHB•tur•RAI•nee•yen] *adj*
unterirdisch

**subtle** [SUH•tl] *adj* fein

**subtract** (pull down; deduct)
[suhb•TRAKT] *vt* abziehen

**subtraction** [suhb•TRAK•shn]
*n* Abziehen N
**suburb** [SUH•burb] *n* Vorort M
**suburban** [suh•BUR•ban] *adj*
vorstädtisch
**subversive** [suhb•VUR•siv] *adj*
umstürzlerisch
**subway** [SUHB•wai] *n*
Untergrundbahn F
**succeed** [suhk•SEED] *vi*
gelingen; (come after) fogen
**success** [suhk•SES] *n* Erfolg M
**successful** [suhk•SES•fl] *adj*
erfolgreich
**succession** [suhk•SES•shn] *n*
Reihenfolge F
**succor** [SUHK•or] *n* Beistand M
**succulent** [SUHK•yoo•lint] *adj*
saftig
**succumb** [suh•KUM] *vi*
zusammenbrechen
**such** [suhch] *adv* solch; *adj*
solche(r)
**suck** [suhk] *vt* saugen
**suction** [SUHK•shn] *n*
Saugen N
**sudden** [SUH•din] *adj* plötzlich
**suddenly** [SUH•din•lee]
plötzlich
**suddenness** [SUH•din•nes] *n*
Plötzlichkeit F
**suds** [suhdz] *n* Seifenwasser N
**sue** [soo] *vt* verklagen
**suet** [SOO•it] *n* Nierenfett N
**suffer** [SUH•fur] *vi* leiden
**suffering** [SUHF•fring] *n*
Leiden N
**suffice** [suh•FUYS] *vi* genügen;
reichen
**sufficiency** [suh•FI•shen•see] *n*
Angemessenheit F

**sufficient** [suh•FI•shent] *adj*
genügend
**suffocate** [SUH•fo•KAIT] *vt*
ersticken
**suffocation** [SUH•fo•KAI•shn]
*n* Ersticken N
**suffrage** [SUH•frij] *n*
Frauenstimmrecht N
**suffuse** [suh•FYUZ] *vt*
überströmen
**sugar** [SHOO•gur] *n* Zucker M
**sugar bowl** [SHUG•gr BOL] *n*
Zuckerdose F
**suggest** [sug•JEST] *vt*
vorschlagen; (hint at)
andeuten; (hint at negatively)
unterstellen
**suggestion** [sug•JES•shn] *n*
Vorschlag M
**suggestive** [sug•JES•tiv] *adj*
anregend
**suicide** [SOO•i•SUYD] *n*
Selbstmord M
**suit** [soot] *n* Anzug M;
(woman's) Kostüm
**suitcase** [soot•KAIS] *n*
Koffer M
**suite** [sweet] *n* (rooms) Suite,
Zimmerflucht F; *n* (of
furniture) Garnitur F
**sulk** [suhlk] *vi* schmollen;
beleidigt sein; *n* Schmollen N
**sullen** [suh•LEN] *adj* mürrisch
**sultan** [suhl•TIN] *n* Sultan M
**sum** [suhm] *n* (total) Summe F;
(of money) Betrag M
**summarize**
[SUHM•muh•RUYZ] *vt*
zusammenfassen
**summary** [SUHM•muh•ree] *n*
Zusammenfassung F

**summer** [SUHM•mur] *n*
Sommer M; *adj* Sommer-
**summit** [SUHM•mit] *n* Gipfel
M; *adj* Gipfel-
**summon** [SUH•mun] *vt*
(meeting) einberufen; (help)
(herbei) rufen
**summons** [SUH•munz] *n*
Vorladung F; *vt* vorladen
**sun** [suhn] *n* Sonne F; *vr* to ~
oneself\ sich sonnen
**sunbathe** [SUHN•baith] *vi*
sonnenbaden
**sunbeam** [SUHN•beem] *n*
Sonnenstrahl M
**sunburn** [SUHN•birn] *n* (tan)
Bräunen F; (painfully)
Sonnenbrand M
**Sunday** [SUHN•dai] *n*
Sonntag M
**sunflower** [SUHN•flouur] *n*
Sonnenblume
**sunglasses** [SUHN•glah•sez]
*npl* Sonnenbrille F
**sunlight** [SUHN•luyt] *n*
Sonnenlicht N
**sunny** [SUHN•nee] *adj* sonnig
**sunrise** [SUHN•ruyz]
Sonnengaufgang
**sunshine** [SUHN•shuyn] *n*
Sonnenschein M
**super** [SOO•pur] *adj*
phantastisch; klasse
**superficial** [SOO•pur•FI•shul]
*adj* oberflächlich
**superintendent**
[SOO•pur•in•TEN•dunt] *n*
Aufsicht F; (police)
Polizeipräsident M
**superior** [soo•PEE•ree•ur] *adj*
besser; (in rank) höher;

(greater) überlegen; *n* (in
rank) Vorgesetzte(r) MF
**superlative** [soo•PUR•la•tiv]
*adj* überragend; *n*
Superlativ M
**supermarket**
[SOO•pur•MAHR•ket] *n*
Supermarkt M
**supernatural**
[SOO•pur•NA•chur•el] *adj*
übernatürlich
**superpower** *n* Supermacht F
**supersede** [SOO•pur•SEED] *vt*
ablösen
**superstition**
[SOO•pur•STI•shun] *n*
Aberglaube M
**supervise** [SOO•pur•VUYZ] *vt*
beaufsichtigen; *vi* Aufsicht
furen; die Aufsicht haben
**supervision** [SOO•pur•VI•zhun]
*n* Aufsicht F; (action)
Beaufsichtigung F
**supper** [SUH•pur] *n*
Abendessen M; to have ~
Abend essen
**supplement** [SUH•pluh•munt]
*n* Ergänzung F; *vt* ergänzen;
(income) aufbessern
**supply** [SUH•pluy] *n*
Versorgung F; *vt* sorgen für;
(want/need) abhelfen
**supplies** [SUH•pluyz] *npl*
Vorräte M
**support** [SUH•paurt] *n* Stütze
F; *vt* stützen; (fig)
unterstützen; ~ oneself\ sich
stützen
**suppose** [suh•POZ] *vt* sich
vorstellen; (assume)
annehmen

**supposed** *adj* vermutet

**supposedly** *adv* angeblich

**suppress** [suh•PRES] *vt* unterdrücken

**supreme** [suh•PREEM] *adj* höchste(r)

**sure** [shoor] *adj* sicher; *adv* (yes) klar!

**surely** [SHOOR•lee] bestimmt; sicher

**surf** [surf] *n* Brandung F; *vi* surfen

**surface** [SUR•fas] *n* Oberfläche F; on the ~\ oberflächlich; *vt* (road) mit einem Belag versehen; *vi* auftauchen

**surge** [surj] *n* (sea) Wogen N; (crowd) eine wogende Menschenmenge; *vi* branden; anschwellen

**surgeon** [SUR•jun] *n* Chirurf(in) M(F)

**surgery** [SUR•jur•ee] *n* Chiurgie F

**surgical** [SUR•ji•kul] *adj* operatuv

**surly** [SUR•lee] *adj* vedrießlich

**surmount** [sur•MOUNT] *vt* überwinden

**surname** [SUR•naim] *n* cognome M

**surpass** [SUR•pas] *vt* übertreffen

**surplus** [SUR•plus] *n* Uberschluß M; *adj* überschüssig

**surprise** [sur•PRUYZ] *n* Überraschung F; *adj* überrasche; *vt* überraschen

**surrealism** [sur•REE•LIZM] *n* Surrealismus M

**surrender** [sur•REN•dur] *vt* to ~ to\ sich ergeben; übergeben; (goods) einlösen .

**surreptitious** [su•REP•ti•SHUS] *adj* heimlich

**surround** [su•ROUND] *vt* umbegen *n* Umrandung F

**surrounding** [su•ROUN•ding] *adj* umliegend

**surroundings** [su•ROUN•dingz] *npl* Umbegung F

**survey 1** [SIR•veh] *n* Vermessung F (study) Überlick M ; *vt* (look at) sich ansehen

**survey 2** [sir•VEH] *vi* (examine) untersuchen; (land) vermessen; inspizieren

**survival** [sur•VUY•vul] *n* Überleben N

**survive** [sur•VUYV] *vi* überleben

**survivor** [sur•VUY•vur] *n* Überlebender M

**susceptibility** [suh•SEP•ti•BI•li•tee] *n* Anfälligkeit F

**susceptible** [suh•SEP•ti•bl] *adj* anfällig

**suspect** [sus•PEKT] *vt* verdächtigen

**suspend** [sus•SPEND] *vt* aufhängen; (stop) einstellen

**suspenders** [sus•SPEN•durz] *npl* Hosenträger

**suspense** [suhs•SPENS] *n* Spannung F

**suspicion** [suhs•SPI•shn] *n* Argwohn M

**sustain** [suh•STAIN] *vt* stützen; (receive injury; etc) erleiden

**sustenance** [SUH•ste•nenz] *n* Unterhalt M

**suture** [SOO•chur] *n* Naht F

**swab** *n* Scheuerlappen M

**swagger** [SWAG•gur] *vi* prahlen

**swain** *n* Bauernbursche M

**swallow** [SWAH•lo] *vt* schlucken

**swallow** [SWAH•lo] *n* Schwalbe F

**swamp** *n* Sumpf M

**swan** [swahn] *n* Schwan M

**swap** [swahp] *vt* austauschen

**swarm** *n* Schwarm M

**swarthy** [SWAUR•thee] *adj* schwärzlich

**swat** *vt* quetschen

**swathe** [swath] *n* Schwaden M

**sway** [swai] *vi* schwanken; (influence) *n* Macht F

**swear** [swair] *vi* schwören

**sweat** [swet] *vi* schwitzen; *n* Schweiß M

**sweater** [SWET•tur] *n* Pullover M

**Swede** [sweed] *n* Schwede Schwedin (i) M

**Sweden** [SWEED•din] *n* Schweden

**Swedish** [SWEED•dish] *adj* schwedisch

**sweep** *vt* säubern; kehren; fegen

**sweeper** [SWEEP•pur] *n* Feger M

**sweeping** [SWEEP•ping] *adj* sausend

**sweet** *adj* süß

**sweet potato** [SWEET po•TAI•to] *n* Süßkartoffel F

**sweetbread** [SWEET•bred] *n* Brieschen N

**sweeten** [SWEET•tin] *vt* süßen

**sweetness** [SWEET•nis] *n* Süßigkeit F

**swell** [swel] *vi* aufschwellen

**swelling** [SWEL•ling] *n* Schwellen N

**swelter** [SWEL•tur] *vi* verschmachten

**swerve** [swurv] *vi* seitwärts wenden

**swift** *adj* schnell

**swiftness** [SWIFT•nes] *n* Schelligkeit F

**swim** *vi* schwimmen

**swimmer** [SWIM•mur] *n* Schwimmer M

**swimming** [SWIM•ming] *n* Schwimmen N

**swimming pool** *n* Schwimmbad Freibad N

**swimsuit** [SWIM•soot] *n* Badeanzug M

**swindle** [SWIN•dl] *vi* betrügen

**swindle** [SWIN•dl] *n* Schwindel N

**swing** *n* (movement, rhythm) Schwung M; *vi* schwingen; (influence) umschlagen lassen

**swipe** [swuyp] *vi* hauen; *n* (blow) Schlag M

**swirl** [swurl] *vi* wirbeln

**Swiss** *n* Schweizer in M

**switch** [swich] *n* Schalter M; *vt* (change) wechseln; ~ off\ ausschlaten

**switchboard** [SWICH•baurd] *n* Schaltbrett N

**Switzerland** [SWIT•zur•land] *n*
Schweiz F

**swivel** [SWI•vul] *n*
Drehzapfen M

**swivel chair** *n* Drehstuhl M

**swoon** *vi* schwinden

**swoop** *vi* herabstoßen

**sword** [sord] *n* Schwert N

**sycamore** [SI•ki•MAUR] *n*
Maulbeerfeigenbaum M

**syllable** [SI•li•bl] *n* Silbe F

**syllogism** [SI•lo•JIZM] *n*
Vernunftschluß M

**symbol** [SIM•buhl] *n* Symbol N

**symbolic** [sim•BAH•lik] *adj*
symbolisch

**symmetrical** [sim•ME•tri•kuhl]
*adj* symmetrisch

**sympathetic**
[SIM•puh•THE•tik] *adj*
mitfühlend

**sympathy** [SIM•puh•thee] *n*
Sympathie F

**symphony** [SIM•fo•nee] *n*
Sinfonie F

**symptom** [SIMP•tum] *n*
Anzeichen N

**symptomatic**
[SIMP•to•MA•tik] *adj*
symptomatisch

**synagogue** [SI•no•GOG] *n*
Synagoge F

**synchronize** [SIN•kro•NUYZ]
*vi* gleichzeitig sein

**syndicate** [SIN•di•kit] *n*
Konsortium N

**synonym** [SI•ni•NIM] *n*
Synonym N

**synonymous**
[si•NAHN•ni•mus] *adj*
synonymisch

**syntax** [SIN•taks] *n* Satzbau M

**synthesis** [SIN•thuh•sis] *n*
Synthese F

**Syria** [SEE•ree•uh] *n* Syrien

**Syrian** [SEE•ree•yen] *n* Syrier
in M

**syringe** [sir•RINJ] *n* Spritze F

**syrup** [SEER•rup] *n* Sirup M

**system** [SIS•tim] *n* System N

**systematic** [SIS•te•MA•tik] *adj*
systematisch

# T

**tab** *n* Rechnung F

**table** [TAI•bl] *n* Tisch M

**table (card)** *n* Kartentisch M

**tablet** [TAB•lit] *n* Täfelchen N

**tableware** [TAI•bl•WAIR] *n*
Tischgeschirr N

**tabloid** [TAB•bloid] *n*
Tablette F

**tabular** [TAB•yoo•lar] *adj*
tafelförmig

**tabulate** [TAB•yoo•LAIT] *vt*
tabellarisieren

**tachometer** [ta•KAH•me•tur] *n*
Tachometer N

**tacit** [TA•sit] *adj*
stillschweigend

**taciturn** [TA•si•TURN] *adj*
schweigsam

**tack** [tak] *n* Stift M

**tackle** [TAK•kl] *vi* angreifen

**tackle (fishing)** *n* Gerät N

**tact** [takt] *n* Takt M

**tactical** [TAK•ti•kul] *adj*
taktisch

**tactics** [TAK•tiks] *n* Taktik F

**tactile** [TAK•tul] *adj* taktil

**tadpole** [TAD•pol] *n*
Kaulquappe F

**taffeta** [TA•fit•tuh] *n* Taft M

**tag** *n* Zipfel M

**tag along** *vi* hinterherlaufen

**tail** *n* Schwanz M

**tailor** [TAI•lur] *n* Schneider M

**taint** *n* Makel M

**take** [taik] *vt* nehmen;
(transport; accompany)
bringen; (course) machen;
(consume) zu sich nehmen;
(photo) machen; (respond)
aufnehmen; (require)
brauchen; (clothes size)
haben; *vi* (fire) angehen; *n*
(film) Aufnahme F

**take along** *vt* mitenhemen

**take away** *vi* schmällern

**take back** sich zurück geben

**take in** (person, etc) hinein
herinbringeng

**take off** *vi* (plane) starten;
(remove) abmachen; (deduct)
abziehen

**take out** *vt* bringen

**take over** *vi* an die Macht
kommen

**talcum** [TAL•kum] *n* Talk M

**tale** [tail] *n* Erzählung F

**talent** *n* Talent N

**talk** [tauk] *vi* reden; *n*
Gespäch N

**talkative** [TAUK•uh•tiv] *adj*
gesprächig

**talker** [TAU•kur] *n*
Sprechender M

**talking** [TAU•king] *n* Reden N

**tall** *adj* groß

**tallow** [TA•lo] *n* Talg M

**tally** [TA•lee] *vt* nachzählen

**tam-o'-shanter** [TAM o'
SHAN•tur] *n* Schottenmütze F

**tame** [taim] *adj* zahm; *vt*
bändigen

**tamper** [TAM•pur] *vt*
herumbasteln

**tan** *n* Sonnenbräunung F; *vt*
(face) bräunen

**tandem** [TAN•dim] *n*
Tandem N

**tangent** [TAN•jent] *n*
Tangente F

**tangerine** [TAN•juh•REEN] *n*
Mandarine F

**tangible** [TAN•juh•bl] *adj*
greifbar

**Tangiers** [tan•JEERZ] *n* Tangier

**tangle** [TANG•gl] *vt* verwirren

**tank** *n* Tank M

**tank (gasoline)** *n* Tank M

**tanker** [TANK•kur] *n* Tanker M

**tannery** [TAN•nur•ree] *n*
Gerberei F

**tantalize** [TAN•tuh•LUYZ] *vi*
peinigen

**tantrum** [TAN•trum] *n* Wut M

**tap 1** *n* Zapfen M; *vt* zapfen;

**tap 2** *n* Klopfen M; *vt* klopfen

**tape** [taip] *n* Band N

**taper** [TAI•pur] *vt* zuspitzen;
(candle) *n* Kerze

**tapestry** [TA•pe•stree] *n* Wandteppich M

**tar** *n* Teer M

**tardy** [TAR•dee] *adj* spät

**tare** [tair] *n* (weed) Unkraut N

**tare** [tair] *n* (weight) Tara F

**target** [TAR•git] *n* Ziel N

**tariff** [TAIR•rif] *n* Zolltarif M

**tarnish** [TAR•nish] *vt* trüben

**tarpaulin** [TAR•puh•lin] *n* Persenning F

**tarry** [TAIR•ree] *vi* zaudern

**tart 1** *adj* sauer

**tart 2** *n* Torte F

**tartar** [TAR•tur] *n* Wüterich M

**task** *n* Aufgabe F

**tassel** [TA•suhl] *n* Quaste F

**taste** [taist] *vi* schmecken; *n* Geshmack

**tasteless** [TAIST•les] *adj* schmacklos

**tasty** [TAI•stee] *adj* schmackhaft

**tattered** [TAT•turd] *adj* abgerissen

**tattle** [TAT•tl] *vt* ausplaudern

**tattle-tale** [TAT•tl•TAIL] *n* Klatschbase F

**tattoo 1** [ta•TOO] *n* (of skin) Zapfenstreich M

**tattoo 2** *n* (drums) Trommeln N

**taught** [taut] *pp* teach gelehrt

**taunt** *vt* verhöhnen

**tavern** [TA•vurn] *n* Lokal N

**tax 1** [taks] *n* Steuer F

**tax 2** (income) *n* Einkommensteuer F

**tax 3** (state tax) *n* Mehrwertssteuer F

**taxi** [TAK•see] *n* Taxi N

**taxpayer** [TAKS•PAI•ur] *n* Steuerzahler M

**tea** [tee] *n* Tee M

**tea party** [TEE PAHR•tee] *n* Teegesellschaft F

**teach** [teech] *vt* unterrichten

**teacher** [TEE•chur] *n* Lehrer in M

**teaching** [TEE•ching] *n* Lehren N

**teacup** [TEE•kup] *n* Tasse F

**teakettle** [TEE•KET•tl] *n* Teekanne F

**teal** [teel] *n* Krickente F

**team** [teem] *n* Mannschaft F

**teamwork** [TEEM•wurk] *n* Zusammenarbeit F

**teapot** [TEE•pot] *n* Teekanne F

**tear 1** [tayr] *vt* (paper etc) zereißen; (~ away) reißen; *n* Riß M

**tear 2** [teer] *n* Träne F

**tear down herunterreißen**

**tease** [teez] *vi* foppen

**teaspoon** [TEE•spoon] *n* Teelöffel M

**technical** [TEK•ni•kul] *adj* technisch

**technician** [tek•NI•shn] *n* Techniker M

**tedious** [TEE•dee•is] *adj* langweilig

**teem** *vi* wimmeln

**teens** [teenz] *npl* Jugendjahre M

**teethe** *vi* zahnen

**telegram** [TEL•le•GRAM] *n* Telegramm N

**telegraph** [TEL•le•GRAF] *n* Telegraph M

**telephone** [TEL•le•FON] *n* Telefon N; *vt* anrufen; telefonierin

**telephone number**
[TEL•le•FON NUM•bur] *n*
Telefonnummer F

**telephone operator**
[TEL•le•FON A•pur•RAI•tur]
*n* Telephonist in M

**telescope** [TEL•le•SKOP] *n*
Fernrohr N

**televise** [TEL•le•VUYZ] *vi* im
Fernsehen bringen

**television** [TEL•le•VI•shn] *n*
Fernsehen N

**television set** [TE•li•VI•shn
SET] *n* Fernseher M

**tell** *vt* (say; order) sagen;
(relate) erzählen; (discern)
wissen

**tell of** ausschimpfen

**teller** [TEL•lur] *n* Erzähler M

**telling** [TEL•ling] *adj*
wirkungsvoll

**telltale** [TEL•tail] *n*
Kennzeichen N

**temerity** [te•MAIR•ri•tee] *n*
Kühnheit F

**temper** [TEM•pur] *n*
Temperament N; *vt* (action)
mäßigen

**temperament** [TEM•pur•ment]
Temperament N

**temperance** [TEM•prenz] *n*
Mäßigkeit F

**temperate** [TEM•pret] *adj*
gemäßigt

**temperature**
[TEM•pruh•CHUR] *n*
Temperatur F

**tempest** [TEM•pest] *n* Sturm M

**tempestuous** [tem•PES•chus]
*adj* stürmisch

**temple 1** [TEM•pl] *n*
Tempel M

**temple 2** *n* (anat) Schläfe F

**temporal** [TEM•pruhl] *adj*
zeitlich

**temporary** [TEM•po•RAI•ree]
*adj* zeitweilig

**temporize** [TEM•po•RUYZ] *vi*
Zeit zu gewinnen suchen

**tempt** *vt* versuchen

**temptation** [tem•TAI•shn] *n*
Versuchung F

**tempting** [TEMP•ting] *adj*
verführerisch

**ten** *num* zehn

**tenable** [TEN•uh•bl] *adj* haltbar

**tenacious** [ten•AI•shus] *adj*
klebrig

**tenacity** [ten•A•si•tee] *n*
Klebrigkeit F

**tenant** [TEN•nant] *n* Mieter M

**tend 1** *vi* (inclination) neigen

**tend 2** *vt* (a machine) bedienen

**tendency** [TEN•den•cee] *n*
Tendenz F

**tender 1** [TEN•dur] *adj* zart

**tender 2** *vt* anbieten

**tender 3** *n* Pfleger in M

**tenderloin** [TEN•dur•LOIN] *n*
Lendenstück N

**tenderness** [TEN•dur•nes] *n*
Zartheit F

**tendon** [TEN•din] *n* Sehne F

**tendril** [TEN•dril] *n* Ranke F

**tenement** [TEN•ne•mint] *n*
Wohnhaus N

**tennis** [TEN•nis] *n* Tennis M

**tenor** [TEN•nor] *n* Tenor M

**tense 1** [tens] *adj* gespannt; *vt*
anspannen

**tense 2** *n* Zeitform F

**tensile** [TEN•sil] *adj* streckbar

**tension** [TEN•shun] *n*
Spannung F

**tent** *n* Zelt N

**tentative** [TEN•tuh•tiv] *adj*
vorläufig

**tenth** *num* zehnte

**tenuous** [TEN•yoo•us] *adj*
dürftig

**tepid** [TE•pid] *adj* lauwarm

**term** [turm] *n* Wort Zeit (f)
Dauer (f) N

**terminal** [TUR•min•nl] *n*
Endstation M

**terminate** [TUR•min•NAIT] *vt*
beendigen

**terrace** [TAIR•res] *n* Terrasse F

**terrain** [tair•RAIN] *n*
Gelände N

**terrestrial** [tair•RES•stree•ul]
*adj* irdisch

**terrible** [TAIR•uh•bl] *adj*
furchtbar; chrecklich

**terrific** [tuhr•RIF•fik]*adj*
kolossal

**terrify** [TAIR•ri•FUY] *vt*
erschrecken

**territory** [TAIR•ri•TO•ree] *n*
Gebiet N

**terror** [TAIR•ror] *n* Schrecken M

**terrorize** [TAIR•ro•RUYZ] *vt*
terrorisieren

**terse** [turz] *adj* knapp

**test 1** *n* Prüfung F; *vt* prüfen; *vi*
einen Test machen

**test 2** (blood) *n* Stichprobe F

**test tube** [TEST TOOB] *n*
Reagenzglas N

**testament** [TES•tuh•mint] *n*
Testament N

**testify** [TES•ti•FUY] *vt*
bezeugen

**testimony** [TES•ti•MO•nee] *n*
Aussage F

**tetanus** [TE•tuh•nes] *n*
Tetanus M

**tether** [TE•thur] *vt* anbinden

**text** [tekst] *n* Text M

**textbook** [TEKST•bok] *n*
Buch N

**textile** [TEKS•tuyl] *npl*
Textilwaren M

**texture** [TEKS•chur] *n*
Textur F

**than** als

**thank** *vt* danken

**thankful** *adj* dankbar

**thankfully** [THANK•fuh•lee]
dankbar

**thankless** [THANK•les] *adj*
undankbar

**thanklessness**
[THANK•les•nes] *n*
Undankbarkeit F

**thanks** *npl* Dank; *interj* danke

**thanksgiving** [thanks•GI•ving]
*n* Dankfest N

**that** *pron* der; die; das; daß;'
welch

**thatch** *n* Dachstroh N

**thaw** [thau] *vi* schmelzen

**the** [thuh] der die das

**theater** [THEE•i•tir] *n*
Theater N

**theatrical** [thee•A•trik•kl] *adj*
theatralisch

**theft** *n* Diebstahl M

**their** [thair] *pron* ihr ihre

**theirs** [thairz] das ihrige

**them** si; e ihnen

**theme** [theem] *n* Thema N

**themselves** [them•SELVZ] *pron* sie; selbst

**then** dann; damals; from ~ on\ von da an; (in that case) dann (furthermore, also) dann außerderm

**theology** [thee•AH•lo•gee] *n* Theologie

**theorem** [THEE•or•em] *n* Theorem N

**theoretical** [THEE•o•RE•tik•kl] *adj* theoretisch

**theory** [THEEU•ree] *n* Theorie F

**therapeutic** [THAIR•uh•PYOO•tik] *adj* therapeutisch

**there** [thair] *prep* da; dort

**thereabouts** [THAIR•uh•BOUTS] da herum

**thereafter** [thair•AF•tur] *adv* danach

**thereby** [thair•BUY] dadurch

**therefore** [thair•FOR] deshalb

**therein** [thair•IN] darin

**thereof** [thair•OF] davon

**thereon** [thair•ON] daran

**thereupon** [THAIR•uh•PON] darauf

**thermal** [THUR•muhl] *adj* wärme

**thermometer** [thur•MAH•me•tur] *n* Thermometer N

**thermostat** [THUR•mo•STAT] *n* Thermostat M

**these** [theez] diese; dieser; dies

**thesis** [THEE•sis] *n* These F

**they** [thai] man

**thick** [thik] *adj* dick

**thicken** [THIK•kin] *vt* verdicken

**thickness** [THIK•nes] *n* Dicke F

**thief** [theef] *n* Dieb M

**thigh** [thuy] *n* Schenkel M

**thimble** [THIM•bl] *n* Fingerhut M

**thin** *adj* dünn

**thing** [thing] *n* Ding N; *npl* ~s (possession) Sachen; *n* (non material) Sache F

**think** *vi* denken

**thinker** [THINK•kur] *n* Denker M

**thinking** [think•king] *n* Denken N

**thinly** [THIN•lee] *adj* dünn

**thinness** [THIN•nes] *n* Dünne F

**third** [thurd] dritte

**thirdly** [THURD•lee] drittens

**thirst** [thurst] *n* Durst M

**thirteen** [thur•TEEN] *num* dreizehn

**thirteenth** [thur•TEENTH] *num* dreizehnte

**thirtieth** [THUR•tee•eth] *num* dreißigste

**thirty** [THUR•tee] *num* dreißig

**thirty-first** [THUR•tee•FURST] ein-und-dreißigste

**this** *article* dieser; diese

**thistle** [THIS•tl] *n* Distel F

**thong** *n* Riemen M

**thorn** *n* Dorn M

**thorough** [THUR•ro] *adj* sorgfältig

**thoroughbred** [THUR•ro•BRED] *adj* reinrassig

**thoroughfare** [THUR•ro•FAIR] *n* Verkehrsstraße F

**thoroughly** [THUR•ro•lee] *adj* völlig

**those** [thoz] dieser

**thou** du

**though** [tho] *adv* obwohl

**thought** [thaut] *n* Gedanke M

**thoughtful** [THAUT•fl] *adj* gedankenvoll

**thoughtfulness** [THAUT•fl•nes] *n* Nachdenklichkeit F

**thoughtless** [THAUT•les] *adj* gedankenlos

**thoughtlessness** [THAUT•les•nes] *n* Gedankenlosigkeit F

**thousand** [THOU•zund] *num* tausend

**thousandth** [THOU•zundth] tausendste

**thrash** *vt* verdreschen

**thread** [thred] *n* Faden M

**threadbare** [THRED•bair] *adj* fadenscheinig

**threat** [thret] *n* Drohung F

**threaten** [THRET•tin] *vt* drohen

**threatening** [THRET•ning] *adj* drohend

**three** *num* drei

**thresh** *vt* dreschen

**threshing** [THRESH•ing] *n* Dreschen N

**threshold** [THRESH•hold] *n* Schwelle F

**thrice** [thruyz] *adv* dreimal

**thrift** *n* Sparsamkeit F

**thrill** *n* Erregung F

**thrive** [thruyv] *vt* gedeihen

**throat** [throt] *n* Hals M

**throb** [thrahb] *vi* pochen

**throne** [thron] *n* Thron M

**throng** *n* Gedränge N

**throttle** [THRAH•tl] *n* Kehle F

**through** [throo] *prep* durch

**throw** [thro] *vi* werfen

**throw out** [thro out] *vi* wegwerfen

**throw up** *vi* erbrechen

**thrush** [thruhsh] *n* Drossel F

**thrust** [thruhst] *vt* stoßen; stecken

**thug** [thuhg] *n* Verbrecher M

**thumb** [thuhmb] *n* Daumen M

**thump** [thuhmp] *vi* plumpsen

**thunder** [THUHN•dur] *n* Donner M

**thunderbolt** [THUHN•dur•BOLT] *n* Blitz M

**thunderclap** [THUHN•dur•KLAP] *n* Donnerschlag M

**thundering** [THUHN•dring] *adj* donnernd

**thunderous** [THUHN•drus] *adj* gewitterschwül

**thunderstorm** [THUHN•dur•STAURM] *n* Gewitter N

**Thursday** [THURZ•dai] *n* Donnerstag M

**thus** [thuhs] so

**thus far** [THUHS FAHR] bis her

**thwart** *vt* vereiteln

**thyme** [tuym] *n* Thymian M

**tiara** [tee•AHR•uh] *n* Tiara F

**tibia** [TI•bee•uh] *n* Schienbein N

**tick 1** [tik] *n* Ticken N; *vi* ticken
**tick 2** *n* (insect) Zecke F
**ticket** [TIK•kit] *n* Fahrkarte F
**ticket office** [TIK•kit AW•fis] *n* Schalter M
**tickle** [TIK•kl] *vt* kitzeln
**TIDAL** [TUY•dl] *adj* Gezeiten
**tide** [tuyd] *n* Ebbe M
**tidiness** [TUY•dee•nes] *n* Sauberkeit F
**tidings** [TUY•dings] *npl* Nachrichten
**tidy** [TUY•dee] *adj* sauber
**tie** [tuy] *n* Kravatte F; *vt* binden
**tie-up** [TUY•uhp] *vt* anbinden
**tier** [teer] *n* Reihe F
**tiger** [TUY•gur] *n* Tiger M
**tight** [tuyt] *adj* dicht
**tighten** [TUY•tin] *vt* zusammenziehen
**tightness** [TUYT•nes] *n* Dichtheit F
**tightwad** [TUYT•wahd] *n* Geizkragen M
**tigress** [TUY•gris] *n* Tigerin M
**tile** [tuyl] *n* Dachziegel M
**till 1** [til] *prep* bis
**till 2** *n* (cash register) Kassenbestand M
**till 3** *vt* (agr) bestellen
**tilt** *vt* kippen; *n* Kippen N
**timber** [TIM•bur] *n* Bauholz N
**time** [tuym] *n* Zeit F; what ~ is it\ wie spät ist?; (occasion) diesmal; dieses mal; have a good ~\ ~ viel Späs!; (multiplication 6 ~s 5\ 6 mal 5
**timekeeper** [TUYM•KEE•pur] *n* Zeitmesser M

**timely** [TUYM•lee] *adj* rechtzeitig
**timepiece** [TUYM•peez] *n* Uhr F
**timer** [TUY•mur] *n* Stoppuhr F
**timetable** [TUYM•TAI•bl] *n* Zeittabelle F
**timid** [TI•mid] *adj* schüchtern
**tin** *n* Zinn N
**tin can** *adj* Blechdose F
**tincture** [TINK•chur] *n* Tinktur F
**tinder** [TIN•dur] *n* Zunder M
**tinfoil** [TIN•foil] *n* Stanniol N
**tinge** [tinj] *vt* färben
**tingle** [TING•gl] *vi* prickeln
**tinkle** [TINK•kl] *vi* klingeln
**tinned** [tind] *adj* verzinnt
**tinsel** [TIN•sul] *n* Flittergold N
**tint** *n* Farbe F; *vt* tönen
**tiny** [TUY•nee] *adj* winzig
**tip** *n* Spitze F
**tipsy** [TIP•see] *adj* beschwipst
**tiptoe** [TIP•to] auf den Zehenspitzen
**tirade** [TUY•raid] *n* Tirade F
**tire 1** [tuyr] *n* Reifen M
**tire 2** (flat) *n* Reifenpanne F
**tire 3** (spare) *n* Zusatzreifen M
**tire 4** *vi* ermüden
**tired** [tuyrd] *adj* müde
**tiredness** [TUYRD•nes] *n* Müdigkeit F
**tireless** [TUYR•les] *adj* unermüdlich
**tiresome** [TUYR•sum] *adj* ermüdend
**tissue** [TI•shyoo] *n* Gewebe N
**tissue-paper** [TI•shyoo PAI•pur] *n* Seidenpapier N
**tithe** [tuyth] *n* Zehnte M

**title** [TUY•tl] *n* Titel M
**titular** [TI•choo•lur] *adj* titular
**to** [too] *prep* (direction) zu; (as far as) bis; (per) pro; ~ and fro\ hin und her
**toad** [tod] *n* Kröte F
**toast** [tost] *n* Toast M
**tobacco** [tuh•BAK•ko] *n* Tabak M
**tobacconist** [tuh•BAK•ko•nist] *n* Tabakhändler M
**toboggan** [tuh•BOG•gin] *n* Toboggan M
**today** [too•DAI] heute
**toe** [to] *n* Zehe F
**toenail** *n* Zehennagel M
**together** [too•GE•thur] *prep* zusammen
**toil** *vi* sich abmühen
**toilet** [TOI•let] *n* Toilette F
**toilet paper** [TOI•let PAI•pur] *n* Toilettenpapier N
**toilet water** [TOI•let WAH•tur] *n* kölnisches Wasser N
**token** [TO•kin] *n* Merkmal N
**told** *pp* tell erzählt
**tolerable** [TAH•lur•uh•bl] *adj* erträglich
**tolerance** [TAH•luh•renz] *n* Duldsamkeit F
**tolerant** [TAH•luh•rent] *adj* geduldig
**tolerate** [TAH•luh•RAIT] *vi* dulden
**toll 1** [tol] *n* (payment) Zoll M
**toll 2** *n* (effect) Todesopfer N
**toll-bridge** [TOL•brij] *n* Zollbrücke F
**tomato** [to•MAI•to] *n* Tomate F
**tomb** [toom] *n* Grab N

**tombstone** [TOOMB•ston] *n* Grabstein M
**tomcat** [TAHM•kat] *n* Kater M
**tomorrow** [too•MAH•ro] morgen
**ton** [tuhn] *n* Tonne F
**tone** [ton] *n* Ton M
**tongs** [taungz] *n* Zange F
**tongue** [tuhng] *n* Zunge F
**tongue-tied** [TUHNG•tuyd] *adj* zungenlahm
**tonic** [TAH•nik] *n* Stärkungsmittel N
**tonight** [too•NUYT] heute abend
**tonnage** [TUH•nij] *n* Tonnage F
**tonsil** [TAHN•sil] *n* Mandel F
**tonsillitis** [TAHN•si•LUY•tis] *n* Mandelentzündung F
**tonsure** [TAHN•shur] *n* Haarschneiden N
**too** auch
**tool** *n* Werkzeug N
**tooth** *n* Zahn M
**toothache** [TOOTH•aik] *n* Zahnweh N
**toothpaste** [TOOTH•paist] *n* Zahnpasta F
**toothpick** [TOOTH•pik] *n* Zahnstocher M
**top** [tahp] *n* Oberteil N; (upper surface) Oberfläche; *adj* (upper) obeere (r,s); *vt* bedecken
**topaz** [TO•paz] *n* Topas M
**topcoat** [TAHP•kot] *n* Überzieher M
**topic** [TAH•pik] *n* Thema N
**topmost** [TAHP•most] *adv* höchst

**topography**
[tah•PAH•grah•fee] *n*
Topographie

**topple** [TAH•pl] *vi* kippen

**topsy-turvy**
[TAHP•zee•TUHR•vee] *adj*
verkehrt

**torch** *n* Fackel F

**torment** [taur•MENT] *vt*
peinigen

**tormentor** *n* Peiniger M

**tornado** [taur•NAI•do] *n*
Tornado M

**torpedo** [taur•PEE•do] *n*
Torpedo M

**torpid** [TAUR•pid] *adj* starr

**torrent** [TAUR•rint] *n*
Wolkenbruch M

**torrid** [TAUR•rid] *adj* brennend
heiß

**tortoise** [TAUR•tus] *n*
Schildkröte F

**tortuous** [TAUR•choo•us] *adj*
gewunden

**torture** [TAUR•chur] *n*
Folterung F

**torturer** [TAUR•chur•rur] *n*
Folterknecht M

**toss** [taus] *vt* werfen

**tot** [taht] *n* Knirps M

**total** [TO•tl] *n* Summe F; *adj*
gesamt

**totalitarian**
[to•TA•li•TAI•ree•yen] *adj*
totalitär

**totality** [to•TA•li•tee] *n*
Gesamtheit F

**totally** [TO•tuh•lee] *adv* ganz

**totter** [TAH•tur] *vi* torkeln

**touch** [tuhch] *vi* berühren

**touching** [TUHCH•ching] *adj*
ergreifend

**touchy** [TUH•chee] *adj*
empfindlich

**tough** [tuhf] *adj* hart

**toughen** [TUH•fin] *vt* zäh
machen

**toughness** [TUHF•nis] *n*
Zähigkeit F

**tour** [toor] *n* Tour F

**tourist** [TOOR•rist] *n* Tourist M

**tournament** [TOOR•nuh•mint]
*n* Turnier N

**tow** [to] *n* Schleppen N; *v*
schleppen

**towards** [TOO•wahrdz] nach

**towel** [TOW•wuhl] *n* Tuch N

**tower** [TOW•wur] *n* Turm M

**towing** [TO•wing] *n*
Schleppen N

**town** [toun] *n* Stadt F

**township** *n* Gemeinde

**toxic** [TAHK•sik] *adj* giftig

**toxin** [TAHK•sin] *n* Toxin N

**toy** [toi] *n* Spielzeug N

**trace** [trais] *n* Spur F; *v*
nachspüren

**tracer** [TRAI•sur] *n*
Aufspürer M

**trachea** [TRAI•kee•uh] *n*
Trachea F

**track** [trak] *n* Spur; (train)
Gleis F

**tract** [trakt] *n* Fläche F

**tractable** [TRAK•tuh•bl] *adj*
fügsam

**traction** [TRAK•shn] *n*
Griffigkeit F

**tractor** [TRAK•tur] *n* Traktor M

**trade** [traid] *n* Handel M

**trade school** [TRAID SKOOL]
*n* Fachschule F

**trade-union** [TRAID
YOON•yun] *n*
Gewerkschaft F

**trademark** [TRAID•mahrk] *n*
Schutzmarke F

**trader** [TRAI•dur] *n* Händler M

**tradesman** [TRAIDZ•man] *n*
Ladeninhaber M

**tradewind** [TRAID•wind] *n*
Passatwinde F

**trading** [TRAI•ding] *n*
Handeln N

**tradition** [truh•DI•shn] *n*
Tradition F

**traffic** [TRAF•fik] *n* Verkehr N

**tragedy** [TRA•ji•dee] *n*
Tragödie F

**tragic** [TRA•jik] *adj* tragisch

**trail** [trail] *n* Pfad M

**trailer** [TRAI•lur] *n*
Wohnwagen M

**train 1** *n* Zug M

**train 2** (express) *n* Eilzug M

**trainer** [TRAI•nur] *n* Trainer M

**training** [TRAI•ning] *n*
Schulung F

**trainman** [TRAIN•man] *n*
Zugleiter M

**trait** *n* Zug M

**traitor** [TRAI•tor] *n* Verräter M

**trajectory** [truh•JEK•to•ree] *n*
Flugbahn F

**tram** *n* Straßenbahn F

**tramp** *n* Luder N

**trample** [TRAM•pl] *vi* trampeln

**trance** [trans] *n* Trance F

**tranquil** [TRAN•kwil] *adj* ruhig

**tranquillity** [tran•KWIL•li•tee]
*n* Ruhe F

**transact** [tranz•AKT] *vt*
abschließen

**transaction** [tranz•AK•shn] *n*
Durchführung F

**transcend** [tran•SEND] *vt*
überschreiten

**transcribe** [tran•SKRUYB] *vt*
abschreiben

**transept** *n* Querschiff N

**transfer** [TRANS•fur] *vt*
hinüberbringen; *n*
Übertragung F

**transform** [trans•FAURM] *vt*
umwandeln

**transformation**
[TRANS•faur•MAI•shn] *n*
Umwandlung F

**transformer** [trans•FAUR•mur]
*n* Umgestalter M

**transfusion** [trans•FYOO•shn]
*n* Umgießen N

**transgress** [trans•GRES] *vt*
übertreten

**transgression** [trans•GRE•shn]
*n* Übertretung F

**transient** [TRAN•zee•int] *adj*
flüchtig

**transit** [TRANS•zit] *n*
Transit M

**transition** [trans•ZI•shn] *n*
Übergang M

**transitive** [TRANS•zi•tiv] *adj*
transitiv

**translate** [trans•LAIT] *vt*
übersetzen

**translation** [trans•LAI•shn] *n*
Übersetzung F

**translator** [trans•LAI•tur] *n*
Übersetzer in M

**translucent** [trans•LOO•sent]
*adj* lichtdurchlässig

**transmission** [trans•MI•shn] *n*
Versand M

**transmit** [trans•MIT] *vt*
übersenden

**transmitter** [trans•MI•tur] *n*
Übersender M

**transom** [TRANS•sum] *n*
Querblende F

**transparent** [trans•PAIR•rent]
*adj* durchsichtig

**transpiration**
[TRANS•pi•RAI•shn] *n*
Ausdünstung F

**transpire** [tran•SPUYR] *vi*
transpirieren

**transplant** [trans•PLANT] *vt*
versetzen

**transport** [TRANS•port] *vt*
transportieren

**transpose** [trans•POZ] *vt*
umstellen

**transverse** [trans•VURZ] *adj*
diagonal

**trap** *n* Falle F; *vt* fangen

**trap-door** [TRAP•DOR] *n*
Klapptür F

**trapeze** [tra•PEEZ] *n* Trapez N

**trappings** [TRAP•pings] *n*
Staatsgeschirr N

**trash** *npl* Abfälle M

**travel** [TRA•vul] *vi* (journey)
reisen; (route) fahren

**travel agency** [TRA•vul
AI•jen•cee] *n* Reisebüro N

**traveler** [TRA•vuh•lur] *n*
Reisender M

**traveling** [TRA•vuh•ling] Reise

**traverse** [tra•VURZ] *vt*
überqueren

**travesty** [TRA•ve•stee] *n*
Travestie F

**tray** [trai] *n* Servierbrett N

**treacherous** [TRE•chur•us] *adj*
verräterisch

**treachery** [TRE•chur•ree] *n*
Verrat M

**tread** [tred] *n* Tritt M

**treason** [TREE•zun] *n*
Verrat M

**treasure** [TRE•shur] *n*
Schatz M

**treasurer** [TRE•shuh•ur] *n*
Finanzabteilung F

**treasury** [TRE•shuh•ree] *n*
Schatzkammer F

**treat** [treet] *vt* behandeln; *n*
besondere Freude

**treatise** (dissertation; essay)
[TREE•tis] *n* Abhandlung F

**treatment** [TREET•mint] *n*
Handlung F

**treaty** [TREE•tee] *n* Vertrag M

**treble** [TRE•bl] dreifach

**treble clef** *n* Diskant M

**treble voice** [TRE•bl VOIS]
Sopran

**tree** *n* Baum M; (family)
Stamm M

**trefoil** [TREE•foil] *n* Klee M

**trellis** [TRE•lis] *n* Gitter N

**tremble** [TREM•bl] *vi* erzittern

**tremendous** [tre•MEN•dus] *adj*
gewaltig

**tremor** [TRE•mur] *n* Zittern N

**tremulous** [TRE•myu•lus] *adj*
žitternd

**trench** *n* Graben M

**trench coat** [TRENCH KOT] *n*
Wettermantel M

**trend** *n* Tendenz F

**trespass** [TRES•pas] *n*
Übertretung F

**trespasser** [TRES•pa•sur] *n*
Unbefugter M

**tress** [tres] *n* Zopf M

**trestle** [TRE•sl] *n* Gestell N

**trial** [truyl] *n* Versuch M

**triangle** [TRUY•an•gl] *n*
Dreieck N

**tribe** [truyb] *n* Volksstamm M

**tribulation** [TRI•byu•LAI•shn]
*n* Leiden N

**tribunal** [truy•BYOO•nl] *n*
Gerichtshof M

**tribune** [TRI•byoon] *n* Tribun M

**tributary** [TRI•byoo•TAI•ree] *n*
Nebenfluß M

**trick** [trik] *n* Trick M; *vt*
hereinlegen

**trickery** [TRIK•ree] *n*
Gaunerei F

**trickle** [TRIK•kl] *vi* tröpfeln

**tricky** [TRIK•kee] *adj* heikel

**trifle** [TRUY•fl] *n* Kleinigkeit F

**trigger** [TRI•gur] *n* Auslöser M

**trill** [tril] *vt* trillern

**trim** *adj* beschneiden

**trinket** [TRINK•kit] *n*
Schmuck M

**trio** [TREE•o] *n* Trio N

**trip** *n* Reise F

**triple** [TRIP•pl] *adj* dreifach

**tripod** [TRUY•pod] *n*
Dreifuß M

**trite** [truyt] *adj* banal

**triumph** [TRUY•uhmf] *n*
Sieg M

**triumphant** [truy•UHM•fint]
*adj* erfolgreich

**triumphantly**
[truy•UHM•fint•lee] *adj*
jubelnd

**trivial** [TRI•vee•ul] *adj*
alltäglich

**trolley** [TRAH•lee] *n*
Straßenbahnwagen M

**trombone** [trahm•BON] *n*
Posaune F

**troop** *n* Trupp M

**trooper** [TROOP•pur] *n*
Polizist M

**trophy** [TRO•fee] *n* Trophäe F

**tropic** [TRAH•pik] *adj* tropisch

**tropics** [TRAH•pik] *npl*
Tropen M

**trot** [traht] *vi* trotten

**trot** *n* Trott M

**trouble** [TRUH•bl] *n*
Belästigung F

**trouble maker** [TRUH•bl
MAI•kur] *n* Unruhestifter M

**trouble shooter** [TRUH•bl
SHOO•tur] *n*
Störungssucher M

**troublesome** [TRUH•bl•suhm]
*adj* beschwerlich

**trough** [trahf] *n* Mulde F

**trousers** [TROU•zurz] *n* Hose F

**trousseau** [TROO•so] *n*
Aussteuer F

**trowel** [TROU•wl] *n* Kelle F

**truant** [TROO•int] *n*
Faulenzer M

**truce** [troos] *n* Waffenruhe F

**truck** [truhk] *n* Güterwagen M;
*vt* transportieren

**trudge** [truhj] *vt* fortschleppen

**true** [troo] *adj* wahr; (acurate)
warheitsgetreu (faithful) treu;
come ~\ wahr weden

**truly** [TROO•lee] *adj* wirklich

**trump** [truhmp] *vt* erdichten

**trumpet** [TRUHM•pit] *n*
Trompete F

**trunk** [truhnk] *n* Koffer M

**truss** [truhs] *n* Bündel N

**trust** [truhst] *vt* vertrauen; *n*
Vertrauen N; (company)
Trust M

**trustee** [truh•STEE] *n*
Verwalter M

**trustworthy**
[TRUHST•wur•thee] *adj*
vertrauenswürdig

**trusty** [TRUH•stee] *adj*
zuverlässig

**truth** [trooth] *n* Wahrheit F

**truthful** [TROOTH•fl] *adj* wahr

**truthfulness** [TROOTH•fl•nes]
*n* Wahrhaftigkeit F

**try** [truy] *vt* versuchen; *n*
Versuch M

**trying** [TRUY•ying] *adj*
schwierig

**tub** [tuhb] *n* Wanne F

**tube** [toob] *n* rohr N

**tubercular** [too•BUR•kyu•lur]
*adj* tuberkulös

**tuberculosis**
[too•BUR•kyu•LO•sis] *n*
Tuberkulose F

**tubing** [TOO•bing] *n* Rohr N

**tuck** [tuk] *n* Falte F; *vt* stecken

**Tuesday** [TOOZ•dai] *n*
Dienstag M

**tuft** [tuhft] *n* Schopf M

**tug** [tuhg] *vt* zerren

**tuition** [TOO•i•shn] *n*
Schulgeld N

**tulip** [TOO•lip] *n* Tulpe F

**tulle** [tool] *n* Tüll M

**tumble** [TUHM•bl] *n* Sturtz M

**tumbler** [TUHM•blur] *n*
Becher M

**tumor** [TOO•mur] *n* Tumor M

**tumult** [TUH•muhlt] *n*
Getöse N

**tumultuous**
[too•MUHL•choo•us] *adj*
lärmend

**tun** *n* Tonne F

**tuna** [TOO•nuh] *n* Thunfisch M

**tune** [toon] *n* Melodie F; *vt*
(~up) stimmen; ~ in\
eintschalten

**tunic** [TOO•nik] *n* Bluse F

**tuning** [TOO•ning] Stimm

**tunnel** [TUH•nuhl] *n* Tunnel M

**turbid** [TUR•bid] *adj*
dickflüssig

**turbine** [TUR•buyn] *n*
Turbine F

**turbulent** [tur•BYU•lint] *adj*
unruhig

**turf** *n* Rasen M

**turgid** [TUR•jid] *adj*
aufgedunsen

**Turk** *n* Türke M

**turkey** [TUR•kee] *n*
Truthahn M

**Turkey** [TUR•kee] *n* die Türkei

**Turkish** *adj* türkisch

**turmoil** [TUR•moil] *n* Unruhe F

**turn** N Kurve F; *vt* drehen; *vi*
sich drenehn; (change
direction) abbiegen

**turn against** *vi* sich wenden
gegen

**turn around (face)** sich
umdrehen

**turn down** (heat etc)
herunterdrehen; (offer)
züruckweisen

**turn up** (arrive) erscheinen
**turnip** n Rübe F
**turnover** [TUR•NO•vur] vt
umsetzen
**turntable** [TURN•TAI•bl] n
Plattenteller M
**turpentine** [TUR•pin•TUYN] n
Terpentin N
**turpitude** [TUR•pi•TOOD] n
Verworfenheit F
**turquoise** [TUR•koiz] n
Türkis M
**turret** [TUR•rit] n Türmchen N
**turtle** [TUR•tl] n Schildkröte F
**tusk** [tuhsk] n Fangzahn M
**tutor** [TOO•tur] n
Privatlehrer M
**tuxedo** [tuk•SEE•do] n
Smoking M
**twang** n Schwirren N
**tweed** n Tweed M
**tweezers** [TWEE•zurz] npl
Pinzette
**twelfth** num zwölfte
**twelve** [twelv] zwölf
**twentieth** [TWEN•tee•ith] num
zwanzigste
**twenty** [TWEN•tee] zwanzig
**twice** [twuys] zweimal
**twig** n Zweig M
**twilight** [TWUY•luyt] n
Dämmerung F
**twin** n Zwilling M

**twine** [twuyn] n Bindfaden M
**twinge** [twinj] n Zwicken N
**twinkle** [TWINK•kl] n
Glitzern N
**twinkling** [TWINK•kling] n
Blinken N
**twirl** vt herumwirbeln
**twist** vt drehen
**twitch** vt zupfen
**twitter** [TWI•tur] vi zwitschern
**two** [too] num zwei
**tympani** [TIM•puh•nee] n
Trommelfell M
**type** [tuyp] n Typ M
**typewriter** [TUYP•RUY•tur] n
Schreibmaschine F
**typhoid** [TUY•foyd] adj typhös
**typhoon** [tuy•FOON] n
Taifun M
**typhus** [TUY•fus] n
Flecktyphus M
**typical** [TI•pi•kl] adj typisch
**typist** [TUY•pist] n
Maschinenschreiber M
**typography**
[tuy•PAH•gruh•fee] n
Buchdruckerkunst F
**tyrannical** [teer•RA•ni•kl] adj
tyrannisch
**tyranny** [TEER•ri•nee] n
Tyrannie F
**tyrant** [TUY•rent] n Tyrann M

# U

**udder** [UH•dur] n Euter N

**ugliness** [UH•glee•nes] n
Häßlichkeit F

**ugly** [UH•glee] *adj* häßlich

**ulcer** [UHL•sur] *n*
Geschwür N

**ulceration** [UHL•sur•RAI•shn]
*n* Geschwürbildung F

**ulterior** [uhl•TEE•ree•ur] *adj*
anderweitig

**ultimate** [UHL•ti•mit] *adj*
äußerst

**ultimately** [UHL•ti•mit•lee] *adj*
schließlich

**umbilicus** [uhm•BI•li•kus] *n*
Nabel M

**umbrage** [UHM•brij] *n*
Anstoß M

**umbrella** [uhm•BREL•luh] *n*
Schirm M

**umpire** [UHM•puyr] *n*
Schiedsrichter M

**un-** [uhn] un

**unable** [uhn•AI•bl] *adj* unfähig

**unaccountable**
[UHN•a•KOUN•tuh•bl] *adj*
nicht verantwortlich

**unaccustomed**
[UHN•a•KUH•stumd] *adj*
ungewohnt

**unacknowledged**
[UHN•ak•NAH•lejd] *adj* nicht
anerkannt

**unaffected** [UHN•a•FEK•ted]
*adj* ungekünstelt

**unanimity**
[YOO•nuh•NI•mi•tee] *n*
Einstimmigkeit F

**unanimous** [yoo•NA•ni•mus]
*adj* einstimmig

**unapproachable**
[UHN•a•PRO•chuh•bl] *adj*
unnahbar

**unarmed** [uhn•ARMD] *adj*
unbewaffnet

**unassailable**
[UHN•a•SAIL•luh•bl] *adj*
unangreifbar

**unassuming**
[UHN•uh•SOO•ming] *adj*
anspruchslos

**unattractive**
[UHN•uh•TRAK•tiv] *adj*
reizlos

**unavailable**
[UHN•uh•VAI•luh•bl] *adj*
nicht verfügbar

**unavoidable**
[UHN•uh•VOI•duh•bl] *adj*
unvermeidlich

**unaware** [UHN•uh•WAIR]
nicht bewußt sein

**unawares** [UHN•uh•WAIRZ]
*adj* versehentlich

**unbalanced** [uhn•BAL•enzd]
aus dem Gleichgewicht
gebracht

**unbearable** [uhn•BAI•ruh•bl]
*adj* unerträglich

**unbecoming**
[UHN•bee•KUH•ming] *adj*
unpassend

**unbelievable**
[UHN•bee•LEE•vuh•bl] *adj*
unglaublich

**unbeliever** [UHN•bee•LEE•vur]
*n* Ungläubiger M

**unbelieving**
[UHN•bee•LEE•ving] *adj*
ungläubig

**unbending** [uhn•BEN•ding] *adj*
unbiegsam

**unbiased** [uhn•BUY•esd] *adj*
unbeeinflußt

**unbounded** [uhn•BOUN•ded]
*adj* unbegrenzt

**unbreakable**
[uhn•BRAI•kuh•bl] *adj*
unzerbrechlich

**unbroken** [uhn•BRO•ken] *adj*
ungebrochen

**unburden** [uhn•BUR•den] *vt*
entlasten

**unbutton** [uhn•BUH•ten] *vt*
aufknöpfen

**uncanny** [uhn•KA•nee] *adj*
unheimlich

**unceasing** [uhn•SEE•sing] *adj*
unaufhörlich

**uncertain** [uhn•SUR•ten] *adj*
unsicher

**unchangeable**
[uhn•CHAIN•juh•bl] *adj*
unveränderlich

**unchanged** [uhn•CHAINJD]
unverändert

**uncharted** [uhn•CHAHR•ted]
auf keiner Landkarte
verzeichnet

**uncivil** [uhn•SI•vil] *adj*
unhöflich

**unclaimed** [uhn•KLAI•med] *adj*
nicht beansprucht

**uncle** [UHN•kl] *n* Onkel M

**unclean** [uhn•KLEEN] *adj*
unrein

**uncomfortable**
[uhn•KUHM•faur•tuh•bl] *adj*
unbequem

**uncommon** [uhn•KAH•men]
*adj* ungewöhnlich

**uncompromising**
[uhn•KAHM•pro•MUY•zing]
*adj* kompromißlos

**unconcerned**
[uhn•KUHN•surnd] *adj*
uninteressiert

**unconditional**
[UHN•kun•DI•shuh•nl] *adj*
unbedingt

**unconquered**
[uhn•KAHN•kurd] *adj*
unbesiegt

**unconscious** [uhn•KAHN•shus]
*adj* unbewußt

**unconsciousness**
[uhn•KAHN•shus•nes] *n*
Unbewußtheit F

**uncontrollable**
[UHN•kuhn•TRO•luh•bl] *adj*
unkontrollierbar

**uncontrolled**
[UHN•kuhn•TROLD] *adj*
unbeaufsichtigt

**unconventional**
[UHN•kuhn•VEN•shuh•nl] *adj*
unkonventionell

**uncork** [uhn•KAURK] *vt*
entkorken

**uncouth** [uhn•KOOTH] *adj*
grob

**uncover** [uhn•KUH•vur] *vt*
aufdecken

**unction** [UHNK•shun] *n*
Salbung F

**unctuous** [UHNK•shus] *adj*
ölig

**uncultured** [uhn•KUL•churd]
*adj* unkultiviert

**undeceive** [UHN•dee•SEEV]
die Augen öffnen

**undecided**
[UHN•dee•SUY•ded] *adj*
unentschieden

**undeniable**
[UHN•dee•NUY•uh•bl] *adj*
unbestreitbar

**under** [UHN•dur] *prep* unter

**underbrush**
[UHN•dur•BRUSH] *n*
Gesträuch N

**undercarriage**
[UHN•dur•KAI•rij] *n*
Fahrwerk N

**underclothes**
[UHN•dur•KLOTHZ] *n*
Unterkleidung F

**underestimate**
[UHN•dur•ES•ti•MAIT] *vt*
unterschätzen

**undergo** [UHN•dur•GO] *vt*
erleben

**undergraduate**
[UHN•dur•GRA•joo•wait] *n*
Student -in M

**underground**
[UHN•dur•GROUND] *adj*
untergrund

**underhanded**
[UHN•dur•HAN•ded] *adj*
heimlich

**underline** [UHN•dur•LUYN] *vt*
unterstreichen

**underlying**
[UHN•dur•LUY•ing] *adj*
darunterliegend

**undermine** [UHN•dur•MUYN]
*vt* unterminieren

**underneath** [uhn•dur•NEETH]
*prep* unter; unterhalb

**underpay** [UHN•dur•PAI]
·schlecht bezahlen

**undersell** [UHN•dur•SEL] *vt*
unterbieten

**undershirt** [UHN•dur•SHURT]
*n* Unterhemd N

**undersigned**
[UHN•dur•SUYND] *n*
Unterzeichneter M

**undersized** [UHN•dur•SUYZD]
unter Normalgröße

**understand**
[UHN•dur•STAND] *vi*
verstehen

**understandable**
[UHN•dur•STAN•duh•bl] *adj*
verständlich

**understanding**
[UHN•dur•STAN•ding] *n*
Verstand M

**understate** [UHN•dur•STAIT]
*vt* abschwächen

**understudy**
[UHN•dur•STUH•dee] *n*
Ersatzmann M

**undertake** [uhn•dur•TAIK] *vt*
unternehmen

**undertaken** [uhn•dur•TAI•ken]
*pp* untergenommen

**undertaker** [UHN•dur•TAI•kur]
*n* Leichenbestatter M

**undertaking**
[UHN•dur•TAI•king] *n*
Unternehmen N

**undertow** [UHN•dur•TO] *n*
Widersee F

**underwear** [UHN•dur•WAIR]
*n* Unterhose F

**underworld**
[UHN•dur•WURLD] *n*
Unterwelt F

**underwrite** [UHN•dur•RUYT]
*vt* versichern

**undeviating**
[UHN•DEE•vee•AI•ting] *adj*
unentwegt

**undiscriminating**
[UHN•di•SKRI•mi•NAI•ting]
*adj* unterschiedslos

**undistinguished**
[UHN•di•STIN•gwishd] *adj*
undeutlich

**undisturbed**
[UHN•di•STURBD] *adj*
ungestört

**undo** [uhn•DO] *vt* aufmachen

**undress** [uhn•DRES] *vi vt* sich
entkleiden

**undue** [uhn•DOO] *adj*
übermäßig

**undulate** [UHN•joo•LAIT] *vi*
wogen

**undying** [uhn•DUY•ing] *adj*
unsterblich

**unearned** [uhn•URN•ed] *adj*
unverdient

**unearth** [uhn•URTH] *vt*
ausgraben

**uneasy** [uhn•EE•zee] *adj*
unruhig

**uneducated**
[uhn•ED•joo•KAI•ted] *adj*
ungebildet

**unemployed**
[UHN•em•PLOID] *adj*
arbeitslos

**unemployment**
[UHN•em•PLOI•ment] *n*
Arbeitslosigkeit F

**unending** [uhn•EN•ding] *adj*
endlos

**unequal** [uhn•EE•kwel] *adj*
ungleich

**uneven** [uhn•EE•ven] *adj*
uneben; (line) ungerade;
(pulse) unreglmäßig

**unexpected**
[UHN•ek•SPEK•tid] *adj*
unerwartet

**unfair** [uhn•FAIR] *adj* unfair;
ungerecht

**unfaithful** [uhn•FAITH•ful] *adj*
untreu; treulos

**unfasten** [uhn•FAS•sin] *vt*
aufmachen

**unfinished** [uhn•FIN•ishd] *adj*
unfertig; unvollendet;
(business) unerledigt

**unfit** [uhn•FIT] *adj* ungeeignet;
untauglich

**unfold** [uhn•FAULD] *vt*
auseinanderfalten (story); sich
abwickeln

**unfortunate**
[uhn•FAUR•tchoo•net] *adj*
unglücklich; (person)
glücklos; (day; event)
unglückselig

**unfriendly** [uhn•FREND•lee]
*adj* unfreundlich

**ungrateful** [uhn•GRAIT•ful]
*adj* undankbar

**unhappy** [uhn•HA•pee] *adj*
unglücklich; traurig

**unhappiness** [uhn•HA•pee•nes]
*n* Traurigkeit F

**unhealthy** [uhn•HEL•thee] *adj*
(person) nicht gesund;
(interest) krankhaft

**unicorn** [YOO•nee•KAURN] *n*
Einhorn N

**unidentified**
[UHN•uh•DEN•ti•FUYD] *adj*
unbekannt

**uniform** [YOO•ni•FAURM] *adj*
einheitlich; *n* Uniform M

**unimportant**
[UHN•im•PAUR•tant] *adj*
unwichtig
**uninterested**
[uhn•IN•ter•ehs•tid] *adj*
intersselos
**union** [YOO•nyuhn] *n*
Vereinigung F
**unique** [yoo•NEEK] *adj* einzig
**unison** [YOO•ni•suhn] *n*
Gleichklang; Einklang M in
~\ unisono; einstimmig
**unit** [YOO•nit] *n* Einheit F;
(math) Einer M
**unite** [yoo•NUYT] *vt* verbinden;
*vi* sich zusammenschließen
**United Kingdom** *n* Vereinigtes
Königreich M
**United Nations** *npl* Vereinte
Nationen F
**United States** *npl* Vereinigte
Statten M
**universe** [YOO•ni•VERS] *n*
Universum N
**universal** [YOO•nee•VER•sal]
*adj* universal; universell
**university**
[YOO•nee•VER•si•tee] *n*
Universität F; *adj*
Universitäts-
**unjust** [uhn•JUHST] *adj*
ungerecht
**unkind** [uhn•KUYND]
adjunfreundlich; lieblos;
gemein; spitz
**unkindess** [uhn•KUYND•nes] *n*
Unfrendlichkeit F
**unknown** [uhn•NOHN] *adj*
unbekannt
**unless** [uhn•LES] *conj* es sei
denn

**unlike** [uhn•LUYK] *adj*
unähnlich; *prep* in Gegesatz
zu
**unlikely** [uhn•LUYK•lee] *adj*
unwahrscheinlich;
unglaubwürdig
**unlimited** [uhn•LIM•i•tud] ad
unbegrenzt; schrankenlos;
(patience) unendlich
**unload** [uhn•LOHD] *vt*
entladen; ausladen; abladen
(cargo) löschen
**unlock** [uhn•LAHK] *vt*
aufschließen
**unlucky** [uhn•LUH•kee] *adj*
unglückselig; to be ~\ Pech
haben
**unmarried** [uhn•MA•reed] *adj*
unverheiratet; ~ mother\
ledige Mutter
**unnatural** [uhn•NA•chur•el] *adj*
unnatürlich
**unnecessary**
[uhn•NE•si•SAI•ree] *adj*
unnötig
**unnoticed** [uhn•NOH•tisd] ad
unbermerkt; to be ~\
unbermerkt bleiben
**unoccupied**
[uhn•AH•kyoo•PUYD] *adj*
unberschäftigt; (place)
unbewohnt; (seat) frei
**unofficial** [uhn•oh•FI•shul] *adj*
inoffiziell
**unpack** [uhn•PAK] *vt vi*
auspacken
**unpaid** [uhn•PAID] *adj*
unbezahlt
**unpleasant** [uhn•PLEH•zunt]
*adj* unangenehm; (person,
remark) unfreundlich

**unpopular** [uhn•PAH•pyoo•lur]
*adj* unbeliebt; (decision)
unpopulär

**unpredictable**
[uhn•pree•DIK•tuh•bul] *adj*
unvorhersehbar

**unqualifed**
[uhn•KWAH•li•FUYD] *adj*
unqualifiziert; (absolute)
uneingeschränkt

**unravel** [uhn•RA•vul] *vi*
afuziehen; entwirren;
(mystery) lösen

**unrealistic**
[uhn•REE•uh•LIS•tik] *adj*
unrealistich

**unreasonable**
[uhn•REE•sohn•uh•bl]
adjüberstreiben; (person)
uneinsichtig; to be ~ about\
kein Verständnis für etwas
zeigen

**unsuccessful**
[UHN•suhk•SES•fl] *adj*
unerfolgreich

**unsuitable** [uhn•SOO•tuh•bl]
*adj* unpassend

**unsuspected**
[UHN•suh•SPEK•ted] *adj*
unverdächtigt

**unsuspecting**
[UHN•suh•SPEK•ting] *adj*
ahnungslos

**unthinkable**
[uhn•THING•kuh•bl] *adj*
undenkbar

**unthinking** [uhn•THING•king]
*adj* gedankenlos

**untidiness** [uhn•TUY•dee•nes]
*n* Unordentlichkeit F

**untie** [uhn•TUY] *vt* aufknoten

**until** [uhn•TIL] *prep* bis

**untimely** [uhn•TUYM•lee] *adj*
unzeitig

**untiring** [uhn•TUYR•ring] *adj*
unermüdlich

**unto** [UHN•too] *prep* zu

**untold** [uhn•TOLD] *adj*
unerzählt

**untouched** [uhn•TUCHD] *adj*
unberührt

**untrained** [uhn•TRAIND] *adj*
ungeschult

**untried** [uhn•TRUYD] *adj*
unerprobt

**untroubled** [uhn•TRUH•bld]
*adj* ungestört

**untrue** [uhn•TROO] *adj* falsch

**unused** [uhn•YOOSD] *adj*
unbenutzt

**unveil** [uhn•VAIUL] *vt*
entschleiern

**unwarranted**
[uhn•WAH•ren•ted] *adj*
ungerechtfertigt

**unwary** [uhn•WAI•ree] *adj*
unvorsichtig

**unwashed** [uhn•WASHD] *adj*
ungewaschen

**unwelcome** [uhn•WEL•kom]
*adj* unwillkommen

**unwholesome** [uhn•HOL•sum]
*adj* ungesund

**unwieldy** [uhn•WEEL•dee] *adj*
schwerfällig

**unwilling** [uhn•WIL•ling] *adj*
widerwillig

**unwillingness**
[uhn•WIL•ling•nes] *n*
Widerwille M

**unwind** [uhn•WUYND] *vt*
loswicklen

**unwise** [uhn•WUYZ] *adj*
unklug

**unworthy** [uhn•WUR•thee] *adj*
unwürdig

**unwrap** [uhn•RAP] *vt*
auswickeln

**unyielding** [uhn•YEEL•ding]
*adj* nicht nachgeben

**up** [uhp] nach oben auf

**up-to-date** [UHP•too•DAIT]
*adj* modern

**upbraid** [uhp•BRAID] *vt*
Vorwürfe machen

**upgrade** [UHP•gräid] *n*
Steigung F

**upheaval** [uhp•HEE•vul] *n*
Erhebung

**uphill** [UHP•hil] *adj* bergauf

**uphold** [uhp•HOLD] *vt*
hochhalten

**upholster** [uh•POL•stur] *vt*
auspolstern

**upholstery** [uh•POL•stree] *npl*
Polsterwaren

**upkeep** [UHP•keep] *n*
Instandhaltung F

**uplift** [uhp•LIFT] *vt*
emporheben

**upon** [uh•PAHN] *prep* darauf

**upper** [UH•pur] *adj* ober

**upright** [UHP•ruyt] *adj*
aufsenkrecht

**uprising** [UHP•ruy•zing] *n*
Aufstehen N

**uproar** [UHP•ror] *n* Aufruhr M.

**upset** [uhp•SET] *vt* umstoßen

**upshot** [UHP•shot] *n* Ende N

**upside** [UHP•suyd] *n*
Oberseite F

**upstairs** [uhp•STAIRZ] die
Treppe hinauf

**upstart** [UHP•start] *n*
Emporkömmling M

**upward** [UHP•wurd] *adv*
aufwärts

**uranium** [yur•AI•nee•um] *n*
Uran N

**urban** [UR•bin] *adj* städtisch

**urchin** [UR•chin] *n* Balg M

**urge** [urj] *vt* anspornen

**urgency** [UR•jen•see] *n*
Dringlichkeit F

**urgent** [UR•jent] *adj* dringend

**urgently** [UR•jent•lee] *adv*
dringend

**urinate** [YUR•in•NAIT] *vi*
urinieren

**urine** [YUR•rin] *n* Urin M

**urn** *n* Urne F

**us** [uhs] *per pron* uns

**usage** [YOO•sej] *n* Brauch M

**use** [yooz] *n vt* Gebrauch
gebrauchen M

**used car** [YOOZD KAHR] *n*
Gebrauchwagen M

**used up** [YOOZD UHP] *adj*
ausgebraucht

**useful** [YOOS•ful] *adj* nützlich

**usefulness** [YOOS•ful•ness] *n*
Nützlichkeit F

**useless** [YOOS•les] *adj*
vergeblich

**uselessness** [YOOS•les•nes] *n*
Zwecklosigkeit F

**usher** [UH•shur] *n*
Platzanweiser M

**usual** [YOO•shoo•ul] *adj*
gewöhnlich

**usually** [YOO•shoo•lee] *adv*
üblich

**usurer** [YOO•zoo•rur] *n*
Wucherer M

**usurp** [yoo•SURP] *vt* sich
bemächtigen
**usury** [YOO•zur•ee] *n*
Wucher M
**utensil** [yoo•TEN•sul] *n*
Gerät N
**utility** [yoo•TI•li•tee] *n*
Nutzen N

**utilize** [YOO•ti•LUYZ] *vt*
verwenden
**utmost** [UHT•most] *adj* äußerst
**utter** [UHT•tur] *vi* äußern
**utterance** [UHT•tur•anz] *n*
Ausdruck M
**uvula** [YOO•vyu•luh] *n*
Zäpfchen N

# V

**vacancy** [VAI•ken•see] *n* freier
Platz M
**vacant** [VAI•kint] *adj* leer
**vacate** [VAI•kait] *vi* räumen
**vacation** [vai•KAI•shn] *n*
Urlaub M
**vaccinate** [VAK•zin•NAIT] *vt*
impfen
**vaccine** [vak•SEEN] Impf
**vacillate** [VA•sil•LAIT] *vi*
schwanken
**vacuum** [VA•kyum] *n*
Staubsauger M
**vagabond** [VA•guh•BAUND] *n*
Vagabund M
**vague** [vaig] *adj* undeutlich
**vain** *adj* eitel; in ~\ umsonst
**vainly** [VAIN•lee] *adv*
bergeblich; vergebens
**valentine** [VA•len•TUYN] *n*
Valentinsgruß M
**valet** [va•LAI] *n*
Kammerdiener M
**valiant** [VA•lee•ent] *adj* tapfer
**valid** [VA•lid] *adj* gültig
**validity** [va•LI•di•tee] *n*
Gültigkeit F

**valise** [va•LEES] *n*
Reisetasche F
**valley** [VAL•lee] *n* Tal N
**valor** [VA•lor] *n* Tapferkeit F
**valorous** [VA•lo•rus] *adj* mutig
**valuable** [VAL•yoo•bl] *adj*
wertvoll
**value 1** [VAL•yoo] *n* Wert M
**value 2** (market) *n*
Handelswert M
**valve** *n* Ventil N
**van** *n* Lastwagen M
**vane** [vain] *n* Wetterfahne F
**vanilla** [vuh•NIL•luh] *n*
Vanille F
**vanish** [VA•nish] *vi*
verschwinden
**vanity** [VA•ni•tee] *n* Eitelkeit F
**vanquish** [VAN•kwish] *vt*
besigen
**vantage** [VAN•tij] *n* Vorteil M
**vapid** [VA•pid] *adj* schal
**vapor** [VAI•por] *n* Dampf M
**vaporize** [VAI•po•RUYZ] *vt*
eindampfen
**variable** [VAIR•ree•uh•bl] *adj*
veränderlich

**variance** [VAIR•ree•ens] n
Abweichung F

**variation** [VAIR•ree•AI•shn] n
Veränderung F

**varied** [VAIR•reed] adj
verschieden

**variegated** [VAI•re•GAI•ted]
adj schekkig

**variety** [vuh•RUY•i•tee] n
Mannigfaltigkeit F

**various** [VAIR•ee•us] adj
verschieden

**varnish** [VAR•nish] n Lack M

**vary** [VAIR•ree] vt verändern

**vase** [vaiz] n Vase F

**vast** adj weit

**vastness** [VAST•nis] n Weite F

**vat** n Faß N

**vaudeville** [VAUD•vil] n
Variete N

**vault** n Gewölbe N; vi springen

**vaunt** vt vi sich rühmen

**veal** [veel] n Kalbfleisch N

**veer** vi umdrehen

**vegetable** [VE•je•tuh•bl] n
Gemüse F

**vegetarian** [VE•je•TAI•ree•en]
n Vegetarier in M

**vegetate** [VE•je•TAIT] vi
wachsen

**vegetation** [VE•je•TAI•shn] n
Pflanzenwelt F

**vehemence** [VEE•him•menz] n
Heftigkeit F

**vehicle** [VEE•hi•kl] n
Fahrzeug N

**veil** [vail] n Schleier M

**vein** [vain] n Vene; Ader F

**velocity** [ve•LAH•si•tee] n
Geschwindigkeit F

**velvet** [VEL•vit] n Samt M

**vendor** [VEN•dur] n
Verkäufer M

**vendor** (street) n Verkäufer M

**veneer** [vuh•NEER] n
Furnierholz N

**venerable** [VE•nur•uh•bl] adj
ehrwürdig

**venerate** [VE•nur•RAIT] vt
verehren

**veneration** [VE•nur•RAI•shn]
n Verehrung F

**vengeance** [VEN•jenz] n
Rache F

**venison** [VE•ni•sun] n
Wildbret N

**venom** [VE•nuhm] n Gift N

**venomous** [VE•nuh•mus] adj
giftig

**vent** n Luftloch N

**ventilate** [VEN•ti•LAIT] vt
belüften

**ventilation** [VEN•ti•LAI•shn] n
Belüftung F

**ventilator** [VEN•ti•LAI•tur] n
Entlüfter M

**venture 1** [VEN•chur] n
Risiko N

**venture 2** (business) n
Unternehmung F

**venue** [VEN•yoo] n Gerichtsort;
Platz M

**verandah** [vur•AN•duh] n
Veranda F

**verb** [vurb] n Verbum N

**verbal** [VER•bul] adj mündlich

**verbose** [vur•BOS] adj
wortreich

**verdict** [VUR•dikt] n
Urteilsspruch M

**verge** [vurj] n Rand M

**verification**
[VAI•ri•fi•KAI•shn] *n*
Nachprüfung F

**verify** [VAI•ri•FUY] *vt*
nachprüfen

**veritable** [VAI•rih•ti•bl] *adj*
echt

**vermin** [VUR•min] *n*
Ungeziefer N

**vernacular** [vur•NAK•kyu•lur]
*adj* mundartlich

**verse** [vurs] *n* Vers M

**versed** [vursd] *adj* versiert

**version** [VUR•shin] *n*
Fassung F

**vertebra** [VUR•ti•bruh] *n*
Wirbel M

**vertical** [VUR•ti•kl] *adj* lotrecht

**vertigo** [VUR•ti•GO] *n*
Schwindelgefühl N

**very** [VAIR•ree] *adv* sehr

**vespers** [VE•spurz] *n*
Abendstern M

**vessel** [VE•sul] *n* Schiff N

**vest** *n* Weste F

**vestibule** [VE•sti•BYUL] *n*
Vestibül N

**vestige** [VE•stij] *n* Spur F

**vestigial** [ve•STI•jul] *adj*
rudimentär

**vestment** [VEST•ment] *n*
Amtstracht F

**vestry** [VES•stree] *n* Sakristei F

**veteran** [VE•tur•rin] *n*
Veteran M

**veterinarian**
[VE•tur•NAI•ree•en] *n*
Tierarzt M

**veterinary** [VE•tur•NAI•ree]
*adj* tierärztlich

**veto** [VEE•to] *n* Veto N

**vex** [veks] *vt* bedrücken

**via** [VEE•yuh] *prep* über

**viaduct** [VUY•uh•DUKT] *n*
Viadukt M

**vial** [vuyl] *n* Fläschchen N

**viands** [VEE•endz] *n*
Lebensmittel N

**viaticum** [vee•A•ti•kum] bei der
letzten Ölung gereichte
Eucharistie

**vibrate** [VUY•brait] *vi* vibrieren

**vibration** [vuy•BRAI•shn] *n*
Vibrieren N

**vice** [vuys] *n* Untugend F

**vice** (tool) [vuys] *n*
Schraubstock M

**vicinity** [ve•SIN•i•tee] *n* Nähe F

**vicious** [VI•shus] *adj* bösartig

**victim** [VIK•tim] *n* Opfer N

**victor** [VIK•tor] *n* Sieger in M

**victorious** [vik•TAU•ree•us] *adj*
siegreich

**victory** [VIK•tree] *n* Sieg M

**victuals** [VIK•chulz] *npl*
Eßwaren

**vie** [vuy] *vi* wetteifern

**view 1** [vyoo] *n* Besichtigung;
Sicht F; (see) betrachen

**view 2** (bird's eye) *n*
Aussicht F

**vigil** [VI•jil] *n* Wachsein N

**vigilant** [VI•ji•lint] *adj*
wachsam

**vigor** [VI•gur] *n* Kraft

**vigorous** [VI•gur•us] *adj*
kraftvoll

**vile** [vuyl] *adj* gemein

**villa** [VI•luh] *n* Villa F

**village** [VI•lij] *n* Dorf N

**villager** [VI•li•jur] *n* Dörfler M

**villain** [VI•lin] *n* Schurke M

**villainous** [VI•lin•nis] *adj*
schurkisch
**villainy** [VI•lin•nee] *n*
Schurkerei F
**vim** *n* Schwung M
**vindicate** [VIN•di•KAIT] *vt*
verteidigen
**vindictive** [vin•DIK•tiv] *adj*
rachsüchtig
**vine** [vuyn] *n* Rebe F
**vinegar** [VI•ni•gur] *n* Essig M
**vineyard** [VIN•yurd] *n*
Weinberg M
**vintage** [VIN•tij] *n*
Weinlesezeit
**violate** [VUY•o•LAIT] *vt*
brechen
**violation** [VUY•o•LAI•shn] *n*
Bruch M
**violence** [VUY•o•lenz] *n*
Gewalt F
**violent** [VUY•o•lent] *adj*
gewaltig
**violet** [VUY•o•let] *n*
Veilchen N
**violin** [VUY•o•lin] *n* Violine F
**violinist** [VUY•o•LI•nist] *n*
Violinist M
**viper** [VUY•pur] *n* Viper F
**virgin** [VUR•jin] *n* Jungfrau F
**virginity** [vur•JI•ni•tee] *n*
Jungfernschaft F
**virile** [VEER•rl] *adj* männlich
**virility** [vur•RI•li•tee] *n*
Männlichkeit F
**virtual** [VUR•choo•ul] *adj*
tatsächlich
**virtually** [VUR•chuh•lee] *adj*
eigentlich
**virulence** [VEER•yoo•lenz] *n*
Virulenz F

**virus** [VUY•rus] *n* Virus N
**visa** [VEE•zuh] *n* Visum N
**visage** [VI•sej] *n* Antlitz N
**viscera** [VI•suh•ruh] *npl*
Eingeweide
**viscosity** [vi•SKAH•si•tee] *n*
Viskosität F
**visibility** [VI•si•bi•li•tee] *n*
Sichtbarkeit F
**visible** [VI•si•bl] *adj* sichtbar
**vision** [VI•shin] *n* Sehkraft F
**visionary** [VI•shin•NAI•ree] *adj*
visionär
**visit** [VI•zit] *n* Besuch M
**visitation** [VI•zi•TAI•shn] *n*
Besuchen N
**visitor** [VI•zi•tur] *n* Besucher
in M
**vista** [VI•stuh] *n* Blick M
**visual** [VI•shoo•ul] *adj* visuell
**visualize** [VI•shoo•LUYZ] *vt*
sich vergegenwärtigen
**vital** [VUY•tl] *adj* lebenswichtig
**vitality** [vuy•TA•li•tee] *n*
Vitalität F
**vitamin** [VUY•tuh•min] *n*
Vitamin N
**vitreous** [VI•tree•us] *adj*
glasartig
**vitriol** [VI•tree•ol] *n* Vitriol N
**vivacious** [vuy•VAI•shus] *adj*
lebhaft
**vivacity** [vuy•VA•si•tee] *n*
Lebhaftigkeit F
**vivid** [VI•vid] *adj* leuchtend
**vocabulary**
[vo•KA•byu•LAI•ree] *n*
Wörterverzeichnis N
**vocal** [VO•kul] *adj* stimmlich
**vocation** [vo•KAI•shn] *n*
Begabung F

**vogue** [vog] *n* Mode F
**voice** [vois] *n* Stimme F
**void** *adj* leer
**volatile** [VAH•li•tl] *adj*
vergänglich
**volcanic** [vol•KA•nik] *adj*
vulkanisch
**volcano** [vol•KAI•no] *n*
Vulkan M
**volley** [VAH•lee] *n*
Flugschlag M
**volt** *n* Volt N
**voltage** [VOL•tej] *n*
Spannung F
**volume** [VAHL•yoom] *n*
Volumen N
**voluntary** [VAH•lun•TAI•ree]
*adj* freiwillig
**volunteer** [VAH•lun•TEER] *n*
Freiwilliger in M
**voluptuous** [vuh•LUP•shus]
*adj* wollüstig

**vomit** [VAH•mit] *vt* erbrechen
**voracious** [vor•RAI•shus] *adj*
gierig
**vote** [vot] *n* Wahlstimme F; *vt*
*vi* wählen
**voter** [VO•tur] *n* Wähler M
**voting** [VO•ting] *n*
Abstimmung F
**vouch** *vi* bürgen
**voucher** [VOU•chur] *n*
Bürge M
**vow** [vou] *n* Schwur M
**vowel** [VOU•wul] *n* Vokal M
**voyage** [VOI•ij] *n* Flugreise F
**vulgar** [VUL•gur] *adj* ordinär
**vulgarity** [vul•GAI•ri•tee] *n*
Pöbelhaftigkeit F
**vulnerable** [VUHL•nur•uh•bl]
*adj* verwundbar
**vulture** [VUHL•chur] *n*
Geier M

# W

**wad** [wahd] *n* Bausch M
**waddle** [WAH•dl] *vi* watscheln
**wade** [waid] *vi* waten
**wafer** [WAI•fur] *n* Waffel F
**waffle** [WAH•fl] *n* Waffel F
**waft** [wahft] *vt* wehen
**wag** *vi* wackeln
**wage** [waij] *n* Lohn M
**wager** [WAI•jur] *vt* wetten
**wagon** [WAG•gin] *n* Wagen M
**waif** *n* verwahrlostes Kind N
**wail** *vi* jammern

**waist** *n* Taille F
**wait** *vi* warten; *n* Wartzeit F
**wait on** (serve) bedienen
**waiter** [WAI•tur] *n* Kellner M
**waiting** [WAI•ting] *n* Warten N
**waiting-room** *n*
Wartezimmer N
**waitress** [WAI•tres] *n*
Kellnerin F
**waive** [waiv] *vt* verzichten auf
**wake 1** [waik] *vi* erwachen
**wake 2** *n* (naut) Kielwasser N

**wake 3** *n* (over corpse)
Totenwache F
**waken** [WAI•kin] *vt* aufwecken
**walk** [wauk] *vi* spazieren
**wall** [waul] *n* Wand F
**walled** [wauld] *adj* eingemauert
**wallet** [WAU•lit] *n*
Brieftasche F
**wallflower**
[WAUL•FLOU•wur] *n*
Mauerblümchen N
**wallop** [WHAH•lop] *vt*
verdreschen
**wallow** [WHAH•lo] *vi* sich
wälzen
**wallpaper** [WAUL•PAI•pur] *n*
Tapete F
**walnut** [WAHL•nut] *n*
Walnuß F
**waltz** [wahlz] *n* Walzer M
**wan** *adj* bleich
**wand** *n* Zauberstab M
**wander** [WAN•dur] *vi* wandern
**wanderer** [WAN•dur•rur] *n*
Wanderer M
**wane** [wain] *vi* abnehmen
**want** [wahnt] *aux verb* wollen
**wanton** [WAHN•tin] *adj*
mutwillig
**war** [waur] *n* Krieg M
**warble** [WAUR•bl] *vt* trillern
**ward** [waurd] *n* Bezirk M
**warden** [WAUR•din] *n*
Wächter M
**wardrobe** [WAUR•drob] *n*
Garderobe F
**ware** [wair] *n* Waren
**warehouse** [WAIR•houz] *n*
Lagerhaus N
**warlike** [WAUR•luyk] *adj*
kriegerisch

**warm** [wahrm] *adj* warm
**warmth** *n* Wärme F
**warn** *vt* warnen
**warning** [WAUR•ning] *n*
Warnung F
**warp** [waurp] *vt* krümmen
**warped** [waurpt] *adj* verzogen
**warrant** [WAUR•rint] *n*
Vollmacht
**warrior** [WAUR•yur] *n*
Krieger M
**wart** [waurt] *n* Warze F
**wary** [WAIR•ree] *adj* vorsichtig
**wash** [wahsh] *vt* waschen
**washer** [WAHSH•ur] *n*
Wäscher M
**washing** [WAH•shing] *n*
Wäsche F
**washing-machine**
[WAH•shing muh•SHEEN] *n*
Waschmaschine F
**wasp** [wahsp] *n* Wespe F
**waste** [waist] *vt* verschwenden
**waste-paper basket**
[WAIST•PAI•pur BA•skit] *n*
Papierkorb M
**wasteful** [WAIST•fl] *adj*
kostspielig
**watch** [wahch] *vt n* beobachten
Armbanduhr F
**watchdog** [WAHCH•daug] *n*
Wachhund M
**watchman** [WAHCH•man] *n*
Nachtwächter M
**water** [WAH•tur] *n* Wasser N;
*vt* (garden) sprengen; *vi*
(mouth) wässern; (eye) tränen
**water sports** [WAH•tur
SPAURTS]
*n* Wassersport M

**watercolor** [WAH•tur KUH•lur] *n* Wasserfarbe F

**waterfall** [WAH•tur•FAL] *n* Wasserfall M

**waterproof** [WAH•tur•PROOF] *adj* wasserdicht

**watertight** [WAH•tur•TUYT] *adj* wasserdicht

**waterway** [WAH•tur•WAI] *n* Wasserstraße F

**watery** [WAH•tur•ree] *adj* wässerig

**wave** [waiv] *n* Welle F; *vt* winken mit; *vi* winken

**wavelength** [WAIV•length] *n* Wellenlänge F

**wavy** [WAIV•vee] *adj* wellig

**wax** [waks] *n* Wachs N

**way** [wai] *n* Weg M; (direction) Richtung F; (method) Art, Weise F; (respect) Hinsicht F; (state) Zustand M

**waylay** [WAI•lai] *vt* auflauern

**wayward** [WAI•wurd] *adj* launisch

**we** [wee] *pers pron* wir

**weak** [week] *adj* schwach

**weaken** [WEE•kin] *vt* schwächen

**weakly** [WEEK•lee] *adj* schwächlich

**wealth** [welth] *n* Reichtum M

**wealthy** [WEL•thee] *adj* reich

**wean** [ween] *vt* entwöhnen

**weapon** [WE•pun] *n* Waffe F

**wear** [wair] *vt* tragen

**weariness** [WEE•ree•ness] *n* Müdigkeit F

**wearisome** [WEE•ree•some] *adj* ermüdend

**weary** [WEE•ree] *adj* müde

**weasel** [WEE•zul] *n* Wiesel N

**weather** [WE•thur] *n* Wetter N

**weather conditions** [WE•thur kun•DI•shns] *n* Wetteraussicht F

**weave** [weev] *vt* weben

**web** *n* Gewebe

**webbing** [WEB•bing] *n* Gewebe N

**wed** *vt* vermählen

**wedded** [WED•ded] *adj* ehelich

**wedding** [WED•ding] *n* Hochzeit F

**wedge** [wej] *n* Keil M

**Wednesday** [WENS•dai] *n* Mittwoch M

**weed** *n* Unkraut N

**weedy** [WEE•dee] *adj* unkrautartig

**week** *n* Woche F

**weekday** [WEEK•dai] *n* Wochentag M

**weekly** [WEEK•lee] *adj* wöchentlich

**weep** *vi* weinen

**weeping** [WEE•ping] *adj* weinend

**weevil** [WEE•vul] *n* Rüsselkäfer M

**weigh** [wai] *vt* wiegen

**weight** [wait] *n* Gewicht

**weighty** [WAI•tee] *adj* schwerwiegend

**welcome** [WEL•kum] *n* Willkommen N

**weld** *vt* verschweißen

**welfare** [WEL•fair] *n* Wohlfahrt F

**well 1** [wel] *adj* gut; wohl; (good health) gesund; (as ~) auch

**well 2** *int* nun

**well 3** (oil) *n* Ölschacht M

**well-being** [WEL•BEE•ing] *n* Wohlgefühl N

**well-bred** [WEL•BRED] *adj* wohlerzogen

**well-to-do** [WEL•too•DOO] *adj* wohlhabend

**welt** *n* Schlag M

**werewolf** [WAIR•wolf] *n* Werwolf M

**west** *n* Westen M

**western** [WES•turn] *adj* westlich

**westerner** [WES•tur•nur] *n* Westländer M

**westward** [WEST•wurd] *adj* westwärts

**wet** *adj* naß

**whack** [wak] *vt* schlagen

**whale** [wail] *n* Wal M

**wharf** [warf] *n* Kai M

**what** [waht] *pron* int was; *adj* welche(r,s)

**whatever** [waht•EV•vur] alles was

**wheat** [weet] *n* Weizen M

**wheel** [weel] *n* Rad N; (push) schieben

**wheelbarrow** [WEEL•BAIR•ro] *n* Schubkarren M

**wheelchair** [WEEL•chair] *n* Rollstuhl M

**wheezy** [WEE•zee] *adj* keuchend

**when** [wen] *adv* wann; *conj* wenn

**whenever** [wen•EV•vur] wann

**where** [wair] *prep* wo; wohin

**whereabouts** [WAIR•uh•BOUTZ] wo ungefähr

**whereas** [wair•AS] *prep* während

**whereby** [wair•BUY] *prep* wodurch

**wherefore** [WAIR•for] *adv* weshalb

**wherever** [wair•EV•vur] wo auch immer

**wherewithal** [WAIR•with•AL] *n* Mittel N

**whet** [wet] *vt* wetzen

**whether** [WE•thur] ob; ~ or not\ ob oder nicht

**which** [wich] welch

**whichever** [wich•EV•vur] welch; auch immer

**whiff** [wif] *n* Hauch M

**while** [wuyl] *n* Weile; *adv conj* während

**whim** [wim] *n* Einfall M

**whimper** [WIM•pur] *vt* wimmern

**whimsical** [WIM•si•kl] *adj* grillenhaft

**whine** [wuyn] *vi* winseln

**whip** [wip] *n* Peitsche F; *vi* wiehern

**whipping** [WIP•ping] *n* Peitschen N

**whir** [wur] *vi* schwirren

**whirl** [wurl] *vi* wirbeln

**whirlpool** [WURL•pool] *n* Strudel M

**whirlwind** [WURL•wind] *n* Wirbelwind M

**whisk** [wisk] *vt* wischen; *n* Wischen N

**whisker** [WIS•kur] *n*
Barthaar N
**whiskey** [WIS•kee] *n*
Whisky M
**whisper** [WIS•pur] *vi* wispern
**whistle** [WIS•sl] *vi* pfeifen
**whit** [wit] bißchen
**white** [wuyt] weiß
**whiten** [WUY•tin] *vi* weiß
werden
**whiteness** [WUYT•nis] *n*
Weise F
**whitewash** [WUYT•wash] *n*
Tünche F
**Whitsuntide** [WIT•zun•tuyd] *n*
Pfingsten N
**whittle** [WIT•tl] *vt*
wegschnitzen
**whiz** [wiz] *vi* sausen
**who** [hoo] wer
**whole** [hol] *adj* ganz
**wholesale** [HOL•sail] *n*
Großhandel M
**wholesome** [HOL•sum] *adj*
gesund
**wholly** [HOL•lee] *adv* völlig
**whom** [hoom] wem; wen
**whomever** [hoom•EV•vur]
welchen
**whoop** [woop] *n* Geschrei N
**whore** [hor] *n* Hure F
**whose** [hooz] wessen
**why** [wuy] warum
**wick** [wik] *n* Docht M
**wicked** [WIK•kid] *adj* böse
**wickedness** [WIK•kid•nes] *n*
Bosheit F
**wicker** [WIK•kur] Weiden
**wicket** [WIK•kit] *n*
Drehkreuz N
**wide** [wuyd] *adj* breit

**wide awake** [WUYD
uh•WAIK] *adj* hellwach
**widely** [WUYD•lee] *adv* weit
**widespread** [WUYD•spred]
*adv* weit verstreut
**widow** [WI•do] *n* Witwe F
**widower** [WI•do•wur] *n*
Witwer M
**width** *n* Breite F
**wield** [weeld] *vt* ausüben
**wife** [wuyf] *n* Frau; Gattin F
**wig** *n* Perücke F
**wild** [wuyld] *adj* wild
**wile** [wuyl] *vt* verlocken
**will** [wil] *vi* werden; *vi* wollen;
*n* Wille M
**willful** [WIL•ful] *adj*
eigenwillig
**willing** [WIL•ling] *adj* gewillt
**willingly** [WIL•ling•lee] *adj*
bereitwillig gern
**willingness** [Wil•ling•nis] *n*
Bereitschaft F
**willow** [WIL•lo] *n* Weide F
**wilt** *vt* verwelken
**wily** [WUY•lee] *adj* listig
**win** *vt* gewinnen
**wince** [winz] *vt*
zusammenzucken
**winch** *n* Haspel M
**wind 1** [wind] *n* Wind M
**wind 2** [wuynd] *v* winden; sich
winden
**windfall** [WIND•fal] *n*
Windschlag M
**winding** [WUYN•ding] *n*
Winden N
**windmill** [WIND•mil] *n*
Windmühle F
**window** [WIN•do] *n* Fenster N

**window shade** [WIN•do SHAID] *n* Fensterladen M

**windowsill** [WIN•do•SIL] *n* Fensterscheibe F

**windshield** [WIND•sheeld] *n* Windschutzscheibe F

**windy** [WIN•dee] *adj* windig

**wine** [wuyn] *n* Wein M

**wine cellar** [WUYN SEL•lur] *n* Weinkeller M

**wineglass** [WUYN•glas] *n* Weinglas N

**wing** *n* Flügel M

**winged** [WING•gid] *adj* geflügelt

**wink** *vi* blinzeln

**winner** [WIN•ner] *n* Gewinner -in M

**winning** [WIN•ning] *adj* siegreich

**winter** [WIN•tur] *n* Winter M

**wintry** [WIN•tree] *adj* wintrig

**wipe** [wuyp] *vt* abwischen

**wiper** [WUY•pur] *n* Wischer M

**wire** [wuyr] *n* Draht

**wireless** [WUYR•les] *adj* drahtlos

**wiry** [WUYR•ree] *adj* drahtig

**wisdom** [WIZ•dom] *n* Weisheit F

**wise** [wuyz] *adj* weise

**wiseacre** [WUYZ•AI•kur] *n* Neunmalklug M

**wisecrack** [WUYZ•krak] *n* witzige Bermerkung F

**wish 1** *n* Wunsch M; *vi* wünschen

**wish 2** *vi* wünschen

**wistful** [WIST•ful] *adj* sehnsüchtig

**wit** *n* Verstand M

**witch** [wich] *n* Hexe F

**with** *prep* mit; (in company) bei

**withdraw** [with•DRAU] *vt* zurückziehen

**withdrawal** [with•DRAU•wul] *n* Zurückziehung F

**withdrawn** [with•DRAUN] *adj* zurückgezogen

**wither** [WITH•thur] *vi* verdorren

**withhold** [with•HOLD] *vt* zurückhalten

**within** [with•THIN] *prep* innerhalb von

**without** [with•THOUT] *prep* ohne

**withstand** [with•STAND] *vt* widerstehen

**witness** [WIT•nes] *n* Zeuge M

**witticism** [WIT•ti•CIZM] *n* Witz M

**witty** [WIT•tee] *adj* witzig

**wizard** [WIZ•zurd] *n* Zauberer M

**woe** [wo] *excl* wehe!; *n* Jammer M

**wolf** *n* Wolf M

**woman** [WUH•man] *n* Frau F; Weib N

**womanhood** [WUH•min•HUD] *n* Weiblichkeit F

**womanly** [WUH•min•lee] *adj* weiblich

**womb** [woom] *n* Gebärmutter F

**won** *pp* win gewann

**wonder** [WUN•dur] *n* Wunder n; *vi* sich verwundern

**wonderful** [WUN•dur•fl] *adj* wunderbar

**wonderfully**
[WUN•dur•ful•lee] *adv*
herrlich

**wont** [wahnt] *adj* gewohnt

**woo** *vt* locken

**wood** [wud] *n* Holz N

**woodland** [WUD•land] *n*
Waldland N

**woodpecker** [WUD•PEK•kur]
*n* Kolibri M

**woodwork** [WUD•wurk] *n*
Holzwerk N

**woodworker**
[WUD•WUR•kur] *n*
Holzarbeiter M

**wool** [wul] *n* (wool)
Schußgarn N

**woolen** [WUH•lin] *n*
Wollstoff M

**woolly** [WUH•lee] *adj* wollig

**word** [wurd] *n* Wort N

**wore** [wor] *pp* wear trug

**work** [wurk] *n* Arbeit F

**workday** [WURK•dai] *n*
Arbeitstag M

**worker** [WURK•ur] *n* Arbeiter
in M

**working** [WUR•king] *n*
Arbeiten N

**workman** [WURK•man] *n*
Facharbeiter M

**workmanship**
[WURK•man•SHIP] *n*
Kunstfertigkeit F

**workshop** [WURK•shop] *n*
Werkstatt F

**world** [wurld] *n* Welt F

**worldly** [WURLD•lee] *adj*
weltlich

**worm** [wurm] *n* Wurm M

**worry 1** [WUR•ree] *vi* sich
kümmern um

**worry 2** *n* (bother) Kummer M

**worse** [wurz] *adj* schlechter

**worship** [WUR•ship] *vt*
verehren; anbeten

**worshipper** [WUR•ship•pur] *n*
Anbeter in M

**worst** [wurst] *adj* schlechtest;
schlimmst

**worth** [wurth] *n* Wert M

**worthless** [WURTH•les] *adj*
wertlos

**worthy** [WUR•thee] *adj* würdig

**would** [wud] *pret* wollten

**wound** [woond] *n* Wunde

**wrangle** [RAN•gl] *vi* sich
zanken

**wrap** [rap] *vt* wicklen

**wrapper** [RAP•pur] *n* Hülle F

**wrapping paper** [RAP•ping
PAI•pur] *n* Packpapier N

**wrath** [rath] *n* Zorn M

**wreath** [reeth] *n* Kranx M

**wreck** [rek] *n* Zerstörung F

**wrench** [rench] *n* Verdrehung;
Schraubenschlüssel (tool) F

**wrest** [rest] *vt* entreißen

**wrestle** [RES•tl] *vi* ringen

**wretch** [retch] *n* Schuft M

**wretched** [RETCH•chid] *adj*
elend

**wring** [ring] *vt* auswringen

**wrinkle** [RINK•kl] *n* Runzel F

**wrist** [rist] *n* Handgelenk N

**writ** [rit] *n* Erlaß M

**write** [ruyt] *vt* schreiben

**writer** [RUY•tur] *n* Schreiber M

**writhe** [ruyth] *vi* sich krümmen

**writing** [RUY•ting] *n*
Schreiben N

**wrong** [rong] *adj* falsch;
  unrichtig

**wrought iron** [RAUT I•urn] *n*
  Schmiede; Schweißeisen N
**wry** [ruy] *adj* schief

# X

**X-ray** [EKS•rai] *n*
  Röntgenstrahl M
**xenophobe** [ZEE•no•fob] *n*
  Xenophobie F

**xylography**
  [zuy•LOG•gruh•fee] *n*
  Xylographie F
**xylophone** [ZUY•luh•FON] *n*
  Xylophon N

# Y

**yacht** [yaht] *n* Segeljacht F
**yank** *vt* heftig ziehen
**yard** [yahrd] *n* Hof M
**yardstick** [YAHRD•stik] *n*
  Maßstock M
**yawn** [yaun] *vi* gähnen
**yea** [yai] ja
**year** [yeer] *n* Jahr N
**yearn** [yurn] *vi* sich sehnen
**yearning** [YUR•ning] *n*
  Sehnsucht F
**yeast** [yeest] *n* Hefe F
**yell** [yel] *vi* gellend
**yellow** [YEL•lo] gelb
**yeoman** [YO•min] *n*
  Gutsbesitzer M
**yes** *n* Jawohl; Ja
**yesterday** [YES•tur•dai] *adv*
  gestern
**yet** *conj* noch

**yield** [yeeld] *vt* ergeben
**yielding** [YEEL•ding] *adj*
  ergiebig
**yoke** [yok] *n* Joch N
**yolk** [yok] *n* Eidotter M
**yonder** [YON•dur] dort drüben
**yore** [yor] *adv* ehedem
**you** [yoo] du Sie
**young** [yung] *adj* jung
**youngster** [YUNG•stur]·*n*
  Junge M
**your yours** [yor yorz] ihr; dein;
  euer
**yourself** [yor•SELF] du; Sie;
  selbst
**youth** [yooth] *n* Jugend F
**youthful** [YOOTH•fl] *adj*
  jugendlich
**Yuletide** [YOOL•tuyd] *n*
  Weihnachtszeit F

# Z

**Zaire** [zah•EER] Zaire
**zeal** [zeel] *n* Eifer M
**zealot** [ZE•lot] *n* Eiferer M
**zealous** [ZE•lus] *adj* eifrig
**zebra** [ZEE•bruh] *n* Zebra N
**zenith** [ZEE•nith] *n*
  Scheitelpunkt M
**zephyr** [ZE•fur] *n* Zephir M
**zeppelin** [ZE•pi•lin] *n*
  Zeppelin M
**zero** [ZEE•ro] Null
**zest** *n* Würze F
**zigzag** [ZIG•zag] *n* Zickzack M
**zinc** [zink] *n* Zihnk N
**zip** *vt* schwirren

**zipper** [ZIP•pur] *n*
  Reißverschluß M
**zither** [ZITH•thur] *n* Zither F
**zodiac** [ZO•dee•ak] *n*
  Tierkreis M
**zodiacal** [zo•DUY•i•kl] *adj*
  tierkreis
**zone** [zon] *n* Gürtel M
**zoo** *n* Zoo M
**zoological**
  [ZOO•uh•LAH•jik•kl] *adj*
  zoologisch
**zoology** [zoo•AH•lo•gee] *n*
  Zoologie F
**zoom** *vi* surren